REVISIONING A PENTECOSTAL THEOLOGY OF WATER BAPTISM
AN ECCLESIAL RITE OF EMBODIED TRANSFORMATION

Revisioning a Pentecostal Theology of

Water Baptism

An Ecclesial Rite Of Embodied
Transformation

Edward D. George, Jr.

Revisioning a Pentecostal Theology of Water Baptism
An Ecclesial Rite of Embodied Transformation

Published by CPT Press
900 Walker ST NE
Cleveland, TN 37311
USA
email: cptpress@pentecostaltheology.org
website: www.cptpress.com

ISBN: 978-1-953358-57-8

Copyright © *2024 CPT Press*
All rights reserved. No part of this book may be reproduced or translated in any form, by print, photoprint, microfilm, microfiche, electronic database, internet database, or any other means without written permission from the publisher.

CONTENTS

Acknowledgements viii
Abbreviations x

Chapter 1: Introduction
Purpose and Focus of the Study 1
Structure and Flow of the Argument 2

Chapter 2: A Pentecostal Approach to Scripture
Introduction 7
Spirit 16
Word 23
Community 26
Conclusion 32

Part I
Hearing the Voices of the Community

Chapter 3: Water Baptism in Pentecostal Perspective(s): 1932 to Present
Introduction 35
Reading Pentecostals on Water Baptism 36
Conclusions 104

Chapter 4: Water Baptism in Early Pentecostal Periodicals: 1906 to 1931
Wesleyan-Holiness Periodicals 107
Finished-Work Pentecostals 192
Oneness Pentecostals 264
Findings and Assessment 297

Part II
Hearing the Voices of The Word

Chapter 5: Reading the New Testament
Introduction 323
The Gospel of Matthew's Witness of Water Baptism 324

Romans 6.1-11 Water Baptism – Death and Life in
   Jesus Christ 350
Conclusion... 365

Part III
Discerning the Holy Spirit

Chapter 6: Embodied Pentecostal Spirituality
Introduction 369
Cognitive Scientific Perspectives 370
Embodied Cognition and Ontological Change in the Hebrew
   Scriptures and Tradition 383
Embodied Pentecostal Soteriology 385
Five-fold Gospel 393
Practical and Ecclesiological Implications 395

Chapter 7: Contributions and Suggestions for Further Research
Contributions 401
Suggestions for Further Research 405
Appendices
   A. The Bridegroom's Messenger: Baptismal Service
      Locations 407
   B. Latter Rain Evangel: Baptismal Service Locations 409
   C. Church of God Evangel: Baptismal Service Locations:
      State/City 411
   D. Church of God Evangel: Baptismal Service Locations:
      Country/City 435
   E. Church of God Evangel: Baptismal Terminology:
      'baptized' 436
   F. Church of God Evangel: Baptismal Terminology:
      'baptized in water' 437
   G. Church of God Evangel: Baptismal Terminology:
      'followed the Lord' 440
   H. Pentecostal Herald: Baptismal Service Locations:
      State/City 442
   I. White Wing Messenger: Baptismal Service Locations:
      State/City 446
   J. White Wing Messenger: Baptismal Service Locations:
      Country/City 453

K. White Wing Messenger: Baptismal Service References 453
L. White Wing Messenger: Baptismal Terminology:
   'followed the Lord' 455
M. White Wing Messenger: Baptismal Terminology:
   'baptized in water' 455
N. Word and Witness: Baptismal Service Locations:
   State/City.. 456
O. Word and Witness: Baptismal Service Locations:
   Country/City.. 460
P. Pentecostal Evangel: Baptismal Service References.............. 461
Q. Pentecostal Evangel: Baptismal Terminology:
   'baptized' and cognates 466
R. Pentecostal Evangel: Baptismal Terminology:
   'immersed'... 470
S. Pentecostal Evangel: Baptismal Terminology:
   'burial language' 471
T. Bridal Call/Bridal Call Foursquare, Foursquare Crusader:
   Baptism Locations... 473
Bibliography 476
Index of Biblical (and Other Ancient) References 493
Index of Authors 499

Acknowledgements

A project like this is not done without sacrifice and collaboration. Glenda, thank you for your love, encouragement, sacrifice, support, and understanding over these past eight years! You have enabled me to complete this labor of love – you are deeply loved. This work is dedicated to you. Jerry K. and Evelyn Adams thank you for your close friendship, unchanging love and support, and my home away from home for over fifty years. I love you both dearly. My 'Kiddo', Kelly Dowdell Folsom, Kody (son-in-law), Dakota and Jaymee, Dusty, Cate, and Krew you bring a smile to my heart whenever I think of you. Thank you for our times together! You remind me that there is more to life than research and writing. I love you!

Chris Thomas, my friend for almost 50 years, you sparked an interest in me that had lain dormant for thirty years, completing a PhD. From the day of that conversation in May 2015 through its completion, your supervision has been exceptional. Thank you for the renewal of our friendship, mentoring, laughter, supervision, challenging conversations, and prayer. The study of the early Pentecostal literature has given me a renewed passion for living a Spirit filled Holy life in the name of the Father, the Son, and the Holy Spirit. Thank you for providing a hospitable and challenging place to reclaim my Pentecostal roots and to be transformed by the Father, Son, and Holy Spirit.

To the other doctoral supervisors, Chris Green, Frank Macchia, Lee Roy Martin, and Robby Waddell: thank you for your insights and encouragement along the way.

To my fellow PhD students, it has been a delight to interact with you and your materials. It is hoped that this contribution lives up to the standard you have set. After eight years, the roster of fellow researchers has grown too long to attempt an exhaustive list; however, there are three colleagues who have made invaluable contributions to my life and this project: Ben Wiles, Chris Rouse, and Jared Runck. Thank you!

The following libraries assisted with the research: the William G. Squires Library of Lee University, Cleveland, TN; Bangor University Library, Bangor, Wales, U.K., The Center for the Study of Oneness Pentecostalism, Florissant, MO; and IPHC Archives and Research Center, Bethany, OK And, a special thanks go to The Consortium of Pentecostal Archives, Cleveland, TN (pentecostalarchives.org) who made most of the early Pentecostal Periodicals reviewed available online.

ABBREVIATIONS

Early Pentecostal Periodicals
AF	*The Apostolic Faith*
BC	*Bridal Call*
BCF	*Bridal Call Foursquare*
CE	*Christian Evangel*
COGE	*Church of God Evangel*
FC	*Foursquare Crusader*
LRE	*Latter Rain Evangel*
MDS	*Meat in Due Season*
PE	*The Pentecostal Evangel*
PH	*Pentecostal Herald*
PHA	*Pentecostal Holiness Advocate*
PT	*Pentecostal Testimony*
PT	*Present Truth*
TBT	*The Blessed Truth*
TBM	*The Bridegroom's Messenger*
TFS	*The Faithful Standard*
TGR	*The Good Report*
TP	*The Pentecost*
TPT	*The Present Truth*
TWT	*The Whole Truth*
WE	*Weekly Evangel*
WW	*Word and Witness*
WWM	*White Wing Messenger*

Other
AB	Anchor Bible
AG	Assemblies of God
AJPS	*Asian Journal of Pentecostal Studies*
ATR	*Anglican Theology Review*
BBR	*Bulletin for Biblical Research*
BEM	*Baptism, Eucharist and Ministry*, Faith and Order Paper No. 111.

BNTC	Black's New Testament Commentary Series
BTC	Brazos Theological Commentary
CBQ	*Catholic Biblical Quarterly*
CCC	Coastal Christian Center
CCSS	Catholic Commentary on Sacred Scripture
COG	Church of God
COGOP	Church of God of Prophecy
CPT	Centre for Pentecostal Theology
DPCM	*Dictionary of Pentecostal and Charismatic Movements*
EBC	Expositor's Bible Commentary
ExpTim	Expository Times
HS	Holy Spirit
ICFG	International Church of the Foursquare Gospel
IBT	Interpreting Biblical Texts
IJST	*International Journal of Systematic Theology*
IVP	InterVarsity Press
JBL	*Journal of Biblical Literature*
JEPTA	*Journal of European Pentecostal Theology Association*
JES	*Journal Ecumenical Studies*
JETS	*Journal of the Evangelical Theological Society*
JPT	*Journal of Pentecostal Theology*
JPTSup	Journal of Pentecostal Theology Supplement
JSNTSup	Journal for the Study of the New Testament Supplement
L&L	Light & Life Fellowship
NAC	New American Commentary
NICNT	New International Commentary on the New Testament
NIDPCM	*The New International Dictionary of Pentecostal and Charismatic Movements*
NT	New Testament
NTT	New Testament Theology Commentary Series
OT	Old Testament
OUP	Oxford University Press
PCNT	Paideia: Commentaries on the New Testament
Pneuma	*Pneuma: The Journal of the Society for Pentecostal Studies*
PTSM	Princeton Theological Monograph Series
SBL	Society of Biblical Literature

TPNTC	Pillar New Testament Commentary Series
USA	United States of America
VVCF	Valley Vineyard Christian Fellowship
WB	Water Baptism

1

INTRODUCTION

Purpose and Focus of the Study

In this monograph, I propose to construct a 'revisioned' Pentecostal[1] theology of WB in response to the call to revision Pentecostal theology by Steven Land in his 1993 groundbreaking *Pentecostal Spirituality: A Passion for the Kingdom*.[2] This study is needed. Several presuppositions undergird the structure and flow of the argument.

It is necessary for a self-consciously Pentecostal theology to be as concerned with method as it is with content. Thus, attention must be given to a Pentecostal hermeneutic that guides and informs Scriptural investigation and theological reflection.

Noted Pentecostal scholar, Walter Hollenweger argues that Pentecostal theology should be informed by the earliest years of the movement since the spirituality of early Pentecostalism represents

---

[1] Throughout this study I am employing 'Pentecostal' to refer to classical Pentecostalism in its various forms, with only slight overlap with the charismatic movement. I am conscious that such a refinement is in some instances impossible to maintain given the fluid exchange that has taken place between the two movements in recent years. I will engage some scholars who speak from and to both contexts, but primarily I will focus on the work of those who self-identify as Pentecostals and who belong to classical Pentecostal churches and/or work in Pentecostal institutions of higher education.

[2] Steven J. Land, *Pentecostal Spirituality: A Passion for the Kingdom* (JPTSup 1; Sheffield: Sheffield Academic Press, 1993). Citations and quotations will be from the 2010 CPT Press version: Steven J. Land, *Pentecostal Spirituality: A Passion for the Kingdom* (Cleveland, TN: CPT Press, 2010), p. 7.

the heart and not the infancy of the movement.³ Since Pentecostalism can and should be revisioned without betraying itself or losing its character, our revisioning will privilege Scripture and be informed by the movement's available early periodical literature (1906-1931) regarding the baptismal practices and theological reflection on WB.⁴ Our revisioning will also consider the more recent Pentecostal thought on WB and sacraments (1932-present) and the findings of the neurosciences and cognitive behavioral sciences in our construction.

Next, owing to the role of Scripture in the tradition, Pentecostal theology should be deeply biblical, rooted in and directed by the reading of Scripture. I will provide a literary/narrative reading of the NT's explicit references in the Gospel of Matthew and Paul's Epistle to the Romans in view of their predominant use by early Pentecostals in their treatments of WB.

Finally, on this foundation I will seek to construct a Pentecostal theology of WB that is also informed by recent findings of the neurosciences and cognitive psychology that challenge Christian Neo-Platonism and argue for an embodied valuation of human existence. I will do the aforementioned in dialogue with contemporary theologians within the Pentecostal tradition.

Structure and Flow of the Argument

Given the assumptions that guide this study, the argument begins with addressing the current state of the question, exploring what Pentecostal scholars and prominent Pentecostal leaders are saying about the sacraments, WB, in particular, in Pentecostal thought and practice, both past and present.

For example, John Christopher Thomas advances an ecclesiology he thinks might 'go some way toward reclaiming and re-appropriating the sacraments' for Pentecostals,⁵ and liturgist Simon Chan posits

---

³ Walter J. Hollenweger, *The Pentecostals* (Peabody, MA: Hendrickson, 1988), p. 551.

⁴ I will concentrate on the first 25 years (1906-1931) of the movement in North America; however, attention will be paid to the movements expansion globally as we retrieve reports from the foreign mission fields.

⁵ John Christopher Thomas, *The Spirit of the New Testament* (Blandford Forum: Deo Publishing, 2005), p. 20.

that Pentecostals stand in need of a 'radical revisioning of the church', including a reconsideration of the sacraments.⁶ Kenneth Archer provides a narrative appropriation of the 'sacramental ordinances', placing them as events within the Pentecostal story.⁷ MayLing Tan-Chow discerns that Pentecostal worship, generally, and the charismatic ministry of signs and wonders, particularly, already are deeply sacramental, even if, in fact, they are not described in this way by Pentecostals.⁸ Chris E.W. Green has recently demonstrated that early North American Pentecostal leaders held a variety of beliefs and practices with regard to the sacraments, in general, and the Lord's Supper, in particular.⁹ Green has constructed a Pentecostal theology of the Lord's Supper in response to the clarion calls of Thomas, Chan, Archer, and Tan-Chow. These examples illustrate the increasing emergence of innovative Pentecostal thinking on the sacraments, albeit with limited attention given to WB.

Chapter 2 investigates one methodology utilized in current Pentecostal hermeneutics, 'Spirit-Word-Community', that will guide our investigation and construction, albeit, in a dissimilar order. More specifically, the project will be divided into three sections that correspond to Community-Word-Spirit. Section I, chapters 3 and 4, will listen to the various voices of the 'Community', past and present; Section II, chapter 5, will listen to the voice(s) of the 'Word'; and Section III, chapter 6, will attempt to discern the voice of the Spirit in revisioning a Pentecostal theology of WB.

Chapter 3 (Community) addresses the current state of the question, following with an examination of the water baptismal practices, teachings, and theological reflections of Pentecostal scholars and denominational leaders between 1932 to the present.

Chapter 4 (Community) includes a careful reading of the early Pentecostal periodical materials, following the model pioneered by Kimberly Ervin Alexander in her investigation of early Pentecostal

---

⁶ Simon Chan, *Pentecostal Theology and the Christian Spiritual Tradition* (JPTSup 21; Sheffield: Sheffield Academic Publishing, 2001), p. 14.

⁷ Kenneth J. Archer, 'Nourishment for our Journey: The Pentecostal Via Salutis and Sacramental Ordinances', *JPT* 13.1 (2004), pp. 79-96.

⁸ MayLing Tan-Chow, *Pentecostal Theology for the Twenty-First Century* (Burlington, VT: Ashgate Publishing, 2007), p. 143.

⁹ Chris E.W. Green, *Toward a Pentecostal Theology of the Lord's Supper: Foretasting the Kingdom* (Cleveland, TN: CPT Press, 2012).

healing practices and soteriologies.[10] Material is covered both in terms of chronology (from 1906-1931) and in terms of the various movements (the WHP, FW, and OP streams) within early Pentecostalism.[11]

In my review of the early literature, I employ an inductive approach to allow two periodicals (*AF* and *TBM*) to speak for themselves and establish the categories that could be employed for reading the remaining periodicals. After the initial review of the extant copies of the *AF*-Los Angeles and the *TBM*, I undertake a second reading to assess if the categories are sufficient to the evidence and if I have overlooked relevant material. Upon refinement, the following categories were established to employ in a close reading[12] of the remaining 19 periodicals: the number of person baptized; the geographical location and the body of water utilized in WB; authorized administrator of WB; qualifications for WB; presence of Pentecostal embodied worship; mode of baptism; baptismal formula; obstacles and commitment to WB; the size of crowds present at baptismal services; use of WB for witness and evangelism; stance on infant baptism; rebaptism; and the meaning of WB. By and large, the categories held throughout the review. Due to the shortage of baptismal reports, sermons, and articles on WB in a few periodicals, categories were combined to reflect the change in reporting.

Chapter 5 (Word) engages the biblical text. Having examined the Pentecostal perspectives and practices on WB in the third and fourth chapters, I turn to the Scriptures, for, owing to Pentecostals' high view of Scripture, an authentically Pentecostal theology of WB must be biblically informed. I offer a literary/narrative reading of Matthew

---

[10] Kimberly E. Alexander, *Pentecostal Healing: Models in Theology and Practice* (JPTSup 29; Dorset, UK: Deo Publishing, 2006). Also, 'The Pentecostal Healing Community', in John Christopher Thomas (ed.), *Toward a Pentecostal Ecclesiology: The Church and the Fivefold Gospel* (Cleveland, TN: CPT Press, 2010), pp. 183-206.

[11] The African American community is largely underrepresented in this project due to the lack of available extant material. *The Whole Truth*, the official periodical of the Church of God in Christ, a predominantly African American Pentecostal denomination led by C.H. Mason, was represented by two extant copies; one from 1910 and the other from 1931. Both issues contained a solitary reference to a baptismal service without commentary.

[12] I read each page of the 21 reviewed periodicals out of a concern that crucial data would be missed by a word search. Only later did I employ a search engine to double-check my close reading.

and Romans in their canonical order, engaging them with a 'Pentecostal ear'.

Chapter 6 (Spirit) is devoted to a constructive Pentecostal theology of WB, addressing in detail those issues that are judged to be especially important to Pentecostals. Building upon the previous chapters, this chapter constructs a Pentecostal theology of WB including engagement with key Pentecostal voices, the biblical witness, and non-Pentecostal assessments of the relationship between the Triune God, embodied persons, and mediated learning in an attempt to hear the voice of the Spirit leading forward.

In this chapter, I propose a Pentecostal way of thinking about and practicing WB. In doing this, I attempt to answer how WB 'narrates' us into the Pentecostal story, guiding us into and along the *via salutis*[13] and is informed by the heart of the Pentecostal tradition.

Steven Land has convincingly demonstrated that the fivefold Gospel encapsulates the heart of traditional Pentecostal theology.[14] Relatedly, Faupel has shown that Pentecostal theology is preeminently eschatological,[15] so that the fifth element in the fivefold Gospel, the expectation of Jesus as coming King, serves as the orienting theme and colors and shapes thinking of Jesus as savior, sanctifier, Spirit-baptizer, and healer. In conversation with Land, Archer, Yong, Damasio, and Feuerstein, I explore an understanding of WB as a divinely mediated learning rite of incorporation into the eschatological community and explore ways in which such an understanding would inform the fivefold Gospel.

Chapter 7 concludes the project with a description of major contributions and makes proposals for further research. I explore various implications for Pentecostal biblical, historical, systematic, and practical theology. In particular, attention is given to Christian discipleship in relation to sanctification. Additionally, I suggest ways in which my work might inform Pentecostal ecclesiology; hermeneutics and theological method; and ethical reflection and praxis.

---

[13] Archer, 'Nourishment for our Journey', pp. 79-96.
[14] Land, *Pentecostal Spirituality*, pp. 125-31.
[15] D. William Faupel, *The Everlasting Gospel: The Significance of Eschatology in the Development of Pentecostal Thought* (JPTSup 10; Sheffield, UK: Sheffield Academic Press, 1996; Dorset, UK; Deo Publishing, 2009).

2

A PENTECOSTAL APPROACH TO SCRIPTURE

Introduction

In this section, I will, following K. Archer, employ a 'narrative-praxis' approach to my theological reflection and constructive Pentecostal theology of WB. Archer's 'narrative-praxis' approach asserts that 'Praxis, as a method, unites practice (doing) and theory (knowing) into the same reflective activity'.[1] His approach supports a critical commitment to theological reflection while acknowledging that our religious experiences shape our beliefs, and our beliefs, in turn, form our activities. Thus, practice and theory are inseparable and mutually informing.

Concerning narrative, Archer stresses the 'importance of understanding Scripture as a grand meta-narrative with the Gospels and Acts as the heart of the Christian story'.[2] Thus, since Jesus Christ is the center and leader of Christianity a narrative theology will stress the priority of the story of Jesus Christ and the resultant significance for the Christian community and for the cosmos.[3] While early Pentecostals referenced several Scriptures in the treating the subject of WB, they relied predominantly on passages from Matthew and Romans 6 in their teaching and preaching on WB. Thus, our theological reflection and construction will privilege the story of Jesus through careful narrative readings of Matthew in conversation

---

[1] Archer, 'Nourishment for our Journey', p. 81.
[2] Archer, 'Nourishment for our Journey', p. 81.
[3] Archer, 'Nourishment for our Journey', p. 81.

with B. Charette and Romans in conversation with N.T. Wright and reflection on Pentecostal experience and practices. Before turning to a narrative reading of the Gospel according to Matthew, attention must be paid to the hermeneutical principles that will guide our reading.

Pentecostals[4] are a storied people who find themselves and their identity located in the metanarrative of Holy Scripture.[5] More specifically, Pentecostals have perceived their very existence as a fulfillment of Acts 2, locating themselves as participants of/in the 'latter rain'[6] inaugurated on the Day of Pentecost. The central

---

[4] For more on the history and impact of the Azusa Street revival and the subsequent Pentecostal movement see Cecil M. Robeck, *The Azusa Street Mission, and Revival: The Birth of the Global Pentecostal Movement* (Nashville, TN: Thomas Nelson, 2006); Harold D. Hunter and Cecil M. Robeck (eds.), *The Azusa Street Revival and Its Legacy* (Cleveland, TN: Pathway Press, 2006); Robert R. Owens, *The Azusa Street Revival: Its Roots and Its Message* (Longwood, FL: Xulon Press, 2005); Eddie Hyatt (ed.), *Fire on the Earth: Eyewitness Reports from the Azusa Street Revival* (Lake Mary, FL: Creation House, 2006); A.C. Valdez, Sr., *Fire on Azusa Street: An Eyewitness Account* (Costa Mesta, CA: Gift Publications, 1980); Dayton, *The Theological Roots of Pentecostalism*; and V. Synan, 'Pentecostalism', in Walter A. Elwell (ed.), *The Evangelical Dictionary of Theology* (Grand Rapids: Baker, 1984).

[5] Kenneth J. Archer, 'Pentecostal Story: The Hermeneutical Filter for the Making of Meaning', *Pneuma* 26.1 (Spring 2004), pp. 36-59 (41-42). I am following Archer's view of metanarrative and narrative. He posits:

> By metanarrative I refer to a grand story by which human societies and their individual members live and organize their lives in meaningful ways. The Christian metanarrative refers to the general Christian story about the meaning of the world, the God who created it, and humanity's place in it. This is a story that begins with a good creation, includes a fall into sin, redemption through the Messiah, Christian community, and final restoration of all creation. The Christian metanarrative is primarily dependent on the Bible for this general narrative.

Additionally, for a basic outline of the 'Storyline' of the Christian metanarrative, see Gabriel Fackre, *The Christian Story: A Narrative of Basic Christian Doctrine*, vol. 1 (3d edn; Grand Rapids, MI: Eerdmans, 1996). Fackre writes that 'Creation, Fall, Covenant, Jesus Christ, Church, Salvation, Consummation, … are acts in the Christian drama', with the understanding that 'there is a God who creates, reconciles, and redeems the word' as 'the 'Storyline', p. 834.

[6] See Faupel, *The Everlasting Gospel*, pp. 19-43 for Faupel's development of this point. See also Edith Blumhofer, *Restoring the Faith: The Assemblies of God, Pentecostalism, and American Culture* (Chicago, IL: University of Illinois Press, 1999), pp. 93-97, for a discussion of the influence of the latter rain concept upon the

concern of the latter rain message was the 'restoration of the Gospel'. The central character of the story was Jesus. As Ken Archer has noted, 'The doctrines being restored, the fivefold Gospel, all have to do with one's understanding of the ministry of Jesus – a soteriological and ecclesiastical concern'.[7] Jackie Johns posits that 'At the core of the Pentecostal worldview is affective experience of God which generates an apocalyptic horizon for reading reality'.[8]

In order to gain perspective on their affective experience, Rick D. Moore asserts that

> in its radical re-ordering of reality, Pentecost might be compared to the divine encounters of the OT prophets in their call narratives. The prophetic experience was an apocalyptic event that deconstructed previously held assumptions and created new theological perceptions and new possibilities for God's people.[9]

Furthermore, Roger Stronstad asserts that Peter's interpretation of the events on the Day of Pentecost as the fulfillment of Joel's promise that servants, sons, daughters, old, and young 'will prophesy' (Acts 2.17) serves to strengthen the connection between Pentecost and the prophetic calling. Thus, the HS's gift is the gift of prophecy; consequently, Pentecost and subsequent SB creates a community of prophets.[10]

In other words, early Pentecostals located themselves in Acts 2 and the Gospels, perceiving they were participants in the closing

---

lifestyle of the early Pentecostals. See the following biblical references used to develop the early and latter rain motif: Deut. 11.10-15; Job 29.29; Prov. 16.15; Jer. 3.3, 5.24; Hosea 6.3; Joel 2.23; Zech. 10.1; and James 5.7.

[7] Archer, 'Pentecostal Story', p. 53. Donald Dayton has demonstrated that the Full Gospel forms the basic gestalt of Pentecostal thought and rhetoric. See Dayton, *Theological Roots of Pentecostalism*, p. 173. The Five-fold (Four-fold Gospel) is the Full Gospel, the very heart of Pentecostal ethos. It is Pentecostals' doxological confession concerning Jesus as Saviour, Sanctifier, Healer, Spirit Baptizer, and Soon Coming King.

[8] Jackie David Johns, 'Pentecostalism and the Postmodern Worldview', *JPT* 7 (1995), pp. 73-96 (87).

[9] Rick D. Moore, 'The Prophetic Calling: An Old Testament Profile and Its Relevance for Today', *JEPTA* 24 (2004), pp. 16-29 (18-21).

[10] Roger Stronstad, *The Prophethood of All Believers: A Study in Luke's Charismatic Theology* (Cleveland, TN: CPT Press, 2010), p. 63. Cf. Larry R. McQueen, *Joel and the Spirit: The Cry of a Prophetic Hermeneutic* (Cleveland, TN: CPT Press, 2009), p. 44.

drama of God's redeeming work, leading them to apprehend they were the eschatological people of God. They saw themselves as channels of Jesus Christ, given form in the community of God, created, and sustained by the HS. This, in turn, propelled them to embrace and proclaim the Fivefold Gospel with Jesus Christ as the center.

As the eschatological prophetic people of God, from the beginning of the movement in the early twentieth century, Pentecostals have relied on Scripture for guidance regarding theology and practice.[11] In keeping with my Pentecostal heritage, it is consistent that a proposed Pentecostal theology of WB is built on the foundation of Scripture, congruent with Pentecostal spirituality, rooted in devotion to God through Jesus Christ in the power of the HS. My aim in this section is to advance a hermeneutical model faithful to the Pentecostal tradition of interpretation. After developing the model, I will provide a close reading/hearing of Mt 3.13-17; 21.25-27; 28.16-20, and Rom. 6.1-11, texts that are crucial to re-visioning the theology and practice of WB. The inclusion of 'hearing' the text embraces the position of Lee Roy Martin who asserts that while 'hearing' and 'reading' are analogous in that both approaches refer to a synchronic, holistic, contextual hermeneutic. The term 'hearing', however, more closely approximates the goals of my Pentecostal hermeneutic because: (1) it is a thoroughly biblical term; (2) it accords with the orality of the biblical and Pentecostal contexts; (3) it is relational, implying the existence of a 'person' who is speaking the Word; (4) it denotes a faithful adherence to the Word, since in Scripture to hear often means to obey; (5) it implies transformation, since the hearing of the Word produces change; and (6) it demands humility because, unlike the process of 'reading' Scripture, 'hearing' entails submission to the authority of the word of God.[12]

Similarly, John Christopher Thomas posits that his proposed Pentecostal hermeneutic deliberately includes a focus on hearing the words of Scripture themselves as couched and presented by the text; an approach informed by the experience of the Pentecostal

---

[11] Green, *Toward a Pentecostal Theology*, p. 182.

[12] Lee Roy Martin, *The Unheard Voice of God: A Pentecostal Hearing of the Book of Judges* (JPTSup 32; Dorset, UK: Deo Publishing, 2008), p. 53.

interpreter but not determined by it; an approach where the text is allowed to preserve its own independent voice; a voice that is allowed to shape and form the interpreter and interpretive community, who/which may or may not share the perspective of a particular text and its world.[13]

Pentecostal hermeneutics has been a topic of discussion for over thirty-five years, with various approaches proffered for consideration.[14] The inquiry revolves around the essential

---

[13] John Christopher Thomas, 'What the Spirit is Saying to the Church – The Testimony of a Pentecostal in New Testament Studies', in K.L. Spawn and A.T. Wright (eds.), *Spirit & Scripture: Examining a Pneumatic Hermeneutic* (London: T&T Clark, 2012), pp. 122-23.

[14] While not exhaustive, see the following articles and books on Pentecostal hermeneutics: Gordon D. Fee, 'Hermeneutics and Historical Precedent – A Major Problem in Pentecostal Hermeneutics', in Russell P. Spittler (ed.), *Perspectives on the New Pentecostalism* (Grand Rapids, MI: Baker Book House, 1976), pp. 118-32; Howard M. Ervin, 'Hermeneutics: A Pentecostal Option', *Pneuma* 3.2 (1981), p. 11; G.T. Sheppard, 'Pentecostalism and the Hermeneutics of Dispensationalism: Anatomy of an Uneasy Relationship', *Pneuma* 6.2 (1984), pp. 5-33; M.D. McLean, 'Toward a Pentecostal Hermeneutic', *Pneuma* 6.2 (1984), pp. 35-56; William W. Menzies, 'The Methodology of Pentecostal Theology: An Essay on Hermeneutics', *Essays on Apostolic Themes: Studies in Honor of Howard M. Ervin*, in Paul Elbert (ed.), (Peabody, MA: Hendrickson Publishers, 1985), pp. 1-14 (5-13); F.L. Arrington, 'Hermeneutics', in S.M. Burgess and G.B. McGee (eds.), *DPCM* (Grand Rapids: Zondervan, 1988), pp. 376-89; R. Stronstad, 'Trends in Pentecostal Hermeneutics', *Paraclete* 22.3 (1988), pp. 1-12; Roger Stronstad, 'The Hermeneutic of Lucan Historiography', *Paraclete* 22.4 (1988), pp. 5-17; R.D. Moore, 'Approaching God's Word Biblically: A Pentecostal Perspective' (Annual Meeting of the Society for Pentecostal Studies, Fresno, CA, 1989); L.V. Newman, 'Pentecostal Hermeneutics: Suggesting a Model, Exploring the Problems' (Annual Meeting of the Society for Pentecostal Studies, Lakeland, FL, 1991); Roger Stronstad, 'Pentecostal Experience and Hermeneutics', *Paraclete* 26.1 (1992), pp. 14-30; J.D. Johns and C. Bridges Johns, 'Yielding to the Spirit: A Pentecostal Approach to Group Bible Study', *JPT* 1 (1992), pp. 109-34; G. Anderson, 'Pentecostal Hermeneutics' (Annual Meeting of the Society for Pentecostal Studies, Springfield, MO, 1992); A.C. Autry, 'Dimensions of Hermeneutics in Pentecostal Focus', *JPT* 3 (1993), pp. 29-50; D. Albrecht, R. Israel, and R. McNally, 'Pentecostals and Hermeneutics: Texts, Rituals and Community', *Pneuma* 15 (1993), pp. 137-61; T.B. Cargal, 'Beyond the Fundamentalist-Modernist Controversy: Pentecostals and Hermeneutics in a Postmodern Age', *Pneuma* 15 (1993), pp. 163-87; J. Byrd, 'Paul Ricoeur's Hermeneutical Theory and Pentecostal Proclamation', *Pneuma* 15.2 (1993), pp. 203-14 (205); F.L. Arrington, 'The Use of the Bible by Pentecostals', *Pneuma* 16 (1994),

pp. 101-107; H.K. Harrington and R. Patten, 'Pentecostal Hermeneutics and Postmodern Literary Theory', *Pneuma* 16 (1994), pp. 109-14; R.P. Menzies, 'Jumping Off the Postmodern Bandwagon', *Pneuma* 16 (1994), pp. 115-20; and G.T. Sheppard, 'Biblical Interpretation after Gadamer', *Pneuma* 16 (1994), pp. 121-41; Kenneth J. A. Archer, 'Pentecostal Hermeneutics: Retrospect and Prospect', *JPT* 4.8 (April 1996), pp. 63-81 (63); Veli-Matti Kärkkäinen, 'Pentecostal Hermeneutics in the Making: On the Way from Fundamentalism to Postmodernism', *JEPTA* 18 (1998), pp. 76-115; Kenneth J. Archer, 'Early Pentecostal Biblical Interpretation: Blurring the Boundaries' (Annual Meeting of the Society for Pentecostal Studies, Kirkland, WA, March 2000); Yongnan Jeon Ahn, 'Various Debates in the Contemporary Pentecostal Hermeneutics', *The Spirit & Church* 2.1 (May 2000), pp. 9-52 (26); Frank D. Macchia, 'The Spirit and The Text: Recent Trends in Pentecostal Hermeneutics', *The Spirit & Church* 2.1 (May 2000), pp. 53-65 (56); Mathew S. Clark, 'Pentecostal Hermeneutics: The Challenge of Relating to (Post)-Modern Literary Theory', *The Spirit & Church* 2.1 (May 2000), pp. 67-93 (90); Matthias Becker, 'A Tenet under Examination: Reflections on the Pentecostal Hermeneutical Approach', *JEPTA* 24.1 (2004), pp. 30-48; Amos Yong, *Spirit-Word-Community: Theological Hermeneutics in Trinitarian Perspective* (Aldershot, UK: Ashgate, 2002); Kenneth J. Archer, *A Pentecostal Hermeneutic for the Twenty-First Century: Spirit, Scripture, and Community* (JPTSup 28; London, UK: T&T Clark, 2004; Cleveland, TN; CPT Press, 2009); John Christopher Thomas, '"Where the Spirit Leads": The Development of Pentecostal Hermeneutics', *Journal of Beliefs & Values: Studies in Religion & Education* 30.3 (December 2009), pp. 289–302; Bradford McCall, 'The Pentecostal Reappropriation of Common Sense Realism', *JPT* 19.1 (January 1, 2010), pp. 59-75; Bradley Truman Noel, *Pentecostal and Postmodern Hermeneutics: Comparisons and Contemporary Impact* (Eugene, OR: Wipf and Stock, 2010); Joel B. Green, *Practicing Theological Interpretation: Engaging Biblical Texts for Faith and Formation* (Grand Rapids, MI: Baker Academic, 2011); L. William Oliverio Jr., *Theological Hermeneutics in the Classical Pentecostal Tradition: A Typological Account* (Global Pentecostal and Charismatic Studies 12; Leiden: Brill, 2012); Kevin L. Spawn and Archie T. Wright (eds.), *Spirit and Scripture: Examining a Pneumatic Hermeneutic* (New York, NY: T&T Clark International, 2012); John Christopher Thomas, 'Pentecostal Biblical Interpretation', in S.L. McKenzie (ed.), *Oxford Encyclopedia of Biblical Interpretation* (Oxford: Oxford University Press, 2013), vol. 2, pp. 89–97; Chris E.W. Green, *Sanctifying Interpretation: Vocation, Holiness, and Scripture* (Cleveland, TN: CPT Press, 2nd edn, 2020); Kenneth J. Archer, 'Pentecostal Hermeneutics and the Society for Pentecostal Studies: Reading and Hearing in One Spirit and One Accord', *Pneuma* 37.3 (2015), pp. 317–39 (327); Lee Roy Martin (ed.), *Pentecostal Hermeneutics: A Reader* (Leiden: Brill, 2013); Melissa L. Archer, *'I Was in the Spirit on the Lord's Day': A Pentecostal Engagement with Worship in the Apocalypse* (Cleveland, TN: CPT Press, 2015), pp. 45–54; Craig S. Keener, *Spirit Hermeneutics: Reading Scripture in Light of Pentecost* (Grand Rapids, MI: Eerdmans, 2016); Rickie Moore, 'Altar Hermeneutics: Reflections of Pentecostal Biblical Interpretation', *Pneuma* 38.2 (2016), pp. 148–59; Peter Althouse and Robby Waddell, 'The Pentecostals and Their

components and approach(es) for a reading/hearing of Holy Scripture to be considered Pentecostal.¹⁵ Over the course of developing a Pentecostal hermeneutic, it has been acknowledged that a Pentecostal hermeneutic rejects any association with the liberal Protestant interpretative tradition.¹⁶ Similarly, while evangelicals share a high view of Scripture with Pentecostals, evangelical interpretative approaches are generally incompatible with Pentecostal strategies due to their rationalistic bias.¹⁷ Influenced by postmodernism with the displacement of reason as the mediating factor in all of life, Cheryl Bridges Johns asserts that both

> Deconstructionism and Pentecostalism are consummatory, apocalyptic movements which dismantle the 'cathedral of modern intellect' and mock all forms of anthropological reductionism. Both mock the modernist conceit that humanity can construct a livable habitation utilizing the skill of rational analysis and problem solving.¹⁸

Scriptures', *Pneuma* 38.1-2 (2016), pp. 115-121; Kenneth J. Archer and L. William Oliverio, Jr. (eds.), *Constructive Pneumatological Hermeneutics in Pentecostal Christianity* (New York: Palgrave Macmillan, 2016), pp. 1–14; L. William Oliverio, 'Reading Craig Keener: On Spirit Hermeneutics: Reading Scripture in Light of Pentecost', *Pneuma* 39.1–2 (2017), pp. 126–45; Dean Deppe, 'Comparing Spirit Hermeneutics by Craig Keener with Classical Pentecostal Hermeneutics', *Calvin Theological Journal* 52.2 (2017), pp. 265–76; and Amos Yong, *Mission After Pentecost: The Witness of the Spirit from Genesis to Revelation* (Grand Rapids, MI: Baker Academic, 2019).

¹⁵ John Christopher Thomas, 'Women, Pentecostals and the Bible: An Experiment in Pentecostal Hermeneutics', *JPT* 5 (1994), pp. 41-56 (43).

¹⁶ Archer, *A Pentecostal Hermeneutic*, p. 22.

¹⁷ Noel, *Pentecostal and Postmodern Hermeneutics*, pp. 122-23. This assertion is disputed by Robert P. Menzies, 'Jumping Off the Postmodern Bandwagon', *Pneuma* 16.1 (1994), p. 119.

¹⁸ Cheryl Bridges Johns, 'Partners in Scandal: Wesleyan and Pentecostal Scholarship', *Pneuma* 21.2 (Fall 1999), pp. 183-97 (192). Also, see the discussion of postmodernism provided in J.K.A. Smith, *Thinking in Tongues: Pentecostal Contributions to Christian Philosophy* (Grand Rapids, MI: Eerdmans, 2010), p. 58 where he asserts that

> Postmodernism rejects the reductionistic picture of human beings as merely thinking things, it also calls into question the privileging of reason and intellect as queen of the faculties. Instead, postmodernism argues that our orientation to the world is not primarily mediated intellectual perception but rather a more fundamental 'passional orientation' and affective comportment to the world

Similarly, postmodern literary theory[19] that focuses on the final form of the text, enables Pentecostal scholars in developing models better aligned with the ethos of the movement.[20] While scholarly consensus relative to *a* Pentecostal hermeneutic continues to be elusive, there is a glimmer of hope found in what appears to be growing agreement regarding the features necessary for a hermeneutic to be Pentecostal.[21] One model offered is the rubric of

---

that 'construes' the world of experience on the basis of 'understanding' that is precognitive.

[19] See the following for helpful discussions of literary criticism: Mark Allen Powell, *What is Narrative Criticism?* (Minneapolis, MN: Fortress Press, 1990), pp. 17-18; M. Davies, 'Literary Criticism,' in R.J. Coggins and J.L. Houlden (eds.), *A Dictionary of Biblical Interpretation* (London: SCM, 1990), pp. 402-405 (404); Hannah K. Harrington and Rebecca Patten, 'Pentecostal Hermeneutics and Postmodern Literary Theory', *Pneuma* 16.1 (Spring 1994), pp. 109-14; E.W. Davies, *Biblical Criticism: A Guide for the Perplexed* (London: Bloomsbury, 2013), pp. 4, 14; Pheme Perkins, 'Crisis in Jerusalem? Narrative Criticism in New Testament Studies', *Theological Studies* 50 (1989), pp. 296-313; and M. Davies, 'Reader-Response Criticism,' in R.J. Coggins and J.L. Houlden (eds.), *A Dictionary of Biblical Interpretation* (London: SCM, 1990), pp. 578-80 (578).

[20] Green, *Toward a Pentecostal Theology*, p. 183. Also, see Rickie D. Moore, 'Canon and Charisma in the Book of Deuteronomy', *JPT* 1 (1992), pp. 75-92 (11) who explains that the combination of literary methods with theological interest offers a helpful approach for the Pentecostal biblical scholar; and Robby Waddell, *The Spirit of the Book of Revelation* (JPTSup 30; Blandford Forum: Deo Publishing, 2006), pp. 39-66, who combines a Pentecostal theological approach with the methodology of intertextuality.

[21] Green, *Toward a Pentecostal Theology*, pp. 182-83 where he identifies the following eight points of general agreement among Pentecostal scholars:

1. The work of the Spirit in making faithful interpretation possible, inspiring the readers to make gospel sense of the texts.
2. The authority and sufficiency of the Scriptures' final, canonical form.
3. The role of the worshipping community in the process of interpreting the Scriptures.
4. The need for confessional, theological readings concerned primarily with how the Scriptures work as God's address to God's people here and now.
5. Respect for the irreducible diversity of theological and literary 'voices' in the Scriptures.
6. Regard for the over-arching 'story' of the history of salvation as a hermeneutical key.

'Spirit, Word, Community' since it appears to be the case that the model is reflected in the early Church's attempt to resolve new questions arising within the embryonic community. John Christopher Thomas has argued that within the Acts 15 account of the Jerusalem Council the HS, community, and Scripture were all operative and dialogical in the discernment and decision-making processes of the Jerusalem Council.[22] The personal experiences, or testimonies, of members of the community were central to the discernment process. It seems the integrative approach at the Jerusalem Council was utilized 'not just to understand a certain biblical text cognitively, rather, the goal is to understand and to be transformed by the biblical text'.[23]

Therefore, it appears that when engaging the Word of God[24] to seek guidance on pressing concerns and personal experiences the best practice is to do so within the community, appealing to the Scripture, under the direction of the HS. The expectation is that readers/hearers will receive guidance and be transformed by the encounter, just as they were at the Jerusalem Council in Acts 15.[25] While each segment of the triad will stand on its own theoretically, the reality is the 'Spirit, Word, Community' are so closely integrated in the Pentecostal ethos that it appears to be next to impossible to separate them. M. Archer posits, 'The Scriptures are a product of the Spirit; the community is formed by the Spirit and shaped by both the Scriptures and the Spirit. Nonetheless, there are important ideas that Pentecostals affirm from Scripture, the community, and the Holy Spirit'.[26]

---

7. The priority of narrative, literary readings of a text over against historical-critical readings.
8. The significance of the history of effects for the contemporary interpretative process.

[22] Thomas, 'Women, Pentecostals and the Bible', pp. 17-40.
[23] Archer, '*I Was in The Spirit*', p. 45.
[24] 'Word of God', has historically been used as a reference to Jesus Christ and Holy Scripture. Unless noted, 'Word of God', 'Word', and 'word of God' will refer to Holy Scripture in this study. References to Jesus Christ as Word of God will be duly noted.
[25] Cheryl Bridges Johns, *Pentecostal Formation; A Pedagogy among the Oppressed* (JPTSup 2; Sheffield, UK: Sheffield Academic Press, 1993; Eugene, OR: Wipf & Stock, 2010), p. 122.
[26] Archer, '*I Was in the Spirit*', pp. 45-46.

It is to a focused exploration of the three-fold framework that we turn our attention, fully cognizant that it will continue to be refined in view of changing contexts and global Pentecostal insights.[27]

Spirit

It should be noted at the outset that attention to the HS's role in the interpretation of Scripture is not a new phenomenon. Leulseged Philemon argues in *Pneumatic Hermeneutics: The Role of the Holy Spirit in the Theological Interpretation of Scripture*[28] that throughout the history of Christianity the major faith traditions of the Eastern Orthodox Church, Roman Catholicism, and Protestantism have all addressed the role of the HS in the theological reading/hearing of Scripture with varying emphases on the priority of the HS in relationship to the ecclesia and Scripture.[29] In regard to the Protestant tradition,

---

[27] This rubric has been employed by a number of Pentecostal scholars including, Moore, 'Canon and Charisma', pp. 75-92; Thomas, 'Women, Pentecostals and the Bible', pp. 41-56; Yong, *Spirit-Word-Community;* Archer, *A Pentecostal Hermeneutic;* Green, *Toward a Pentecostal Theology;* Archer, 'I *Was in the Spirit*'; and McQueen, *Joel and the Spirit.*

[28] Leulseged Philemon, *Pneumatic Hermeneutics: The Role of the Holy Spirit in the Theological Interpretation of Scripture* (Cleveland, TN: CPT Press, 2019). While Philemon's focus is on the HS's role in theological interpretation, he provides an excellent introduction to the current debate regarding theological interpretation. See Kevin J. Vanhoozer (ed.), *Dictionary for Theological Interpretation of the Bible* (Grand Rapids: Baker Academic, 2005); Daniel J. Treier, *Introducing Theological Interpretation of Scripture: Recovering a Christian Practice* (Grand Rapids, MI: Baker Academic, 2008); Stephen E. Fowl (ed.), *The Theological Interpretation of Scripture: Classic and Contemporary Readings* (Blackwell Reading in Modern Theology; Oxford: Blackwell, 1997); Stephen E. Fowl, *Theological Interpretation of Scripture* (Cascade Companions; Eugene: OR, Cascade, 2009); Joel B. Green, *Practicing Theological Interpretation: Engaging Biblical Texts for Faith and Formation* (Theological Explorations for the Church Catholic; Grand Rapids, MI: Baker Academic, 2011); Craig G. Bartholomew and Heath A. Thomas (eds.), *A Manifesto for Theological Interpretation* (Grand Rapids, MI: Baker Academic, 2016). Also, see the *Journal of Theological Interpretation* (ed. Joel B. Green, Winona Lake, IN: Eisenbrauns), and the following commentary series: Brazos Theological Commentary on the Bible; Belief: A Theological Commentary on the Bible; the Two Horizons New Testament Commentary; and the Two Horizons Old Testament Commentary.

[29] Philemon, *Pneumatic Hermeneutics,* pp. 75-129. Philemon asserts that the pneumatological priority in the Eastern Orthodox tradition distinguishes its biblical interpretation as a contemplative, prayerful practice rather than an intellectual engagement. Moreover, Philemon asserts

Philemon provides an analysis of the views held by John Calvin, John Owen, and John Wesley, demonstrating their, similar, yet diverse, perspectives on the role of the HS in relation to the inspiration,

> Reading the Bible in the Eastern tradition is a divine encounter that eventually leads to a profound inward transformation of the human spirit. The aspiration to perceive divine truth beyond the reality of this world orients the deep-seated pneumatic character of biblical interpretation within Orthodox Christianity. Its theology strongly affirms the Church and tradition as the proper context within which the spirits interpretive guidance takes place. The Spirit provides illumination of Scripture through the Church's tradition and its liturgical setting, so it experiences and enjoys the divine truth and reality. (p. 96).

While the Roman Catholic approach also deems the Church the appropriate context for interpretation, the Roman Catholic approach yields more interpretative authority to the Church than its counterpart, Eastern Orthodoxy. Philemon posits that

> Based on the dogmatic Constitution of divine revelation, the Roman Catholic spiritual interpretation involves Christological, ecclesial, and theological elements. The Christological concern maintains that Christ is the unifying principle of the biblical canon and knowledge of him through Scripture is the ultimate goal of spiritual reading. The orally transmitted ecclesial tradition as reflected in the beliefs and worship of the Church is another key issue in the churches spiritual exegesis. The 'rule of faith', in which the Spirit guides the church's journey of faith seeking understanding through the sacred texts is also a significant theological concern in Roman Catholicism. There is a mutual influence between the Spirit's interpretive work and these three elements that maintain the principle of the Roman Catholic spiritual interpretation. As de Lubac's spiritual exegesis suggests, the spirit guides the church to listen to God's voice beyond reading the literal historical sense of Scripture. This is illustrated by the practice of Lectio Divina as listening to the Spirit through the reading of Scripture (pp. 96-97).

In contrast to the Roman Catholic and Eastern Orthodox views, the sixteenth-century Reformers and subsequent Protestant movements asserted *sola Scriptura* to mirror their view of Scripture as the supreme authority in all matters of doctrine and practice in early Protestantism. The essence of this claim arose from the Reformers' deep conviction that Scripture does not require the teaching authority of the Church to make it meaningful and understandable because of its competence for self-interpretation. Based on their doctrine of the perspicuity or clarity of Scripture, the Reformers insist that the meaning of biblical texts can be clear to the ordinary reader without seeking the interpretive framework of church tradition (pp. 100-101).

Moreover, the relation of the Scripture to the HS is valued in the doctrine of inspiration and the promise of Jesus in Jn 16.13 that the Spirit will guide Jesus' followers into all truth.

illumination, and interpretation of Scripture.[30] Of particular importance to Pentecostals is the position of John Wesley, the 'grandfather of Pentecostalism' from whom the holiness and Pentecostal movement sprang in the late nineteenth and early twentieth centuries.[31] Wesley stresses the importance of prayer as a means to aid the inspiration of readers for a faithful reading/hearing of the written Word of God. In regard to the Spirit's role in biblical interpretation, Wesley asserts the HS 'awakens and inspires the reader of Scripture through a prayerful reading and response to the guidance of the Spirit through the words of Scripture'.[32] The work of the Spirit is not limited to individual readers/hearers. The

---

[30] Philemon, *Pneumatic Hermeneutics*, pp. 75-129. Per Philemon, John Calvin's elucidation of the doctrine of divine illumination extends beyond rational apprehension of the meaning of the Scriptures. In addition to cognitive knowledge, the HS generates obedience. Per Philemon, Calvin teaches,

> There is no purpose in reading or hearing Scripture unless the Spirit in his illumination 'effectually appears into our hearts' and regulates our lives to make it possible 'to walk in that righteousness the law enjoins'. In doing so, Calvin shows that the illumination of the Spirit aims ultimately to produce an obedient Christian life that 'discerns the light of life that God manifests by his word' and that 'humbles us to contemplate with admiration' and 'to convince us the more of our need of the grace of God, to comprehend the mysteries, which surpass our limited capacity'.

Calvin's view on the witness of the Spirit and divine illumination, assists in establishing one Protestant understanding of the Spirit's role in biblical interpretation (pp. 109-10).

John Owen, who is viewed as both a Puritan and Reformed theologian, approaches the role of the HS in biblical interpretation by positing that divine illumination consists of two parts:

> The first has to do with the Spirit's work and enabling us to believe in the divine nature of Scripture is the word of God. This is the internal testimony and affirmation that the Spirit provides about the divine status of the Bible. It is the Holy Spirit who generates faith, the assurance of truth of the divine origin of the Bible. 'Indeed', Owen writes, 'that all which is properly called faith, with respect unto divine revelation, and is accepted with God as such, with respect unto divine revelation, and is accepted with God as such, is the work of the Spirit of God in us, or is bestowed on us by him'. The second part of divine illumination is the opening of the mind to understand the truth of the biblical texts. It is the actual work of the spirit to illuminate the mind so it can be able to see what God reveals in his written text (p. 113).

[31] See Dayton, *Theological Roots of Pentecostalism*, pp. 35-60.
[32] Philemon, *Pneumatic Hermeneutics*, pp. 127-28.

inspiration of the community by the Spirit is also incorporated in Wesley's view. Prayer allows the HS to be active in the work of the biblical interpreter and in the entire sanctification experience of the Church as an interpretive community.

While Wesley fully affirms the HS's constant illumination or inspiration to provide direction and aid in the Christian life, he often insists that Scripture is reliable and trustworthy as the origin of God's self-revelation. To press forward his view, Wesley distinguishes between Scripture as a 'rule' and the Spirit as a 'guide' in our lives. In doing so, Wesley shows caution, introducing a significant restriction on this understanding of the Spirit's influence on the interpretation to prevent the danger of 'enthusiasm', which he describes as 'a religious madness arising from some falsely imagined influence or inspiration of God'.[33] Wesley's distinction contributes helpful guidance and illumination to how readers/hearers engage the HS in the theological reading of Scripture.

The brief survey of the major Christian movements and representative Protestant theologians regarding the role of the HS in the inspiration, illumination, and interpretation of Scripture provides sufficient evidence that before the ascent of the historical-critical method, the HS was viewed as having an integral role when interpreting Scripture and applying it to daily life.[34] The ecclesial bodies also held a crucial role in the interpretation of Scripture, while each movement configured the interplay between the HS, Scripture, and community quite differently. In summary, it appears, then, that acknowledging and relying on the HS when engaged in theological reading/hearing of Scripture is not a new phenomenon. Rather, integrating the HS with an emphasis on inspiration and illumination of the Scriptures for knowledge, direction, and personal transformation in relation to ecclesia and the larger world is in full accord with historic Christian tradition, of which the Pentecostal movement drinks deeply.

Relative to the role of the HS in Pentecostal hermeneutics, Lee Roy Martin provides a linkage between modern Pentecostalism and the early Church when he asserts 'The hermeneutics of the apostles

---

[33] Philemon, *Pneumatic Hermeneutics*, pp. 127-28.
[34] See the content of fn. 29, 30 for summaries of Philemon's treatments.

changed on the Day of Pentecost'.[35] While the apostles continued to employ many accepted Jewish interpretative practices, their approach to Scripture was radically altered by four new contextual factors:

> 1. the life, teachings, and resurrection of Jesus; 2. the gift of the Holy Spirit poured out on the Day of Pentecost; 3. the mission of spreading the gospel, which demanded that the disciples go with haste into the world; 4. the eschatological nature of Jesus' kingdom, which required the disciples to wait patiently for the return of Jesus.[36]

Similarly, early twentieth-century Pentecostals found it incumbent to revise their hermeneutics in the light of their experiences of being baptized with the HS. Their use of the Bible Reading Method,[37] inherited from the holiness movement, was altered by the new reality of HS baptism.

In general, Pentecostals apprehend and value the presence and work of the HS from the formation of the interpreter within the community to the creation of the interpretative community. Moreover, the HS is perceived to be engaged at every juncture of interpretation, from the discernment of the diverse voices in Scripture to the formation of the gathered canon of Scripture.[38] Pentecostals also understand that the role of the HS in the interpretation of Scripture is 'to lead and guide the community in understanding the present meaningfulness of Scripture',[39] empowering us to read/hear the text with a 'new clarity that could

---

[35] Martin (ed.), *Pentecostal Hermeneutics: A Reader*, pp. 285-90.

[36] Martin (ed.), *Pentecostal Hermeneutics: A Reader*, pp. 285-90.

[37] Archer, *A Pentecostal Hermeneutic*, p. 268. Archer defines Bible Reading Method in the following terms:
> A synchronic commonsensical interpretive method that relied upon commonsense inductive and deductive reasoning. The method was used to trace key themes and topics throughout Scripture and then synthesize this biblical information into a doctrine. The Bible Reading Method was the primary exegetical method used by early Pentecostals in its formation of doctrine.

[38] Thomas, 'What the Spirit is Saying to the Church', pp. 128-29.

[39] Archer, *A Pentecostal Hermeneutic*, p. 248. See Clark Pinnock, 'The Work of the Holy Spirit from the Perspective of a Charismatic Biblical Theologian', *JPT* 18 (2009), pp. 157-71.

not be possible without this aid'.⁴⁰ Land describes the authority and efficacy of Scripture as finally dependent on the relation of the Spirit to Christ. This means that the Word and Spirit are wed so that no thought or action is truly scriptural if it is not 'communicated out of the fullness of the Spirit'. It is this that makes the Scriptures authoritatively effective 'as the Spirit formed Christ in Mary, so the Spirit uses Scripture to form Christ in believers and vice-versa'.⁴¹ Additionally, Mark Cartledge suggests, 'Pneumatology provides the link between text and community, since the Spirit has both inspired the original text and inspires the reading of the text today'.⁴² Similarly, Clark Pinnock posits Scripture is a gift of the HS that is at the disposition of the HS for new and subtle uses.⁴³ As a creation of the Spirit, the community attends to and anticipates the HS to inspire the Scriptures for their *Sitz im Leben*.⁴⁴ Reliance on the HS by Pentecostals reflects their 'radical openness to the invasion and intervention of God's Spirit in our daily lives'.⁴⁵ The intervention by the HS leads to transformation when the triad of Spirit-Word-Community is engaged.⁴⁶ As the ultimate interpreter of the Word of God, the HS is dependent upon the community of readers/hearers and the Scriptures for the creation of new meaning.⁴⁷

---

⁴⁰ John W. McKay, 'When the Veil Is Taken Away: The Impact of Prophetic Experience on Biblical Interpretation', *JPT* 5 (1994), pp. 17-40 (21).

⁴¹ Land, *Pentecostal Spirituality*, p. 94.

⁴² Mark J. Cartledge, 'Text-Community-Spirit: The Challenges Posed by Pentecostal Theological Method to Evangelical Theology', in K.L. Spawn and A.T. Wright (eds.), *Spirit & Scripture: Examining a Pneumatic Hermeneutic* (London: T&T Clark, 2012), p. 140.

⁴³ Clark Pinnock, 'The Work of the Spirit in the Interpretation of Scripture from the Perspective of a Charismatic Biblical Theologian', Martin, Lee Roy (ed.), *Pentecostal Hermeneutics: A Reader* (Leiden: Brill, 2013), pp. 233-48.

⁴⁴ John Wesley wrote, 'The Spirit of God not only once inspired those who wrote the Bible but continually inspires those who read it with earnest prayer'. Cited in Clark Pinnock, 'The Work of the Holy Spirit in Hermeneutics', *JPT* 2 (1993), pp. 3-23 (4).

⁴⁵ Terry L. Cross, 'The Divine-Human Encounter: Towards a Pentecostal Theology of Experience', *Pneuma* 31 (2009), pp. 3-34 (6).

⁴⁶ Cross, 'The Divine-Human Encounter', p. 7.

⁴⁷ Archer, *A Pentecostal Hermeneutic*, p. 247.

Pentecostals view the HS's ministry as an extension of the crucified, resurrected, and glorified Christ's[48] ministry that extends to all persons, the community of faith, and the world. As the extension of Christ, the HS operates in numerous ways within the community. Pentecostals testify to feeling the presence of God/HS/Jesus in the worshiping community.[49] The Spirit's presence is perceived within the corporate body through community worship, preaching, prayer, testimonies, anointed singing, glossolalia, and the operation of the gifts of the Spirit.[50] Discerning the Spirit's presence and leading evokes diverse responses from persons in the community; namely, hand-raising, audible praise, clapping, shouting, weeping, falling prostrate, dancing, and running. These embodied acknowledgments of the HS's presence and leading are valued to be in concert with responses to God expressed in the worship of Israel, especially in the Psalms. Since embodied worship is contained within Scripture, twentieth-century Pentecostals deem precedent has been set and is valid and apropos for the community.

Pentecostals discern the HS is not restricted to working in the worshiping community alone. Rather, the HS is active in faith communities outside the realm of the Pentecostal movement. The unifying impulse of the HS compels Pentecostals to establish relational connections and dialogue in order to discern points of continuity and discontinuity in order to advance ecumenical, as well as inter-faith, dialogue. Similarly, since the Spirit is operative throughout the world, 'Pentecostals will discern what the Spirit is saying to them from outside their community, which may be both typical and yet surprising for the Pentecostal community'.[51]

Generally, Pentecostals maintain the HS is no less active in present-day biblical interpretation than in the ancient composition of these texts. Clark Pinnock dismisses altogether the distinction of 'inspiration' and 'illumination,' insisting they are only two modes of the same inspiration – 'contemporary' and 'original'.[52] In any case,

---

[48] See John 13-17, in the farewell discourse of Jesus, where he explicates the crucial role of the HS in the life of the Christian community and the larger society.

[49] Land, *Pentecostal Spirituality*, pp. 3-9; Archer, 'I Was in The Spirit', p. 54.

[50] Archer, *A Pentecostal Hermeneutic*, p. 249.

[51] Archer, *A Pentecostal Hermeneutic*, p. 250.

[52] Clark Pinnock, 'The Work of the Holy Spirit in Hermeneutics', *JPT* 2 (1993), pp. 3-23.

the witness of countless Pentecostals indicates that the interpretive process is a supernatural event due to the presence of the HS.[53]

Word

Pentecostals have held and continue to hold a high view of the Christian Bible, viewing the Word of God as the graciously-given written revelation of God to humanity, bearing witness to the revelation of Jesus Christ.[54] Ellington characterizes the role of Scripture within the Pentecostal community as 'the basic rule of faith and practice' which provides 'the corrective and interpretive authority for all religious experience'.[55] He then argues that Pentecostals do not base their understanding of biblical authority on a doctrine of inspiration. Rather, biblical authority is established by their experience of God. Holy Scripture then 'adds language to the relationship which exists between the believer and God'. The Bible serves as 'the word of God' because Pentecostals experience God in the Scripture. Therefore, 'what the Bible says is identical with what God said'.[56]

As 'people of the Book' Pentecostals find themselves located in the metanarrative of Scripture and read their Bible with an appreciation and apprehension of the entire narrative. More specifically, the Hebrew Bible and the NT are regarded as one story unfolding the revelation of Jesus Christ as the focal point of God's engagement with all creation.[57]

---

[53] McKay, 'When the Veil is Taken Away', pp. 17-40 (21), offers the following regarding Pentecostals and the interpretive process:
> They tell of passages illuminated in many ways, of texts that take on new meaningfulness, of verses that burned themselves into the memory, of completely new appreciations of whole books of the Bible, of a positive urge to read page after page of the text, of exciting new discoveries about God's self-revelation in Scripture, and so forth.

[54] C.H. Pinnock, *The Scripture Principle* (San Francisco: Harper & Row, Publishers, 1984), p. xix.

[55] Ellington, 'Pentecostalism and the Authority of Scripture', *JPT* 4.9 (1996), pp. 16-38 (21).

[56] Ellington, 'Pentecostalism and the Authority of Scripture', p. 21.

[57] Green, *Toward a Pentecostal Theology*, p. 188, posits

The apprehension of their place in the metanarrative of God's revelation informs Pentecostals of the fundamental narrativity of the Word. As the essential story and guide on orthodoxy (right belief), but also on orthopraxy (right action), and orthopathy (right affections),[58] it is incumbent on Pentecostal interpreters to read/hear the Scriptures narratively to appreciate and apprehend the drama of *Heilsgeschichte*. J.K.A. Smith posits that 'Pentecostal spirituality is perhaps perfectly attuned to narrative as a fundamental and irreducible mode of understanding and is uniquely situated to hear Scripture testify of the overall plot of God's rescue of his creation'.[59]

Again, the interdependent dialogical nature of interpretation depends on the Word being made alive through the presence and power of the HS to assist singular persons and the community to discern the voice of God and apply the same. The Spirit is 'centrally valued in the creation, transmission, reception, and application of the text'.[60]

Thus, as Pentecostals read/hear the Word, it becomes 'an event of the Spirit in which the reader is transformed and made to experience what the Bible puts forth as living truth'.[61] On the one hand, for Pentecostals, the fact that the Word was originally reported in a different historical context does not restrain its applicability. On the other hand, Macchia avers that for Pentecostals, there is a 'certain "present-tenseness" to the events and words of Scripture, so that

---

A growing number of Pentecostals are distancing themselves from traditional evangelical descriptions of the nature and authority of Scripture, including the notion of *sola Scriptura*. This move is not intended to undermine the authority of Scripture, but to avoid reductionistic accounts of how that authority works. By playing up the importance of the Spirit's and community's shared roles in interpretation, Pentecostals are seeking to avoid treating Scripture as an object rather than a living word which interprets us and through which the Spirit flows in ways that we cannot dictate, calculate, or program. The aim is to allow Scripture to be truly God's Word.

[58] Land, *Pentecostal Spirituality*, pp. 1, 30-37.

[59] Smith, *Thinking in Tongues*, p. 69.

[60] Keith Warrington, *Pentecostal Theology: A Theology of Encounter* (London: T&T Clark, 2008), p. 199.

[61] F.D. Macchia, 'Theology, Pentecostal', in S.M. Burgess and E.M. van der Maas (eds.), *NIDPCM* (Grand Rapids: MI, 2002), pp. 1120-41 (1122).

what happened then happens now'.⁶² Therefore, Pentecostals read/hear the Word of God as participants in the stories, not as observers. 'In this way Pentecostals have an *experiential* relationship with Scripture as they relate to and participate in the *world* of the text'.⁶³ John McKay emphasizes this point when he offers an analogy from 'the world of drama, the academic being in some ways like the reviewer whose task is to analyse, criticize and comment on the play, the charismatic more like the producer or the performer on stage'.⁶⁴

Pentecostals gravitate toward focusing on the final canonical form of the Word. The concerns of the historical-critical method, focusing on the world behind the text, are not as important to Pentecostals as the world within and in front of the text.⁶⁵ It is the canonical form of the biblical narrative that shapes the reader/hearer enabling them to establish a praxis-oriented understanding of life.⁶⁶ As such, the Scriptures are to be read/heard as one coherent story; namely, the 'drama of salvation history'.⁶⁷ Due to the understanding of the biblical narrative as story, Pentecostals are drawn to and privilege narrative sections of the Word.⁶⁸ 'As readers and hearers, they become caught up in the stories of Scripture and, as a result, they are invited to experience transformation'.⁶⁹

---

⁶² Macchia, 'Theology, Pentecostal', p. 1122. Also, Cross, 'The Divine-Human Encounter', p. 5, where Cross asserts that 'At least part of what we are claiming when we say we have experienced God is that the God of the Bible is the one who encounters us in the history of our own lives'.

⁶³ Archer, '*I Was in The Spirit*', p. 47. Emphasis original.

⁶⁴ McKay, 'When the Veil is Taken Away', pp. 1-40 (19).

⁶⁵ Martin, *The Unheard Voice of God*, p. 14.

⁶⁶ Archer, *A Pentecostal Hermeneutic*, p. 228.

⁶⁷ Green, *Toward a Pentecostal Theology*, p. 189.

⁶⁸ Warrington, *Pentecostal Theology*, p. 191.

⁶⁹ Pinnock, 'The Work of the Holy Spirit in the Interpretation of Scripture', p. 170:

> [T]he Spirit bears unique testimony to the living God as revealed in Jesus Christ. Readers get caught up and get lost in the text and are changed. Scripture is less the demand to submit to God than it is an invitation to indwell the narrative of God's grace. The task is not an attempt to adapt the words of Scripture to our reality but an invitation to make sense of our reality within its purview of new creation. The reader, by means of interpretation, enters into and appropriates the world of meaning that the text projects. The text creates a space into which the reader is being invited for transformation.

Community

The strategic move to include the community as a core element of a Pentecostal hermeneutic appears to reflect two concerns: first, to adopt the model of Word-Community-Spirit demonstrated by John Christopher Thomas, Rick D. Moore, Lee Roy Martin, Melissa Archer, Chris E.W. Green, and Larry McQueen,[70] and second, to limit the practice of 'private interpretation' noted heretofore. Melissa Archer asserts, 'The effects of distortions of the Word seem to have shifted the focus from private interpretation to a communal context'.[71] To this point, Chris E.W. Green asserts, 'Increasingly, Pentecostal scholars are insisting on the authoritative role of the community and the interpretive process. So much so that a consensus seems to have emerged: interpretation is ultimately a communal undertaking.'[72]

The gathered community is then viewed as the 'social-cultural context in which interpretation takes place'.[73] Therefore, of necessity, it is 'in the community's discussion of Scripture that God's intended meaning is negotiated'.[74] In other words, since the community is created by the Spirit, it is within the community that the Word is interpreted through the leading of the same Spirit. The interdependence of the Spirit, community, and the Word enables the

---

[70] Moore, 'Canon and Charisma', pp. 75-92; Thomas, 'Women, Pentecostals and the Bible', pp. 41-56; Yong, *Spirit-Word-Community*; Archer, *A Pentecostal Hermeneutic*; Green, *Toward a Pentecostal Theology*; Archer, 'I Was in The Spirit'; and McQueen, *Joel and the Spirit*.

[71] Archer, '*I Was in The Spirit*', pp. 48-49:
Reading the Scriptures within the community of believers helps guard against interpretations that are dogmatic, divisive and thus ultimately and fundamentally flawed. It is the community of faith which facilitates the uniting of a myriad of contrasting, individual lives, context utilized applications of meaning and an arena of mutual coherence and significance.

[72] Green, *Toward a Pentecostal Theology*, p. 190. See Archer's, 'Pentecostal Story', p. 37: 'The hermeneuts and the methods are not isolated islands. Both the methods and the hermeneuts are socially, culturally, and theologically shaped entities that contribute to the making of meaning. In order for interpretation to take place, the reader must participate.'

[73] Archer, 'Pentecostal Story: The Hermeneutical Filter for the Making of Meaning', pp. 36-59 (39). Also see Archer, *A Pentecostal Hermeneutic*, p. 213.

[74] Green, *Toward a Pentecostal Theology*, p. 190.

apprehension of the meaning of Scripture for the present-day context due to the dialogical nature of the text and the community of readers/hearers. It is this dialogue about the Word in view of community members' shared experiences that the HS makes a right interpretation feasible.[75]

Kenneth Archer asserts that a communication event occurs when the community reads/hears the biblical text. The text desires to be understood and the community desires to hear the text, allowing the Word to fulfill its dialogical role in the communicative event. The receptivity to the Word by the Pentecostal community proceeds from the collective valuation of the Bible as 'sacred revelation – the inspired, authoritative word of God' that can speak 'clearly and creatively as the word of God to the contemporary Pentecostal community's situation and needs'.[76] The above approach empowers the community 'to live faithfully before and with the living God'.[77]

The current Pentecostal attention given to the history of effects (*Wirkungsgeschichte*)[78] in relation to the interpretative endeavor flows

---

[75] See Green, *Toward a Pentecostal Theology*, p. 186 for his assertion that 'Apart from the Spirit's help, the faithful, and effective reading of Scripture as God's Word is, quite simply, impossible'.

[76] Archer, *A Pentecostal Hermeneutic*, p. 214.

[77] Archer, *A Pentecostal Hermeneutic*, p. 214.

[78] The initial call for Pentecostals to utilize *Wirkungsgeschichte* came from J.C. Thomas, 'Pentecostal Theology in the Twenty-First Century', *Pneuma* 20 (1998), pp. 3–19. For attempts of this approach, see L.R. McQueen, *Joel and the Spirit*, pp. 69–89; H.L. Landrus, 'Hearing 3 John 2 in the Voices of History', *JPT* 11.1 (2002), pp. 70–88; J.C. Thomas and K.E. Alexander, '"And the Signs are Following": Mark 16.9–20 – A Journey into Pentecostal Hermeneutics', *JPT* 11.2 (2003), pp. 147–70; J.C. Thomas, 'Healing in the Atonement: A Johannine Perspective', *JPT* 14.1 (2005), pp. 175–89; Alexander, *Pentecostal Healing*, pp. 64–194; L.R. McQueen, *Toward a Pentecostal Eschatology: Discerning the Way Forward* (JPTSup 39; Dorset: Deo Publishing, 2012), pp. 60–199; Green, *Toward a Pentecostal Theology*, pp. 74–181; J.S. Lamp, 'New Heavens and New Earth: Early Pentecostal Soteriology as a Foundation for Creation Care in the Present', *Pneuma* 36.1 (2014), pp. 64–80; Archer, *'I Was in the Spirit on the Lord's Day'*, pp. 68–118; H.O. Bryant, *Spirit Christology in the Christian Tradition: From the Patristic Period to the Rise of Pentecostalism in the Twentieth Century* (Cleveland, TN: CPT Press, 2015), pp. 464–508; L.R. Martin, 'The Function and Practice of Fasting in Early Pentecostalism', *JPT* 96 (2015), pp. 1–19; D.R. Johnson, 'The Mark of the Beast, Reception History, and Early Pentecostal Literature', *JPT* 25.2 (2016), pp. 184–202; A.R. Jackson, 'Wesleyan Holiness and Finished Work Pentecostal Interpretations of Gog and Magog Biblical Texts', *JPT* 25.2 (2016), pp. 168–83.

seamlessly from the emphasis on the role of the community. John Christopher Thomas correlates attending to the history of effects with hearing 'voices from the church with regard to a given book is like hearing testimonies of the effect this or that book has had in the church'.[79] Most notably demonstrated by Ulrich Luz, *Wirkungsgeschichte* attempts to discern the impact or effect that biblical texts have had on the Church and society throughout the centuries, as well as how the various traditions have impacted the interpretation of the biblical texts.[80] On the one hand, Luz avows the 'historical-critical method does deal with the area of experience, but it is the experience of persons in the past'.[81] On the other hand, picking up on the position of Eugen Drewemann, Luz asserts that in itself, the historical-critical method 'cannot lead to a theological insight in the *lasting* significance of the text.[82]

Christianity has a relationship with Scripture as its sacred text, the history between the texts and its reader cannot be separated because this history 'is an expression of the text's own power'.[83]

> Whatever we say about the biblical texts presupposes that we already have a relationship with them – directly, because we already know, love, or hate them; or indirectly, because we take part in a culture dominated by Christianity and speak a language formed by the Bible. We too are a product of the affective history of the Bible.[84]

The history of effects approach abandons the futile attempt of seeking to approach the text from a purely objective, positivistic, distant, and neutral posture.

Interpreters employing a historical-critical approach alone argue the text can have only one intended meaning. To the contrary, Luz asserts that '*There is no uniquely true interpretation of a text*'.[85] Pressing his point, Luz posits that *Wirkungsgeschichte* '*describes* the ditch between

---

[79] Thomas, 'Pentecostal Theology in the Twenty-First Century', pp. 3-19 (16).
[80] Luz follows Gadamer, who is the first to use the term. Ulrich Luz, *Matthew in History: Interpretation, Influence, and Effects* (Minneapolis: Fortress Press, 1994).
[81] Luz, *Matthew in History*, p. 9.
[82] Luz, *Matthew in History*, p. 9. Emphasis original.
[83] Luz, *Matthew in History*, p. 24.
[84] Luz, *Matthew in History*, p. 25.
[85] Luz, *Matthew in History*, p. 26. Emphasis original.

past and present and makes clear that there was never an interpretation of a text that did not bear the mark of the historical situation of its interpreter'.[86]

While the text itself is stable and fixed, interpretations of texts are revisioned as they are read in new contexts or as a consequence of new experiences in the life of the interpreter or the experiences of a community.[87]

These new experiences and dynamic occurrences stimulate hearers/readers to study and interpret texts in fresh and meaningful ways, albeit with some limits. A text cannot become pliable to the point of serving as the recipient of projections and biases of the interpreter or community. Texts have been and (continue to be) misinterpreted. This, too, is an important part of effective history.[88]

A vital contribution of the *Wirkungsgeschichte* approach to Scripture is that it stresses the power biblical texts possess as expressions of 'the living Christ'. Commenting on the fruit of patristic interpreters, Luz avers that their Christological and pneumatic exegesis offers the following outcomes:

1. When all the biblical texts are expressions of a present reality, the living Christ, then every interpretation is guided by our experience and understanding of this living Christ. There is an element of personal identity and personal faith that belongs to all interpretations of biblical texts. They are not 'alien' to the interpreter.

2. When the biblical texts become expressions of the living Christ, the barrier between past and present that we experience is eliminated. Christ, about whom the texts speak, never is merely past reality. There is no possibility of a 'mere' past that has nothing to do with us.

3. When the biblical texts become expressions of the living Christ, they speak with one voice, the voice of the living Christ of faith. Therefore they do not fall apart into many different, unconnected,

---

[86] Luz, *Matthew in History*, p. 26. Emphasis original.
[87] Luz, *Matthew in History*, p. 26.
[88] Luz, *Matthew in History*, p. 28.

or even contradicting testimonies of different biblical witnesses, between which modern interpreters have to choose.[89]

Consequently, Scripture is held in utmost regard as a living word for the present, rather than a static book of regulations belonging to the past. Biblical interpretation, then, as informed by the living Christ, continues to bring the power of Scripture to bear on the ever-changing milieu and situations in the Church's life.

Emerson Powery views *Wirkungsgeschichte* as a beneficial approach for Pentecostals in their reading/hearing of texts because it 'requires that we examine the effects of different interpretations, including our own, as a basis for judging the validity of particular readings of the sacred texts'.[90] Furthermore, Powery asserts that Pentecostals should be concerned with 'the effects our readings have had throughout our history and in the present-day on the Pentecostal movement'.[91] The history of effects approach complements the Spirit-Word-Community rubric as an integral dialogue partner in reading/hearing the canonical form of the biblical text. Similarly, M. Archer rightly states that an *Wirkungsgeschichte* approach that engages early Pentecostal literature 'holds much promise for connecting the movement with its historical and theological roots and enabling contemporary Pentecostals[92] to be in 'experiential continuity' with early Pentecostalism as they hear the testimonies of their spiritual ancestors.[93]

---

[89] Luz, *Matthew in History*, pp. 36-37.

[90] Emerson B. Powery, 'Ulrich Luz's *Matthew in History*: A Contribution to Pentecostal Hermeneutics?' *JPT* 14 (1999), pp. 3-17. (15).

[91] Powery, 'Ulrich Luz's *Matthew in History*', p. 15.

[92] Archer, '*I Was in The Spirit*', p. 60. Land, *Pentecostal Spirituality*, p. 221 proffers the following challenge to Pentecostals: 'Contemporary Pentecostals should explore what it would mean to be in experiential continuity with the early movement in light of the claim to be in continuity with the apostolic church'.

[93] For the foundational role that testimonies play in Pentecostal Spirituality, see Johns, *Pentecostal Formation*, pp. 126-27:

> Testimony is the means of you meshing the realities of life with the ongoing story of the faith community. Among Pentecostals, testimony can serve as a way of 'decoding reality' in order to analyze it for further action and reflection. It serves as a corporate liturgy, in which all are invited to speak, for each person has a testimony – a story – which when offered to the community serves to

The community holds a crucial role in the interpretation of Scripture. Consequently, a self-reflective mindset needs to be maintained to avoid projecting interpretations onto the biblical text. While not intended to serve as a cautionary warning, the groundbreaking work by Rick D. Moore serves to guide the community in its interpretative work. Moore discerns in Deuteronomy a Pentecostal 'theology of Revelation' that allows for 'two revelatory channels, that of canonical writing and charismatic speech'.[94] Moore contends that 'Spirit-impelled *speech* is divinely purposed to keep Israel from losing touch with the God who speaks and is spoken of in the *written* texts'.[95] While he readily acknowledges that a 'close linkage' remains between the scripted Word and the 'charismatic utterance', Moore believes Deuteronomy teaches that each revelation medium would have its own respective function.[96]

Deuteronomy here seems to see the essential and distinct contribution of charismatic revelation in terms of the manifesting of God's nearness in a way that counters an idolatrous manufacturing of divine presence, on one hand, and a legalistic distancing of divine word, on the other.[97]

Moore's analysis argues for the necessity of holding Word and Spirit in creative tension to avoid 'a Spirit-less Word (rationalism), on the one hand, and a Word-less Spirit (subjectivism), on the other'.[98] In other words, Pentecostal hermeneutics depends, in part, on the

---

empower others ... [Testimonies] offer alternative realities when placed in dialogue with the Christian story. When a person has experienced an encounter with God, they are usually asked to testify. This serves to submit individual experience to corporate judgment (with Scripture being held as the final authority) and to allow for experience to be given interpretive meaning.

See also Thomas, 'What the Spirit is Saying to the Church', p. 118, who advocates that the testimonies of early Pentecostals must also be heard within the present-day Pentecostal community: 'I would suggest that for the Pentecostal interpreter the hearing of testimonies should not be limited to the contemporary voices of the Pentecostal community but be extended by means of *Wirkungsgeschichte* to include the voices of those who have preceded us in discerning their way on this narrative journey'.

[94] Moore, 'Canon and Charisma', p. 79.
[95] Moore, 'Canon and Charisma', p. 82.
[96] Green, *Toward a Pentecostal Theology*, pp. 189-95.
[97] Moore, 'Canon and Charisma', p. 89.
[98] Moore, 'Canon and Charisma', p. 91.

willingness and ability to allow the Spirit's '*dynamic* word' expressed through the charismata, to illuminate the '*enduring* word' of the biblical texts.[99]

Conclusion

In summary, through the reading/hearing of Scripture within a Spirit-led community, Pentecostals experience nothing less than 'theophany, a divine encounter, a revelation, and experience with the living God'.[100] It is via the reading/hearing of Scripture that believers anticipate being formed by the HS into Christ's image as members of the body of Christ. Moreover, Pentecostals trust that God's revelatory Word will be provided when gathering as a Spirit-led community, appealing to the Scriptures in search of guidance and discernment.

---

[99] Moore, 'Canon and Charisma', p. 89. Emphasis original.
[100] Green, *Toward a Pentecostal Theology*, p. 183.

PART I
HEARING THE VOICES OF THE COMMUNITY

Wirkungsgeschichte avers that before engaging in a close reading of Matthew and Romans 6 it is necessary to apprehend how the Pentecostal community interpreted the selected texts, reflected theologically on WB, and was, in turn, effected by those interpretations. Thus, before proceeding to Matthew and Romans 6, we will first attempt to hear the voices of the modern (1932 to present) Pentecostal community regarding their interpretation of the texts, subsequent theological constructions, and praxis before hearing the voices of the early Pentecostals.

3

WATER BAPTISM IN PENTECOSTAL PERSPECTIVE(S): 1932 TO PRESENT

Introduction

It is commonly believed, both within and without the movement, that Pentecostals have given relatively little attention to sacramental practice and theology. The facts are that Pentecostals have often employed the via negativa when speaking about the sacraments, focusing on what they do not believe rather than stating their beliefs in a positive manner. However, this is not the whole of the story. Since Steven J. Land's *Pentecostal Spirituality*[1] was published in 1993, scholars have devoted increased attention to the sacraments, on occasion with the intent of developing a self-consciously Pentecostal theology of the sacraments.

Specifically, Chris E.W. Green recently published his PhD thesis[2] in which he makes the case for the Lord's Supper as sacrament. He examines the state of Pentecostal theological reflection with regard to the sacraments, generally, and the Lord's Supper, in particular. With the above developments in mind, this chapter examines the state of Pentecostal theological reflection, focusing on WB alone. By and large, this chapter focuses on engagement with *scholarly* Pentecostal works and those written by key Pentecostal leaders of the classical Pentecostal denominations. While not exhaustive in scope,

---

[1] Land, *Pentecostal Spirituality*.
[2] Green, *Toward a Pentecostal Theology*.

the chapter attempts to engage the aforementioned works from various strands of the Pentecostal movement. These works are engaged in chronological order, ranging from 1932 to the present day. This chapter, then, is dedicated to engagement of Pentecostal theological scholarship, while a separate chapter is devoted to the literature of the first generation of Pentecostals (1906-1931).

Reading Pentecostals on Water Baptism

Myer Pearlman

In 1937 Pearlman, a faculty member of Central Bible Institute and a prolific author,[3] published *Knowing the Doctrines of the Bible*,[4] a volume read and studied by several generations of AG ministers. According to AG historian Edith Blumhofer, 'For many years his books (especially *Knowing the Doctrines of the Bible*) were standard texts in Assemblies of God schools'.[5] In chapter 10, entitled 'Church' Pearlman sets forth his view of WB under the rubric, 'The Ordinances of the Church'. For Pearlman NT Christianity is not a ritualistic religion since the heart of it is humanity's direct encounter with God through the HS.

Nonetheless, Pearlman first asserts that these two ceremonies are ordinances since they are divinely ordained: namely, the Lord's Supper and WB. He allows that due to their sacred character the two ceremonies are sometimes described as sacraments.[6] Second, they 'are also referred to as ordinances because they are ceremonies "ordained" by the Lord Himself'.[7] Pearlman offers that WB is the rite of entrance into the church based on faith in Jesus Christ and is therefore to be administered only once since there can be only one

---

[3] William W. Menzies, *Anointed to Serve: The Story of the Assemblies of God* (Springfield, MO: Gospel Publishing House, 1971), pp. 172-73; G.W. Gohr, 'Pearlman, Myer', in Stanley M. Burgess and Eduard M. van der Maas (eds.), *NIDPCM* (rev. and exp. edn; Grand Rapids, MI: Zondervan, 2002), p. 959.

[4] Myer Pearlman, *Knowing the Doctrines of the Bible* (Springfield, MO: Gospel Publishing House, 1937). Revised 1981.

[5] Edith L. Blumhofer, *The Assemblies of God: A Chapter in the Story of American Pentecostalism*, vol. 1 (Springfield, MO: Gospel Publishing House, 1989), pp. 318-19.

[6] Pearlman, *Knowing the Doctrines*, p. 352.

[7] Pearlman, *Knowing the Doctrines*, p. 353.

beginning of life in Christ Jesus.[8] Third, he posits that they be valued as 'means of grace' through which we may grow spiritually, assuming we participate 'intelligently' and discern the spiritual realities 'beyond' the ceremonies.[9] In his usage of 'means of grace' Pearlman appears to reflect Wesleyan influence on his thought.

Addressing the 'mode' of WB, Pearlman writes that the preferred means is immersion since Greek scholars and church historians confirm that 'baptize' used in the formula 'means literally to dip or to immerse'.[10] While Pearlman acknowledges the evolution of sprinkling and pouring as accepted practice, he reminds his readers that 'The Scriptural, original mode is by immersion, which is true to the symbolical meaning of baptism, namely death, burial, and resurrection. Rom. 6.1-4.'[11]

Writing to address issues relevant to the proper baptismal 'formula' Pearlman rejects the position of the Pentecostal Assemblies of the World (Oneness) that Acts 2.38, 'Be baptized every one of you in the name of Jesus Christ' is the proper baptismal formula. Rather, he asserts that it is 'a statement that such persons were baptized as (they) acknowledged Jesus to be Lord and Christ'.[12] Citing the 'Didache', Pearlman asserts the Trinitarian formula, 'Baptizing them in the name of the Father, and of the Son, and of the Holy Ghost' (Mt. 28.19) is the prescribed formula.[13] While the Trinitarian formula is to be employed by the officiant the candidate is to be immersed only once despite the fact that there are some Pentecostals groups that practice triple immersion in correspondence to the Trinitarian formula.[14]

---

[8] Pearlman, *Knowing the Doctrines*, p. 353.

[9] Pearlman, 'The Bread and Blood Covenant', p. 2.

[10] Pearlman, *Knowing the Doctrines*, p. 353.

[11] Pearlman, *Knowing the Doctrines*, p. 354.

[12] Pearlman, *Knowing the Doctrines*, p. 354. Cf. D. William Faupel, *The Everlasting Gospel: The Significance of Eschatology in the Development of Pentecostal Thought* (JPTSup 10; Sheffield: Sheffield Academic Press, 1996), pp. 228-306 for an excellent discussion of the history, dynamics, theological implications, and divisiveness within the movement around this issue.

[13] Pearlman, *Knowing the Doctrines*, p. 354.

[14] Cf. Cecil M. Robeck, Jr. and Jerry L. Sandidge, 'The Ecclesiology of Koinonia and Baptism: A Pentecostal Perspective', *JES* 27.3 (Summer 1990), pp. 511-12 who assert that 'numerous groups ... among them the Apostolic Faith Mission of South

From the preceding it is no surprise that Pearlman limits qualified recipients of baptism to persons who have 'sincerely repent[ed] of their sins and exercise a living faith in the Lord Jesus Christ'.[15] Yet in itself WB has no saving power. Rather, 'people, are baptized not in order to be saved but because they are saved'.[16] Therefore, while baptism is not absolutely essential for salvation, Pearlman opines that 'we may insist that it is essential to full obedience'.[17] While Pearlman advocates for *infant dedication* based on Mt. 19.13, 14, he flatly rejects the practice of infant baptism. Infants are logically excluded from baptism since they have no sins of which to repent and cannot exercise faith.[18]

In unpacking the meaning of WB Pearlman employs the following four theological categories: salvation, experience, regeneration, and testimony. He offers that baptism is a 'sacred drama' illustrating the fundamentals of the gospel. Specifically, the lowering of the convert

---

Africa and various African Independent Churches … immerse three times, employing the Trinitarian formula'. Jerome declared the triune-immersionist emphasis to be an established tradition in his day (400 C.E.) and this clearly separates it from 'Jesus' Name' or 'Oneness' Pentecostals in South Africa by emphasizing the Trinitarian nature of baptism. The origins for this baptismal practice probably lie with the Christian Apostolic Church in Zion, IL, John Alexander Dowie's work. Tom Hezmalhalch and John G. Lake, founders of the Apostolic Faith Mission Church in South Africa, both spent time in Zion with Dowie, a triple immersionist, before going to Africa. Apparently, Charles F. Parham practiced triple-immersion baptism for a while before rejecting the practice.

[15] Pearlman, *Knowing the Doctrines*, p. 355.
[16] Pearlman, *Knowing the Doctrines*, p. 355.
[17] Pearlman, *Knowing the Doctrines*, p. 355.
[18] Pearlman, *Knowing the Doctrines*, p. 355. Emphasis added. A noteworthy exception to the rejection of infant baptism among classical Pentecostals is the International Pentecostal Holiness Church (IPHC). They have no formal statement on the Lord's Supper or WB in their 'Articles of Faith'. They are; however, addressed in a section of the 'Bylaws' under the rubric 'Ordinances'. Apparently, it is a general statement, in keeping with the concerns of founder J.H. King that does not stipulate a specific mode to be employed in baptism. The discussion of mode occurs in a book authored by Paul F. Beacham in 1950. Endorsed by J.A. Synan, then chair of the denomination's leadership General Board of Administrators, Beacham argues that the Bible is ambiguous regarding mode of baptism and offers that 'All candidates for baptism shall have the right of choice in the various modes as practiced by evangelical denominations'. To date, this remains the official position on the mode of WB held by the (IPHC). The preceding cited from Robeck and Sandidge, 'The Ecclesiology of *Koinonia* and Baptism', p. 510.

portrays the accomplishment of Christ's death; the immersion of the candidate speaks of his or her death ratified; and the raising symbolizes the resurrection of Christ or the conquering of death.[19]

Ernest Swing Williams

In the final volume of his three-volume *Systematic Theology*,[20] Williams, an AG theologian, educator, and churchman,[21] devotes a full chapter to the 'ordinances of the church'. He names WB and the Lord's Supper as the only prescribed 'rites or ceremonies' of the church.[22] Published in 1953, Williams' *Systematic Theology*, 'the first systematic theology by a Pentecostal',[23] provides insight to the AG's position on the ordinances. Noteworthy in his treatment of these two ordinances is the fact that Williams writes less than one page on the Lord's Supper, while dedicating five pages to WB.

After addressing baptism in the OT and the baptism of John, Williams characterizes NT baptism as an ordinance instituted by our Lord Jesus Christ, citing Mt. 28.19. Per Williams, WB signifies our identification with Christ (Gal. 3.27). 'This identification is (1) In salvation (Acts 2.30); (2) In death to sin (Rom. 6.3-6); (3) In resurrection unto holiness (Col. 2.12).'[24]

Baptism is to be by immersion; sprinkling is to be rejected. Per Williams, others practice sprinkling through an erroneous application of OT passages to NT baptism.[25]

Williams offers that the 'one baptism' of Eph. 4.5 is probably Christian WB as opposed to the numerous baptisms or washings of the Jews. He rejects baptism as a saving ordinance, insisting that baptism and repentance go together and that baptism 'is an outward sign of an inward work' and 'the answer of a good conscience toward

---

[19] Pearlman, *Knowing the Doctrines*, p. 356.
[20] Ernest Swing Williams, *Systematic Theology* (3 vols.; Springfield, MO: Gospel Publishing House, 1953).
[21] Edith L. Blumhofer, *The Assemblies of God*, p. 261.
[22] Williams, *Systematic Theology*, III, p. 149.
[23] C.M. Robeck, Jr., 'Williams, Ernest Swing', in Stanley M. Burgess and Eduard M. van der Maas (eds.), *NIDPCM* (rev. and exp. edn; Grand Rapids, MI: Zondervan, 2002), pp. 1197-98.
[24] Williams, *Systematic Theology*, III, p. 150.
[25] Williams, *Systematic Theology*, III, p. 152.

God', quoting 1 Pet. 3.21.[26] Citing numerous Scriptures[27] that contain 'Repent ye and be baptized', he asserts that 'Baptism therefore follows, or accompanies repentance and salvation'.[28]

Since repentance and baptism go together, Williams rejects infant baptism as unscriptural since they 'know nothing about repentance and faith'.[29] Furthermore, Williams argues that since children are saved if they die in infancy because they die before accountability, baptism makes no change in their position. Somewhat ironically, Williams offers appreciation for the thoughtfulness of 'those who teach infant baptism in the dedication of children as the public sign of covenant relation', affirming the educational value for parents at such occasions.[30] It may be due to his earlier experience in Free Methodism[31] that allowed Williams to state that 'Were it not that infant baptism has become looked upon as a saving ordinance, we would have no objection to the use of water in connection with the dedication of children'.[32] When it comes to baptismal formula, Williams affirms those who practice triune immersion since they honor the Father, the Son, and the HS, opining that God honors the sincerity of their hearts.

He quickly adds that triune immersion is erroneous since baptism signifies identification with Christ and should therefore be single in act, signifying that 'For all of you who were baptized into Christ have clothed yourselves with Christ'. Gal. 3.27.[33]

M.A. Tomlinson

In 1961, while serving as general overseer of the COGOP, headquartered in Cleveland, TN, M.A. Tomlinson published *Basic Bible Beliefs*,[34] a collection of sermons previously delivered on the *Voice of Salvation* radio program. The author, the son of A.J.

---

[26] Williams, *Systematic Theology*, III, pp. 150-51.
[27] John 3.2, 6, 11; Mt. 28:19, 20; Mk 16.16; Acts 2.38; Rom. 6.3, 4.
[28] Williams, *Systematic Theology*, III, p. 153.
[29] Williams, *Systematic Theology*, III, p. 151.
[30] Williams, *Systematic Theology*, III, p. 153.
[31] Robeck and Sandidge, 'The Ecclesiology of *Koinonia* and Baptism', p. 513. Williams, *Systematic Theology*, III, p. 153.
[32] Williams, *Systematic Theology*, III, p. 153.
[33] Williams, *Systematic Theology*, III, pp. 151-52.
[34] M.A. Tomlinson, *Basic Bible Beliefs* (Cleveland, TN: White Wing Publishing House and Press, 1961).

Tomlinson and brother of Homer Tomlinson,[35] dedicates one sermon each to WB, footwashing, and Holy Communion. Noteworthy is the fact both footwashing and the Lord's Supper are identified as ordinances by Tomlinson,[36] while no such appellation is attached to WB. Nonetheless, after reading the sermon, there is little doubt that Tomlinson viewed WB as an ordinance. Tomlinson establishes the importance of WB on the basis of Jesus' submission to John's baptism in order to 'fulfill all righteousness' Mt. 3.13-15 and the commissioning of the eleven by Jesus to teach and to baptize as they engaged in missionary expansion Mt. 28.19, 20.[37] While baptism is vitally important and should occur as quickly as possible after conversion; baptism does not effect salvation. There is no room for baptismal regeneration or infant baptism in Tomlinson's teaching. Baptism is to be administered only after a conversion or born-again experience has made the person a new creature in Jesus Christ. Baptism is to follow repentance and avowal of faith in God. Moreover, citing 1 Pet. 3.21, Tomlinson posits that 'baptism is the outward manifestation to the world that the person is a new creature in Christ and has left the old sinful life and taken on a new life in Christ'.[38]

Regarding mode of baptism and the appropriate formula to be employed, Tomlinson considers immersion to be the only legitimate means along with a clear Trinitarian statement, 'exactly as set out in the command Jesus gave the disciples'.[39] Appearing to address some concerns pertinent to the necessity of WB prior to receiving the baptism of the HS, Tomlinson asserts that it is not the case, citing NT examples of persons being baptized with the HS prior to being baptized in water.[40] Tomlinson also addresses a question on which both Pearlman and Williams are silent in the texts previously reviewed. Namely, what is the requirement for persons who have once known the Lord, failed God and gone back into sin? Tomlinson

---

[35] H.D. Hunter, 'Tomlinson, Milton Ambrose', in Stanley M. Burgess and Eduard M. van der Maas (eds.), *NIDPCM* (rev. and exp. edn; Grand Rapids, MI: Zondervan, 2002), p. 1147.
[36] Tomlinson, *Basic Bible Beliefs*, pp. 19-23, 54-58, and 59-63.
[37] Tomlinson, *Basic Bible Beliefs*, pp. 19-23.
[38] Tomlinson, *Basic Bible Beliefs*, p. 20.
[39] Tomlinson, *Basic Bible Beliefs*, p. 22.
[40] Tomlinson, *Basic Bible Beliefs*, p. 22.

is unequivocal in his response, stating that 'it is necessary for him to be baptized again when he repents and returns to God'.[41] To support his point, he cites Rev. 2.5, 'Therefore remember from where you have fallen, and repent and do the deeds you did at first; or else I am coming to you and will remove your lampstand out of its place – unless you repent'. Tomlinson reasons that since WB is one of the first works it is necessary to be baptized in water again.[42]

James L. Slay

James L. Slay, pastor, 'preacher's preacher', missionary, churchman, and college instructor, authored *This We Believe*,[43] a text that served as an official training course for the COG, headquartered in Cleveland, TN. Prior to the publication of *This We Believe* in 1963, the COG had not issued a systematized statement of theology and practice beyond its Declaration of Faith.[44] Slay addresses WB, The Lord's Supper, and feet washing [sic] in chapter IV, 'The Doctrine of Church Ordinances'. After a brief exhortation regarding the supremacy of spontaneous worship as opposed to 'liturgical form' Slay focuses on defining the meaning of baptism before identifying the approved mode. Slay makes the effort to note that 'baptism' is derived from the Greek *baptizo* that carries the primary connotation 'to dip'. He then notes that it means much more than to immerse, surmising that 'since to dip one must put in and then take out, while to immerse one merely puts under and does not necessarily have to take out'. He then cites three NT examples of 'dipping' to make his point. Ironically, when he moves to stipulate there is no room for sprinkling or pouring, Slay makes no use of 'dipping' language. Rather, it is the language of immersion.[45] It appears that Slay begins his treatment with some sensitivity to a dispute that had arisen within the COG dating back to 1910 when objections were raised to the inclusion of

---

[41] Tomlinson, *Basic Bible Beliefs*, p. 20.
[42] Tomlinson, *Basic Bible Beliefs*, p. 20.
[43] James L. Slay, *This We Believe* (Cleveland, TN: Pathway Press, 1963).
[44] Slay, *This We Believe*, pp. 7-8.
[45] Slay, *This We Believe*, pp. 98-99.

'immersion' in the COG Teachings since it was not in the Bible[46] and then quickly abandons it for sake of clarity.

Regarding the proper baptismal formula Slay appeals to Mt. 28.19, 20 and opts for a Trinitarian formula while acknowledging Acts 2.38 as a theological statement that the new converts recognized Jesus the Christ 'was to be their Lord and Master and that the rite of baptism was a recognition of His work and authority'.[47] For Slay WB has no saving efficacy. 'People are baptized, not in order to be saved, but to show others that they are really saved.'[48] While baptism is not essential to salvation it is necessary to demonstrate obedience to Christ's command. To be clear about the need for obedience Slay asserts 'an individual can be saved without being baptized, but only if he has not had the opportunity of being baptized'.[49] Slay argues vehemently against infant baptism as being unscriptural and as being detrimental to the child's later spiritual life. 'The child who has been baptized as an infant will hardly ever believe in the truth of personal obedience to God's commands.'[50] In contradistinction to paedobaptism and baptismal regeneration Slay argues for believer's baptism since it is through the act of baptism that the baptized person proclaims to his or her community or 'world' that he or she has died to sin and is raised to a new spiritual life in Christ. 'For all of you who were baptized into Christ have clothed yourselves with Christ' (Gal. 3.27).

Furthermore, according to Slay, 'Baptism symbolizes the union of all believers in Christ'.[51] In closing, Slay states that baptism 'is an

---

[46] Cf. C.T. Davidson, *Upon This Rock* (3 vols., Cleveland, TN: White Wing Publishing House and Press, 1973-76), I, p. 380. and Charles W. Conn, *Like A Mighty Army: A History of the Church of God 1886-1996* (Cleveland, TN: Pathway Press, 2008), pp. 139-40.

[47] Slay, *This We Believe*, pp. 100-101.

[48] Slay, *This We Believe*, p. 101.

[49] Slay, *This We Believe*, p. 101.

[50] Slay, *This We Believe*, p. 103. Slay goes to great effort to solidify his position that only the regenerated are appropriate candidates for baptism, arguing against those who practice baptismal regeneration. In a rather pointed fashion directed toward the followers of Alexander Campbell he asserts that 'In the Church of God, we baptize Christians; in the Church of Christ, sinners are baptized thinking the rite makes them Christians'.

[51] Slay, *This We Believe*, p. 105.

obedient act portraying symbolically the work of regeneration in the life of the believer'.[52]

Walter Hollenweger

Walter J. Hollenweger, Swiss theologian and scholar of Pentecostalism and intercultural theology, broke new ground with the publication of his 10-volume *Handbuch der Pfingstbewegung* in 1969.[53] In the English translation, *The Pentecostals*,[54] made available in 1972, Hollenweger devotes chapter 27 to the early Pentecostals' views on the Lord's Supper, WB, and footwashing.[55] With regard to WB Hollenweger asserts that 'most Pentecostals hold a view of baptism close to that of the Baptists'.[56] According to him, baptism is a public testimony of repentance from sin and evidence of conversion. Baptism is an outward sign or expression of an internal spiritual identification with Christ's death, burial, and resurrection.[57] Moreover, most Pentecostals hold that baptism is by immersion, utilizing the Trinitarian baptismal formula. While there are Pentecostals who practice sprinkling and infant baptism, they are the minority, according to Hollenweger. Additionally, there are some who have lost sight of the original significance of baptism as a single unique act and transformed it into a rite of purification that is routinely repeated.[58]

Hollenweger reports that Pentecostals are not unanimous in their rejection of infant baptism or insistence on immersion. In particular, he notes the Chilean Pentecostals who trace their origins to the Methodist church practice both infant and adult baptism, by sprinkling and immersion. The preferred method for adult baptism is still sprinkling. Baptism by sprinkling is practiced by Apostolowo Fe Dedefia Habobo, Musama Christo Disco Church, other African churches, and certain German and Yugoslavian churches such as the

---

[52] Slay, *This We Believe*, p. 106.
[53] D.D. Bundy, 'Hollenweger, Walter Jacob', in Stanley M. Burgess and Eduard M. van der Maas (eds.), *NIDPCM* (rev. and exp. edn; Grand Rapids, MI: Zondervan, 2002), p. 729.
[54] Walter J. Hollenweger, *The Pentecostals: The Charismatic Movement in the Churches* (Minneapolis, MN: Augsburg Publishing House, 1972).
[55] Hollenweger, *The Pentecostals*, pp. 385-98.
[56] Hollenweger, *The Pentecostals*, p. 390.
[57] Hollenweger, *The Pentecostals*, p. 390.
[58] Hollenweger, *The Pentecostals*, pp. 393-94.

Mulheim Association of Christian Fellowships and Kristova Duhovna Crkva 'Malkrstenih', per Hollenweger.[59] In an effort to mediate polarization within Pentecostalism over WB, Hollenweger offers that by maintaining both kinds of baptism the Chileans express the two essential themes of baptism: God's unconditional promise to humanity and humanity's profession of faith in this promise to God. Theologically, the retaining of infant baptism with believer's baptism assures that the promise of God to humanity is not dependent upon humankind's response.[60]

J. Lancaster

In 1976 J. Lancaster, an Elim Pentecostal Church minister, contributed a chapter entitled 'The Ordinances' to *Pentecostal Doctrines*,[61] edited by P.S. Brewster, prominent Elim Pentecostal Church minister in Wales and active participant in the Pentecostal World Conference.

Lancaster identifies four ordinances of the Elim Pentecostal Church: the Lord's Supper, WB, the Laying on of Hands, and the Anointing of the Sick. Lancaster reminds readers that disputes over baptism and the Lord's Supper have raged since the Reformation with Zwingli maintaining the two ordinances were symbolic in nature, while Calvin opted for viewing them as a means of grace. Luther understood them to be a channel through which the 'real presence' of Jesus Christ was communicated to the participant. Lancaster asserts that the 'older Pentecostal churches' have leaned towards the Zwinglian view that a sacrament is 'an outward and visible sign of an inward and spiritual grace'.[62] They would not, however, go so far as to say that the sacraments are a channel of grace. They would argue that the baptism that effectually introduces a believer into the Body of Christ is the inner work of the HS at the heart of which WB is but the external sign Rom. 6.1-4; 1 Cor. 12.13.[63]

---

[59] Hollenweger, *The Pentecostals*, p. 391, nn. 45-47.
[60] Hollenweger, *The Pentecostals*, p. 395
[61] J. Lancaster, 'The Ordinances', in P.S. Brewster (ed.), *Pentecostal Doctrines* (Cheltenham: Elim, 1976), pp. 79-92. Cf. D.W. Cartwright, 'Brewster, Percy Stanley', in Stanley M. Burgess and Eduard M. van der Maas (eds.), *NIDPCM* (rev. and exp. edn; Grand Rapids, MI: Zondervan, 2002), p. 442.
[62] Lancaster, 'The Ordinances', p. 80.
[63] Lancaster, 'The Ordinances', p. 80.

Lancaster offers that the term 'ordinance' is employed intentionally over sacrament due to the ethos of the movement with its rejection of the formalism and deadness of the institutionalized Church. 'With roots going back into the soil that nurtured early Methodism',[64] Pentecostals' fervent desire to avoid the lifeless ceremonies of a stilted formalism in preference for a direct encounter with the Living God drove them to reject anything that smacked of mechanical means.[65]

Surveying modern scholarship of the day, Lancaster cites NT scholar James D.G. Dunn who states 'Paul knew nothing of a sacramental grace as such'.[66] While Dunn concedes that the Lord's Supper and WB are present in Paul's teaching he adds, 'to attempt somehow to depict the sacraments in Paul as the chief or sole channels of grace would be to fly in the face of all the evidence'.[67] Similarly, systematic theologian Emil Brunner, according to Lancaster, posits, 'Properly speaking New Testament Christianity knows nothing of the word "sacrament", which belongs essentially to the heathen world of the Graeco-Roman empire'.[68] Contrary to Dunn and Brunner, NT scholar and theologian Rudolf Bultmann argues, 'in earliest Christianity, the sacrament was by no means a symbol, but a miracle-working rite'.[69] In the face of the contradictory opinions Lancaster asserts 'Someone must be wrong'![70]

Before moving on to discuss WB, Lancaster makes it a point to remind readers that the Early Church experienced what has been called its 'pneumatic condition' or vivid sense of Christ's presence. The promise of Christ to be in the midst of two or three gathered was realized not by sacramental rites, but through the dynamic activity of the promised HS. It was only after the presence of the HS began to wane that the sacraments rose to a place of prominence. 'Visible and tangible signs become more important when the invisible moving of the Spirit is not known as powerfully as previously'.[71] The

---

[64] Lancaster, 'The Ordinances', p. 80.
[65] Lancaster, 'The Ordinances', pp. 80-82.
[66] Lancaster, 'The Ordinances', p. 81.
[67] Lancaster, 'The Ordinances', p. 81.
[68] Lancaster, 'The Ordinances', p. 81.
[69] Lancaster, 'The Ordinances', p. 81.
[70] Lancaster, 'The Ordinances', p. 81.
[71] Lancaster, 'The Ordinances', p. 82.

return of the HS to people's daily lives and worship, however, brings a spiritual immediacy with a deeper awareness of God's presence. This in turn invites simpler forms of worship due to the diminished dependence on the physical senses to apprehend God's presence.[72]

Lancaster cites Christ's commission to the disciples as the necessity for baptism (Mt. 28.18-20; Mk 16.15, 16). He then points to the following numerous passages: Acts 2.38; 8.12, 36-38; 9.18; 10.47, 48; 16.33; 19.5 as evidence that 'baptism was accepted as the normal, outward response for those who were converted through the evangelism of the Early Church'.[73]

Following the lead of NT scholar G.R. Beasley-Murray,[74] Lancaster posits that the real roots of Christian baptism are found in the baptism of John the Baptist. John's baptism had two foci: first, 'it marked the "turn" (repentance means conversion) of a Jew to God, associating him with the penitent people and assuring him of forgiveness and cleansing';[75] second, it 'anticipated the Messianic baptism with Spirit and fire, assuring him a place in the kingdom'.[76] Per Lancaster, by submitting to John's baptism Christ was intentionally, publicly identifying Himself with sinful humanity and 'acknowledging their need for repentance before they could be restored to fellowship with God'.[77] For Lancaster the events of Jesus' baptism; namely, the descent of the HS and the voice from Heaven did more than mark Jesus' identity as God's Son and verify the Father's divine approval of the Son's faithful obedience. It also 'gave "official" recognition to Him as the Lamb of God, the divinely-appointed means of salvation Mt. 3.13-16; Jn. 1.29-36'.[78]

Therefore, the baptism of Jesus sets a model of obedience as well as provides clues as to the meaning of baptism. It points to the necessity of repentance and the centrality of Jesus as the focal point of the saving activity of God. It anticipates Paul's definition of the ideal response to the gospel as 'repentance toward God and faith in

---

[72] Lancaster, 'The Ordinances', p. 82.
[73] Lancaster, 'The Ordinances', p. 82.
[74] G.R. Beasley-Murray, *Baptism in the New Testament* (London: McMillan & Co, 1963).
[75] Lancaster, 'The Ordinances', p. 82.
[76] Lancaster, 'The Ordinances', p. 82.
[77] Lancaster, 'The Ordinances', pp. 82-83.
[78] Lancaster, 'The Ordinances', pp. 82-83.

our Lord Jesus Christ' Acts 20.21. 'This is why baptism in the name of Jesus was required of those who had already been subject to John's baptism (Acts 19.3-5).'[79] While the 'baptismal formula' of Mt. 28.19 is set out in the three-fold name of the Trinity the format in the Book of Acts is consistently 'in the name of Jesus'. It is not to draw any distinctions between persons of the Trinity. Rather, it is to emphasize that it is only through faith in Jesus Christ and his redeeming work that a sinner can enter into fellowship with the Triune God.[80]

For Lancaster repentance, confession of sin, and faith in Jesus Christ are requisite for baptism. Consequently, there is no allowance for baptismal regeneration in his view. 'Unless water baptism points to an inner event which has either preceded it or is taking place simultaneously it has no validity.'[81] To be baptized 'into Christ' means 'putting on' Christ Gal. 3.27, but this is only possible once a person has become a child of God through faith Gal. 3.26.

According to Lancaster WB by immersion expresses outwardly the inward cleansing effected by the Word and the HS (Eph. 5.26; Titus 3.5) as well as the believer's identification with the death, burial, and resurrection of Christ. Furthermore, it is a 'sign and seal' of a transaction between God and a believer in which both have pledged themselves to each other. 'In the waters of baptism, the believer ratifies His commitment to Christ and God confirms through the inner witness of the Holy Spirit His acceptance and approval of that faith.'[82] Per Lancaster, baptism then becomes a means of grace and source of profound joy to those who meet the demands with sincere hearts. In view of this, Pentecostals 'cannot accept the implications of infant baptism'.[83] Infant Dedication, lacking theological or biblical warrants, is encouraged in lieu of infant baptism.

---

[79] Lancaster, 'The Ordinances', p. 83.
[80] Lancaster, 'The Ordinances', p. 83.
[81] Lancaster, 'The Ordinances', p. 84.
[82] Lancaster, 'The Ordinances', p. 85.
[83] Lancaster, 'The Ordinances', p. 84. With regard to the argument that infants and children were included in the 'household baptisms' referred to in Acts 18.18 Lancaster argues that 'there is no direct evidence whatever in "household baptisms" that children were included'.

Raymond M. Pruitt

Raymond M. Pruitt published *Fundamentals of the Faith*[84] in 1981. Pruitt, a bishop in the COGOP, with a distinguished ministry as a pastor, missionary, state overseer, and college instructor, published the denomination's first systematic outline of doctrine since its formation.[85] In the book's Foreword, General Overseer M.A. Tomlinson writes positively that the book is a 'rather comprehensive work' as an introduction to doctrinal studies, adding the caveat that the book has been 'reviewed by the Church's committee on history, polity and doctrine, but it is not being published with the thought of setting forth the Church's official stand on each subject covered'.[86] The ordinances are addressed in chapter 32 'The Membership, Function, and Destiny of the Church' and identified as WB, the Lord's Supper and feet washing [sic].

Before addressing the ordinances, Pruitt speaks to the limitations of human language to describe encounters with the ineffable as well as experiences with other Christians. Since it is in our nature to commune with God as beings created in God's image, we have been provided a means wherein we may communicate with God and others.[87] It is through the means of signs and symbols since words alone 'are inadequate to express the deeper meanings, even in human relationships, to say nothing of those transcendent, indescribable relationships with God'.[88] Pruitt asserts that a solitary 'tear coursing down the cheek expresses sorrow better than ten thousand words'.[89] Moreover, 'the experiences of the soul and spirit are best expressed in the universal language of signs and symbols'.[90] Per Pruitt, 'The Lord has given the Church such a means of expression in the ordinances, or sacraments, which he instituted'.[91] He makes it clear that the signs and symbols are expressions of what has been imparted

---

[84] Raymond M. Pruitt, *Fundamentals of the Faith* (Cleveland, TN: White Wing Publishing House and Press, 1981).
[85] Pruitt, *Fundamentals of the Faith*, p. 3.
[86] Pruitt, *Fundamentals of the Faith*, p. 5.
[87] Pruitt, *Fundamentals of the Faith*, p. 364.
[88] Pruitt, *Fundamentals of the Faith*, pp. 364-65.
[89] Pruitt, *Fundamentals of the Faith*, p. 365.
[90] Pruitt, *Fundamentals of the Faith*, p. 365.
[91] Pruitt, *Fundamentals of the Faith*, p. 365.

through a person's relationship with Christ and that there is no impartation of grace through the ordinances.[92]

According to Pruitt, WB replaces the Jewish rite of circumcision, which served to identify one with the people of God under the old covenant. It is the rite that identifies one with Jesus Christ. Pruitt is a strong proponent of total immersion, arguing from the original Greek that 'pour' and 'sprinkle' are not allowed by the text nor does sprinkling convey the meaning intended by the sign or symbol. The sign of WB signifies death, burial, and resurrection Rom. 6.1-4. Moreover, it means we are immersed into Christ and that our new life is in the risen Lord Gal. 3.27.[93] Pruitt argues for the baptismal formula of Mt. 28.19 as the correct one since it 'signifies that those who are baptized are acknowledging that they have been immersed into spiritual communion with the Triune God'.[94]

Guy Duffield and N.M. Van Cleave

In 1983 Guy P. Duffield and N.M. Van Cleave, members of the ICFG and faculty members of L.I.F.E Bible College, co-authored *Foundations of Pentecostal Theology*.[95] Their finished work prompted Dr. Jack Hayford, a prominent leader in the Foursquare Gospel organization, Pentecostal minister, and Chancellor of King's University, to assert that 'There can hardly be found as complete and functional a doctrinal study from within the Pentecostal movement'.[96] In the preface the authors assert the Pentecostal movement is grounded upon the entire Bible as the Word of God and is not just an inspirational experience. Speaking for Pentecostals, they offer that 'we are a Bible-believing people. We subscribe to "all the counsel of God" (Acts 20.27).'[97] Consequently, the approach taken by Duffield and Van Cleave in their book is 'to compile the Scriptural teachings concerning the great doctrines of our faith as contained in this book'.[98]

---

[92] Pruitt, *Fundamentals of the Faith*, p. 365.
[93] Pruitt, *Fundamentals of the Faith*, pp. 365-66.
[94] Pruitt, *Fundamentals of the Faith*, p. 366.
[95] Guy P. Duffield and Nathaniel M. Van Cleave, *Foundations of Pentecostal Theology* (San Dimas, CA: L.I.F.E. Bible College, 1983).
[96] Duffield and Van Cleave, *Foundations of Pentecostal Theology*, p. x.
[97] Duffield and Van Cleave, *Foundations of Pentecostal Theology*, p. xv.
[98] Duffield and Van Cleave, *Foundations of Pentecostal Theology*, p. xv.

When it comes to addressing the ordinances of the church under chapter eight, 'The Doctrine of the Church', Duffield and Van Cleave identify WB and the Lord's Supper as ordinances or sacraments. They are named ordinances since they are outward rites or symbolic observances commanded by Jesus. They also set forth essential Christian truths and are understood as the outward sign of an inward work or the visible sign of an invisible work. Evidence for the establishment of WB by Jesus is found in both Mt. 28.19 and Mk 16.16. Similarly, Peter called for it on the Day of Pentecost Acts 2.38, 41. Utilization of the Trinitarian baptismal formula is established by Mt. 28.19 and called for in the Foursquare *Declaration of Faith,* per Duffield and Van Cleave. The manner of baptism is by immersion, symbolizing that we have been buried with Him into his death and that we have been raised up with Him to walk in newness of life.[99]

John Bond

In 1989 two University of South Africa professors, Henry Lederle and M.S. Clark, co-authored *What is Distinctive about Pentecostal Theology?*[100] In Appendix A of the volume, John Bond, a South African AG pastor and churchman of some stature, offers what he believes are the distinctive marks of Pentecostal theology in the classical sense.[101] Bond posits that, speaking generally, 'all Pentecostal theology is conservative and fundamentalist' and has been inherited from Evangelical traditions.[102]

---

[99] Duffield and Van Cleave, *Foundations of Pentecostal Theology,* p. 436.

[100] M.S. Clark and H.I. Lederle (eds.) *What is Distinctive about Pentecostal Theology?* (Pretoria: University of South Africa, 1989).

[101] John Bond, 'What is Distinctive about Pentecostal Theology', in M.S. Clark and H.I. Lederle (eds.), *What is Distinctive about Pentecostal Theology?* (Pretoria: University of South Africa, 1989), pp. 133-42.

[102] Bond, 'What is Distinctive about Pentecostal Theology', p. 134. One major distinction noted by Bond is the belief that 'the baptism of the Holy Ghost is a second experience to salvation and that it should be or can be accompanied by speaking in tongues (real languages unknown to the speakers)'. Additionally, he notes the operation of the miraculous and the availability and operation of the gifts of the Spirit enumerated in 1 Cor. 12.7-11. Highlighting the impact of the baptism of the HS, Bond takes special note to differentiate between the proper language ('upon baptism') employed by classical Pentecostals when speaking of the baptism of the HS as an outpouring coming from above as opposed to charismatics of the sacramental school who employ 'release of something already within' when making

Per Bond, a distinctive of Pentecostal theology relates to epistemology. For Pentecostals, experience of the acts of God holds primacy over theology. According to Bond, Pentecostals eschew the thought of truth merely as abstraction or conceptualized in a theory. Rather, truth must be experienced with power, or it is invalid and a mere form of religion. Pentecostal thinking prefers the dynamic as opposed to that which appears to be formalized and tightly structured.[103] While experience plays a powerful role for Pentecostals so does the high view of the Bible. Bond asserts 'the Bible is accepted as verbally inspired and as the all-sufficient guide for doctrine and practice'.[104] He posits that it is the 'greatest strength of the Pentecostal churches. They are people of the Book.'[105] It is no surprise then when Bond begins to address WB and the Lord's Supper that he has no truck for sacramentalism. While he employs the term sacrament he clearly views the two rites as memorials. Bond is a strong proponent of believer's baptism by total immersion and has no countenance for pouring, sprinkling, or infant baptism. Baptism is viewed as an act of obedience and a rite of Christian initiation; however, it is not necessary for salvation or a means of regeneration.[106]

---

reference to infant baptism or sprinkling. Another distinctive relates to the spiritual affinities of Pentecostalism. Bond posits that Pentecostal theology is neither Catholic nor Protestant and that Pentecostals will have to recognize how it differs from them in obvious points of conflict such as WB and in its philosophical distance from Western Christianity. Moreover, Bond offers that 'there are those who would assert that the spiritual affinities of Pentecostals are more with the mystical theology of the Eastern Church than with either Western Protestantism or Catholicism'.

[103] Bond, 'What is Distinctive about Pentecostal Theology', p. 135. According to Bond, 'formal theology failed in the beginning of the revival when it sat in judgment on the charismatic experiences which were manifested'. Consequently, historically speaking, the formally structured church 'became the enemy of Pentecostal experience by outlawing and driving out its protagonists'.

[104] Bond, 'What is Distinctive about Pentecostal Theology', p. 138.

[105] Bond, 'What is Distinctive about Pentecostal Theology', p. 139.

[106] Bond, 'What is Distinctive about Pentecostal Theology', pp. 134-39.

William Menzies, Stanley Horton, and Michael Dusing

In 1993 Stanley M. Horton published *Bible Doctrines: A Pentecostal Perspective*,[107] a revised and expanded version of *Understanding Our Doctrine*, originally published in 1971 by William W. Menzies as a unit in a training course for Sunday school workers in the AG. While the structure of the book follows the Statement of Fundamental Truths as posited by the AG, the authors' stated intent is not to indoctrinate readers with AG doctrines. Rather, the intent is to set forth the biblical basis and applications of the doctrines being examined.[108] We have seen the same basic approach employed by Pearlman, Williams, Tomlinson, Slay, Duffield and Van Cleave, and Pruitt to a lesser degree.

It comes as no surprise in the opening paragraph of chapter six, 'Ordinances of the Church', to read that 'Biblical Christianity is not ritualistic or sacramental. Sacramentalism is the belief that special grace is bestowed on participants who engage in certain prescribed rituals.'[109] Menzies and Horton further assert that the view is typically espoused by sacramental churches that grace is received by participants in WB and the Lord's Supper regardless of whether they have active or believing faith or not. A person only has to go through the form or rite.[110] They further remark that the two ordinances that Jesus initiated and commanded have no special merit attached to them; however, they are to be followed in obedience to Christ's command. The Lord's Supper and WB are to be viewed as memorials alone since there is no saving efficacy in them. Any blessing to be experienced will be God's blessing of the person's heart at God's initiative.[111]

More specifically, for Menzies and Horton WB is a symbolic public declaration through a ceremony of a person's identification with Jesus Christ in his death and resurrection since it is through these divine acts that one has new life in Jesus Christ, Rom. 6.1-4. Furthermore, WB is to be by immersion for those who have repented

---

[107] William W. Menzies and Stanley M. Horton, *Bible Doctrines: A Pentecostal Perspective* (Springfield, MO: Logion Press, 1993).
[108] Menzies and Horton, *Bible Doctrines*, pp. 7-8.
[109] Menzies and Horton, *Bible Doctrines*, p. 111.
[110] Menzies and Horton, *Bible Doctrines*, p. 111.
[111] Menzies and Horton, *Bible Doctrines*, p. 111.

of their sins and expressed faith in Christ Acts 2.38. Since WB is for believers who have reached the age of accountability, infant baptism is unthinkable. Lastly, Menzies and Horton assert that the Triune baptismal formula found in Mt. 28.19 is the correct one, echoing all of their predecessors except Williams.[112]

In 1994 Stanley Horton served as editor of the AG's *Systematic Theology*.[113] The revised edition was published in 1995. The volume is basically an update and rewrite of *Bible Doctrines* by specialists who write in more detail. The Lord's Supper and WB are addressed in chapter sixteen, 'The New Testament Church' by Michael L. Dusing.[114] One contribution Dusing makes to the discussion relates to the history of the debate about WB and the Lord's Supper. He states that since the Reformation, Protestantism has rejected the sacramental nature of all rites except WB and the Lord's Supper. Furthermore, since Augustine's time the view has been held that both WB and the Lord's Supper serve as 'outward and visible signs of an inward and spiritual grace'.[115]

A critical issue focuses on how to interpret their meaning as an 'inward and spiritual grace'. Historically, these rites have been called sacraments and ordinances. According to Dusing, most Pentecostals and evangelicals prefer the use of 'ordinance' to express their understanding of WB and the Lord's Supper in order to avoid the 'somewhat magical connotation accompanying the use of the term 'sacrament'.[116] Similarly, most evangelicals and Pentecostals do not perceive WB and the Lord's Supper as effecting spiritual change. Rather, they are understood as ordained and commanded by Jesus Christ and participated in as acts of obedience and discipleship. 'They serve as symbols or forms of proclamation of what Christ has already spiritually effected in the believer's life'.[117] Dusing posits that while baptism symbolizes a significant spiritual reality (salvation and

---

[112] Menzies and Horton, *Bible Doctrines*, pp. 112-15.
[113] Stanley M. Horton, (ed.) *Systematic Theology* (Springfield, MO: Logion Press, rev. edn, 1995).
[114] Michael L. Dusing, 'The New Testament Church', in Stanley M. Horton, (ed.) *Systematic Theology* (Springfield, MO: Logion Press, rev. edn, 1995), pp. 525-66.
[115] Dusing, 'The New Testament Church', pp. 556-58.
[116] Dusing, 'The New Testament Church', p. 557.
[117] Dusing, 'The New Testament Church', p. 558.

new life in Jesus Christ), 'the symbol itself should never be elevated to the level of that higher reality'.[118]

John Christopher Thomas

In *Footwashing in John 13 and the Johannine Community*,[119] first published in 1991 and revised in 2014, John Christopher Thomas argues than in all probability footwashing was practiced by the Johannine community as a religious rite.[120] He further posits that footwashing symbolizes the cleansing of believers from post-conversion sin. Thomas, a COG (Cleveland, TN) minister, seminary professor, NT scholar, and Pentecostal biblical theologian supports his argument through a survey of the traditional and critical readings of John 13.1-20 and his own literary and exegetical analysis of the text. Thomas further engages other Johannine and NT scholars around the issue of sacramentalism and footwashing within the highly debated issue of the Fourth Gospel and sacramentalism. He notes that since Jesus' baptism and the institution of the Lord's Supper are both absent from the Fourth Gospel several scholars have concluded that John is either anti- or non-sacramental. Thomas offers another option for consideration, namely, that John 'purposefully withholds the sacraments in certain expected contexts in order to reinterpret or correct the current view about them'.[121] He employs a number of examples to make his point. Two illustrations will suffice. First is John 6 where the Eucharistic overtones are clear and rich while the overt language is absent; second is John 13.10 where baptismal imagery is vibrant and rich and *Baptizo* and cognates do not occur. The second point is particularly germane to our investigation. Thomas moves on to posit that 'it may safely be assumed that both baptism and Eucharist had their place'[122] and 'may be identified as sacraments for the Johannine community'.[123] With regard to footwashing Thomas asserts, 'In light of footwashing's place in the Fourth Gospel and the limited relevant evidence from the early church, it may be concluded

---

[118] Dusing, 'The New Testament Church', p. 557.
[119] John Christopher Thomas, *Footwashing in John 13 and the Johannine Community* (2nd edn; Cleveland, TN: CPT Press, 2014).
[120] Thomas, *Footwashing in John 13*, p. 177.
[121] Thomas, *Footwashing in John 13*, p. 178.
[122] Thomas, *Footwashing in John 13*, p. 181.
[123] Thomas, *Footwashing in John 13*, p. 182.

that footwashing functioned, alongside baptism and Eucharist, as a "sacrament" for the Johannine community'.[124]

Speaking to the rationale for the author's deliberate withholding of the sacraments by name, Thomas proposes that perhaps it was as a corrective to the over-realistic view of the sacraments that surfaced as early as the mid-fifties. Apparently, the church at Corinth had developed a quasi-magical view of the sacraments that the Apostle Paul was challenged to address in 1 Cor. 10.1-11. It also appears that Ignatius held to a quasi-magical view of the sacraments.[125] It is by placing the account of the footwashing in the place normally occupied by the Last Supper that John attempts to emphasize the true nature of the sacraments and correct the quasi-magical view held by Ignatius and some of the Corinthians. Viewed in the light of the Fourth Gospel, the traditional Pentecostal rite of footwashing is truly sacramental and not a magical or quasi-magical rite. The same may be said for the Lord's Supper and WB through John's eyes.[126] All three are sacramental in that 'they are signs of God's gracious action based upon the death of Jesus. Such rites do not stand alone but must be accompanied by faith.'[127]

In his 1998 Society for Pentecostal Studies presidential address,[128] Thomas offers a proposal for consideration regarding a possible 'paradigm' to pursue in the twenty-first century. This proposed paradigm, 'A Pentecostal Approach to Ecclesiology', grows out of his dialogue with Steven Land and Donald Dayton[129] from whom he gains the strong conviction 'that standing at the theological heart of Pentecostalism is the fivefold gospel: Jesus is Savior, Sanctifier, Holy Ghost Baptizer, Healer, and coming King'.[130] He further proposes that reflection about the nature, identity, and mission of the church would be contained within each of the five treatments, concluding

---

[124] Thomas, *Footwashing in John 13*, p. 185.
[125] Thomas, *Footwashing in John 13*, pp. 186-87.
[126] Thomas, *Footwashing in John 13*, p. 189.
[127] Thomas, *Footwashing in John 13*, p. 189.
[128] John Christopher Thomas, 'Pentecostal Theology in the Twenty-First Century', *Pneuma* 20.1 (1998), pp. 3-19.
[129] Donald W. Dayton, *Theological Roots of Pentecostalism* (Peabody, MA: Hendrickson Publishers, 1991).
[130] Thomas, 'Pentecostal Theology in the Twenty-First Century', p. 17.

each section with implications for the faith community and its life.¹³¹ Thomas' hope is that adapting the above paradigm would advance the reclamation and re-appropriation of the sacraments by Pentecostals who have been uncertain about them and their place in the worship of the faith community.¹³² Moreover, this approach to the church would further clarify for Pentecostals 'the dynamic relationship that should exist between these signs and the experience of salvation itself'.¹³³ Lastly, it might lead Pentecostals to reconsider the nature and number of sacraments and to discover that there is a sign to accompany each aspect of the fivefold gospel: water baptism for salvation, footwashing for sanctification, glossolalia for Spirit baptism, anointing with oil for healing, and the Lord's Supper for the second coming.¹³⁴

J. Rodman Williams

J. Rodman Williams, Presbyterian theologian, pastor, and educator was an early participant in the charismatic renewal of the late 1960's and early 70's. In 1972, he became founding president and professor of theology at Melodyland School of Theology located in Melodyland, CA. During that time Williams also participated in the International Roman Catholic-Pentecostal Dialogue.¹³⁵ Between 1988 and 1992 he completed his three-volume *Renewal Theology*,¹³⁶ a significant study in systematic theology from a charismatic perspective. Williams addresses the Lord's Supper and WB in chapter six 'Ordinances' of volume three of *Renewal Theology*. While he acknowledges that many churches in the Anabaptist tradition affirm footwashing as an additional ordinance, Williams holds it questionable to view it in the same way as the Lord's Supper and WB. He employs the terms ordinance and sacrament, prefers ordinance, and eschews any sense of sacramentalism.¹³⁷ Williams contextualizes

---

¹³¹ Thomas, 'Pentecostal Theology in the Twenty-First Century', p. 18.
¹³² Thomas, 'Pentecostal Theology in the Twenty-First Century', p. 18.
¹³³ Thomas, 'Pentecostal Theology in the Twenty-First Century', p. 18.
¹³⁴ Thomas, 'Pentecostal Theology in the Twenty-First Century', pp. 18-19.
¹³⁵ C.M. Robeck, Jr., 'Williams, J. Rodman', in Stanley M. Burgess and Eduard M. van der Maas (eds.), *NIDPCM* (rev. and exp. edn; Grand Rapids, MI: Zondervan, 2002), pp. 1197-98. (p. 1198)
¹³⁶ J. Rodman Williams, *Renewal Theology: The Church, the Kingdom, and Last Things* (Grand Rapids: MI: Zondervan Publishing House, 1992), III, pp. 221-63.
¹³⁷ Williams, *Renewal Theology* III, pp. 221-25.

WB as a key component of the Great Commission positing that 'baptism is a vital part of the Great Commission. It is just as much a part of it as are both the preceding "Go ... and make disciples of all nations" and the ensuing "teaching them to observe all that I have commanded you"'.[138] Baptism is vitally related to discipleship and following Jesus Christ as Lord and Savior. Consequently, WB is for believers – persons who are capable of making life-long commitments to Jesus Christ since baptism is a once in a lifetime event. Like many of his predecessors, Williams holds that baptism relates to the forgiveness of sins, regeneration, being buried and raised with Christ, engagement to be the Lord's, incorporation into the body of Christ, and unity with other believers.[139] Williams argues for usage of the Trinitarian baptismal formula but allows for baptism in the name of Jesus. After citing Rom. 6.3, Gal. 3.27, and Col. 2.12, he offers the following mediating wisdom: 'It is clear that whatever the exact formula, Christ is the central reality'.[140]

For Williams total immersion is the correct mode of WB even though sprinkling and pouring is widely practiced throughout Western Christendom. Considering the decline of total immersion, a 'very unfortunate development', Williams asserts that 'Immersion much needs to be reinstated as the normal mode of baptism, and therefore as the regular practice in all Christian churches'.[141] It follows, then, that Williams opposes infant baptism and finds no scriptural justification for its practice. At the close of his consideration of the major arguments in favor of infant baptism Williams clearly asserts that 'my concern is to call those churches that practice infant baptism to seriously reconsider what they are doing and make every effort to reinstate the baptism of believers'.[142]

Departing from those who understand baptism to be a memorial or a purely external sign of an invisible internal work, on the one hand, and those who espouse baptismal regeneration or baptism as effecting salvation, on the other hand, Williams offers a third alternative. For Williams, WB is best understood as a means of grace

---

[138] Williams, *Renewal Theology* III, p. 136.
[139] Williams, *Renewal Theology* III, p. 223-34.
[140] Williams, *Renewal Theology* III, p. 222-23.
[141] Williams, *Renewal Theology* III, p. 228.
[142] Williams, *Renewal Theology* III, p. 239.

in addition to being understood as a seal and sign.[143] Williams offers the following explication of his view:

> Not only is God's grace of salvation signified and sealed in baptism, but also baptism is a channel of that grace. For example, Paul's words about 'the washing of regeneration' imply that in the washing, which relates to water baptism, regeneration occurs. Through the act of baptism God's grace is given. It is not that the act of baptism regenerates but that baptism may be the channel, or means, by which the grace of regeneration is applied and received.[144]

Similarly, burial with Christ is not affected by immersion in the water since 'such burial is a profoundly spiritual experience of dying to self'.[145] Nonetheless, the visible and tangible experience of going under the water can be a channel of God's grace in spiritual death and resurrection. Lastly, to 'put on Christ' is essentially an act of repentance and faith, and baptism may act as a channel or means of grace in which the putting off of the old self and the putting on of the new occurs.[146]

French L. Arrington

French L. Arrington, an ordained COG (Cleveland, TN) minister, respected Bible scholar, biblical theologian, and teacher at both the collegiate and seminary levels, authored his three-volume *Christian Doctrine: A Pentecostal Perspective*[147] between 1992 and 1994. Arrington writes from a decidedly classical Pentecostal perspective, offering a biblical and practical presentation of Christian doctrine in a fashion reminiscent of Myer Pearlman's *Knowing the Doctrines*. The ordinances of the Lord's Supper, WB, and footwashing are addressed in volume three, chapter eleven, 'The Worship of the Church'.[148] Arrington never employs the term sacrament, nor does he offer alternative perspectives to the views being presented. For Arrington, 'ordinances

---

[143] Williams, *Renewal Theology* III, p. 224.
[144] Williams, *Renewal Theology* III, p. 224.
[145] Williams, *Renewal Theology* III, p. 224.
[146] Williams, *Renewal Theology* III, p. 224.
[147] French L. Arrington, *Christian Doctrine: A Pentecostal Perspective* (3 vols., Cleveland, TN, Pathway, 1992-94).
[148] Arrington, *Christian Doctrine*, III, pp. 201-17.

of the church are visible signs of the saving work of Jesus Christ' and while they are external 'representations of the great realities of salvation and confirm the divine promise' they are more than that.[149] He posits that for believers they are a means of God's strengthening grace.[150]

Thus, WB is more than a mere sign pointing to something else and it is less than the effecting agent of the sacramentalists. Arrington's expanded view of ordinance reflects some of the fullness of meaning conveyed by Myer Pearlman's 'means of grace'. Water baptism is most assuredly a sign and a means of grace for those who have expressed saving faith in Jesus Christ.

As one might anticipate, Arrington asserts the only proper candidates for baptism are those who have accepted Christ as their Savior, having repented of their sins. Their baptism is to be by total immersion, employing the Triune baptismal formula. While baptismal regeneration and infant baptism are categorically rejected as unscriptural, infant dedication is welcomed and encouraged as a proper practice to keep Christ at the center of all things.[151]

Lastly, Arrington asserts that WB is 'a once-for-all public witness of our conversion and entry by repentance and faith into the Christian life'.[152] In this assertion Arrington appears to be taking a contrary position to the one held by other classical Pentecostals who require rebaptism after returning to the 'fold'. For example, as recent as 1961 M.A. Tomlinson had asserted that when a backslider returns to God 'it is necessary for him to be baptized again when he repents and returns to God'.[153]

Consistent with his Pentecostal perspective in his treatment of WB, Arrington gives particular attention to differentiate between the various 'baptisms' that are spoken of in the biblical text. Arrington offers that in addition to WB there is baptism simultaneous with conversion, and then there is the baptism of the HS subsequent to conversion.[154] In contrast to E.S. Williams, who proposes Eph. 4.5

---

[149] Arrington, *Christian Doctrine*, III, pp. 208.
[150] Arrington, *Christian Doctrine*, III, pp. 208.
[151] Arrington, *Christian Doctrine*, III, pp. 209-11.
[152] Arrington, *Christian Doctrine*, III, p. 211.
[153] Tomlinson, *Basic Bible Beliefs*, p. 20.
[154] Arrington, *Christian Doctrine*, III, p. 209.

refers to WB[155] Arrington interprets Eph. 4.5 in the same manner that 1 Cor. 12.13 is interpreted, namely, as that baptism which is the unique act of the HS by which repentant sinners become members of the Body of Christ after their conversion. Distinguishing this baptism from WB and Christ baptizing believers with the HS, Arrington asserts that 'there is only one baptism that incorporates the believer into the church, Christ's body, and that is administered by the Holy Spirit at conversion'.[156]

Cecil M. Robeck, Jr. and Jerry L. Sandidge

Cecil Robeck and Jerry Sandidge, AG ministers, church historians, Pentecostal theologians, educators, and committed ecumenists co-authored 'The Ecclesiology of *Koinonia* and Baptism: A Pentecostal Perspective'[157] in the summer 1990. According to Roman Catholic theologian Fr. Donald Gelpi, 'the most serious doctrinal differences dividing Catholic charismatics and Protestant Pentecostals lie in the area of sacramental theology'.[158] The authors opine the same could be said of Roman Catholics and Pentecostals in general and that one aspect of sacramental theology, baptism, had caused more than a little strife in the movement.

Consequently, the authors propose 'to look at the church-dividing issue of water baptism within the context of an ecclesiology of *koinonia* from the perspectives of various Pentecostal bodies'.[159]

The method of their inquiry is to 1) demonstrate the wide diversity of praxis within classical Pentecostalism, 2) provide a theological assessment of the data, and 3) provide observations and recommendations in order to move the Roman Catholic/Pentecostal Dialogue forward. Their summative report on the result of the 1974 meeting is instructive for our study.[160] In summary form, the following points were made:

---

[155] Williams, *Systematic Theology*, III, pp. 150-51.

[156] Arrington, *Christian Doctrine*, III, pp. 209-10.

[157] Robeck and Sandidge, 'The Ecclesiology of *Koinonia* and Baptism', pp. 504-34. The article was a paper originally delivered at the international Roman Catholic/Pentecostal Dialogue in Emmetten, Switzerland in 1988.

[158] Quoted in Robeck and Sandidge, 'The Ecclesiology of *Koinonia* and Baptism', p. 505.

[159] Robeck nd Sandidge, 'The Ecclesiology of *Koinonia* and Baptism', p. 505.

[160] Robeck and Sandidge, 'The Ecclesiology of *Koinonia* and Baptism', pp. 506-507.

1. Water baptism is related to movement from the kingdom of darkness to the kingdom of Christ.

2. The NT reflects the missionary situation of the apostolic generation and does not reflect the historical situation of later Christians.

3. In the NT, baptism by immersion is reflected as the ideal form of baptism, and it occurs in a constellation of other initiatory phenomena including proclamation, faith, repentance, and the reception of the HS.

4. While progress in understanding was made, agreement was not reached on the subject of paedobaptism.

5. Sacraments are in no sense magical but must be appropriated by faith. As such, where paedo or infant baptism is practiced, it gains meaning only within the context of a faith community.[161]

The authors report that the problematic issues regarding baptism had not resolved by 1988.[162] Robeck and Sandidge further assert that the pastoral and theological ambiguity of Pentecostals regarding baptism 'appears clearly when they encounter a spiritual tradition that has a well-defined theology of baptism and where a primary role is given to the practice of baptism at a pastoral level'.[163]

---

[161] Robeck and Sandidge, 'The Ecclesiology of *Koinonia* and Baptism', p. 507.

[162] Per Robeck and Sandidge, 'The Ecclesiology of *Koinonia* and Baptism', p. 508, offer the following assessment: 1) Lack of sufficient mutuality and trust established between and among participants before engaging in discussion of sensitive and complicated topics in more pastoral and theological terms; 2) Polarization and a sense of betrayal over believer's baptism between classical Pentecostals and Protestant charismatics. Apparently, the traditional Protestant charismatics who practice infant baptism gravitated toward the Roman Catholic position and abandoned the Pentecostals who championed believer's baptism. 3) The strong conviction among many Pentecostals against paedobaptism and continuing distrust of Roman Catholics in spite of disclaimers that infant baptism is not an 'automatic' means of salvation. 4) The issue of re-baptism was not resolved in 1974 at the pastoral level. Apparently, there was a press release for this to occur but it went no further. 5) The historical and theological self-understanding and the diverse practices within the Pentecostal community make dialogue on WB difficult.

[163] Robeck and Sandidge, 'The Ecclesiology of *Koinonia* and Baptism', p. 508.

After surveying Pentecostal baptismal practice, the authors provide a theological assessment of the data and conclude with the following eight observations and recommendations for advancing discussion between Pentecostals and Roman Catholics: 1) Genuine reflective dialogue among the Pentecostal movement on the issue of WB needs to take place. 2) All Pentecostals agree that baptism is mandated by Jesus and that it is vital for Jesus' disciples to fulfill his command; however, at times the import of baptism is debated. All Pentecostals agree that faith in Jesus Christ must be related to baptism, but the sequence of the relationship is variously understood and debated. The majority view is that faith must precede baptism.[164] 3) Pentecostals tend to view WB 'as best practiced/understood to be a one-time, nonrepeatable event, undertaken at the point of entry into the Christian life'.[165] Dialogue needs to take place among Pentecostals, addressing the rationale and biblical justification of 're-baptism' and whether all previous baptisms are invalid. 4) The Pentecostal groups that practice both believer's and infant baptism or allow for alternative modes of baptism besides immersion may be 'particularly useful in interchurch discussions on the subject of baptism' since they appear to have been 'least affected by "restorationist" thinking and biblical literalism'. Moreover, they may serve as primary connectors between many Pentecostal churches and mainline churches. Examples of the Pentecostal groups that practice believer's baptism and infant baptism include the IPHC, The Iglesia Pentecostal de Chili, and the Iglesia Methodista Pentecostal (Chile).[166] 5) Pentecostals are urged to rediscover the theological roots of their own traditions by exploring the Lutheran, Reformed, Methodist, and Holiness traditions in an effort to gain a greater level of self-understanding of their own practices, especially WB. 6) Overall, Pentecostal churches would benefit from a concerted effort to rediscover the significance of WB for the faith community as related to Christian *koinonia*. Similarly, Pentecostals are encouraged to investigate WB as a sacrament and not just an ordinance to be obeyed because it is commanded by Jesus. Failure to consider WB as a sacrament tends 'to overlook the real presence of the Sovereign

---

[164] Robeck and Sandidge, 'The Ecclesiology of *Koinonia* and Baptism', p. 532.
[165] Robeck and Sandidge, 'The Ecclesiology of *Koinonia* and Baptism', p. 532.
[166] Robeck and Sandidge, 'The Ecclesiology of *Koinonia* and Baptism', p. 532.

whose death, burial, and resurrection are remembered (*amamnesis*) in the act of obedience'.¹⁶⁷ 7) In view of the WB discussions that arose concerning 'issues of time, of the sequence of events in any perceived order of salvation, and questions of subsequence'¹⁶⁸ the authors caution the biblical witness seems 'to view a number of initiatory events without the nuanced concerns for sequence that Pentecostals, because of historical and experiential concerns, have given them'.¹⁶⁹ Robeck and Sandidge assert that the Oneness denominations appear to grasp this point better than most other Pentecostal groups. In view of Christian *koinonia* Trinitarian and Oneness Pentecostal groups would be well served to dialogue around issues of timing and subsequence relative to WB.¹⁷⁰ 8) The lack of mutual recognition of baptismal practices within the visible Church does not bear witness to one body but to many. All Pentecostals who participated in the International Roman Catholic/Pentecostal Dialogue are encouraged to have their denominations respond formally to the *BEM* study.¹⁷¹

Harold D. Hunter

Harold Hunter, a Pentecostal theologian, educator, archivist, and ecumenist, broke ground in 1983 with the publication of his PhD dissertation under the title, *Spirit-Baptism: A Pentecostal Alternative*.¹⁷² Since that time he has taken an active role in ecumenical discussions in various spheres as reflected in his response¹⁷³ to the *BEM*. Hunter begins his response noting that it appears 'virtually all major traditions and most parts of the world have found this discriminating work of Faith and Order worthy of serious interaction'.¹⁷⁴ Also, Pentecostals from around the world offer that classical Pentecostals should have some of their fears allayed by the 'welcome opportunity'

---

¹⁶⁷ Robeck and Sandidge, 'The Ecclesiology of *Koinonia* and Baptism', p. 533.
¹⁶⁸ Robeck and Sandidge, 'The Ecclesiology of *Koinonia* and Baptism', p. 533.
¹⁶⁹ Robeck and Sandidge, 'The Ecclesiology of *Koinonia* and Baptism', p. 533.
¹⁷⁰ Robeck and Sandidge, 'The Ecclesiology of *Koinonia* and Baptism', p. 533.
¹⁷¹ Robeck and Sandidge, 'The Ecclesiology of *Koinonia* and Baptism', p. 533.
¹⁷² Harold D. Hunter, *Spirit-Baptism: A Pentecostal Alternative* (Lanham, MD: University Press of America, 1983).
¹⁷³ Harold D. Hunter, 'Reflections by a Pentecostalist on Aspects of *BEM*', *JES* 29.3-4 (1992), pp. 317-45.
¹⁷⁴ Hunter, 'Reflections by a Pentecostalist', p. 318.

to participate in the future of the conciliar movement based on the ability of the *BEM* to arrive at important 'convergences'.[175]

Speaking to the issue of WB, Hunter takes note of the dearth of resource material available to Robeck and Sandidge as they prepared their reflection paper for presentation to the Roman Catholic/Pentecostal Dialogue in 1988.[176] While he stops short of fully endorsing the *BEM,* Hunter strongly encourages Pentecostals to take note of the mutually exclusive views of WB among their own ranks and sounds a clarion call to 'give a careful reading of approaches that differ in substance'.[177] Acknowledging that Pentecostals will not entertain a view of sacramental efficacy that is independent of the participant's faith, Hunter challenges Pentecostals to broaden their acceptance of baptism at variance with their own views. He hopefully asserts that Pentecostals can learn that it is unnecessary 'to deny that salvation is conveyed *ex opera operato,* given the delicate handling of fundamental biblical themes in theological systems once summarily dismissed because of post-apostolic motifs'.[178] He encourages Trinitarian Pentecostals to consider the following consensus achieved by the 1977-1984 Evangelical-Roman Catholic Dialogue on Mission:

> We agree that baptism must never be isolated, either in theology or in practice, from the context of conversion. It belongs essentially to the whole process of repentance, faith, regeneration by the Holy Spirit, and membership of the covenant community, the Church.
>
> ... We rejoice together that the whole process of salvation is the work of God by the Holy Spirit. And it is in this connection that

---

[175] One shortcoming noted by Hunter 'may be the lack of redress by *BEM* to anything like the Pentecostal ethos' especially since 'Pentecostal praxis anticipated Bonhoeffer's concept of "cheap grace"'. Hunter, 'Reflections by a Pentecostalist', p. 318.

[176] Hunter, 'Reflections by a Pentecostalist', pp. 329-30. Hunter expresses admiration and gratitude for their scholarship and their attempt to forge new ground without official ecclesial support. Hunter acknowledges that his subsequent remarks on baptism are based largely on interaction with the Robeck-Sandidge paper.

[177] Hunter, 'Reflections by a Pentecostalist', p. 329.

[178] Hunter, 'Reflections by a Pentecostalist', pp. 329-30.

Roman Catholics understand the expression *ex opera operato* in relation to baptism. It does not mean that the sacraments have a mechanical or automatic efficacy. Its purpose rather is to emphasize that salvation is a sovereign work of Christ, in distinction to a Pelagian or semi-Pelagian confidence in human ability.[179]

Per Hunter, there is one significant exception to the aforementioned Pentecostal rejection of baptismal regeneration. Namely, one arm of the Oneness Pentecostals has linked 'faith and repentance with water baptism in the name of the Lord Jesus Christ by immersion and initial evidence of Spirit baptism'.[180] Hunter further asserts that Pentecostals will value the 'dispelling of magical ingredients' sometimes injected into this sacrament by declaring WB to be 'both God's gift and our human response'.[181] Hunter offers that since Evangelicals have typically defended the primacy of the spoken word as a means of grace while the 'high church' traditionalists have tended to emphasize the sacramental acts, 'Pentecostals have been inclined, in practice, to look to multiple manifestations of deity'.[182]

The preceding is typical of Hunter's positive interaction with the *BEM* and serves to supplement his treatment of the 'Ordinances, Pentecostal'[183] that is analytical and descriptive rather than prescriptive and constructive. The article focuses on classical Pentecostal positions on the ordinances, excluding Protestant and Roman Catholic charismatic positions that tend to hold to far more sacramental traditions. However, Hunter argues that there is not one uniform Pentecostal position in regard to the Lord's Supper, WB, and footwashing. In fact, some groups do not consider foot-washing in the same class as WB and the Lord's Supper that are generally held to be external rites mandated by Scripture and observed by the gathered community of faith.[184]

---

[179] Hunter, 'Reflections by a Pentecostalist', p. 330.
[180] Hunter, 'Reflections by a Pentecostalist', p. 331.
[181] Hunter, 'Reflections by a Pentecostalist', p. 331.
[182] Hunter, 'Reflections by a Pentecostalist', p. 331.
[183] H.D. Hunter, 'Ordinances, Pentecostal', in Stanley M. Burgess and Eduard M. van der Maas (eds.), *NIDPCM* (rev. and exp. edn; Grand Rapids, MI: Zondervan, 2002), pp. 947-49.
[184] Hunter, 'Ordinances, Pentecostal', p. 947.

Steven J. Land

Steve Land, COG (Cleveland, TN) minister, theologian, pastor, and seminary professor and president published his seminal work, *Pentecostal Spirituality*, in 1993 calling for a revisioning of the Pentecostal tradition. His revisioning views the first ten years of the movement as the heart of its spirituality and not the infancy. Moreover, Land identifies the theological heart of the tradition as the fivefold gospel that proclaims, Jesus is Savior, Sanctifier, Holy Ghost Baptizer, Healer, and Soon Coming King.[185] Land posits that from the outset the early Pentecostals saw themselves as recovering and reentering the same 'new phase of the salvation-history drama of redemption' that had been ushered in on the first day of Pentecost.[186] For the early Pentecostals to abide in the Word was equated to abiding in Jesus and the written Word, per Land. Furthermore, 'the redemption events live in the believers and the believers live in them, because they are in Christ and Christ is in them by the power of the Spirit'.[187] Consequently, 'to abide in the Word was to use it as the norm for evaluating beliefs and practices'.[188] In the face of fanaticism and speculation, daily guidance was open to the HS, often providing new insights into familiar Scriptures; however, 'the beliefs, affections, and practices would all have to be tested by the Word'.[189]

Per Land, the point of Pentecostal spirituality is 'to experience life as part of a biblical drama of participation in God's history'. 'Thus their concern was not so much with an *ordo salutis* as a *via salutis*. The narrative of salvation provided the structure for formation within the missionary movement.'[190] According to Land, the entire congregation was engaged in the formation process. Furthermore, all the elements of corporate worship – singing, preaching, testifying, witnessing, and the ordinances of WB, the Lord's Supper, and footwashing, altar calls, prayer meetings, and the exercise of the gifts of the Spirit – contributed to preparing people to be called to new birth, sanctification, HS baptism, and a life of missionary engagement and

---

[185] Land, *Pentecostal Spirituality*, p. 182.
[186] Land, *Pentecostal Spirituality*, pp. 62-64.
[187] Land, *Pentecostal Spirituality*, p. 66.
[188] Land, *Pentecostal Spirituality*, p. 66.
[189] Land, *Pentecostal Spirituality*, p. 67.
[190] Land, *Pentecostal Spirituality*, p. 67.

witness.[191] Land asserts that 'these ways of remembering the biblical Word mediated the biblical realities in a kind of Pentecostal sacramentality'[192] 'where learning about God and directly experiencing God perpetually inform and depend upon one another'.[193]

Learning about God and directly experiencing God were body-mind-spirit engagements with the HS. The total bodily dedication was necessary since spirituality encompassed the person's whole being, every aspect of his or her personhood. Moreover, 'the correspondence between Spirit and body is evident in a great variety of psychomotor celebration'.[194] Land posits that 'when the congregation gathered for worship they moved as one body-mind-spirit in response to the Holy Spirit'.[195] Spirit-body correspondence was also evidenced in the ordinances of the Lord's Supper, WB, and footwashing.

For the early Pentecostals WB was performed in acknowledgment of an individual's conversion and that all righteousness had been fulfilled Mt. 3.15. Great joy and celebration attended the baptisms as the HS would come close and those gathered would praise God for another person had come to join them on the missionary journey to the kingdom of God. Per Land, baptism was not a converting sacrament of initiation; however, it was viewed as a means of grace in that it represented following Jesus Christ in public solidarity with the church as one started out on his or her journey with the Lord. Infants were not baptized but were dedicated. It was believed that they would not be lost if they died before baptism.

Baptism was individual as well as corporate since it was a death and resurrection ritual of remembrance and hope while serving as the public acceptance of the call to become a holy witness in the power of the HS. In keeping with the Anabaptist tradition, baptism was repeated if persons had been baptized before conversion or if they had backslidden.[196]

---

[191] Land, *Pentecostal Spirituality*, p. 67.
[192] Land, *Pentecostal Spirituality*, p. 67.
[193] R.D. Moore, 'A Pentecostal Approach to Scripture', *The Seminary Viewpoint* 8.1 (1987), pp. 1-2.
[194] Land, *Pentecostal Spirituality*, pp. 108-109.
[195] Land, *Pentecostal Spirituality*, p. 108.
[196] Land, *Pentecostal Spirituality*, pp. 109-10.

The word sacrament was viewed by early Pentecostals as a non-biblical term of Roman Catholic derivation that was associated with mechanical ritual. While the word ordinance was also non-biblical, it was closer to the concept of obeying the commands of Jesus.

Caricaturing the ordinances as mere remembrance and obligation would be to miss the fullness of the actual practice. 'To eat, drink, baptize, and wash feet was to do it unto the Lord; and he was present in, with, under, and through these acts'.[197]

For Land, living in the presence of God is vital to Christian spirituality and Pentecostal piety, in particular. Also, 'the passion for the kingdom is the ruling affection of Pentecostal spirituality and not the mere love of experience for experience's sake'.[198] While this does not mean mere mental exercise or living with certain constant sensations, it does mean participating in community. For Land, Pentecostal spirituality is developed in community, not isolation. Living in God's presence entails placing oneself at the disposal of the HS as the source and direction of daily life. 'Moral integration will be an ongoing, daily gift of grace through all the means of grace (prayer, Scripture, worship, fellowship, counsel, confession, Lord's Supper, footwashing, and so on).'[199]

Peter Hocken
Father Peter Hocken, a charismatic Roman Catholic theologian and historian of the movement, has written several books as well as pieces in both scholarly and popular journals, while maintaining strong ecumenical participation.[200] In 'The Holy Spirit Makes the Church More Eschatalogical',[201] Hocken reports that prior to his involvement with the charismatic movement, he believed in but had given little thought to the second coming of Jesus. He states that 'at best, eschatology was a theological topic that could be interesting, as long

---

[197] Land, *Pentecostal Spirituality*, p. 112.
[198] Land, *Pentecostal Spirituality*, p. 177.
[199] Land, *Pentecostal Spirituality*, p. 204.
[200] C.M. Robeck Jr., 'Hocken, Peter Dudley', in Stanley M. Burgess and Eduard M. van der Maas (eds.), *NIDPCM* (rev. and exp. edn; Grand Rapids, MI: Zondervan, 2002), p. 723.
[201] Peter Hocken, 'The Holy Spirit Makes the Church More Eschatological', in William K. Kay and Anne E. Dyer, *Pentecostal and Charismatic Studies: A Reader* (London: SCM Press, 2004), pp. 43-46.

as it avoided all fundamentalism and naivety'.²⁰² After he experienced a deep renewal of his faith through the charismatic movement, his indifference began to erode as he became vibrantly alive to God's future of the second coming of Jesus Christ.²⁰³

Hocken states that the key that unlocked the truth and power of the second coming was Paul's teaching on the gift of the HS as *arrabon* (deposit) and *aparche* (first fruits). Both of these terms convey the greatness of the present gift of the HS as well as point to what is to come in the fullness of time. Moreover, as believers welcome the gift of the HS in this life, they experience a desire for the fullness of the gift of the HS in the resurrection to come. The HS alone, according to Hocken, can birth this new awakening and longing for the second coming.²⁰⁴

He reports that the Spirit awakens hope of the second coming in the Church as well as the individual Christian. Hocken quickly realized how this longing for the Parousia permeates Roman Catholic liturgy. Of particular interest is the impact of the second coming on the Catechism sections that address the sacraments. Per Hocken, 'the sacramental signs – the baptismal bath, the eucharistic banquet, the anointing with oil for healing – all symbolize and prepare for the glory of the age to come'.²⁰⁵ Through the liturgy and the sacramental signs, the HS makes the Church more eschatological as the Spirit restores the fullness of the NT hope. This blessed hope promises total salvation, the deliverance of all creation from decay and death, and our resurrection in glorified spiritual bodies. The last will enable total communion with all the saints in perfect peace and eternal life of the Father, Son, and HS.²⁰⁶

---

[202] Hocken, 'The Holy Spirit Makes the Church More Eschatological', p. 43.
[203] Hocken, 'The Holy Spirit Makes the Church More Eschatological', p. 43.
[204] Hocken, 'The Holy Spirit Makes the Church More Eschatological', p. 44.
[205] Hocken, 'The Holy Spirit Makes the Church More Eschatological', pp. 44-45.
[206] Hocken, 'The Holy Spirit Makes the Church More Eschatological', pp. 45-46.

Frank D. Macchia

In 1993, Frank Macchia,[207] a Basel-trained systematician and professor of theology at Vanguard University, an AG institution, located in Costa Mesa, CA, published 'Tongues as a Sign: Towards a Sacramental Understanding of Pentecostal Experience'.[208] While the article focuses on tongues the argument mounted by Macchia may have implications for rethinking a Pentecostal theology of WB. Macchia readily acknowledges that most Pentecostals are uncomfortable with the term 'sacrament' due to the association of the term with the 'institutionalization' of the HS and with formal and dead liturgical traditions and the accompanying fear that the use of the term 'sacrament' would imply 'an understanding of sacramental efficacy as necessitated by a causative dynamic intrinsic to the elements'.[209] Nonetheless, Macchia calls for Pentecostals to reconsider usage of the term 'sacrament' in light of theological shifts made recently by contemporary Catholic theologians Karl Rahner and Edward Schillebeeckx who have questioned the neo-scholastic Catholic understanding of the sacraments. In general, this more recent Catholic sacramental theology views the sacraments primarily as occasions for a personal encounter between God and the 'sign value' of the sacrament.[210] Macchia offers the following to support his perspective:

> For Rahner, the reality signified becomes present and is experienced through the visible sign in the process of signification. The reality signified is actually made present in the process of signification, in a way analogous to how we as 'souls' are made present as 'bodies.' Through sacramental signification, the eschatological presence of God is realized among believers.[211]

Macchia asserts that tongues function for Pentecostals in a way similar to Rahner's description of sacrament and that there is

---

[207] Green, *Toward a Pentecostal Theology*, p. 34. According to Pentecostal theologian Chris Green, 'Few Pentecostals or charismatics have made more creative contributions to sacramental theology than Frank Macchia'.

[208] Frank D. Macchia, 'Tongues as a Sign: Towards a Sacramental Understanding of Pentecostal Experience', *Pneuma* 15.1 (1993), pp. 61-76.

[209] Macchia, 'Tongues as a Sign', pp. 61-62.

[210] Macchia, 'Tongues as a Sign', p. 62.

[211] Macchia, 'Tongues as a Sign', pp. 62-63.

'nothing essentially alien in such understandings of sacramental signification to a Pentecostal understanding of the role of tongues as initial evidence of Spirit baptism'.[212]

In the process of embracing the sacramentality of tongues, Macchia urges Pentecostals not to disregard their discomfort with liturgical traditions since glossolalia is a different kind of sacrament than that which is conveyed in formalized and structured liturgies. 'Glossolalia accents the free, dramatic, and unpredictable move of the Spirit of God.'[213] Per Macchia, while reactivity to liturgical worship may be one-sided, it reveals a needed emphasis on the freedom of the HS in worship. Pentecostal worship is characterized by an embryonic sacramentality in that it was formed in reaction to the objectification of the Spirit in formalized rites. Still, in spite of the differences between Pentecostals and Roman Catholics regarding liturgical worship, Macchia is hopeful that his proposal regarding tongues as sacrament may provide a new point of dialogue.[214]

When it comes to Macchia's section entitled 'Tongues and Ecclesial Sacraments', the complexity of the issues compound with a more dynamic and personalistic understanding of sacramental worship in tension with the Protestant principle of the freedom of the Spirit. In the face of this tension Macchia calls for greater exploration for the future of Pentecostal theology. He offers that 'the kind of Pentecostal sacramental spirituality implied in tongues as initial sign arises from a theology that seems more "theophanic" than incarnational'.[215] Consequently, to be 'consistent with Pentecostal theology would be a dynamic notion of the incarnation that portrays Christ as the primary locus of God's active presence'.[216] Once again, a possible solution to fruitful ecumenical discussions is to be found along personalistic versus metaphysical categories when addressing the sacraments of WB and the Lord's Supper.[217]

---

[212] Macchia, 'Tongues as a Sign', p. 63.
[213] Macchia, 'Tongues as a Sign', p. 63.
[214] Macchia, 'Tongues as a Sign', pp. 62-63.
[215] Macchia, 'Tongues as a Sign', p. 73.
[216] Macchia, 'Tongues as a Sign', p. 73.
[217] Macchia, 'Tongues as a Sign', p. 73.

In his essay 'Is Footwashing the Neglected Sacrament? A Theological Response to John Christopher Thomas',[218] Macchia acknowledges that as Pentecostals 'we have developed a sacramental tradition that is not the same as other communions traditionally held to be sacramental'.[219] On the one hand, we observe the Lord's Supper and WB, treating them theologically as acts of symbolic remembrance and repentance rather than as 'sacraments' in the sense that the dynamic presence of Christ through the HS is encountered by the participants. On the other hand, we employ the term 'ordinances' for these rites since Jesus established them. The implication is that they are celebrated only out of obedience. To the contrary, Macchia asserts that thankfully and fortunately 'we have usually experienced baptism and eucharist as occasions for God's redemptive presence through the power of the Spirit, meaning that our theology of the sacraments must still "catch up" to our experience of them'.[220]

Macchia praises Thomas for challenging him as a Pentecostal to rethink how we view WB and the Lord's Supper, and 'how we might approach these "principal" sacraments consistently in a way similar to those powerful encounters with God that we have in glossolalia, footwashing, or healing'.[221] Before discussing the theological import of Thomas' book, Macchia offers a clarifying definition of 'sacrament'. Per Macchia, 'Simply put, "sacrament" in the early church referred to a visible sign of grace'.[222] Similarly, Paul Tillich refers to a sacrament as a 'kairos' event 'in which the visible or audible sign is integrally connected with the divine self-disclosure'.[223] Thus, Macchia picks up on the same argument employed in 'Tongues as a

---

[218] Frank D. Macchia, 'Is Footwashing the Neglected Sacrament? A Theological Response to John Christopher Thomas', *Pneuma* 19.2 (1997), pp. 239-49.

[219] Macchia, 'Is Footwashing the Neglected Sacrament?', p. 241.

[220] Macchia, 'Is Footwashing the Neglected Sacrament?', p. 241.

[221] Macchia, 'Is Footwashing the Neglected Sacrament?', p. 242. This is of particular interest for Macchia given his passion for keeping the ecumenical discussion viable and vibrant between Pentecostals and Roman Catholics and between Pentecostals and members of the Reformed tradition.

[222] Macchia, 'Is Footwashing the Neglected Sacrament?', p. 245. Contrary to medieval Catholic theologian Thomas Aquinas, who argued that sacraments cause what they signify, Karl Rahner and Edward Schillebeeckx locate the power of the sacrament in its sign value.

[223] Macchia, 'Is Footwashing the Neglected Sacrament?', p. 246.

Sign: Towards a Sacramental Understanding of Pentecostal Experience'[224] to support footwashing as a sacrament and for a reconsideration of WB and the Lord's Supper to be revisioned as sacraments in the fullest sense of the term.

Supporting Thomas' view of the sacramentality of footwashing from John 13, Macchia asserts that a possible response to the Johannine message might be to view the footwashing as a link between baptism and the eucharist, interpreting the ongoing significance of baptism for us and preparing us for the eucharist. The footwashing as primarily a sanctifying experience can bridge the original confession of faith found in baptism with the eucharistic meal that celebrates the cross by looking ahead explicitly to the messianic banquet. The fact that the footwashing also points to the cross and implies eschatological significance allows it to play this role as a bridge between baptism and eucharist.[225]

In *Baptized in the Spirit*[226] Macchia addresses the sacraments, WB in particular, in chapter five entitled 'Signs of Grace in a Graceless World: TOWARD A SPIRIT-BAPTIZED ECCLESIOLOGY'. Acknowledging the ambivalence of Pentecostals toward the sacraments, Macchia appears to advance his position by assuming the value of WB as a sacrament or 'visible sign of grace' when addressing the relationship between WB and Spirit baptism: 'Because Christ came into solidarity with us as the man of the Spirit in the baptismal waters, we can by the same Spirit come into solidarity with Christ in our baptism.'[227] Because we are buried with him in baptism it means that our death is now in solidarity with his death Rom. 6.3, 4. Furthermore, just as Christ' death was 'an act of the pouring out of a life through the eternal Spirit (Heb. 9:14) that was shown to be indestructible and victorious (7:16), so our death "with him" takes on the supreme act of an indestructible life poured out for God's

---

[224] Macchia, 'Tongues as a Sign', pp. 61-76.

[225] Macchia, 'Is Footwashing the Neglected Sacrament?', p. 249.

[226] Frank D. Macchia, *Baptized in the Spirit: A Global Pentecostal Theology* (Grand Rapids: Zondervan, 2006).

[227] Macchia, *Baptized in the Spirit*, p. 249. Also see Frank D. Macchia, *Justified in the Spirit: Creation, Redemption, and the Triune God* (Grand Rapids, MI: Eerdmans, 2010), pp. 282-92 for a discussion of the sacraments, WB, in particular, in relationship to justification.

kingdom as well'.[228] Similarly, to complete the sacrament, WB compels us to rise up from the water in newness of life just as Christ rose from the dead to fulfill the will of God on earth. We rise from the water for the same purpose of seeing the kingdom come! Lastly, baptism anticipates the resurrection of the dead 'by the Spirit of holiness' Rom. 1.4.[229]

For Macchia, the purpose of the 'entire performance in baptism of our regeneration by faith in the gospel is to hear this word of the gospel again so that we can publicly perform our conversion to Christ and its fulfillment in resurrection'.[230] In view of this position, Macchia finds infant baptism difficult to justify. In addition to this argument is the lack of evidence from the NT to support infant baptism.

Richard Bicknell

In 1998 Keith Warrington edited and published *Pentecostal Perspectives*,[231] a collection of papers surveying the history, beliefs, practices, and developments of two significant British classical Pentecostal denominations (AG and Elim Pentecostal Church). Within the volume, Richard Bicknell, an Elim theologian, and minister, addresses the thought and practice related to the Lord's Supper and WB under 'The Ordinances: The Marginalized Aspects of Pentecostalism'. Like Robeck and Sandidge, *et al.*, Bicknell attempts to articulate the characteristic shape of the Pentecostal ordinance of baptism. He posits that Pentecostals have historically affirmed a purely symbolic view of the ordinances and eschewed sacramental language with its intimation that 'baptism and the eucharist are sure channels of grace conveying that which they signify'.[232] In fact, Pentecostals avoid sacrament and employ

---

[228] Macchia, *Baptized in the Spirit*, p. 249.
[229] Macchia, *Baptized in the Spirit*, p. 249.
[230] Macchia, *Baptized in the Spirit*, p. 249.
[231] Richard Bicknell, 'The Ordinances: The Marginalized Aspects of Pentecostalism', in Keith Warrington (ed.), *Pentecostal Perspectives* (Carlisle: Paternoster, 1998), pp. 204-22. The volume contains several chapters that address significant issues that have impacted Pentecostalism.
[232] Bicknell, 'The Ordinances', p. 205.

ordinance in order to avoid any sense that 'grace is somehow conveyed to the recipient through the rite itself'.[233]

Accordingly, WB does not affect salvation and should only follow a person's declaration of faith in Christ as an act of obedience to the command of Christ. Since infants cannot make a personal response, paedobaptism is to be rejected.[234] Baptism is viewed, according to Bicknell, as a confession of 'personal salvation' and 'as a sign, baptism expresses "pictorially" a believer's "dying and rising" with Christ'.[235] In the face of questions regarding the necessity of baptism, Bicknell argues that Pentecostals' 'understanding baptism in terms of obedience and disobedience derives from its status as a command of Jesus'.[236] Thus, participation is both expected and encouraged. According to Bicknell, Pentecostals argue that while WB is not essential for salvation, it is required to fulfill obedience to Christ's command.[237]

Echoing Pearlman and Arrington, Bicknell argues that baptism can be a means of grace, while rejecting any concept of a mechanical transfer of saving grace. Bicknell, citing J. Lawrence, Elim Pentecostal theologian, argues that in WB, the believer ratifies his or her commitment to Christ and God confirms through the inner witness of the Spirit God's acceptance and approval of that faith. In this, it becomes a means of grace and a source of great joy to those who meet its demands sincerely.[238]

After setting forth the characteristic thought and practice of the Pentecostal ordinances, Bicknell asserts that overall, 'the content of the Pentecostal discussion of the ordinances, like much of Pentecostal theology, has followed an evangelical agenda'.[239]

---

[233] Bicknell, 'The Ordinances', p. 205.
[234] Bicknell, 'The Ordinances', p. 205.
[235] Bicknell, 'The Ordinances', p. 206.
[236] Bicknell, 'The Ordinances', p. 206.
[237] Bicknell, 'The Ordinances', p. 206.
[238] Bicknell, 'The Ordinances', p. 207.
[239] Bicknell, 'The Ordinances', p. 211-12. More specifically, Bicknell offers that for the past 150 years evangelicals have focused on the need for personal faith response to the gospel as a reaction to the overemphasis on the action of the sacraments. Their understanding of the ordinances grows out of this 'reactionary' environ with the consequential polemical debates that tend to polarization on the historical evangelical/sacramental lines of the debate.

Bicknell notes that while Pentecostals have historically emphasized the practice of the ordinances, detailed discussion of the nature of the ordinances has been lacking. Moreover, Pentecostals tend to focus on the effects or practical benefits from celebrating the ordinances, instead of reflecting on them doctrinally. Consequently, the discussion of ordinances has tended to be descriptive and prescriptive, dependent entirely upon exegesis of Scripture, rather than constructive. Bicknell acknowledges Pentecostal resistance to theological reflection given the long-held association with the 'dry and dead' intellectualism of the 'Established churches'.[240]

Per Bucknell, most Pentecostals today are anti-sacramentalist in spite of the fact that in the early days of the British Pentecostal movement it was ecumenical in character. Moreover, many of the participants came from differing theological traditions that were sacramentalist in practice' however, the 'ecumenical spirit' did not last long. After the pioneers of the movement passed from the scene, new leadership arose that soon adopted the evangelical agenda and forever shifted the stance toward the ordinances.[241]

Moving forward, Bicknell suggests that Pentecostals reclaim a true Pentecostal theology/understanding of the ordinances by focusing on their practices. 'That which at first sight appears to be an "undeveloped theology" might simply signal a different "pragmatic" approach to theology, one which makes practice its defining statement.'[242]

More specifically, Pentecostals have tended to focus on the 'result' of an ordinance; for example, 'tangible' communion with Christ, restoration, and revitalization are all associated with participation in the ordinances.[243] In sum, the Pentecostal ordinances should retain an almost exclusively salvific reference with an awareness of the presence of the HS. Similarly, Pentecostal ordinances should be celebrated with a keen awareness of the larger faith community that is bearing witness to the baptism of new believers.[244]

---

[240] Bicknell, 'The Ordinances', p. 213.
[241] Bicknell, 'The Ordinances', pp. 214-15.
[242] Bicknell, 'The Ordinances', p. 216.
[243] Bicknell, 'The Ordinances', p. 216.
[244] Bicknell, 'The Ordinances', pp. 216-17.

Simon Tan

In his 2003 essay, 'Reassessing Believer's Baptism in Pentecostal Theology and Practice',[245] Simon Tan, an AG minister and theologian, calls for Pentecostals to reconsider their stance against infant baptism. He explains his interest in the baptismal ordinance arose after being questioned regarding the lack of infant baptisms in the local AG churches. Further reflection led Tan to study the reasons for withholding baptism from infants that then compelled him to call for a reassessment.

According to Tan there are two main approaches to WB. One emphasizes the necessity of a faith response prior to the believer being baptized. This is often called the subjective view.[246] However, the objective view sees 'baptism simply as an expression of the reality of the grace of God in the life of the individual'.[247]

Tan's study reflects the evangelical versus sacramentalist arguments just addressed in Bicknell without a distinctive Pentecostal contribution. While Tan appears to understand and appreciate the subjective position, he argues for and sides with the objective, finding infant baptism to be preferred. Since he finds no clear evidence in Scripture, either explicitly for or against infant baptism, Tan raises the objection that 'an independent individualism as expressed in believer's baptism is a uniquely American and modern western phenomenon'[248] and does not fit with Asian culture's valuation of family, lineage, and society. Moreover, Tan is concerned that believer's baptism leads Pentecostals further down the road to collapse into subjectivism and the 'heroics' demanded of a faith response.[249] Infant baptism, however, does not oppose biblical teachings, fits well with Asian culture, respects the grace of God, and is 'grounded not in human will or doing but solely in the will and word of God'.[250] Tan rejects infant dedication due to the lack of biblical and theological warrant and closes by asserting, 'I personally believe that infant baptism is biblically warranted, and to baptize them is to respond

---

[245] Simon G.H. Tan, 'Reassessing Believer's Baptism in Pentecostal Theology and Practice', *AJPS* 6.2 (2003), pp. 219-34.
[246] Tan, 'Reassessing Believer's Baptism', pp. 219-20.
[247] Tan, 'Reassessing Believer's Baptism', p. 219.
[248] Tan, 'Reassessing Believer's Baptism', p. 230.
[249] Tan, 'Reassessing Believer's Baptism', p. 233.
[250] Tan, 'Reassessing Believer's Baptism', p. 233.

faithfully to God's word of grace'.²⁵¹ I believe Tan has, perhaps unknowingly, argued for the merits of infant baptism based on the subjective valuation of his cultural preferences and the silence of Scripture over against Christ's clear command of believers to be baptized in water (Mt. 28.19).

Daniel E. Albrecht

In *Rites in the Spirit*²⁵² published in 1999, Daniel Albrecht, then Professor of Christian History and Spirituality at Bethany College, an AG institution, located in Santa Cruz, CA, attempts to understand more fully Pentecostal/charismatic spirituality by describing, analyzing, and constructively interpreting it through the lens of ritual or Sunday morning corporate worship.²⁵³ Albrecht and his team of researchers employ participant observation and ethnographic interviews to gather information from their subjects. Albrecht then performs the final analysis of three Pentecostal/charismatic communities,²⁵⁴ with special attention given to their appropriation/ reappropriation of Pentecostal symbols. Albrecht concludes his research asserting that 'members of each of the three congregations manifest a typical Pentecostal propensity for mystical experiences of the Spirit both in liturgy and in personal life'.²⁵⁵ More specifically, he asserts

---

²⁵¹ Tan, 'Reassessing Believer's Baptism', p. 234.

²⁵² Daniel E. Albrecht, *Rites in the Spirit: A Ritual Approach to Pentecostal/ Charismatic Spirituality* (JPTSup 17; Sheffield: Sheffield Academic Press, 1999).

²⁵³ Albrecht asserts that although classical Pentecostals and charismatics share a basic experience of the HS, charismatics are more likely than classical Pentecostals to desire and formulate a sacramental theology, because the former come from traditions that practice the sacraments regularly. In fact, this is a key distinctive of the charismatic movement.

²⁵⁴ All three of these 'faith communities' are located in Sea City, CA: CCC, a classical Pentecostal church of the AG denomination; L&L, an 'untraditional' and 'creative' community of the Foursquare denomination; and VVCF, a charismatic church and member of The Community of Vineyard Churches, USA. None of the three churches represent what their own denominations consider 'ethnic', 'non-English speaking', or 'African-American' congregations. Also, Albrecht chose churches that reflect a more baptistic or reformed style of Pentecostalism as opposed to the Wesleyan type. Lastly, he chose churches that maintain a Trinitarian theology as opposed to a Unitarian view of Pentecostalism. Cf. Albrecht, *Rites in the Sprit*, pp. 72-73, n. 5.

²⁵⁵ Albrecht, *Rites in the Sprit*, p. 118.

experiencing God is the fundamental goal of the pentecostal [sic] service. This experiencing or encountering God is often symbolized as felt presence of the divine. The sense of the divine presence is a primary component, an aim, of spirituality Pentecostal efforts to develop and maintain pathways into the presence points to the centrality of the mystical element in pentecostal [sic] spirituality.[256]

Albrecht's summary on the meaning of the use of 'altar space' by the three congregations reveals that the 'altar space functions symbolically as an *axis mundi* in Pentecostal spirituality, a sacred place, a place for meeting God, a place for humans to make self-offerings in prayers, actions and ministry rites'.[257] Albrecht states the communion table is 'traditionally centered below the pulpit on the main floor below the platform in Pent/Char churches'.[258] It is no longer a permanent fixture in the ritual space of CCC and it never was in the newer churches, L&L and VVCF. Apparently, the communion table appears regularly once a month when the eucharist is celebrated. According to Albrecht, 'this is further minimization of the table as a ritual center within the altar space. Pentecostals, CCC included, have not traditionally focused on the sacrament of communion.'[259] Also, the baptismal font is another minimized center. While all three of the churches practice adult/believer's baptism, only the CCC has a baptistry. Albrecht posits this may be due to L&L and VVCF holding services in buildings not originally constructed for worship but it may 'also point to a relative de-emphasis on baptism as a Christian community boundary'.[260] Despite the lack of communion tables and baptismal fonts and the 'relative de-emphasis' of WB and the Lord's Supper in relationship to other practices, Albrecht states that it is not his intent to intimate that these three 'churches are not interested in the sacramental dimensions of worship. Though they seldom use the sacramental language, they

---

[256] Daniel E. Albrecht, 'Pentecostal Spirituality: Looking Through the Lens of Ritual', *Pneuma* 14.2 (1992), pp. 107-25 (114).
[257] Albrecht, *Rites in the Sprit*, p. 133.
[258] Albrecht, *Rites in the Sprit*, p. 132.
[259] Albrecht, *Rites in the Sprit*, p. 132.
[260] Albrecht, *Rites in the Sprit*, p. 132.

certainly believe and experience their God's gracious acts.'[261] Per Albrecht, Pentecostal and charismatic sacramentality is unique given the situating of their spirituality within the Christian mystical tradition.[262]

Albrecht's claim to the sacramentality of the three churches under observation appears to be based on their individual and collective encounters of the divine presence, despite the minimization of WB and the Lord's Supper. One is made to wonder about the theological content and parameters of mystical encounters when the theological moorings appear to have been diminished.

Amos Yong

Amos Yong, a licensed AG minister and now Director of the Center for Missiological Research and Professor of Theology and Mission at Fuller Theological Seminary, Pasadena, CA, is a prolific writer and one of the foremost Pentecostal theologians of the twenty-first century. In *The Spirit Poured Out on All* Flesh[263] Yong attempts to develop and articulate a 'world theology' through the perspective of Pentecostal experiences and practices in conversation with the classical and disparate contemporary theological and philosophical viewpoints.

Yong writes from a Trinitarian theological perspective, employing 'pneumatological imagination' throughout his work. His reflection on WB is found in chapter three entitled 'The Acts of the Apostles and

---

[261] Albrecht, *Rites in the Sprit*, p. 132.

[262] Daniel E. Albrecht, 'Pentecostal Spirituality: Ecumenical Potential and Challenge', *Cyberjournal for Pentecostal-Charismatic Research* 2 (July 1997), <http://www.pctii.org/cyberj/cyberj2/albrecht.html>. Albrecht goes on to assert that

> in a very real sense the Sunday services of all of our focus churches are designed to provide a context for a mystical *encounter*, an experience with the divine … The primary rites of worship and altar/response are particularly structured to sensitize the congregants to the presence of the divine and to stimulate conscious experience of God. The worship and praise rite especially functions as a framing context for certain mystical experiences of God. At least in part, the apparent goal of the worship service is to allow the worshippers to have a heightened sense of the presence of the divine. The gestures, ritual actions, and symbols all function within this context to speak of the manifest presence.

[263] Amos Yong, *The Spirit Poured Out on All Flesh: Pentecostalism and the Possibility of Global Theology* (Grand Rapids, MI: Baker Academic, 2005).

of the Holy Spirit: Toward a Pneumatological Ecclesiology'.[264] Before addressing WB, in particular, Yong asserts that 'Pentecostal sacramentality should *not* be considered in the classical sense, whereby salvation is mediated through the priesthood, through baptism or through the (other) sacraments'.[265] Rather, he avers that Pentecostals strongly believe that the 'Spirit who resides within and presides over the church is the same Spirit who anointed Jesus of Nazareth and that the Spirit is truly encountered and manifest palpably and tangibly in the lives of individuals who constitute the church'.[266] The HS is made manifest 'through tongues, healings, the shout, the dance – the Spirit's reality is mediated through the particularly embodied experiences of the community of saints'.[267] Consequently, there is a different or unique form of sacramentality at work, according to Yong. He posits that it is 'an experiential and incarnational logic that acknowledges the Spirit's being made present and active through the materiality of personal embodiment and congregational life'.[268]

With the preceding cautionary note and expanded view of sacramentality on record Yong moves to set forth his views on WB in 'Born of Water and the Spirit: Toward a Pneumatological Theology of Baptism'. Along the way, he notes traditional views, problematic issues, and navigates his way through the quagmire while holding forth his pneumatological ecclesiological view of baptism. First, Yong opines that both the biblical and patristic witnesses posit an unquestionable connection between WB and SB. He rejects baptismal regeneration 'if understood to refer to the baptismal waters' magically washing away sins 1 Pet. 3:21, but can be accepted if understood pneumatically and mystically as an action of the Spirit (e.g., Titus 3:5) that includes the faith response of believers'.[269]

Second, per Yong, 'the theology and practices of Oneness Pentecostals also hold water and Spirit baptism together in ways consistent with the early church but with the explicit rejection of

---

[264] Yong, *The Spirit Poured Out on All Flesh*, pp. 121-66.
[265] Yong, *The Spirit Poured Out on All Flesh*, p. 136. Emphasis original.
[266] Yong, *The Spirit Poured Out on All Flesh*, p. 136.
[267] Yong, *The Spirit Poured Out on All Flesh*, p. 136.
[268] Yong, *The Spirit Poured Out on All Flesh*, p. 136.
[269] Yong, *The Spirit Poured Out on All Flesh*, p. 157.

baptismal regeneration magically understood'.²⁷⁰ Yong writes supportively of OP views, citing their adherence to the apostolic model in the book of Acts. He is not without critique, stating 'they also oftentimes go further than the traditional soteriological view of baptism ... full salvation includes repentance, baptism in water, and the reception of the Holy Spirit ... evidenced by speaking in other tongues'.²⁷¹ Yong parts ways regarding the soteriological significance of tongues-speech asserting, 'Any dogmatic stance of evidential tongues as salvific is dubious precisely because such dogmatism runs counter to the dynamic, holistic, and eschatological dimensions of Christian life and experience'.²⁷²

Yong posits the key elements of a Pentecostal and pneumatological theology of WB can be articulated with the assistance of the ecumenical *BEM*. First and foremost, the invocation of the HS at the time of the celebration of the Christian rite of WB should declare the event as explicitly Christian and locate the sacramentality in the presence, power, and activity of the HS and not in the materiality of the consecrated water.²⁷³

A second point highlighted by the *BEM* is that WB 'enacts our participation in the death and resurrection of Christ and our conversion/cleansing but also represents our reception of the gift of the Holy Spirit'.²⁷⁴ According to Yong, 'Baptism is, in this sense, a concrete experiencing of the death and life of Jesus (the body of Christ) (cf. Rom. 6:4; Gal. 3:27; Col. 2:12). It is both an invitation to identify with the death and life of Jesus and an actualization of this reenactment.'²⁷⁵ To employ Wesleyan and Pentecostal language WB becomes the 'crisis experience' or the historical point in time when one experiences the life of Jesus Christ by the power of the HS. Empowered by the HS, believers are equipped to follow in the footsteps of Jesus and to do what he did.²⁷⁶

Yong's final point is that if the preceding 'sketch has any validity, Pentecostals can cease to be suspicious of sacramental language

---

[270] Yong, *The Spirit Poured Out on All Flesh*, p. 157.
[271] Yong, *The Spirit Poured Out on All Flesh*, p. 157.
[272] Yong, *The Spirit Poured Out on All Flesh*, p. 158.
[273] Yong, *The Spirit Poured Out on All Flesh*, p. 158.
[274] Yong, *The Spirit Poured Out on All Flesh*, p. 159.
[275] Yong, *The Spirit Poured Out on All Flesh*, p. 159.
[276] Yong, *The Spirit Poured Out on All Flesh*, p. 159.

regarding baptism'.[277] He argues that at the least, there is a protosacramental character to baptism as Christian initiation if baptism is understood to be obedient participation in the death of Christ and realization of new life in Christ through the power of the HS. On the other extreme, if WB is understood as a 'living and transformative act of the Spirit of God on the community of faith, then baptism is not only protosacramental but fully sacramental in the sense of enacting the life and grace of God to those who need and receive it by faith'.[278] Yong's comments are designed to challenge his Pentecostal colleagues and churches to move beyond 'a purely symbolic view of the ordinances'. He believes his proposal is consistent with 'pentecostal [sic] intuitions regarding the Spirit's presence and activity in the worshipping community'.[279]

Most recently, (2014) in his *Renewing Christian Theology*, Yong 'seeks to provide a summary exposition of central teachings of the Christian faith relevant to the twenty-first-century global renewal context'.[280] Yong's order of presentation follows the World AG Fellowship's Statement of Faith with one notable exception – he puts eschatology as his first chapter after the introduction. Yong asserts that 'eschatology provides the initial thrust and orientation for renewal thinking rather than being relegated, as historically, to an afterthought'[281] as the rationale.

Yong's treatment of WB is found in chapter six entitled 'Ordinances and Sacraments: *Practicing the Christian Life*'. He includes the World AG Fellowship Statement of Faith – Article 7: The Ordinances of the Church for reference. The relevant portion pertaining to WB follows: 'We believe that baptism in water by immersion is expected of all who have repented and believed. In so doing they declare to the world that they have died with Christ and

---

[277] Yong, *The Spirit Poured Out on All Flesh*, p. 160.
[278] Yong, *The Spirit Poured Out on All Flesh*, p. 160.
[279] Yong, *The Spirit Poured Out on All Flesh*, p. 160.
[280] Amos Yong with Jonathan A. Anderson, *Renewing Christian Theology: Systematics for a Global Christianity* (Waco, TX: Baylor University Press, 2014), pp. xxiii, 20. His 'wager' is that 'the Christian theological tradition as a whole has something to gain from engaging especially with renewal voices and perspectives and may even be revitalized in such a discussion'.
[281] Yong and Anderson, *Renewing Christian Theology*, p. xxiii.

been raised with Him to walk in newness of life (Matthew 28:19; Acts 10:47-48; Romans 6:4).'[282]

Yong notes well how the Article 7 language of 'ordinances' signals the contentious debate launched during the Reformation, which has resurfaced with a vengeance within the renewal movement. After a descriptive historical account of how the tensions between the 'ordinance' and 'sacramental' perspectives came to exist within the Pentecostal and charismatic movements, and an excursus into the history of Christian initiation, Yong offers a way forward via a renewed Christian theology of the sacraments.

Preferring to refer to them as Christian practices, Yong attests that the Trinitarian character of baptism, the Lord's Supper, and the renunciation of evil have to be noted and maintained. More specifically, concerning WB, the Christological, pneumatological, and relational core has to be kept in focus. While baptism is followed on the basis of Jesus' command Mt. 28.19 and apostolic injunction Acts 2.38, Jesus' example of being baptized by John Mt. 3.16; Mk 1.10; Luke 3.22; Jn. 1.32-34 and reception of the Spirit are paradigmatic for Christian practice.

Moreover, it is consistent with his teaching of Nicodemus that one must be born of water and the Spirit.[283] 'More importantly, Jesus' own Spirit-baptized life is the reality into which his followers are invited, precisely through their own baptism in, with, and by the Holy Spirit.'[284] It is crucial for Yong that in addition to focusing on the Christological and pneumatological aspects of the Christian practices it is remembered that there 'is identification of the trinitarian [sic] God as the one who has initiated such charismatic and redemptive encounters for human beings and has chosen to reveal himself in precisely these events'.[285] Consequently, 'this means that the practices precede individual participation ... and that these ecclesial practices of the body of Christ and the fellowship of the Spirit ... constitute the normal matrix within or through which people encounter God's saving actions'.[286] 'So there is something sacramental about these

---

[282] Yong and Anderson, *Renewing Christian Theology*, p. 131.
[283] Yong and Anderson, *Renewing Christian Theology*, pp. 153-54.
[284] Yong and Anderson, *Renewing Christian Theology*, p. 154.
[285] Yong and Anderson, *Renewing Christian Theology*, p. 154.
[286] Yong and Anderson, *Renewing Christian Theology*, p. 154.

practices insofar as they are occasions through which salvific grace meets human creatures'.[287] Grace-filled encounters occur not because certain words, formulas or actions are performed. Rather, God's saving power is made manifest to the body of Christ as long as they are represented relationally in Jesus Christ through the power of the HS.

Yong avers that while the triune God initiates the Christian practices, their reception by human creatures must be involved to maintain their relational character. Therefore, there is a performative aspect to the practices in general and WB, in particular. By baptizing in the name of Jesus Acts 2.38; 8.16; 10.48 or in the name of the Triune God Mt. 28.19 'Christians as historically embodied creatures are tangibly and kinesthetically both receiving from God and simultaneously bearing witness to the world'.[288] Thus, Yong argues that 'there are both iconic and symbolic aspects to the practices. As Jesus himself … so also can the body of Christ be understood iconically as announcing the arrival of God's reign and mediating the good news of that reign through its various practices.'[289] The import of an iconic representation is that it expedites access to what lies behind or beyond the icon. The salient point is not that this or that material is iconic. Rather, 'the world as created can always be a medium of revelation regarding the Creator'.[290]

Kenneth J. Archer

In 'Nourishment for our Journey: The Pentecostal *Via Salutis* and Sacramental Ordinances',[291] Kenneth J. Archer, Professor of Theology at Southeastern University (an AG institution), located in Lakeland, FL, an ordained Bishop in the COG (Cleveland, TN), follows up and further develops John Christopher Thomas' 'insightful suggestion to connect a Sacrament with each of the theological themes of the five-fold gospel'.[292] Archer anchors his essay in a 'narrative-praxis' approach to doing theology. More specifically, 'Praxis, as a method, unites practice (doing) and theory

---

[287] Yong and Anderson, *Renewing Christian Theology*, p. 154.
[288] Yong and Anderson, *Renewing Christian Theology*, p. 155.
[289] Yong and Anderson, *Renewing Christian Theology*, p. 155.
[290] Yong and Anderson, *Renewing Christian Theology*, p. 155.
[291] Archer, 'Nourishment for our Journey', pp. 79-96.
[292] Archer, 'Nourishment for our Journey', pp. 81-82 n. 5.

(knowing) into the same reflective activity'.[293] This type of approach supports a critical commitment to theological reflection while acknowledging that our religious experiences shape our beliefs, and our beliefs, in turn, form our activities. Thus, practice and theory are inseparable and mutually informing. Concerning narrative Archer intends 'to highlight the importance of understanding Scripture as a grand meta-narrative with the Gospels and Acts as the heart of the Christian story'.[294] Hence, 'Jesus Christ is the center and leader of Christianity; therefore, a narrative theology will emphasize the priority of the story of Jesus Christ and its significance for the Christian community and for the world'.[295]

Archer argues that the worshipping community is the rightful contextual arena for the discussion of theology and that the sacraments should be placed within the theological framework of the way of salvation since the Pentecostal *via salutis* is a dynamic pneumatic soteriology.[296] According to Archer, 'The sacraments are significant symbolic signs that bring transformative grace by bringing people into closer contact with the saving action of Jesus'.[297]

With the preceding in view, the author asserts that Pentecostalism from its very inception has intentionally placed Jesus Christ and the full gospel at the center of its beliefs and practices. The 'full gospel' or 'fivefold gospel' is Jesus proclaimed as Savior, Sanctifier, Spirit Baptizer, Healer, and Soon-Coming King. He, therefore, calls for a revisioning of the 'historical' 'Pentecostal understanding of ordinances into 'sacramental' ordinances 'because in Pentecostal worshipping communities these rites provide sacramental experiences for the faith-filled participants'.[298] These are redemptive experiences since they provide ongoing spiritual formation of being conformed to the image of Christ through the participatory reenactment of various parts of the story of Jesus Christ.

With Christ at the center as the ultimate sacrament, Archer argues for employing 'sacramental' ordinances concerning WB and the

---

[293] Archer, 'Nourishment for our Journey', p. 81.
[294] Archer, 'Nourishment for our Journey', p. 81.
[295] Archer, 'Nourishment for our Journey', p. 81.
[296] Archer, 'Nourishment for our Journey', pp. 81-82.
[297] Archer, 'Nourishment for our Journey', p. 82.
[298] Archer, 'Nourishment for our Journey', p. 85.

Lord's Supper. Here Archer follows the lead of evangelical scholar Stanley Grenz, who argues for retaining the term ordinance and asserts the ordinances are channels for the HS to work in the lives of Christians, thereby serving as more than memorial rites.[299]

To the dismay of Archer, there are some Pentecostals who 'deny any "real grace" being mediated through the participatory ordinance to the community'.[300] Consequently, these 'mysteries' are reduced to memorial rituals for cognitive reflection and emotional machinations devoid of the HS's presence and power.

Per Archer, 'the sacramental ordinances become means of grace for the receptive individuals-in-community'.[301] Moreover, they are not 'magical actions' or 'symbols of human response'. Rather, the sacramental ordinances are 'effective means of grace when inspired by the Holy Spirit and received by genuine human response in faith'.[302]

Following the schema suggested by Thomas of connecting a sacrament with each of the theological themes of the fivefold gospel, Archer links WB with Jesus as Savior. In his sketch of the connections between WB and Jesus as Savior, Archer employs the narrative theology approach to ground the believer's story in the story of Jesus.

Jesus is our Savior. According to Archer, Jesus, our atoning sacrifice, has ransomed us from the kingdom of spiritual darkness and reconciled us to God the father. He is the pioneer and perfecter of our faith, per Heb. 12.2. Persons are saved when they call upon the name of Jesus, repenting from their sin and turning to God. These persons experience justification and regeneration by the grace of God. 'They are born again and have the Holy Spirit. All future redemptive experiences spring forth from the seed sown in the initial experience of salvation'.[303]

The sacramental ordinance that publicly proclaims a person's new identity in Jesus Christ and his community of disciples is WB. New converts are baptized by immersion in water because Jesus

---

[299] Archer, 'Nourishment for our Journey', p. 84.
[300] Archer, 'Nourishment for our Journey', p. 84.
[301] Archer, 'Nourishment for our Journey', p. 86.
[302] Archer, 'Nourishment for our Journey', p. 86.
[303] Archer, 'Nourishment for our Journey', p. 91.

commanded his followers to do so Mt. 28.18-20.³⁰⁴ Archer posits that 'Water baptism recapitulates the protection of Noah and his family from divine judgment sent upon the wicked (Gen, 6-9; 1 Pet. 3.20-21) and also the Israelites' exodus deliverance through the waters of the Red Sea.'³⁰⁵ Through their deliverance from the Red Sea, they emerged as 'a people belonging to God on "the way" to the promised land. Water baptism is the sacramental sign initiating one into the cooperate *via salutis*.'³⁰⁶

While the focus of WB is on the candidate, it is not on the candidate alone. The community members witness the candidate's baptism and are also beckoned by the HS to relive their own initiatory salvific experiences. Thus, they are called to re-identify themselves as part of the redemptive community – the body of Jesus Christ. Archer offers that baptism also functions to direct us to the 'ultimate goal of salvation – glorification and the redemption of creation. It is a promise that creates hope and reshapes our identity as we proleptically participate in the redemptive experience.'³⁰⁷ Archer states that 'We are the eschatological community of God and, as this community, we function as a redemptive sacrament for the world – the body of Christ broken for the healing of the nations'.³⁰⁸

Simon Chan

Simon Chan, an AG minister, systematician, and liturgist is the former Earnest Lau Professor of Systematic Theology and Dean of Studies at Trinity Theological College, Singapore. In his *Spiritual Theology*³⁰⁹ under the rubric, 'The Nature of the Visible Church', Chan asserts that 'Present-day Protestantism must return to its sacramental heritage if it hopes to discover an authentic spirituality that goes beyond individualistic piety'.³¹⁰ Two years later, addressing concerns within Pentecostalism, Chan posits that for the 'Pentecostal church

---

³⁰⁴ Archer, 'Nourishment for our Journey', p. 91. It is 'by immersion' since it best reenacts 'the salvific experience of identifying with the death and resurrection of Jesus (Rom. 6.4) for the forgiveness of sins (Acts 2.38).
³⁰⁵ Archer, 'Nourishment for our Journey', p. 91.
³⁰⁶ Archer, 'Nourishment for our Journey', p. 91.
³⁰⁷ Archer, 'Nourishment for our Journey', p. 91.
³⁰⁸ Archer, 'Nourishment for our Journey', p. 91.
³⁰⁹ Simon Chan, *Spiritual Theology: A Systematic Study of the Christian Life* (Downers Grove, IL: InterVarsity Press, 1998).
³¹⁰ Chan, *Spiritual Theology*, p. 109.

to be an effective bearer of its own tradition, there needs to be a radical revisioning of the church'.[311] He argues that the church should not be viewed primarily as a functional entity for the sake of organizational effectiveness, existing within time and space. Rather, the Church should be understood as this and more. The church is 'supremely a spiritual reality, though existing in space and time, transcends space and time'.[312] Furthermore, the church is not the total of all Christians. Rather, the church exists prior to individual Christians. Chan asserts that 'To understand the church in this way, we need to reconsider the place of the sacraments and pneumatology'.[313] Moreover, 'Pentecostals need to see beyond a doctrine of the Spirit as "my personal Comforter" to one that sees the Spirit as first and foremost the Spirit for the *church* coming from *beyond* history'.[314] Chan opines that the implications of this approach for Pentecostal worship are far-reaching and that Pentecostals can learn much from Eastern Orthodoxy. Lastly, he asserts that the radical revisioning of the church, as proposed above, will aid Pentecostals in recovering a genuine sense of solidarity with all Christians just as the original Pentecostal pioneers manifested an ecumenical impulse in spite of racial, ethnic, educational, cultural, and socio-economic differences.

Chan's summons to reconsider the place of the sacraments in the church appears to focus primarily on the Lord's Supper or Eucharist. In response to 'What, then, makes for a sound, holistic worship which enlivens a sound, holistic theology?' Chan responds, 'I would like to suggest that it is worship where the eucharist is the organizing centre'.[315] Nonetheless, he also addresses the import of WB in the life of the church. Chan avers that the church is most clearly 'the church as it celebrates baptism and the Eucharist. Baptism incorporates new members into the body of Christ, and the Eucharist reveals the communal nature of the Christian life (Acts

---

[311] Chan, *Pentecostal Theology and the Christian Tradition*, p. 14.
[312] Chan, *Pentecostal Theology and the Christian Tradition*, p. 14.
[313] Chan, *Pentecostal Theology and the Christian Tradition*, p. 14.
[314] Chan, *Pentecostal Theology and the Christian Tradition*, p. 14. Italics original.
[315] Chan, *Pentecostal Theology and the Christian Tradition*, p. 37. Chan's passion for the Eucharist as an organizing center for worship finds its fullest treatment in Simon Chan, *Liturgical Theology: The Church as Worshiping Community* (Downers Grove, IL: InterVarsity Press, 2006).

2:42-47).[316] 'It is in that living organism called the church that we receive our true identity.'[317]

In addition to the church being a sacramental community, it is also an eschatological community. He argues that it is in the sacraments that the 'transcendent and historical poles of the church's being are brought into dialectical relationship. Baptism is incorporation into the *new* creation in Christ; the Eucharistic celebration is a constant reminder that Christ is present and also to come (1 Cor. 11:26).'[318] For Chan, the 'signs of the sacramental community are also the signs of an eschatological community: a community on the move, whose life and mission are always directed toward the future, the *visio Dei*'.[319] Consequently, the 'fellowship of Jesus Christ' to which God has called the baptized is an exacting community, a costly fellowship. The demands of discipleship call for spiritual development of which prayer is a primary component. Prayer, according to Chan, is by divine initiative and an outworking of WB:

> Prayer, like everything else about the Christian life, begins with the fact of our incorporation into Christ. Prayer, as Gregory of Sinai (mid-fourteenth century) puts it, is the manifesting of baptism. It arises out of the basic fact that we have been baptized into the body of Christ and that we share the life of Christ and his Word in the body. Prayer is essentially the human response to the Word. We do not originate prayer; prayer is already going on in us. God's Word has the initiative; we are simply the listeners.[320]

In *Liturgical Theology* Chan examines WB more closely in a chapter entitled 'The Catechumenate'.[321] He provides a brief review of the history of the catechumenate, pre, and post-Constantine, and asserts that 'the key to the making of a real Christian is still the catechumenate',[322] arguing that it must be intentionally connected to the liturgy and worship of the church. Chan avers that after persons have completed training, and 'after the catechumens have been

---

[316] Chan, *Spiritual Theology*, p. 112.
[317] Chan, *Spiritual Theology*, p. 208.
[318] Chan, *Spiritual Theology*, pp. 112-13.
[319] Chan, *Spiritual Theology*, p. 113.
[320] Chan, *Spiritual Theology*, p. 128.
[321] Chan, *Liturgical Theology*, pp. 101-25.
[322] Chan, *Liturgical Theology*, p. 105.

satisfactorily "scrutinized" concerning their way of life in accordance with the creed, the Ten Commandments, and the Lord's Prayer, they are ready for baptism'.[323] 'If the catechumenate is the process of weaning the Christian from the world, the flesh and the devil, then baptism constitutes the final break with the three enemies of the soul.'[324]

For Chan, WB has both individual and cosmic implications since WB is also the occasion for Spirit baptism. He argues that 'Christian baptism is unlike John's baptism in that it is Jesus' baptizing with the Spirit. Thus, the water ritual can be understood only in relation to the gift of the Spirit'.[325] Alluding to Peter's response in Acts 2.38 Chan asserts that 'The world needs to be transformed into church through a radical break with the past (repentance) and incorporation into the body of Christ (baptism)'.[326] Citing Col. 1.13, Eph. 5.8, 1 Pet. 2.9-10, 20-21, and 1 Cor. 10.2, he illustrates the various portrayals of transformation employed by NT writers. According to Chan, the cosmic dimension of baptism referenced in 2 Cor. 5.17 (immersion into death and rising into new life in the new creation) does not infer a loss of one's unique identity. Rather, 'It is the old self that is buried, and out of the old emerges the new self. Our true personal identity is revealed in Christ. As members of Christ's body, we are unique persons with very distinctive functions.'[327]

Wesley Scott Biddy

In his 2005 *Pneuma* article, 'Re-envisioning the Pentecostal Understanding of the Eucharist: An Ecumenical Proposal',[328] Wesley Scott Biddy asserts a resounding 'yes' to the question, 'Is there any such thing' as a 'distinctively Pentecostal sacramentology'?[329] While the answer is affirmative, Biddy admits 'it is largely undeveloped' and 'many Pentecostals are uncomfortable with the word *sacrament* because they associate it with a "High Church" liturgical worship

---

[323] Chan, *Liturgical Theology*, p. 117.
[324] Chan, *Liturgical Theology*, p. 117.
[325] Chan, *Liturgical Theology*, p. 119.
[326] Chan, *Liturgical Theology*, p. 118.
[327] Chan, *Liturgical Theology*, p. 118.
[328] Wesley Scott Biddy, 'Re-envisioning the Pentecostal Understanding of the Eucharist: An Ecumenical Proposal', *Pneuma* 28.2 (2006), p. 228.
[329] Biddy, 'Re-envisioning the Pentecostal Understanding', p. 230.

format that they consider frozen'.³³⁰ Nonetheless, he believes the 'resources latent in Pentecostal spirituality hold much potential for developing a conscious theological appreciation of the sacramental character of worship in general'.³³¹ Of particular interest to Biddy are 'those ecclesial rituals that have historically been explicitly recognized as "sacraments" in particular'.³³² With the preceding in view, Biddy's goal is to investigate the inherent latent potential in order 'to demonstrate how, if shaped in a certain way, this area of Pentecostal theology can aid doctrinal rapprochement between Pentecostals and other groups of Christians'.³³³ With an ecumenical agenda in clear view, Biddy focuses his investigation on the Eucharist as his starting point. While Biddy's study lies outside our focus on WB, his line of reasoning for re-envisioning the sacramental nature of Pentecostal worship with its particular ecclesial rituals has much to offer for consideration.

Biddy begins his investigation by citing the Council of Trent definition of a sacrament as 'a symbol of something sacred, a visible form of invisible grace, having the power of sanctifying'.³³⁴ Dismissing the last phrase as the most disputable, he employs 'symbol' as the focal point, reinterpreting it using Tillichian categories of sign/symbol.

According to Tillich, a sign 'bears no necessary relation to which it points'³³⁵ whereas a 'symbol participates in the reality of that for which it stands ... Therefore, the religious symbol, the symbol which points to the divine, can be a true symbol only if it participates in the power of the divine to which it points'.³³⁶ In a similar vein, Biddy cites Edward Schillebeeckx, Roman Catholic theologian, who observes that theologians post-World War II have recognized that 'the sacraments are first and foremost symbolic acts of activity as signs'.³³⁷ From Tillich and Schillibeeckx Biddy asserts that a

---

³³⁰ Biddy, 'Re-envisioning the Pentecostal Understanding', p. 228. Emphasis original.
³³¹ Biddy, 'Re-envisioning the Pentecostal Understanding', p. 228.
³³² Biddy, 'Re-envisioning the Pentecostal Understanding', p. 228.
³³³ Biddy, 'Re-envisioning the Pentecostal Understanding', p. 228.
³³⁴ Biddy, 'Re-envisioning the Pentecostal Understanding', pp. 228-29.
³³⁵ Biddy, 'Re-envisioning the Pentecostal Understanding', p. 229.
³³⁶ Biddy, 'Re-envisioning the Pentecostal Understanding', p. 231.
³³⁷ Biddy, 'Re-envisioning the Pentecostal Understanding', p. 231.

'Pentecostal sacramentology will have to begin with an account of the sacraments as *events of a divine-human encounter that take place through symbols*.'[338]

Biddy restates from Frank Macchia's work on glossolalia[339] two key concepts in 'sacramentology: (1) that divine-human encounters take place in, with and under *signs*, and (2) that these encounters may rightly be regarded as moments in which God dispenses *grace*',[340] as long as grace is not limited to refer only to the forgiveness of sins. After all, most Pentecostals reject the idea that the forgiveness of sins comes through the sacraments. According to Biddy, there is 'nothing inherently resistant in Pentecostalism to the idea that God grants the Church blessings beyond that of forgiveness of sins'.[341] Pentecostal worship experience and theological reflection both attest to divine-human encounters after justification. The 'second blessing' of sanctification and the 'third blessing' of baptism in the HS with the evidence of speaking in tongues are two examples of subsequence. Furthermore, Biddy asserts that two (SB and divine healing for all under the Atonement) of the five theological motifs of the fivefold gospel '*explicitly* involve *signs* of God's work in the believer, and both are regarded as pointing to'[342] the Second Coming of Jesus Christ, which is typically viewed as an imminent event – they are eschatological signs.

Since many Pentecostals have historical connections to the Wesleyan Holiness movement and a significant body of Pentecostals remain Wesleyan theologically, Biddy opines that engaging John Wesley as an ecumenical dialogue partner about the Eucharist is a logical and wise choice. Wesley is a logical choice since he eschews an *ex opere operato* understanding of sacramental efficacy, consistently stressing the rites accomplish nothing without faith.

Furthermore, for Wesley, faith does not cause the dispensing of God's grace. 'Grace, being what it is, comes strictly and directly from

---

[338] Biddy, 'Re-envisioning the Pentecostal Understanding', p. 231.

[339] Frank D. Macchia, 'Tongues as a Sign: Towards a Sacramental Understanding of Pentecostal Experience', *Pneuma* 15.1 (1993), pp. 61-76; also see his 'Sighs Too Deep for Words: Towards a Theology of Glossolalia', *JPT* 1 (1992), pp. 47-73. Emphasis original.

[340] Biddy, 'Re-envisioning the Pentecostal Understanding', p. 230.

[341] Biddy, 'Re-envisioning the Pentecostal Understanding', p. 230.

[342] Biddy, 'Re-envisioning the Pentecostal Understanding', p. 239.

God.'³⁴³ In other words, Wesley regards the Eucharist as a 'means of grace'. He defines 'means of grace' as 'outward signs, words or actions, ordained of God, and appointed for this end, to be the ordinary channels whereby He might convey to men, preventing, justifying, or sanctifying grace'.³⁴⁴ Wesley names the following as means of grace: prayer, the reading of Scripture, preaching, WB, and the Eucharist.³⁴⁵

Keith Warrington

In 2008, Keith Warrington, British Pentecostal theologian, Elim churchman, former Vice Principal and Director of Doctoral Studies, Regent Theological College, UK, published *Pentecostal Theology: A Theology of Encounter*.³⁴⁶ Warrington discusses the Pentecostal ordinances in Chapter 4 entitled 'The Church', asserting that many Pentecostals avoid employing the terms 'sacrament', 'ritual', and even 'ordinance' for their core practices lest some persons understand the procedures contain self-inducing powers. He further asserts that 'Pentecostals believe that without faith on the part of the recipient, participation in these ceremonies has little, if any, benefit'.³⁴⁷ Per Warrington, the administration of ordinances is not restricted to the clergy by scriptural mandate while it appears to be limited to them in practice.

Warrington, writing descriptively of WB, asserts that most Pentecostals submit to baptism by immersion out of their desire to emulate the baptism of Jesus (Mk 1.10) and to be obedient to his command (Mt. 28.19). He avers that Pentecostals deny that the water is 'charged with any supernatural properties' or that it 'confers salvation'.³⁴⁸ While most Pentecostals believe baptism is not essential for salvation, WB is 'regarded as normative practice' and expected as a sign of obedience.³⁴⁹ Oneness Pentecostals are the exception since

---

³⁴³ Biddy, 'Re-envisioning the Pentecostal Understanding', p. 239.
³⁴⁴ Biddy, 'Re-envisioning the Pentecostal Understanding', p. 239.
³⁴⁵ Biddy, 'Re-envisioning the Pentecostal Understanding', p. 239.
³⁴⁶ Keith Warrington, *Pentecostal Theology: A Theology of Encounter*, (London: T&T Clark, 2008).
³⁴⁷ Warrington, *Pentecostal Theology*, p. 162.
³⁴⁸ Warrington, *Pentecostal Theology*, p. 162.
³⁴⁹ Warrington, *Pentecostal Theology*, pp. 162-63.

they view baptism in the name of Jesus as effecting salvation.[350] Per Warrington, the Trinitarian formula of Mt. 28.19 is invoked over the candidate prior to the act of baptism. This formula is amended by Oneness Pentecostals by the substitution of the name of 'Jesus Christ' (Acts 2.38; 10.48) or 'the Lord Jesus' (Acts 8.16; 19.5)'.[351] Typically, baptism occurs after a brief period of instruction regarding essentials of the Christian life. Some argue that baptism should occur immediately after conversion based on Acts 16.33.

Water baptism by total immersion is viewed by many as symbolizing a clear break with their former life and an opportunity to proclaim their allegiance to Jesus Christ, in which the pictorial 'dying and rising' metaphors of Rom. 6.1-4 refer to the renunciation of their lives outside the Lordship of Jesus. Warrington posits that 'baptism is intended to signify repentance, the forgiveness of sins, salvation and the integration of the believer and Christ (Gal. 3.27) though there is no suggestion that such a relationship is initiated during baptism'.[352] On the contrary, baptism is the 'public affirmation of a previous integration into the family of God at salvation (1 Cor. 12.13; Eph. 4.5)'.[353] Overall, Pentecostals do not believe WB is the time for the candidate to receive the baptism of the HS. They find support for this position in Acts 19.5-6 that is the only occasion for this occurrence in the NT. On occasion, those being baptized have experienced physical healing or the baptism of the HS.[354] Consequently, Warrington reports that one scholar suggests that WB may be understood as a 'sacramental encounter such that the moment of baptism becomes a moment of encounter with the Divine'.[355]

Quoting Bicknell, Warrington argues that 'By concentrating its efforts upon personal faith over against corporate identity … the Pentecostal understanding of the ordinances may have been robbed of corporate significance'.[356] Consequently, Warrington opines that

---

[350] Warrington, *Pentecostal Theology*, p. 163.
[351] Warrington, *Pentecostal Theology*, p. 163.
[352] Warrington, *Pentecostal Theology*, p. 163.
[353] Warrington, *Pentecostal Theology*, p. 163.
[354] Warrington, *Pentecostal Theology*, p. 164.
[355] Warrington, *Pentecostal Theology*, p. 163.
[356] Warrington, *Pentecostal Theology*, p. 163.

the value of person's incorporation into the Body of Christ is worthy of increased emphasis.

Water baptism is administered primarily to adults and sometimes with children. Infant baptism is rejected by most Pentecostals since the act would be devoid of repentance and a personal act of faith on the part of the candidate. However, there are some Pentecostal denominations like the Methodist Pentecostal Church of Chile that practice infant baptism. Warrington reports that Tan argues for the value of baptizing the infants of believing parents in an Asian setting where more prominence is placed on the social construct of the family.

Warrington opines that while few Pentecostals will accept Tan's argument, 'it demonstrates a flexible Pentecostalism that is prepared to explore alternative views and to recognize the value of culture in one's hermeneutic'.[357]

Veli-Matti Kärkkäinen

Veli-Matti Kärkkäinen, Pentecostal theologian, ecumenist, and an ordained minister of the Full Gospel Churches of Finland, is Professor of Systematic Theology at the School of Theology, Fuller Theological Seminary, Pasadena, CA, and also holds a teaching position at the University of Helsinki as Docent of Ecumenics. A prolific author, Kärkkäinen has written or edited about twenty books in English (and seven in his native language, Finnish) as well as more than 150 articles that have appeared in international scholarly journals. Much of Kärkkäinen's writing serves to summarize and assess the work of others without clearly asserting his position. In *The Lord's Supper: Five Views*[358] he provides the Pentecostal view in comparison to the Roman Catholic, Lutheran, Reformed, and Baptist views. While the focus of our inquiry is Kärkkäinen's view on WB, it appears that his treatment of the Lord's Supper may be as close as we may come to his thinking about the sacraments in general and WB, in particular. He acknowledges that historically Pentecostals have given little attention to the constructive theology of sacraments even though a clear and well-developed pattern of Eucharistic

---

[357] Warrington, *Pentecostal Theology*, p. 164.
[358] Veli-Matti Kärkkäinen, 'The Pentecostal View' in Gordon T. Smith (ed.), *The Lord's Supper: Five Views* (Downers Grove, IL: IVP Academic, 2008), pp. 117-35.

devotion and practice exists. 'More work has been done with regard to water baptism since it has emerged as an issue of contention in the Pentecostal and evangelistic and missionary work in relation to members of established churches with a different baptismal practice'.[359] Kärkkäinen echoes the warning of a Pentecostal leader against minimizing the import of the Lord's Supper and WB as meaningful practices of the Christian life in the face of anti-sacramental sentiment in the Pentecostal movement.

Kärkkäinen concludes his article by applauding the work of a new generation of Pentecostal scholars who are engaged in constructive theology relative to the sacraments. He takes special note of the way scholars are saying 'that nothing in Pentecostal spirituality or theology necessarily makes talk about sacraments problematic'.[360] He questions 'whether the terminology of sacraments will establish itself among Pentecostal theologians'.[361]

Telford C. Work

Telford Work, Professor of Theology at Westmont College, located in Santa Barbara, CA, a member of the ICFG, and ecumenical systematician, asserts that 'Baptismal death and rebirth are not just metaphors'.[362] In fact, Christian symbolism is eschatological in nature. Work further posits that 'charismatic and sacramental signs are significant only if they are symbols of things that last'.[363] Baptism is significant because it symbolizes resurrection.

Commenting on God's command for Israel to cross over the brook Zered Deut. 2.13, Work asserts that WB as 'Christian initiation is a figure of the real end and new beginning of Israel at the edge of the wilderness'.[364] Furthermore, 'In baptism God declares an end to the reign of the lie in us and we embrace the truth of all things in light of his revelation in Jesus Christ, vowing to abide in him that we may know his truth and gain our freedom'.[365] The commitment to

---

[359] Kärkkäinen, 'The Pentecostal View', p. 132.
[360] Kärkkäinen, 'The Pentecostal View', p. 132.
[361] Kärkkäinen, 'The Pentecostal View', p. 133.
[362] Telford Work, *Deuteronomy* (BTC; Grand Rapids: Brazos Press, 2009), p. 45.
[363] Telford Work, *Ain't Too Proud to Beg: Living through the Lord's Prayer* (Grand Rapids, MI: Eerdmans, 2007), p. 74.
[364] Work, *Deuteronomy*, p. 45.
[365] Work, *Ain't Too Proud to Beg*, p. 183.

God is no mere ceremonial rite. Rather, for Work, 'Baptism is the revolution that overthrows evil by turning away from the devil and his works ... confessing trust in the Triune God of love, and entering into Jesus' death and resurrection for his befriended adversaries'.[366] Since people are prone to ideological idolatries like Marxism and colonialism Work argues that 'The call to baptism confronts us with a definitive end to futility (Eph. 4:17)'.[367] Similarly, 'The baptismal church accepts God's righteous rejection of our "former way of life" (4:22) and lives through sharing Jesus's resurrection'.[368]

Wolfgang Vondey

Vondey, a classically trained systematic theologian, directs the Centre for Pentecostal and Charismatic Studies with teaching and supervision responsibilities in the Department of Theology and Religion at the University of Birmingham, UK. In *People of Bread*[369] he proposes a 'theology of bread' that seeks to elucidate 'the significance of bread *beyond* its role at the Lord's Supper'.[370] Vondey avers that beyond its central role in the Christian liturgy 'the biblical story of bread also reveals the social nature and moral responsibility of the people of God, the mission of the Church, its sacramental nature, ecumenical purpose, and eschatological vision'.[371] For Vondey, the sacramental nature of the Church as the community of bread 'depends on the most crucial aspect of the breaking of the bread: the continuing presence of Christ'.[372] While he does not mention WB explicitly in *People of Bread,* he seems to indicate a sacramental view of baptism when speaking of the present process of creation's transformation. He proffers 'One may even speak of the "sacramentality of creation" and consider the natural elements, such as water, wine, or bread, as manifestations of the divine grace'.[373] The linkage of water to wine and bread appear to refer to WB.

---

[366] Work, *Ain't Too Proud to Beg*, p. 201.
[367] Work, *Deuteronomy*, p. 143.
[368] Work, *Deuteronomy*, pp. 143-44.
[369] Wolfgang Vondey, *People of Bread: Rediscovering Ecclesiology* (Mahwah, NJ: Paulist Press, 2008).
[370] Vondey, *People of Bread*, p. 3. Italics original.
[371] Vondey, *People of Bread*, p. 3.
[372] Vondey, *People of Bread*, p. 160.
[373] Vondey, *People of Bread*, p. 247.

A strong advocate for ecumenism and engagement with diverse cultures, Vondey envisions a future Global Pentecostalism 'that does not propose one particular (Pentecostal) structure but suggests that ecclesiality is experienced most concretely in a diversity of liturgical rhythms where church and culture meet in a mutual movement that shapes the ecclesial community in that particular context'.[374] In order for this to occur Pentecostal churches will need to become more ecumenical in their perspectives. Vondey posits that distribution of the ecumenical document, *The Nature and Mission of the Church*, to the churches and faith communities of the Pentecostal traditions could well speak to the import of the ecumenical communion. Moreover, it could 'call Pentecostals to consider the significance of baptism, Eucharist, as ministry in a way that has not been achieved by previous ecumenical documents'.[375] He avers this to be true despite their distinct emphases regarding the 'predominance of sacramental categories in the ecclesiology of the NMC'.[376]

Mark J. Cartledge

Mark Cartledge is Principal, Professor of Practical Theology at the London School of Theology, London, UK. He is a minister (priest) ordained in the Church of England (UK) for over twenty-five years and describes himself as a 'Charismatic Evangelical Anglican' or 'Renewal Anglican'. In 2010, Cartledge published *Testimony in the Spirit*,[377] his exploration of the beliefs and practices of Pentecostal and charismatic Christians in relationship to the HS by studying one classical Pentecostal congregation in the UK. More specifically, his study is 'an investigation into the contribution that ordinary discourse makes in the construction of a practical-theological account of Pentecostal identity'.[378] He asserts that 'the central aim of this study

---

[374] Wolfgang Vondey, *Beyond Pentecostalism: The Crisis of Global Christianity and the Renewal of the Theological Agenda* (Grand Rapids, MI: Eerdmans, 2010), p. 170.

[375] Wolfgang Vondey, 'Pentecostal Contributions to The Nature and Mission of the Church' in Wolfgang Vondey (ed.), *Pentecostalism and Christian Unity: Ecumenical Documents and Critical Assessments* (Eugene, OR: Pickwick Publications, 2010), pp. 256-68 (266).

[376] Vondey, 'Pentecostal Contributions to The Nature and Mission of the Church', p. 266.

[377] Mark J. Cartledge, *Testimony in the Spirit: Rescripting Ordinary Pentecostal Theology* (Burlington, VT: Ashgate Publishing Company, 2010).

[378] Cartledge, *Testimony in the Spirit*, p. 10.

is to listen to, record and reflect upon the "ordinary theology" of congregational members in relation to a number of key themes'.[379] The identified themes are worship, conversion, baptism in the Spirit, healing, life and witness, world mission and the second coming, and the sacraments.

In his exploration of conversion Cartledge employs a multi-disciplinary theory of religious conversion approach to 'listen to' the data he has collected in the form of testimonies and interviews. In particular, he employs the seven-stage framework of Lewis R. Rambo to explicate the nature of conversion. Rambo regards conversion as a process rather than an event. He acknowledges that sudden conversion does happen. He also asserts that 'all conversions are mediated through people, institutions, communities and groups'.[380] Rambo also 'advocates a process model of conversion that is multi-dimensional – that is, containing various elements that are 'interactive and accumulative over time'.[381] The seven stages of the model offered by Rambo and adopted by Cartledge are context, crisis, quest, encounter, interaction, commitment, and consequences.

It is within the commitment stage that a 'specific step is made by the convert in which a decision to follow a new path or orientation is made'.[382] Cartledge avers that in several religions there is an important ritual that symbolizes this commitment and participation in the ritual can serve to consolidate the decision. The power of ritual is particularly true for new converts to Christianity and WB is an example of such a ritual. It is through WB that 'the convert says both "no" to the past and "yes" to the future. It functions to sustain loyalty to the group and is a symbolic act of "bridge burning", creating boundaries between converts and the outside world'.[383]

In his section entitled 'Rescripting Ordinary Theology' addressing the theme of conversion, Cartledge asserts, 'It is important that lay leaders and not just the pastors recognize the importance and role that they have as advocates in the process of conversion' in an attempt to press forward the process nature of conversion and that

---

[379] Cartledge, *Testimony in the Spirit*, p. 10.
[380] Cartledge, *Testimony in the Spirit*, p. 63.
[381] Cartledge, *Testimony in the Spirit*, p. 64.
[382] Cartledge, *Testimony in the Spirit*, p. 68.
[383] Cartledge, *Testimony in the Spirit*, p. 68.

it occurs within the context of the larger community of faith. While he contends that rites of commitment are important for conversion, he also posits that these may vary dependent upon the background of those desiring to convert. 'It may be that rites other than baptism, such as reception into fellowship, might assist in "institutional transitions", which would appear to make up the majority of those joining Pentecostal churches'.[384]

Daniel Tomberlin
Tomberlin is Assistant Professor of Pastoral Ministries at Pentecostal Theological Seminary, Cleveland, TN. An ordained bishop in the COG (Cleveland, TN), Tomberlin has over 35 years of pastoral ministry and denominational leadership experience. In 2010, Tomberlin published *Pentecostal Sacraments: Encountering God at the Altar*,[385] his argument for the sacramental nature of WB, the Lord's Supper, Footwashing and anointed touch. Tomberlin's line of reasoning rests upon a Pentecostal theology/spirituality of Christo-Pneumatic encounter and the perspective that the four sacraments are means through which 'all believers ... encounter God's salvific grace'.[386]

Per Tomberlin, WB is a '*visible* sign of *invisible* grace'[387] and should be construed as an act of worship and discipleship, following the precedent of Jesus' baptism in the Jordan. Since Christ is the effectual cause of regeneration, both repentance and WB must be acts of faith, effectively disallowing baptismal regeneration. Nonetheless, WB is, in some fashion, salvific and a key event on the *via salutis*. Also, WB is paradigmatic for the believer's participation in the redemptive work in Christ and believers are therefore said to be 'in Christ'. Since believers are 'in Christ' or in union with him, the HS and the power of the resurrected Christ are present within all believers. Thus, a believer may anticipate his/her own bodily resurrection, just as Christ

---

[384] Cartledge, *Testimony in the Spirit*, p. 79.
[385] Daniel Tomberlin, *Pentecostal Sacraments: Encountering God at the Altar* (Cleveland, TN: Cherohala Press, rev. edn, 2019).
[386] Tomberlin, *Pentecostal Sacraments*, pp. 2-3.
[387] Tomberlin, *Pentecostal Sacraments*, p. 138. Italics original.

was raised from the dead.[388] Per Tomberlin, while WB and SB are not collateral, they are closely related.

Regarding ecclesiastical practices, Tomberlin posits that the church should insist that baptismal candidates submit to church membership and those seeking church membership should be baptized.[389] Similarly, Pentecostals should structure programs of discipleship to facilitate the sanctifying process provided through ongoing theological and ethical catechesis. With regard to baptismal formula, Tomberlin offers, 'Even as the Trinitarian formula is preferred, we must concede that baptism "in the name of Jesus" is attested in the Acts of the Apostles as a biblical baptismal formula'.[390] Last, while total immersion appears to be Tomberlin's preferred mode of WB, he acknowledges sprinkling as an acceptable alternative.

Andrew Ray Williams
Williams, ordained minister of the ICFG, author, professor, and Lead Pastor at Church on the Hill, Waynesboro, VA, published *Washed in the Spirit: Toward a Pentecostal Theology of Water Baptism*[391] in 2021, in an attempt to 'construct a distinctly Pentecostal theology of water baptism explicitly concerned with renewing Pentecostal teaching and practice, as well as engage ecumenical engagement'.[392] To accomplish his objective, Williams seeks to intersect the theological contributions of three historic Pentecostal denominations based in the USA: the ICFG, the IPHC, and the Pentecostal Assemblies of the World,[393]

---

[388] Pertaining to the impact of WB on the whole person, Tomberlin asserts

The cleansing of the spiritual heart of a person has a sanctifying effect upon the physical body because spirit, soul, and body are three components of the human self. Spirit and water are a means of salvific grace whereby human spirit and body are cleansed so that the whole human person – body, soul, and spirit – may be a temple of the Holy Spirit. Tomberlin, *Pentecostal Sacraments*, p. 150.

[389] Tomberlin, *Pentecostal Sacraments*, pp. 164-65.

[390] Tomberlin, *Pentecostal Sacraments*, p. 170.

[391] Andrew Ray Williams, *Washed in the Spirit: Toward a Pentecostal Theology of Water Baptism* (Cleveland, TN: CPT Press, 2021).

[392] Williams, *Washed in the Spirit*, p. 1.

[393] Per Williams, *Washed in the Spirit*, p. 6, the three classic Pentecostal denominations represent white and black Pentecostals, WHP, and FW Pentecostals, and Trinitarian and Oneness Pentecostals and provide a cross-section of early Pentecostalism.

with the 'ordinary theology,' following Cartledge, of early and contemporary Pentecostals, key biblical texts (Rom. 6.1-11 and Acts 2.37-40), and the formal theology of Pentecostal scholars and denominations.

Based on his research, Williams offers several suggestions for reformulating Pentecostal apprehension of WB. First, per Scripture, WB and 'the forgiveness of sins are indeed related and connected'.[394] Second, WB is more than a symbolic representation and believers actively participate in the life of Jesus Christ through WB.[395] Consequently, Pentecostals need to consider adopting participatory language and abandoning representative language. Third, the adoption of participatory language beckons for a change in missional practices, in that, since we share in Christ's life believers also share in his mission to those outside the church. Fourth, privileging Christ's baptism and his reception of the HS, 'the unity of water and Spirit baptism should be understood as paradigmatic for the Christian'.[396]

Williams posits the following points relative to baptismal practice. First, while immersion is preferred, pouring is the best alternative, since it calls attention to the pouring out of the Spirit in baptism. Second, the Trinitarian baptismal formula is recommended; however, in view of the ongoing dialogue with OPs, 'trinitarian Pentecostals might consider the best way forward to be including "Jesus Christ" within the trinitarian formula'.[397] Third, Williams asserts Pentecostals should consider the legitimacy of both believer's and infant baptism, and that rebaptism be discontinued. Fourth, since WB is a rite of incorporation into the body of Christ, baptism should take place within the context of the church as a community of faith.

Conclusions

The above survey reveals a radical development within Pentecostalism during the last ninety years. From 1932 to the early 1990s, the majority of reviewed perspectives, characterized by Pearlman, J.R. Williams, Tomlinson, Slay, Pruitt, Duffield, Van Cleave, Menzies,

---

[394] Williams, *Washed in the Spirit*, p. 197.
[395] Williams, *Washed in the Spirit*, p. 198.
[396] Williams, *Washed in the Spirit*, p. 237.
[397] Williams, *Washed in the Spirit*, p. 276.

Horton, Dusing, and Arrington, reflect a view of WB as an ordinance to be commemorated out of obedience to Christ. Moreover, WB was deemed a memorial act, bearing symbolic value that served to declare the believers' identification with the death, burial, and resurrection of Jesus Christ. Some, but not all, valued WB as a means of receiving God's grace. In the early 1990s, some Pentecostal scholars began to argue for the sacramental value of WB based on the Pentecostal-Roman Catholic dialogues, namely, Robeck, Sandidge, and Hunter. Subsequent scholars have advanced the implications of the dialogue relative to WB, notably, Chan, Macchia, Archer, Yong, Tomberlin, and A.R. Williams.

4

WATER BAPTISM IN EARLY PENTECOSTAL PERIODICALS: 1906-1931

The Wesleyan-Holiness Pentecostal Periodicals

The Apostolic Faith

Introduction

In the summer of 1906, revival erupted in the newly formed congregation meeting at the small, run-down Apostolic Faith Mission at 312 Azusa Street in Los Angeles. Critics attacked the assembly because of its mild-mannered black Holiness preacher, William J. Seymour, who preached racial reconciliation and the restoration of biblical spiritual gifts. The Azusa Street Revival, as it became known, soon became a local sensation, attracting thousands of curiosity seekers and pilgrims from around the world. The spiritual intensity of the revival was red hot for over three years, making Azusa Street one of the most important Pentecostal centers in the early 20th century.[1]

The Azusa Street Mission published a newspaper, *The Apostolic Faith*,[2] which reported on the revival in Los Angeles and the emerging

---

[1] Walter J. Hollenweger, *Pentecostalism: Origins and Developments Worldwide* (Peabody, MA: Hendrickson Publishers, Inc., 1997), pp. 18-20. Also, C.M. Robeck Jr., 'Seymour, William Joseph' in Stanley M. Burgess and Eduard M. van der Maas (eds.), *NIDPCM* (rev. and exp. edn; Grand Rapids, MI: Zondervan, 2002), pp. 1053-58.

[2] The collection features thirteen issues published between September 1906 and May 1908.

Pentecostal movement. The newspaper, which featured letters and articles from around the world, shared the excitement and passion of these early Pentecostals. *AF* and the other periodicals of the first 25 years of the movement are an indispensable guide in enabling readers to gain an informed understanding of the people, events, backgrounds, theological issues addressed, and the accompanying conflicts that helped shape the contours of the nascent Pentecostal movement.

The AF Movement, according to Seymour, 'Stands for the restoration of the faith once delivered unto the saints – the old-time religion, camp meetings, revivals, missions, street and prison work and Christian unity everywhere'.[3] At the core of the restoration movement stood the teaching that 'The Baptism with the Holy Ghost is a gift of power upon the sanctified life; so when we get it we have the same evidence as the Disciples received on the Day of Pentecost (Acts 2:3,4), in speaking in new tongues'.[4] Seymour further asserts that 'We are not fighting men or churches, but seeking to displace dead forms and creeds and wild fanaticisms with living, practical Christianity'.[5]

The movement spread rapidly, widely, and fervently due to the missionary zeal of people newly empowered by the HS as new people received the message of Pentecost and received the Baptism of the Holy Ghost with the evidence of speaking in new tongues. *AF* serves both to report the response to the Pentecost message and an 'evangelistic' tool to spread the message to those who had not yet heard the message preached to them.[6]

The centrality of the Pentecost message is captured in the most concise explication of the *via salutis* found in *AF*:

> Before you can receive the baptism with the Holy Ghost, you must have a thorough, definite experience of justification and

---

[3] *AF* 1.1 (September 1906), p. 2.
[4] *AF* 1.1 (September 1906), p. 2.
[5] *AF* 1.1 (September 1906), p. 2.
[6] From the first edition, *AF* was published free of charge and without a subscription fee. Offerings were encouraged and received by the publisher to cover the costs of publication. Extra copies were printed of each edition to be distributed as 'samples' as a method of outreach and evangelism. See *AF* 1.1 (September 1906), pp. 2, 4.

sanctification, which are through the Blood of Jesus, and they are two distinct acts of grace. First, what God has done for you; second, what God has wrought within you. Then and only then are you prepared to receive your baptism from the Father, by Jesus Christ His Son. And when you have received your baptism, He, the Holy Ghost, will speak through you in tongues, and not before.[7]

While there is no mention of WB in the *via salutis* or the 'statement of faith'[8] it would be a mistake to assume that The Apostolic Faith Movement placed little to no import on WB. A close reading of *AF* reveals the opposite to be the case.

The Practice of Water Baptism

Reporters from the field submit detailed accounts of WBs conducted at the end of revival services and camp meetings that Seymour then includes in all but two of the thirteen extant issues.[9] Significantly, these eleven issues contain fifteen articles reporting WBs. Given the fact that no explicit theological rationale for detailed reporting is supplied by the reporters or offered by Editor Seymour, it appears to be the case that WB was assumed to be a vital part of Christian discipleship to be followed after conversion. The following citation is typical of references to baptismal practice found in the *AF*:

> Before closing the meeting, they gave the altar call, and there was such a rush to the altar that some fell over the seats and one woman nearly knocked the stove down. Twenty-seven in all came

---

[7] *AF* 1.7 (April 1907), p. 3. Lengthier treatments by Seymour are found in *AF* 1.1 (September 1906), pp. 2, 3; *AF* 1.3 (November 1906), p. 3; *AF* 1.5 (January 1907), p. 2; *AF* 1.6 (February-March 1907), p. 7; *AF* 1.10 (September 1907), p. 2; *AF* 1.11 (October-January 1908, pp. 2, 3; *AF* 1.12 (January 1908), p. 2; and *AF* 2.12 (May 1908), pp. 2, 3.

[8] *AF* 1.1 (September 1906) p. 2.

[9] *AF* 1.1 (September 1906), p. 4; *AF* 1.2 (October 1906), p. 4; *AF* 1.4 (December 1906), p. 1; *AF* 1.5 (January 1907), p. 1; *AF* 1.6 (February-March 1907), p. 4; *AF* 1.7 (April 1907), p. 1; *AF* 1.8 (May 1907), p. 4; *AF* 1.9 (June-August 1907), p. 1; *AF* 1.10 (September 1907), p. 1; *AF* 1.12 (January 1908), p. 1; and *AF* II.13 (May 1908), p. 1. No reports of WB are found in *AF* 1.3 (November 1906) and *AF* 1.11 (October-December 1907). Only two issues of the paper, *AF* 1.3 (November 1906) and *AF* 1.11 (October-December 1907), contain no reports of WB.

to the altar and 22 of them got saved ... On Sunday they had water baptism and 14 were baptized in the creek by immersion. One lady fell under the power of God just after she came out of the water. In these meetings there was no preaching. God Himself did the work.[10]

The reader is left to ponder the disparity between the number of those reported 'saved', and the number later baptized in water that appears in the reports.

Administration

Noteworthy is Seymour's assertion regarding the administrator of WB. He posits that 'It should be administered by a disciple who is baptized with the Holy Ghost Acts 1:4'. He argues, 'But we find that they were first to tarry for the promise of the Father which would qualify them'.[11]

Exact Reporting

The importance of WB is highlighted by including detailed numerical reporting of those baptized in water.[12] Only one report omits an exact count of those baptized in water.[13] Noteworthy is the fact that no instance of rebaptism is mentioned. This may account for the disparity between the number of persons 'saved' and those baptized.

Widely Practiced

Apparently, WB is valued and practiced widely as the reports originate in Los Angeles, CA,[14] Seattle, WA,[15] Bonsoll, CA,[16]

---

[10] *AF* 1.6 (February-March 1907), p. 4.

[11] *AF* 1.10 (September 1907), p. 2.

[12] *AF* 1.1 (September 1906), p. 4; *AF* 1.2 (October 1906), p. 4; *AF* 1.4 (December 1906), p. 1; *AF* 1.5 (January 1907), p. 1; *AF* 1.6 (February-March 1907), p. 4; *AF* 1.7 (April 1907), p. 1; *AF* 1.8 (May 1907), p. 4; *AF* 1.9 (June-August 1907), p. 1; *AF* 1.10 (September 1907), p. 1; *AF* 1.12 (January 1908), p. 1; and *AF* 2.13 (May 1908), p. 1.

[13] *AF* 1.12 (January 1908), p. 1.

[14] *AF* 1.1 (September 1906), p. 4; *AF* 1.2 (October 1906), p. 4; *AF* 1.4 (December 1906), p. 1; AF 1.10 (September 1907), p.1; and *AF* 2.13 (May 1908), p. 1.

[15] *AF* 1.5 (January 1907), p. 1.

[16] *AF* 1.6 (February-March 1907), p. 4.

Bellingham, WA,[17] Denver CO,[18] Santa Rosa and San Jose, CA,[19] Portland, OR,[20] Minneapolis, MN,[21] Winnipeg, Manitoba, Canada,[22] Arcadia, FL,[23] and Sweden.[24]

Mode of Baptism

The mode of WB as practiced by The Apostolic Faith Movement appears to be immersion. Six[25] of the fifteen reports from practitioners in the field employ 'immersion' as the mode of WB utilized. Three of the remaining nine articles use burial language to report on WB: 'buried in the likeness of His death',[26] 'followed Jesus in baptism, and came out of the water praising God',[27] and 'been baptized in water, buried in baptism, that is the Bible way'.[28] Four of the remaining six reports identify the body of water utilized for the baptismal service: 'Eighty-five were baptized in the ocean',[29] 'We had a wonderful service out on Puget Sound and I baptized about thirty, young and old',[30] 'Fourteen converts have been baptized in the bay',[31] and 'He was baptized down at the ocean and shouted and jumped in the water and out of the water'.[32] The last two reports state the candidates were baptized *in water*. The article from Sweden simply states that 'twenty-three were baptized *in water* in the name of Jesus

---

[17] *AF* 1.7 (April 1907), p. 1.
[18] *AF* 1.7 (April 1907), p. 4.
[19] *AF* 1.8 (May 1907), p. 4.
[20] *AF* 1.8 (May 1907), p. 4. and *AF* 1.9 (June-August 1907), p. 1.
[21] *AF* 1.9 (June-August 1907), p. 1.
[22] *AF* 1.9 (June-August 1907), p. 1.
[23] *AF* 1.12 (January 1908), p. 1.
[24] *AF* 2.13 (May 1908), p. 1.
[25] *AF* 1.1 (September 1906), p. 4; *AF* 1.4 (December 1906), p. 1; *AF* 1.6 (February-March 1907), p. 4; *AF* 1.7 (April 1907), p. 7; *AF* 1.8 (May 1907), p. 4; and *AF* 1.9 (June-August 1907), p. 1.
[26] *AF* 1.9 (June-August 1907), p. 1.
[27] *AF* 1.10 (September 1907), p. 1.
[28] *AF* 1.12 (January 1908), p. 1.
[29] *AF* 1.2 (October 1906), p. 4.
[30] *AF* 1.5 (January 1907), p. 1.
[31] *AF* 1.7 (April 1907), p. 1.
[32] *AF* 2.13 (May 1908), p. 1.

Christ'.³³ A report from Portland reads, 'Sixty-seven were baptized *in water* one day'.³⁴

Sufficient Water

An essential feature of the baptismal reports is the attention given to the locations of baptismal services. On only one occasion is a church baptistry noted.³⁵ Three reports detail baptismal services occurring in the ocean.³⁶ The following locations are mentioned once by reporters: Puget Sound,³⁷ a creek,³⁸ the bay,³⁹ a pool formed by the creek,⁴⁰ a suburban lake,⁴¹ Assiniboine River,⁴² and a stream.⁴³ It seems the reporters and Seymour want readers to know that sufficient water is available for immersion. The not insignificant bodies of water used for WB highlight the public nature of the venue for the worship service of the faith community, allowing for the baptismal service to become proclamation by word and deed.

Pentecostal Worship

In keeping with fervent Pentecostal spirituality, reports of shouting, singing, joyful worship, Spirit of God manifestations, people praising God, and speaking in tongues are contained in ten of fifteen reports.⁴⁴

---

[33] *AF* 2.13 (May 1908), p. 1. Emphasis added.
[34] *AF* 1.9 (June-August 1907), p. 1. Emphasis added.
[35] *AF* 1.4 (December 1906), p. 1.
[36] *AF* 1.1 (September 1906), p. 4; *AF* 1.2 (October 1906), p. 4; and *AF* 2.13 (May 1908), p. 1.
[37] *AF* 1.5 (January 1907), p. 1.
[38] *AF* 1.6 (February-March 1907), p. 4.
[39] *AF* 1.7 (April 1907), p. 1.
[40] *AF* 1.10 (September 1907), p. 1.
[41] *AF* 1.9 (June-August 1907), p. 1.
[42] *AF* 1.9 (June-August 1907), p. 1.
[43] *AF* 1.10 (September 1907), p. 1.
[44] *AF* 1.1 (September 1906), p. 4; *AF* 1.2 (October 1906), p. 4; *AF* 1.4 (December 1906), p. 1; *AF* 1.5 (January 1907), p. 1; *AF* 1.6 (February-March 1907), p. 4; *AF* 1.7 (April 1907), p. 1; *AF* 1.8 (May 1907), p. 4; *AF* 1.9 (June-August 1907), p. 1; *AF* 1.10 (September 1907), p. 1; and *AF* 2.13 (May 1908), p. 1.

Formula

In general, reports neglect to identify the baptismal formula employed. The exception is a report from Sweden that refers to persons being baptized 'in the name of Jesus Christ'.[45]

Meaning of Water Baptism

Seymour underlines their importance by providing detailed explanations of the three ordinances of foot washing, WB, and the Lord's Supper to allay any suspicion regarding the movement's valuation of the ordinances.[46]

On WB, Seymour employs a straightforward reading of the biblical text. He asserts that WB is to be received in obedience to the resurrected Christ (Mk 16.16), and the proper mode is single immersion (Mt. 3.13, Acts 8.38-39). Citing Rom. 6.3-5 and Gal. 3.27, Seymour posits that WB 'sets forth the believer with Christ in death, burial, and resurrection'. Water baptism has no saving power and is to be followed in obedience to the command of Jesus Christ (Mk 16.16; Acts 2.28). Moreover, 'It is "Not the putting away of the filth of the flesh, but the answer of a good conscience toward God." 1 Pet. 3.21. It is obedience to the command of Jesus, following saving faith. We believe every true believer will practice it.'[47]

Finally, Seymour asserts that 'We believe that we should teach God's people to observe all things whatsoever He has commanded us, practicing every command and living by every word that proceedeth out of the mouth of God. This is a full Gospel.'[48]

The following month, Seymour further emphasizes the importance and place of WB in the *via salutis* by the assertion that 'The principles of the doctrine of Christ are: Repentance; Faith in our Lord and Saviour Jesus Christ; Water Baptism; Sanctification; The Baptism of the Holy Spirit; Second coming of our Lord Jesus Christ; and Final white throne judgment'.[49]

---

[45] *AF* 2.13 (May 1908), p. 1.
[46] *AF* 1.10 (September 1907) pp. 1, 2.
[47] *AF* 1.10 (September 1907), p. 2.
[48] *AF* 1.10 (September 1907), p. 2.
[49] *AF* 1.11 (October-December 1907), p. 4.

The Bridegroom's Messenger

Introduction

The Bridegroom's Messenger (*TBM*)[50] was first published in 1907 by evangelist G.B. Cashwell.[51] Cashwell, along with A.G. Garr, Charles H. Mason, D.J. Young, and others, brought the Pentecostal message from the Azusa Street revival in Los Angeles to the southeastern USA. Elizabeth A. Sexton succeeded Cashwell as editor in 1908. Contributing editors included leaders of what would become the COG (Cleveland, TN), the International Pentecostal Holiness Church (IPHC), and the Pentecostal Free Will Baptist Church. The periodical included articles, reports, and letters from the USA and mission endeavors outside the continental USA. Hattie M. Barth, who with her husband co-pastored the Pentecostal Mission, became editor in 1924. Under her leadership, *TBM* became the official organ of the Association of Pentecostal Assemblies (APA), a small fellowship organized in 1921 by Pentecostal churches in the Southeast.[52]

The Practice of Water Baptism

Ministers, missionaries, and religious workers routinely submitted ministry reports to the publication's editor, who then includes them to document the revival fires spread over the USA and foreign countries as the Good News is spread. No explicit theological rationale for detailed reporting of WB is supplied by the reporters or offered by the editor until May 1908.[53] In addition to *TBM*'s formal declaration of WB as an ordinance, The Apostolic Faith Mission in Bombay, India, affirms the importance of WB as one of the

---

[50] I reviewed 265 issues of *TBM*, published between October 1907 and September 1931.

[51] H.V. Synan, 'Cashwell, Gaston Barnabas' in Stanley M. Burgess and Eduard M. van der Maas (eds.), *NIDPCM* (rev. and exp. edn; Grand Rapids, MI: Zondervan, 2002), pp. 457-58.

[52] W.E. Warner, 'International Pentecostal Church of Christ' in Stanley M. Burgess and Eduard M. van der Maas (eds.), *NIDPCM* (rev. and exp. edn; Grand Rapids, MI: Zondervan, 2002), pp. 797-98.

[53] In *TBM* 2.37 (May 1909), p. 1, the editor includes an article outlining the various doctrines of the movement, naming WB as an ordinance supported by Mt. 28.19. The doctrinal statement is reiterated in *TBM* 3.60 (April 1910), p. 1; *TBM* 5.109 (May 1912), p. 1; and *TBM* 9.185 (August 1916), p. 1.

Pentecostal truths for which they have always stood. Specifically, they aver that this mission stands for:

> An unlimited salvation for body, soul and spirit through the sacrifice on Calvary; Baptism by immersion on confession of faith in Jesus Christ; The honoring of the precious blood; The baptism of the Holy Spirit; Divine healing and health; and The soon coming of Jesus in the air for His saints.[54]

The only exception to the considerable attention given WB as an ordinance and critical doctrine of the Pentecostal movement is a curious omission in the report from the Association of Pentecostal Assemblies ninth meeting. Water baptism, the Lord's Supper, and footwashing are all absent from the report that enumerates 'the cardinal points of our faith'.[55]

It appears to be the case that WB was assumed to be a vital part of Christian discipleship to be followed after one's public confession of faith. The following citation is typical of references to baptismal practice found in *TBM* during the first year of publication:

> On Sunday afternoon, May 31, 1908, over 500 people gathered on the shores of a beautiful little lake to witness a baptismal service. Amid songs, shouts, and rejoicing, the candidates were plunged beneath the surface of the water in obedience to the command of Jesus, our Lord, and Savior. Several others are yet to be baptized.[56]

Twenty-three years later, in June 1931, the following account is provided from Shanghai, China, by Walter and Eva Turner:

> We feel we dare not close the Hart Road Mission for twenty-seven new converts have just been buried with Him by WB and these converts are but babes in Christ and need to have the precious Word rightly divided into them.[57]

---

[54] *TBM* 6.136 (July 1913), p. 3.
[55] *TBM* 22.273 (July-September 1929), p. 7.
[56] *TBM* 1.16 (June 15, 1908), p. 1.
[57] *TBM* 29.278 (October-December 1930), p. 9.

Exact Reporting

The emphasis placed on WB is highlighted by including detailed numerical reporting of those baptized in water by the editor.[58] The

---

[58] *TBM* 1.2 (November 1, 1909), p. 2; *TBM* 1.12 (April 15, 1908), p. 2; *TBM* 1.15 (June 1, 1908), p. 1; *TBM* 2.33 (March 1, 1909), p. 2; *TBM* 3.49 (November 1, 1909), p. 2: *TBM* 3.51 (December 1, 1909), pp. 3, 4; *TBM* 3.52 (December 15, 1909), p. 1; *TBM* 3.53 (January 1, 1910), p. 4; *TBM* 3.54 (January 15, 1910), p. 2; *TBM* 3.60 (April 15, 1910), p. 4; *TBM* 3.61 (May 1, 1910), p. 2; *TBM* 3.62 (May 15, 1910), pp. 1, 2; *TBM* 3.64 (June 15, 1910), p. 4; *TBM* 3.65 (July 1, 1910), p. 4; *TBM* 3.67 (August 1, 1910), p. 3; *TBM* 3.68 (August 15, 1910), p. 3; *TBM* 3.69 (September 1, 1910), p. 3; *TBM* 3.70 (September 15, 1910), pp. 1, 4; *TBM* 3.71 (October 1, 1910), p. 4; *TBM* 4.72 (October 15, 1910), p. 2; *TBM* 4.74 (November 15, 1910), pp. 1, 3, and 4; *TBM* 4.75 (December 1, 1910), p. 2, 4; *TBM* 4.76 (December 15, 1910), p. 4; *TBM* 4.81 (March 1, 1911), p. 4. *TBM* 4.83 (April 1, 1911), pp. 1, 4; *TBM* 4.85 (May 1, 1911), p. 1; *TBM* 4.94 (September 15, 1911), p. 3; *TBM* 5.96 (October 15, 1911), pp. 2, 3; *TBM* 5.98 (November 15, 1911), p. 4; *TBM* 5.102 (January 15, 1912), p. 3; *TBM* 5.104 (February 15, 1912), p. 4; *TBM* 5.105 (March 1, 1912), p. 2; *TBM* 5.106 (March 16, 1912), p. 1; *TBM* 5.115 (August 1, 1912), p. 1; *TBM* 5.119 (October 15, 1912), p. 2; *TBM* 6.125 (January 15, 1913), p. 1; *TBM* 6.132 (May 1, 1913), p. 4; *TBM* 6.133 (May 15, 1913), p. 2; *TBM* 6.134 (June 1, 1913), p. 1; *TBM* 6.135 (June 15, 1913), p. 3; *TBM* 6.136 (July 1, 1913), pp. 2, 3; *TBM* 6.137 (August 1, 1913), pp. 2, 3; *TBM* 6.140 (September 15, 1913), pp. 1, 3; *TBM* 7.141 (October 1, 1913), p. 1; *TBM* 7.145 (December 1, 1913), p. 1; *TBM* 7.147 (January 1, 1914), p. 1; *TBM* 7.148 (January 15, 1914), p. 2; *TBM* 7.150 (February 15, 1914), p. 3; *TBM* 7.156 (June 1, 1914), pp. 2, 3; *TBM* 7.160 (August 15, 1914), p. 2; *TBM* 8.164 (November 1, 1914), p. 2; *TBM* 8.165 (December 1, 1914), p. 1; *TBM* 8.167 (February 1, 1915), pp. 1, 3; *TBM* 8.168. (March 1, 1915), p. 3; *TBM* 8.172 (July 1, 1915), p. 2; *TBM* 8.173 (August 1, 1915), p. 3; *TBM* 8.174 (September 1, 1915), p. 3; *TBM* 8.175 (October 1, 1915), p. 5; *TBM* 9.177 (December 1, 1915), p. 2; *TBM* 9.185 (August 1, 1916), p. 3; *TBM* 9.186 (September 1, 1916), p. 4; *TBM* 9.187 (October 1, 1916), p. 3; *TBM* 10.191 (February 1, 1917), p. 3; *TBM* 10.199 (May 1, 1917), p. 3; *TBM* 10.200 (June 1, 1917), p. 3; *TBM* 12.215 (July-August 1, 1919), p. 2; *TBM* 12.216 (September 1, 1919), p. 3; *TBM* 14.226 (October-November 1, 1920), p. 3.; *TBM* 14.229 (April-May 1, 1921), p. 3; *TBM* 18.253 (September-November 1, 1924), p. 3; *TBM* 18.256 (June-September 1, 1925), pp. 3, 4; *TBM* 19.257 (October-December 1925), p. 2; *TBM* 19.258 (January-February 1926), p. 3; *TBM* 19.259 (March-May 1926), p. 3; *TBM* 20.261. (September-October 1926), p. 3; *TBM* 20.263 (March-April 1927), p. 4; *TBM* 21.266 (November-December 1927), p. 1; *TBM* 21.268 (March-April 1928), p. 3; *TBM* 21.269 (May-August 1928), pp. 3, 4; *TBM* 22.270 (September-December 1928), p. 4; *TBM* 22.271 (January-March 1929), pp. 10, 16; *TBM* 22.272 (April-June 1929), p. 11; *TBM* 23.275 (January-March 1930), p. 12; *TBM* 23.277 (July-September 1930), p. 12; *TBM* 24.278 (October-December 1930), p. 9; and *TBM* 24.280 (April-June 1931), p. 6.

importance of WB for the recipients is noted in their testimonies.⁵⁹ Even when the editor's reports of baptismal events do not note an exact number of recipients reports from the field are included.⁶⁰ Also included in reports are occasions of inquirers seeking after WB as a natural progression in the *via salutis*.⁶¹

Widely Practiced

Water baptism is valued and practiced widely worldwide as the reports originate from foreign mission stations in South Africa, India, China, Guatemala, Ceylon, Australia, Salvador, West Africa, and Japan. Also, submitted reports originate from North America: Alabama, North Carolina, Maryland, Canada, Kansas, New Jersey, Florida, Tennessee, Georgia, Ohio, Texas, Arkansas.⁶²

Mode of Baptism

In *TBM*, dated May 1, 1909, the editor outlines the critical doctrines of the movement, asserting that WB is to be 'by immersion on confession of faith in Jesus Christ'.⁶³ The verse cited for the practice is Mt. 28.19. According to reports, the mode of WB as practiced on the field appears to be immersion.

Baptismal reports from practitioners in the field employ 'immersed' or a derivative thereof as the mode of WB more than 25 times.⁶⁴ The phrase 'baptized in water', 'baptism in water', 'received

---

⁵⁹ *TBM* 1.2 (November 1, 1909), p. 2; *TBM* 1.16 (June 15, 1908), p. 3.

⁶⁰ *TBM* 2.29 (January 1, 1909), p. 1; *TBM* 2.42 (July 15, 1909), p. 3; *TBM* 5.112 (June 15, 1912), p. 4; *TBM* 7.150 (February 15, 1914), p. 4; *TBM* 9.179 (February 1, 1916), p. 3; and *TBM* 9.180 (March 1, 1916), p. 3.

⁶¹ *TBM* 3.49 (November 1, 1909), p. 2.

⁶² Please see Appendix A for a compilation of locations, including city, nation/state, and reference.

⁶³ In *TBM* 2.37 (May 1909), p. 1. The doctrinal statement is reiterated in *TBM* 3.60 (April 1910), p. 1, *TBM* 5.109 (May 1912), p. 1, and *TBM* 9.185 (August 1916), p. 1.

⁶⁴ *TBM* 3.70 (September 15, 1910), p. 4; *TBM* 3.70 (September 15, 1910), p. 4; *TBM* 4.72 (October 15, 1910), p. 2; *TBM* 4.85 (May 1, 1911), p. 1; *TBM* 5.96 (October 15, 1911), p. 3; *TBM* 5.96 (October 15, 1911), p. 3; *TBM* 5.119 (October 15, 1912), p. 2; *TBM* 6.136 (July 1, 1913), p. 3; *TBM* 7.147 (January 1, 1914), p. 1; *TBM* 7.156 (June 1, 1914), p. 3; *TBM* 8.167 (February 1, 1915), p. 3; *TBM* 9.176 (November 1, 1915), p. 1; *TBM* 9.180 (March 1, 1916), p. 3; *TBM* 9.186 (September 1, 1916), p. 4; *TBM* 10.191(February 1, 1917), p. 3; *TBM* 10.199 (May 1, 1917), p. 3;

water baptism', and 'baptized in a specific body of water' occurs more than 50 times.⁶⁵ Images of burial in water and following Christ's example in WB are employed in 20 reports.⁶⁶ While there is no mention of water, immersion, burial imagery, or following Jesus' example in the articles, there are 28 additional reports that chronicle baptismal activity.⁶⁷ According to reports from the field, total

---

TBM 10.200 (June 1, 1917), p. 3; *TBM* 12.215 (July-August 1919), p. 2; *TBM* 19.257 (October-December 1925), p. 2; *TBM* 20.263 (March-April 1927), p. 4; *TBM* 21.266 (November-December 1927), p. 1; *TBM* 21.269 (May-August 1928), p. 3; and *TBM* 21.269 (May-August 1928), p. 4

⁶⁵ *TBM* 1.15 (June 1, 1908), p. 1; *TBM* 2.29 (January 1, 1909), p. 1; *TBM* 2.33 (March 1, 1909), p. 2; *TBM* 2.42 (July 15, 1909), p. 3; *TBM* 3.49 (November 1, 1909), p. 2; *TBM* 3.51 (December 1, 1909), p. 3; *TBM* 3.51 (December 1, 1909), p. 4; *TBM* 3.52 (December 15, 1909), p. 1; *TBM* 3.62 (May 15, 1910), p. 2; *TBM* 3.64 (June 15, 1910), p. 4; *TBM* 3.67 (August 1, 1910), p. 3; *TBM* 3.68 (August 15, 1910), p. 3; *TBM* 3.68 (August 15, 1910), p. 3; *TBM* 3.70 (September 15, 1910), p. 1; *TBM* 4.74 (November 15, 1910), pp. 1, 3, and 4; *TBM* 4.75 (December 1, 1910), pp. 2, 4; *TBM* 4.76 (December 15, 1910), p. 4; *TBM* 4.94 (September 15, 1911), p. 3; *TBM* 5.96 (October 15, 1911), p. 2; *TBM* 5.112 (June 15, 1912), p. 4; *TBM* 6.133 (May 15, 1913), p. 2; *TBM* 6.136 (July 1, 1913), p. 2; *TBM* 6.137 (August 1, 1913), p. 3; *TBM* 7.141 (October 1, 1913), p. 1; *TBM* 7.145 (December 1, 1913), p. 1; *TBM* 7.150 (February 15, 1914), p. 3; *TBM* 7.156 (June 1, 1914), p. 2; *TBM* 7.160 (August 15, 1914), p. 2; *TBM* 8.165 (December 1, 1914), p. 1; *TBM* 8.167 (February 1, 1915), pp. 1, 3; *TBM* 8.168. (March 1, 1915), p. 3; *TBM* 8.172 (July 1, 1915), p. 2; *TBM* 8.173 (August 1, 1915), p. 3; *TBM* 8.175 (October 1, 1915), p. 5; *TBM* 9.177 (December 1, 1915), p. 2; *TBM* 9.179 (February 1, 1916), p. 3; *TBM* 9.185 (August 1, 1916), p. 3; *TBM* 9.187 (October 1, 1916), p. 3; *TBM* 10.200 (June 1, 1917), pp. 3, 4; *TBM* 12.216 (September 1919), p. 3; *TBM* 14.226 (October-November 1920), p. 3; *TBM* 18.253 (September-November 1924), p. 3; *TBM* 18.256 (June-September 1925), pp. 3, 4; *TBM* 19.258 (January-February 1926), p. 3; *TBM* 19.259 (March-May 1926), p. 3; *TBM* 21.268 (March-April 1928), p. 3; *TBM* 22.270 (September-December 1928), p. 4; *TBM* 23.277 (July-September 1930), p. 12.

⁶⁶ *TBM* 1.16 (June 15, 1908), p. 1; *TBM* 3.61 (May 1, 1910), p. 2; *TBM* 3.62 (May 15, 1910), p. 1; *TBM* 4.72 (October 15, 1910), p. 2; *TBM* 4.83 (April 1, 1911), p. 1; *TBM* 5.98 (November 15, 1911), p. 4; *TBM* 5.105 (March 1, 1912), p. 2; *TBM* 6.125 (January 15, 1913), p. 1; *TBM* 6.134 (June 1, 1913), p. 1; *TBM* 6.135 (June 15, 1913), p. 3; *TBM* 7.156 (June 1, 1914), p. 3; *TBM* 8.164 (November 1, 1914), p. 2; *TBM* 8.165 (December 1, 1914), p. 1; *TBM* 8.167 (February 1, 1915), p. 3; *TBM* 8.167 (February 1, 1915), p. 3; *TBM* 18.256 (June-September 1925), p. 3; *TBM* 22.271 (January-March 1929), p. 10; *TBM* 22.272 (April-June 1929), p. 11; *TBM* 24.280 (April-June 1931), p. 6; *TBM* 9.278 (October-December 1930), p. 9.

⁶⁷ *TBM* 1.12 (April 15, 1908), p. 2; *TBM* 3.49 (November 1, 1909), p. 2; *TBM* 3.51 (December 1, 1909), p. 4; *TBM* 3.51 (December 1, 1909), p. 4; *TBM* 3.64

immersion as the only acceptable mode of baptism for believers appears to have been widely accepted in all locales and cultures. The demand for total immersion is met with requests for the same from the recently converted, restored, and newly Spirit-filled.[68]

The explicit position of total immersion implicitly denies the validity and acceptability of infant or paedo-baptism. This is underscored throughout *TBM* by several accounts of persons previously baptized seeking total immersion as the preferred mode to fulfill Christ's command. The following three reports illustrate this dynamic. First, from Quebec, Canada, we read that three Roman Catholics were immersed in a baptismal service. Many, after they were saved, realized they had been making an empty profession. They said: 'We thought we were all right ... We were on the road to hell and didn't know it until you dear brethren came up here and preached a full gospel to us in power'.[69] Second, a letter from Sister Wood, serving in Argentina, South America, reports that Don Juan Mayans, a Christian man for over twenty-five years and baptized in the HS became convinced 'he needed more than his infant baptism in the Catholic church, and asked to be immersed'. Mayans was taken to the river and baptized by brother Sorensen in accord with the command of Jesus.[70] Last, a letter from Mrs. Lillie Doll-Maltby in Kandy, Ceylon provides immersion being practiced by converts from various

---

(June 15, 1910), p. 4; *TBM* 4.81 (March 1, 1911), p. 4; *TBM* 4.83 (April 1, 1911), p. 4; *TBM* 5.104 (February 15, 1912), p. 4; *TBM* 5.106 (March 16, 1912), p. 1; *TBM* 5.115 (August 1, 1912), p. 1; *TBM* 6.132 (May 1, 1913), p. 4; *TBM* 6.136 (July 1, 1913), p. 3; *TBM* 6.136 (July 1, 1913), p. 3; *TBM* 6.140 (September 15, 1913), pp. 1, 3; *TBM* 7.145 (December 1, 1913), p. 1; *TBM* 8.164 (November 1, 1914), p. 2; *TBM* 8.174 (September 1, 1915), p. 3; *TBM* 9.183 (June 1, 1916), p. 4; *TBM* 9.185 (August 1, 1916), p. 1; *TBM* 10.199 (May 1, 1917), p. 3; *TBM* 14.229 (April-May 1921), p. 3; *TBM* 15. 237 (April-May 1922), p. 3; *TBM* 19.258 (January-February 1926), p. 3; *TBM* 20.261. (September-October 1926), p. 3; *TBM* 22.271 (January-March 1929), p. 16; *TBM* 23.275 (January-March 1930), p. 12; and *TBM* 24.280 (April-June 1931), p. 6.

[68] *TBM* 3.49 (November 1, 1909), p. 2; *TBM* 4.76 (December 15, 1910), p. 4; *TBM* 4.83 (April 1, 1911), p. 4; *TBM* 6.125 (January 15, 1913), p. 1; *TBM* 6.136 (July 1, 1913), p. 3; *TBM* 6.125 (January 15, 1913), p. 1; *TBM* 6.140 (September 15, 1913), p. 3; *TBM* 7.144 (November 15, 1913), p. 1; *TBM* 8.164 (November 1, 1914), p. 2; *TBM* 8. 64 (November 1, 1914), p. 2; and *TBM* 15. 237 (April-May 1922), p. 3.

[69] *TBM* 7.147 (January 1, 1914), p. 1.

[70] *TBM* 10.191 (February 1, 1917), p. 3.

religious backgrounds and nationalities: 'Three were Singhalese, four Lamils and three Malayalams, two had been Hindus, one a Mohammedan, two Catholics, two Buddhist'.[71]

Sufficient Water

An important feature of the baptismal reports is the attention given to the bodies of water utilized for baptismal services of immersion. The following locations are mentioned at least once by reporters: the Pease River,[72] a 'beautiful little lake',[73] the Scioto river,[74] an unnamed river,[75] a dam,[76] Black Creek,[77] the River Choptank,[78] a large mine dam,[79] the Shao river,[80] a tank,[81] the sea,[82] the 'historic Potomac river,'[83] the open-air baptistry,[84] and a baptismal pool.[85] It seems the reporters aspire for readers to know that sufficient water is available for immersion. The notably large bodies of water used for WB highlight the public nature of the venue, whereby the baptismal service becomes an opportunity for the proclamation of the Gospel.[86] The estimated attendance of worshipping witnesses, detached observers, and documentation of large crowds at occasions

---

[71] *TBM* 19.259 (March-May 1926), p. 3.
[72] *TBM* 1.15 (June 1, 1908), p. 1.
[73] *TBM* 1.16 (June 15, 1908), p. 1.
[74] *TBM* 2.29 (January 1, 1909), p. 1.
[75] *TBM* 2.33 (March 1, 1909), p. 2; *TBM* 3.62 (May 15, 1910), p. 2; *TBM* 3.67 (August 1, 1910), p. 3; *TBM* 4.83 (April 1, 1911), p. 4; *TBM* 4.94 (September 15, 1911), p. 3; *TBM* 5.102 (January 15, 1911), p. 3; *TBM* 9.186 (September 1, 1916), p. 4; and *TBM* 19.259 (March-May 1926), p. 3.
[76] *TBM* 3.62 (May 15, 1910), p. 1.
[77] *TBM* 3.67 (August 1, 1910), p. 3.
[78] *TBM* 5.96 (October 15, 1911), p. 3.
[79] *TBM* 5.105 (March 1, 1912), p. 2.
[80] *TBM* 5.112 (June 15, 1912), p. 4.
[81] *TBM* 7.145 (December 1, 1913), p. 1.
[82] *TBM* 7.150 (February 15, 1914), p. 4.
[83] *TBM* 8.164 (November 1, 1914), p. 2.
[84] *TBM* 9.185 (August 1, 1916), p. 3.
[85] *TBM* 22.270 (September-December 1928), p. 4.
[86] *TBM* 2.33 (March 1, 1909), p. 2; *TBM* 3.49 (November 1, 1909), p. 2; *TBM* 7.156 (June 1, 1914), p. 3; and *TBM* 20.263 (Mar-April 1927), p. 4.

of WB is noted numerous times, apparently to support WB as proclamation or evangelism by word and deed.[87]

Formula

According to reports from the field, it appears the preferred formula to be utilized in WB is the Trinitarian formula. Namely, persons are to be 'immersed in the name of the Father, and of the Son, and of the Holy Spirit'.[88] Water baptism, employing the Trinitarian formula, is consistent with the Foundational Truths of the movement, according to the citation of Mt. 28.19.[89] In an editorial titled, 'In the Likeness of His Death', the author explicitly argues against utilization of the 'Jesus only' baptismal formula and the need for Christians to be rebaptized with the formula.[90]

Pentecostal Worship

Throughout the organ, illustrating fervent embodied Pentecostal spirituality, are reports of participants receiving the baptism of the HS, speaking in tongues, rejoicing, shouting, singing, joyful worship, manifestations of the Spirit of God, visions, persons being shaken by the HS, and people praising God, during baptismal services.[91] From the June 15, 1908, issue, A.J. Tomlinson reports that on May 31, over 500 people gathered to witness a baptismal service. In the

---

[87] *TBM* 1.15 (June 1, 1908), p. 1; *TBM* 1.16 (June 15, 1908), p. 1; *TBM* 2.29 (January 1, 1909), p. 1; *TBM* 2.33 (March 1, 1909), p. 2; *TBM* 4.72 (October 15, 1910), p. 2; *TBM* 20.263 (March-April 1927), p. 4; and *TBM* 21.268 (March -April 1928), p. 3.

[88] *TBM* 9.186 (September 1, 1916), p. 4; *TBM* 18.256 (June-September 1, 1925), p. 3.

[89] *TBM* 9.185 (August 1, 1916), p. 1.

[90] *TBM* 8.171 (June 1, 1915), p. 1.

[91] *TBM* 1.15 (June 1, 1908), p. 1; *TBM* 3.51 (December 1, 1909), p. 4; *TBM* 3.67 (August 1, 1910), p. 3; *TBM* 3.68 (August 15, 1910), p. 3; *TBM* 3.70 (September 15, 1910), p. 1; *TBM* 4.72 (October 15, 1910), p. 2; *TBM* 4.74 (November 15, 1910), pp. 1, 4; *TBM* 4.76 (December 15, 1910), p. 4; *TBM* 5.105 (March 1, 1912), p. 2; *TBM* 6.137 (August 1, 1913), p. 3; *TBM* 7.145 (December 1, 1913), p. 1; *TBM* 7.148 (January 15, 1914), p. 2; *TBM* 7.156 (June 1, 1914), p. 3; *TBM* 8.167 (February 1, 1915), p. 3; *TBM* 8.174 (September 1, 1915), p. 3; *TBM* 9.179 (February 1, 1916), p. 3; *TBM* 9.185 (August 1, 1916), p. 3; *TBM* 9.186 (September 1, 1916), p. 4; *TBM* 10.200 (June 1, 1917), p. 3; *TBM* 12.216 (September 1919), p. 3; *TBM* 19.259 (March-May 1926), p. 3; *TBM* 21.268 (March-April 1928), p. 3; *TBM* 22.270 (September-December 1928), p. 4; and *TBM* 22.272 (April-June 1929), p. 11.

midst of 'songs, shouts and rejoicing the candidates were plunged beneath the surface of the water in obedience to the command of Jesus, our Lord and Savior'.[92] In a 1909 issue, the following account from Chillicothe, OH is provided by M.L. and S.L. Otterman:

> The last Sunday we held meetings the ordinance of baptism was observed in the Scioto river, about twelve hundred persons witnessed the scene ... but never before did we see such power of God manifested as at this one. One young sister preached to the people as she stood in the water, and there such spirit in her words and her face beaming with the light of heaven that scores were brought under conviction and tears streamed down their cheeks while the shouts from the saints filled the air.[93]

Embodied Pentecostal spirituality was also evidenced in the baptismal services in Petersburg, Transvaal, South Africa, per a report from Elias Kgobe:

> On May 23, 1913, have again three young men baptized in water, and one of them he received the other tongues, his name Michack. The Spirit shake many people. It was many joy, wonderful joy, and Josaes he received the other tongue on time with Michack. Praise God for His power with His people. The work are greater here now. I have the names of the people, 18 wanted to be baptized. I pray to God to open for me the way to go baptize that people.[94]

From Tokyo, Japan, Frank and Mary Gray report that a young girl was saved on October 14, 1915, and then buried with Christian baptism on November 23. As they traveled to the river for the baptismal service, and she understood anew baptism as taught in Romans 6,

> her little face beamed with holy joy as she clapped her hands almost danced in the street. When she rose to walk in newness of life, her throat was swollen by the operation of the Spirit; and soon she said happily: 'Inaba is buried; Rebecca is resurrected.' Saturday, three of these dear young disciples and one other were

---

[92] *TBM* 1.16 (June 15, 1908), p. 1.
[93] *TBM* 2.29 (January 1, 1909), p. 1.
[94] *TBM* 6.137 (August 1, 1913), p. 3.

immersed, while we sang ... The Spirit of God so rested upon some of them that it was difficult to get them up the bank.[95]

In addition, favorite phrases, 'a blessed time', 'a blessed feast to our souls', 'a blessed service', and 'a sweet heavenly service' are employed as shorthand to communicate the presence and activity of the HS in the baptismal worship services.[96]

Meaning of Water Baptism

The Bridegroom's Messenger reflects a literal reading of the biblical text, positing that WB, an ordinance of the Church, is to be offered and received in obedience to the risen Christ's command (Mt. 28.19).[97] The proper mode is immersion (Mt. 3.13, Acts 8.38-39).[98] Baptism is understood as 'the outward sign of the believer's identification with Christ in his death and resurrection (Rom. 6.3-4; Gal. 3.27; Col. 2.12).[99] In addition to the above meaning, one reporter in Bombay, India, writes he teaches immersion 'to all who are converted because I can see it is like the Red Sea which divided the children of Israel from the land of Egypt and closed the way back. It is a separation from the old life.'[100]

Moreover, WB by immersion is also viewed as an outward expression of sanctification, an inner work, since it is a sign of death

---

[95] *TBM* 8.167 (February 1, 1915), p. 3.

[96] *TBM* 3.51 (December 1, 1909), p. 3; *TBM* 3.52 (December 15, 1909), p. 1; *TBM* 3.62 (May 15, 1910), p. 2; *TBM* 3.67 (August 1, 1910), p. 3; *TBM* 3.68 (August 15, 1910), p. 3; and *TBM* 7.156 (June 1, 1914), p. 3.

[97] *TBM* 2.37 (May 1, 1909), p. 1; *TBM* 9.185 (August 1, 1916), p. 1.

[98] *TBM* 7.156 (June 1, 1914), p. 3; *TBM* 9.180 (March 1, 1916), p. 3; *TBM* 16.242 (January 1923), p. 1. Also, see *TBM* 3.70 (September 15, 1910), p. 4; *TBM* 3.70 (September 15, 1910), p. 4; *TBM* 4.72 (October 15, 1910), p. 2; *TBM* 4.85 (May 1, 1911), p. 1; *TBM* 5.96 (October 15, 1911), p. 3; *TBM* 5.96 (October 15, 1911), p. 3; *TBM* 5.119 (October 15, 1912), p. 2; *TBM* 6.136 (July 1, 1913), p. 3; *TBM* 7.147 (January 1, 1914), p. 1; *TBM* 8.167 (February 1, 1915), p. 3; *TBM* 9.176 (November 1, 1915), p. 1; *TBM* 9.186 (September 1, 1916), p. 4; *TBM* 10.191(February 1, 1917), p. 3; *TBM* 10.199 (May 1, 1917), p. 3; *TBM* 10.200 (June 1, 1917), p. 3; *TBM* 12.215 (July-August 1919), p. 2; *TBM* 19.257 (October-December 1925), p. 2; *TBM* 20.263 (March-April 1927), p. 4; *TBM* 21.266 (November-December 1927), p. 1; *TBM* 21.269 (May-August 1928), p. 3; and *TBM* 21.269 (May-August 1928), p. 4.

[99] *TBM* 9.183 (June 1, 1916), p. 4. Also, see *TBM* 5.105 (March 1, 1912), p. 2; *TBM* 8.167 (February 1, 1915), p. 3; *TBM* 9.176 (November 1, 1915), p. 1; *TBM* 9.183 (June 1, 1916), p. 4; and *TBM* 16.242 (January 1923), p. 1.

[100] *TBM* 9.180 (March 1, 1916), p. 3.

'to the world, to the self-life, to friends and even to loved ones, forsaking all for Jesus'. However, it also symbolizes new life since we are 'risen with our Lord to walk with Him in newness of life'.[101]

Water baptism follows conversion and serves as a public acceptance of Christ and evidence that a person is 'born again'.[102] Public acceptance of Jesus Christ as evidenced through WB could be physically dangerous and life-threatening,[103] as well as precipitate the loss of 'family, friends, position, money, in fact, everything'.[104] Persons administering WB without authorization from government officials were liable for fines and imprisonment in some locales.[105] At the same time, some new converts use the occasion of WB to identify themselves with Jesus Christ through the adoption of Christian names. One letter reports that Brother Norton baptized twelve women and girls, and four boys. After the service, 'some of these young girls gave up their heathen names and took Christian names, such as Rebekah, Leah and Rachael'.[106]

While not widely reported, there are some requirements to be met before candidates are baptized. For example, from Middelburg, Transvaal, South Africa, we read of one young man who had 'given up his beer and tobacco, this is a necessary condition which must be met by all of our candidates'.[107] While not explicitly stated, similar requirements are implied in a report from South India:

> Our dear Lord has done a mighty work in the hearts of several coolly people, some of them have gotten their salvation and left

---

[101] *TBM* 16.242 (January 1923), p. 1. Also, see *TBM* 9.176 (November 1, 1915), p. 1.

[102] *TBM* 3.53 (January 1, 1910), p. 4; *TBM* 4.74 (November 15, 1910), pp. 1, 4; *TBM* 4.76 (December 15, 1910), p. 4; *TBM* 6.125 (January 15, 1913), p. 1; *TBM* 6.132 (May 1, 1913), p. 4; *TBM* 7.156 (June 1, 1914), p. 3; *TBM* 8.167 (February 1, 1915), p. 3; *TBM* 8.174 (September 1, 1915), p. 3; *TBM* 6.125 (January 15, 1913), p. 1; and *TBM* 15. 237 (April-May 1922), p. 3.

[103] *TBM* 6.125 (January 15, 1913), p. 1; *TBM* 8.174 (September 1, 1915), p. 3; *TBM* 7.156 (June 1, 1914), p. 3; and *TBM* 15. 237 (April-May 1922), p. 3.

[104] *TBM* 7.144 (November 15, 1913), p. 1. Also see *TBM* 4.74 (November 15, 1910), pp. 1, 4; *TBM* 4.76 (December 15, 1910), p. 4; *TBM* 6.125 (January 15, 1913), p. 1; *TBM* 6.132 (May 1, 1913), p. 4; and *TBM* 8.174 (September 1, 1915), p. 3.

[105] *TBM* 7.156 (June 1, 1914), p. 3.

[106] *TBM 3.62* (May 15, 1910), p. 2.

[107] *TBM* 5.115 (August 1, 1912), p. 1.

their bad habits of drinking, tobacco, snuffing, etc., and promised to live for Christ ... Two days before I left that place, we ten members went to a hill to wait upon God. Oh, it was a blessed time. God sent his power among us and shook all of us. After that they asked me to baptize them. All glory be to God.[108]

In Argentina, South America, 'The day of the baptisms was one of fasting and prayer, and God graciously met us'.[109]

Latter Rain Evangel

Introduction

The *Latter Rain Evangel* (*LRE*) was published monthly, between 1908 to 1939, by the Stone Church, the influential early Pentecostal congregation in Chicago founded by William Hamner Piper. The Stone Church became Pentecostal in 1907 and hosted the second General Council of the AG in November 1914 and the 1919 General Council.[110] From May 15-29, 1910, The Stone Church hosted a Pentecostal Convention, focusing on world missions, that began to meet semiannually for missionary support, strategic planning, and addressing problems on the field.[111]

The Practice of Water Baptism

The Stone Church employed the *LRE* to disseminate information relative to the expanding missionary and evangelistic endeavors in the USA and foreign soil. While the editor supplies no explicit rationale for detailed reporting of WB, regular reports from the field, sermons, and articles reveal the vital importance of WB for all engaged with advancing the Gospel message.[112] It appears to be the case that WB

---

[108] *TBM* 8.164 (November 1, 1914), p. 2.

[109] *TBM* 10.200 (June 1, 1917), p. 3.

[110] Allan Anderson, '"To All Points of the Compass": The Azusa Street Revival and Global Pentecostalism', *Enrichment: A Journal for Pentecostal Ministry* 11.2 (2006), pp. 164-172. Also, see E.L. Blumhofer, 'Piper, William Hamner' in Stanley M. Burgess and Eduard M. van der Maas (eds.), *NIDPCM* (rev. and exp. edn; Grand Rapids, MI: Zondervan, 2002), pp. 989-90.

[111] H.D. Curtis, 'Pentecostal Missions and the Changing Character of Global Christianity', *International Bulletin of Missionary Research* 36.3 (2012), pp. 122-26, 128.

[112] *LRE* 6.4 (January 1914), pp. 20-21; *LRE* 6.5 (February 1914), pp. 17-18; *LRE* 6.8 (May 1914), pp. 10-12; *LRE* 6.10 (July, 1914), p. 4; *LRE* 6.12 (September

was assumed to be a crucial aspect of Christian discipleship to be followed after catechesis,[113] examination,[114] public confession of faith,[115] and evidence of a changed life.[116] The following citation is a typical report of WB by immersion found in the *LRE*: 'A blessed baptismal service was held on this same day, in which about thirty candidates were immersed into the name of the Triune God'.[117] Water baptism by immersion is also viewed as necessary to those who receive the Good News, as the following report by Wm. H. Johnson, writing from Africa, attests:

> We went down into the water and baptized forty-five, one being an old woman over seventy years of age who had walked about seventy-five miles to be baptized. We had a meeting in her section and she happened to be away at the time, so she came all that distance although she was far from well. The king was also baptized and how he rejoiced and shouted praises to God.[118]

In July 1931 WB by immersion continues to hold a central place in the praxis of evangelists, missionaries, and converts. Mrs. Frank Nicodem of Rupaidiha, North India, provides the following of a baptismal service:

> Seven had asked for baptism, but after they had gone into the water and came out again with radiant faces, the invitation was

---

1914), p. 6; *LRE* 7.9 (June 1914), p. 16; *LRE* 9.6 (March 1917), pp. 3-5; *LRE* 9.7 (April 1917), p. 13; *LRE* 9.9 (June 1917), p. 18; *LRE* 10.3 (December 1917), p. 16; *LRE* 10.6 (March 1918), pp. 19-21; *LRE* 10.9 (June 1918), p. 9; *LRE* 11.4 (January 1919), p. 9; *LRE* 11.6 (March 1919), p. 8; *LRE* 13.4 (January 1921), p. 8; *LRE* 13.5 (February 1921), p. 10; *LRE* 20.7 (April 1928), p. 21; *LRE* 20.12 (September 1928), pp. 14-15; and *LRE* 23.10 (July 1931), p. 22.

[113] *LRE* 6.3 (December 1913), p. 7; *LRE* 9.9 (June 1917), p. 18; *LRE* 12.10 (July 1920), p. 17; *LRE* 17.5 (February 1925), p. 13; *LRE* 18.4 (January 1926), p. 4; *LRE* 19.2 (November 1926), p. 17; and *LRE* 20.12 (September 1928), pp. 14-15.

[114] *LRE* 11.6 (March 1919), p. 8; *LRE* 13.8b (May 1921), p. 22; *LRE* 19.1 (October 1926), p. 13; *LRE* 20.11 (August 1928), p. 15; and *LRE* 20.12 (September 1928), p. 15.

[115] *LRE* 8.10 (July 1916), p. 9; *LRE* 9.6 (March 1917), p. 3; *LRE* 12.10 (July 1920), p. 17; *LRE* 17.5 (February 1925), p. 13; and *LRE* 23.8 (May 1931), p. 21.

[116] *LRE* 12.10 (July 1920), p. 17; *LRE* 20.7 (April 1928), p. 21; and *LRE* 20.12 (September 1928), p. 14.

[117] *LRE* 7.9 (June 1914), p. 16.

[118] *LRE* 10.9 (June 1918), pp. 8-9.

extended to any standing on the bank ... before we left the place, instead of seven there were twenty-two who obeyed the Lord in baptism ... We do not class them as Christians until they proclaim it openly ... through water baptism ... this dear old man tottered forward and made his way down the bank, and there was such a witness in our hearts as we saw him come up out of the water with the joy of the Lord upon his face.[119]

In sharp contrast to the evident zeal to provide and the eagerness to receive WB, the practice could be vehemently opposed by those outside the faith community. Missionary Grunner Vingren, reporting on the outpouring of the HS in Brazil, writes of a mob with knives drawn prohibiting him from baptizing. In addition, 'They had a great stick up a tree ready to fall on my head, but a sister asked the Lord not to permit the stick to fall, and the Lord helped us to perform the baptism unharmed, even in the face of knives.'[120]

Administration

It appears only duly authorized males perform the proper administration of WB by immersion; however, exceptions could be made. During the Second World-Wide Missionary Conference of Pentecostal Missionaries, ministers and workers met at The Stone Church, Chicago, May 12-19. While addressing issues and problems in the foreign mission field, the following position is stated relative to baptizing native converts when male missionaries or ordained workers were not available. A concession was made 'by the brethren that women could, in perfect accord with the spirit of the Gospel, baptize natives, administer the Lord's Supper and bury the dead, but these were exceptions and not the rule'.[121]

Exact Reporting

The editor of the *LRE* places stress on WB by the inclusion of exact numerical reporting of those baptized in water.[122] Even when the

---

[119] *LRE* 23.10 (July 1931), p. 22.
[120] *LRE* 8.4 (January 1916), pp. 14-16. Also, see *LRE* 14.3 (December 1921), p. 19; *LRE* 17.6 (March 1925), p. 23; and *LRE* 18.4 (January 1926), p. 5.
[121] *LRE* 10.9 (June 1918), pp. 12-16.
[122] *LRE* 5.7 (April 1913), p. 15; LRE 5.12 (September 1913), p. 16; *LRE* 6.5 (February 1914), pp. 11, 14, 23; *LRE* 6.8 (May 1914), pp. 10, 12; *LRE* 6.11 (August

precise number of recipients of WB is not provided, reports of baptismal events are included by the editor from the field. Also included in reports are occasions of inquirers seeking after WB as a natural progression in the *via salutis*.

1914), p. 17; *LRE* 6.12 (September 1914), p. 6; *LRE* 7.4 (January 1915), p. 15; *LRE* 7.9 (June 1915), p. 16; *LRE* 8.3 (December 1915), p. 12; *LRE* 8.4 (January 1916), p. 16; *LRE* 8.11 (August 1916), pp. 10, 13; *LRE* 9.3 (December 1916), p. 15; *LRE* 9.7 (April 1917), p. 13; *LRE* 9.9 (June 1917), p. 18; *LRE* 9.10 (July 1917), p. 14; *LRE* 10.9 (June 1918), p. 9; *LRE* 11.1 (October 1918), p. 9; *LRE* 11.4 (January 1919), p. 9; *LRE* 11.6 (March 1919), pp. 8, 16; *LRE* 11.9 (June 1919), p. 15; *LRE* 11.11 (August 1919), p. 14; *LRE* 12.1 (October 1919), p. 10; *LRE* 12.4 January 1920 p. 16; *LRE* 12.4 (January 1920), p. 16; *LRE* 12.5 (February 1920), pp. 15, 19; *LRE* 12.6 (March 1920), p. 14; *LRE* 12.10 (July 1920), pp. 15, 17; *LRE* 12.12 (September 1920), p. 20; *LRE* 13.4 (January1921), p. 18; *LRE* 13.5 (February 1921), p. 10; *LRE* 13.6 (March 1921), p. 11; *LRE* 13.8b (May 1921), p. 22; *LRE* 13.10 (July 1921), p. 15; *LRE* 14.3 (December 1921), p. 19; *LRE* 14.5 (February 1922), p. 18; *LRE* 14.7 (April 1922), p. 12; *LRE* 15.3 (December, 1922), pp. 13, 23; *LRE* 15.9 (June 1923), pp. 18; *LRE* 15.10 (July 1923), p. 20; *LRE* 15.11 (August 1923), p. 17; *LRE* 16.7 (April 1924), p. 2; *LRE* 16.12 (September 1924), pp. 14-16; *LRE* 17.2 (November 1924), p. 22; *LRE* 17.3 (December, 1924), p. 15; *LRE* 17.4 (January 1925), p. 21; *LRE* 17.5 (February 1925), p. 13; *LRE* 17.7 (April 1925), p. 14; *LRE* 17.8 (May 1925), p. 16; *LRE* 17.10 (July 1925), p. 23; *LRE* 17.11 (August 1925), pp. 15, 17; *LRE* 18.1 (October 1925), p. 23; *LRE* 18.4 (January 1926), pp. 4-5, 15; *LRE* 18.5 (February1926), pp. 5-6; *LRE* 18.6 (March 1926), pp. 14-16; *LRE* 18.9 (June 1926), p. 12; *LRE* 18.10 (July 1926), p.12; *LRE* 18.11 (August 1920), p. 22; *LRE* 18.12 (September 1926), p. 11; *LRE* 19.2 (November 1926), p. 17; *LRE* 19.5 (February 1927), p. 11; *LRE* 19.6 (March 1927), p. 12; *LRE* 19.8 (May 1927), p. 16; *LRE* 19.9 (June 1927), pp. 8, 12; *LRE* 19.12 (September 1927), pp. 3, 17-18; *LRE* 20.2 (November 1927), pp. 6, 11; *LRE* 20.3 (December, 1927), pp. 4, 15, 17; *LRE* 20.6 (March 1928), p. 17; *LRE* 20.7 (April 1928), pp. 21-22; *LRE* 20.8 (May 1928), pp. 20, 23; *LRE* 20.10 (July 1928), p. 20; *LRE* 20.11 (August 1928), pp. 12, 15; *LRE* 20.12 (September 1928), pp. 13-16, 18; *LRE* 21.1 (October 1928), p. 15; *LRE* 21.2 (November 1928), p. 14; *LRE* 21.7 (April 1929), pp. 13-14; *LRE* 21.8 (May 1929), p. 12; *LRE* 21.10 (July 1929), p. 11; *LRE* 21.11 (August 1929), p. 17; *LRE* 21.12 (September 1929), p. 9; *LRE* 22.1 (October 1929), pp. 20-21; *LRE* 22.4 (January 1930), pp. 14, 21; *LRE* 22.5 (February 1930), p. 19; *LRE* 22.6 (March 1930), p. 10; *LRE* 22.10 (July 1930), p. 19; *LRE* 22.11 (August 1930), pp. 15-16; *LRE* 23.4 (January 1931), p. 18; *LRE* 23.5 (February 1931), pp. 17-18, 20-21; *LRE* 23.6 (March 1931), p. 19; *LRE* 23.7 (April 1931), pp. 7, 21; *LRE* 23.8 (May 1931), p. 21; *LRE* 23.10 (July 1931), p. 22; *LRE* 23.12 (September 1931), p. 22; and *LRE* 24.1 (October 1931), p. 14.

Widely Practiced

Water baptism is valued and practiced globally as the reports originate from foreign mission stations in Egypt, South Africa, India, China, North China, Ceylon, Fiji and Solomon Islands, Congo, East Africa, Norway, Persia, Argentina, South Africa, Bulgaria, Tanzania, Peru, North India, Venezuela, Greece, Nicaragua, South India, El Salvador, South China, British West Indies, West Africa, and Japan. Also, submitted reports originate from North America: Canada, Illinois, Washington, South Dakota, and Pennsylvania.[123]

Mode of Baptism

Reviewed issues of the *LRE* are replete with reports of baptismal services, employing a wide variety of phrases to recount baptismal events and communicate the meaning of WB and the preferred mode of WB, immersion. 'Baptized in water',[124] 'baptized',[125] 'baptismal

---

[123] Please see Appendix B for a compilation of locations, including city, nation/state, and reference.

[124] *LRE* 5.2 (November 1912), p. 13; *LRE* 6.5 (February 1914), p. 11; *LRE* 6.10 July 1914 pp. 3-4; *LRE* 12.12 (September 1920), p. 20; *LRE* 13.4 (January1921), p. 18; *LRE* 13.5 (February 1921), p. 10; *LRE* 15.3 (December, 1922), p. 23; *LRE* 15.11 (August 1923), p. 17; *LRE* 16.12 (September 1924), p. 15; *LRE* 17.11 (August 1925), p. 15; *LRE* 18.1 (October 1925), p. 23; *LRE* 18.4 (January 1926), pp. 5, 15; *LRE* 18.6 (March 1926), p. 16; *LRE* 19.6 (March 1927), p. 12; *LRE* 19.8 (May 1927), p. 16; *LRE* 19.9 (June 1927), p. 12; *LRE* 19.12 (September 1927), pp. 3, 17-18; *LRE* 20.2 (November 1927), p. 6; *LRE* 20.3 (December, 1927), p. 17; *LRE* 20.8 (May 1928), p. 20; *LRE* 20.8 (May 1928), p. 23; *LRE* 21.11 (August 1929), p. 17; *LRE* 21.12 (September 1929), p. 9; *LRE* 22.1 (October 1929), p. 20; *LRE* 22.1 (October 1929), p. 21; *LRE* 22.5 (February 1930), p. 19; *LRE* 22.10 (July 1930), p. 9; *LRE* 22.11 (August 1930), p. 15; *LRE* 23.5 (February 1931), p. 18; *LRE* 23.5 (February 1931), pp. 20-21; *LRE* 23.6 (March 1931), p. 19; *LRE* 23.10 (July 1931), p. 22; and *LRE* 23.12 (September 1931), p. 22.

[125] *LRE* 8.11 (August 1916), pp. 10, 13; *LRE* 11.1 (October 1918), pp. 9-10; *LRE* 11.6 (March 1919), p. 16; *LRE* 12.10 (July 1920), p. 17; *LRE* 13.10 (July 1921), p. 15; *LRE* 11.9 (June 1919), p. 15; *LRE* 14.5 (February 1922), p. 18; *LRE* 12.1 (October 1919), p. 10; *LRE* 12.5 (February 1920), p. 15; *LRE* 12.5 (February 1920), p. 19; *LRE* 12.6 (March 1920), p. 14; *LRE* 14.7 (April 1922), p. 12; *LRE* 15.9 (June 1923), pp. 18; *LRE* 15.10 (July 1923), p. 20; *LRE* 16.12 (September 1924), pp. 14-15; *LRE* 17.2 (November 1924), p. 22; *LRE* 17.3 (December, 1924), p. 15; *LRE* 23.7 (April 1931), p. 7; *LRE* 17.4 (January 1925), p. 21; *LRE* 17.11 (August 1925), p. 17; *LRE* 18.12 (September 1926), p. 11; *LRE* 18.6 (March 1926), pp. 15-16; *LRE* 18.11 (August 1920), p. 22; *LRE* 19.2 (November 1926), p. 17; *LRE* 19.5 (February

service',[126] and 'immersed'[127] or variations of 'immersion'[128] are the most frequently utilized phrases.

Highlighting immersion as the preferred mode, reporters employ burial language alluding to Rom. 6.1-4, 'buried with Christ in the waters of baptism', to commemorate public confession of Jesus as Lord.[129] The only exception to WB by immersion is reported by B.S. Moore of Japan in her story of a country evangelist who 'baptized' his wife, daughter, and son by pouring gallons of water over them.

1927), p. 11; *LRE* 20.11 (August 1928), p. 12; *LRE* 20.12 (September 1928), pp. 13-14, 16, 18; *LRE* 21.1 (October 1928), p. 15; *LRE* 21.2 (November 1928), p. 14; *LRE* 21.7 (April 1929), p. 13; *LRE* 21.7 (April 1929), p. 14; *LRE* 22.4 (January 1930), p. 14; *LRE* 22.6 (March 1930), p. 10; *LRE* 16.7 (April 1924), p. 2; *LRE* 22.10 (July 1930), p. 19; *LRE* 22.11 (August 1930), p. 15; *LRE* 23.4 (January 1931), p. 18; *LRE* 23.5 (February 1931), pp. 14, 17-18, 22; *LRE* 23.10 (July 1931), p. 22; and *LRE* 23.12 (September 1931), p. 22.

[126] *LRE* 10.9 (June 1918), p. 9; *LRE* 11.6 (March 1919), p. 16; *LRE* 11.11 (August 1922), p. 14; *LRE* 12.4 (January 1920), p. 16; *LRE* 13.5 (February 1921), p. 10; *LRE* 13.8b (May 1921), p. 22; *LRE* 14.3 (December, 1921), p. 19; *LRE* 14.7 (April 1922), p. 12; *LRE* 15.3 (December, 1922), p. 13; *LRE* 19.2 (November 1926), p. 17; *LRE* 19.3 (December, 1926), p. 8; *LRE* 19.6 (March 1927), p. 12; *LRE* 19.12 (September 1927), p. 17; *LRE* 20.2 (November 1927), p. 6; *LRE* 20.6 (March 1928), p. 17; *LRE* 21.1 (October 1928), p. 15; *LRE* 21.8 (May 1929), p. 12; *LRE* 22.4 (January 1930), pp. 14, 21; *LRE* 22.10 (July 1930), p. 19; *LRE* 22.11 (August 1930), p. 16; *LRE* 23.5 (February 1931), pp. 20-21; and *LRE* 23.10 (July 1931), p. 22.

[127] *LRE* 6.8 (May 1914), p. 11; *LRE* 7.9 (June 1915), p. 16; *LRE* 8.8 (May 1916), p. 13; *LRE* 9.6 (March 1917), pp. 17-18; *LRE* 11.11 (August 1922), p. 14; *LRE* 12.4 (January 1920), p. 16; *LRE* 15.3 (December 1922), p. 13; *LRE* 18.10 (Jul 1926), p. 12; *LRE* 19.7 (April 1927), p. 23; and *LRE* 20.3 (December 1927), p. 4.

[128] *LRE* 6.10 (July 1914), p. 4; *LRE* 10.3 (December 1917), p. 16; *LRE* 12.6 (March 1920), p. 15; *LRE* 16.4 (January 1924), p. 22; *LRE* 18.9 (June 1926), p. 12; and *LRE* 20.12 (September 1928), p. 15.

[129] *LRE* 4.9 (June 1912), p. 18; *LRE* 8.1 (October 1915), p. 17; *LRE* 8.3 (December, 1915), p. 12; *LRE* 9.10 (July 1917), p. 14; *LRE* 9.11 (August 1917), p. 22; *LRE* 11.10 (July 1919), pp. 21-22; *LRE* 12.10 (July 1920), p. 15; *LRE* 13.4 (January 1921), p. 8; *LRE* 13.6 (March 1921), p. 11; *LRE* 14.3 (December, 1921), p. 19; *LRE* 15.10 (July 1923), p. 20; *LRE* 17.6 (March 1925), p. 13; *LRE* 17.10 (July 1925), p. 23; *LRE* 18.6 (March 1926), p. 14; *LRE* 18.9 (June 1926), p. 12; *LRE* 19.7 (April 1927), p. 23; *LRE* 19.9 (June 1927), p. 8; *LRE* 20.2 (November 1927), p. 11; *LRE* 20.5 (February 1928), p. 23; *LRE* 20.6 (March 1928), p. 17; *LRE* 20.8 (May 1928), p. 20; *LRE* 20.11 (August 1928), p. 15; *LRE* 21.8 (May 1929), p. 12; *LRE* 21.10 (July 1929), p. 11; *LRE* 22.4 (January 1930), p. 21; *LRE* 23.5 (February 1931), p. 21; *LRE* 23.7 (April 1931), pp. 7, 21; and *LRE* 23.10 (July 1931), p. 22.

She opined, 'That surely was a new formula of baptism, and I believe it was acceptable with God'.[130]

Even those who had been sprinkled as children or adults felt compelled to be immersed. The compulsion came from external influence as well internal. More than a few persons lived the scenario like the one described by a missionary in Uska Bazar, India:

> The Spirit led our Sister Bernice Lee, to talk on the subject of immersion under a great anointing, and God worked. Three days later they all walked through the fields to a pool where five, who had formerly been sprinkled, were immersed. The Spirit of God descended upon their Bible woman who was the first to go into the water, and as she came out she shouted and praised God, her face shining with His glory.[131]

In his sermon, 'Divine Healing in the Path of Obedience: The Signs Following the Word', preached in Flint, MI on November 10, 1917, Evangelist A.T. Rape argues that some are not healed because of their disobedience. Following Christ in WB by immersion, he argues, is one commandment people resist. By implication, it is the reason healing eludes them.

> Some people do not obey the Lord's command in baptism ... This was one of the hardest lessons for me to learn ... My wife was baptized before I was and told me I ought to be, but I insisted that I had been. She said, 'You were sprinkled.' 'Well,' I said, 'Is not that enough'? ... She asked me for the Scripture, and though I searched my Bible I could not find anything. I finally saw the truth and was baptized. The fire of God burned within me as I came up out of the water.[132]

Sufficient Water

References to the bodies of water employed for baptismal services are significantly reduced compared to the publications already reviewed. The following locations are mentioned at least once by

---

[130] *LRE* 14.3 (December 1921), pp. 19-20.
[131] *LRE* 10.3 (December 1917), pp. 16-17.
[132] *LRE* 10.6 (March 1918), pp. 19-22.

reporters: a reservoir,[133] a creek,[134] 'baptismal waters',[135] a river,[136] a lake,[137] a fount,[138] a pool,[139] water,[140] a stream,[141] the North River,[142] the 'sea of Athens',[143] a canal,[144] the Nile River,[145] a baptistry 'out under the beautiful trees',[146] a water tank,[147] and the Matagalpa River.[148] While the references are reduced in number, it appears the reporters desire for readers to know that sufficient water is available for immersion.

Formula

According to reports from the field, it appears the preferred formula to be utilized in WB is the Trinitarian formula.[149] Namely, persons are to be 'immersed in the name of the Father, and of the Son, and of the Holy Spirit'. Positions for employing the Trinitarian formula are provided in highly charged polemics against the proponents of 'the new theology' based on 'special revelation', with the resultant 'degradation of our Lord rather than His Exaltation'.[150] Pastor Andrew L. Fraser's sermon, 'The New Theology: After the Rudiments of Men but not after Christ', preached on April 25, 1915, in The Stone Church, Chicago, IL is typical of the apologetic for

---

[133] *LRE* 4.10 (July 1912), p. 10.
[134] *LRE* 6.12 (September 1914), p. 6.
[135] *LRE* 8.1 (October 1915), p. 17; *LRE* 8.3 (December 1915), p. 12.
[136] *LRE* 8.4 (January 1916), pp. 15, 16; *LRE* 15.11 (August 1923), p. 17; *LRE* 19.2 (November 1926), p. 17; and *LRE* 20.3 (December 1927), p. 15.
[137] *LRE* 9.6 (March 1917), pp. 3, 4.
[138] *LRE* 9.11 (Aug 1917), p. 22.
[139] *LRE* 10.3 (December 1917), p. 16.
[140] *LRE* 7.4 (January 1915), p. 15; *LRE* 10.9 (June 1918), p. 9; and *LRE* 12.1 (October 1919), p. 10.
[141] *LRE* 6.12 (September 1914), p. 3; *LRE* 11.10 (July 1919), p. 21.
[142] *LRE* 14.3 (December 1921), p. 19.
[143] *LRE* 18.11 (August 1920), p. 22.
[144] *LRE* 19.3 (December 1926), p. 8.
[145] *LRE* 20.2 (November 1927), p. 6.
[146] *LRE* 22.1 (October 1929), p. 20.
[147] *LRE* 23.5 (February 1931), p. 17.
[148] *LRE* 23.7 (April 1931), p. 7.
[149] *LRE* 7.9 (June 1915), p. 16; *LRE* 8.4 (January 1916), p. 16; *LRE* 8.8 (May 1916), p. 13; *LRE* 12.1 (October 1919), p. 10; *LRE* 13.10 (July 1921), p. 15; and *LRE* 23.5 (February 1931), p. 17.
[150] *LRE* 7.8 (May 1915), pp. 2-7; *LRE* 11.8 (May 1919), pp. 18-19.

utilization of the Trinitarian formula as opposed to the 'Jesus only' formula. Fraser asserts the new teaching attempts to 'demolish the doctrine of the Trinity' by the rejection of Mt. 28.19 and the use of an alternate formula, 'in the name of Jesus Christ'. Furthermore, adherents of the new teaching 'insist that the name is one and not three' and until their day Christians have been guilty of worshipping three gods. Since they have received 'special revelation' they believe it is 'their high privilege to disabuse our minds of this tritheistic idea'. Adherents posit the formula of Mt. 28.19 was temporary and 'that its telic import' was later communicated to the Apostles through special revelation who then utilized the same formula espoused by the new teaching. Fraser reports adherents of the new teaching 'oppose and disfellowship all who have been baptized according to Mt. 28:19' because they have not been baptized as Jesus commanded. Last, per Fraser, 'they practically insist upon rebaptism in the name of Jesus Christ'.[151]

Moreover, evidence suggests the controversy adversely impacts ministers in the mission field. One report disavows being affected by the new doctrine since they have not been accepted. Yet, the report quickly adds there has been an adverse financial impact.[152]

Pentecostal Worship

Distributed throughout the official organ of the *LRE*, illustrating fervent embodied Pentecostal spirituality, are reports of participants receiving the baptism of the HS, speaking in tongues, rejoicing, shouting, singing, joyful worship, manifestations of the Spirit of God, visions, and people praising God, during baptismal services.[153] From the May 1914 issue, Elizabeth Sisson reports from Dallas, TX that before fifteen candidates had all been immersed the power of God fell and that audience members who had not planned to be baptized 'began to rise and go to the dressing rooms to prepare for the ceremony'. The power of God fell on these and as many of the

---

[151] *LRE* 7.8 (May 1915), pp. 2-9.
[152] *LRE* 9.3 (December 1916), p. 15.
[153] *LRE* 9.6 (March 1917), pp. 3-5; *LRE* 9.7 (April 1917), p. 13; *LRE* 10.3 (December 1917), p. 16; *LRE* 11.4 (January 1919), p. 9; *LRE* 16.12 (September 1924), p. 16; *LRE* 17.7 (April 1925), p. 14; *LRE* 18.4 (January 1926), p. 4; *LRE* 19.3 (December 1926), p. 8; *LRE* 23.5 (February 1931), pp. 17-18; and *LRE* 23.10 (July 1931), p. 22.

candidates came out of the water 'drunk with the Spirit, some shouted, some danced in the water, and the same blessed power of God and of rejoicing came all through the audience'.[154]

The following accounts provide similar reports of embodied Pentecostal spiritual worship before, during, and after baptismal services. Mrs. Neely, writing from Liberia, reports that during a service where 16 were buried in baptism, 'the power fell; some while on the bank and some while in the water, especially after we had baptized them'.[155] Mrs. I.D. Shakley, reporting on the ministry among the Kru tribe in Africa to The Stone Church, May 19, 1924 reports experiencing 'wonderful outpourings of the Spirit' and after a year several baptismal services were held when 'the power of God rested upon those people as they went down into the water and arose into newness of life'.[156] Also, Miss Erickson, writing from Africa, reported the following incident in September 1924 of a woman's experience when she was baptized in the HS:

> She spoke in tongues a long time, and oh! how she did rejoice, saying over and over again, 'Glory to Jesus ! Hallelujah !' ... Together with fifteen others she was one of the happy candidates that day. The spirit fell upon her at the water side and she was prostrated on the ground, praising the Lord with a loud voice.[157]

Meaning of Water Baptism

The *LRE* reflects a literal reading of the biblical text, asserting that WB is to be received in obedience to the command of the risen Christ as found in Mt. 28.19.[158] The dissemination of teaching relative to Christ's command appears to generate seekers for WB among

---

[154] *LRE* 6.8 (May 1914), p. 10.
[155] *LRE* 11.4 (January 1919), p. 9.
[156] *LRE* 16.12 (September 1924), p. 16.
[157] *LRE* 17.7 (April 1925), p. 14.
[158] *LRE* 1.6 (March 1909), pp. 22-23; *LRE* 6.4 (January 1914), pp. 20-21; *LRE* 6.8 (May 1914), pp. 10-11; *LRE* 9.7 (April 1917), p. 13; *LRE* 10.6 (March 1918), pp. 19-21; *LRE* 13.4 (January 1921), p. 8; *LRE* 17.6 (March 1925), p. 23; *LRE* 17.7 (April 1925), p. 14; *LRE* 17.8 (May 1925), p. 16; *LRE* 20.8 (May 1928), pp. 20, 23; and *LRE* 23.10 (July 1931), p. 22.

converts.[159] The proper mode is immersion (Mt. 3.13, Acts 8.38-39).[160] While it does not appear that evangelists mandate rebaptism for those previously sprinkled, missionary reports suggest that believers new to the Pentecostal message and experience found themselves desirous of WB by immersion. Three baptismal services were held; 'Methodists, United Brethren, Congregationalists, Catholics and new converts, twenty or thirty in all, have been baptized in water'.[161] Water baptism is understood to mean the believer is 'buried with Christ in death to the "old life" and raised with Him to "walk in newness of life"',[162] based on the confession of sin and professing faith and trust in the redeeming person and work of Jesus Christ.[163] While specific verses are not cited, it appears the following texts inform the burial imagery employed: Rom. 6.3-4; Gal. 3.27; and Col. 2.12.[164] The *LRE* unequivocally denies that WB has any saving efficacy through the consistent emphasis placed on

---

[159] *LRE* 6.3 (December 1913), p.7; *LRE* 14.3 (December 1921), p. 20; *LRE* 20.12 (September 1928), p. 15; *LRE* 22.5 (February 1930), p. 19; *LRE* 23.8 (May 1931), p. 21; and *LRE* 23.10 (July 1931), p. 22.

[160] *LRE* 6.8 (May 1914), p. 11; *LRE* 6.10 (July 1914), p. 4; *LRE* 7.9 (June 1915), p. 16; *LRE* 8.8 (May 1916), p. 13; *LRE* 9.6 (March 1917), pp. 3, 17-18; *LRE* 9.9 (June 1917), p. 18; *LRE* 10.3 (December 1917), p. 16; *LRE* 10.6 (March 1918), pp. 19-21; *LRE* 11.11 (August 1922), p. 14; *LRE* 12.4 (January 1920), p. 16; *LRE* 12.6 (March 1920), p. 15; *LRE* 13.8b (May 1921), p. 22; *LRE* 15.3 (December 1922), p. 13; *LRE* 16.4 (January 1924), p. 22; *LRE* 18.9 (June 1926), p. 12; *LRE* 18.10 (July 1926), p. 12; *LRE* 19.7 (April 1927), p. 23; *LRE* 20.3 (December 1927), p. 4; and *LRE* 20.12 (September 1928), p. 15.

[161] *LRE* 14.7 (April 1922), p. 12.

[162] *LRE* 6.4 (January 1914), pp. 20-21; *LRE* 6.8 (May 1914), pp. 10-11; *LRE* 9.6 (March 1917), p. 3; and *LRE* 11.10 (July 1919), p. 22.

[163] *LRE* 8.10 (July 1916), p. 9; *LRE* 20.12 (September 1928), p. 15; and *LRE* 23.10 (Jul 1931), p. 22.

[164] *LRE* 4.9 (June 1912), p. 18; *LRE* 8.1 (October 1915), p. 17; *LRE* 8.3 (December 1915), p. 12; *LRE* 9.10 (July 1917), p. 14; *LRE* 9.11 (August 1917), p. 22; *LRE* 11.10 (July 1919), pp. 21-22; *LRE* 12.10 (July 1920), p. 15; *LRE* 13.4 (January 1921), p. 8; *LRE* 13.6 (March 1921), p. 11; *LRE* 14.3 (December 1921), p. 19; *LRE* 15.10 (July 1923), p. 20; *LRE* 17.6 (March 1925), p. 13; *LRE* 17.10 (July 1925), p. 23; *LRE* 18.6 March 1926 p. 14; *LRE* 18.9 (June 1926), p. 12; *LRE* 19.7 (April 1927), p. 23; *LRE* 19.9 (June 1927), p. 8; *LRE* 20.2 (November 1927), p. 11; *LRE* 20.5 (February 1928), p. 23; *LRE* 20.6 (March 1928), p. 17; *LRE* 20.8 (May 1928), p. 20; *LRE* 20.11 (August 1928), p. 15; *LRE* 21.8 (May 1929), p. 12; *LRE* 21.10 (July 1929), p. 11; *LRE* 22.4 (January 1930), p. 21; *LRE* 23.5 (February 1931), p. 21; *LRE* 23.7 (April 1931), pp. 7, 21; and *LRE* 23.10 (July 1931), p. 22.

confession of sin and profession of faith in Christ as the requisites for reconciliation with God.[165]

Church of God Evangel

Introduction

The *Church of God Evangel* (*COGE*) was initially a monthly periodical with the first issue published on February 1, 1910, in Cleveland, TN.[166] Under the editorial purview of A.J. Tomlinson,[167] the *COGE* made the eventual transition to a weekly publication. Tomlinson served as editor until he was relieved of his editorial duties and replaced by J.S. Llewellyn in December 1922.[168] The *COGE* continues to be published by the COG, headquartered in Cleveland, TN.

The Practice of Water Baptism

A.J. Tomlinson utilized the *COGE* from the outset to accomplish the following: facilitate communication; disseminate information regarding evangelistic endeavors, church expansion, ministerial and congregational activity; foster fellowship; and inspire readers. In the third issue of the publication, Tomlinson delivers the following invitation and charge:

> We believe it would be good for every minister to write a few words occasionally and let the readers of the paper know your whereabouts and where you are laboring this year. Give reports of any revivals that may be in progress, any baptizings [sic] or

---

[165] *LRE* 8.10 (July 1916), p. 9; *LRE* 9.6 (March 1917), p. 3; *LRE* 12.10 (July 1920), p. 17; *LRE* 17.5 (February 1925), p. 13; and *LRE* 23.8 (May 1931), p. 21.

[166] C.W. Conn, 'Church of God (Cleveland, TN)' in Stanley M. Burgess and Eduard M. van der Maas (eds.), *NIDPCM* (rev. and exp. edn; Grand Rapids, MI: Zondervan, 2002), pp. 530-34. I reviewed 904 issues of the *COGE* published during 1910 – 1931.

[167] H.D. Hunter, 'Tomlinson, Ambrose Jessup' in Stanley M. Burgess and Eduard M. van der Maas (eds.), *NIDPCM* (rev. and exp. edn; Grand Rapids, MI: Zondervan, 2002), pp. 1143-45. In addition to the *COGE*, A.J. Tomlinson published *The Faithful Standard* as a for-profit magazine-style monthly periodical in 1922. The majority of the content was compiled by Homer Tomlinson, eldest son of A.J. Tomlinson. The extant eight issues contain no references to WB.

[168] *COGE* 13.46 (November 11, 1922), p. 2.

communion services you may have. Let us all keep in touch and fellowship with each other through the paper.[169]

Tomlinson's explicit request for reports of baptisms and communion services appears linked to the position that both are sacred ordinances along with Foot Washing.[170] As sacred ordinances commanded by Christ, it would be vital to the spiritual life and health of believers and local assemblies to be obedient to Christ's commands. Coupled with obedience to Christ is Tomlinson's desire to publicize and track the movements' advance of the Gospel and the messages of sanctification and baptism with the Holy Ghost with the evidence of speaking in tongues in various regions. Thus, the *COGE* became a vehicle for both evangelism of non-Christians and edification of disciples of Christ. Moreover, it appears to be the case that WB was assumed to be a crucial aspect of Christian discipleship to be followed after conversion. 'Water Baptism by Immersion' first appears in the August 15, 1910, issue of the *COGE* as one of the COG Teachings. The following Bible verses are cited to support the practice: 'Mt. 28:19, Mk. 1:9, 10, John 3:22, 23, Acts 8:36-38'.[171]

The call to WB is taken seriously by hearers so that even cold water, mud, and snow do not serve as deterrents to candidates. A report from Belmont, NC, states the following: 'In the last three Sunday nights ... Sunday evening at 3 p.m. a number of the brethren went thru the snow and mud to the place where the baptizing took place'.[172]

The following citation found in the *COGE* provided by L.L. Turner, reporting on a tent meeting at Poplar Camp, VA, is a typical report of 'results' from evangelistic endeavors, including WB: 'Twelve were baptized with the Holy Ghost, eighteen were added to the church, thirteen baptized in water, many healed and some saved and sanctified'.[173] The reports also include unique details like the ages of baptismal candidates. The youngest person baptized was age

---

[169] *COGE* 1.3 (April 1, 1910), p. 4.
[170] *COGE* 1.14 (September 15, 1910), p. 5; *COGE* 1.12 (August 15, 1910), p. 3; *COGE* 6.28 (July 10, 1915), p. 4; *COGE* 8.19 (May 19, 1917), p. 2; and *COGE* 14.34 (August 25, 1923), p. 2.
[171] *COGE* 1.12 (August 15, 1910), p. 3.
[172] *COGE* 20.50 (February 22, 1930), p. 4; *COGE* 21.22 (July 26, 1930), p. 3.
[173] *COGE* 6.43 (October 23, 1915), p. 4.

three,[174] and the oldest was ninety-three years of age.[175] While the editor stresses the importance of WB for the COG and finds support by ministers in the field, an aggregate WB report is absent from the periodical.

Exact Reporting

The *COGE* editor accentuates the import of WB by including specific statistical reporting of those baptized in water.[176] When the precise number of recipients of WB is not provided, reports of baptismal events are still included.[177] The omission of a precise count from the report proves to be the exception to the rule. Also included in the *COGE* are reports of inquirers seeking after WB as a natural progression in the life of a disciple of Jesus Christ.[178] Water baptism is valued and practiced widely across the USA, but most baptisms are reported from Alabama, Arkansas, Florida, Georgia, and Tennessee.[179] To a lesser degree, reports are submitted from a handful of other countries where the COG has made inroads. The Caribbean islands of Jamaica and The Bahamas dominant the number of baptismal reports from foreign countries.[180]

---

[174] *COGE* 21.27 (August 30, 1930), p. 3.

[175] *COGE* 20.28 (September 7, 1929), p. 1.

[176] See the footnotes under the Mode of Baptism section below for all references with exact numbers.

[177] *COGE* 1.16 (Oct 15, 1910), p. 7; *COGE* 1.18 (November 15, 1910), p. 8; *COGE* 8.32 (August 18, 1917), p. 4; *COGE* 9.28 (July 13, 1918), p. 2; *COGE* 11.27 (July 3, 1920), p. 4; *COGE* 11.44 (Oct 30, 1920), p. 3; *COGE* 12.22 (May 28, 1921), p. 3; *COGE* 12.25 (June 18, 1921), p. 3; *COGE* 12.26 (June 25, 1921), p. 2; *COGE* 12.34 (August 20, 1921), p. 3; *COGE* 12.38 (September 17, 1921), p. 2; *COGE* 13.34 (August 26, 1922), p. 2; *COGE* 13.44 (November 11, 1922), p. 1; *COGE* 15.36 (September 20, 1924), p. 3; *COGE* 16.35 (August 29, 1925), p. 3; *COGE* 17.20 (May 22, 1926), p. 4; *COGE* 17.37 (September 18, 1926), p. 3; *COGE* 17.40 (Oct 9, 1926), p. 1; *COGE* 18.39 (September 24, 1927), p. 1; *COGE* 19.47 (December 1, 1928), p. 4; *COGE* 20.2 (March 9, 1929), p. 1; *COGE* 20.28 (September 7, 1929), p. 2; *COGE* 20.30 (September 21, 1929), p. 4; *COGE* 20.50 (February 22, 1930), p. 4; *COGE* 21.12 (May 17, 1930), p. 3; and *COGE* 21.22 (July 26, 1930), p. 3.

[178] *COGE* 16.23 (June 6, 1925), p. 4; *COGE* 17.23 (June 12, 1926), p. 2; and *COGE* 20.34 (Oct 19, 1929), p. 2.

[179] Please see Appendix C for a breakdown of the locations in the case of the USA. The sites are listed in alphabetical order according to state and city.

[180] Please see Appendix D for a breakdown of the locations according to country. The sites are listed in alphabetical order according to country and city.

Widely Practiced

References to specific bodies of water utilized for baptismal services are significantly reduced compared to the publications already reviewed. The following locations are mentioned at least once by reporters: a 'bathtub',[181] the Atlantic Ocean,[182] creeks,[183] lakes,[184] pond,[185] pool,[186] various rivers,[187] streams,[188] and 'the water's edge'.[189] The significant reduction of specific bodies of water may be accounted for by the fact that almost every report of WB includes a reference to water. It seems to be the case that readers of the *COGE* would have understood sufficient water for immersion was available when the rite was performed. Hence, there was no need to add specific details to the reports. Another possibility to explain the limited specifics may be an editorial attempt to standardize the reports while allowing for exceptions.

---

[181] *COGE* 6.30 (July 24, 1915, p. 3.

[182] *COGE* 16.5 (January 31, 1925), p. 1; *COGE* 18.28 (July 9, 1927), p. 2; and *COGE* 19.15 (April 14, 1928), p. 4.

[183] *COGE* 11.44 (Oct 30, 1920), p. 3; *COGE* 13.36 September 9, 1922), p. 2; *COGE* 18.35 (August 27, 1927), p. 3; and *COGE* 21.12 (May 17, 1930), p. 3.

[184] *COGE* 5.42 (Oct 17, 1914), p. 4; *COGE* 9.47 (November 23, 1918), p. 3; *COGE* 12.26 (June 25, 1921), p. 2; *COGE* 12.31 (July 30, 1921), p. 2; *COGE* 14.27 (July 7, 1923), p. 4; *COGE* 18.39 (September 24, 1927), p. 1; *COGE* 21.6 (April 5, 1930), p. 4; *COGE* 21.24 (August 9, 1930), p. 3; and *COGE* 21.28 (September 6, 1930), p. 3

[185] *COGE* 12.31 (July 30, 1921), p. 2.

[186] *COGE* 17.28 (July 17, 1926), p. 3.

[187] *COGE* 6.18 (May 1, 1915), p. 4; *COGE* 6.28 (July 10, 1915), p. 2; *COGE* 8.34 (September 1, 1917), p. 2; *COGE* 11.46 (November 20, 1920), p. 2; *COGE* 12.20 (May 14, 1921), p. 2; *COGE* 12.22 (May 28, 1921), p. 3; *COGE* 12.31 (July 30, 1921), p. 2; *COGE* 21.34 (Oct 18, 1930), p. 2; *COGE* 12.40 (Oct 1, 1921), p. 2; *COGE* 13.34 (August 26, 1922), p. 2; *COGE* 16.28 (July 11, 1925), p. 1; *COGE* 17.39 (Oct 2, 1926), p. 4; *COGE* 18.28 (July 9, 1927), p. 1; *COGE* 18.34 (August 20, 1927), p. 2; *COGE* 19.33 (August 18, 1928, p. 1; *COGE* 19.37 (September 15, 1928), p. 1; *COGE* 21.10 (May 3, 1930), p. 4; *COGE* 21.15 (June 7, 1930), p. 3; *COGE* 21.22 (July 26, 1930), p. 3; *COGE* 21.28 (September 6, 1930), p. 2; and *COGE* 21.30 (September 20, 1930), p. 1.

[188] *COGE* 15.36 (September 20, 1924), p. 3; *COGE* 16.36 (September 5, 1925), pp. 1-2.

[189] *COGE* 11.28 (July 10, 1920), p. 3; *COGE* 15.30 (August 9, 1924), p. 3; *COGE* 17.39 (Oct 2, 1926), p. 1; *COGE* 19.18 (May 15, 1928), p. 4; *COGE* 20.30 (September 21, 1929), p. 4; *COGE* 21.33 (Oct 11, 1930), p. 4; and COGE 22.26 (August 29, 1931), p. 2.

Modes of Baptism

The reports of baptismal services employ various phrases to recount baptismal events and communicate the meaning of WB and the preferred mode of WB, immersion. It appears that immersion was practiced without exception and that sermons, reports, and testimonies were employed to offer a rejection of sprinkling as an acceptable mode of baptism and an apologia for strict adherence to the practice.[190] In addition to employing 'immerse', variants of the word or other imagery connoting immersion,[191] and burial language are also employed to describe being baptized in water.[192]

'Baptized',[193] 'baptized in water',[194] and 'followed the Lord in water baptism'[195] are the most frequently employed phrases. Additionally, the following terms are also utilized in varying frequency: 'baptized with water',[196] 'followed Jesus in water baptism',[197] 'followed Christ by being baptized',[198] 'followed their Savior in water baptism',[199] and 'baptized unto repentance'.[200]

The proper mode of WB is immersion.[201] In a 1916 article titled 'What About Baptism', the author, A.J. Tomlinson, asserts that 'When we, the Church of God, refer to water baptism at all it is always immersion, and no other form is recognized as baptism'. He

---

[190] *COGE* 7.17 (April 22, 1916), pp. 1-2; *COGE* 8.22 (June 9, 1917), p. 2; *COGE* 8.40 (Oct 13, 1917), p. 4; and *COGE* 11.24 (June 12, 1920), p. 4.

[191] *COGE* 1.15 (Oct 1, 1910), p. 5; *COGE* 5.8 (February 21, 1914), pp. 5, 8; *COGE* 8.32 (August 18, 1917), p. 2; *COGE* 10.28 (July 12, 1919), p. 3; *COGE* 12.31 (July 30, 1921), p. 2; *COGE* 16.36 (September 5, 1925), pp. 1-2; and *COGE* 21.22 (July 26, 1930), p. 3.

[192] *COGE* 5.37 (September 12, 1914), p. 5; *COGE* 6.24 (June 12, 1915), p. 2; *COGE* 7.21 (May 20, 1916), p. 2; *COGE* 9.47 (November 23, 1918), p. 3; *COGE* 10.8 (February 22, 1919), p. 2; *COGE* 11.39 (September 25, 1920), p. 2; *COGE* 11.40 (Oct 2, 1920), p. 2; *COGE* 13.25 (June, 24, 1922), p. 2; *COGE* 14.34 (August 25, 1923), p. 2; *COGE* 16.42 (Oct 17, 1925), p. 1; *COGE* 17.39 (Oct 2, 1926), p. 1; *COGE* 22.12 (May 23, 1931), p. 4; and *COGE* 22.26 (August 29, 1931), p. 2.

[193] See Appendix E for all references to 'Baptized'.

[194] See Appendix F for all references to 'baptized in water'.

[195] See Appendix G for a list of all references to 'followed the Lord in WB'.

[196] *COGE* 1.18 (November 15, 1910), p. 8.

[197] *COGE* 6.3 (January 16, 1915), p. 3.

[198] *COGE* 22.35 (November 7, 1931), p. 3.

[199] *COGE* 1.12 (August 15, 1910), p. 3.

[200] *COGE* 7.17 (April 22, 1916), pp. 1-2.

[201] *COGE* 5.40 (Oct 4, 1914), p. 5; *COGE* 7.10 (March 4, 1916), p. 4.

allows the only reason immersion is employed is due to the confusion experienced by persons who have been sprinkled or had water poured on them and call it baptism. To ensure proper understanding, he states, 'it becomes necessary to use the word immersion as a means of explanation'.[202]

Administration

Proper administration of WB by immersion was crucial in the movement from the outset.[203] It is to be performed by a 'duly credentialed minister' who has been baptized in the Holy Ghost with the evidence of speaking tongues. In 1915, M.S. Lemons argued that the administrator must be baptized in the HS, citing Scriptural examples of John the Baptist and Jesus. He states,

> If it makes no difference who baptizes you; why then did God give John the Baptist the Holy Ghost so early in life, and why did Jesus command His disciples to tarry first in the city, and why did Paul baptize a dozen men over, before he laid his hands on them that they might receive the Holy Ghost?[204]

In 1927, F.J. Lee reiterated the above position in an article titled, 'Water Baptism Enjoined – THE PROPER ADMINISTRATOR', when he asserts that before his Ascension, Jesus instructed his followers to tarry until endued with power from on high, thus showing that no one is to be recognized as legal administrator of baptism until they have received the Holy Ghost.[205] It seems to be the case that the phrase, 'duly credentialed minister', carried the requirement that the minister is *male*. Baptismal reports from March 1916 through July 1931 illustrate the necessity of WB being performed by a credentialed *male*.[206] The following report captures the dynamics in play during this era of the COG. After Sister Shumaker conducted a revival and had candidates for WB, 'Brother Simmons, come to baptize and receive followers into the great

---

[202] *COGE* 7.17 (April 22, 1916), pp. 1-2.
[203] *COGE* 5.40 (Oct 4, 1914), p. 5; *COGE* 7.10 (March 4, 1916), p. 4.
[204] *COGE* 6.22 (May 29, 1915), p. 2.
[205] *COGE* 18.35 (August 27, 1927), pp. 1, 3.
[206] *COGE* 7.10 (March 4, 1916), p. 4; *COGE* 18.37 (September 10, 1927), p. 3; *COGE* 19.28 (July 14, 1928), p. 1; *COGE* 20.26 (August 24, 1929), p. 2; *COGE* 21.9 (April 26, 1930), p. 2; and *COGE* 22.21 (July 25, 1931), p. 4.

Church of God. Fourteen obeyed Christ in WB and such a wonderful time as was had.'[207]

A.J. Tomlinson supported the need for rebaptism in July 1917. Without explicit reference to the 'New Issue' or 'New Light' doctrine, it appears the controversy provoked a question to the then moderator of the Seventh General Assembly. While minimizing the use of the correct 'formula', Tomlinson provides permission for the practice of rebaptism in his response:

> In reference to the question about re-baptizing, will say that it is not so much the formula or ceremony used in baptism that counts as the act itself. It may be good to rebaptize people sometimes, but it should not be done merely because of the use or non-use of words in the ceremony. – Ed.[208]

Tomlinson does not provide criteria for when it might be 'good' to rebaptize a person. It appears that the question was left to be answered at the discretion of ministers and persons desirous of being baptized again. In 1924 a question relative to the requirements for restoration of 'backslidden' persons was submitted for consideration by a committee:[209] 'Question 5. If he backslides, can he be reclaimed and receive the Holy Ghost again without being baptized again in water?'[210] The committee answers with the following: 'He can receive the Holy Ghost again, but should be baptized again the same as any other soul that repents.'[211] Again, no rationale is offered for the response.

Reports reveal that after 'backsliders' have been 'reclaimed', they are rebaptized. A reporter from Parkersburg, WV provides the following account: 'Fourteen followed the Lord in water baptism;

---

[207] *COGE* 21.9 (April 26, 1930), p. 2. Also see *COGE* 7.10 (March 4, 1916), p. 4; *COGE* 18.37 (September 10, 1927), p. 3; *COGE* 19.28 (July 14, 1928), p. 1; *COGE* 20.26 (August 24, 1929), p. 2; *COGE* 21.9 (April 26, 1930), p. 2; and *COGE* 22.21 (July 25, 1931), p. 4.

[208] *COGE* 8.29 (July 28, 1917), p. 4.

[209] The heavy load assumed by F.J. Lee when elected General Overseer required him to delegate responsibilities to ministerial colleagues. A committee of three persons was formed to reply to the questions submitted for review. The committee consisted of J.M. Baldree, W.L. Hindman, and R.C. Mullen.

[210] *COGE* 15.8 (February 23, 1924), p. 3.

[211] *COGE* 15.8 (February 23, 1924), p. 3.

some of this number had been backsliders and were reclaimed, and some were members of other churches. The Lord manifested His approval in the baptismal service by His presence, and by richly blessing His people.'[212]

Providing greater detail of what faith groups are represented by candidates for baptism and rebaptism is the following report from Louisville, KY: 'Twenty-nine followed the Lord in water baptism. Some had been Baptists, Methodists, Free Methodists, and some Catholics, but thank God, when He shall bring again Zion, we shall all see eye to eye. Praise God'.[213] Lastly, the first-hand testimony by Nettie Renfroe from Tarpon Springs, FL, provides insight into the internal psychological, and spiritual processes of persons transitioning from another faith group to the COG:

> There were eighteen joined the dear old Church of God Sunday night, but as our minister told us what it took to join I failed to join ... I had once been baptized in the Christian Church I didn't feel the need of being rebaptized ... but next day I was under such awful conviction until I said, 'yes, Lord, I am willing to be baptized.' He showed me how the door of the church was open and I was unable to enter on account of not obeying, so the Lord willing I will be baptized with the rest, and by the help and favor of the most high God, I want to be ready always to obey His Word and be a faithful child of God.[214]

Rebaptism also seemed to follow significant religious experiences. The personal testimony by J.H. Ralstin from Nashville, TN, illustrates the practice:

> I will be baptized in the river here soon. I was baptized in a pond when I was converted, and when I was sanctified, I was baptized in the Wabash, and now since I have the Holy Ghost, I would like to be baptized in the ocean, but as I can't, I'll take the river.[215]

---

[212] *COGE* 15.46 (December 6, 1924), p. 2.
[213] *COGE* 11.27 (July 3, 1920), p. 3.
[214] *COGE* 6.33 (August 14, 1915), p. 4.
[215] *COGE* 7.26 (June 24, 1916), p. 3. Also see *COGE* 10.42 (October 18, 1919), p. 3.

Water baptism was passionately sought and practiced by hundreds of people within the growing Pentecostal movement; however, not everyone was amenable to the practice or supportive of family members being baptized. J.W. Allen reports severe opposition, inspired by the Devil, from Mater, KY, when an 18-year-old young woman was saved and planned to be baptized. Her 'people' opposed her baptism and 'tied her with a rope and cut up her clothes to keep her from going, but she came on anyway'. The woman's uncle informed her that her brother would kill her and the preacher if she followed through with the baptism. Undeterred, the woman was baptized.[216]

Sharing the perspective of the preceding report that opposition to new believers and the practice of WB is genuinely Satanic, the following story from Cocoanut Grove, FL, captures opposition from the spouse of a convert who objected to his wife being baptized. 'Despite his protest, she was baptized "tho" he was real mad'. The report further offers that 'The Lord blessed and the people shouted. We are glad for the people who will stand for God in spite of the devil.'[217]

In addition to the external opposition received from those alienated from God, there was also opposition to the COG's stance on WB from fellow Pentecostals. This took form in the 'New Light' or 'New Issue' doctrine that was being promulgated. It appears the new doctrine was first confronted and rebuffed by A.J. Tomlinson in mid-1917 when he asserts that 'it is not so much the formula or ceremony used in baptism that counts as the act itself'.[218] The controversy is first named in May 1919 in a letter by E.L Pinkley of Evadale, AR, in a report on his experience in Truman, AR: 'I have just come through Truman and preached two nights. The saints have just come through a great war with "New Light" and "Finished Work" doctrine but the storm has ceased and God's people are calm and still standing true'.[219] The following report from Abilene, TX, provides an account of what the above 'storm' may have been like

---

[216] *COGE* 16.14 (April 4, 1925), p. 3.
[217] *COGE* 21.13 (May 24, 1930), p. 3.
[218] *COGE* 8.29 (July 28, 1917), p. 4.
[219] *COGE* 10.21 (May 24, 1919), p. 2.

for the saints in Arkansas after two people were baptized with the HS:

> the enemy stepped in in the form of man and began to try to get in his 'Jesus only and redemption stuff' and told them to go and be baptized in Jesus' name and they would have the promise of the Father after they already had it, for we heard them speak with tongues, Acts 2:4. Immediately we loaded David's slingshot with the Word of God and ... openly rebuked him and pretty soon we had the enemy on flight. I think the people in this part of the country are beginning to find out that Church of God folks won't stand for just any old thing.[220]

Early reports from the field reflect the preferred formula for WB is the Trinitarian formula. Namely, persons are to be 'immersed in the name of the Father, and of the Son, and of the Holy Spirit'.[221] Several articles published between 1921 to 1931 fill the pages of the *COGE* pointedly defending the doctrine of the Trinity and the use of the Trinitarian formula and refuting and attacking the opposition's arguments.[222] Apparently, the apologetics in the *COGE* provided spiritual support and theological clarity for ministers and members on the field to the effect that the 'New Light' doctrine did not adversely impact the COG.

Pentecostal Worship and Witness

Despite internal and external opposition COG congregations and ministers drank deeply from the spiritual stream that enlivened their daily lives and corporate worship. This was especially true when celebrating WB. Dispersed throughout the *COGE*, recounting passionate embodied Pentecostal spirituality, are reports of worshippers receiving the baptism of the HS, speaking in tongues, rejoicing, shouting, singing, joyful worship, manifestations of the

---

[220] *COGE* 18.35 (August 27, 1927), p. 1.
[221] *COGE* 5.37 (September 12, 1914), p. 5; *COGE* 6.32 (August 7, 1915), p. 2.
[222] *COGE* 12.30 (July 23, 1921), p. 3; *COGE* (August 27, 1921), p. 3; *COGE* 12.38 (September 17, 1921), p. 3; *COGE* 12.45 (November 12, 1921), p. 2; *COGE* 12.46 (November 19, 1921), p. 3; *COGE* 13.8 (February 25, 1922), p. 2; *COGE* 13.38 (September 23, 1922), p. 3; *COGE* 14.21 (May 26, 1923), p. 1; *COGE* 15.45 (November 29, 1924), pp. 1, 3; *COGE* 20.41 (December 14, 1929), pp. 1, 3; *COGE* 21.33 (Oct 11, 1930), pp. 1, 3; and *COGE* 21.44 (January 10, 1931), pp. 1, 3.

Spirit of God, visions, and people praising God, during and after baptismal services.²²³ From the October 1, 1910 issue, the author from Coalburg, AL, writes of seven little girls marching to the water to be baptized: 'some of them speaking in tongues, and were baptized one by one. The Lord gave us great victory and joy as we obeyed His commission, "teach and baptize".'²²⁴

The following report from Brewster, FL provides an account of Pentecostal spiritual worship that is displayed before, during, and after a baptismal service held for a woman seeking baptism:

> As we were preparing to baptize her she began to talk in tongues. As she went into the water the power lifted her up and she floated there under the power for some time. Finally, she was baptized and she came out on the bank. She looked like an angle. [sic] She stretched her arms out and turned her head to one side like Jesus on the cross when he gave up the Ghost.²²⁵

Other reports note the permeating presence and power of the HS that is experienced during baptismal services without describing the activity of the people as the HS is manifested. The essence of the service is captured by the words 'wonderful', 'sweetest', and 'beautiful'.²²⁶ Preaching and teaching about WB before and during the baptismal service were also practiced according to numerous reports. It appears to be the case that the ministers viewed the occasion to preach and teach about WB as an evangelistic opportunity to share the Good News and explain the meaning of WB.²²⁷ This was

---

²²³ *COGE* 1.15 (October 1, 1910), p. 5.
²²⁴ *COGE* 1.15 (October 1, 1910), p. 5.
²²⁵ *COGE* 5.38 (September 19, 1914), p. 8.
²²⁶ *COGE* 5.37 (September 12, 1914), p. 5; *COGE* 6.18 (May 1, 1915), p. 4; *COGE* 6.22 (May 29, 1915), p. 3; *COGE* 6.24 (June 12, 1915), p. 2; *COGE* 6.30 (July 24, 1915, p. 3; *COGE* 6.35 (August 28, 1915), p. 4; *COGE* 6.36. (September 4, 1915), p. 4; *COGE* 6.36. (September 4, 1915), p. 4; *COGE* 9.31 (August 3, 1918), p. 2; *COGE* 9.47 (November 23, 1918), p. 3; *COGE* 20.3 (March 16, 1929), p. 4; *COGE* 21.9 (April 26, 1930), p. 2; *COGE* 21.12 (May 17, 1930), p. 1; *COGE* 21.16 (June 14, 1930), p. 4; *COGE* 21.17 (June 21, 1930), p. 1; *COGE* 21.36 (November 8, 1930), p. 3; *COGE* 22.22 (August 1, 1931), p. 1; and *COGE* 22.26 (August 29, 1931), p. 2.
²²⁷ *COGE* 1.5 (May 1, 1910), p. 7; *COGE* 6.18 (May 1, 1915), p. 4; *COGE* 8.22 (June 9, 1917), p. 2; *COGE* 13.34 (August 26, 1922), p. 2; *COGE* 16.44 (Oct 31, 1925), p. 4; *COGE* 19.18 (May 15, 1928), p. 4; *COGE* 21.16 (June 14, 1930), p. 4; *COGE* 21.17 (June 21, 1930), p. 1; and *COGE* 22.33 (Oct 24, 1931), p. 4.

especially true since the baptismal services drew large crowds to observe and participate in baptismal services.²²⁸

Meaning of Water Baptism

The *COGE* reflects a literal reading of the biblical text, positing that the ordinances (WB, the Lord's Supper, and footwashing) are to be followed in obedience to the words of Christ, which are understood to be commands.²²⁹ Water baptism is to be received in obedience to the command of the risen Christ found in Mt. 28.19. Tomlinson asserts that he 'was bent on perfect obedience to Jesus'. He avers he was aware that some taught WB was 'a symbol of a death and burial and resurrection and was an outward sign of an inward work wrought in the heart'; however, he offers that the teaching never appealed to him. Rather, 'the only thing that gave me comfort and satisfaction was the fact that Jesus said be baptized. That was enough for me – obedience to Jesus was what impressed me most.'²³⁰

The meaning attached to WB as an act of obedience echoes in reports from the field that utilize the following phrases to emphasize submission to Jesus Christ: 'command of Jesus obeyed', 'obeyed His commission, teach and baptize', and 'obeyed the Lord in water baptism'.²³¹ The desire to be obedient to Christ's command appeared to stimulate new believers to feel compelled to be baptized as soon as possible. In contrast, others worried that failure to receive WB would hurt their standing with God.²³² Also, WB meant literally to follow the example of Jesus Christ in baptism, just as John baptized

---

[228] *COGE* 5.32 (August 8, 1914), p. 8; *COGE* 6.18 (May 1, 1915), p. 4; *COGE* 6.30 (July 24, 1915, p. 3; *COGE* 6.40 (Oct 2, 1915), p. 4; *COGE* 7.38 (September 16, 1916), p. 3; *COGE* 8.22 (June 9, 1917), p. 2; *COGE* 8.26 (July 7, 1917), p. 4; *COGE* 11.40 (Oct 2, 1920), p. 2; *COGE* 12.31 (July 30, 1921), p. 2; *COGE* 13.12 (March 25, 1922), p. 4; *COGE* 19.18 (May 15, 1928), p. 4; *COGE* 22.14 (June 6, 1931), p. 1; and *COGE* 22.21 (July 25, 1931), p. 3.

[229] *COGE* 8.17 (May 5, 1917), p. 1.

[230] *COGE* 8.17 (May 5, 1917), p. 1.

[231] *COGE* 1.9 (July 1, 1910), p. 7; *COGE* 1.15 (Oct 1, 1910), p. 5; *COGE* 10.20 (May 17, 1919), p. 3; *COGE* 14.35 (September 1, 1923), p. 3; *COGE* 19.42 (Oct 20, 1928), p. 4; *COGE* 20.5 (March 30, 1929), p. 4; *COGE* 20.50 (February 22, 1930), p. 4; and *COGE* 21.9 (April 26, 1930), p. 2.

[232] *COGE* 5.40 (Oct 4, 1914), p. 5; *COGE* 6.30 (July 24, 1915), p. 3; *COGE* 6.33 (August 14, 1915), p. 1; and *COGE* 7.10 (March 4, 1916), p. 4.

him in the Jordan.²³³ A report from Bradentown, FL reflects this perspective: 'Here fifteen were baptized *in* water as Jesus was baptized of John *in* Jordan. Not for, but because of the remission of their sins.'²³⁴ In addition to the meanings of WB noted above, WB by immersion is also valued to signify the believer is 'buried with Christ in death to the "old life" and raised with Him to "walk in newness of life," following Col 2:12 and Romans 6'.²³⁵ While this valuation appears to be a minority position reflected in the issues of the *COGE* reviewed, it does seem to be a meaning held by some in the COG. Conversely, F.J. Lee responds to a question about the meaning of Gal. 3.27, 'For as many of you as have been baptized into Christ have put on Christ' posits that 'Baptized into Christ means more than water baptism. It means to be completely immersed in Christ not the water, but absorbed in Him, swallowed up in Him.'²³⁶

The *COGE* eschews baptismal regeneration and the notion that WB has any saving efficacy. Instead, a consistent emphasis is placed on confession of sin and the profession of faith in Christ as the prerequisites for reconciliation with God.²³⁷

Pentecostal Herald

Introduction

Chicago Pentecostal leader, George Brinkman, founded the *Pentecostal Herald* in 1915 as an independent Pentecostal paper to serve as an evangelistic tool to spread the Gospel of Jesus Christ. In the fourth issue of the paper, Brinkman posits that he has 'no new doctrine to promulgate'. Instead, he desires to spread the simple Gospel, which

---

²³³ *COGE* 5.8 (February 21, 1914), pp. 5, 8; *COGE* 6.30 (July 24, 1915), p. 3; *COGE* 21.30 (September 20, 1930), p. 1; and *COGE* 22.26 (August 29, 1931), p. 2.

²³⁴ *COGE* 5.8 (February 21, 1914), pp. 5, 8. Emphasis original.

²³⁵ *COGE* 5.48 (December 5, 1914), p. 6; *COGE* 10.28 (July 12, 1919), p. 3. See *COGE* 14.2 (January 13, 1923), p. 3; *COGE* 21.46 (January 24, 1931), p. 3. F.J. Lee cites a marginal reading of Rom 6.3, arguing that 'The margin says instead of were baptized, "are" baptized, "are" baptized, now, not yesterday or twenty years ago but now baptized, so this is evident to my mind that it means full salvation, and hid away in Jesus'. He does not comment on the relationship to WB.

²³⁶ *COGE* 14.2 (January 13, 1923), p. 3.

²³⁷ *COGE* 5.8 (February 21, 1914), pp. 5, 8; *COGE* 6.4 (January 23, 1915), pp. 1, 4; *COGE* 6.28 (July 10, 1915), p. 4; *COGE* 14.2 (January 13, 1923), p. 3; and *COGE* 21.46 (January 24, 1931), p. 3.

is the death and resurrection of Jesus Christ. He requests those who will contribute articles to bear his intent in mind, avoid being 'taken up with hair-splitting theories, and always trying to dig up some new thing'. Brinkman proffers that he has printed several old articles by W.H. Durham in the *PH* because they are 'far ahead of most articles written these days'. Brinkman reasserts that 'What we want is not a new gospel for the old crowd, but the old Gospel for a new crowd'.[238]

In December 1919, a group gathered in Chicago to attempt uniting 'their resources for the purpose of spreading the Gospel'. The group became known as the Pentecostal Assemblies of the USA. George C. Brinkman was elected secretary. The newly formed group accepted Brinkman's offer and adopted the *PH* as the official organ of the newly formed fellowship. In February 1922, a reorganization meeting was held, and the name of the fellowship was changed to the Pentecostal COG. The final issue of the *PH* was published on October 10, 1923.[239]

From the outset, Brinkman solicited articles from Pentecostal writers with the intent to 'have the very best obtainable on all subjects pertaining to the full Gospel as experienced and taught by the Pentecostal people'. Water baptism was identified as the second on a list of 25 possible subjects recommended by Brinkman.[240]

The Practice of Water Baptism

It appears to be the case that WB held an essential position in the theology of Brinkman and the newly formed organization since the first baptismal report is found in the February 1918 issue of the *PH*.[241] Consistent with the pattern observed in previously reviewed Pentecostal publications, the *PH* documents the importance of WB by including detailed reports of baptismal activity on the field. More than eighty reports of baptismal services are contained in the fifty-

---

[238] *PH* 1.4 (July 1915), p. 2.
[239] W.E. Warner, 'Pentecostal Church of God' in Stanley M. Burgess and Eduard M. van der Maas (eds.), *NIDPCM* (rev. and exp. edn; Grand Rapids, MI: Zondervan, 2002), pp. 965-66.
[240] *PH* 1.4 (July 1915), p. 2.
[241] *PH* 3.10 (February 1918), p. 3.

three issues available for review.²⁴² Additionally, both the announcements of future baptismal services and the stated intent to baptize unnamed people are included.²⁴³

Exact Reporting, Widely Practiced with Sufficient Water

The reports contain precise numbers of persons baptized and geographical locations where the baptisms occurred.²⁴⁴ The second feature provides evidence that WB was widely practiced in the USA and beyond its borders. The location, name, and type of water employed for a particular baptismal service are provided sparingly. The bodies of water identified include a creek,²⁴⁵ river,²⁴⁶ lake,²⁴⁷ also, ice.²⁴⁸ While the mention of water and the specific naming of bodies of water inclines readers to anticipate baptism by immersion as the proper mode of WB, the issue is settled without question once a review of the baptismal language is completed.

---

²⁴² *PH* 3.10 (February 1918), p. 3; *PH* 4.4 (August 1918), pp. 1, 3; *PH* 4.4 (August 1918), pp. 3, 4; *PH* 4.5 (September 1918), pp. 3, 4; *PH* 4.6 (October 1918), pp. 3, 4; *PH* 4.7 (November 1918), pp. 2, 3; *PH* 4.12 (April 1919), p. 4; *PH* 5.1 (May 1919), p. 3.; *PH* 5.3 (August 1919), pp. 3, 4; *PH* 5.4 (September 1919), pp. 1, 3, and 4; *PH* 5.5 (October 1919), pp. 1, 3, and 4; *PH* 5.6 (November 1919), pp. 1, 3, and 4; *PH* 5.7 (December 1919), pp. 3, 4; *PH* 5.9 (February 1920), p. 3; *PH* 6.3 (June 1920), pp. 2, 3, and 4; *PH* 6.10 (January 1921), p. 4; *PH* 6.11 (February 1921), pp. 1, 2, and 3; *PH* 7.4 (June 1921), pp. 2, 4; *PH* 8.9 (January 1, 1922), p. 1; *PH* 8.15 (April 15, 1922), pp. 3, 4; *PH* 8.16 (May 1, 1922), p. 4; *PH* 8.17 (May 15, 1922), p. 4; *PH* 8.18 (June 1, 1922), pp. 1, 2, and 3; *PH* 8.20 and 21 (July 1 and 15, 1922), p. 4; *PH* 8.22 (August 1, 1922), p. 4; *PH* 9.9 (August 15, 1922), p. 3; *PH* 9.10 (September 1, 1922), p. 1; *PH* 9.11 (September 15, 1922), p. 4; *PH* 9.13 (November 1, 1922), p. 3; *PH* 9.15 (January 1, 1923), p. 4; *PH* 10.2 (April 1, 1923), p. 4; *PH* 10.3 (May 1, 1923), p. 5; *PH* 10.4 (June 1, 1923), pp. 5, 6; *PH* 10.7 (September 1, 1923), p. 7; *PH* 10.9 (October 1, 1923), p. 5; and *PH* 10.18 (March 1, 1923), p. 4.

²⁴³ *PH* 4.4 (August 1918), p. 1; *PH* 6.3 (June 1920), pp. 3, 4; *PH* 7.4 (June 1921), p. 4; *PH* 8.22 (August 1, 1922), p. 4; *PH* 9.10 (September 1, 1922), p. 1; and *PH* 10.18 (March 1, 1923), p. 4.

²⁴⁴ Please see footnote 242 above for the references containing exact reporting. For a listing of the places named see Appendix H.

²⁴⁵ *PH* 9.9 (August 15, 1922), p. 3.

²⁴⁶ *PH* 4.6 (October 1918), p. 4; *PH* 8.17 (May 15, 1922), p. 4; *PH* 9.9 (August 15, 1922), p. 3; and *PH* 9.13 (November 1, 1922), p. 3.

²⁴⁷ *PH* 4.4 (August 1918), p. 1; *PH* 4.7 (November 1918), p. 2; *PH* 7.4 (June 1921), p. 4; *PH* 9.10 (September 1, 1922), p. 1; and *PH* 10.2 (April 1, 1923), p. 4.

²⁴⁸ *PH* 3.10 (February 1918), p. 3; *PH* 8.17 (May 15, 1922), p. 4; *PH* 9.11 (September 15, 1922), p. 4; and *PH* 10.2 (April 1, 1923), p. 4.

Mode of Baptism

The favorite phrase employed to report WB is 'baptized in water', which occurs approximately 35 times.[249] On ten occasions, either 'immersed in water' or 'baptized by immersion' are used to describe WB.[250] Burial language, alluding to Rom. 6.3-4, is well represented in the reports with the following phrases: 'buried', 'buried with Christ', 'buried in water baptism', 'buried in the watery grave', 'baptized into His death', 'and 'going down into his death'.[251] Burial language is complemented by resurrection language with phrases like 'arose again to walk in newness of life', 'raised up out of the water', 'came up from their watery grave', 'coming up to walk in newness of life', 'raised up out of the water', and 'and raise again, by the Grace of God, to live in the resurrection power of our risen Lord, the life of victory over sin, death and hell'.[252]

In addition to the preceding, WB is practiced out of obedience to Jesus Christ's command in Mt. 28.19. 'Obeyed the Lord in water baptism', 'followed the Lord in water baptism', and 'follow Him in the divine ordinance of baptism' are the phrases most often

---

[249] *PH* 3.10 (February 1918), p. 3; *PH* 4.4 (August 1918), pp. 3, 4; *PH* 4.5 (September 1918), p. 3; *PH* 4.6 (October 1918), p. 3; *PH* 4.7 (November 1918), p. 3; *PH* 4.12 (April 1919), p. 4; *PH* 4.12 (April 1919), p. 4; *PH* 5.1 (May 1919), p. 3; *PH* 5.3 (August 1919), pp. 3, 4; *PH* 5.4 (September 1919), p. 4; *PH* 5.5 (October 1919), pp. 1, 3, and 4; *PH* 5.7 (December 1919), p. 4; *PH* 6.3 (June 1920), p. 2; *PH* 6.10 (January 1921), p. 4; *PH* 6.11 (February 1921), pp. 1, 2, and 3; *PH* 7.4 (June 1921), p. 2; *PH* 7.4 (June 1921), p. 4; *PH* 8.15 (April 15, 1922), pp. 3, 4; *PH* 8.16 (May 1, 1922), p. 4; *PH* 8.17 (May 15, 1922), p. 4; *PH* 8.18 (June 1, 1922), p. 3; *PH* 8.20 and 21 (July 1 and 15, 1922), p. 4; *PH* 9.9 (August 15, 1922), p. 3; *PH* 9.10 (September 1, 1922), p. 1; *PH* 9.11 (September 15, 1922), p. 4; *PH* 9.13(November 1, 1922), p. 3; *PH* 10.4 (June 1, 1923), p. 5; *PH* 10.7 (September 1, 1923), p. 7; *PH* 10.9 (October 1, 1923), p. 5; and *PH* 10.18 (March 1, 1923), p. 4.

[250] *PH* 4.4 (August 1918), p. 1; *PH* 4.5 (September 1918), p. 3; *PH* 4.6 (October 1918), p. 4; *PH* 5.9 (February 1920), p. 3; *PH* 8.15 (April 15, 1922), pp. 3, 4; *PH* 8.18 (June 1, 1922), p. 3; *PH* 8.22 (August 1, 1922), p. 4; *PH* 10.2 (April 1, 1923), p. 4; and *PH* 10.18 (March 1, 1923), p. 4.

[251] *PH* 4.7 (November 1918), p. 2; *PH* 5.3 (August 1919), p. 4; *PH* 5.4 (September 1919), pp. 1, 3; *PH* 5.5 (October 1919), p. 1; *PH* 5.7 (December 1919), p. 3; *PH* 8.18 (June 1, 1922), pp. 1, 2; *PH* 9.9 (August 15, 1922), p. 3; *PH* 9.10 (September 1, 1922), p. 1; and *PH* 10.4 (June 1, 1923), p. 6.

[252] *PH* 4.5 (September 1918), p. 3; *PH* 5.4 (September 1919), pp. 1, 3; *PH* 8.18 (June 1, 1922), pp. 1, 2; *PH* 9.10 (September 1, 1922), p. 1; and *PH* 10.4 (June 1, 1923), p. 6.

employed to signify WB as an act of submission to Jesus Christ.[253] The commitment to practice WB as an act of obedience to Jesus Christ is powerfully illustrated by four reports that rehearse WB being carried out in icy weather conditions. First, from Davis City, IA, we read, 'ten were baptized in water through a hole cut in the ice'.[254] Second, we read from Van Wert, IA, that 'On February 12 we went to the river and baptized 10 in water baptism, cutting the ice which was two feet thick. The intense cold prevented many from being baptized.'[255] From Freemont, NE, Mrs. Lulu E. Lane testifies that 'I was determined to be one of God's chosen, and so on December 4, 1921, the ice was broken and I was baptized in water'.[256] Lastly, from Superior, CO, we read: 'The other day, I cut the ice on a lake near town and conducted baptismal services, at which time a number were immersed in obedience to Christ's command'.[257]

Formula

Baptismal reports in the *PH* provide evidence that the trinitarian formula was employed when baptizing candidates at the Woodworth-Etter Tabernacle. They are baptized 'in the name of the Father, and of the Son, and of the Holy Ghost', according to Mt. 28.19.

> By this form of service we recognize the fatherhood of God, the deity and sonship of Jesus Christ, as well as the work of the Holy Spirit, and are keeping out of the apostasy that is fast taking hold of Pentecost. The Holy Spirit is wonderfully poured out in these services. This service needs to be seen in order to be fully appreciated.[258]

A report from Ramsey, IL, in October 1919 confirms the use of the Trinitarian formula. Also included in the report is a confirmation provided by the HS via a message in tongues followed by the interpretation that the trinitarian formula is the correct formula to be employed.

---

[253] *PH* 4.4 (August 1918), p. 3; *PH* 4.5 (September 1918), p. 4; *PH* 4.6 (October 1918), p. 4; and *PH* 4.10 (February 1919), p. 4.
[254] *PH* 3.10 (February 1918), p. 3.
[255] *PH* 8.17 (May 15, 1922), p. 4.
[256] *PH* 9.11 (September 15, 1922), p. 4.
[257] *PH* 10.2 (April 1, 1923), p. 4.
[258] *PH* 10.3 (May 1, 1923), p. 5.

The Lord gave a wonderful manifestation of His presence at the baptismal service, by pouring out His Spirit on the candidates, as they came up out of the water, and giving a powerful message in other tongues thru Sister Ridgeway. Then the interpretation came, confirming this mode of baptism; which was in the name of the Father, Son and Holy Ghost.[259]

While the Trinitarian formula appears to be the preferred formula per reports, the inclusion of separate apologetic articles by A.H. Argue[260] and Aimee Semple McPherson[261] provides evidence that the New Issue continued to impact adversely the congregations and fellowships affiliated with the *PH* well into the first decade of the twentieth century.

In addressing the 'question of formula', Argue presents a well-reasoned apologetic emphasizing the priority of the trinitarian formula. More importantly, reflecting an irenic spirit, he emphasizes that 'THE TRUE VALUE OF WATER BAPTISM TO THE CANDIDATE SHOULD NOT DEPEND SO MUCH UPON THE WORDS OF THE BAPTIZER AS ON WHAT BAPTISM REALLY MEANS TO THE ONE BEING BAPTIZED'.[262]

In addition to incorporating articles and reports that reiterate the correct usage of the Trinitarian formula, Brinkman also provides resources that address the theological underpinnings of the New Issue movement. For instance, Brinkman included the 1918 'A Statement of Fundamental Truths Approved of and Adopted by the Indian Assemblies of God',[263] in which 'The Essentials as to the Godhead' are enumerated. Challenging the Modalistic Monarchianism of the New Issue adherents the 'Essentials' assert the distinction and relationship in the Godhead, holding the unity of the one being of Father, Son, and HS while asserting the identity of three persons co-operating in the Godhead. In a similar vein an article, 'Triune God: Being Three in One', by Pastor E.G. Hurt of Hoopeston, IL asserts the following:

---

[259] *PH* 5.5 (October 1919), p. 3; *PH* 4.10 (February 1919), p. 4.
[260] *PH* 4.10 (February 1919), p. 3.
[261] *PH* 4.12 (April 1919), p. 1.
[262] *PH* 4.10 (February 1919), p. 3. The emphasis is in the original.
[263] *PH* 5.1 (May 1919), p. 3.

> A study of the divine titles as they are used in God's Word will convince any person who is willing to be convinced that while the Godhead is one so far as nature and essence are concerned, there are in the Godhead a plurality of persons ... there are three that bear record in heaven, the Father, the Word, and the Holy Ghost: and these three are one (1 John 5:7).[264]

While rebaptism is not overtly addressed in the *PH*, it appears to have occurred when believers experienced doubt and anxiety relative to the merits or validity of their previous baptism and the formula employed. One account is chronicled from the Woodworth-Etter Tabernacle in the September 1919 issue of the *PH*:

> The power of God fell like big drops of rain all morning and in the afternoon there was a down pour [sic] of the Latter Rain ... The Lord suddenly spoke to three of these dear ones after preparation was being made for the baptizing and showed them to be baptized also ... One of these, a sister with credentials as a minister, and who had been baptized in the new way has been attending these meetings for some time, but was in doubt as to whether this was the right way or not. God suddenly spoke to her and said, 'Now or never.' When this revelation came she ran to the house to get her baptismal robe and was soon back ready for the baptism. During this time she was praying, 'If this is right, manifest thyself.' She went into the water praying and as she was raised up out of the water she saw shining steps go from the water right into heaven and all around the water was white cloud. She then heard a voice say, 'This is the way, walk ye in it.'[265]

Administration

The question of the proper administrator for WB is not distinctly addressed in the *PH*. From the Minutes of the Pentecostal Assemblies of Canada, we learn that women may 'act as Evangelists, Missionaries, or Deaconesses, but not as Pastors or Elders'.[266] Since Pastors or Elders were the only persons eligible to administer WB, the implication is that only ordained males were authorized to

---

[264] *PH* 8.17 (May 15, 1922), pp. 2, 3.
[265] *PH* 5.4 (September 1919), p. 3.
[266] *PH* 5.4 (September 1919), p. 3.

baptize. However, it seems to be the case that necessity and zeal were instrumental in setting aside established guidelines. Of note is the story of a young woman who acted independently in obedience to the leading of the HS as told in 'Entering the Kingdom of Heaven: Testimony of an Italian Sister'.[267]

The young woman tells of her conversion at the Italian Full Gospel Mission in Chicago five years prior, followed by WB and her quest for the baptism of the HS. Her father stood in opposition to her faith commitment and her desire to minister to her siblings. Regardless of his opposition, four of her siblings were converted and desirous of WB. They could not go to the priest, nor were their men available for baptizing. 'Consequently, I took them out to a little creek that ran by the farm, and there I asked God to give me grace to baptize them, so I baptized four of them.' Within three months, the young woman and five of her brothers 'received the Holy Ghost – all spoke in tongues'. After her five-year-old sister 'came under the power', the young woman took her to the creek for baptism, too. The young woman testifies that 'When I baptized the others, I thought she was too small, but the Lord put me to shame in this case'.[268]

Qualification for baptism is abundantly clear. Anyone who has 'really repented and in their hearts have truly believed on Christ as Savior and Lord'[269] is eligible for WB.

Pentecostal Worship

In keeping with vibrant Pentecostal spirituality, baptismal reports catalog passionate embodied worship enumerating the same activities identified in previously reviewed publications. A report from Cool Springs, TN, captures the vitality of one baptismal service:

> The power of God rested over the watery scene and ... As Brother Jayner and Graves waded out into the mightiest deep, it seemed as if the angels of heaven were singing, with the echo resting on the water's edge, while the saints were standing with uplifted hands toward heaven, praising Him in the highest. Waves of power and glory would roll over the audience. Many said they

---

[267] *PH* 2.11 (March 1917), p. 2.
[268] *PH* 2.11 (March 1917), p. 2.
[269] *PH* 5.1 (May 1919), p. 3.

felt the power of God as soon as they got on the ground. Sinners said they never heard such singing before.[270]

From the Northwest Kansas Camp Meeting of 1918 we read that while eight or ten were being baptized, 'Heaven opened and the power of God mightily fell and there was great rejoicing and shouting'. After they came up out of the water, others were 'convinced that "to obey is better than sacrifice," went down into the water and were baptized', until about 26 or 27 had been baptized.[271]

Reports from the Woodworth-Etter Tabernacle located in Indianapolis, IN, provide in-depth descriptions of baptismal services held in one of the few indoor baptisteries in the Pentecostal movement.

> A large number have been baptized into his death, by following Him in the ordinance of water baptism ... At the first baptismal service held in the tabernacle the power fell so that people lay like dead around the baptistry. Messages with interpretations came forth, which were in the substance, that God's blessing will greatly rest upon this tabernacle work, if His people will only keep humble before Him.[272]

Another feature of embodied Pentecostal spirituality present in the baptismal reports are testimonies of divine healing.[273] Two testimonies are reported in some detail. First, from Portland, OR, we read in the October 1918 issue of the *PH* of a dying sister who came from Bellingham, WA, after being operated on for cancer and given no hope by the physicians.

> She had heard about the Pentecostal Mission and kept saying: 'Oh, if I could but get word to the mission, I would be healed' ... I had just risen to me feet to give the message when the mother arose, interrupted me and made her request. We immediately and unitedly prayed. The next day a visit was made to the hospital and we found she slept like a baby. In another few days she was in a

---

[270] *PH* 5.7 (December 1919), p. 3.
[271] *PH* 4.5 (September 1918), p. 3.
[272] *PH* 4.5 (September 1918), p. 3; *PH* 4.10 (February 1919), p. 4; *PH* 5.1 (May 1919), p. 3; *PH* 5.6 (November 1919), pp. 1, 3; and *PH* 8.18 (June 1, 1922), pp. 1, 2.
[273] *PH* 4.6 (October 1918), p. 4.

wheel chair, [sic] and on the last day of the camp meeting was at the services, ten days after the operation ... At this time she could not raise her arm without the aid of the other because of the leaders being cut, but after being prayed for she immediately raised it without aid, glorifying and praising God. The next day she followed her Lord and Savior in water baptism perfectly healed.[274]

From Indianapolis, IN, we read of one sister who saw a band of angels as she was carried out under the power. Another sister came in unsaved, dying of cancer. She had been operated on for internal cancer, had another cancer growing on her side, and had been unable to lie down for several months. The doctor gave her six months to live. After Sister Etter prayed for her she could sleep on either side. She went home that night and slept all the rest of the night. She improved and also received the baptism of the HS with speaking in other tongues as the evidence, according to the writer.[275]

Meaning of Water Baptism

Water baptism is viewed as an ordinance of the Church in the *PH*.[276] In the article 'Go Teach and Preach', Elder W.V. Kneisley grounds the ordinance of WB in the Great Commission contained in Mt. 28.19 and Mk 16.16, asserting that Jesus was able to do so because 'all authority and all power in heaven and in earth is given unto him'. Just as his disciples were commissioned to go into all the world and make disciples of all nations ... Jesus teaches us 'to observe all things whatsoever I have commanded you even unto the end of the world'. Thus, it is our duty to obey and do the things he specified:

We are to go to all nations.
We are to teach them.
We are to baptize all believers.
We are to bury them with Christ.
We are to baptize in the name of the Father and of the Son and of the Holy Ghost.
We are to instruct them to observe (do) all things commanded.

---

[274] *PH* 4.6 (October 1918), p. 4.
[275] *PH* 5.6 (November 1919), p. 3.
[276] *PH* 4.5 (September 1918), p. 3; *PH* 4.10 (February 1919), p. 4; and *PH* 5.4 (September 1919), p. 3.

We are to go into all the world.
We are to preach the Gospel to every creature.
Repentance and remission of sins is to be preached In His name. Luke 14:47.[277]

The importance and meaning of WB are clearly expressed in the 'Statement of Fundamental Truths Approved of and Adopted by the Indian Assemblies of God, 1918'. Paragraph 11 informs readers that

> The Ordinance of Baptism by a burial in water which Christ should be observed as commanded in the Scriptures, by all who have really repented and in their hearts have truly believed on Christ as Savior and Lord. In so doing, they have the body washed in pure water as an outward symbol of cleansing while their heart has already been sprinkled with the Blood of Christ as an inner cleansing. Thus they declare to the world that they have died with Jesus and that they have also been raised with Him to walk in newness of life. – Mt. 28:19; Acts 10:47-48; Rom. 6:4; Acts 20:21; Heb. 10:22.[278]

It appears from the above statements that WB is practiced out of obedience to God since Jesus Christ commanded it. It has no salvific import by itself since it is an external symbol of the internal spiritual cleansing resulting from true repentance from sin and authentic faith in Jesus Christ as Lord and Savior.

Moreover, WB is a symbolic public proclamation that a person has identified with Jesus Christ in his death and resurrection. The significance of identification with Christ's death and resurrection in the act of WB receives emphasis in various articles in the *PH*. In the September 1, 1922 issue of the *PH*, an unnamed author asserts that 'According to God's Word, we only find one mode of water baptism'. Romans 6.4-5 is quoted with the additional comment, 'As we go down in the watery grave a symbol of the burial and resurrection of Christ and also a sign of an inward cleansing'.[279]

Leroy Baxter of Blair, NE, rejects baptismal regeneration while emphasizing the importance and meaning of Rom. 6.3, asserting that 'Immersion is at once the picture of Jesus' death, burial, and

---

[277] *PH* 2.11 (March 1917), p. 2.
[278] *PH* 5.1 (May 1919), p. 3.
[279] *PH* 9.10 (September 1, 1922), p. 3.

resurrection, and of our identification with Him in all these particulars'.

Furthermore, Baxter posits that 'Our real union with Christ in His death will insure our participation in His resurrection'. In terms of priority, Blair argues that the 'first thing for the one seeking eternal life is that he must die to his life of sin, or the old Adamic nature'. Only then is the person fit to be buried. Jesus, our example, was first crucified and then buried in the sepulcher, after he was dead. Similarly, believers must be buried with Him after we are dead to sin. 'They that are Christ's have crucified the flesh with the affections and lusts. We are buried into His death, burial and resurrection through the Name of the Father and of the Son and of the Holy Ghost.' Blair avoids naming the acceptable mode of WB and encourages readers to depend on the HS for guidance in the matter, but he is clear that repentance must precede WB. 'Immersion is the outward symbol. The Holy Ghost does the cleansing within.'[280]

The meaning of WB as a reflection of sanctification echoes from Johannesburg, South Africa, in Wilford E. Lake's article, 'Delivered from Temptation'.[281] Lake, commenting on Romans 6, asserts that 'Paul teaches in Romans 6 that nature which I inherited from the fall is to be crucified or put to death. Not gradually but at one time; not just one or more members of that sinful nature, but the whole body.' Lake rejects any notion that God gives power to overcome besetting sin(s) or say no to sinful desires. Rather, he holds the existence of the desire to sin is evidence that the body of sin has not been crucified. Moreover, referring to Romans 6, Lake posits that 'Paul says we are to bury it with Christ in baptism. So now, it is not only dead, but it is buried. That which is dead and buried is no more – it is finished with forever.'[282]

Pentecostal Holiness Advocate

Introduction

The *Pentecostal Holiness Advocate* served as the official organ of the newly formed Pentecostal Holiness Church created by the 1911 merger of the Fire-Baptized Holiness Church and the Holiness

---

[280] *PH* 9.16 (January 15, 1923), p. 4.
[281] *PH* 6.10 (January 1921), p. 2.
[282] *PH* 6.10 (January 1921), p. 2.

Church of North Carolina. Rev. G.F. Taylor was named editor and business manager of the organ during the Third General Conference of the PHC in Abbeville, SC, on January 23-29, 1917. The first issue of the *PHA* was printed on May 3, 1917, by the Falcon Publishing Company in Falcon, NC. Taylor resigned in 1925 and was replaced by Rev. J.H. King, who served as editor from 1925-1929. Taylor returned to serve as editor in 1929.[283]

The issues of the *PHA* contain editorials, sermons, missionary updates, deaths, WBs, testimonies, and announcements of future meetings in response to the editor's request in the inaugural issue of the *PHA*:

> For this paper to be the Official Organ of The Pentecostal Holiness Church, properly speaking, it must contain information that the church needs. Apart from the contributions, reports from evangelists, pastors and other workers, apart from official announcements, testimonies, obituaries, and other items of interest, the church stands in great need of statistical facts, relating to our work at home and abroad, as well as a great variety of facts concerning the Christian world in general.[284]

While eager to disseminate the latest news from the field, the editor states that he will exert editorial authority to maintain doctrinal integrity and foster spiritual vitality through the organ. The gravity of the editorial task is forcefully articulated in the following statement where the editor speaks of himself in the third person:

> All contributed matter must pass his examination. He is to be the judge as to what should enter the paper, and what should be left out. Sometimes whole contributions may be published just as they are submitted, at other times whole contributions must be thrown into the waste basket, [sic] at other times part of a contribution must be published, and a part rejected. The editor must be the

---

[283] H.V. Synan, 'Taylor, George Floyd' in Stanley M. Burgess and Eduard M. van der Maas (eds.), *NIDPCM* (rev. and exp. edn; Grand Rapids, MI: Zondervan, 2002), pp. 1115-16.

[284] *PHA* 1.1 (May 3, 1917), p. 9.

judge in all such cases ... It is my purpose to edit the paper, not in name only, but in deed and in truth.[285]

The number of statistical reports regarding outcomes from evangelistic meetings, church meetings, and camp meetings is limited compared to those found in the previously reviewed publications. Consequently, there are significantly fewer references to explore the mode of WB, the formula employed, and the atmosphere of baptismal services. On the other hand, from the outset, the PHC established clearly defined positions on the practice of WB. Additionally, when questions on the field arose relative to the method and meaning of WB, various respondents provided questions via the 'Question Box', and, later, the 'Question Drawer', regular features in the official organ of the PHC. Employing the *PHA* as a vehicle to respond to questions from the field is established before the first issue of the periodical by the following invitation: 'Have you a question you would like to ask concerning the Bible, concerning your church, concerning any other church, or touching any other religious topic? There is a question department in The Advocate.'[286]

The Practice of Water Baptism

Water baptism was not required for admission to membership. It seems to be the case the PHC took this stance to minimize barriers that could prohibit persons from admission to the Holiness Church of North Carolina. Specifically, this decision appears to have been made to accommodate Quakers who had embraced holiness teaching. According to the editor, the Holiness Church received members with/without WB since the Quakers do not believe in WB. 'The Holiness Church was so organized as to let that class in, as many of them in North Carolina were enjoying the experience of holiness'.[287]

Mode

After the formation of the Pentecostal Holiness Church, WB was made a requirement for those desiring to join a local congregation. However, the mode of WB was left to the candidate. Again, the

---

[285] *PHA* 1.1 (May 3, 1917), p. 9.
[286] *PHA* 1.1 (May 3, 1917), p. 1.
[287] *PHA* 4.47 (March 24, 1921), p. 9.

editor provides the history of the 1909 decision: 'This Convention made water baptism essential to membership; but the candidate was left free to choose his own mode of baptism, as had been the case from the beginning, and is so to this day'.[288] In the December 8, 1927 issue of the *PHA*, justification for practicing various modes of baptism is also provided, primarily 'because the Bible does not define the mode. We may be sure that if the mode was the important thing in baptism, the Lord or some of the Apostles would have made it clear.' Furthermore, it is stated that the 'most important thing in water baptism is, what it signifies, and not the manner in which it is administered'.[289]

While the official position of the PHC embraced immersion, pouring, and sprinkling as acceptable modes of WB, it appears there were persons on the field reticent to accept modalities besides immersion. In the Q & A exchange from June 30, 1921, *PHA* asks if an ordained minister of the PHC can be loyal to the movement and consistent with the church's discipline and refuse to administer sprinkling or pouring as options for receiving members into the church. The response is a display of wisdom and even-handedness, asking in return if the minister can refuse to administer baptism by immersion and be loyal? On the one hand, 'If he can refuse to immerse and be loyal, he can refuse to sprinkle and pour and be loyal'. On the other hand, 'if his refusal to immerse would be disloyal, his refusal to sprinkle or pour would be disloyal'. The respondent reiterates that while the PHC discipline affords all baptismal candidates the right to choose the preferred mode, however, the discipline provides no guidance relative to the 'choice of the preacher who is to do the baptizing'.[290]

While it seems to be the case that there was no disagreement about WB being an ordinance or sacrament of the Church, there arose some confusion on the field regarding baptismal regeneration and the PHC's stance on the issue. In response to the complexity, Taylor asserts, 'We are not commanded to baptize any one [sic] in order that he may be saved, but we are commanded to baptize them after they

---

[288] *PHA* 4.47 (March 24, 1921), p. 9.
[289] *PHA* 5.9 (June 30, 1921), pp. 9-10.
[290] *PHA* 11.32 (December 8, 1927), p. 1.

are saved. No Christian should be denied the rite of baptism.'²⁹¹ Similarly, in response to the inquiry regarding the meaning of Mk 16.16, we read the text is speaking of WB, the outward sign of the Christian profession. Yet, WB is not 'absolutely necessary' to salvation as faith is. 'All believers should receive water baptism as the symbol of their faith, but it is faith and not baptism that really saves'.²⁹²

A related theological issue focused on the necessity of WB for salvation. The question regularly appears between 1917 to 1931. It seems to be the case that readers were either confused by the responses they received or were hoping they would be provided with an authoritative word to settle an un-named dispute. It may be that the un-named disagreement arose with the change in membership requirements after the Union of the two groups mentioned earlier. Additionally, some ambiguous and seemingly contradictory responses contributed to the confusion. For example, in his 1917 exposition of the 'Basis of Union' in a section titled, 'Pardon', G.F. Taylor asserts that WB

> is a Scriptural term which includes far more than water baptism, and the Scriptures do not teach that every man must receive water baptism in order to be pardoned. The thief on the cross was pardoned without water baptism, and Cornelius received the Baptism of the Spirit before he received the water baptism. (Acts 10:44-48.) ... and I mean to say that works and faith are the conditions on our part to be met before pardon is granted. So we conclude that pardon is merited through the blood of Jesus alone, but granted to us on the conditions of works and faith.²⁹³

While Taylor is unclear about the meaning of 'works and faith' as the necessary condition for salvation, he proffers that WB is not essential. Less than a year later, Taylor's editorial remarks on Mk 16.19-20, appear to support the essentiality of WB for salvation:

---

²⁹¹ *PHA* 3.10 (July 3, 1919), pp. 2-3. Also, see *PHA* 1.35 (December 27, 1917), p. 16; *PHA* 5.5 (June 2, 1921), p. 10; *PHA* 8.31 (November 27, 1924), pp. 4-5; and *PHA* 15.8 (June 18, 1931), p. 10.
²⁹² *PHA* 15.20 (September 10, 1931), p. 10.
²⁹³ *PHA* 1.29 (November 15, 1917), pp. 4-5.

One must be baptized in order to be saved. Water baptism is an ordinance to be observed by every Christian. I do not believe that one could wilfully [sic] neglect water baptism, if he sees it as an ordinance, and retain his experience very long ... Jesus has commanded it, and we should cheerfully comply with the command. However, I do not think any one [sic] should receive water baptism until he is saved. Jesus here puts baptism a condition of being saved.[294]

An apparent opposite position to the preceding appears in 1920 in response to a reader's inquiry: 'Will a person that has not been baptized by any mode of baptism be saved? If so please explain the verse, Except ye be baptized with water and the Spirit, ye cannot enter the kingdom of heaven.' The respondent writes that 'There is no such verse as you quote'. Rather, 'Jesus said to Nichodemus [sic], "Except a man be born of water and of the Spirit, he can not [sic] enter into the kingdom of God." (John 3:5)'. Taylor states that it is his understanding 'that this water is the "Water of Life"'. Taylor goes on to posit his belief 'that all Christians should receive water baptism; but I do not believe one would be kept out of heaven for not receiving it, unless he failed to receive it through disobedience'. Taylor concludes his response with a strong statement on the question: 'Water baptism is a Christian duty, but it is not a part of the atonement. To teach otherwise is to say that the death of Jesus is in itself insufficient.'[295]

In 1930, ten years after the previous Q & A exchange, the question of the essentiality of WB for salvation is asked again to be met with a resounding NO! The respondent states that the PHC 'does not teach that water baptism is essential to salvation in the sense that faith is'. Instead, 'baptism is the privilege and duty of every true believer to receive baptism when the opportunity is afforded, according to the command of Jesus Christ'.[296]

In an open letter to Brother Taylor and the Advocate Family, John W. Wilson picks up on the thread of WB as an act of obedience in the latter portion of his letter:

---

[294] *PHA* 2.18 (August 29, 1918), pp. 8-11.
[295] *PHA* 3.42 (February 12, 1920), p. 9.
[296] *PHA* 14.7 (June 12, 1930), p. 9.

As a great many people seem not to understand the proper baptism, it is a Christian's privilege to be baptized in the water, should they deem it necessary to make the race successful to heaven, for we find in Matthew the 3rd chapter that our Savior came to John to be baptized of him, and told him to suffer it now, for thus it becomes us to fill all righteousness. Glory to God. We must not forget the law of doing this, not only in baptism, but in every respect as our Christian duties.[297]

Understandably, readers would be confused by the seemingly contradictory 'yes and no' responses to their questions, as well as the assertions made in editorials and sermons that seem to support the essentiality of WB for salvation. In contrast, others deny the necessity of WB. Closer examination reveals the responses are an unequivocal NO; WB is not essential to salvation. The confusion seems to appear concerning the actual practice of WB and a perception that it was optional when allowed an opportunity to be obedient to Christ's command. The following questions and answers provide clear examples of the NO relative to the essentiality of WB while affirming the need to be obedient to Christ's command. First is Question 582 that asks if WB is essential to salvation? The answer is, 'The Bible does not teach, that one cannot be saved without water baptism'. However, the author cautions that although the sacraments 'are outward, and may be observed in a sense without receiving the grace of salvation, but this is no reason why true believers should neglect them'. To neglect willfully what God has commanded may lead to backsliding.[298] Second, Question 731 requests an explanation of Acts 16.31 and asks if WB is essential for salvation. Again, 'No, water baptism is not essential to salvation, in the sense that one cannot be saved without it' is the response, followed by the exhortation that everyone who has saving faith 'should be baptized as a testimony and confession of faith, before the world' in keeping with the Great Commission in Mt. 28.19. Regarding the Philippian jailer, the respondent replied, 'he believed on Christ and was saved,

---

[297] *PHA* 3.46 (March 11, 1920), p. 16.
[298] *PHA* 12.20 (September 13, 1928), p. 8. Also, *PHA* 1.7 (June 15, 1917), pp. 2-4; *PHA* 14.31 (November 27, 1930), p. 9; *PHA* 12.20 (September 13, 1928), p. 3; *PHA* 13.50 (April 18, 1929), p. 8; and *PHA* 15.20 (September 10, 1931), p. 10.

but it was also his privilege and duty to receive Christian baptism, which he did. – Acts 16:33'.[299]

In his open letter to Brother Taylor and readers of the *PHA,* John W. Wilson asserts that obedience to God and reliance on the Scriptures may be the cure for some of the disputations occurring within the PHC, including debates concerning the essentiality of WB as well as mode. Wilson urges readers to remember that preachers 'are only witnesses of Him that is to come, and that all are called to 'be true to the Word and get the baptism of the Holy Ghost and fire (Matthew 3)'. He opines that if this counsel is followed, 'Then there will not be so much dispute if we do not get sprinkled'.[300]

Because of the preceding references, it appears that respondents embrace the following two points: 1. Water baptism has no saving efficacy and is not essential for salvation; 2. The restored relationship to God, through Jesus Christ, and empowered by the HS requires obedience to the commands of Christ to continue in that relationship. Consequently, the ongoing inquiries and responses place in relief the tension between PHC doctrine and call to discipleship with personal preferences and previously held beliefs.

Administration

Concerning the proper authority for the administration of WB, it appears to be the case that only ordained ministers (male) were authorized to administer the ordinance. Nonetheless, one woman seems to have exercised authority to administer WB in the absence of ordained males. The following account of Sister Maggie Simmons Smith's baptism captures the event:

> Truly of her it can be said, 'She went about doing good.' She took all things to God in prayer, and in the sweet simple faith of a child, she asked to be guided in every step, and the dear Father revealed to her what He would have her do. She prayed over her baptism, and said it was revealed to her that her pastor, Sister Josie Williams, should immerse her, so accompanied by Sister Annie Bolinger, the three went to a little stream near Sister Smith's home, and she was immersed. The power fell on all three, and the blessing that filled

---

[299] *PHA* 13.46 (March 21, 1929), p. 9.
[300] *PHA* 3.46 (March 11, 1920), p. 16.

their souls made them like Peter of old on the mount of Transfiguration exclaim, 'It is good for us to be here.'[301]

In addition to the approval of sprinkling and pouring as acceptable modes of WB, the newly formed PHC also embraced infant baptism as an approved practice. Only one baptismal service of infants is reported. Mrs. J.N. Sanders, writing from Monroe, GA says: 'Seven baptized by immersion, seven sprinkled including three babies, and eighteen joined the church'.[302] It appears that questions from the field about the validity of infant baptism and the Scriptural justification for the practice persisted despite being thoughtfully addressed as early as 1918. The Q & A exchange from May 9, 1918, *PHA* reflects one inquiry (Question 202) regarding the Scriptural basis for baptizing infants. The respondent acknowledges proponents for both positions can find Scriptural grounds for their positions; however, he is quick to concede the question has caused strife and division. The respondent provides the following reminder and counsel:

> The framers of our discipline knowing this, said, 'Christian parents and guardians shall have liberty of conscience in the baptism of their children.' (Page 9 of 1917 edition.) Here is where I shall let the matter rest. My advice is, if you desire to baptize your children, do so, but do not try to force others to do it; if you do not want to baptize your children, do not do so, but let others alone who do so desire it.[303]

A similar inquiry and response, recorded in 1929, demonstrates the issue was far from settled in the minds of some. In response to Question 982: 'Do we have any Bible on sprinkling babies'? the respondent asserts the following verses can be interpreted to justify infant baptism: 'Gen. 17:9-14; I Sam. 1:28; Prov. 22:6; Mt. 19:13-15; Mk. 10:13-16; Luke 18:15-17; I Cor. 7:14; 10:1, 2'.[304]

---

[301] *PHA* 2.2 (May 9, 1918), pp. 10-11.
[302] *PHA* 3.27 (October 30, 1919), p. 14. The practice of infant baptism is inextricably linked to the concept of original sin in *PHA* 3.10 (July 3, 1919), p. 10.
[303] *PHA* 2.2 (May 9, 1918), p. 16.
[304] *PHA* 13.32 (December 5, 1929), p. 10.

Widely Practiced with Sufficient Water

With the elevation of WB as a requirement for membership, reports of WBs from the field were reflected in the *PHA*. For the period 1917 to 1931, 15 years inclusive, there are slightly more than 100 baptismal reports[305] contained in the 742 issues reviewed, providing the geographical location and the number of persons baptized. The majority of baptisms appear to have occurred in South Africa, Oklahoma, and Virginia. While some of the bodies of water utilized for the baptismal services are identified, namely, stream,[306] baptismal

---

[305] *PHA* 1.4 (May 24, 1917), p. 13; *PHA* 1.9 (June 28, 1917), p. 6; *PHA* 1.51 (April 18, 1918), p. 6; *PHA* 2.2 (May 9, 1918), p. 10-11; *PHA* 2.16 (August 15, 1918), pp. 6-7, 10-11, and 12; *PHA* 2.18 (August 29, 1918), p. 5; *PHA* 2.27 (October 31, 1918), p. 12; *PHA* 2.33-34 (December 19-26, 1918), pp. 14-15; *PHA* 3.12-13 (July 17-24, 1919), pp. 6-7; *PHA* 3.21 (September 18, 1919). p. 15; *PHA* 3.27 (October 30, 1919), p. 14; *PHA* 3.30 (November 20, 1919), pp. 11-12; *PHA* 3.46 (March 11, 1920), p. 10; *PHA* 4.8 (June 24, 1920), p. 14; *PHA* 4.8 (June 24, 1920), p. 14; *PHA* 4.14 (August 5, 1920), p. 15; *PHA* 4.17 (August 26, 1920), pp. 6-7; *PHA* 4.25 (October 21, 1920), pp. 6, 15; *PHA* 4.44/45 (March 3, 10, 1921), pp. 5, 6-7, and 13; *PHA* 5.15 (August 11, 1921), p. 11; *PHA* 5.21 (September 22, 1921), pp. 6-7; *PHA* 5.22 (September 29, 1921), p. 6; *PHA* 5.31 (December 1, 1921), p. 3; *PHA* 5.33 (December 15, 1921), pp. 4, 6; *PHA* 5.37 (January 12, 1922), p. 12; *PHA* 5.8 (June 22, 1922), p. 10, 1; *PHA* 6.32 (December 7, 1922), pp. 7, 15; *PHA* 7.5 (May 31, 1923), pp. 7, 10, 11, 12, and 13; *PHA* 7.16 (August 16, 1923), p. 6; *PHA* 7.26 (October 25, 1923), p. 11; *PHA* 7.27 (November 1, 1923), p. 11; *PHA* 7.31 (November 29, 1923), pp. 6-7; *PHA* 8.22 (September 25, 1924), p. 5; *PHA* 8.29 (November 13, 1924), pp. 12-13; *PHA* 8.44 (February 26, 1925), p. 11; *PHA* 9.30 (November 26, 1925), pp. 11-12; *PHA* 9.35 (January 7, 1926), pp.12-13; *PHA* 9.45 (March 18, 1926), pp. 6, 7; *PHA* 10.8 (June 24, 1926), p. 14; *PHA* 11.44 (March 8, 1928), p. 11; *PHA* 12.10 (July 5, 1928), pp. 12, 13; *PHA* 12.14 (August 2, 1928), p. 13; *PHA* 12.33 (December 13, 1928), pp. 5, 7; *PHA* 12.45 (March 14, 1929), p. 13; *PHA* 13.37 (January 17, 1929), pp. 4-5; *PHA* 13.42 (February 20, 1930), p. 14; *PHA* 13.45 (March 13, 1930), pp. 7, 12-13; *PHA* 13.50 (April 17, 1930), p. 5; *PHA* 13.52 (May 1, 1930), p. 8; *PHA* 14.5 (May 29, 1930), pp. 3-5, 10-12; *PHA* 14.15 (August; 7, 1930), pp. 11-12; *PHA* 14.16 (August 14, 1930), pp. 7, 15; *PHA* 14.22 (September 25, 1930), p. 11; *PHA* 14.24 (October 9, 1930), p. 7; *PHA* 14.28 (November 6, 1930), p. 7; *PHA* 14.41 (February 12, 1931), p. 5; *PHA* 15.5 (May 28, 1931), p. 12; *PHA* 15.7 (June 11, 1931), pp. 6, 7; *PHA* 15.19 (September 3, 1931), p. 11; *PHA* 15.20 (September 10, 1931), p. 12; *PHA* 15.23 (October 1, 1931), pp. 6-7; *PHA* 15.27 (October 29, 1931), pp. 14-15; *PHA* 15.33 (December 10, 1931), pp. 10-11; *PHA* 15.34 (December 17, 1931), pp. 3-4; and *PHA* 15.35 (December 24, 1931), pp. 7, 11-12.

[306] *PHA* 2.2 (May 9, 1918), pp. 10-11.

pool,[307] The Atlantic Ocean,[308] river,[309] and pond,[310] the majority of the reports identify 'water' alone as the medium. The lack of specificity regarding bodies of water may be due to the acceptance of sprinkling[311] as an acceptable mode of WB. The endorsement of sprinkling may have diminished the perceived need to demonstrate sufficient water for immersion found in other Pentecostal publications. The importance of WB is further evidenced by the inclusion of baptismal service announcements in the *PHA*.[312]

While a variety of modes were deemed acceptable, it appears to be the case that baptism by immersion was the most widely used mode. The frequently employed phrases support this assertion. 'Baptize(d) in water' with the variants 'baptized (in water), and baptizing' are the terms used predominantly.[313] Similarly, 'immerse(d)'

---

[307] *PHA* 13.10 (July 4, 1929), pp. 10-12.

[308] *PHA* 15.19 (Sep 3, 1931), p. 11.

[309] *PHA* 1.4 (May 24, 1917), p. 13; *PHA* 1.51 (April 18, 1918), p. 6; *PHA* 3.21 (Sep 18, 1919). p. 15; *PHA* 4.17 (Aug 26, 1920), pp. 6-7; *PHA* 4.44/45 (March 3, 10, 1921), p. 13; *PHA* 13.23 (Oct 3, 1929), p. 7; *PHA* 13.50 (April 17, 1930), p. 5; *PHA* 15.7 (June 11, 1931), p. 7; and *PHA* 15.23 (Oct 1, 1931), pp. 6-7.

[310] *PHA* 13.23 (Oct 3, 1929), p. 12.

[311] *PHA* 2.16 (August 15, 1918), pp. 10-11; *PHA* 3.27 (October 30, 1919), p. 14.

[312] *PHA* 1.4 (May 24, 1917), p. 13; *PHA* 1.51 (April 18, 1918), p. 6; *PHA* 3.21 (September 18, 1919). p. 15; *PHA* 4.17 (August 26, 1920), pp. 6-7; *PHA* 4.44/45 (March 3, 10, 1921), p. 13; *PHA* 13.23 (October 3, 1929), p. 7; *PHA* 13.50 (April 17, 1930), p. 5; *PHA* 15.7 (June 11, 1931), p. 7; and *PHA* 15.23 (October 1, 1931), pp. 6-7.

[313] *PHA* 1.4 (May 24, 1917), p. 13; *PHA* 1.9 (June 28, 1917), p. 6; *PHA* 1.51 (April 18, 1918), p. 6; *PHA* 2.2 (May 9, 1918), pp. 10-11; *PHA* 2.16 (August 15, 1918), pp. 6-7, 10-11, and 12; *PHA* 2.18 (August 29, 1918), p. 5; *PHA* 2.27 (October 31, 1918), p. 12; *PHA* 2.33-34 (December 19-26, 1918), pp. 14-15; *PHA* 3.12-13 (July 17-24, 1919), pp. 6-7; *PHA* 3.21 (September 18, 1919). p. 15; *PHA* 3.27 (October 30, 1919), p. 14; *PHA* 3.30 (November 20, 1919), pp. 11-12; *PHA* 3.46 (March 11, 1920), p. 10; *PHA* 4.8 (June 24, 1920), p. 14; *PHA* 4.8 (June 24, 1920), p. 14; *PHA* 4.14 (August 5, 1920), p. 15; *PHA* 4.17 (August 26, 1920), pp. 6-7; *PHA* 4.25 (October 21, 1920), pp. 6, 15; *PHA* 4.44/45 (March 3, 10, 1921), pp. 5, 6-7, and 13; *PHA* 5.15 (August 11, 1921), p. 11; *PHA* 5.21 (September 22, 1921), pp. 6-7; *PHA* 5.22 (September 29, 1921), p. 6; *PHA* 5.31 (December 1, 1921), p. 3; *PHA* 5.33 (December 15, 1921), pp. 4, 6; *PHA* 5.37 (January 12, 1922), p. 12; *PHA* 5.8 (June 22, 1922), p. 10, 1; *PHA* 6.32 (December 7, 1922), pp. 7, 15; *PHA* 7.5 (May 31, 1923), pp. 7, 10, 11, 12, and 13; *PHA* 7.16 (August 16, 1923), p. 6; *PHA* 7.26

and 'immersion' is used to report WBs.[314] The language of obedience is reflected in 'followed the Lord in water baptism' to describe being baptized.[315] Burial language is the second most frequently used metaphor to describe the baptismal event. 'Buried with Christ/their Lord'[316] and 'go in and out of their watery graves/buried beneath the yielding wave'[317] reflect the use of the Pauline imagery found in Romans 6.

Exact Reporting

While precise numbers are provided for those baptized, a notable lack is found in the baptismal reports relative to the size of the crowds in attendance and the presence of embodied Pentecostal worship. First,

---

(October 25, 1923), p. 11; *PHA* 7.27 (November 1, 1923), p. 11; *PHA* 7.31 (November 29, 1923), pp. 6-7; *PHA* 8.22 (September 25, 1924), p. 5; *PHA* 8.29 (November 13, 1924), pp. 12-13; *PHA* 8.44 (February 26, 1925), p. 11; *PHA* 9.30 (November 26, 1925), pp. 11-12; *PHA* 9.35 (January 7, 1926), pp.12-13; *PHA* 9.45 (March 18, 1926), pp. 6, 7; *PHA* 10.8 (June 24, 1926), p. 14; *PHA* 11.44 (March 8, 1928), p. 11; *PHA* 12.10 (July 5, 1928), pp. 12, 13; *PHA* 12.14 (August 2, 1928), p. 13; *PHA* 12.33 (December 13, 1928), pp. 5, 7; *PHA* 12.45 (March 14, 1929), p. 13; *PHA* 13.37 (January 17, 1929), pp. 4-5; *PHA* 13.42 (February 20, 1930), p. 14; *PHA* 13.45 (March 13, 1930), pp. 7, 12-13; *PHA* 13.50 (April 17, 1930), p. 5; *PHA* 13.52 (May 1, 1930), p. 8; *PHA* 14.5 (May 29, 1930), pp. 3-5, 10-12; *PHA* 14.15 (August, 7, 1930), pp. 11-12; *PHA* 14.16 (August 14, 1930), pp. 7, 15; *PHA* 14.22 (September 25, 1930), p. 11; *PHA* 14.24 (October 9, 1930), p. 7; *PHA* 14.28 (November 6, 1930), p. 7; *PHA* 14.41 (February 12, 1931), p. 5; *PHA* 15.5 (May 28, 1931), p. 12; *PHA* 15.7 (June 11, 1931), pp. 6, 7; *PHA* 15.19 (September 3, 1931), p. 11; *PHA* 15.20 (September 10, 1931), p. 12; *PHA* 15.23 (October 1, 1931), pp. 6-7; *PHA* 15.27 (October 29, 1931), pp. 14-15; *PHA* 15.33 (December 10, 1931), pp. 10-11; *PHA* 15.34 (December 17, 1931), pp. 3-4; and *PHA* 15.35 (December 24, 1931), pp. 7, 11-12.

[314] *PHA* 2.2 (May 9, 1918), pp. 10-11; *PHA* 2.16 (August 15, 1918), pp. 10-11; *PHA* 3.27 (October 30, 1919), p. 14; *PHA* 4.44/45 (March 3, 10, 1921), p. 13; *PHA* 5.37 (January 12, 1922), p. 12; and *PHA* 8.22 (September 25, 1924), p. 5

[315] *PHA* 1.4 (May 24, 1917), p. 13; *PHA* 1.51 (April 18, 1918), p. 6.

[316] *PHA* 2.27 (October 31, 1918), p. 12; *PHA* 2.33-34 (December 19-26, 1918), pp. 14-15; *PHA* 3.30 (November 20, 1919), pp. 11-12; *PHA* 5.31 (November 30, 1922), pp. 11-12; *PHA* 7.31 (November 29, 1923), pp. 6-7; *PHA* 8.22 (September 25, 1924), p. 5; *PHA* 9.30 (November 26, 1925), pp. 11-12; *PHA* 9.45 (March 18, 1926), pp. 6, 7; *PHA* 13.37 (January 17, 1929), pp. 4-5; *PHA* 13.10 (July 4, 1929), pp. 10-12; *PHA* 13.31 (November 28, 1929), pp. 4-5; *PHA* 15.5 (May 28, 1931), p. 12; *PHA* 15.19 (September 3, 1931), p. 11; and *PHA* 15.35 (December 24, 1931), pp. 7, 11-12.

[317] *PHA* 2.27 (October 31, 1918), p. 12; *PHA* 13.10 (July 4, 1929), pp. 10-12.

there are no estimates of the crowd sizes present for WBs. The vague descriptor, 'largest crowd', is employed once in reports.[318] Secondly, only five of the 100 reports capture manifestations of the HS's presence and influence during baptismal services. S.W. Sublett reports from Mont Calm, WV that on 'Sunday evening there were eight baptized in water. God gave witness to and blessed the same. Praise the Lord for the sweetness of His sacred presence.'[319] From Randfontein, Transvaal, South Africa, Joe, and V.E. Rhodes offer, 'At Randfontein we baptized six in water on the first Sunday in May. The services were real good, and both those who were baptized and those who attended the services seemed to be blessed.'[320] K.E.M. Spooner writing from Rustenburg, Transvaal, South Africa, provides two accounts of worship. First is the service conducted on Sunday, August 18, 1918:

> the whole town followed us to the river, as we went to carry out the last command of the Master as is found in Mt. 28:19. It was indeed one of the most blessed baptismal services that we have had as yet. Thirty-one were buried with Christ, and it was blessed to watch them go in and out of their watery graves. Hallelujah![321]

Second, Spooner reported in 1925:

> Rev. Brooks gave a short talk to the candidates for baptism, after which we took our way to the river at which time sixty-three were buried with Christ in baptism. This is the biggest baptismal service we have had as yet, we have baptized as many as sixty-one at one service, but we rejoice that we are going forward instead of backwards.[322]

Finally, Ella Whitaker, reporting from Gibson, SC, provides an account of a lively baptismal service when 150 who were blessed during the baptismal service at Pate's Mill Pond. She states, 'There were twenty-seven baptized by Bro. Leviner. The power of God sure

---

[318] *PHA* 4.8 (June 24, 1920), p. 14.
[319] *PHA* 2.16 (August 15, 1918), pp. 6-7.
[320] *PHA* 5.21 (September 22, 1921), pp. 6-7.
[321] *PHA* 2.27 (October 31, 1918), p. 12.
[322] *PHA* 9.30 (November 26, 1925), pp. 11-12.

did fall. The candidates went in the water shouting and praising God.'[323]

A possible rationale for the lack of evidence of embodied spirituality may be found in G.F. Taylor's account of PH history. In rehearsing B.H. Irwin's contribution to the movement, Taylor states,

> However, I will say that Rev. B.H. Irwin was originally from Missouri. He was educated for a lawyer, but became a Baptist preacher. He was turned out of the Baptist Church for preaching holiness. About the year 1896 he became a prominent contributor to 'The Way of Faith,' of Columbia, S.C. He was then preaching in the middle West and South, and great revivals attended his preaching, and thousands of souls were saved and sanctified in his meetings. They claimed to receive the baptism of the Holy Ghost, the baptism of fire, and the baptism of dynamite; that is, many of them did. It is reported that many of his meetings were somewhat on the wild order.[324]

The noteworthy scarcity enables the editor to present a more restrained view of worship than the meetings of Irwin that 'were somewhat on the wild order'. This scarcity, in turn, may be an attempt to assuage persons from within the holiness movement who were ill at ease with more effusive praise and worship. Former Quakers who were now members of the PHC may have reflected the desire for more restraint.

While not falling under the strict category of 'embodied Pentecostal worship' sufficient evidence documents occurrences of healing taking place during and after WBs.[325] Examples from South Africa by two different missionaries demonstrate God's healing power. First, reported by J.O. Lehman from Johannesburg, we read, 'God is working in our midst. In Bloemhof, 21 were baptized in water and a number of precious healings took place.'[326] Then, writing from Rustenburg, K.E.M. Spooner reports that 'we baptized seven persons … consecrated six children which made a total of fourteen children

---

[323] *PHA* 13.23 (October 3, 1929), p. 12.
[324] *PHA* 4.40 (February 3, 1921), pp. 8-9.
[325] *PHA* 3.12-13 (July 17-24, 1919), pp. 6-7; *PHA* 4.17 (August 26, 1920), pp. 6-7; and *PHA* 14.15 (August 7, 1930), pp. 11-12; and *PHA* 14.41 (February 12, 1931), p. 5.
[326] *PHA* 3.12-13 (July 17-24, 1919), pp. 6-7.

consecrated, and thirty-six baptized in water, many healed, and one clear baptism in the Spirit'.[327]

On the one hand, it seems to be the case that education regarding the meaning and import of WB before baptismal services was not a priority in the USA. There is no evidence in the reports to indicate otherwise. On the other hand, baptismal candidates in China, India, and South Africa appear to have been educated about the meaning of WB before the event. Additionally, candidates appear to have been examined to verify understanding and engagement of the Christian faith.[328] The rationale for providing teaching before baptism appears to be related to the consequences of candidates after baptism. A report from Hyderabad, Afghanistan, by Rev. J.T. Perkins of the Methodist Mission in Hyderabad tells of a Muslim who had expressed belief in Jesus but was afraid to undergo WB out of fear that he would lose his property which consists of two villages. Moreover, his wife was not willing to become a Christian. Consequently,

> The moment he is baptized, she will be divorced from him, according to Mohammedan law, and he will not be allowed to look upon her face. Even if she would consent to live with him after his baptism, Mohammedan Law would hold her as living in adultery. This makes work among Mohammedan families difficult. We do not wish to break up their families.[329]

Reports from previously reviewed Pentecostal publications indicate that ostracism from families, castes, and communities with the corresponding surrender of earthly treasure was a reality faced by persons who converted to the Christian faith from Hindu, Muslim, and Buddhist religions. It stands to reason that the same fate would have been visited upon persons converted under the banner of the Pentecostal Holiness Church. The preparatory teaching and examination of new believers appear to operate on this assumption, and that new converts needed to be able to count the cost and make informed decisions.

---

[327] *PHA* 4.17 (August 26, 1920), pp. 6-7.
[328] *PHA* 3.30 (November 20, 1919), pp. 11-12; *PHA* 5.37 (January 12, 1922), p. 12; *PHA* 9.35 (January 7, 1926), pp. 12-13; and *PHA* 13.23 (October 3, 1929), p. 7.
[329] *PHA* 12.33 (December 13, 1928), p. 5.

Formula

Before the formation of the PHC, William H. Durham's Finished Work teaching/preaching was embraced within the nascent Pentecostal movement, most notably by the AG. Groups in the movement most resistant to the Finished Work theology held to the holiness doctrine of sanctification as a second definite work of grace after being 'saved'. The PHC was a champion of the second work theology. Consequently, when the 'New Issue' or 'New Light' controversy erupted in 1914, the PHC leadership took a clear, unequivocal stand in opposition to the 'Jesus' name' baptismal formula. During the first year of publication, the editor, in an article on 'The Sabbath' provides the following comment:

> There were baptisms in the Old Testament times. (See Heb. 6:2; and in Heb. 9:10, the word 'washings' in the Greek is Baptisms.) However, the water used was mingled with blood and ashes; but in the New Dispensation, the water is pure, and baptism must be administered with the formula, 'In the name of the Father, and of the Son, and of the Holy Ghost.' All of this is entirely ceremonial, but it is ceremony of the New Dispensation.[330]

The editor then provided a challenge to the New Issue position in May 1918 in his reflection on Acts 2.38. He posits that those who are teaching a 'one name baptism' are doing nothing more than reviving Unitarianism which is intended to destroy the doctrine of the Trinity. Further, he offers that once it is accepted 'that there are three Persons in the Godhead, one name baptism must go' since 'Jesus commanded us to baptize "In the name of the Father, and of the Son, and of the Holy Ghost." (Mt. 28:19)'. To accentuate his argument, the editor references the Basis of Union, where Unitarianism is rejected on the basis that the 'principle point of their doctrine is the unipersonality of God, and we are utterly opposed to such doctrine because the general tenor of the Scriptures is against it'.[331]

The *PHA* documents the ongoing struggle with the New Light teaching in 1925 as F.M. Britton reports on his ministry in Mobile, AL, where the so-called 'one God, one name baptism' has caused much confusion. Britton laments the proponents' substitution of

---

[330] *PHA* 1.18 (August 30, 1917), pp. 4-5.
[331] *PHA* 2.2 (May 9, 1918), p. 3.

WB in 'the name of Jesus only' for the blood of Jesus. Lastly, they posit 'that in being baptized in that way they get rid of sin.' Britton offers that he believes 'This I believe to be an awful error.'[332]

Similarly, the debate continued to be rebuffed in December 1929 as the Q & A column was employed to counter baptism in the name of 'Jesus only'. The following answer was in response to Question 991 regarding the meaning of Acts 2.38: Does the verse 'mean that people were to be baptized in water in the name of Jesus Christ? Is the name of Jesus Christ the name of the Father, and the Son, and the Holy Ghost, Mt. 28:19'? The answer moves beyond quoting Mt. 28.19 to the second level of discourse to explain that 'in receiving Christian baptism, they were to recognize Jesus as the Christ, the Son of God'. Moreover, 'To be sound in Christian faith, we must duly recognize and confess the three personalities of the God-head, and baptism must be administered in the name of the Triune God.'[333]

Despite the challenges of the New Light movement faced by the PHC, there is scant evidence of persons rebaptized by PHC ministers. Only one report alludes to rebaptism, and the context and rationale are absent. A.H Butler recounts from Kinston, NC, that 'Two were sprinkled and twelve were immersed, and the others had been baptized before'.[334]

Finally, changes were affected in the Discipline of the PHC to provide substantive support to the Trinitarian baptismal formula:

> On page 32, under the paragraph 'Water Baptism,' after the word 'denominations' shall be inserted the following: And baptism shall be administered according to the divine command of our blessed Lord: 'In the name of the Father, and of the Son, and of the Holy Ghost.' Mt. 28:19, 20.[335]

The Meaning of Water Baptism

While the article, 'That Spiritual Drink', was not published until the August 14, 1930, issue of the *PHA*, the valuation placed on 'signs and symbols' by G.F. Taylor provides insight into his theological

---

[332] PHA 9.22 (October 1, 1925), p. 14.
[333] PHA 13.33 (December 12, 1929), p. 9. Also, PHA 14.28 (November 6, 1930), p. 10.
[334] PHA 2.16 (August 15, 1918), pp. 10-11.
[335] PHA 13.5 (May 30, 1929), p. 9.

perspective and the lenses through which he interpreted and applied Scripture. First, Taylor regards God's use of material things as vehicles to convey spiritual truth, especially concerning the sacraments. He employs the word sacrament 'in the sense of a thing that is to be received by the child of God, conveying with it the spiritual benefits, such as water baptism, or the Lord's Supper'. According to Taylor, it is in the sacraments that we 'receive the highest spiritual benefits from material things'. Second, he observes that 'spiritual blessings derived from sacraments are only received in proportion to the faith exercised by the recipient'. Per Taylor, sacraments become emptied of spiritual grace without accompanying faith. He also asserts 'that Christ is present in a sacrament to all who believe ... we mean that Christ is with the sacrament to feed the soul of all who believe in Him'. In sum, Taylor offers that 'there is a connection somehow between the spiritual and the material, and though it may be difficult to find, Christ has been pleased to represent to us the heavenly blessings under signs, symbols, and sacraments'. However, these are of no use unless they are received in faith. Nonetheless, 'Christ is present in them to all who have faith in Him'. Despite all our failures and short-comings, 'we may all drink together of that spiritual drink if we forgive one another, even as God for Christ's sake has forgiven us'.[336]

In his July 1919 Sunday School lesson on WB, G.F. Taylor elucidates the meaning of Mt. 28.18-20 and Mk 1.1-11; 8.26-40, asserting that WB is the 'first ordinance of the church. It is the sign of allegiance to Christ. The New Testament church began with John the Baptist, and ... We do not find where this ordinance has been repealed.'[337] While Taylor's view that the early church began with John the Baptist and that John's baptism is identical to the baptism commanded by Jesus[338] is open to dispute, there is virtual unanimity

---

[336] *PHA* 14.16 (August 14, 1930), pp. 1, 8.

[337] *PHA* 3.10 (July 3, 1919), pp. 2-3.

[338] Taylor was not alone in this view. See *PHA* 12.28 (November 8, 1928), p. 8 in which Paul F. Beacham responds to a request to explain the differences between the baptisms of John the Baptist and Jesus Christ. He responds with the following:

> I suppose you mean the baptism administered by Christ, through the apostles, John 4:1-2, during His earthly ministry. It appears that Christ during the early

that WB is the first ordinance of the Church, signifying the new birth or being 'converted or saved'.[339] Also, WB is commanded by Christ as a public witness that one has become a disciple of Christ.[340]

Addressing the meaning of WB in the January 7, 1926, issue of the *PHA,* R.H. Lee echoes Taylor, seven years later, when he posits that 'Water baptism is the step in outward testimony to an inward work. Being born of water is typical of the Spiritual birth, or the birth from above.' Just as John baptized Jesus before beginning his public

---

months of His ministry in Judea, labored as the colleague of John the Baptist, His preaching and baptism were the same. However, Christ did not administer water baptism except through His disciples, as is shown in John 4:2. His ministry and their baptizing met with such success that some of John's disciples became uneasy about the reputation of their teacher, but when they reported it to John, he only rejoiced in the progress of their work. – John 3:20-30; 4:12. John's preaching and baptism was a call to the Jewish nation, to repentance. And the ministry of Christ and His disciples was the same until after the resurrection. Their commission was to go to the 'lost sheep of the house of Israel.' After the resurrection Christ commanded them to preach to all nations, and baptize believers in the name of the Father, and of the Son, and of the Holy Ghost. This as a matter of fact gave to baptism a new dignity and a greater significance. The contrast between his baptism and that of Christ, of which John spoke, was not in water. It was a contrast between the baptism of John with water, and the Pentecostal baptism with the Holy Ghost and fire which Christ administers. However, we are not to understand the fire to be a baptism distinct from the Holy Spirit. The fire is a symbol of the work, and influence of the Spirit. The baptism with the Spirit gives heavenly illumination, and kindles a flame of holy zeal in the hearts of those who receive Him. This is the significance of the 'tongues like as of fire,' on the day of Pentecost.

Similarly, see *PHA* 12.45 (March 14, 1929), p. 9:

Question 718: Did John the Baptist belong to the Baptist church? Answer. – No, there was not any Baptist church until many hundred years, after the days of John the Baptist. He was called John the Baptist, or the baptizer, because of his ministry of baptism. The ministry of other prophets, had not been accompanied by the administration of baptism. But John was the forerunner of a new dispensation, and it was suitable that he should adminster [sic] this rite, as an outward sign of true repentance and faith, in the coming Messiah.

For a competing view see *PHA* 1.23 (October 4, 1917), pp. 2-3, 6.

[339] *PHA* 4.40 (February 3, 1921), pp. 8-9. The author asserts:

The pardon of sin, justification, regeneration, and the witness of the Spirit are all separate acts, and yet the holiness movement included them all when it spoke of being saved. Conversion means a complete change in one's manner of life, a turning around, and so all these acts of God are but the first work of grace in saving a soul from his actual sins. The holiness people called it being converted or saved.

[340] *PHA* 3.10 (July 3, 1919), pp. 2-3.

ministry, so too are believers 'buried with Christ in baptism in obedience to His command'. Water baptism marks our setting apart and consecration to the Master's service with our 'entire being'.[341]

The spiritual foundation for pledging allegiance to Christ is through the atonement of Jesus Christ and the repentance and godly sorrow of those beleaguered by sin. The editor employs the deliverance from Egyptian bondage and crossing the Red Sea as types for Christ's atoning work and WB, respectively. According to the editor, the only way to a relationship with God is through repentance or godly sorrow for sin. It is through 'God coming down into your heart and eradicating sin with the blood of our Christ. Not until then can sin be removed.' The editor stresses that the 'blood-sprinkled way is the way of eternal life, the way of the atonement of Jesus' and that Israel's deliverance from Egyptian bondage is a good type of justification. In the deliverance from Egyptian bondage, God demonstrated his power when the death angel passed over and not one person who was 'under the blood' lost their life. Afterward, Israel was led by God through the Red Sea, 'a perfect type of water baptism, for the Word says they were baptized unto Moses in the cloud and in the sea'.[342]

The exact position is reflected in the 'Q & A' exchanges published spanning 1921 through 1931. In June 1921, the respondent emphasized the atoning work of Christ and employed the Ark as a type of Christ, as he explains 1 Pet. 3.21:

> The parenthetical expression refers to water baptism, and this has its place, and is right and proper, but mere water baptism alone has no saving virtue. The baptism that counts is the inward work of grace, the regenerating forces and virtues of the atonement and resurrection of Jesus Christ. The Ark was a type of Christ, and those saved in it are prophetical of those who are saved by the grace of God.[343]

---

[341] *PHA* 9.35 (January 7, 1926), pp. 6-7.
[342] *PHA* 5.15 (August 11, 1921), p. 2. Also, see *PHA* 1.29 (November 15, 1917), pp. 4-5; *PHA* 8.31 (November 27, 1924), pp. 4-5.
[343] *PHA* 5.5 (June 2, 1921), p. 10.

Another request to explain the same passage, almost ten years later, receives similar treatment with the typology expanded to include the water in which the Ark floated as a symbol of WB:

> Answer: 'It is here declared that Christ in the person of the Holy Spirit was in Noah and enabled him to preach to the disobedient people of his day while he was building the Ark. And the salvation of Noah by means of the Ark is referred to as a type of our salvation through the death and resurrection of Jesus Christ. The water floating the Ark which saved Noah and his family from destruction, is also taken as a symbol of Christian baptism, which is the outward sign of the inner work of the Spirit regenerating, and cleansing the soul by virtue of the blood of Christ. There is no ground here for the idea that water baptism actually saves and cleanses the soul. Peter rather shows, that while water has power to cleanse the body outwardly, that there must be the inward work of the Spirit to renew and purge the conscience, and this only comes through appropriating faith in the death and resurrection of Christ. Water baptism is all right as far as it goes, but it cannot save without that inner 'good conscience' which answers to the demand of God.[344]

More so than any of the previously reviewed publications, the *PHA* attaches the symbolism of WB to the doctrine of sanctification. Sanctification is understood as 'the eradication of the carnal mind from the heart of a regenerated believer, and puts him in the same state as man was placed before he transgressed in the garden'.[345] This 'deeper meaning' of WB is gained through interpreting Rom. 6.3-6 as the second definite work of grace which is understood to describe 'the eradication of the carnal mind'. L.R. Graham illustrates this perspective in his 1917 sermon on Rom. 6.3-6 when he asserts, 'This baptism does away with our old man, the cause of division, thereby answering Christ's prayer in the 17th of John, that was found in the one hundred and twenty when they went to the upper room'. In conclusion, Graham posits the results of this baptism: 'Negatively, it looses from sin: absence of the old man and

---

[344] *PHA* 14.7 (June 12, 1930), p. 9.
[345] *PHA* 3.3 (May 15, 1919), pp. 5-6.

his deeds. Positively, one accord; great joy; continual praises to God.'[346]

The interpretation of various scriptures through reading Romans 6 as referring to sanctification then follows as seen in Question 199, which inquires if Acts 19.5 refers to WB. The reply is, 'Water baptism may be implied, but I am sure it refers more directly to the baptism of Romans 6:3-7, which means a crucifixion of the old man'.[347] A second exchange is found in September 29, 1921, *PHA*, where explanations and clarifications are requested for Jn. 3.5 and Mk 16.16. The respondent avers the 'water in John 3:5 refers to the water of life mentioned in John 3:10'. The 'Baptism of Mk. 16:16 refers to crucifixion of the old man (Rom. 6:6), and may also take in the Baptism of the spirit'. The writer concludes with 'I have no objection to the interpretation that includes water baptism with the others in Mk. 16:16'.[348] Third, from the December 12, 1929, *PHA*, we read that 'A deeper significance of baptism as it relates to Christian experience, is found in Romans 6:3-6, where it is shown that in addition to pardon and regeneration, we are sanctified or the old man is crucified'. According to the author, 'This experience precedes the gift of the Holy Ghost, and is implied in Acts 2:38'. He reasons that this has to be the case; if it were false, WB would be 'essential to receiving the baptism with the Spirit, which certainly is not the case as people are often saved, sanctified, and receive the Gift of the Holy Ghost before receiving water baptism', according to the scenario is found in Acts 10.47.[349]

J.H. King's interpretation of Romans 6 provides the final example of the same approach. Originally published as Chapter 15 in *From Passover to Pentecost*,[350] King's treatment is published in the October 20, 1927, *PHA*. King interprets Romans 6 through the lens of sanctification. King makes significant use of typology in equating WB with sanctification as a second definite work of grace. Moreover, his argument hinges on equating 'the body of sin' with the 'old man'

---

[346] *PHA* 1.7 (June 15, 1917), pp. 2-4.
[347] *PHA* 2.2 (May 9, 1918), p. 16.
[348] *PHA* 5.22 (September 29, 1921), p. 6.
[349] *PHA* 13.33 (December 12, 1929), p. 9.
[350] J.H. King, *From Passover to Pentecost* (Franklin Springs, GA: Publishing House of the Pentecostal Holiness Church, 1955).

in Rom. 6.6. According to King, WB is designed to symbolize 'purification of heart and life'. The entire person is immersed in water, 'which typifies a completeness of the inward work', and the whole person is symbolically raised, signifying resurrection, 'a walking in newness of life'. Baptism is analogous to Christ's death 'as a means of removing "the sin of the world" judicially, out of sight'. King references Adam's adverse impact on all creation and asserts that Christ 'gathered up all the sin of the world upon himself, and went down into death, and all the unrighteousness of the old creation sank with him beneath the waves of death. It was buried forever in His vicarious death.' In Christ's resurrection, 'Everything that came up with Christ belonged to the new creation, not one vestige of the old arose with Him. The new creation only can live unto God, the old is dead.' Thus, for King, the death and resurrection of Christ 'was all judicial, vicarious, representative, and the Holy Spirit has come to translate the whole into human experience'.[351]

According to King, WB 'is not a proclamation of the fact that the inward death has been fully accomplished'. Paul called the Roman Christians 'to reckon themselves to be dead indeed unto sin because they had passed through it symbolically, in baptism'. In baptism, 'the "old man," "body of sin," rolls off us into death, his element, the old creation, and we come up with not one vestige of it clinging to our hearts'. Per King, 'the Holy Spirit is the baptizing agent, we are the subjects, death is the element into which we are plunged, the effect is the death and burial of the "old man," the resurrection to a life wholly renewed in God's image of holiness, the result'.[352]

For King, the disposal of the carnal principle, the 'old man,' the 'body of sin' is accomplished through the judicial act of Christ's death and resurrection. King posits the Roman Christians 'had been justified and baptized into His death, symbolically … they were to go down into death spiritually, by reckoning themselves to be dead with Christ, to sin, and rise to holiness of life, in the new creation with Christ'. In like manner, 'The same process must take place with, and in us. We are justified then to go down with Christ into death unto death to all sin, and live unto God in the purity of a new walk.'[353]

---

[351] *PHA* 11.25 (October 20, 1927), pp. 9-11.
[352] *PHA* 11.25 (October 20, 1927), pp. 9-11.
[353] *PHA* 11.25 (October 20, 1927), pp. 9-11.

Interpreting Rom. 6.3-6 as a second definite work of grace appears to restrict the meaning of the text to other interpretative possibilities and incline interpreters to a misreading of parallel passages. An example of this is found in Taylor's article on 'Crucifixion', where he treats Gal. 2.20 in relation to Rom. 6.6, arguing that the two passages refer to two different crucifixions. After quoting Gal. 2.20, Taylor asserts that the crucifixion referred to in Gal. 2.20 occurs after cleansing and that 'it has no reference to the crucifixion of Rom. 6:6'. Instead, the crucifixion in Galatians is 'crucifixion of self, subsequent to cleansing'. To illustrate his point, Taylor cites the conflict between Peter and Paul recounted in Galatians 2, interpreting Peter's difficulty as one of the self-life, namely, that Peter was still habituated to old ways of thinking and acting. Similarly, Paul's need to die daily is cited to support the need for the 'self-life' ongoing crucifixion.[354]

As mentioned under 'The Practice of Baptism', the PHC both endorsed and practiced infant baptism. Theologically, the practice was rooted in the doctrines of original sin, the atonement, and sanctification, as we see from Taylor's December 24, 1931, editorial entitled 'Crucifixion'. Taylor summarizes his argument in answering, 'When does this eradication take place in the dying infant?' First, Taylor states 'the infant does not receive any divine life through natural generation; but each infant is brought under the benefits of the atonement at the moment of conception'. The benefits, as mentioned above, 'impart eternal life, or regeneration; otherwise, Jesus could not have said that little children belong to the kingdom of heaven'. To maintain the doctrine of sanctification as a second definite work of grace, Taylor asserts, 'The atonement, however, does not sanctify the infant at conception, nor at birth necessarily, for then children would be born without inward sin'. Jeremiah's sanctification (Jer. 1.5) is understood to mean a 'call of God to the office of prophet'. For Taylor, since John the Baptist was filled with the HS from birth (Lk. 1.15), the implication is that 'he was sanctified also from birth'. To forestall objections to his position, Taylor counsels readers to 'Let those cases stand by themselves, and we will take the masses of infants as having original sin, though regenerated, belonging to the kingdom of God'.

---

[354] *PHA* 2.7 (June 13, 1918), pp. 8-10.

Taylor concludes his article with what appears to be a reversal of an earlier statement: 'If in that condition the child arrives at death, we claim that Adamic sin is eradicated by the atonement before his death; that means that as all die in Adam, even so in Christ all are made alive'.[355] Taylor's argument appears to be a well-intended attempt to provide pastoral care and support for those who have experienced the death of an infant while laboring within the bounds of accepted doctrines that fail to address the difficulties of life and death in the kingdom of God.

White Wing Messenger

Introduction

The *White Wing Messenger* (*WWM*) was initially a bi-monthly periodical with the inaugural issue published by A.J. Tomlinson on September 15, 1923, in Cleveland, TN, less than ten months after being relieved of his duties as General Overseer of the COG.[356]

Tomlinson served as Editor and Publisher until his death on October 2, 1943.[357] The *WWM* continues to be published by the COGOP, headquartered in Cleveland, TN.

Practice of Water Baptism

A.J. Tomlinson utilized the *WWM* from the outset, as he had employed the *Church of God Evangel* earlier. Namely, to disseminate information and inspire readers. In the first issue of the publication, Tomlinson states the following charge and invitation: 'We invite all the workers to send in reports of interest from the battlefield. Help us make "The White Wing Messenger" a medium of information as well as a spiritual blessing.'[358]

While Tomlinson does not explicitly request reports of WBs in the inaugural edition, it appears ministers on the field understood they were to continue reporting as they had before his departure as editor of the *COGE*.[359] That this was the case is supported by the plethora of WB reports contained in the organ, in addition to the

---

[355] *PHA* 15.35 (December 24, 1931), pp. 1, 8, and 9.
[356] *COGE* 13.46 (November 11, 1922), p. 2. See Hunter, 'Tomlinson, Ambrose Jessup', p. 1145.
[357] *WWM* 20.20 (October 2, 1943), p. 1.
[358] *WWM* 1.1 (September 15, 1923), pp. 1, 2, and 3.
[359] *COGE* 13.46 (November 11, 1922), p. 2.

results of evangelistic and missionary endeavors. The first baptismal reports are found in the second issue of the *WWM*.[360] Similarly, there appears to be no change in the valuation of WB as a critical component of Christian discipleship, as the contents of the reports demonstrate.

The following report from A.J. Lawson occurs in 1927. Lawson's comments appear to represent the same position held by Tomlinson before 1923 regarding the import of WB. Lawson posits that the most significant thing in the ceremony of WB is that the 'candidate dedicates himself or herself to the Father, to the Son and to the Holy Ghost, and that is just an outward declaration that they really believe in the three of the one God head [sic]'.[361]

The following citations provided by unnamed sources are typical of baptismal reports found in the *WWM*. From Willisburg, KY, we read, 'Thirteen followed the Lord in water baptism'.[362] A writer from Altavista, VA, reports that 'Sunday morning we had preaching, Sunday afternoon fourteen followed the Lord in water baptism, and the Lord blessed in this service'.[363] Lastly, Parkers Landing, PA's representative, writes, 'We had baptismal services last Sunday at the river. Ten were baptized There was a large attendance.'[364]

Widely Practiced

Water baptism is valued and practiced widely across the USA. The majority of the baptisms are reported from the southeastern USA: Alabama, Georgia, Kentucky, Tennessee, Virginia, and West Virginia.[365] Reports are also submitted from a handful of other countries, including the Bahamas, Barbados, Jamaica, Virgin Islands, and China.[366]

---

[360] *WWM* 1.2 (September 29, 1923), pp. 1, 2, and 3.
[361] *WWM* 4.10 (May 7, 1927), pp. 1, 2.
[362] *WWM* 1.2 (September 29, 1923), p. 1.
[363] *WWM* 2.11 (May 23, 1925), p. 1.
[364] *WWM* 1.20 (June 28, 1924), p. 3.
[365] Please see Appendix I for a breakdown of the locations in the case of the USA. The sites are listed in alphabetical order according to state and city.
[366] Please see Appendix J for a breakdown of the locations according to country. The sites are listed in alphabetical order according to country and city.

Exact Reporting

The editor of the *WWM* accentuates the import of WB by the inclusion of specific statistical reporting of those baptized in water.[367] Also included in the *WWM* are announcements of future baptismal services so that those desiring to follow Christ in baptism may be prepared for participation.[368]

Sufficient Water

Following the pattern of previously reviewed periodicals, references to specific water bodies utilized for baptismal services are identified; however, references are limited. The following locations are mentioned at least once by reporters: a 'tank',[369] the Atlantic Ocean,[370] various rivers,[371] lakes,[372] Tangier Sound,[373] Savannah Sound,[374] 'the water's edge/water side',[375] 'at the beach/down to the beach',[376] also, 'down to the water/went under the water/ out in the water'.[377]

---

[367] Please see Appendix K for the references for statistical reporting.

[368] *WWM* 2.20 (October 10, 1925), p. 4; *WWM* 3.18 (August 28, 1926), p. 3; *WWM* 3.19 (September 11, 1926), p. 4; *WWM* 3.22 (October 22, 1926), p. 1; *WWM* 7.19 (September 27, 1930), p. 1; *WWM* 8.17 (August 15, 1931), p. 1; and *WWM* 4.1 (January 1, 1927), p. 2.

[369] *WWM* 8.18 (August 29, 1931), p. 1.

[370] *WWM* 2.18 (August 29, 1925), p. 4; *WWM* 3.19 (September 11, 1926), p. 4; *WWM* 3.22 (October 23, 1926), p. 3; *WWM* 4.6 (March 12 ,1927), p. 4; and *WWM* 7.17 (August 16, 1930), p. 2.

[371] *WWM* 1.20 (June 28, 1924), p. 3; *WWM* 1.21 (July 12, 1924), p. 3; *WWM* 1.22 (July 26, 1924), p. 4; *WWM* 1.24 (August 23, 1924), p. 3; *WWM* 2.6 (March 14, 1925), p. 4; *WWM* 2.17 (August 15, 1925), p. 2; *WWM* 3.20 (September 25, 1926), p. 4; *WWM* 4.14 (July 2, 1927), p. 1; *WWM* 4.16 (July 30, 1927), p. 4; *WWM* 6.19 (October 12, 1929), p. 4; *WWM* 7.17 (August 16, 1930), p. 1; *WWM* 8.1 (January 3, 1931), p. 1; *WWM* 8.15 (July 18, 1931), p. 1; *WWM* 8.17 (August 15, 1931), p. 1; and *WWM* 8.23 (November 21, 1931), p. 4.

[372] *WWM 1.22* (July 26, 1924), p. 4; *WWM* 6.18 (September 28, 1929), p. 2.

[373] *WWM* 4.11 (May 21, 1927), p. 1.

[374] *WWM* 6.13 (July 6, 1929), p. 3.

[375] *WWM* 1.20 (June 28, 1924), pp. 1, 2; *WWM* 2.11 (May 23, 1925), p. 2; *WWM* 5.27 (December 15, 1928), p. 3; *WWM* 8.24 (December 5, 1931), p. 4; and *WWM* 8.19 (September 26, 1931), p. 2.

[376] *WWM 3*.25 (December 4, 1926), p. 1; *WWM* 4.6 (March 12 ,1927), p. 3; and *WWM* 7.19 (September 27, 1930), p. 2.

[377] *WWM* 3.21 (October 9, 1926), p. 4; *WWM* 4.11 (May 21, 1927), p. 1; *WWM* 5.20 (August 18, 1928), p. 1; and *WWW* 8.24 (April 28, 1928), pp. 2, 4.

The reduction of naming specific bodies of water may be accounted for by the belief that readers of the *WWM* would have understood sufficient water for immersion was available when the rite was performed. Hence, there was no need to add specific details to the reports. Another possibility to explain the limited specifics may be an editorial attempt to standardize the descriptions while allowing for exceptions. This same practice was evident in the *COGE*, edited by Tomlinson.

Mode of Baptism

It appears that immersion was practiced without exception and that reports, sermons, and testimonies were utilized to offer a rejection of sprinkling as an acceptable mode of baptism and an apologia for strict adherence to the practice. For example, the importance of WB is reiterated by the editor in the following comment on the proper mode of baptism:

> The same comparison and analogy will apply to being a member of the Baptist church, which is strong for baptism by immersion, and attending a Methodist or Presbyterian church and help support them by his presence and putting in the collections when they oppose immersion and teach baptism otherwise. Only lukewarm, undecided, unconcerned people will divide themselves in any such way.[378]

The editor responds in like fashion to a question on the permissibility of admission to the COG by a person who believes in WB by sprinkling and is satisfied with that mode of baptism. The answer is brief and unequivocal, asserting that 'Sprinkling is not water baptism'. Furthermore, 'The Church of God stands for water baptism by immersion and recognizes nothing else as baptism'. According to the editor, it is inconceivable that a person 'be a loyal member of the Church of God and claim, believe and teach sprinkling as water baptism'. Thus, such a person should not be received into church membership.[379]

Similarly, a photograph of Brother J.O. Hamilton, overseer of the state of Mississippi, conducting a baptismal service is titled:

---

[378] *WWM* 5.9 (April 28, 1928), p. 4.
[379] *WWM* 4.7 (March 26, 1927), p. 2.

'Baptizing in the Old Time Way' with the following caption: 'He is seen above engaged in a glorious baptismal service in South Mississippi, with a number of happy saints ready to be buried with the Lord in water baptism'.[380]

Baptism by immersion was also practiced as the movement spread outside the continental USA. From China, one missionary's commitment to baptism by immersion is recounted in an inspirational story that reflects the ingenuity of persons who desire to be faithful to the command of Christ amid multiple obstacles. The story begins one week before June 28; the day planned to conduct a baptismal service. There had been no rain and the heat was stifling. Inside the house, the temperature was 105, and outside it was guessed to be 120. Despite the 'extreme heat the attendance in the mission was good', and there were 'sixty candidates to be baptized'. Additional challenges faced the missionaries since the mission hall was a rented place without room to build a baptismal tank or fill it with water since it relied on well water. Furthermore, a new law prohibited the use 'of the small river here and the Chinese women object(ed) to public baptism'. On the 21st, Peter, the missionary, proposed building a tank in his yard and filling it with well water. The tank was built in the sweltering heat, but there was no water available on the day before the planned baptism since the well had run dry. On top of that, Peter had contracted cholera a week before he was to baptize 60 candidates. People prayed, and God spared his life. After soul-wrenching supplication and at the very last minute 'a man came and offered us water from his well and just as the first hymn was sung, the last pail of water was poured in the tank'. With four and one-half feet of water in the tank, 53 men and women were buried with Christ to rise in the newness of life.[381]

The commitment to baptism by immersion was not one-sided on the part of ministers and missionaries. Many reports testify to the resolve of new converts desirous of baptism by immersion. From Akron, OH, the writer offers that 'On February 20 we had a baptismal service, although there was about six inches of snow on the ground'.[382]

---

[380] *WWM* 1.2 (September 29, 1923), p. 1.
[381] *WWM* 8.18 (August 29, 1931), p. 1.
[382] *WWM* 4.7 (March 26, 1927), p. 1.

Reporting in January 1931 from Burnside, KY, the author reports with gratitude that age was not a barrier in baptizing his mother and father: 'My father will be 90 years old in June and mother 64 years in April. A large crowd was gathered on the river banks to see the baptism. Brother Durham and brother Abbott did the baptizing.'[383] A report from Oneida, TN informs readers that three were baptized despite the snow and ice-cold water: 'There was snow on the ground, but the brother and two sisters walked right down into the icy water and came out shouting. I praise God for His mighty power.'[384] Finally, a report from Deals Island Beach, MD, posted on May 21, 1927, paints the scene of 300-350 present for the baptismal service conducted by Rev. Mario Wilson. He baptized three persons by immersion in Tangier Sound. The commitment and resolve of all persons are captured by the reporter who states, 'The weather was extremely cold, the wind blowing from the northwest and the waves were quite boisterous ... all came out of the water with their faces shining and showing their inward joy'.[385]

To remove any doubt regarding immersion as the proper mode of baptism, the reports of baptismal services use two phrases to describe baptismal events. 'Followed the Lord in water baptism' is employed over 100 times, emphasizing the aspect in obedience to Christ's command in Mt. 28.19 as well as emulating the example of Christ being baptized by immersion at the hands of John the Baptist.[386] The phrase 'baptized in water' occurs approximately 200 times, highlighting immersion as the acceptable mode.[387] Burial language is employed less than five times in the issues reviewed.[388]

Administration

The proper administrator of WB receives passing mention in the issues reviewed, and then only concerning the ministerial authority of a person recommended to the office of deacon. The respondent

---

[383] *WWM* (January 3, 1931), p. 1.
[384] *WWM* 4.6 (March 12 ,1927), p. 1.
[385] *WWM* 4.11 (May 21, 1927), p. 1.
[386] Please see Appendix L for the references employing 'followed the Lord in water baptism'.
[387] Please see Appendix M for the references employing 'baptized in water'.
[388] *WWM* 1.2 (September 29, 1923), p. 1; *WWM* 1.31 (December 6, 1924) p. 1; and *WWM* 8.18 (August 29, 1931), p. 1.

avers that such a person has no authority until he is ordained. After ordination, the person 'has authority to baptize, set churches in order, administer the Lord's Supper, the washing of the saints' feet, etc'.[389]

It seems to be the case that Tomlinson continues to adhere to the practice of granting authority to baptize only to those who are ordained, which meant only *males*. Baptismal reports from September 1923 through December 1931 provide no evidence of a woman performing WB. If WB is needed after a woman evangelist has held a revival meeting for a woman pastor, it seems that a male minister had to be called to perform the baptism(s). The report from Moorman, KY, illustrates this pattern. After the evangelists, Sister Damie St. Clair and Clara Miller, closed a ten-day revival here, seven were baptized in water. 'Brother Settles came and baptized for us and took the members into the church.'[390]

It appears that the practice of rebaptism continued in the Tomlinson COG.[391] Lacking a clear statement on the topic, the following reports from the field provide evidence that rebaptism was practiced. One report from an unnamed writer in Arkansas asserts that while new converts were baptized, presumably for the first time, 'the other saints got a renewal baptism'.[392]

Another report originating from New York, NY by Homer A. Tomlinson recounts rebaptism occurred at Ocean Beach,

> the same place where we have baptized before, twenty-four followed the Lord in baptism. Among these was Sister Quitsch, who had been baptized as a child, but felt that she would like to be baptized now when she had a full realization of the depths of meaning in water baptism. There are a dozen or so more to be baptized, and these will be baptized a little later.[393]

Pentecostal Worship

Consistent with the periodicals previously reviewed, passionate embodied Pentecostal spirituality is well-represented in the *WWM*.

---

[389] *WWM* 4.11 (May 21, 1927), p. 2.
[390] *WWM* 6.17 (August 31, 1929), p. 1.
[391] Explanation of Tomlinson COG. Legal name changed in 1953 due to a court order.
[392] *WWM* 3.26 (December 18, 1926), p. 1.
[393] *WWM* 3.19 (September 11, 1926), p. 4.

Reports are found of worshippers experiencing services described as 'glorious',[394] 'wonderfully blessed',[395] 'great',[396] and 'wonderful'.[397] Baptismal services are marked by 'much shouting and praising God in the water'.[398] Also, celebrants are tangibly experiencing the HS. A report from Sapulpa, OK, from October 24, 1931, relates the following account with about 2500 onlookers:

> Some of the converts shouted before they were baptized and some shouted after they were baptized and some shouted almost all the way out of the water and then we marched right on to the church that night and took the sacrament and had feet washing. There must have been about fifty who engaged in this service.[399]

A report from Whipple, WV, recounts embodied worship during the baptismal service on May 31 when the HS 'power fell and the saints began dancing and Jesus was seen in the midst hanging on the cross, with angels dancing in the midst of the saints ... Tears were shed for joy as God set His approval on the work.'[400]

From the June 20, 1925, issue, the author from Kennesaw, GA, offers the following account, which illustrates the convicting, humbling, and reconciling work of the HS within the worship context of a baptismal service:

> In the service on Sunday, the power fell in a wonderful way, two men were broken down and they ended an old envious feud, families were reunited and two more received the full blessing. We then returned to the water for another baptizing. Glory to His dear name! Others made confessions to the Church and begged forgiveness. Truly the Saints are on fire for God.[401]

---

[394] *WWM* 1.31 (December 6, 1924) p. 1.
[395] *WWM* 2.13 (June 20, 1925), p. 3.
[396] *WWM* 2.18 (August 29, 1925), p. 4.
[397] *WWM* 2.14 (July 4, 1925), p. 4; *WWM* 3.21 (October 9, 1926), p. 4; *WWM* 4.13 (June 18, 1927), p. 1; *WWM* 6.13 (July 6, 1929), p. 3; *WWM* 7.19 (September 27, 1930), p. 2; *WWM* 8.15 (July 18, 1931), p. 1; and *WWM* 8.24 (December 5, 1931), p. 4.
[398] *WWM* 8.24 (December 5, 1931), p. 4.
[399] *WWM* 8.21 (October 24, 1931), p. 3.
[400] *WWM* 1.20 (June 28, 1924), p. 1.
[401] *WWM* 2.13 (June 20, 1925), p. 3.

Preaching about WB at the occasion of the baptismal service was practiced, according to a report from Eleuthera, Bahamas: 'three followed the Lord in water baptism. We had a wonderful time at the beach. Brother Frank and Brother Hermis preached the baptismal service and it was wonderful.'[402]

Sermons were preached at baptismal services and were viewed as opportunities for evangelism since they attracted large crowds to observe and participate in baptismal services.[403]

While not explicitly mentioning rebaptism, a report from Morgan City, LA, implies that those who had been previously baptized in the Roman Catholic Church were rebaptized after conversion in a Pentecostal meeting: 'five Catholics were saved and baptized in water. You ought to have seen the people come to see the baptizing'.[404]

Meaning of Water Baptism

The *WWM* contains limited exposition on the meaning of WB. The most explicit elucidation is reflected in comments on Mk 1.1-11, which focuses on the baptism of Jesus. The author posits that WB is still essential and that the church should emphasize that everyone 'who is saved should be baptized as soon as convenient and not wait to get sanctified and filled with the Holy Ghost before they are baptized'. Water baptism has no salvific effect, but it is 'fulfilling righteousness' and the answer of a good conscience toward God. Simply put, the author asserts that 'water baptism is an outward sign of inward purity, and this should follow repentance'. It appears to be the case that the importance of WB is connected to being obedient to the command of Christ to be baptized. It is assumed that 'in every case where the individual gets real salvation there will be a longing for water baptism'.[405]

Following Christ in WB as an act of obedience finds further emphasis in the following exchange relative to the necessity of WB for salvation before one dies. In response to such an inquiry, the

---

[402] *WWM* 7.19 (September 27, 1930), p. 2.
[403] *WWM* 1.21 (July 12, 1924), p. 3; *WWM* 1.22 (July 26, 1924), p. 4; *WWM* 2.14 (July 4, 1925), p. 2; *WWM* 4.11 (May 21, 1927), p. 1; *WWM* 4.14 (July 2, 1927), p. 1; *WWM* 6.19 (October 12, 1929), p. 4; *WWM* 7.19 (September 27, 1930), p. 2; and *WWM* 8.21 (October 24, 1931), p. 3.
[404] *WWM* 1.22 (July 26, 1924), p. 4.
[405] *WWM* 1.21 (July 12, 1924), p. 2.

respondent offers an affirmative reply within specific parameters: 'Yes, a converted person can live right if he will. One would be saved if he dies provided he is saved before he dies and remains saved up to death.' Emphasizing that WB does not save a person, the author avers that 'it is so closely connected with salvation that everyone should be baptized'.[406] Similarly, obedience to Christ appears to inform the casuistry of two exchanges regarding WB and persons living in adultery.[407] In 1926 it was asked if a person living in adultery should be baptized? The response is conditional: 'Provided he forsakes the adultery which he evidently promises God he will do before he gets saved so he is eligible to baptism'.[408] The same question is answered again in 1930 with the same proviso: 'Provided he forsakes the adultery, which he evidently promises God he will do before he gets saved'.[409]

Finished Work Pentecostal Periodicals

Word and Witness

Introduction

The *Word and Witness* (*WW*), published by E.N. Bell, served as the first periodical of the Church of God in Christ (COGIC). At times it was referred to as COGIC [white] to distinguish it from Bishop Charles H. Mason's predominantly African American organization, which went by the same name. Most members of the COGIC (white) were located in the South and initially consisted of ministers who held credentials with Charles Parham's Apostolic Faith Movement. Sometime after mid-1907, this group of ministers left Parham to form their own organization. The new organization continued using the name Apostolic Faith Movement, and its periodical continued the name and enumeration of Parham's publication, *The Apostolic Faith*.

---

[406] *WWM* 4.11 (May 21, 1927), p. 2.

[407] The topic of divorce and remarriage received considerable attention in the Pentecostal movement. It was hotly debated in the COG as early as 1914 and continues to be a point of tension to the present day.

[408] *WWM* 3.16 (July 31, 1926), p. 3

[409] *WWM* 7.25 (December 20, 1930), pp. 2, 4.

In late 1910 or 1911, this group changed its name to the COGIC. In 1911 or 1912, Bell changed the name of the periodical to *WW*.[410]

In the December 20, 1913, issue of *WW*, Bell published 'the call' to Hot Springs, AR, which was an open invitation for Pentecostal ministers to attend the April 1914 founding convention of the AG USA. Delegates at the first General Council elected Bell to serve as chairman, and J.R. Flower was installed as the new editor of *WW*.[411] The *WW* became one of two official periodicals of the AG, along with the Christian Evangel (*CE*).

Later, the *CE* was renamed *Weekly Evangel* (*WE*).[412] The *WW* merged into the *WE* on January 1, 1916. From June 1, 1918, to October 4, 1919, *WE* appeared as the *CE*. The name of the organ was changed to the *Pentecostal Evangel* (*PE*) in 1919, with the first issue appearing on October 18, 1919.[413]

The Practice of Water Baptism

The *WW* emphasizes WB through various articles that assert the practice is an ordinance and to be practiced out of obedience to Jesus Christ. First, it is an ordinance of Christ:

> What is an ordinance? It is a LAW. It does not say you MAY, it is GOOD to do so or you OUGHT. It COMMANDS you. It says thou SHALT, and if you do not, some fine or penalty is attached.
>
> BAPTISM — In His final commission when Jesus commanded us to make disciples of all the nations we find the phrase, 'Baptizing them,' Mt. 28:19. The word also says, 'He gave COMMANDMENTS THROUGH HIS APOSTLES,' and He did. After the the [sic] Holy Ghost Even was received, the Apostle Peter

---

[410] W.E. Warner, 'Bell, Eudorus N.' in Stanley M. Burgess and Eduard M. van der Maas (eds.), *NIDPCM* (rev. and exp. edn; Grand Rapids, MI: Zondervan, 2002), p. 369; W.E. Warner, 'Church of God in Christ (White)' in Stanley M. Burgess and Eduard M. van der Maas (eds.), *NIDPCM* (rev. and exp. edn; Grand Rapids, MI: Zondervan, 2002), p. 537.

[411] *WW* 10.5 (May 20, 1914), p. 1. *WW* made official organ by General Council.

[412] *WW* 12.11 (November 1915), p. 4.

[413] *WW* 12.11 (November 1915), p. 3. An announcement that *WW* would be discontinued, effective January 1, 1916. *WW* was published in Malvern, AR, 1912-June 1914; Findlay, OH, July 1914-January 1915; and St. Louis, MO, February 1915-December 1915.

'COMMANDED them to be baptized.' Acts 10:48. So then Water Baptism is one of the ORDINANCES of Christ's Church.[414]

A sole report employs the language of 'the ordinance of baptism'.[415] One minister, writing from Portland, OR personalized the command of Christ 'to baptize' to the degree that he claimed it as the only authority he had to baptize: 'We have a large baptismal service … according to our Saviour's [sic] express command found in Mt. 28:19. This being the only authority I have to baptize the people, this is my commission which I gladly obey.'[416] As an ordinance of Christ, WB is, therefore, an ordinance of the Church: 'ORDINANCES of CHURCH. We believe in baptism-in being "buried through baptism" Rom. 6:4, just as Paul puts it.'[417]

The reception of WB at the hands of others finds expression with 'received water baptism'[418] and 'baptism was administered to'.[419] The phrase 'obeyed the Lord in water baptism' is employed to capture the sense that obedience to Christ's command to be baptized is of paramount importance.[420]

The importance of WB as an ordinance receives further attention by A.P. Collins in his article, 'Wise Above That Which Is Written' in the May 20, 1914, issue of the *WW*. Collins' rebuttal engages the assertions of 'Some mistaken preachers and would-be teachers [who] claim to have a revelation from the Holy Spirit that water baptism and the Lord's Supper are not to be observed any more'.[421] Citing NT evidence of WB occurring after the crucifixion of Christ, Collins asserts:

> How and when was the 'handwriting of ordinances that was contrary to us' blotted out? The same verse answers, 'Nailing it to the cross,' 2:14. Then it was by the crucifixion of Christ and done

---

[414] *WW* 9.6 (June 20, 1913), p. 2. Capitalized words appear in the original.
[415] *WW* 12.5 (May 1915), p. 8.
[416] *WW* 12.9 (September 1915), p. 7.
[417] *WW* 10.5 (May 20, 1914), p. 1; *WW* 12.9 (September 1915), p. 2. Capitalized words appear in the original.
[418] *WW* 10.7 (July 1914), p. 4; *WW* 12.5 (May 1915), p. 8.
[419] *WW* 12.5 (May 1915), p. 8.
[420] *WW* 9.11 (November 20, 1913), p. 2; *WW* 12.5 (May 1915), p. 7; and *WW* 12.8 (August 1915), p. 1.
[421] *WW* 10.5 (May 20, 1914), p. 3.

at the cross. This makes it absolutely certain that this 'handwriting of ordinances' was the writing in the law of Moses and the ordinances removed were those that existed BEFORE the cross, and not to water baptism and the supper which were commanded AFTER the crucifixion. He could not command to baptize after his resurrection, as he did, if his death had just removed water baptism.[422]

Width of Practice and Mode

The centrality of WB in the COGIC (white) is established through the numerous reports[423] of baptismal services held throughout the USA[424] and Canada, South America, Asia, and Africa.[425] The reports, as mentioned above, contain the exact numbers of those baptized during each baptismal service.

The accepted mode of WB appears to have been immersion.[426] A tentative assertion is offered due to the lack of a clear position statement regarding the mode of WB. Instead, the claim is proffered on the bases of direct references to immersion in the baptismal reports as well as the inferential language. More specifically,

---

[422] *WW* 10.5 (May 20, 1914), p. 3. Capitalized words appear in the original.

[423] *WW* 8.6 (August 20, 1912), p. 3; *WW* 8.8 (October 20, 1912), pp. 1, 2, and 3; *WW* 9.1 (January 20, 1913), p. 3; *WW* 9.2 (February 20, 1913), p. 3; *WW* 9.3 (March 20, 1913), p. 3; *WW* 9.5 (May 20, 1913), pp. 2, 3; *WW* 9.6 (June 20, 1913), pp. 1, 5, and 8; *WW* 9.7 (July 20, 1913), p. 1; *WW* 9.8 (August 20, 1913), pp. 1, 3; *WW* 9.9 (September 20, 1913), pp. 1, 3, and 4; *WW* 9.10 (October 20, 1913), pp. 2, 3; *WW* 9.11 (November 20, 1913), pp. 1, 2, 3, and 4; *WW* 9.12 (December 20, 1913), p. 3; *WW* 10.1 (January 20, 1914), pp. 1, 3; *WW* 10.3 (March 20, 1914), p. 1; *WW* 10.4 (April 20, 1914), pp. 3, 4; *WW* 10.5 (May 20, 1914), p. 3; *WW* 10.7 (July 1914), pp. 1, 2, and 4; *WW* 10.8 (August 1914), pp. 2, 3; *WW* 10.10 (October 1914), pp. 1, 2, and 4; *WW* 12.5 (May 1915), pp. 3, 7, and 8; *WW* 12.6 (June 1915), pp. 3, 5, 6, and 8; *WW* 12.7 (July 1915), pp. 1, 2, 3, 5, 6, and 7; *WW* 12.8 (August 1915), pp. 1, 3, 5, 7, and 8; *WW* 12.9 (September 1915), pp. 1, 2, 3, 4, 5, 6, 7, and 8; *WW* 12.10 (October 1915), pp. 1, 2, 5, 6, 7, and 8; and *WW* 12.11 (November 1915), pp. 3, 4, and 5.

[424] Please see Appendix N for a breakdown of the locations in the case of the USA. The sites are listed in alphabetical order according to state and city.

[425] Please see Appendix O for a breakdown of the locations according to the country. The sites are listed in alphabetical order according to country and city.

[426] *WW* 12.6 (June 1915), p. 2; *WW* 12.7 (July 1915), pp. 2, 3.

'immersed in water',[427] 'buried in water' or 'buried in baptism'[428] and 'followed the Lord in the watery grave of baptism'[429] all utilize burial language, inferring immersion as the accepted mode of baptism.

Lastly, review of the periodical reveals the expressions 'baptized in water' and 'baptizing in water' are the most frequently utilized by reporters.[430] The numerous references to 'in water' underscore the medium of baptism, water. When the general phrase 'in water' is not utilized in reports, a reference to a body of water is employed.[431] Specifically, the following bodies of water are cited with the apparent desire to communicate that sufficient water was present for complete immersion of the baptismal candidate: rivers,[432] nonspecific waters' edge,[433] and baptistries.[434] It appears that only two Pentecostal churches, one in Dallas, TX, and the other in St. Paul, MN, possessed

---

[427] *WW* 9.9 (September 20, 1913), p. 3; *WW* 9.11 (November 20, 1913), pp. 1, 3; *WW* 10.7 (July 1914), p. 1; *WW* 12.8 (August 1915), p. 3; and *WW* 12.9 (September 1915), pp. 3, 6.

[428] *WW* 9.8 (August 20, 1913), p. 3; *WW* 9.10 (October 20, 1913), p. 3; *WW* 9.11 (November 20, 1913), p. 4; *WW* 10.7 (July 1914), p. 2; *WW* 10.10 (October 1914), p. 4; *WW* 12.8 (August 1915), pp. 3, 7, and 8; and *WW* 12.10 (October 1915), p. 7.

[429] *WW* 9.5 (May 20, 1913), p. 3; *WW* 9.11 (November 20, 1913), p. 4.

[430] *WW* 8.6 (August 20, 1912), p. 3; *WW* 8.8 (October 20, 1912), pp. 1, 2, and 3; *WW* 9.1 (January 20, 1913), p. 3; *WW* 9.2 (February 20, 1913), p. 3; *WW* 9.3 (March 20, 1913), p. 3; *WW* 9.5 (May 20, 1913), pp. 2, 3; *WW* 9.6 (June 20, 1913), pp. 1, 5, and 8; *WW* 9.7 (July 20, 1913), p. 1; *WW* 9.8 (August 20, 1913), pp. 1, 3; *WW* 9.9 (September 20, 1913), pp. 1, 3, and 4; *WW* 9.10 (October 20, 1913), pp. 2, 3; *WW* 9.11 (November 20, 1913), pp. 1, 2, 3, and 4; *WW* 9.12 (December 20, 1913), p. 3; *WW* 10.1 (January 20, 1914), pp. 1, 3; *WW* 10.3 (March 20, 1914), p. 1; *WW* 10.4 (April 20, 1914), pp. 3, 4; *WW* 10.5 (May 20, 1914), p. 3; *WW* 10.7 (July 1914), pp. 1, 2, and 4; *WW* 10.8 (August 1914), pp. 2, 3; *WW* 10.10 (October 1914), pp. 1, 2, and 4; *WW* 12.5 (May 1915), pp. 3, 7, and 8; *WW* 12.6 (June 1915), pp. 3, 5, 6, and 8; *WW* 12.7 (July 1915), pp. 1, 2, 3, 5, 6, and 7; *WW* 12.8 (August 1915), pp. 1, 3, 5, 7, and 8; *WW* 12.9 (September 1915), pp. 1, 2, 3, 4, 5, 6, 7, and 8; *WW* 12.10 (October 1915), pp. 1, 2, 5, 6, 7, and 8; and *WW* 12.11 (November 1915), pp. 3, 4, and 5.

[431] See footnote 429 for references.

[432] *WW* 9.6 (June 20, 1913), p. 5; *WW* 10.1 (January 20, 1914), p. 1; *WW* 10.3 (March 20, 1914), p. 1; and *WW* 10.10 (October 1914), pp. 2 and 4; and *WW* 12.9 (September 1915), pp. 3, 6, and 7.

[433] *WW* 9.9 (September 20, 1913), p. 1; *WW* 12.9 (September 1915), p. 3.

[434] *WW* 9.8 (August 20, 1913), p. 3; *WW* 12.5 (May 1915), p. 3.

a baptistry during the era spanning 1912-1915. Other congregations were dependent on the availability of natural bodies of water.[435]

Authority and Requirements

The reception of WB at the hands of others finds expression by 'received water baptism'[436] and 'baptism was administered to'.[437] The phrase 'obeyed the Lord in water baptism'[438] is employed to capture the sense that obedience to Christ's command to be baptized is of paramount importance.

It appears to be the case that only ordained Elders were authorized to baptize candidates.

The editor provides insight relative to who may administer the ordinances of Christ by referencing a report from Pastor J.W. Bell, Panama City Canal Zone who reports that Jas. M. Parkinson of that same location has been 'disfellowshipped for disorderly conduct in assuming, without ordination or authority, and against the advice of the pastor, to administer baptism, the Lord's supper, etc'.[439]

While the ministry of women was valued within the movement, women were not authorized to administer the ordinances of WB and the Lord's Supper. The General Council meeting held in Hot Springs, AR, Apr 2 to 12, 1914 issued the following statement on 'Women in the Ministry':

> It was recommended that in view of the fact that the scriptures speak of women prophesying in the Gospel, (Acts 2:17) and as helpers to Paul in the same (Rom. 16:3) and that they are still a welcome force in the hands of God for advancing the kingdom – in view of these things it was resolved that we recommend to ministers and assemblies the right of [sic] women called of God, to be ordained, not as Elders with authority, but as evangelists of

---

[435] *WW* 8.8 (October 20, 1912), p. 3; *WW* 9.8 (August 20, 1913), p. 3; *WW* 9.9 (September 20, 1913), p. 3; *WW* 12.5 (May 1915), p. 3; and *WW* 12.11 (November 1915), p. 5.

[436] *WW* 10.7 (July 1914), p. 4; *WW* 12.5 (May 1915), p. 8.

[437] *WW* 12.5 (May 1915), p. 8.

[438] *WW* 9.11 (November 20, 1913), p. 2; *WW* 12.5 (May 1915), p. 7; and *WW* 12.8 (August 1915), p. 1.

[439] *WW* 10.7 (July 1914), p. 4.

missionaries, after being duly tried and approved according to the scriptures.[440]

The bias against granting women the same authority as men to administer the sacraments appears to reflect the society, culture, and attitudes of the day. The June 1915 *WW* reflects one business authority's attitude toward women in the following 'Notice to Women Missionaries':

> This is to request all the women home missionaries with credentials from the Assemblies of God, not to make applications for clergy rates over the railroads. Those who already have rates may keep them till personally asked to return their book. The Clergy Bureau has just definitely decided that they will not in new cases grant these women missionaries rates over the railroads, on the ground that these women do not receive a guaranteed salary … We are very sorry of this, but the Railroads make these rules and not ourselves. Let the women take notice of this, and trust God for full fare. This does not apply to men who are properly ordained nor to foreign women missionaries. – H.A. Goss, Hot Springs, AR.[441]

The mandated requirement for candidates presenting themselves for WB was repentance and faith in Jesus Christ.[442] Minimum age requirements for receiving baptism are not found in the *WW*. Similarly, there are no age limitations observed. One reporter provides the exact age of one candidate who was baptized in the Matagalpa River in Guatemala to emphasize the efficacy of the Gospel with the people, regardless of their age: 'We baptized a man yesterday who is over eighty years old. His dear old face lighted up with the glory of God as he was led into the water.'[443]

---

[440] *WW* 10.5 (May 20, 1914), p. 1.

[441] *WW* 12.6 (June 1915), p. 5. There appears to have been some sensitivity to the negative impact the notice would have on the affected women missionaries. The *WW* 12.9 (September 1915), p. 1 provides a notification that 'the sisters will be recognized' during the General Council meeting in St. Louis, MO from October 1 to 10.

[442] *WW* 9.10 (October 20, 1913), p. 2; *WW* 10.5 (May 20, 1914), pp. 2, 3; and *WW* 12.9 (September 1915), p. 2.

[443] *WW* 10.10 (October 1914), p. 4.

Baptismal Formula

It appears that prior to the 1913 California camp meeting declaration that WB was to occur 'in the name of Jesus only', there was no preferred formula to be utilized in WB.[444] It was not until the August 1915 issue of *WW* that reference to Mt. 28.19 is made about baptism. Even then, it is unclear if the reference to the verse focuses on the proper formula, or if it refers to the commission to baptize. Moreover, as the 'Jesus only' movement gained a following in the

---

[444] During a Pentecostal camp meeting in California, 1913, one of the participants, John G. Scheppe, experienced the power of the name of Jesus. Large numbers accepted his revelation, and they found support for their belief in 'Jesus Only' baptism in Jn 3.5 and Acts 2.38. This led to the denial of the doctrine of the Trinity and to the claim that Jesus is the sole Person in the Godhead. This controversy split the nascent Pentecostal group and led to the establishment of a new movement. The theological variances related to the disruption within the COGIC were two in number. First, the baptismal formula, 'in Jesus name only' vs. 'in the name of the Father, the Son, and the Holy Spirit'. Second, a trinitarian understanding of the nature of God vs a Modalistic Monarchianism view. It is beyond the scope of this study to explore the controversy in detail. Moreover, the debate has received detailed treatment in the following work: David A. Reed, *'In Jesus Name': The History and Beliefs of Oneness Pentecostals* (JPTSup 31; Blandford Forum: Deo, 2008). See the following numerous references for the arguments proffered by those in the COGIC (white): *WW* 12.5 (May 1915), p. 4; *WW* 12.5 (May 1915), pp. 2-3 'To Act in the Name of Another' by E.N. Bell; *WW* 12.6 (June 1915), pp. 2-3. 'The Sad New Issue: Over the Baptism Formula in the Name of Christ only. Is the Issue Really New? The New Claims in the Light of Historic Facts', *WW* 12.7 (July 1915), pp. 1-2. 'The "Acts" on Baptism in Christ's Name Only by E. N. Bell', *WW* 12.6 (June 1915), p. 1. 'Preliminary Statement on New Issue: Concerning the Principles Involved in the New Issue by the Presbytery', *WW* 12.6 (June 1915), p. 1. 'Editorial Explanation on Preliminary Statement Which Appears Above', *WW* 12.6 (June 1915), p. 4. 'A Statement. By the Presbytery', *WW* 12.7 (July 1915), pp. 3, 6. 'Scriptural Varieties of Baptismal Formula by E.N. Bell', *WW* 12.9 (September 1915), p. 5. *PE* 103 (August 14, 1915), p. 1. 'Who is Jesus Christ? Jesus Christ Being Exalted As The Jehovah Of The Old Testament And The True God of the New. A New Realization Of Christ As The Mighty God', *WW* 12.10 (October 1915), p. 1. 'There is Safety in Counsel' Editor E.N. Bell tells why He was baptized in the Name of the Lord Jesus Christ and shows the Necessity for the Brethren to meet together in General Council, *WW* 12.10 (October 1915), p. 4. 'A Statement by the Presbyters', and *WW* 12.10 (October 1915), p. 4. 'Personal Statement: For the Benefit of our readers we print below a Declaration of the Attitude of a number of Presbyters in regard to some matters which will come up for consideration at the approaching Council to be held in St. Louis, Mo., October 1st to 10.'

early COGIC, the leadership of the COGIC (white) responded with an irenic approach that resisted a dogmatic position on WB and sought to allow individual preference to prevail. This stance appears to have been motivated by the view that the General Council was not a denomination and had no legislative power. As the leaders of the COGIC (white) and the 'Jesus only' movement became more polarized, readers were informed via the *WW* in October 1915 of a forthcoming 'Declaration of the Attitude' regarding baptism. The clergy convening would consider the 'Declaration' in St. Louis, MO, October 1 to 10, 1915 that argued against 1. Declaring a baptism invalid based on the use/nonuse of a specified formula, 2. Rebaptism, and 3. Violating one's conscience regarding baptism/rebaptism.[445] The outcome of the General Council relative to WB is unclear from the existing issues of the *WW*. J.R. Flower was

---

[445] *WW* 12.10 (October 1915), p. 4. The four components of the 'Declaration of the Attitude' are:

> That the essential thing in Christian baptism is the burial, in obedience to the command of Christ, through baptism, of a person who has repented and believed, in water with Christ in the likeness of His death and resurrection (Acts 2.38; Rom, 6:3, 4); and that its validity should not be repudiated simply because of some slight variation in the formula repeated over him In the act; that the use, in connection with baptism, or any of the following passages of Scripture should be accepted: Mt. 28:19; Acts 2:38; 8:16; 10:48; or 19:5.
>
> That the Scriptures give no example of any one [sic], who has once had Christian baptism ever being re-baptized.
>
> That, therefore, re-baptizing of converts who have been once buried with Christ in baptism should be discouraged, and that ministers should respect, as a rule, such baptisms performed by their fellow ministers.
>
> That in the case of individual conscience, each minister or candidate should have full liberty to be personally baptized with any words he prefers, long as he stays within the Scriptures on the subject; and it is hereby understood that nothing herein said shall hinder any minister from dealing, as he sees best, with cases whose consciences are not satisfied with their former baptism, only he should not go into any congregation not under his care, except at the invitation of its pastor or those in rightful authority to extend such invitation, and that even when so invited it would be wrong to so emphasize anyone [sic] scriptural phrase on baptism above another scriptural phrase on the same subject as to lead saints by the wholesale, to believe any one set phrase to be repeated over the candidate is essential to Christian baptism. All division or strife over mere phrases, as that there should be a fixed or invariable formula, is wrong on both sides of the question; but this does not prevent anyone from setting forth his own conviction on this matter in the proper spirit and where authorized to do so.

announced as the new editor, and the *WW* was discontinued at the end of 1915.[446]

Pentecostal Worship and Witness

From Benton, AR to Shanghai, China, reports from the field provide informative descriptions of the baptismal services.[447] Regarding attendance, several articles report large crowds being present for the services. Typically, the reports employ the descriptors 'big, great, and large' to assess crowd size.[448] Numerical estimates of crowd size are provided on a few occasions, ranging from '300 or more being present'[449] at Vinson, MO to Ottumwa, IA, where 'Thousands of people from the city were in attendance, especially for the baptismal service in the afternoon'.[450]

A second descriptor in the reports concerns the worship atmosphere during and after the baptismal service. Numerous reports highlight the presence and power of God amid the worshipping community. The following phrases paint an inspiring portrait: The 'power of God was present in a mighty way';[451] 'The sweet presence of the Lord was with us all day';[452] 'the power fell';[453] 'The glory of the Lord came upon us';[454] 'the Spirit set His approval on the service by pouring forth at intervals a deluge of glory upon the saints';[455] 'blessed time and blessed service';[456] and 'the Lord

---

[446] *WW* 12.10 (October 1915), p. 4.

[447] *WW* 8.8 (October 20, 1912), p. 3; *WW* 9.2 (February 20, 1913), p. 3; *WW* 9.3 (March 20, 1913), p. 3; *WW* 9.5 (May 20, 1913), p. 3; *WW* 9.6 (June 20, 1913), pp. 1, 5; *WW* 9.9 (September 20, 1913), pp. 1, 3; *WW* 9.10 (October 20, 1913), p. 3; *WW* 10.7 (July 1914), pp. 1, 2; *WW* 12.8 (August 1915), pp. 1, 3, 7, and 8; *WW* 12.9 (September 1915), pp. 1, 3, 6, 7, and 8; and *WW* 12.10 (October 1915), pp. 3, 5, and 8.

[448] *WW* 8.8 (October 20, 1912), p. 3; *WW* 9.2 (February 20, 1913), p. 3; *WW* 9.9 (September 20, 1913), p. 3; *WW* 10.7 (July 1914), p. 1; and *WW* 12.8 (August 1915), p. 3.

[449] *WW* 12.8 (August 1915), p. 3.

[450] *WW* 8.8 (October 20, 1912), p. 3.

[451] *WW* 8.8 (October 20, 1912), p. 3; *WW* 12.8 (August 1915), p. 3.

[452] *WW* 12.8 (August 1915), p. 3.

[453] *WW* 9.10 (October 20, 1913), p. 3; *WW* 12.8 (August 1915), p. 1; and *WW* 12.9 (September 1915), pp. 1, 7.

[454] *WW* 10.10 (October 1914), p. 4.

[455] *WW* 12.8 (August 1915), p. 8.

[456] *WW* 9.9 (September 20, 1913), p. 1.

working with us, confirming the word with signs following'.[457] The 'signs following' included visions[458] and healings.[459] The presence and power of the HS stirred those present to worship with their entire being. Their worship was marked by 'shouting praises to God';[460] 'rejoicing';[461] 'dancing in the Spirit';[462] and 'talking in tongues'.[463] A report from South Africa captures several of the other descriptors:

> A man was slain under the power of the Spirit during the communion service and after a few hours arose speaking in tongues. He was from Ladybrand, O.F.S. and had seen in a vision the semi-circular motto 'Jesus Christ the same yesterday and today and forever.' and the Lord told him to come and be baptized in water and in the Holy Ghost. He really looked like a drunken man as he was looking at the motto and praising God in tongues. The fire fell in the evening and a young girl was baptized and her mother and sister were saved. Three others were under the power until midnight.[464]

The gathered worshipping communities also employed baptismal services as opportunities to 'give them the Gospel' by word and witness.[465] Similarly, the services bore witness to the reconciling ministry of Jesus Christ that compelled the redeemed to follow Christ in WB, thus, identifying with him through the symbolism of burial and resurrection.[466] In one instance, several persons attended a baptismal service unprepared to be baptized, and after witnessing the baptisms of others and feeling prompted by the HS, responded to

---

[457] *WW* 12.9 (September 1915), p. 3.

[458] *WW* 9.3 (March 20, 1913), p. 3; *WW* 9.6 (June 20, 1913), p. 5; and *WW* 12.9 (September 1915), p. 8.

[459] *WW* 12.8 (August 1915), p. 3; *WW* 12.10 (October 1915), pp. 5, 8.

[460] *WW* 9.3 (March 20, 1913), p. 3; *WW* 9.5 (May 20, 1913), p. 3; *WW* 9.8 (August 20, 1913), p. 3; *WW* 9.9 (September 20, 1913), p. 3; and *WW* 12.8 (August 1915), p. 1.

[461] *WW* 9.5 (May 20, 1913), p. 3; *WW* 10.7 (July 1914), p. 1; *WW* 12.9 (September 1915), p. 3; and *WW* 12.10 (October 1915), p. 5.

[462] *WW* 10.7 (July 1914), p. 1.

[463] *WW* 10.7 (July 1914), p. 1.

[464] *WW* 12.9 (September 1915), p. 8.

[465] *WW* 8.8 (October 20, 1912), p. 3; *WW* 10.7 (July 1914), p. 1; *WW* 10.10 (October 1914), p. 4; and *WW* 12.9 (September 1915), p. 2.

[466] *WW* 12.8 (August 1915), pp. 3, 5, 8; *WW* 12.10 (October 1915), p. 5.

the invitation to be baptized, since they had not previously followed Christ into the waters of baptism. W.O. Kim, reported from Pleasant View, AR that

> We had a baptismal service in water, according to Rom. 6:4, Sunday, Jun 13, at which 23 were buried with Him in baptism. At the beginning 14 were candidates for baptism and the Spirit set His approval on the service by pouring forth at intervals a deluge of glory upon the saints which was manifested by shouts of victory both in our natural tongues and in other tongues. After the fourteen were baptized, the invitation was extended to any child of God who was not baptized, and nine more came and the glory of the Lord witnessed to every heart.[467]

Commitment and Consequences

The reports from the field also document the ministers' commitment to baptizing persons requesting the same, regardless of the hardships or difficulties encountered by those commissioned to baptize. Ayad Abdel Malik provides the following account from Minya, Egypt:

> They sent for us to come baptize them. Yesterday Jesse Baker and I rode 4 hours on donkeys going there, and we baptized eleven. One of them was a WOMAN filled with the Spirit, the first woman in all Egypt in the Pentecostal work to be baptized in water.[468]

The commitment to WB was not one-sided. Rather, candidates endured harsh circumstances like illness and severe weather to follow Christ in WB. One writer, reporting the death of his sister, identifies her as his 'invalid sister, whom you saw in the invalid chair at the Hot Springs Convention. She was also baptized in water in her invalid chair, just a few months ago'.[469] Snow, cold water, and inclement weather failed to deter some candidates as the following account from Chelsea, MA attests:

> Last Sunday five followed the Lord in water baptism. The cold day and falling snow did not deter them from following the Lord. As

---

[467] *WW* 12.8 (August 1915), p. 8.
[468] *WW* 9.6 (June 20, 1913), p. 1.
[469] *WW* 10.10 (October 1914), p. 4.

the service was going on in the river, five white geese passed over their heads forming the shape of a cross. The power of the Spirit fell on one of the young ladies in the water who had the baptism and she had to be carried out. Three of the five who were baptized have been called into the work. After they came out of the water hands were layed on the three men who had not received the Spirit, in the name of the Lord for the reception of the Holy Ghost and one of them at once received the Spirit.[470]

Similarly, E.J. Emery reports from Wausau, WI, that he 'Had the privilege also of immersing two, having to break the ice to do so'.[471]

It seems that in addition to overcoming illness and bad weather to follow Christ in WB, some persons suffered severe repercussions for their faithfulness. This was especially true in India, according to Sister Denny, who provides the following account:

> Last Sunday 2 [sic] Hindu men of some prominence gave their hearts to Jesus, and expect to be baptized next Sunday. Water baptism is the real 'reproach of the cross' to these people. They don't care for one believing and confessing Christ, so long as he is not baptized, for until then they have a hope that he will come out alright, but when one is baptized before all the world, he is disgraced forever, and cast out at once. So a willingness to be baptized is the surest proof, in view of this fact, that God has really saved their souls.[472]

The Meaning of Water Baptism

In his editorial, E.N. Bell asserts, 'The most important thing under heaven is to get men saved from sin'.[473] Eschewing the teaching of sanctification as a second definite work of grace and championing the Finished Work position,[474] Bell avers the next step is the 'baptism in the Spirit' followed by 'the daily living of a holy life'.[475] In contrast to 'the delusions of the day and of modern backslidden Christianity

---

[470] *WW* 10.4 (April 20, 1914), p. 3.
[471] *WW* 9.12 (December 20, 1913), p. 3.
[472] *WW* 9.11 (November 20, 1913), p. 4.
[473] *WW* 8.6 (August 20, 1912), p. 2.
[474] Bell was not alone in affirming the Finished Work position. See *WW* 9.9 (September 20, 1913), p. 3; *WW* 10.4 (April 20, 1914), p. 4.
[475] *WW* 8.6 (August 20, 1912), p. 2.

is "joining the church" through some formal ceremony of man, just like they join lodges and the like',[476] Bell proffers that to join 'God's true church' a person 'must be "born from above," [and] must be by regeneration "created in Christ" (Eph. 2:10), and so "added unto the Lord" (Acts 11:24)'.[477]

For Bell, it is then that persons are to be in a 'likeness' or symbolically 'baptized into Christ' (Rom. 6.3) and so by God's ordained ceremony formally take on the name of Christ or Christian, just as in a marriage ceremony a woman takes on the name of the man she marries. Christ is our Bridegroom, and 'as a chaste virgin' we are espoused unto Christ (2 Cor. 11.2). Then 'by one Spirit,' better 'in one Spirit are we all baptized into one body (1 Cor. 12:13), which is the church' (Col. 1.24). No ceremony by man can put you into Christ or into his Church.[478]

J.R. Flowers echoes Bell when he contrasts WB with the Lord's Supper:

> Water baptism typifies the death, burial and resurrection of Christ, which is performed once for all, just as Christ died once for all and rose once for all. We die with Him in the likeness of His resurrection, and then go on to perfection. This is not to be repeated lest we put Christ to an open shame. He died and rose again once, and so we are planted into the likeness of His death and resurrection once. But the Lord's Supper is different. It typifies a continual partaking of the Life of Jesus though He had been slain freshly for us a continual sacrifice, freshly killed, for we need the fresh sacrifice to be made real to us continually, to cover us and protect us from the enemy.[479]

Water baptism, then, has no salvific effect, nor was it viewed sacramentally by Bell and Flowers. Noteworthy is the fact that references to Rom. 6.3-6 are not understood univocally to refer to WB. Contrary to Bell and Flowers, B.F. Lawrence, in an article

---

[476] *WW* 8.6 (August 20, 1912), p. 2.
[477] *WW* 8.6 (August 20, 1912), p. 2. Words in bold font appear in the original.
[478] *WW* 8.6 (August 20, 1912), p. 2; *WW* 9.8 (August 20, 1913), p. 3. Words in bold font appear in the original.
[479] *WW* 12.8 (August 1915), p. 5.

entitled 'Assembly of God' asserts that baptism in Rom. 6.3-6 refers to Spirit baptism:

> The baptism that is, baptism by the HS into the death, burial and resurrection of Jesus Christ; or, concretely expressed, 'into one body.' 1 Cor. 12:12-13; Rom. 6:3-6; Gal. 3:27. (Many Pentecostal preachers hold that 1 Cor. 12:13 refers to the baptism with the Holy Ghost. – Ed.)[480]

Pentecostal Testimony

Introduction

William H. Durham, of Chicago, IL, became pastor of Chicago's North Avenue Mission in 1901. Upon hearing of the outpouring of the HS at the Azusa Street Mission in Los Angeles, CA, Durham travelled to Azusa Street and received the baptism of HS on March 2, 1907. It appears to be the case that as a Baptist minister, Durham's theology was formed without the overt influence of the holiness and Pentecostal teaching of sanctification as a second definite work of grace.[481]

Recounting his early theological misgivings regarding sanctification as a second definite work and the recent clarity he had received from the HS concerning the matter, Durham avers that

> Soon the Spirit began to reveal in my heart the finished work of Christ on the Cross of Calvary, but it was so contrary to all that I had taught, and been taught, that I dared not admit, even to myself, that I could find nothing in the Word of God to establish the doctrine that sanctification was a definite, second work of grace. Still the Spirit kept revealing in my heart the precious Gospel as preached by the Apostles: identification with Jesus Christ in His death, burial and resurrection.[482]

At the 1910 Pentecostal convention in Chicago, IL, Durham delivered a message in which he sought to 'nullify the blessing of sanctification as a second definite work of grace' and debut his

---

[480] *WW* 10.5 (May 20, 1914), p. 3.
[481] R.M. Riss, 'Durham, William H.', in Stanley M. Burgess and Eduard M. van der Maas (eds.), *NIDPCM* (rev. and exp. edn; Grand Rapids, MI: Zondervan, 2002), pp. 594-95.
[482] *PT* 2.3 (June 1912), p. 14.

teaching, 'The Finished Work'. Durham asserted the 'finished work' of Christ on the cross, both objectively and subjectively, are made available to believers on the occasion of their justification. Moreover, Durham asserted the benefits of Calvary are available subjectively to appropriate over the course of one's life.[483]

The Practice of Water Baptism

While the primary thrust of Durham's *Pentecostal Testimony* focused on the 'Finished Work' teaching, he and his followers were attentive to the place and importance of WB in the *via salutis*.[484] Moreover, Durham asserted that WB was a requisite for a group to call itself a church. In the January 1912 issue of the *PT*, he states that from a Scriptural standpoint, a church 'is a company of people who are called out of the world, made new creatures in Christ Jesus, *buried with Him by baptism into death,* and filled with the Holy Spirit'.[485]

Durham's emphasis on WB is understandable given the fact that he considered the Lord's Supper and WB, symbols of God's grace, to be the only ordinances of the Church. He posits that, on the one hand, WB symbolizes being 'buried by baptism into His death' or 'getting into Christ'. On the other hand, in celebrating the Lord's supper, 'We commune of the body and blood of the Lord' which symbolizes 'our partaking of Christ, or of His coming into us'.[486]

Breadth of Practice and Mode

The *PT* contains baptismal reports from Columbus, OH; Chicago, IL; and Ottawa, Canada. The terms employed to report WB were

---

[483] Riss, 'Durham, William H.', pp. 594-95. According to D.A. Reed, 'Oneness Pentecostalism', in Stanley M. Burgess and Eduard M. van der Maas (eds.), *NIDPCM* (rev. and exp. edn; Grand Rapids, MI: Zondervan, 2002), pp. 936-44, Durham was attempting to shift from the pneumatological focus of the early Pentecostals with their multiple experiences to a Christological center. He desired to return to the 'simple gospel' that focused on the grace of God available through the atoning work of Christ.

[484] *PT* 1.5 (July 1, 1910), pp. 11, 15; *PT* 1.8 (1911), pp. 3-4; *PT* 2.1 (January 1912), pp. 11-12; and *PT* 2.3 (June 1912), p.16; See *PT* 1.8 (1911), pp. 3-4. 'I preach the finished work of Calvary, that we come into Christ and are fully saved in conversion, and that the next step is to be baptized in water, and then in the Holy Spirit'.

[485] *PT* 2.1 (January 1912), p. 13. Italics added.

[486] *PT* 1.5 (July 1, 1910), p. 15. Durham rejected anointing with oil, laying on of hands, and foot-washing as ordinances, while allowing they were Scriptural.

'baptized'[487] and 'immerse/immersion'.[488] Sparse in number, the reports provide the number baptized, the geographical site of the baptisms, and the names of the reporters. The number of persons baptized ran from 25 to 52. Durham estimated that in Chicago, IL over one thousand people had been baptized in a period of three years.[489]

Regarding the mode of baptism, Durham was clearly committed to 'the single immersion of the whole body of a believer in water'.[490] He stood in opposition to the teaching and practice of triune immersion where candidates were dipped or plunged beneath the water three times in accordance with the words of Jesus in Mt 28.19, baptizing converts 'Into the name of the Father and of the Son and of the Holy Ghost'. Durham posits that since WB represents a burial, a single immersion is sufficient. With tongue in cheek, he offers that 'No one is buried and dug up and buried over two or three times'.[491]

Authority and Requirements

The requirements for persons desiring to be baptized are clear and unequivocal. The requisites are identical to those periodicals previously reviewed, confession of sin, repentance, and faith in Jesus Christ.[492]

Relative to the question of authority to baptize, the *PT* provides no perspective. While the below statement on WB is used analogically to make a point regarding HS baptism, it avoids identifying the qualification of the 'administering agent'.

> Because, just as in water baptism the administering agent is a *person* and the element 'in' or 'with' water, so in the baptism in the Spirit, the Agent, the Baptizer, is Christ, and the element is 'in' or 'with'

---

[487] *PT* 1.5 (July 1, 1910), p. 15; *PT* 1.8 (1911), pp. 3, 5, and 6; *PT* 2.1 (January 1912), pp. 3, 11-12; *PT* 2.2 (1912), pp. 6, 7; and *PT* 2.3 (1912), pp. 3, 16.
[488] *PT* 1.5 (July 1, 1910), p. 15. *PT* 2.1 (January 1912), pp. 9-10; and *PT* 2.2 (1912), p. 7.
[489] *PT* 1.5 (July 1, 1910), p. 15.
[490] *PT* 1.5 (July 1, 1910), p. 15; *PT* 2.2 (1912), pp. 6, 7.
[491] *PT* 2.2 (May 1912), pp. 6-7.
[492] *PT* 1.8 (1911), pp. 2, 5-7; *PT* 2.2 (May 1912), pp. 6-7.

the Holy Spirit. It is when we are 'baptized with the Spirit' that we are 'sealed with the Spirit.'[493]

Baptismal Formula

Durham was unabashedly against baptism in the name of 'Jesus only'. In an article identifying false doctrines, he states that the 'Jesus only' teaching 'should be classed as false'. Citing the instructions of Jesus in Mt. 28.19, Durham opines that 'there is no conflict between this plain command and those passages in Acts where it is only mentioned that they were baptized into the Name of Jesus'.[494] Positively, he affirmed usage of the trinitarian formula when baptizing.[495]

Durham's position on the 'Jesus only' baptismal teaching appears to predate the 'revelation' of the 'truth' that occurred in 1913 in Oakland, CA and Conrad, AR. This suggests that the concept of the 'Jesus only' baptismal formula was circulating prior to the historic camp meetings. It is ironic that historians attribute the 'Finished Work' teaching of Durham as the hotbed for birthing the 'Jesus only' movement when he was an ardent opponent and the teaching predated 1913.

Pentecostal Worship and Witness

The *PT* provides a solitary record of Pentecostal worship and witness. The account asserts

> We had three baptismal services during the convention and altogether twenty-five were baptized in water. These were most beautiful services, indeed, as the power of the Spirit was much

---

[493] *PT* (March 1909), p. 12.

[494] *PT* 2.2 (May 1912), pp. 6-7. Durham also avers that 'One who is baptized into the Name of the Father, Son and HS is baptized into the Name of Jesus. The words of Jesus quoted above are sufficient for me'. The third 'false doctrine' opposed by Durham concerns the Trinity:

> One form of this teaching is to the effect that, as in Christ dwells all the fulness of the Godhead bodily, and as Christ is received when a man is saved, all who receive Christ at the same time receive the Holy Spirit. In other words they claim that it means one and the same thing to receive Christ, and to receive the Holy Spirit. This is a false interpretation of Scripture. The truth is, sinners receive Christ, and believers, and believers only, receive the Holy Spirit. Many of Us received the Blessed Christ and years later received the Holy Spirit.

[495] *PT* 2.2 (May 1912), pp. 6-7.

upon us and He witnessed that God was well pleased to have His children thus identify themselves with Christ in His burial and resurrection.[496]

The periodical provides but one descriptor of the service, beautiful. It lacks any description of Pentecostal worship, including the reactions of persons to the presence of the HS. This is a point of divergence from previously reviewed periodicals.

Commitment and Consequences

It seems to be the case that the identified commitment to receive WB was repentance, confession, and faith in Christ. Durham offers the connection between these acts with WB in the following statement:

> But the moment a man believes on Jesus Christ he is made a new creature. He passes out of death – the natural state of all men – into life, and life is actually imparted unto him. This makes him a candidate for water baptism, which is the only thing required of him between conversion and the baptism in the Holy Spirit.[497]

There are no accounts of persons receiving instruction to the meaning of WB prior to being baptized. Similarly, the available issues of the *PT* provide no reports of opposition to those baptized. It may be that Durham's message of the 'Finished Work' received the primary focus of the periodical and minimized other points of concern for researchers.

The Meaning of Water Baptism

Durham proffers that those who receive WB are symbolically baptized into the death of Christ and raised up to walk in newness of life with Jesus Christ. Identification with Jesus Christ, per Durham, 'is the plain teaching of this Scripture, We are dead with Christ, buried with Him, and raised up to walk in newness of life with Him'.[498]

---

[496] *PT* 2.1 (January 1912), pp. 11-12.
[497] *PT* 1.8 (1911), pp. 5-7.
[498] *PT* 2.1 (January 1912), p. 3.

Building on the concept of Federal Headship[499] with his focus on identification, Durham provides commentary on the substitutionary death of Christ where Christ is made a substitute for fallen humanity. Moreover, 'Christ has taken our place judicially, and died in our stead; so that in the eyes of the law we are dead, that is dead in the person of our substitute'.[500]

Positively speaking, Durham asserts that by immersion in water our identification with Christ also includes the resurrection of Jesus Christ, and the capacity to live by the power, guidance, and influence of the HS. Since believers are buried with Christ, they are raised up with him.[501] Consequently, believers are invited and challenged to live lives unto God through the HS.[502]

Pentecostal Evangel

Introduction

The *Pentecostal Evangel*, the weekly magazine of the AG USA, has been one of the prominent Pentecostal periodicals in the world. J. Roswell and Alice Flower started the publication in July 1913 as the *CE*, which served primarily a small regional Pentecostal network of churches,

---

[499] See *PT* 2.3 (June 1912), p. 6. Durham captures his understanding of Federal Headship in the following statement:

> The simple truth is that a sinner is identified with Adam. A believer is identified with Jesus Christ. No man is identified with Adam the first and Adam the second at the same time. A sinner is in Adam and Adam is in a sinner. A believer is in Christ and Christ is in a believer. A sinner is condemned in Adam. A believer is free from condemnation in Christ. A sinner has condemnation and a believer has peace. A man is not in Adam and Christ at the same time. Christ and Adam are not in a man at the same time. When Adam fell the old creation was dragged down with him. When Christ arose from the dead, the new creation came up with Him. A sinner is in the kingdom of darkness and sin. A believer is in the kingdom of Jesus Christ. Before conversion a man is in 'nature's darkness.' In conversion he is translated out of nature's darkness into the Kingdom of God's dear Son. It is in conversion that a man receives Jesus Christ, the glorious Son of God, and is made a new creature in Him, and old things pass away and all things become new. As these glorious truths grip our souls they put real strength in us, and we become established in our Blessed Lord and Savior, Jesus Christ. These are the real truths of the Gospel. The Spirit witnesses to them when they are preached. The signs follow when this Gospel is preached.

[500] *PT* 2.1 (January 1912), pp. 9-10.
[501] *PT* 2.1 (January 1912), pp. 9-10.
[502] *PT* 2.1 (January 1912), pp. 9-10.

known as the Association of Christian Assemblies. In April 1914, J. Roswell Flower helped to lead this network into the newly formed AG. He was elected to serve as the first secretary and gave the *CE* to the AG, just as E.N. Bell (the first chairman) also gave his periodical, *WW*, to the Fellowship.

The first issue (July 19, 1913) of the *CE* featured interracial content (three articles were by or about Garfield T. Haywood, the African American pastor of the largest Pentecostal congregation in Indianapolis). The first masthead read, 'The simplicity of the gospel, in the bonds of peace, the unity of the spirit, till we all come to the unity of the faith'. This language, which affirmed the possibility of spiritual unity despite a lack of unity of the faith, found its way into the preamble of the organizational document of the AG.

Publishing the *CE* weekly was quite an undertaking. The name was changed to the *WE* in 1915, drawing attention to this fact. On January 1, 1916, *WW* merged into the *WE*. The title changed back to *CE* in 1918 becoming a biweekly publication. In 1919 the current title, *PE*, was adopted. The magazine returned to a weekly publication in 1923.

The *PE*, particularly in its earlier decades, was a rich source of theological essays, news articles, missionary letters, and revival reports. The *PE* is one of the essential primary sources for the study of the AG and the broader Pentecostal movement.

The Practice of Water Baptism

The various iterations of the *PE*[503] accentuate WB and contend the practice is an ordinance to be practiced out of obedience to Jesus Christ. The first mention of baptism as an ordinance is in the October 26, 1913 issue of the *PE* where a report from Milwaukee, WI, recounts that 'Bro. (John G.) Lake preached a fine message on the ordinances of baptism and the Lord's Supper'.[504] In the November 27, 1915 issue of the *PE* WB and the Lord's Supper are both identified as the ordinances of the Church.[505]

---

[503] To maintain a sense of chronology and continuity the *Christian Evangel*, the *Weekly Evangel* will be subsumed under the *Pentecostal Evangel*.
[504] *PE* (October 26, 1913), p. 8.
[505] *PE* 117 (November 27, 1915), p. 3.

Given some of the questions submitted to the *PE* for clarification, it seems to be the case that the necessity of WB was called into question on the field. In the May 6, 1916, issue, inquiry 52 is posed: 'Now that Christ has come does this do away with baptism in water? Some tell us the ordinances were to be observed only 'till He come,' and since He has come they are done away now'.[506] The respondent employs the occasion as an opportunity to clarify and provide instruction:

> Ans. This Is Ignorance or false teaching. True it is we are to do these things 'till He comes;' but He has not come yet in the sense here meant. He had already come in the Spirit on the day of Pentecost when Paul in 1 Cor. 11:26, says by partaking of the supper we 'show forth the Lord's death till He come.' If this 'coming' referred to the outpouring of the Spirit, why would Paul, 20 years after this outpouring, still enjoin the keeping of the ordinances 'till He come,' which was still future? Nay, this coming is the personal second coming of our Lord, and since this has not yet taken place, it is our duty still to baptize in water and to observe the Lord's Supper.[507]

Controversy regarding the baptismal formula and the nature of the Godhead continued to polarize laity and clergy and the leadership of the AG crafted the Fundamental Truths in an attempt to distinguish their identity from the adherents of the 'Jesus Only' teachings. The General Council of the AG in October 1916, approved a statement of Fundamental Truths with the following proviso:

> This statement of Fundamental Truths is not intended as a creed for the Church, nor as a basis of fellowship among Christians, but only as a basis of unity for the ministry alone (i.e., that we all speak the same thing, I Cor. 1:10; Acts 2:42). The human phraseology employed in such a statement is not inspired nor contended for, but the truth set forth in such phraseology is held to be essential to a full Gospel ministry.[508]

---

[506] *PE* 138 (May 6, 1916), p. 8.
[507] *PE* 138 (May 6, 1916), p. 8; *PE* 161 (October 21, 1916), p. 4.
[508] *PE* 170 (December 23, 1916), p. 8.

Concerning WB, the General Council clearly established it as an ordinance:

> The Ordinance by a burial with Christ should be observed as commanded in the Scriptures, by all who have really repented and in their hearts have truly believed on Christ as Saviour and Lord. In doing so, they have the body washed in pure water as an outward symbol of cleansing, while their heart has already been sprinkled with the blood of Christ as an inner cleansing. Thus they declare to the world that they have died with Jesus and that they have also been raised with Him to walk in newness of life. Matth. [sic] 28:19; Acts 10:47-48; Rom. 6:4; Acts 20:21; Heb.10:22.[509]

Periodically, questions were submitted regarding the ordinances of the Church. It is unclear if the inquiries were asked and answered to provide instruction, posed to settle a dispute regarding foot washing, or published to refute false teaching. Regardless of the reason, the AG maintained a consistent position on the NT ordinances. According to an exchange in the July 22, 1922, issue of the *PE*, the answer to a question regarding the ordinances of the Church is 'Water Baptism and the Lord's Supper'. The respondent then addresses an unarticulated question on whether foot-washing is an ordinance. The editor argues the position that foot-washing is an example, not an ordinance because it was not 'commanded'.[510]

In addition to being recognized as an ordinance, WB holds a critical place in the *via salutis*. In response to questions from the field regarding the order of reconciliation with God through Jesus Christ, the following answer is provided:

> The normal order is repentance, faith and baptism in water; them [sic] to receive the Spirit. This should be the order taught where God gives a chance so to teach and seek. But God has a right to baptize them with the Spirit any time He sees fit, as He did at the house of Cornelius. Many, soundly repentant, may and will at once receive the Spirit, if exhorted to look up and believe. If one can get saved and filled with the Spirit in the same service, I would not discourage him, but encourage him to do so. But any sinner who

---

[509] *PE* 170 (December 23, 1916), p. 8.
[510] *PE* 454/455 (July 22, 1922), p. 8.

repents and accepts Christ as Savior and does not receive the Spirit in the same service, should, if possible, be baptized in water before the next service, then prayed for to receive the Spirit and kept pressing on until he does receive.[511]

Breadth of Practice and Mode

The importance of WB in the fellowships that amalgamated to become the newly formed AG is confirmed through the scores of reports of baptismal services held throughout South America, Asia, Africa, Canada, and the USA. The reports contain the location and a precise number of those baptized during each baptismal service.[512] A review of the periodical reveals that the following expressions were used interchangeably and most frequently to report baptisms: 'baptized', 'baptized in water', and 'baptizing'.[513]

According to the *PE*, the accepted mode of WB seems to have been total immersion. The official stance on the mode of baptism is confirmed through the following means: the 'Question and Answer' forum,[514] various articles[515] in the organ, and the phrases employed in reports from the field. Regarding the last point, a broad array of phrases is utilized to describe the baptismal events reported in the *PE*. The phrase 'immersed in water'[516] explicitly points to immersion. Similarly, burial language implies total immersion. Specifically, 'buried

---

[511] *PE* 96 (June 26, 1915), p. 3; *PE* 161 (October 21, 1916), p. 4; *PE* 210 (October 13, 1917), p. 7; *PE* 262/263 (November 16, 1918), p. 5; and *PE* 306/307 (September 20, 1919), p. 9.

[512] See Appendix P for a complete list of references to WB in the *PE*.

[513] See Appendix Q for a complete list of references to 'baptized', 'baptized in water', and 'baptizing' in the *PE*.

[514] *PE* 181 (March 17, 1917), p. 9; *PE* 308/309 (October 4, 1919), p. 5; *PE* 324/325 (January 24, 1920), p. 5; and *PE* 348/349 (July 10, 1920), pp. 6-7.

[515] *PE* 83 (March 27, 1915), pp. 1, 3; *PE* 306/307 (September 20, 1919), p. 9; *PE* 520 (November 3, 1923), p. 3; and *PE* 889 (March 14, 1931), pp. 1, 9. Also, see *PE* 660 (August 14, 1926), p. 4, where A.H. Argue provides support of immersion by citing the works of the Justin Martyr and Athenagoras.

[516] See Appendix R for a complete list of references to immersion in the *PE*.

in baptism',[517] 'buried in water' or 'buried in the waters of baptism',[518] 'buried by baptism',[519] 'buried in the watery grave' and 'baptized in the water grave',[520] 'buried them in water baptism',[521] and 'buried beneath the waters of baptism',[522] all employ burial language that portrays baptism by immersion as the only plausible explanation. Additionally, burial language is coupled with identification with the person of Jesus Christ and his death and resurrection as the focus and meaning of WB is emphasized: 'Buried with Christ in baptism',[523] 'buried with Christ in the water',[524] 'baptized' or 'buried with our

---

[517] *PE* 464/465 (September 30, 1922), p. 11; *PE* 466/467 (October 14, 1922), p. 8; *PE* 597 (May 16, 1925), p. 12; *PE* 619 (October 24, 1925), p. 17; *PE* 721 (November 5, 1927), p. 10; *PE* 829 (January 4, 1930), p. 13; *PE* 871 (November 1, 1930), p. 12; and *PE* 891 (March 28, 1931), p. 11.

[518] *PE* 567 (October 11, 1924), p. 12; *PE* 580 (January 17, 1925), p. 9; *PE* 601 (June 13, 1925), p. 13; *PE* 669 (October 23, 1926), p. 9; *PE* 730 (January 14, 1928), p. 13; *PE* 742 (April 7, 1928), p. 12; *PE* 756 (July 21, 1928), p. 12; *PE* 767 (October 6, 1928), p. 12; *PE* 779 (January 5, 1929), p. 11; *PE* 803 (June 22, 1929), p. 12; *PE* 822 (November 9, 1929), p. 12; and *PE* 832 (January 25, 1930), p. 12.

[519] *PE* 464/465 (September 30, 1922), p. 11; *PE* 466/467 (October 14, 1922), p. 8; *PE* 597 (May 16, 1925), p. 12; *PE* 619 (October 24, 1925), p. 17; *PE* 721 (November 5, 1927), p. 10; *PE* 829 (January 4, 1930), p. 13; *PE* 871 (November 1, 1930), p. 12; and *PE* 891 (March 28, 1931), p. 11.

[520] *PE* 288/289 (May 17, 1919), p. 7; *PE* 422/423 (December 10, 1921), p. 28; *PE* 488/489 (March 17, 1923), p. 14; *PE* 904 (June 27, 1931), p. 19; and *PE* 926 (December 5, 1931), p. 19.

[521] *PE* 292/293 (June 14, 1919), p. 9; *PE* 298/299 (July 26, 1919), p. 10; *PE* 310/311 (October 18, 1919), p. 14; *PE* 338/339 (May 1, 1920), p. 13; *PE* 350/351 (July 24, 1920), p. 14; *PE* 478/479 (January 6, 1923), p. 10; *PE* 495 (May 5, 1923), p. 14; *PE* 521 (November 10, 1923), p. 13; *PE* 568 (October 18, 1924), p. 12; *PE* 571 (November 8, 1924), p. 12; *PE* 614 (September 12, 1925), p. 12; *PE* 615 (September 19, 1925), p. 13; *PE* 616 (September 26, 1925), p. 12; *PE* 632 (January 30, 1926), p. 10; *PE* 655 (July 10, 1926), p. 20; *PE* 662 (August 28, 1926), p. 14; *PE* 856 (July 12, 1930), p. 11; and *PE* 910 (August 8, 1931), p. 12.

[522] *PE* 513 (September 8, 1923), p. 15.

[523] *PE* 2.19 (May 9, 1914), p. 6; *PE* 49 (July 11, 1914), p. 3; and *PE* 50 (July 18, 1914), p. 3.

[524] See Appendix S for a complete list of references to 'buried with Christ in the water' in the *PE*.

Lord',[525] 'followed the Lord in the watery grave of baptism',[526] 'buried with Jesus in water baptism',[527] 'buried with the Lord Jesus',[528] 'buried into His death',[529] 'buried with Christ in the watery grave',[530] 'buried with Christ in water' or 'buried with Christ',[531] 'buried with our Lord in the liquid grave',[532] 'buried with the Master in water baptism',[533] 'buried with our Lord by baptism',[534] 'buried as in Romans 6:4',[535] 'buried into the likeness of His death',[536] 'buried with the Lord in water',[537] 'buried into death with Christ by baptism',[538] 'baptized' or 'buried' with Christ in immersion',[539] and 'we buried them in the waters of a running brook in the likeness of the death'.[540]

Several phrases were employed to reflect converts' obedience to Christ's command to be baptized and follow him: 'followed the Lord' and 'followed Christ' in baptism',[541] 'followed their Lord in this

---

[525] *PE* 312/313 (November 1, 1919), p. 23; *PE* 452/453 (July 8, 1922), p. 4; *PE* 661 (August 21, 1926), p. 10; *PE* 916 (September 26, 1931), p. 8; and *PE* 669 (October 23, 1926), p. 8.

[526] *PE* 901 (June 6, 1931), p. 13; *PE* 911 (August 15, 1931), p. 13; and *PE* 918 (October 10, 1931), p. 15.

[527] *PE* 585 (February 21, 1925), p. 13.

[528] *PE* 861 (August 16, 1930), p. 9; *PE* 915 (September 12, 1931), pp. 15, 16

[529] *PE* 595 (May 2, 1925), p. 13.

[530] *PE* 508 (August 4, 1923), p. 13; *PE* 868 (October 11, 1930), p. 11; *PE* 870 (October 25, 1930), p. 12; *PE* 880 (January 10, 1931), p. 12; *PE* 916 (September 26, 1931), p. 16; and *PE* 917 (October 3, 1931), p. 18.

[531] *PE* 559 (August 16, 1924), p. 7; *PE* 566 (October 4, 1924), p. 12; *PE* 590 (March 28, 1925), p. 13; *PE* 607 (July 26, 1925), p. 12; *PE* 610 (August 15, 1925), p. 11; *PE* 640 (March 27, 1926), p. 10; *PE* 656 (July 17, 1926), p. 12; *PE* 687 (March 5, 1927), p. 19; *PE* 720 (October 29, 1927), p. 20; *PE* 816 (September 21, 1929), p. 12; *PE* 900 (May 30, 1931), p. 12; and *PE* 912 (August 22, 1931), p. 13.

[532] *PE* 759 (August 11, 1928), p. 12. *PE* 758 (August 4, 1928), p. 12.

[533] *PE* 758 (August 4, 1928), p. 12.

[534] *PE* 530 (January 19, 1924), p. 13; *PE* 536 (March 8, 1924), p. 13.

[535] *PE* 49 (July 11, 1914), p. 3.

[536] *PE* 506 (July 21, 1923), p. 10.

[537] *PE* 572 (November 15, 1924), p. 12.

[538] *PE* 584 (February 14, 1925), p. 12.

[539] *PE* 868 (October 11, 1930), p. 12; *PE* 920 (October 24, 1931), p. 14.

[540] *PE* 755 (July 7, 1928), p. 15.

[541] *PE* 905 (July 4, 1931), p. 12; *PE* 906 (July 11, 1931), p. 12; *PE* 915 (September 12, 1931), p. 15; *PE* 916 (September 26, 1931), pp. 6, 8, 15, and 16; *PE* 917 (October 3, 1931), pp. 16, 17, and 18; *PE* 918 (October 10, 1931), p. 16, 18; *PE* 919 (October

way',[542] 'followed the Master',[543] 'followed Jesus in water baptism',[544] 'followed the Saviour in baptism',[545] 'obeying the Lord in fulfilling all righteousness',[546] 'obeyed the Lord in water baptism',[547] 'witnessed their faith by Christian baptism',[548] 'went through the water',[549] 'buried in Christian baptism',[550] and 'followed the Lord in Christian baptism' or 'received Christian baptism'.[551]

The numerous references to 'in water' underscore the medium of baptism, water. When the general phrase 'in water' is not utilized in reports, a reference to a body of water is employed. Specifically, the following bodies of water are cited with the apparent desire to communicate that sufficient water was present for total immersion of candidates: brooks,[552] the waters' edge,[553] varying

---

17, 1931), pp. 16, 17, and 18; *PE* 920 (October 24, 1931), p. 13; *PE* 921 (October 31, 1931), pp. 16, 17; *PE* 922 (November 7, 1931), p. 16; *PE* 923 (November 14, 1931), pp. 16, 17; *PE* 925 (November 28, 1931), pp. 17, 20; and *PE* 926 (December 5, 1931), p. 20.

[542] *PE* 922 (November 7, 1931), p. 16.
[543] *PE* 911 (August 15, 1931), p. 13.
[544] *PE* 912 (August 22, 1931), p. 10.
[545] *PE* 919 (October 17, 1931), p. 16.
[546] *PE* 64 (October 24, 1914), p. 2.
[547] *PE* 914 (September 5, 1931), p. 16; *PE* 916 (September 26, 1931), p. 16.
[548] *PE* 925 (November 28, 1931), p. 19.
[549] *PE* 549 (June 7, 1924), p. 13.
[550] *PE* 896 (May 2, 1931), p. 12; *PE* 900 (May 30, 1931), p. 12; and *PE* 923 (November 14, 1931), p. 16.
[551] *PE* 900 (May 30, 1931), p. 12; *PE* 901 (June 6, 1931), pp. 12, 13; *PE* 902 (June 13, 1931), p. 16; *PE* 903 (June 20, 1931), pp. 12, 13; *PE* 904 (June 27, 1931), pp. 19, 20, and 21; *PE* 905 (July 4, 1931), p. 12; *PE* 906 (July 11, 1931), pp. 12, 13; *PE* 907 (July 18, 1931), p. 12; *PE* 908 (July 25, 1931), pp. 11, 12; *PE* 909 (August 1, 1931), pp. 10, 11; *PE* 910 (August 8, 1931), p. 12; *PE* 911 (August 15, 1931), p. 12; *PE* 912 (August 22, 1931), pp. 11, 12; *PE* 913 (August 29, 1931), p. 9; *PE* 916 (September 26, 1931), p. 15; *PE* 916 (September 26, 1931), p. 17; *PE* 918 (October 10, 1931), p. 16, 18; *PE* 920 (October 24, 1931), p. 15; *PE* 921 (October 31, 1931), p. 13; *PE* 923 (November 14, 1931), pp. 16, 17; *PE* 924 (November 21, 1931), p. 18; *PE* 925 (November 28, 1931), pp. 20, 21; and *PE* 927 (December 12, 1931), p. 12.
[552] *PE* 630 (January 16, 1926), p. 10; *PE* 755 (July 7, 1928), p. 15.
[553] *PE* 657 (July 24, 1926), p. 13; *PE* 659 (August 7, 1926), p. 12; *PE* 665 (September 18, 1926), p. 14; *PE* 667 (October 2, 1926), p. 13; *PE* 713 (September 3, 1927), p. 12; *PE* 729 (January 7, 1928), p. 11; *PE* 858 (July 26, 1930), p. 13; *PE* 860 (August 9, 1930), p. 12; *PE* 870 (October 25, 1930), p. 12; *PE* 910 (August 8, 1931), p. 12; and *PE* 916 (September 26, 1931), p. 17.

oceans,[554] riverbank and riverside,[555] Puget Sound,[556] stream,[557] creeks;[558] diverse seas;[559] various lakes;[560] assorted rivers;[561] and baptistries.[562]

---

[554] *PE* 240/241 (May 18, 1918), p. 14; *PE* 244/245 (June 15, 1918), p. 16; *PE* 330/331 (March 6, 1920), p. 13; *PE* 332/333 (March 20, 1920), p. 14; *PE* 493 (April 21, 1923), p. 10; and *PE* 604 (July 4, 1925), p. 13.

[555] *PE* 165 (November 18, 1916), p. 12; *PE* 248/249 (July 27, 1918), p. 10; *PE* 474/475 (December 9, 1922), p. 10; *PE* 614 (September 12, 1925), p. 12; and *PE* 860 (August 9, 1930), p. 12.

[556] *PE* 57 (September 5, 1914), p. 1.

[557] *PE* 286/287 (May 3, 1919), p. 14; *PE* 575 (December 6, 1924), p. 13; *PE* 640 (March 27, 1926), p. 10; *PE* 759 (August 11, 1928), p. 3; and *PE* 855 (July 5, 1930), p. 11.

[558] *PE* 124 (January 22, 1916), p. 16; *PE* 145 (June 24, 1916), p. 15; *PE* 150 (July 29, 1916), p. 14; *PE* 181 (March 17, 1917), p. 16; *PE* 197 (July 7, 1917), p. 14; *PE* 242/243 (June 1, 1918), p. 14; *PE* 342/343 (May 29, 1920), p. 14; *PE* 452/453 (July 8, 1922), p. 9; *PE* 452/453 (July 8, 1922), p. 14; *PE* 494 (April 28, 1923), p. 10; *PE* 497 (May 19, 1923), p. 14; *PE* 500 (June 9, 1923), p. 10; *PE* 502 (June 23, 1923), p. 10; *PE* 575 (December 6, 1924), p. 12; *PE* 584 (February 14, 1925), p. 12; *PE* 607 (July 26, 1925), p. 12; *PE* 615 (September 19, 1925), p. 12; *PE* 621 (November 7, 1925), p. 12; *PE* 628 (January 2, 1926), p. 6; *PE* 629 (January 9, 1926), p. 12; *PE* 653 (June 26, 1926), p. 12; *PE* 661 (August 21, 1926), p. 13; *PE* 788 (March 9, 1929), p. 11; *PE* 869 (October 18, 1930), p. 13; *PE* 877 (December 13, 1930), p. 12; and *PE* 911 (August 15, 1931), p. 13.

[559] *PE* 51 (July 25, 1914), p. 4; *PE* 240/241 (May 18, 1918), p. 11; *PE* 296/297 (July 12, 1919), p. 11; *PE* 388/389 (April 16, 1921), p. 13; *PE* 428/429 (January 21, 1922), p. 13; *PE* 434/435 (March 4, 1922), p. 13; *PE* 454/455 (July 22, 1922), p. 13; *PE* 551 (June 21, 1924), p. 9; *PE* 561 (August 30, 1924), p. 14; *PE* 612 (August 29, 1925), p. 10; *PE* 654 (July 3, 1926), p. 10; *PE* 658 (July 31, 1926), p. 11; *PE* 780 (January 12, 1929), p. 10; *PE* 795 (April 27, 1929), p. 10; *PE* 810 (August 10, 1929), p. 6; *PE* 821 (November 2, 1929), pp. 10-11; *PE* 842 (April 5, 1930), p. 13; and *PE* 856 (July 12, 1930), p. 11.

[560] *PE* 55 (August 22, 1914), p. 3; *PE* 102 (August 7, 1915), p. 1; *PE* 107 (September 11, 1915), p. 1; *PE* 132 (March 25, 1916), p. 14; *PE* 139 (May 13, 1916), pp. 14, 15; *PE* 146/147 (July 8, 1916), p. 11; *PE* 200 (July 28, 1917), p. 14; *PE* 258/259 (October 19, 1918), p. 1; *PE* 302/303 (August 23, 1919), p. 14; *PE* 412/413 (October 1, 1921), p. 15; *PE* 452/453 (July 8, 1922), p. 14; *PE* 464/465 (September 30, 1922), p. 11; *PE* 498 (May 26, 1923), p. 10; *PE* 513 (September 8, 1923), p. 15; PE 542 (April 12, 1924), p. 14; *PE* 559 (August 16, 1924), p. 9; *PE* 605 (July 11, 1925), p. 12; *PE* 619 (October 24, 1925), p. 16; *PE* 669 (October 23, 1926), pp. 5, 9, and 12; *PE* 712 (August 27, 1927), p. 12; *PE* 728 (December 24, 1927), p. 10; *PE* 735 (February 18, 1928), p. 3; *PE* 759 (August 11, 1928), p. 3; *PE* 816 (September

21, 1929), p. 12; *PE* 865 (September 13, 1930), p. 12; *PE* 873 (November 15, 1930), p. 16; *PE* 899 (May 23, 1931), p. 12; and *PE* 914 (September 5, 1931), p. 7.

⁵⁶¹ *PE* 66 (November 7, 1914), p. 4; *PE* 90 (May 15, 1915), p. 1; *PE* 103 (August 14, 1915), p. 4; *PE* 104 (August 21, 1915), p. 3; *PE* 106 (September 4, 1915), p. 3; *PE* 123 (January 15, 1916), p. 13; *PE* 131 (March 18, 1916), p. 14; *PE* 139 (May 13, 1916), p. 12; *PE* 148 (July 15, 1916), p. 15; *PE* 163 (November 4, 1916), p. 8; *PE* 198 (July 14, 1917), p. 14; *PE* 199 (July 21, 1917), p. 14; *PE* 204 (August 25, 1917), p. 12; *PE* 211 (October 20, 1917), p. 14; *PE* 212 (October 27, 1917), pp. 2, 3; *PE* 216 (November 24, 1917), p. 14; *PE* 224 (January 26, 1918), p. 10; *PE* 238/239 (May 4, 1918), p. 9; *PE* 246/247 (June 29, 1918), p. 11; *PE* 252/253 (August 24, 1918), pp. 14, 15; *PE* 254 (September 7, 1918), p. 5; *PE* 256/257 (October 5, 1918), pp. 1, 14; *PE* 270/271 (January 11, 1919), p. 1; *PE* 280/281 (March 22, 1919), p. 10; *PE* 288/289 (May 17, 1919), p. 14; *PE* 292/293 (June 14, 1919), p. 14; *PE* 304/305 (September 6, 1919), pp. 10, 14; *PE* 308/309 (October 4, 1919), p. 12; *PE* 312/313 (November 1, 1919), p. 23; *PE* 326/327 (February 7, 1920), p. 13; *PE* 334/335 (April 13, 1920), p. 14; *PE* 340/341 (May 15, 1920), p. 14; *PE* 346/347 (June 26, 1920), p. 13; *PE* 356/357 (September 4, 1920), pp. 9, 14; *PE* 392/393 (May 14, 1921), p. 9; *PE* 396/397 (June 11, 1921), p. 13; *PE* 408/409 (September 3, 1921), p. 15; *PE* 410/411 (September 17, 1921), p. 15; *PE* 414/415 (October 15, 1921), p. 12; *PE* 414/415 (October 15, 1921), p. 12; *PE* 442/443 (April 29, 1922), p. 21; *PE* 458/459 (August 19, 1922), p. 13; *PE* 472/473 (November 25, 1922), p. 27; *PE* 476/477 (December 23, 1922), p. 14; *PE* 478/479 (January 6, 1923), p. 12; *PE* 502 (June 23, 1923), p. 11; *PE* 512 (September 1, 1923), p. 11; *PE* 517 (October 13, 1923), p. 11; *PE* 550 (June 14, 1924), p. 13; *PE* 551 (June 21, 1924), p. 12; *PE* 552 (June 28, 1924), p. 9; *PE* 557 (August 2, 1924), p. 13; *PE* 559 (August 16, 1924), p. 11; *PE* 563 (September 13, 1924), p. 12; *PE* 566 (October 4, 1924), pp. 9, 11, and 12; *PE* 567 (October 11, 1924), p. 14; *PE* 570 (November 1, 1924), p. 12; *PE* 571 (November 8, 1924), p. 13; *PE* 572 (November 15, 1924), p. 9; *PE* 580 (January 17, 1925), pp. 9, 12; *PE* 596 (May 9, 1925), p. 12; *PE* 598 (May 23, 1925), p. 12; *PE* 603 (June 27, 1925), p. 13; *PE* 604 (July 4, 1925), p. 13; *PE* 608 (August 1, 1925), p. 10; *PE* 609 (August 8, 1925), p. 9; *PE* 610 (August 15, 1925), p. 12; *PE* 614 (September 12, 1925), p. 11; *PE* 615 (September 19, 1925), p. 12; *PE* 645 (May 1, 1926), p. 12; *PE* 650 (June 5, 1926), p. 7; *PE* 655 (July 10, 1926), p. 21; *PE* 663 (September 4, 1926), pp. 5, 12; *PE* 667 (October 2, 1926), p. 13; *PE* 671 (November 6, 1926), p. 13; *PE* 687 (March 5, 1927), p. 2; *PE* 695 (April 30, 1927), p. 9; *PE* 707 (July 23, 1927), p. 12; *PE* 709 (August 6, 1927), p. 18; *PE* 710 (August 13, 1927), p. 8; *PE* 713 (September 3, 1927), p. 11; *PE* 715 (September 17, 1927), p. 12; *PE* 721 (November 5, 1927), p. 10; *PE* 735 (February 18, 1928), p. 3; *PE* 750 (June 2, 1928), p. 12; *PE* 751 (June 9, 1928), p. 12; *PE* 759 (August 11, 1928), p. 3; *PE* 778 (December 22, 1928), p. 13; *PE* 779 (January 5, 1929), p. 11; *PE* 809 (August 3, 1929), p. 14; *PE* 811 (August 17, 1929), p. 12; *PE* 818 (October 12, 1929), p. 17; *PE* 829 (January 4, 1930), p. 12; *PE* 859 (August 2, 1930), p. 12; *PE* 860 (August 9, 1930), p. 12; *PE* 870 (October 25, 1930), p. 10; *PE* 891 (March 28, 1931), p. 11; *PE* 897 (May 9, 1931), p. 12; *PE* 905 (July 4, 1931), p. 12; *PE* 907 (July 18, 1931), p. 13; *PE* 915 (September 12, 1931), p. 15; *PE* 916 (September 26, 1931), p. 15; *PE* 919 (October 17, 1931), p. 17; *PE* 922 (November 7, 1931), p. 16; and *PE* 928 (December 19, 1931), p. 12.

⁵⁶² *PE* 85 (April 10, 1915), p. 4; *PE* 85 (April 10, 1915), p. 4; *PE* 106 (September 4, 1915), p. 3; *PE* 126 (February 12, 1916), p. 12; *PE* 174 (January 27, 1917), p. 16;

While immersion is identified as the requisite mode of baptism, questions still arose regarding the validity of 'sprinkling' as an acceptable mode. When the question was posed to the 'Question and Answer' forum, the response was an unqualified rejection of sprinkling. In the July 10, 1920 issue of the *PE* one reader queries 'Is sprinkling of water on the head a scriptural way for baptism in water? If so, where can it be found in the scriptures? Does the word sprinkle in Ezek. 36:25 mean WB?' The reply is a clear 'No, the word for baptism in the Greek is *bapto*, or *baptizo*, but the word for sprinkle is *rantizo*. There is not a single place in the New Testament where the word *rantizo* (sprinkle) is translated to baptize.'[563] The respondent then offers a tongue-in-cheek picture of a body being buried by sprinkling over a few grains of sand over a body. An explanation of the meaning of Ezek. 36.25 completes the reply.

Infant baptism was also rejected. Anecdotal evidence was invoked to refute the validity of infant baptism. For instance, Grace Perley offered the following witness in the March 14, 1931 issue:

> My third find is a more recent one and I wonder that I have been so long in finding it. *WATER BAPTISM*. I was brought up to believe that infant baptism (sprinkling) was sufficient, but the Lord showed me differently from Col. 2:12. In December, I was 'buried with Him in baptism,' and as I came up out of the water, this verse was given me: 'Ye are complete in Him which is the head of all principality and power.'[564]

Close to a decade earlier, another writer provided a similar report:

> I believe that everyone should be baptized by immersion and that the last part of him, his head, should go down and be buried in baptism unto death. As I said before, I was brought up in an Episcopal Church and the minister put on his gown and made a little outward, visible sign on top of my head which was supposed

---

PE 238/239 (May 4, 1918), p. 15; *PE* 320/321 (December 27, 1919), p. 9; *PE* 580 (January 17, 1925), p. 12; *PE* 589 (March 21, 1925), p. 12; *PE* 613 (September 5, 1925), p. 11; *PE* 648 (May 22, 1926), p. 13; *PE* 655 (July 10, 1926), p. 17; *PE* 716 (September 24, 1927), p. 13; *PE* 738 (March 10, 1928), p. 13; *PE* 814 (September 7, 1929), p. 13; and *PE* 927 (December 12, 1931), p. 13.

[563] *PE* 348/349 (July 10, 1920), pp. 6-7.
[564] *PE* 889 (March 14, 1931), pp. 1, 9.

to be an indication of an inward spiritual grace which I did not get. That little drop of water on my head was all I had, but when God gave me the light on His Word it wasn't long before I obeyed Him in baptism.[565]

Also, several questions were posed in the 'Question and Answer' forum seeking clarification on the issue as early as 1923. In each instance, the response was in the negative, typically invoking the argument that a person had to be able to repent, and infants are unable to repent of their sin. Ernest S. Williams responded with the following in the May 4, 1929. issue of the *PE*: 'The wrong in baptizing infants is in making such a saving ordinance. The Bible says, "Repent ye and be baptized." An infant cannot repent'.[566] While infant baptism was rejected, there appears to be no minimum age restriction placed on baptismal candidates. Once again, Ernest S. Williams guides readers: Question 55. 'What is the usual age when a young person may be baptized? Answer: As soon, having become conscious of committing sin, he repents and believes the gospel'.[567]

Authority to Baptize and Candidate Requirements

Questions concerning who was authorized to administer the ordinances of WB, the Lord's Supper, and perform marriages appear to have been points of contention during the first fifteen years of the movement. It seems to be the case that only ordained Elders were authorized to baptize candidates.[568] In special circumstances, 'An exhorter or Deacon, filled with the Holy Ghost, in the absence of others more customary, and if approved so to do by their brethren, might baptize converts without violating any scripture command or precept'.[569] Also, questions arose regarding the validity of baptism if a minister was not filled with the Spirit. The Question and Answer forum in the July 12, 1919 issue of the *PE* provides an exchange:

> Question 711: Since God introduced water baptism through John who was filled with the Holy Ghost from birth and continued it

---

[565] *PE* 520 (November 3, 1923), p. 3.
[566] *PE* 796 (May 4, 1929), p. 9; *PE* 478/479 (January 6, 1923), p. 8.
[567] *PE* 796 (May 4, 1929), p. 9.
[568] *PE* 121 (January 1, 1916), p. 8; *PE* 330/331 (March 6, 1920), p. 5; *PE* 418/419 (November 12, 1921), p. 5; and *PE* 499 (June 2, 1923), p. 8;
[569] *PE* 121 (January 1, 1916), p. 8.

through the apostles after they were filled with the Spirit, would water baptism be valid and the fulfillment of righteousness if ministered by a man not filled with the Spirit?

Answer: See John 3:26 and 4:1-2 and note that the disciples administered baptism before Pentecost and before they were filled with the Spirit. If it had not been valid, Jesus would not have used them then. But since Pentecost the normal condition of all church officers is 'full of the Spirit.' Any not so filled are in an abnormal condition.[570]

While allowances were made for un-ordained clergy to baptize, the same privilege was not granted to women ministers except for 'special cases of emergency or in the absence of an elder'.[571] This reply did not settle the question. Another question from the field concerning the difference between the ministerial credentials for men and women evoked the following response that argued against women baptizing along the lines of 'official' functioning and the 'exercise of authority':

> In both cases alike, there [sic} call from God to testify, to evangelize and preach the word is recognized. In this respect there is no difference. The difference comes as soon as one approaches ministerial acts of an OFFICIAL nature, or the exercise of AUTHORITY.
>
> The ordained man there's authorized 'to administer the ordinances of the church and to perform marriage ceremonies in accordance with the laws of the state where he resides.' Now please note two things here. First, that credentials given to women do not contain these clauses to administer church ordinances and to celebrate marriage. If she does either of these things, she does so without the authority of the Assemblies of God, and in most cases would be subject to a heavy fine under the law at the hands of the courts, if it is reported to them.[572]

When confronted with the shortage of ordained ministers on the field, questions continued to be submitted to the organ, requesting

---

[570] *PE* 296/297 (July 12, 1919), p. 5.
[571] *PE* 244/245 (June 15, 1918), p. 5.
[572] *PE* 330/331 (March 6, 1920), p. 5.

resolution. One pointed inquiry is contained in the January 8, 1921 issue of the *PE*:

> If ordained women preachers are not given the same authority as ordained men to administer baptisms and communion, what must the small assemblies in the out of way places do, which have only a woman preacher? Must they go without baptism in water and without communion just because they are too poor to send for a man preacher, or will you brethren send a man at your own expense to baptize us, and administer the communion to us?[573]

The negative response to this inquiry was supported by an appeal to the silence of the NT, supplying an example of a woman baptizing anyone and the absence of a command for women to baptize.[574] The second line of argument employed was placing the responsibility for fulfilling the administration of ordinances back on the congregation and the denial of the General Council's responsibility for meeting the needs of congregations on the field.[575]

E.N. Bell clearly articulated the stated obligation for candidates presenting themselves for WB in the March 27, 1915 issue of the *PE*:

> People should repent of their sin and commit themselves to a personal surrender to Jesus Christ with faith in Him for salvation before being baptized in water, and when one has given a credible

---

[573] *PE* 374/375 (January 8, 1921), p. 10. Also, see *PE* 418/419 (November 12, 1921), p. 5.
[574] *PE* 374/375 (January 8, 1921), p. 10.
[575] *PE* 374/375 (January 8, 1921), p. 10.

The General Council leaves both the woman and the local congregation free in these matters, but it does not take upon itself responsibility for their doing anything the scriptures do not tell a woman to do. In the United States there are few cases where it would be really necessary for a band of saints to go without baptism or the Lord's Supper or have them administered by a woman. If they have ordained deacons, and this is satisfactory to the congregation, the congregation might order the deacons to attend to these things. If the sister who is preaching is experienced in such matters, and capable of taking care of them, and it is the desire of the assembly and of the candidates that she baptize them, there is no specific law on the part of the General Council which directly forbids it. The fact is the scriptures do not positively say that baptism can only be administered by an ordained preacher. But such is customary and agreeable to all, and it is usually safer to follow the accepted custom in religious matters unless there is some special emergency that demands of us to do otherwise or the scripture direct otherwise.

profession of repentance toward God and faith in the Lord Jesus Christ he should be accepted, without hesitation, as a candidate for baptism and be baptized.[576]

Three years later, in the March 9, 1918 issue of the *PE* Bell reasserts the vital connection between repentance and WB for those considering WB:

> It never was designed that anyone should profess to have repented and not be baptized. In the early days they thus practiced what they preached, and God expects all to do the same today. They did not separate theory and practice, or doctrine from life and salvation. All went hand in hand.[577]

There do not appear to have been minimum age requirements for receiving baptism according to the *PE*. It was common for children to be among the group eager for WB, and bold enough to request baptism and have their request honored.[578] Moreover, there were no specified upper age limits observed. Accounts of persons, ranging from 77 to 105, provide a sample of this age group celebrating WB by immersion.[579] Being able to testify to one's confession and repentance of sin, and faith in Jesus Christ were the criteria.[580]

Commitment and Consequences

It seems to be the case that in the USA, candidates for WB were not examined closely nor recipients of instruction concerning the meaning and import of WB. This was not the case on foreign soil

---

[576] *PE* 83 (March 27, 1915), p. 1.

[577] *PE* 230 (March 9, 1918), p. 2.

[578] *PE* 81 (March 13, 1915), p. 3; *PE* 83 (March 27, 1915), p. 4; *PE* 127 (February 19, 1916), p. 12; *PE* 170 (December 23, 1916), p. 13; *PE* 250/251 (August 10, 1918), p. 14; *PE* 502 (June 23, 1923), p. 13; *PE* 561 (August 30, 1924), p. 12; *PE* 717 (October 8, 1927), p. 10; and *PE* 916 (September 26, 1931), p. 6.

[579] *PE* 138 (May 6, 1916), p. 14; *PE* 561 (August 30, 1924), p. 12; and *PE* 654 (July 3, 1926), p. 10.

[580] See *PE* 294/295 (June 28, 1919), p. 8 for a reaction to the 'Doctrinal Statement of the World Conference on Christian Fundamentals'. On the one hand, the author endorsed the World Conference's rejection of 'Modernism'. On the other hand, reservations were expressed in the following lines: 'We would like to have seen in this statement a word showing the importance of repentance, for there is no real moral, saving faith in Christ until there has been repentance towards God. It will also be noticed that there is no reference to either baptism and water or of the baptism of the Holy Ghost in this statement.'

where missionaries worked to ensure candidates were fully informed and committed to following Jesus.[581] The following account from India illustrates the process employed to address the level of commitment while counting the cost of discipleship:

> A young man presented himself for baptism. I then told him to wait a little longer until I have had opportunity to talk with him about the seriousness of the steps he is taking and also the consequences that would follow, and that he would be made an outcaste by his co-religionists. He replied, 'My mother is now willing for me to become a Christian, but she will remain and die in the Hindoo religion.' He was very disappointed that I did not baptize him then with the others. However, praise God, in the meantime his mother has also surrendered to the Lord, and they have boldly confessed Christ together in baptism in the little creek that flows at the bottom of our mission compound.[582]

Similarly, we read of the close scrutiny of those seeking WB in the following report from Peru, South America:

> According to the Sunday School Times, last year Pastor Schwerin had a baptismal class of 1200 of which 522 were finally accepted. At present he has the oversight of a church of 1161 members, with 600 in his baptismal class, and 600 more have been accepted for baptism. One convert has been killed by enemies of the gospel and others have been imprisoned and hung by their fingers to prison rafters.[583]

---

[581] *PE* 146/147 (July 8, 1916), pp. 7, 11; *PE* 148 (July 15, 1916), p. 15; *PE* 175 (February 3, 1917), p. 15; *PE* 260/261 (November 2, 1918), p. 10; *PE* 316/317 (November 29, 1919), p. 13; *PE* 354/355 (August 21, 1920), p. 9; *PE* 418/419 (November 12, 1921), p. 13; *PE* 436/437 (March 18, 1922), p. 11; *PE* 472/473 (November 25, 1922), p. 27; *PE* 550 (June 14, 1924), p. 10; *PE* 639 (March 20, 1926), p. 7; *PE* 675 (December 4, 1926), p. 19; *PE* 681 (January 22, 1927), p. 4; *PE* 709 (August 6, 1927), p. 19; *PE* 735 (February 18, 1928), p. 3; *PE* 779 (January 5, 1929), p. 11; *PE* 786 (February 23, 1929), p. 10; *PE* 788 (March 9, 1929), p. 11; *PE* 793 (April 13, 1929), p. 10; *PE* 829 (January 4, 1930), p. 11; *PE* 837 (March 1, 1930), p. 11; *PE* 839 (March 15, 1930), p. 11; and *PE* 917 (October 3, 1931), p. 6.

[582] *PE* 788 (March 9, 1929), p. 11.

[583] *PE* 639 (March 20, 1926), p. 7.

On occasion, plans to conduct a baptismal service were canceled due to the candidates' failures to pass the examination. A report from Tachikawa, Japan by Harriet Dithridge rehearses the event:

> We had a water baptismal service on the second Sunday in October; but none of the Tachikawa church people were baptized. We thought some of them were ready for baptism as we examined them, but at the last minute they were not ready to come. Two from Kokubunji outstation, and some of the Bible school girls were baptized.[584]

Also, the missionaries' commitment to teaching and examining candidates for baptism to ensure that new believers understood the significance of the ordinance is reflected in the following concern relative to the 'mass movements' taking place in their areas:

> In the districts where the 'mass movement' is on more people are asking for baptism then the missionaries can take in. In the old days the missionary had to go to the people, but now the people are coming to the missionaries, and they are coming in such numbers that there are not enough Christians to teach them.[585]

There can be little doubt of the baptismal candidates' commitment[586] to WB in the face of opposition. They faced

---

[584] *PE* 786 (February 23, 1929), p. 10.

[585] *PE* 8.21 (June 2, 1917), p. 6.

[586] *PE* 58 (September 12, 1914), p. 2; *PE* 102 (August 7, 1915), p. 1; *PE* 132 (March 25, 1916), pp. 13, 14; *PE* 150 (July 29, 1916), p. 12; *PE* 155 (September 2, 1916), p. 13; *PE* 158 (September 23, 1916), p. 4; *PE* 163 (November 4, 1916), p. 8; *PE* 167 (December 2, 1916), p. 12; *PE* 170 (December 23, 1916), p. 13; (January 20, 1917), p. 14; *PE* 181 (March 17, 1917), p. 16; *PE* 212 (October 27, 1917), pp. 2, 3; and 14: *PE* 215 (November 17, 1917), p. 14; *PE* 238/239 (May 4, 1918), p. 10; *PE* 240/241 (May 18, 1918), p. 11; *PE* 294/295 (June 28, 1919), p. 10; *PE* 302/303 (August 23, 1919), p. 14; *PE* 310/311 (October 18, 1919), p. 11; *PE* 324/325 (January 24, 1920), p. 12; *PE* 332/333 (March 20, 1920), p. 13; *PE* 338/339 (May 1, 1920), p. 13; *PE* 350/351 (July 24, 1920), p. 13; *PE* 354/355 (August 21, 1920), p. 10; *PE* 366/367 (November 13, 1920), pp. 9, 10; *PE* 370/371 (December 11, 1920), p. 13; *PE* 384/385 (March 19, 1921), p. 15; *PE* 438/439 (April 1, 1922), p. 14; *PE* 502 (June 23, 1923), pp. 11, 13; *PE* 547 (May 17, 1924), p. 11; *PE* 553 (July 5 1924), p. 9; *PE* 58 (September 12, 1914), p. 2; *PE* 102 (August 7, 1915), p. 1; *PE* 132 (March 25, 1916), pp. 13, 14; *PE* 150 (July 29, 1916), p. 12; *PE* 155 (September 2, 1916), p. 13; *PE* 158 (September 23, 1916), p. 4; *PE* 163 (November 4, 1916), p. 8; *PE* 167

challenges and opposition[587] in the forms of inclement weather marked by severely cold temperatures, freezing water, and frozen ground,[588] familial opposition,[589] loss of social status,[590] physical

---

(December 2, 1916), p. 12; *PE* 170 (December 23, 1916), p. 13; (January 20, 1917), p. 14; *PE* 181 (March 17, 1917), p. 16; *PE* 212 (October 27, 1917), pp. 2, 3; and 14: *PE* 215 (November 17, 1917), p. 14; *PE* 238/239 (May 4, 1918), p. 10; *PE* 240/241 (May 18, 1918), p. 11; *PE* 294/295 (June 28, 1919), p. 10; *PE* 302/303 (August 23, 1919), p. 14; *PE* 310/311 (October 18, 1919), p. 11; *PE* 324/325 (January 24, 1920), p. 12; *PE* 332/333 (March 20, 1920), p. 13; *PE* 338/339 (May 1, 1920), p. 13; *PE* 350/351 (July 24, 1920), p. 13; *PE* 354/355 (August 21, 1920), p. 10; *PE* 366/367 (November 13, 1920), pp. 9, 10; *PE* 370/371 (December 11, 1920), p. 13; *PE* 384/385 (March 19, 1921), p. 15; *PE* 438/439 (April 1, 1922), p. 14; *PE* 502 (June 23, 1923), pp. 11, 13; *PE* 547 (May 17, 1924), p. 11; *PE* 553 (July 5 1924), p. 9; *PE* 555 (July 19, 1924), p. 3; *PE* 584 (February 14, 1925), p. 12; *PE* 604 (July 4, 1925), p. 13; *PE* 605 (July 11, 1925), p. 9; *PE* 607 (July 26, 1925), p. 10; *PE* 612 (August 29, 1925), p. 10; *PE* 613 (September 5, 1925), p. 11; *PE* 616 (September 26, 1925), p. 12; *PE* 619 (October 24, 1925), p. 17; *PE* 628 (January 2, 1926), p. 6; *PE* 630 (January 16, 1926), p. 10; *PE* 631 (January 23, 1926), p. 12; *PE* 645 (May 1, 1926), p. 12; and *PE* 709 (August 6, 1927), p. 18; *PE* 741 (March 31, 1928), p. 13; *PE* 755 (July 7, 1928), pp. 14, 15; *PE* 766 (September 29, 1928), p. 15; *PE* 779 (January 5, 1929), p. 11; *PE* 795 (April 27, 1929), p. 10; *PE* 817 (October 5, 1929), p. 11; and *PE* 824 (November 23, 1929), pp. 5-6.

[587] *PE* 56 (August 29, 1914), p. 4; *PE* 69 (December 5, 1914), p. 4; *PE* 159 (September 30, 1916), p. 4; *PE* 258/259 (October 19, 1918), p. 11; *PE* 260/261 (November 2, 1918), p. 10; *PE* 280/281 (March 22, 1919), p. 11; *PE* 282/283 (April 5, 1919), p. 10; *PE* 502 (June 23, 1923), p. 13; *PE* 294/295 (June 28, 1919), p. 10; *PE* 296/297 (July 12, 1919), p. 11; *PE* 298/299 (July 26, 1919), p. 10; *PE* 304/305 (September 6, 1919), p. 10; *PE* 334/335 (April 13, 1920), p. 13; *PE* 338/339 (May 1, 1920), p. 13; *PE* 350/351 (July 24, 1920), p. 13; *PE* 366/367 (November 13, 1920), pp. 9, 10; *PE* 458/459 (August 19, 1922), p. 13; *PE* 580 (January 17, 1925), p. 9; *PE* 634 (February 13, 1926), p. 11; *PE* 645 (May 1, 1926), p. 11; *PE* 695 (April 30, 1927), p. 9; *PE* 728 (December 24, 1927), p. 10; *PE* 811 (August 17, 1929), p. 11; and *PE* 817 (October 5, 1929), p. 11.

[588] *PE* 102 (August 7, 1915), p. 1; *PE* 132 (March 25, 1916), p. 13; *PE* 158 (September 23, 1916), p. 4; *PE* 181 (March 17, 1917), p. 16; *PE* 212 (October 27, 1917), pp. 2, 3; *PE* 238/239 (May 4, 1918), p. 10; *PE* 240/241 (May 18, 1918), p. 11; *PE* 438/439 (April 1, 1922), p. 14; *PE* 628 (January 2, 1926), p. 6; *PE* 631 (January 23, 1926), p. 12; and *PE* 755 (July 7, 1928), p. 14.

[589] *PE* 258/259 (October 19, 1918), p. 11.

[590] *PE* 56 (August 29, 1914), p. 4; *PE* 366/367 (November 13, 1920), p. 10; and *PE* 634 (February 13, 1926), p. 11.

assault,[591] threat of destruction of homes, forfeiture of earthly possessions, and verbal assault and persecution.[592]

After facing persecution, peril, and loss, newly baptized converts in India, China, and Japan often requested to be known by a 'new name'[593] within the Christian community. From February 20, 1915, *PE*, we read the testimony of Inaba Sand from Japan: 'That day, as is written in Romans 6, I was buried with Jesus in baptism and became a new creation and offered myself to God. I received the name Rebecca and was so happy I truly could not tell it.'[594]

Baptismal Formula

The disruption that ensued following the 1913 declaration that WB was to occur 'in the name of Jesus only' was addressed in the *PE*, starting with the very first issue. As the 'Jesus only' movement gained adherents, the leadership of the COGIC (white) sought to allow individual preference to prevail, resisting a dogmatic position on WB. As antagonism between the two movements increased and the leaders of the COGIC (white) and the 'Jesus only' adherents became more antagonistic, readers were informed of the decision regarding the 'Declaration of the Attitude' considered in St. Louis, MO, October 1 to 10, 1915:[595]

> 1. That the essential thing in Christian baptism is the burial, in obedience to the command of Christ, through baptism, of a person who has repented and believed, in water with Christ in the likeness of His death and resurrection (Acts 2.38; Rom, 6:3, 4); and that its validity should not be repudiated simply because of some sleight [sic] variation in the formula repeated over the candidate in the act: that the use in connection with baptism of

---

[591] *PE* 69 (December 5, 1914), p. 4; *PE* 366/367 (November 13, 1920), p. 9.

[592] *PE* 69 (December 5, 1914), p. 4; *PE* 159 (September 30, 1916), p. 4; *PE* 282/283 (April 5, 1919), p. 10; *PE* 298/299 (July 26, 1919), p. 10; *PE* 338/339 (May 1, 1920), p. 13; *PE* 350/351 (July 24, 1920), p. 13; *PE* 458/459 (August 19, 1922), p. 13; *PE* 502 (June 23, 1923), p. 13; *PE* 580 (January 17, 1925), p. 9; and *PE* 811 (August 17, 1929), p. 11.

[593] *PE* 78 (February 20, 1915), p. 3; *PE* 547 (May 17, 1924), p. 11; *PE* 717 (October 8, 1927), p. 10; and *PE* 758 (August 4, 1928), p. 5.

[594] *PE* 78 (February 20, 1915), p. 3. Also, see *PE* 109 (September 25, 1915), p. 1; *PE* 115 (November 13, 1915), p. 1.

[595] *PE* 111 (October 16, 1915), p. 1.

any of the following passages of Scripture should be acceptable so far as this council sees it. Matt. 28:19; Acts 2:38; 8:16; 10:48; 19:5.

2. That the Scriptures give no example of anyone who has once had Christian baptism ever being re-baptized.

3. That the matter, therefore, of general re-baptizing should not be pressed upon the saints by the preacher; that the only reason for baptizing any person is that his former baptism, taken as a whole, is to the conscience of the candidate, not Christian baptism; that in such cases of individual conscience, any minister or other person should have full personal liberty to be baptized in any name as he sees fit, so long as he stays within the Scriptures on the subject; and it is hereby understood that nothing herein said shall hinder any minister from dealing, as he sees best, with cases whose consciences are not satisfied with their former baptism, only he should not go into any congregation not under his care, except at the invitation of its pastor or those in rightful authority to extend such invitation, and that even when so invited it would be wrong to so emphasize anyone [sic] scriptural phrase on baptism above another scriptural phrase on the same subject as to lead saints by the wholesale, to believe any one set phrase to be repeated over the candidate is essential to Christian baptism. All division or strife over mere phrases, as that there should be a fixed or invariable formula, is wrong on both sides of the question; but this does not prevent anyone from setting forth his own conviction on this matter in the proper spirit and where authorized to do so.[596]

According to the editor, the resolution was well-received, adopted, and 'the brethren seem to forget straightway that there had been any differences'.[597] Unfortunately, the tension between the two camps continued beyond the St. Louis meeting. The polarization of the two groups reached its peak in 1917 when it was announced that a new Pentecostal organization had been formed by the brethren who met at Eureka Springs, Ark., during the holiday season to be called 'The

---

[596] *PE* 111 (October 16, 1915), pp. 1, 2.
[597] *PE* 111 (October 16, 1915), p. 2.

General Assembly of Apostolic Assemblies', with Daniel C.O. Opperman as chairman; Lee Floyd, secretary; Howard A. Goss, treasurer. The new organization was built along similar lines as the General Council, with the same plan of issuing credentials, organizing district assemblies, etc. The credential committee consisted of Daniel C.O. Opperman, Howard A. Goss, and H.G. Rodgers. The new organization had no written statement of truths which it approved but was practically unanimous in its stand against the General Council's position on the Trinity, holding that there was only one person in the Godhead and that person is Lord Jesus Christ.[598] Controversy and polemics continued to fill the pages of the *PE* for several years between 1915 and 1931.[599]

---

[598] *PE* 173 (January 20, 1917), p. 15.

[599] The disruption that ensued following the 1913 declaration that WB was to occur 'in the name of Jesus only' continued to be addressed in the *PE*, starting with the very first issue of the *PE*. The Trinitarian controversy, closely coupled the debate over the baptismal formula, was also engaged in the *PE*. Most often, the two issues were addressed together in the following articles: *PE* 88 (May 1, 1915), pp. 1-2. 'To Act in the Name of Another' by E.N. Bell; *PE* 93 (June 5, 1915), pp. 1, 3. 'The Sad New Issue: Over the Baptism Formula in the Name of Christ only. Is the Issue Really New? The New Claims in the Light of Historic Facts' by E.N. Bell; *PE* 94 (June 12, 1915), pp. 1, 3. 'The "Acts" on Baptism in Christ's Name Only' by E. N. Bell; *PE* 97 (July 3, 1915), pp. 1, 3. 'Scriptural Varieties of Baptismal Formula' by E.N. Bell; *PE* 99 (July 17, 1915), p. 2; *PE* 103 (August 14, 1915), p. 1. 'Who is Jesus Christ? Jesus Christ Being Exalted as The Jehovah Of The Old Testament And The True God of the New. A New Realization of Christ as the Mighty God' by E.N. Bell; *PE* 108 (September 18, 1915), p. 1; *PE* 109 (September 25, 1915), p. 1. 'Where no Counsel is, the People Fall: but in the Multitude of Counsel there is Safety. – Prov. 11:14'; *PE* 114 (November 6, 1915), p. 1. 'Bro. Bell on the Trinity: The One God Manifested in Three Persons Taught in the Word. The Son Specially Being Exalted in this Age'; *PE* 129 (March 4, 1916), pp. 6, 7. 'We all Agree' by Pastor D.W. Kerr; *PE* 143 (June 10, 1916), p. 8; *PE* 161 (October 21, 1916), p. 4; *PE* 168 (December 9, 1916), p. 8. 'A Practical Application of the Doctrine of the Holy Trinity' by AP Collins; *PE* 170 (December 23, 1916), p. 15; *PE* 171 (January 6, 1917), p. 8; *PE* 172 (January 13, 1917), p. 8; *PE* 200 (July 28, 1917), p. 9; *PE* 208 (September 29, 1917), p. 7; *PE* 210 (October 13, 1917), p. 7; *PE* 213 (November 3, 1917), p. 9; *PE* 223 (January 19, 1918), p. 9; *PE* 230 (March 9, 1918), p. 9; *PE* 242/243 (June 1, 1918), p. 9; *PE* 244/245 (June 15, 1918), p. 5; *PE* 248/249 (July 27, 1918), pp. 9, 14; *PE* 264/265 (November 30, 1918), p. 8; *PE* 276/277 (February 22, 1919), p. 5; *PE* 276/277 (February 22, 1919), p. 5;

Pentecostal Worship and Witness

Reports from hundreds of baptismal services around the globe were submitted to the *PE* in order to chronicle the spread and impact of the gospel of Jesus Christ. Overall, reports tended to capture the size of the crowds, number baptized, and the evidence of the HS's impact on worshippers and others witnessing the services.[600] Relative to

---

PE 276/277 (February 22, 1919), p. 14; *PE* 284/285 (April 19, 1919), p. 9; *PE* 288/289 (May 17, 1919), pp. 5, 6, and 7; *PE* 292/293 (June 14, 1919), p. 10; *PE* 298/299 (July 26, 1919), pp. 6-7; *PE* 300/301 (August 9, 1919), pp. 1-2, 5; *PE* 302/303 (August 23, 1919), pp. 8, 9. 'Elohim, God's Name' by Hope G Tiffany; *PE* 304/305 (September 6, 1919), pp. 6-7; *PE* 310/311 (October 18, 1919), p. 4; *PE* 316/317 (November 29, 1919), p. 7; *PE* 324/325 (January 24, 1920), pp. 6, 7; *PE* 370/371 (December 11, 1920), pp. 8, 9; *PE* 436/371 (December 11, 1920), p. 8; *PE* 378/379 (February 5, 1921), p. 1; *PE* 382/383 (March 5, 1921), p. 8; *PE* 390/391 (April 30, 1921), p. 10; *PE* 478/479 (January 6, 1923), p. 8; *PE* 492 (April 14, 1923), p. 6; *PE* 501 (June 16, 1923), p. 5; *PE* 604 (July 4, 1925), p. 6; and *PE* 667 (October 2, 1926), p. 12.

[600] *PE* 2.19 (May 9, 1914), pp. 6, 8; *PE* 33 (May 9, 1914), p. 10; *PE* 50 (July 18, 1914), p. 3; *PE* 56 (August 29, 1914), p. 1; *PE* 57 (September 5, 1914), p. 1; *PE* 59 (September 19, 1914), p. 1; *PE* 60 (September 26, 1914), p. 4; *PE* 62 (October 10, 1914), p. 3; *PE* 64 (October 24, 1914), p. 2; *PE* 65 (October 31, 1914), p. 4; *PE* 69 (December 5, 1914), p. 4; *PE* 95 (June 19, 1915), p. 3; *PE* 99 (July 17, 1915), p. 1; *PE* 100 (July 24, 1915), p. 4; *PE* 101 (July 31, 1915), p. 1; *PE* 102 (August 7, 1915), p. 1; *PE* 103 (August 14, 1915), p. 4; *PE* 104 (August 21, 1915), pp. 1, 3; *PE* 105 (August 28, 1915), pp. 2, 4; *PE* 106 (September 4, 1915), pp. 1, 2, and 3; *PE* 109 (September 25, 1915), p. 1; *PE* 110 (October 2, 1915), p. 3; *PE* 115 (November 13, 1915), p. 1; *PE* 123 (January 15, 1916), p. 13; *PE* 125 (February 5, 1916), p. 14; *PE* 126 (February 12, 1916), p. 12; *PE* 131 (March 18, 1916), p. 14; *PE* 136 (April 22, 1916), p. 11; *PE* 138 (May 6, 1916), p. 14; *PE* 139 (May 13, 1916), pp. 14, 15; *PE* 142 (June 3, 1916), p. 12; *PE* 143 (June 10, 1916), p. 7; *PE* 145 (June 24, 1916), p. 15; *PE* 146/147 (July 8, 1916), p. 15; *PE* 149 (July 22, 1916), p. 11; *PE* 150 (July 29, 1916), p. 14; *PE* 152 (August 12, 1916), p. 11; *PE* 159 (September 30, 1916), p. 14; *PE* 171 (January 6, 1917), p. 14; *PE* 172 (January 13, 1917), p. 16; *PE* 181 (March 17, 1917), p. 16; *PE* 195 (June 23, 1917), p. 14; *PE* 198 (July 14, 1917), p. 14; *PE* 200 (July 28, 1917), p. 13; *PE* 201 (August 4, 1917), pp. 13, 14, and 16; *PE* 204 (August 25, 1917), pp. 12, 14, and 16; *PE* 209 (October 6, 1917), p. 14; *PE* 211 (October 20, 1917), p. 14; *PE* 212 (October 27, 1917), pp. 2, 3, and 14; *PE* 214 (November 10, 1917), pp. 12, 14; *PE* 215 (November 17, 1917), p. 14; *PE* 224 (January 26, 1918), p. 10; *PE* 246/247 (June 29, 1918), p. 11; *PE* 248/249 (July 27, 1918), p. 10; *PE* 252/253 (August 24, 1918), p. 15; *PE* 256/257 (October 5, 1918), p. 1; *PE* 268/269 (December 28, 1918), p. 8; *PE* 288/289 (May 17, 1919), p. 7; *PE* 296/297 (July 12, 1919), pp. 14, 15; PE 298/299 (July 26, 1919), p. 10; *PE* 300/301 (August 9, 1919),

p. 8; *PE* 304/305 (September 6, 1919), p. 14; *PE* 306/307 (September 20, 1919), p. 13; *PE* 308/309 (October 4, 1919), p. 12; *PE* 310/311 (October 18, 1919), pp. 12, 14; *PE* 312/313 (November 1, 1919), p. 23; *PE* 316/317 (November 29, 1919), pp. 13, 15; *PE* 326/327 (February 7, 1920), p. 13; *PE* 330/331 (March 6, 1920), p. 13; *PE* 334/335 (April 13, 1920), pp. 13, 14; *PE* 352/353 (August 7, 1920), pp. 10, 14; *PE* 354/355 (August 21, 1920), pp. 10, 13; *PE* 356/357 (September 4, 1920), p. 9; *PE* 364/365 (October 30, 1920), p. 14; *PE* 366/367 (November 13, 1920), p. 10; *PE* 376/377 (January 22, 1921), p. 12; *PE* 436/437 (March 18, 1922), p. 11; *PE* 442/443 (April 29, 1922), p. 21; *PE* 452/453 (July 8, 1922), p. 9; *PE* 456/457 (August 5, 1922), p. 9; *PE* 460/461 (September 2, 1922), p. 13; *PE* 472/473 (November 25, 1922), p. 27; *PE* 474/475 (December 9, 1922), p. 10; *PE* 495 (May 5, 1923), p. 14; *PE* 497 (May 19, 1923), p. 14; *PE* 501 (June 16, 1923), p. 11; *PE* 530 (January 19, 1924), p. 13; *PE* 532 (February 2, 1924), p. 12; *PE* 534 (February 16, 1924), p. 10; *PE* 536 (March 1, 1924), p. 12; *PE* 547 (May 17, 1924), p. 13; *PE* 558 (August 9, 1924), p. 12; *PE* 559 (August 16, 1924), p. 9; *PE* 560 (August 23, 1924), p. 11; *PE* 561 (August 30, 1924), p. 14; *PE* 566 (October 4, 1924), pp. 8, 12; *PE* 571 (November 8, 1924), p. 13; *PE* 575 (December 6, 1924), p. 13; *PE* 579 (January 10, 1925), p. 12; *PE* 587 (March 7, 1925), p. 12; *PE* 595 (May 2, 1925), p. 13; *PE* 607 (July 26, 1925), p. 12; *PE* 612 (August 29, 1925), p. 10; *PE* 625 (December 5, 1925), p. 18; *PE* 645 (May 1, 1926), pp. 12, 13; *PE* 648 (May 22, 1926), p. 11; *PE* 650 (June 5, 1926), p. 7; *PE* 654 (July 3, 1926), p. 10; *PE* 655 (July 10, 1926), pp. 20, 21; *PE* 657 (July 24, 1926), p. 13; *PE* 663 (September 4, 1926), p. 12; *PE* 667 (October 2, 1926), p. 13; *PE* 669 (October 23, 1926), p. 12; *PE* 676 (December 11, 1926), p. 13; *PE* 690 (March 26, 1927), p. 18; *PE* 700 (June 4, 1927), p. 9; *PE* 702 (June 18, 1927), p. 11; *PE* 708 (July 30, 1927), pp. 8, 11, and 12; *PE* 715 (September 17, 1927), p. 12; *PE* 745 (April 28, 1928), p. 12; *PE* 750 (June 2, 1928), p. 12; *PE* 751 (June 9, 1928), p. 12; *PE* 754 (June 30, 1928), p. 9; *PE* 758 (August 4, 1928), pp. 11, 12; *PE* 759 (August 11, 1928), p. 3; *PE* 774 (November 24, 1928), p. 12; *PE* 779 (January 5, 1929), p. 11; *PE* 780 (January 12, 1929), p. 10; *PE* 786 (February 23, 1929), p. 10; *PE* 816 (September 21, 1929), p. 12; *PE* 821 (November 2, 1929), pp. 10, 11; *PE* 855 (July 5, 1930), p. 11; *PE* 858 (July 26, 1930), p. 13; *PE* 860 (August 9, 1930), p. 12; *PE* 862 (August 23, 1930), p. 10; *PE* 865 (September 13, 1930), p. 12; *PE* 869 (October 18, 1930), pp. 12, 13; *PE* 870 (October 25, 1930), p. 12; *PE* 871 (November 1, 1930), p. 12; *PE* 873 (November 15, 1930), p. 16; *PE* 874 (November 22, 1930), p. 20; *PE* 875 (November 29, 1930), p. 17; *PE* 877 (December 13, 1930), p. 8; *PE* 880 (January 10, 1931), pp. 6-7, 9; *PE* 887 (February 28, 1931), p. 10; *PE* 890 (March 21, 1931), p. 16; *PE* 897 (May 9, 1931), p. 11; *PE* 899 (May 23, 1931), p. 12; *PE* 905 (July 4, 1931), p. 12; *PE* 910 (August 8, 1931), p. 12; *PE* 912 (August 22, 1931), p. 10; *PE* 916 (September 26, 1931), pp. 6, 17; *PE* 921 (October 31, 1931), p. 13; *PE* 923 (November 14, 1931), p. 16; and *PE* 927 (December 12, 1931), p. 8.

attendance, various reports describe large crowds being present for the services.[601] One such account provides details of an event held in Frostburg, MD. In the October 2, 1915, *PE* the reporter posits that

> Last Sunday was one of the greatest days, that has been witnessed in the East for many a day, this was the day that we met to Baptize in water. People came for miles, and automobiles, to witness the scene.

> It was estimated by many, that three thousand people witnessed the service. The different papers stated that there were fully two thousand people there. The Lord made it a very sacred meeting, as we baptized thirty-eight in water and many more to follow soon. Truly the Lord is blessing His Word.[602]

The worship atmosphere during and after the baptismal service provide another descriptor in the reports. The worship was saturated with 'shouts of/shouting for joy'.[603]

---

[601] *PE* 57 (September 5, 1914), p. 1; *PE* 95 (June 19, 1915), p. 3; *PE* 123 (January 15, 1916), p. 13; *PE* 139 (May 13, 1916), p. 15; *PE* 146/147 (July 8, 1916), p. 11. *PE* 209 (October 6, 1917), p. 14; *PE* 211 (October 20, 1917), p. 14; *PE* 212 (October 27, 1917), pp. 2, 3, and 14; *PE* 214 (November 10, 1917), p. 12; *PE* 288/289 (May 17, 1919), p. 7; *PE* 300/301 (August 9, 1919), p. 8; *PE* 304/305 (September 6, 1919), p. 14; *PE* 308/309 (October 4, 1919), p. 12; *PE* 474/475 (December 9, 1922), p. 10; *PE* 501 (June 16, 1923), p. 11; *PE* 566 (October 4, 1924), p. 8; *PE* 571 (November 8, 1924), p. 13; *PE* 650 (June 5, 1926), p. 7; *PE* 700 (June 4, 1927), p. 9; *PE* 715 (September 17, 1927), p. 12; *PE* 750 (June 2, 1928), p. 12; *PE* 759 (August 11, 1928), p. 3; *PE* 821 (November 2, 1929), pp. 10, 11; *PE* 860 (August 9, 1930), p. 12; *PE* 865 (September 13, 1930), p. 12; *PE* 870 (October 25, 1930), p. 12; and *PE* 899 (May 23, 1931), p. 12.

[602] *PE* 110 (October 2, 1915), p. 3.

[603] *PE* 2.19 (May 9, 1914), p. 6; *PE* 101 (July 31, 1915), p. 1; *PE* 181 (March 17, 1917), p. 16; *PE* 211 (October 20, 1917), p. 14; *PE* 212 (October 27, 1917), pp. 2, 3; *PE* 215 (November 17, 1917), p. 14; *PE* 298/299 (July 26, 1919), p. 10; *PE* 310/311 (October 18, 1919), p. 12; *PE* 436/437 (March 18, 1922), p. 11; *PE* 456/457 (August 5, 1922), p. 9; *PE* 501 (June 16, 1923), p. 11; *PE* 530 (January 19, 1924), p. 13; *PE* 587 (March 7, 1925), p. 12; *PE* 595 (May 2, 1925), p. 13; *PE* 645 (May 1, 1926), p. 13; *PE* 702 (June 18, 1927), p. 11; *PE* 751 (June 9, 1928), p. 12; *PE* 758 (August 4, 1928), p. 12; *PE* 862 (August 23, 1930), p. 10; *PE* 905 (July 4, 1931), p. 12; *PE* 910 (August 8, 1931), p. 12; *PE* 921 (October 31, 1931), p. 13; and *PE* 927 (December 12, 1931), p. 8.

Two reports recount the responses to the HS during the first baptismal services. First, from Sparksville, IN, we read 'A large attendance of saints, quite a number leaving their wheat harvest to attend. Those who were baptized came out rejoicing, others danced in the Spirit, some prayed and talked in tongues'.[604] Secondly, a report from Millport, KY says 'as we made a circle in the water, the power (was) falling, the saints (were) shouting and dancing. One received the baptism in the water. Just as she came up out of the water she began speaking in tongues'.[605] In addition to the preceding responses to the HS are healings[606] and visions[607] in the context of baptismal services.

Before, during, and after the WB services, the preachers and teachers used the occasions to proclaim and teach the Gospel to the uninitiated.[608] One story from Matagalpa, Nicaragua, Central America, printed in the September 26, 1914, *PE* captures the glory of a baptismal service and the power of the preached Word of God. The reporter asserts

> Yesterday we had a glorious baptismal service in the Matagalpa River. Six were buried with Christ in baptism. The glory of the Lord came upon us, while the sinner looked on in wonder and amazement, for Matagalpa had never seen such a scene before. We took the opportunity to give them the Gospel. Never before has that word been so dear to us as now, 'El Evangello' (The Gospel). In this country one learns the meaning of Paul's word, 'I am not ashamed of the Gospel of Christ.' We baptized a man

---

[604] *PE* 50 (July 18, 1914), p. 3.

[605] *PE* 56 (August 29, 1914), p. 1.

[606] *PE* 96 (June 26, 1915), p. 1; *PE* 102 (August 7, 1915), p. 1; *PE* 141 (May 27, 1916), p. 15; *PE* 159 (September 30, 1916), p. 4; *PE* 298/299 (July 26, 1919), p. 8; *PE* 438/439 (April 1, 1922), p. 14; and *PE* 460/461 (September 2, 1922), p. 13.

[607] *PE* 56 (August 29, 1914), p. 1; *PE* 146/147 (July 8, 1916), p. 15; *PE* 306/307 (September 20, 1919), p. 13; *PE* 645 (May 1, 1926), p. 13; and *PE* 648 (May 22, 1926), p. 11.

[608] *PE* 123 (January 15, 1916), p. 13; *PE* 149 (July 22, 1916), pp. 9, 11; *PE* 214 (November 10, 1917), p. 12; *PE* 248/249 (July 27, 1918), p. 10; *PE* 260/261 (November 2, 1918), p. 10; *PE* 558 (August 9, 1924), p. 12; *PE* 560 (August 23, 1924), p. 11; *PE* 654 (July 3, 1926), p. 10; *PE* 766 (September 29, 1928), p. 15; *PE* 780 (January 12, 1929), p. 10; *PE* 816 (September 21, 1929), p. 12; and *PE* 858 (July 26, 1930), p. 13.

yesterday who is over eighty years old. His dear old face lighted up with the glory of God as he was led into the water.[609]

It was not uncommon for Christians and the unconverted to attend baptisms and be so moved by the sights before them and the influence of the HS to act and receive WB without prior preparation. Pastor W.O. McKim from Pleasant View, AR, reported that a baptismal service was held, according to Rom. 6.4, and 23 were buried with Christ in baptism.

> At the beginning 14 were candidates for baptism and the Spirit set candidates for baptism and the Spirit set His approval on the service by pouring forth at intervals a deluge of glory upon the saints which was manifested by shouts of victory both in our natural tongues and in other tongues. After the fourteen were baptized, the invitation was extended to any child of God who was not baptized, and nine more came and the glory of the Lord witnessed to every heart.[610]

The Meaning of Water Baptism

One outcome of the 1913 'disruption' is that both sides clarified and codified their respective understandings relative to the practice and meaning of WB. Previous portions of this section have captured the various foci of Pentecostal WB, according to the practices of the AG. The various editorials, articles, and reports found in the *PE* also serve to elucidate the meaning of WB.

In his March 27, 1915 editorial, 'Baptized Once for All', E.N. Bell responds to numerous questions concerning WB.[611] After reiterating repentance and personal surrender or commitment to Christ are the requirements for baptism, Bell asserts that candidates need be baptized only once and that baptismal regeneration is to be rejected.[612] Positively, alluding to Rom. 6.1-14, Bell claims the Apostle Paul was teaching WB as a figure or likeness of burial into the death of Jesus Christ. It is the blood of Christ by the power of the HS that

---

[609] *PE* 60 (September 26, 1914), p. 4
[610] *PE* 99 (July 17, 1915), p. 1.
[611] *PE* 83 (March 27, 1915), pp. 1, 3. Also, see *PE* 230 (March 9, 1918), p. 2, where E.N. Bell addresses similar issues in 'The New Testament and Water Baptism'. Also, *PE* 306/307 (September 20, 1919), p. 9.
[612] *PE* 83 (March 27, 1915), pp. 1, 3.

removes our sin and condemnation and our sins are figuratively washed away in the ordinance of WB.[613]

The rationale for providing a ceremony or the public symbolic act of WB is to provide a definitive dividing line in which a person may severe ties with self-idolatry and old allegiances and reorient their life to the God who has created and redeemed them. According to Bell, a person accomplishes this by identifying with Jesus Christ in his death. More specifically, it is through

> Recognizing that he and his old life have been crucified in Christ and put to death, he stands up and is publicly buried, figuratively into Christ's death. He thus publicly owns himself dead as to his old man and old manner of life before the entire community. As he is raised in the likeness of Christ's resurrection from the watery grave, we see in this act a declaration that he is alive unto God. He is no more to be known by the old name 'sinner' but henceforth as a saint; no more as a child of the devil but as a child of God. He has been espoused under Christ and has put on His name and

---

[613] *PE* 83 (March 27, 1915), pp. 1, 3; *PE* 176 (February 10, 1917), p. 9; *PE* 306/307 (September 20, 1919), p. 9; *PE* 484/485 (February 17, 1923), p. 8; *PE* 601 (June 13, 1925), p. 3; and *PE* 851 (June 7, 1930), p. 2. The meaning of water in Jn. 3.5 is uncertain. Questions were often posed to the Q & A Forum. See *PE* 121 (January 1, 1916), p. 8; *PE* 202 (August 11, 1917), p. 9; *PE* 302/303 (August 23, 1919), p. 5; *PE* 368/369 (November 27, 1920), p. 10; and *PE* 798 (May 18, 1929), p. 9 for treatments of the question. The most thoroughly informed response is found in *PE* 121 (January 8, 1916), p. 8; *PE* 202 (August 11, 1917), p. 9; *PE* 302/303 (August 23, 1919), p. 5; *PE* 368/369 (November 27, 1920), p. 10; and *PE* 798 (May 18, 1929), p. 9:

> All church fathers and preachers from the second century up to John Calvin in the 16th Century, held (Jn 3.5) it referred to water baptism. (See Hastings Bible Dictionary on baptism.) Calvin denied this historic and traditional interpretation. Two other views are held. One is that the natural birth is referred to. This view is supported by the fact that Jesus goes right on in the next verse to speak of the birth of 'the flesh'. Still another view is that the 'washing of the water by the Word' is referred to. See Eph. 5:26. Since Calvin, till recent years, most Protestants have followed Calvin while the Episcopal and Catholic churches have followed still the ancient view that it referred to water baptism. Alexander Campbell, in the last century, and all his followers since, have held it referred to baptism. In recent years many Baptists have deserted Calvin and hold with Campbell on it, but not with as much emphasis on the water as he. Pentecostal saints, most generally, have denied the ancient and Campbell view, but more recently, many hold that it refers to water baptism as an external purifying symbol while the real internal birth is done by the Holy Spirit.

the name Christian. It is thus publicly and officially denied his former worldly crowd and publicly acknowledged his identification with Christ and His people.[614]

Bell also addresses the relationship between WB and Spirit baptism and astutely declares that 'No one can ever enter into all that is implied in Christian baptism without the quickening presence of the Holy Ghost'. While allowing that being baptized in the HS typically follows WB, there are biblical examples of the reverse order.[615] Nonetheless, the HS plays a vital role in WB. The exact nature of the HS's role is not elucidated.[616]

It appears to be the case that contemporaries of Bell were equating WB as Christian circumcision with Jewish circumcision. He asserts the comparison would not adhere since Jewish circumcision was the type of spiritual circumcision, according to Ezek. 36.25-27:

> So then, outward circumcision in the flesh was only a type, only a token, a seal or sign of the inner cutting or changing of the heart and one who becomes thereby a child of God. God has promised saying, 'From all your filthiness and from all your idols I will cleanse you. A new heart also will I give you, and a new spirit will I put within you; and I will take away the stony hear ... And I will

---

[614] *PE* 83 (March 27, 1915), pp. 1, 3.

[615] *PE* 230 (March 9, 1918), p. 2.

[616] Bell also argues that many have not received the Baptism of the HS due to their disobedience in first being baptized in water. See *PE* 230 (March 9, 1918), p. 2:

> No hint is given in the New Testament after Pentecost of any soul who wholeheartedly repented of his sins, who in faith cast Himself unreservedly upon Jesus for mercy and salvation, arose and was baptized in water with wholehearted obedience and then properly dealt with for the receiving of the Spirit that did not receive without all this waiting, struggling and hanging around the altar for months. Only some sorcerer or hypocrite like Simon Magus ever failed. God's plan was certain, the road plain and all who obeyed received according to God's promise. Why not so now? Has God changed? Our trouble may not all be at one point. We may have a lot of unclean sorcerers, as it were, seeking the Holy Ghost who need to repent, get under the blood and get a clean heart. But if we see this error, this wrong method, this wrong order, this unscriptural practice, why not quit it? The altar is all right. But a man has no business there for months before obeying God. For souls who have the light and do not need instruction, the order is repent, believe, be baptized, be prayed with for the Holy Ghost and get Him at once. Why not believe, obey and receive?

give you a heart of flesh. And I will put my Spirit within you'. Ezek. 36:25-27.[617]

The sign of WB is now the new symbol or token of the changed or circumcised heart.[618] Bell references several passages providing a *via salutis* for readers of the NT:

> Paul, speaking of our being made full or complete in Christ, says, 'In whom ye were also circumcised with a circumcision not made with hands, and the putting off of the body of the flesh, and the circumcision of Christ; having been buried with Him in baptism, wherein ye were also raised with Him through faith in the working of God'. Col. 2:11-12.
>
> In another place he speaks of the 'washing (the laver) of regeneration and the renewing of the Holy Ghost.' Tit. 2:5. Again he says, 'Having our hearts sprinkled from an evil conscience and our body washed in pure water.' Heb. 10:22. Again, 'Arise, and be baptized and wash away thy sins, calling on the name of the Lord.' Acts 22:16. Again, 'Repent, and be baptized in (upon) the name of Jesus Christ for (to or in reference to) the remission of sins, and ye shall receive the gift of the Holy Ghost.' Acts 2:38.[619]

Bell concludes this portion of his article, alerting readers to exercise caution concerning the above passages since 'there is a reference both to the water baptism and to the work of the Spirit, a reference to the outward token and to the inward reality'. These two lines should be kept separate so they are not confused. It is vital that

---

[617] *PE* 118 (December 4, 1915), p. 3.
[618] *PE* 118 (December 4, 1915), p. 3.
[619] *PE* 118 (December 4, 1915), p. 3. The same point is made in *PE* 202 (August 11, 1917), p. 9, where Acts 2.38 and Col. 2.12 are understood accordingly:

> Water baptism is referred to in both; but faith that appropriates the blood is implied as previously exercised. Then the washing of the body in pure water symbolizes the internal washing with the blood. Remember, in Apostolic days. baptism was performed at once when one repented and believed, so that faith and baptism went close together, not weeks or years apart as often is the case now. Hence conversion and baptism were regarded as practically one event in those days. But the real work was within by the Spirit, and not accomplished by the water.

we see the outward sign and not lose sight of the inward work of the Spirit.[620]

While Narver Gortner supported the writings of J.N. Bell, Stanley J. Fordsham, and others, Gortner provides a noteworthy emphasis on the symbolism of WB as a memorial to the resurrection of Jesus Christ. This is in counterpoint to the Lord's Supper serving as a memorial to his death. Gortner offers a variant interpretation of 1 Cor. 15.29 since it is often misunderstood and misinterpreted, according to him.

> The apostle argues that baptism of believers is an indication that Christ has risen. Not only His death and burial, but His resurrection also, is signified by the baptism of the believer. If Christ has not risen the believer should go down under the water and stay there. But Christ has risen. Therefore the believer not only goes down under the water, but he rises therefrom. Thus, as the holy communion is a memorial of the death of Christ, the baptism of the believer is a memorial of His resurrection. He died and rose again. Identification with Christ in His death, in His burial, and in His resurrection! Thank God! How great is the privilege of the believer! And how significant is the ordinance of baptism! May it henceforth have a new meaning for each of us![621]

Additional articles and sermons emphasized the 'throne life' or 'union with Christ' as a result of repentance, faith in Christ, and WB. Romans 6.1-14 plays a central role in their thoughts. For instance, an article in the *PE* of April 2, 1921, 'All Things New in Union with Christ', the author claims that

> if it were only the union with Christ in His death, we would still be in our sins (1 Cor. 15:13-19, especially verse 17). But there is a wonderful relation that results from being baptized into His death and that is being baptized into His life through union with Him in His resurrection. That like as Christ was raised from the dead through the glory of the Father, so we also might walk in newness of life (Rom. 6:4). He did not remain dead; He did not remain in

---

[620] *PE* 118 (December 4, 1915), p. 3. Lack of unity also exists in the understanding of Gal. 3.27 regarding whether 'Christ is put on' in WB. See *PE* 386/387 (April 2, 1921), pp. 2-3; *PE* 390/391 (April 30, 1921), p. 10.

[621] *PE* 559 (August 16, 1924), pp. 2-3.

the tomb, for the divine life was in Him. And like as He was raised from the dead through the power of the life of God, so we also are raised by this same power of the life of God to walk in newness of life.⁶²²

Bridal Call/Bridal Call Foursquare/Foursquare Crusader

Introduction

The original edition of the *Bridal Call* was published in June 1917 by F.A. Hess, Savannah, GA, under the stated editorial purview of Bro. and Sis. H.S. McPherson of New York, NY.⁶²³ After her separation from H.S. McPherson in 1918, the monthly periodical was edited solely by Aimee Semple McPherson.⁶²⁴

The rationale for the publication was 'to get the present day [sic] truths to all the people possible before Jesus comes'. Distribution was to occur at McPherson's meetings, enabling the ministry 'to give out hundreds and thousands in our meetings alone as the Lord provides the means to supply paper'. McPherson reports God's blessing on the endeavor since the 'Lord has laid it upon the heart of the dear brother in Savannah to give his time and labor freely'.⁶²⁵ Seven months later, the purpose of the *BC* was sharpened to disseminating the Foursquare message of 'Salvation, the baptism of the Holy Ghost, Divine Healing, and the Soon coming of Jesus'.⁶²⁶ In December 1923, the *BC* was renamed the *Bridal Call Four Square* (*BCF*) and published as a monthly paper.⁶²⁷

On November 25, 1926, the first edition of a new weekly paper, the *Foursquare Crusader* (*FC*), was published.⁶²⁸ Sister Aimee expressed gratitude for the fact 'At last we have our own real newspaper ... the Foursquare Crusader, an eight-page newspaper' that provides a way

---

⁶²² *PE* 386/387 (April 2, 1921), pp. 2-3. See *PE* 805 (July 6, 1929), pp. 6-9.

⁶²³ *BC* 1.1 (June 1917), p. 1.

⁶²⁴ *BC* 2.2 (August 1918), p. 1. For an introduction to the life, ministry, and publications of McPherson see C.M. Robeck Jr. 'McPherson, Aimee Semple' in Stanley M. Burgess and Eduard M. van der Maas (eds.), *NIDPCM* (rev. and exp. edn; Grand Rapids, MI: Zondervan, 2002), pp. 856-59.

⁶²⁵ *BC* 1.1 (June 1917), p. 2.

⁶²⁶ *BC* 1.8 (January 1918), p. 2.

⁶²⁷ *BCF* 7.7-8 (December-January 1924), p. 5.

⁶²⁸ *FC* 1.1 (November 25, 1926), p. 1.

'to tell the world all about the great, big, wonderful things we are doing here in Angelus Temple'.[629]

The Practice of Water Baptism

Because the role of women was highly restricted by society, in general, and in ministry, in particular, one might conjecture that WB would not receive even minimal attention from Aimee Semple McPherson in practice. Similarly, it is unfathomable that WB would hold a place of prominence in the writings of Aimee Semple McPherson.[630] The conjecture will prove to be in error. It appears to be the case, that according to the sheer number of references to WB and baptismal activity in three publications the rite held a place of great import in McPherson's theology and practice throughout the tenure of her ministry and the growth of the nascent ICFG.[631] An

---

[629] *FC* 1.1 (November 25, 1926), p. 1. See C.M. Robeck Jr, 'Angelus Temple' in Stanley M. Burgess and Eduard M. van der Maas (eds.), *NIDPCM* (rev. and exp. edn; Grand Rapids, MI: Zondervan, 2002), pp. 314-15.

[630] The 19th Amendment to the USA Constitution, which gave women the right to vote, was not passed by Congress until June 4, 1919, and ratified on August 18, 1920. Of course, being given the legal right to vote did little to elevate the role of women in religious circles and society.

[631] *BC* 1.2 (July 1917), p. 4; *BC* 1.9 (February 1918), p. 2; *BC* 1.20 (July 1917), p. 4; *BC* 2.2 (July 1918), p. 10; *BC* 2.10 (March 1919), p. 10; *BC* 2.11 (April 1919), p. 16; *BC* 2.12 (May 1919), p. 15; *BC* 4.4 (September 1920), pp. 3, 5; *BC* 5.4 (September 1921), p. 6; *BC* 5.5 (Oct 1921), p. 7, 8, and 9; *BC* 5.10 (March 1922), p. 12; *BC* 6.2, 3 (July and August 1922), pp. 9-10, 13-14; *BC* 6.4 (September 1922), p. 10; *BC* 6.9 (February 1923), p. 18; *BC* 6.12 (May 1923), p. 25; *BC* 7.1 (June 1923), pp. 14, 15, and 19; *BC* 7.4 (September 1923), p. 14; *BC* 7.6 (November 1923), p. 19; *BCF* 8.3 (August 1924), p. 26; *BCF* 8.4 (September 1924), pp. 19-22, 30; *BCF* 8.5 (Oct 1924), p. 11; *BCF* 8.6 (November 1924), pp. 29, 32; *BCF* 8.7 (December 1924), p. 28; *BCF* 8.8 (January 1925), p. 31; *BCF* 8.9 (February 1925), p. 28; *BCF* 8.10 (March 1925), p. 29; *BCF* 8.11 (April 1925), p. 28; *BCF* 9.2 (July 1925), p. 30; *BCF* 9.3 (August 1925), p. 20; *BCF* 9.9 (February 1926), pp. 10-12; *BCF* 9.10 (March 1926), pp. 10-13; *BCF* 10.4 (September 1926), pp. 26, 32; *BCF* 10.7 (December 1926), pp. 16, 25-26; *BCF* 10.9 (February 1927), p. 26; *BCF* 10.11 (April 1927), p. 30; *BCF* 11.1 (June 1927), pp. 15-16, 30; *BCF* 11.2 (July 1927), p. 5; *BCF* 11.3 (August 1927), p. 23; *BCF* 11.5 (Oct 1927), pp. 11-12, 34; *BCF* 11.6 (November 1927), p. 26; *BCF* 12.2 (February 1928), p. 31; *BCF* 12.3 (March 1928), p. 17; *BCF* 12.5 (May 1928), p. 10; *BCF* 12.4 (September 1928), p. 25; *BCF* 12.6 (November 1928), p. 17; *BCF* 12.7 (December 1928), p. 17; *BCF* 12.8 (January 1929), p. 36; *BCF* 12.12 (May 1929), pp. 8, 18; *BCF* 13.1 (June 1929), p. 20; BCF 13.4 (September 1929), p. 24; *BCF* 13.10 (March 1930), pp. 11, 12, and 32; *BCF* 14.3 (August 1930), pp. 5, 15-16, and 31; *BCF* 14.4 (September 20,1930), p. 20; *BCF* 14.12 (May 1931), p. 27; *BCF* 14.14 (July 1931), pp. 6, 26-27; *BCF* 15.5 (Oct 1931), p. 16; *BCF* 15.6 (November 1931), p. 32;

indicator of the importance WB held for Aimee Semple McPherson was the advertisement of a tract by her titled, 'Regarding Water Baptism' for a cost of fifty cents. The advertisement was carried in the 1920 editions of the BC, published in Los Angeles, CA.[632]

In the July 1917 issue of the *BC,* the editors published thirteen points of 'What We Believe and Teach' to clarify for readers the theology and practices espoused by them. They assert that WB is 'an outward sign of an inward work' because we have 'reckoned ourselves and our old sinful lives nailed to the cross, we long to be identified with Him not only in His death but in His burial also. Rom. 6:3-5; Acts 2:38; 10:47, 48; 19;4, 5; Mk 16:16; Mt. 28:19'.[633]

Water baptism by immersion was understood to have been commissioned by Christ[634] and designated an ordinance or sacrament

---

FC 1.1 (November 25, 1926), p. 8; *FC* 1.4 (December 16, 1926), p. 1; *FC* 1.6 (January 1, 1927), pp. 2, 6; *FC* 1.7 (January 8, 1927), pp. 2, 8; *FC* 1.18 (March 26, 1927), p. 1; *FC* 1.22 (April 23, 1927), pp. 2, 8; *FC* 1.24 (May 7, 1927), pp. 2, 3; *FC* 1.25 (May 14, 1927), pp. 2, 5; *FC* 1.28 (June 4, 1927), p. 2, 5; *FC* 1.29 (June 11, 1927), pp. 2, 3; *FC* 1.33 (July 9, 1927), pp. 2, 3-5, and 8; *FC* 1.35 (July 23, 1927), p. 2; *FC* 1.36 (July 30, 1927), pp. 2, 5; *FC* 1.39 (August 17, 1927), p. 2, 3-4; *FC* 1.40 (August 24, 1927), pp. 2, 4, and 8; *FC* 1.45 (September 28, 1927), pp. 1, 2; *FC* 1.49 (Oct 26, 1927), pp. 2, 4; *FC* 1.51 (November 9, 1927), pp. 2, 5, and 8; *FC* 2.2 (December 7, 1927), pp. 2, 5; *FC* 2.4 (December 21, 1927), p. 2; *FC* 2.6 (January 4, 1928), pp. 2, 4, and 5; *FC* 2.7 (January 11, 1928), pp. 2, 8; *FC* 2.12 (February 15, 1928), pp. 2, 3; *FC* 2.21 (April 18, 1928), pp. 4, 8; *FC* 2.24 (May 9, 1928), pp. 2, 3, and 7; *FC* 2.25 (May 23, 1928), pp. 1, 2, and 3; *FC* 2.34 (July 1928), pp. 1, 2; *FC* 2.47 (Oct 17, 1928), p. 2; *FC* 3.4 (December 19, 1928), pp. 2, 8, and 12; *FC* 3.13 (February 20, 1929), pp. 2, 5, and 7; *FC* 3.18 (March 27, 1929), pp. 2, 8; *FC* 3.19 (April 3, 1929), pp. 1, 2; *FC* 3.23 (May 1, 1929), pp. 2, 8, and 13; *FC* 3.25 (May 15, 1929), pp. 2, 5, and 8; *FC* 3.35 (July 24, 1929), pp. 1, 2; *FC* 3.41 (September 4, 1929), pp. 1, 2, and 12; *FC* 3.43 (September 18, 1929), pp. 1, 2, and 7; *FC* 3.46 (Oct 9, 1929), pp. 1, 2, 9, and 11; *FC* 4.5 (December 25, 1929), pp. 1, 2, and 5; *FC* 5.2 (February 26, 1930), pp. 1-2; *FC* 4.16 (March 12, 1930), pp. 1, 2; *FC* 4.18 (March 26, 1930), pp. 2, 7; *FC* 4.23 (April 30, 1930), pp. 7, 8; *FC* 2.35 (July 23, 1930), pp. 1, 5; *FC* 4.41 (September 3, 1930), p. 1; *FC* 5.2 (December 3, 1930), pp. 1, 3, and 11; *FC* 5.12 (February 11, 1931), pp. 1, 4, 5, and 11; *FC* 5.13 (February 18, 1931), pp. 1, 8; *FC* 5.14 (February 25, 1931), pp. 1, 4, and 5; *FC* 5.18 (March 25, 1931), pp. 1, 6; *FC* 5.19 (April 1, 1931), pp. 9, 11; *FC* 5.21 (April 15, 1931), pp. 1, 7; *FC* 5.23 (April 29, 1931), pp. 1, 2, 5, and 6; *FC* 5.24 (May 7, 1931), p. 7; *FC* 5.27 (May 27, 1931), p. 1; *FC* 5.33 (July 8, 1931), pp. 3, 11; *FC* 5.35 (July 22, 1931), p. 5; *FC* 5.36 (July 29, 1931), pp. 2, 4, and 5; *FC* 5.38 (August 12, 1931), pp. 2, 4; *FC* 5.42 (September 9, 1931), pp. 1, 8; *FC* 5.50B (Oct 10, 1931), p. 1; *FC* 6.5 (November 18, 1931), pp. 3, 5, and 8; *FC* 6.8 (December 9, 1931), p. 3; *FC* 6.9 (December 16, 1931), p. 6; and *FC* 6.11 (December 30, 1931), pp. 3, 7.

[632] *BC* 3.8 (January 1920), p. 2; *BC* 3.9 (February 1920), p. 2; *BC* 3.10 (March), p. 2; *BC* 3.11 (April 1920), p. 2; and *BC* 4.4 (September 1920). p. 2.

[633] *BC* 1.2 (July 1917), p. 4. Also, *BC* 1.9 (February 1918), p. 2.

[634] *FC* 1.33 (July 9, 1927), pp. 3-5; *FC* 2.47 (Oct 17, 1928), p. 2.

of the Church, along with the Lord's Supper or Communion, according to a Sunday School lesson from February 1927. In WB 'A dead body is buried, hence as we accept Christ and become dead to the old world life, it is very proper that we evidence this by creatures in Christ'. Again, according to Rom. 6.1-14, baptism is an outward symbol of an inner change.[635]

In May 1919, support for her doctrinal stance and preaching/teaching was provided by Pastor Robert J. Craig, who had the first-hand experience of her ministry in San Francisco, CA:

> All the people who follow Sister McPherson's sound doctrinal teaching will obey their Lord in the teaching of the new birth, water-baptism, the baptism of the Holy Spirit, and the preparation of the Bride, and will be bound to land right. The Spirit has made her sound to the core, and is a safe teacher to follow these dark days of erroneous leadership.[636]

Rev. Geo. A. Bale provides a similar testimonial in the November 1923 issue of the *BC*. He proffers, 'One of the things that has impressed me is the place and prominence of water baptism. Every Thursday night ... this year there has been a baptismal service, and from forty to eighty ... are buried with Christ in baptism each evening'.[637]

In addition to the teaching of sound doctrine, the administration of WB was widely and routinely practiced by other ministers as they served under the ICFG banner, as the following study substantiates.

Widely Practiced and Sufficient Water

While the number of references to WBs between 1917 to 1922, inclusive, is limited, reports of WBs are contained in the *BC*, which signal the import of WB for McPherson during her early ministry. Most of these reports are from Alton, IL,[638] Denver, CO,[639] San

---

[635] *FC* 3.13 (February 20, 1929), p. 7. Additional references to WB as an ordinance or sacrament are found in the ICFG publications from 1923 to 1931: *BC* 7.6 (November 1923), p. 19; *FC* 1.33 (July 9, 1927), pp. 3-5; *FC* 5.12 (February 11, 1931), pp. 4, 5; and *FC* 6.8 (December 9, 1931), p. 7.

[636] *BC* 2.12 (May 1919), p. 15. Also, *BC* 7.6 (November 1923), p. 19.

[637] *BC* 7.6 (November 1923), p. 19.

[638] *BC* 4.4 (September 1920), pp. 7, 9.

[639] *BC* 6.2, 3 (July and August 1922), pp. 9-10, 13-14.

Francisco, CA,[640] and San Jose, CA.[641] Typically, these early reports reflect the location and number baptized.[642] In some instances, the reports reflect only the geographical location.[643] Several reports identify the body of water utilized for the baptisms. The swimming pool located in Idora Park of Oakland, CA, is mentioned once.[644] An unidentified river is named once;[645] while the Mississippi River is named twice.[646]

It appears that church baptistries[647] were widely utilized by McPherson and her ministerial colleagues during the years before the erection of Angelus Temple (AT) in 1923. The use of church baptistries was not new for the Pentecostal movement. Church baptistries had been utilized in locales where the early Pentecostals found favor with the ministers and congregants of mainline churches. One example of such a collaboration is between Dr. William Keeney Towner, pastor of the First Baptist Church, San Jose, CA, and McPherson. Their partnership resulted in a spiritual harvest for the kingdom of God and problematic consequences of abundant usage of a baptistry and baptismal robes. According to Sister Aimee, a baptismal service was held daily 'until the overworked baptistry [sic] sprung a leak and had to rest two or three days until being repaired'. The pastor asserted that 'this was the first time he ever heard of this happening in a Baptist Church'. Due to the remarkable number of baptisms, candidates were urged to bring their apparel for baptism since the baptismal robes could not be dried quickly enough. Dr. Towner humorously opined 'that instead of the usual difficulty of

---

[640] *BC* 2.11 (April 1919), p. 15.

[641] *BC* 5.4 (September 1921), p. 11; *BC* 5.5 (Oct 1921), pp. 7, 8-9.

[642] *BC* 2.11 (April 1919), p. 15; *BC* 4.4 (September 1920), pp. 7, 9; *BC* 5.4 (September 1921), p. 11; *BC* 5.5 (Oct 1921), pp. 7, 8-9; *BC* 5.10 (March 1922), p. 12; *BC* 6.2, 3 (July and August 1922), pp. 9-10, 13-14; and *BC* 6.4 (September 1922), pp. 10-11.

[643] *BCF* 12.2 (February 1928), pp. 20, 22; *BCF* 12.3 (March 1928), pp. 9, 27; *FC* 3.25 (May 15, 1929), p. 8; and *FC* 5.18 (March 25, 1931), p. 2.

[644] *BC* 6.4 (September 1922), p. 10.

[645] *FC* 1.35 (July 23, 1927), p. 8.

[646] *BC* 4.4 (September 1920), pp. 7, 8.

[647] *BC* 5.4 (September 1921), p. 11; *BC* 5.5 (Oct 1921), pp. 7, 8-9; *BC* 5.10 (March 1922), p. 12; and *BC* 6.2, 3 (July and August 1922), pp. 9-10, 13-14.

getting the robes wet, 'twas now an utter impossibility to get them dried quickly enough'.[648]

As Pentecostal faith communities grew and were financially capable, new churches with baptistries were erected and utilized. It does not appear that other Pentecostal churches gave WB and a baptistry the prominent roles they were to play in the ministry of Aimee Semple McPherson and the churches of the ICFG.

After several years of itinerant ministry, McPherson settled in the Echo Park area of Los Angeles, CA, where the AT was constructed and formally dedicated on January 1, 1923.[649] From that date forward, the number of baptismal reports multiplied exponentially.[650] There are several reasons for the increased number of reports related to the AT.

---

[648] *BC* 5.5 (Oct 1921), p. 7. Also, see *BC* 6.2, 3 (July and August 1922), pp. 13-14 for the account of a baptistry constructed when one was not available:

> We built a baptistry [sic] about 12 feet long, 6 feet wide and 4 feet deep. The water it contained was provided from the city waterworks and the necessary warmth provided from the great hot-water tanks of the auditorium. This baptistry [sic] was beautifully adorned on every side with plants and flowers. An arched canopy top was wound with beautiful red roses.

[649] *BC* 6.4 (September 1922), p. 10; *BC* 6.7 (December 1922), pp. 10-11.

[650] *BC* 6.9 (February 1923), p. 18; *BC* 6.12 (May 1923), p. 25; *BC* 7.1 (June 1923), pp. 19, 14-15; *BCF* 8.6 (November 1924), p. 27; *BCF* 8.8 (January 1925), p. 23; *BCF* 8.9 (February 1925), p. 28; *BCF* 8.10 (March 1925), p. 20; *BCF* 8.11 (April 1925), p. 28; *BCF* 9.3 (August 1925), p. 20; *BCF* 10.4 (September 1926), pp. 26, 32; *BCF* 10.9 (February 1927), p. 26; *BCF* 10.11 (April 1927), pp. 15-16; *BCF* 11.6 (November 1927), pp. 27, 32; *BCF* 12.2 (February 1928), pp. 22; *BCF* 12.12 (May 1929), p. 18; *BCF* 14.4 (September 1930), p. 20; *FC* 1.22 (April 23, 1927), p. 2; *FC* 1.25 (May 14, 1927), p. 5; *FC* 1.28 (June 4, 1927), p. 5; *FC* 1.33 (July 9, 1927), p. 4; *FC* 1.35 (July 23, 1927), p. 8; *FC* 1.49 (Oct 26, 1927), p. 4.; *FC* 2.4 (December 7, 1927), p. 5; *FC* 2.6 (January 4, 1928), p. 5; *FC* 2.7 (January 11, 1928), p. 2; *FC* 2.12 (February 15, 1928), p. 3; *FC* 2.24 (May 9, 1928), p. 4; *FC* 2.25 (May 23, 1928), pp. 3, 7; *FC* 3.13 (February 20, 1929), p. 6, 7; *FC* 3.18 (March 27, 1929), p. 8; *FC* 3.19 (April 3, 1929), p. 2; *FC* 3.23 (May 1, 1929), p. 8; *FC* 3.25 (May 15, 1929), p. 2; *FC* 3.35 (July 24, 1929), pp. 1, 2; *FC* 3.41 (September 4, 1929), p. 7; *FC* 3.46 (Oct 9, 1929), pp. 5, 14; *FC* 4.5 (December 25, 1929), p. 9; *FC* 4.18 (March 26, 1930), p. 2; *FC* 4.23 (April 30, 1930), p. 8; *FC* 2.35 (July 23, 1930), pp. 1, 5; *FC* 5.2 (December 3, 1930), pp. 3, 5; *FC* 5.12 (February 11, 1931), pp. 4, 5; *FC* 5.14 (February 25, 1931), p. 5; *FC* 5.18 (March 25, 1931), p. 2; *FC* 5.19 (April 1, 1931), p. 9; *FC* 5.23 (April 29, 1931), pp. 2, 5, and 6; *FC* 5.24 (May 7, 1931), pp. 2, 5; *FC* 5.36 (July 29, 1931), p. 5; *FC* 5.42 (September 9, 1931), p. 1; *FC* 5.50B (Oct 10, 1931), pp. 4, 5; *FC* 6.5 (November 18, 1931), pp. 5, 8; *FC* 6.8 (December 9, 1931), p. 5; *FC* 6.9 (December 16, 1931), p. 6; and *FC* 6.11 (December 30, 1931), p. 3.

First, the baptistry was erected to replicate the Jordan River scene where John baptized Jesus.[651] The physical location of the baptistry appears to have served as a visual reminder of the importance of WB. One observer, commenting on the uniqueness of the AT baptistry, provided the following comments:

> When the velour curtains are swept aside and the lights of the Temple are lowered, a miniature River Jordan meets the gaze. With delight and surprise one sees the water flowing, foaming over the rocks, tumbling into the baptistery in the forground [sic]. Electric lights have been so arranged outside the stained glass windows themselves afford practical enough light for the audience and make the baptistery, which is itself specially lighted, stand out in sharp relief.[652]

Mode

In conjunction with the visual reminder, it appears to be the case that immersion was the only accepted mode of WB. The use of 'immerse'[653] and 'immersion'[654] figure prominently in the reports, as

---

[651] *FC* 6.11 (December 30, 1931), p. 6.

[652] *BC* 7.4 (September 1923), p. 14.

[653] *BCF* 8.6 (November 1924), p. 27; *BCF* 11.7 (November 1927), p. 22; *FC* 2.25 (May 23, 1928), p. 3; *FC* 3.25 (May 15, 1929), p. 2; *FC* 3.35 (July 24, 1929), p. 2; *BCF* 13.10 (March 1930), pp. 11, 12, and 32; *FC* 4.18 (March 26, 1930), pp. 1, 7; *FC* 5.19 (April 1, 1931), p. 9; *FC* 5.23 (April 29, 1931), p. 2; *FC* 5.36 (July 29, 1931), p. 5; and *FC* 5.50B (Oct 10, 1931), p. 2. The mode of baptism employed by McPherson during the nascent years of her ministry also appears to have been immersion, according to the unambiguous language employed. For a fuller discussion, see: *BC* 4.4 (September 1920), pp. 7, 9; *BC* 5.4 (September 1921), p. 11; *BC* 5.5 (Oct 1921), p. 7; *BC* 5.5 (Oct 1921), pp. 8-9; *BC* 5.10 (March 1922), p. 12; *BC* 6.2, 3 (July and August 1922), pp. 9-10; *BC* 6.2, 3 (July and August 1922), pp. 13-14; and *BC* 6.4 (September 1922), pp. 10-11.

[654] *BCF* 9.4 (September 1925), p. 11; *BCF* 9.10 (March 1926), p. 17; *BCF* 9.11 (April 1926), p. 27; *BCF* 10.3 (August 1926), p. 13; *FC* 1.33 (July 9, 1927), pp. 3, 5; *FC* 1.39 (August 17, 1927), p. 3; *FC* 3.4 (December 19, 1928), p. 12; *FC* 3.37 (August 7, 1929), p. 3; *FC* 3.50 (November 6, 1929), p. 9; *BCF* 13.1 (June 1929), p. 20; *FC* 4.6 (January 1, 1930), p. 7; *BCF* 13.10 (March 1930), p. 17; *FC* 4.23 (April 30, 1930), p. 6; *BCF* 14.4 (September 1930), p. 12; *FC* 4.32 (July 1, 1931), p. 7; *BCF* 14.14 (July 1931), p. 14; *BCF* 15.3 (August 1931), p. 33; *FC* 4.42 (September 9, 1931), p. 8; *BCF* 15.5 (Oct 1931), p. 7; and *FC* 6.8 (December 9, 1931), p. 4.

does burial language.⁶⁵⁵ 'Following the Lord'⁶⁵⁶ and 'obedience to Christ's command'⁶⁵⁷ are also employed by reporters. The acceptable mode of WB appears to have been a perennial issue given the question posed and answered in the December 1931 issue of the *FC*. The response is framed by citing the NT narrative of Jesus' baptism, Greek usage of *baptizo*, biblical exegesis of Romans 6, and church history:

> During the first century AD, in fact for the first 150 years, immersion was the only mode of baptism in use. The question may arise as to whether baptism should be by sprinkling or immersion, but the answer is not difficult. From the meaning of the word and the example of scripture, the history of the ordinance, the testimony of scholars and the concession of eminent men in all denominations, it is clear that the original method was immersion in water.⁶⁵⁸

---

⁶⁵⁵ *BC* 6.9 (February 1923), p. 18; *BC* 6.12 (May 1923), p. 25; *BC* 7.1 (June 1923), pp. 14-15; *BC* 7.6 (November 1923), p. 19; *BCF* 8.8 (January 1925), p. 22; *BCF* 9.3 (August 1925), p. 20; *BCF* 9.9 (February 1926), pp. 10-12; *BCF* 10.4 (September 1926), pp. 26, 32; *BCF* 10.9 (February 1927), p. 26; *BCF* 13.10 (March 1930), pp. 11, 12, and 32; *BCF* 14.3 (August 1930), pp. 15-16; *FC* 1.22 (April 23, 1927), p. 2; *FC* 1.25 (May 14, 1927), p. 5; *FC* 1.28 (June 4, 1927), p. 5; *FC* 1.33 (July 9, 1927), pp. 3-5; *FC* 1.35 (July 23, 1927), p. 8; *FC* 1.49 (Oct 26, 1927), p. 4; *FC* 1.51 (November 9, 1927), pp. 3, 5; *FC* 2.4 (December 4, 1927), p. 5; *FC* 2.6 (January 4, 1928), p. 5; *FC* 2.7 (January 11, 1928), p. 2; *FC* 2.25 (May 23, 1928), p. 3; *FC* 2.47 (Oct 17, 1928), p. 2; *FC* 3.13 (February 20, 1929), pp. 2, 5, and 7; *FC* 3.19 (April 3, 1929), p. 2; *FC* 3.23 (May 1, 1929), pp. 8, 13; *FC* 3.35 (July 24, 1929), p. 1; *FC* 3.41 (September 4, 1929), p. 3; *FC* 5.2 (February 26, 1930), pp. 1-2; *FC* 4.18 (March 26, 1930), p. 7; *FC* 2.35 (July 23, 1930), p. 5; *FC* 5.12 (February 11, 1931), p. 5; *FC* 5.19 (April 1, 1931), p. 9; *FC* 5.24 (May 7, 1931), p. 2; *FC* 5.38 (August 12, 1931), p. 4; *FC* 6.5 (November 18, 1931), p. 5; and *FC* 6.8 (December 9, 1931), p. 7.

⁶⁵⁶ *FC* 1.33 (July 9, 1927), p. 4; *BCF* 8.6 (November 1924), p. 27; *FC* 2.35 (July 23, 1930), p. 5; *BCF* 10.4 (September 1926), pp. 26, 32; *FC* 1.49 (Oct 26, 1927), p. 4; *FC* 5.2 (December 3, 1930), p. 3; *FC* 5.23 (April 29, 1931), p. 2; and *FC* 6.9 (December 16, 1931), p. 6.

⁶⁵⁷ *BCF* 8.8 (January 1925), p. 22; *FC* 1.33 (July 9, 1927), pp. 3-5; *FC* 1.40 (August 24, 1927), p. 4; *FC* 1.51 (November 9, 1927), p. 3; and *FC* 5.50B (Oct 10, 1931), p. 5.

⁶⁵⁸ *FC* 6.8 (December 9, 1931), p. 7.

Given the preceding, 'sprinkling' was not an acceptable mode.[659] Consequently, infant baptism was rejected outright.[660] Following the OT example of Hannah, who dedicated infant Samuel to God, baby dedication served as an acceptable alternative to infant baptism for parents desiring God's oversight of their children.[661] The following theological rationale undergirded the support for baby dedication since christening babies was too akin to baptism, and WB was reserved for persons 'who have repented and intelligently accepted the Lord as Saviour'. Children are dedicated to Christ by 'bringing them to Him that He may lay His hands upon them in blessing as in the days of old when mothers brought their little ones to Him when He walked the earth'.[662]

Second, a regularly scheduled baptismal service, officiated by Sister Aimee, was conducted every Thursday at 7.30 pm with a sermon by McPherson or a notable preacher. Reports indicate that by September 1930, more than 21,000 persons had been baptized during this service.[663]

Third, drinking deeply from the well of the dramatic arts, Sister Aimee was gifted with the ability to paint vivid, captivating word portraits that invited readers and KSMG radio-listeners to picture themselves in the baptistry following Jesus in obedience at AT. Her description of a Thursday evening baptismal service provides insight into her approach and ability to evoke responses from her readers and hearers:

> Just back of the speaker's platform, the heavy velour curtains are swept aside, revealing the scene of the River Jordan, which apparently stretches away and away in the distance. From out the foreground of the river a stream of water is flowing, pouring over rocks and pebbles into the baptistry [sic] below. Palms bend low on either side, trunks of trees gnarled and twisted. The baptistry

---

[659] *BCF* 10.7 (December 1926), pp. 25-26; *FC* 1.33 (July 9, 1927), pp. 3-5; *FC* 3.13 (February 20, 1929), p. 2; and *FC* 5.2 (February 26, 1930), pp. 1-2.
[660] *FC* 3.25 (May 15, 1929), p. 5; *FC* 4.18 (March 26, 1930), p. 7.
[661] *BCF* 8.6 (November 1924), p. 29; *FC* 3.23 (May 1, 1929), p. 8; *FC* 3.25 (May 15, 1929), pp. 5, 8; *FC* 6.8 (December 9, 1931), p. 7; and *FC* 6.11 (December 30, 1931), p. 3.
[662] *FC* 3.25 (May 15, 1929), p. 5.
[663] *BCF* 14.4 (September 1930), p. 20.

[sic] itself is of shining white tile. The water is almost completely covered with pink and white roses and white carnations – which have been brought by those whose loved ones are to be buried in baptism – and emptied upon the waters, making this truly 'a watery grave.' Hundreds are saying to each other, 'Oh, I never saw anything so beautiful!' 'It is glorious, Praise the Lord.' One family of eleven are baptized. Later a father with four manly sons fill the pool. Then comes a whole row of husbands and wives. They also are buried together in baptism. One time a family of four composed of husband, wife, mother-in-law and son were baptized at the same time. Truly, it is a grand religion that can cause a man to be baptized with this mother-in-law and to come up with a radiant face and clasp the whole family in his arms, promising God that life, love, home, all are held for His glory from this time forth.[664]

A fourth element contributing to numerous reports from AT was the frequent numerical reports, references, and the regularly scheduled weekly baptismal service that publicized in the *BC*, *BCF*, and *FC*.[665] The constant promotion kept before readers the

---

[664] *BC* 7.1 (June 1923), pp. 14-15.

[665] *BC* 6.9 (February 1923), p. 18; *BC* 6.12 (May 1923), p. 25; *BC* 7.1 (June 1923), pp. 14-15, 19; *BC* 7.4 (September 1923), p. 14; *BC* 7.6 (November 1923), p. 19; *BCF* 8.3 (August 1924), p. 26; *BCF* 8.4 (September 1924), p. 30; *BCF* 8.5 (Oct 1924), p. 11; *BCF* 8.6 (November 1924), pp. 29, 32; *BCF* 8.7 (December 1924), p. 28; *BCF* 8.8 (January 1925), p. 31; *BCF* 8.10 (March 1925), p. 29; *BCF* 8.11 (April 1925), p. 28; *BCF* 9.3 (August 1925), p. 20; *BCF* 9.9 (February 1926), pp. 10-12; *BCF* 10.4 (September 1926), pp. 26, 32; *BCF* 10.7 (December 1926), pp. 25-26; *BCF* 10.11 (April 1927), p. 30; *BCF* 12.8 (January 1929), p. 36; *BCF* 12.12 (May 1929), p. 18; *BCF* 13.1 (June 1929), p. 20; *BCF* 13.10 (March 1930), pp. 11, 12, and 32; *BCF* 14.4 (September 1930), p. 20; *FC* 1.1 (November 25, 1926), p. 8; *FC* 1.4 (December 16, 1926), p. 1; *FC* 1.6 (January 1, 1927), p. 2; *FC* 1.7 (January 8, 1927), p. 2; *FC* 1.18 (March 26, 1927), p. 1; *FC* 1.22 (April 23, 1927), p. 8; *FC* 1.24 (May 7, 1927), p. 2; *FC* 1.25 (May 14, 1927), pp. 2, 5; *FC* 1.28 (June 4, 1927), p. 2, 5; *FC* 1.29 (June 11, 1927), p. 2; *FC* 1.33 (July 9, 1927), pp. 2, 3, 4, and 5; *FC* 1.35 (July 23, 1927), p. 2; *FC* 1.36 (July 30, 1927), pp. 2, 5; *FC* 1.39 (August 17, 1927), p. 2; *FC* 1.40 (August 24, 1927), pp. 2, 4, and 8; *FC* 1.45 (September 28, 1927), pp. 1, 2; *FC* 1.49 (Oct 26, 1927), pp. 2, 4; *FC* 1.51 (November 9, 1927), pp. 2, 8; *FC* 2.2 (December 7, 1927), p. 2; *FC* 2.4 (December 21, 1927), p. 2; *FC* 2.6 (January 4, 1928), p. 2; *FC* 2.7 (January 11, 1928), p. 2; *FC* 2.12 (February 15, 1928), pp. 2, 3;

importance of following Christ in obedience.⁶⁶⁶ In addition, future baptismal services were publicized⁶⁶⁷ along with special baptismal services for identified groups.⁶⁶⁸ Lastly, a running total of those baptized at AT was routinely provided for readers.⁶⁶⁹

In contrast to the plethora of locales reported, both at home and abroad, the practice of WB reported in the organs of the ICFG is mainly circumscribed to AT.⁶⁷⁰ However, WB was not limited to

---

FC 2.21 (April 18, 1928), p. 4; *FC* 2.24 (May 9, 1928), pp. 2, 3; *FC* 2.25 (May 23, 1928), p. 1; *FC* 2.47 (Oct 17, 1928), p. 2; *FC* 3.4 (December 19, 1928), pp. 2, 8, and 12; *FC* 3.13 (February 20, 1929), p. 2; *FC* 3.18 (March 27, 1929), pp. 2, 8; *FC* 3.19 (April 3, 1929), p. 2; *FC* 3.23 (May 1, 1929), pp. 2, 8; *FC* 3.25 (May 15, 1929), p. 2; *FC* 3.35 (July 24, 1929), p. 1; *FC* 3.41 (September 4, 1929), pp. 1, 2; *FC* 3.43 (September 18, 1929), pp. 1, 2; *FC* 3.46 (Oct 9, 1929), pp. 1, 2; *FC* 4.5 (December 25, 1929), pp. 1, 2; *FC* 5.2 (February 26, 1930), pp. 1-2; *FC* 4.16 (March 12, 1930), p. 2; *FC* 4.18 (March 26, 1930), pp. 2, 7; *FC* 4.23 (April 30, 1930), pp. 7, 8; *FC* 2.35 (July 23, 1930), p. 1; *FC* 4.41 (September 3, 1930), p. 1; *FC* 5.2 (December 3, 1930), p. 1; *FC* 5.12 (February 11, 1931), pp. 1, 11; *FC* 5.13 (February 18, 1931), p. 1; *FC* 5.14 (February 25, 1931), p. 1; *FC* 5.18 (March 25, 1931), p. 1; *FC* 5.19 (April 1, 1931), p. 9; *FC* 5.21 (April 15, 1931), p. 1; *FC* 5.23 (April 29, 1931), p. 1; *FC* 5.27 (May 27, 1931), p. 1; *FC* 5.33 (July 8, 1931), p. 3; *FC* 5.36 (July 29, 1931), p. 2; *FC* 5.38 (August 12, 1931), p. 2; *FC* 5.42 (September 9, 1931), p. 1; *FC* 6.5 (November 18, 1931), p. 3; and *FC* 6.11 (December 30, 1931), p. 4.

⁶⁶⁶ *FC* 5.19 (April 1, 1931), p. 9.

⁶⁶⁷ *BCF* 8.6 (November 1924), p. 27; *FC* 1.40 (August 24, 1927), p. 8; *FC* 1.51 (November 9, 1927), p. 5; *FC* 2.6 (January 4, 1928), p. 4; *FC* 3.19 (April 3, 1929), p. 2; *FC* 5.2 (December 3, 1930), p. 5; *FC* 5.12 (February 11, 1931), p. 5; *FC* 5.38 (August 12, 1931), p. 4; *FC* 5.42 (September 9, 1931), p. 1; *FC* 6.5 (November 18, 1931), p. 8; *FC* 6.8 (December 9, 1931), p. 5; and *FC* 6.11 (December 30, 1931), p. 3.

⁶⁶⁸ *FC* 1.51 (November 9, 1927), p. 5; *FC* 2.4 (December 4, 1927), p. 5; and *FC* 2.6 (January 4, 1928), p. 4.

⁶⁶⁹ *BC* 7.1 (June 1923), p. 19; *BCF* 8.6 (November 1924), p. 27; *BCF* 8.8 (January 1925), p. 23; *BCF* 10.4 (September 1926), pp. 26, 32; *BCF* 11.6 (November 1927), p. 27; and *BCF* 14.4 (September 1930), p. 20.

⁶⁷⁰ *BC* 6.9 (February 1923), p. 18; *BC* 6.12 (May 1923), p. 25; *BC* 7.1 (June 1923), pp. 14-15, 19; *BC* 7.4 (September 1923), p. 14; *BC* 7.6 (November 1923), p. 19; *BCF* 8.4 (September 1924), pp. 19-22; *BCF* 8.6 (November 1924), p. 27; *BCF* 8.8 (January 1925), pp. 22, 23; *BCF* 8.9 (February 1925), p. 28; *BCF* 8.10 (March 1925), p. 20; *BCF* 8.11 (April 1925), p. 28; *BCF* 9.3 (August 1925), p. 20; *BCF* 10.4 (September 1926), pp. 26, 32; *BCF* 10.9 (February 1927), p. 26; *BCF* 11.6 (November 1927), p. 27; *BCF* 12.2 (February 1928), p. 20; *BCF* 12.3 (March 1928), pp. 9, 27; *BCF* 12.12 (May 1929), p. 18; *BCF* 14.4 (September 1930), p. 20; *FC* 1.22 (April 23, 1927), p. 2;

AT.[671] Indeed, WB was practiced and reported from as far away as London, England,[672] and the Philippines.[673] It is unclear if the predominance of WBs was held at AT due to practicality matters or the strategic use of WB as a means of initiation and assimilation into a local congregation while establishing and maintaining organizational coherence with the 'mother church'. It may be that it was a combination of both.

Shortly after AT was dedicated on January 1, 1923, McPherson founded the Lighthouse of International Foursquare Evangelism Bible Training School to educate Christian workers and ministers. After a year-and-a-half of training, the students were deployed to areas surrounding Los Angeles to hold tent and camp meetings to preach the Gospel. The meetings bore fruit, and new congregations were established in the following California cities: Torrance,[674] Willowbrook,[675] El Segundo,[676] Lankershim,[677] Ontario,[678] South Gate,[679] Culver City,[680] Riverside,[681] and Corona.[682]

The delay between establishing a local church and buying or building a church with a baptistry is expected. During the interim, WBs were conducted at Angeles Temple due to its central location.

FC 1.25 (May 14, 1927), p. 5; *FC* 1.28 (June 4, 1927), p. 5; *FC* 1.33 (July 9, 1927), pp. 4, 8; *FC* 1.49 (Oct 26, 1927), p. 4; *FC* 1.51 (November 9, 1927), pp. 3, 5, and 8; *FC* 2.4 (December 4, 1927), pp. 4, 5; *FC* 2.6 (January 4, 1928), p. 5; *FC* 2.7 (January 11, 1928), p. 2; *FC* 2.12 (February 15, 1928), p. 3; *FC* 2.25 (May 23, 1928), p. 3; *FC* 2.35 (July 23, 1930), p. 1; *FC* 3.13 (February 20, 1929), p. 7; *FC* 3.19 (April 3, 1929), p. 2; *FC* 3.23 (May 1, 1929), p. 8; *FC* 3.25 (May 15, 1929), p. 2; *FC* 3.35 (July 24, 1929), p. 1; *FC* 3.46 (Oct 9, 1929), pp. 5, 14; *FC* 4.18 (March 26, 1930), pp. 2, 7; *FC* 4.23 (April 30, 1930), p. 8; *FC* 5.2 (December 3, 1930), p. 3; *FC* 5.14 (February 25, 1931), p. 5; and *FC* 5.19 (April 1, 1931), p. 9.

[671] See Appendix T for a list of the states and cities.

[672] *FC* 3.35 (July 24, 1929), p. 2. This report is from the Elim Church led by Jeffries.

[673] *FC* 6.8 (December 9, 1931), p. 5; *FC* 6.11 (December 30, 1931), p. 3.

[674] *BCF* 10.9 (February 1927), p. 26.

[675] *FC* 1.40 (August 24, 1927), p. 4.

[676] *FC* 1.49 (Oct 26, 1927), p. 4.

[677] *FC* 1.40 (August 24, 1927), p. 4.

[678] *FC* 3.18 (March 27, 1929), p. 8.

[679] *FC* 3.23 (May 1, 1929), p. 8.

[680] *FC* 5.18 (March 25, 1931), p. 2.

[681] *FC* 2.25 (May 23, 1928), p. 7.

[682] *FC* 2.25 (May 23, 1928), p. 7.

On the one hand, it appears to have been a matter of practicality. On the other hand, it was more than practicality. Nearby streams, lakes, and ponds could have been easily accessed as they were by other Pentecostals of the time. It is unclear if the 'branch' churches were required to have converts baptized at AT or if the leaders did so of their own volition. What is known is that at AT, new converts were baptized during the regularly scheduled Thursday evening baptismal service, customarily conducted by Aimee Semple McPherson. These special nights were known as 'Branch Night'.[683]

As previously discussed, the Thursday evening service was visually and aurally dramatic, spiritually vibrant, and permeated by the presence and power of the HS. Being baptized by Sister Aimee, candidates would have created a strong identification with her and commitment to her, the Foursquare Gospel, and AT. McPherson's followers' loyalty aids in understanding the strong support for her during and after her 'disappearance' in 1926.[684] This point is not meant to diminish the power and impact the powerful initiatory rite would have on a candidate. It appears to be the case that being baptized by Aimee Semple McPherson was both a matter of practicality and a means employed to connect new converts to Jesus Christ and the leader of the ministry at the hub of the organization, AT.

As 'branch churches' became established and were able to secure facilities with baptisteries, there were fewer trips to AT. A collaborative spirit was found among the 'branches' that were situated nearby. When one of the 'branches' secured a baptistry, the sister 'branches', would gather at that locale for WB.[685] For example,

---

[683] *BCF* 10.9 (February 1927), p. 26; *FC* 1.25 (May 14, 1927), p. 5; *FC* 1.40 (August 24, 1927), p. 4; *FC* 1.49 (Oct 26, 1927), p. 4; *FC* 1.51 (November 9, 1927), p. 8; *FC* 3.18 (March 27, 1929), p. 8; *FC* 3.23 (May 1, 1929), p. 8; *FC* 4.18 (March 26, 1930), p. 2; and *FC* 5.12 (February 11, 1931), p. 11.

[684] During the height of her popularity and the rapid growth of the ICFG, Sister Aimee disappeared from a California beach on May 18, 1926. She resurfaced five weeks later on June 23 in Mexico. She asserted that she had been kidnapped, held for ransom, and then miraculously released. Her disappearance and reappearance fueled the tabloids and appeared to have endeared her even more to her supporters. Lawsuits and legal battles followed the episode; however, charges were dropped due to lack of evidence. See the following for evidence of support and defense of McPherson during and after her disappearance: *BCF* 10.1 (June 1926), pp. 4, 13-17, 18-19.

[685] *FC* 2.25 (May 23, 1928), p. 7; *FC* 5.23 (April 29, 1931), p. 2.

Riverside church was the location of a Union Water Baptismal service when the Foursquare churches of San Bernardino, Corona, and Riverside gathered. 'Twenty-six candidates were baptized by Rev. Alderman of the Riverside church, assisted by Rv. Smith of the San Bernardino church. Riverside candidates numbered 15, San Bernardino 8 and Corona 3'.[686]

The passion for the construction of a baptistry was not limited to North America. A report from Brother and Sister Sigler, missionaries in Belgian Congo, Africa, provides an update on how work is progressing and the establishment of a permanent mission station. Their building efforts include establishing a water source for the garden and baptismal pool:

> much preparatory work must be done before a garden can be planted. The forest must be cleared away; for some time we have had men felling trees and digging out roots, and building a dam which will serve for a baptismal pool as well as a swimming pool; also irrigation for our garden.[687]

Administration

McPherson resisted alignment with one particular denomination or movement to appeal to a broader audience and maintain independence because of the societal, cultural, and restraints placed on women by various faith traditions. Instead, she employed an ecumenical approach to WB, not limited to one tradition. Her approach is most clearly captured in the September 1922 issue of the *BC*. Writing about the baptismal service conducted at Idora Park (Oakland, CA), in the sizeable out-door swimming pool, after the evangelistic campaign, McPherson proffers the following description

> Climbing a ladder, thus mounting to a high platform, easily seen by all, we bring a simple, direct message, descriptive of the symbol, water baptism, and bid those who have not yet made Jesus Christ their Savior make this the day of decision, and now they are singing again. Scores of men and women are stepping into the waters of baptism. Five clergymen, Baptist, Methodist, United

---

[686] *FC* 1.25 (May 14, 1927), p. 5; *FC* 2.25 (May 23, 1928), p. 7.
[687] *FC* 3.43 (September 18, 1929), p. 3.

Brethren, Christian and Missionary Alliance and Congregational are immersing the candidates.[688]

Upon forming the ICFG, McPherson supported, encouraged, authorized, and appointed women to serve in every ministerial capacity that a man could hold in the ICFG. This was remarkable given the social, political, and cultural climate of 1920-1931. McPherson and the ICFG appointed women to serve as evangelists,[689] pastors,[690] and missionaries[691] with all the faculties necessary to provide the sacraments of the church and minister without restrictions. When a question arose in 1931 relative to the propriety of women baptizing, Sister Aimee responded with the following answer that focused on baptisms being performed by ministers and avoided entering a gender debate on the propriety of women baptizing. She concludes by offering that 'the scriptures do not say who should do the baptizing and probably a godly person could perform the ceremony and it would be alright'.[692] This perspective appears to have been central to Sister Aimee's self-understanding as a minister and the elevation of women within her sphere of influence.

The stipulated requirements to receive WB were consistent throughout the ICFG literature reviewed. From the beginning, candidates presenting themselves for WB were to show repentance and faith in Jesus Christ.[693] While 'sprinkling' and 'infant baptism' were not practiced, there appears to have been no minimum age requirement. Apparently, the same requirement of repentance and faith in Jesus Christ was the same standard across the age spectrum.

---

[688] *BC* 6.4 (September 1922), p. 10.

[689] *FC* 1.35 (July 23, 1927), p. 8; *FC* 6.11 (December 30, 1931), p. 5.

[690] *FC* 6.11 (December 30, 1931), p. 5; *FC* 5.23 (April 29, 1931), pp. 2, 6; and *FC* 5.38 (August 12, 1931), p. 4.

[691] *FC* 6.11 (December 30, 1931), p. 3.

[692] *FC* 5.19 (April 1, 1931). p. 11.

[693] *BC* 2.10 (March 1919), p. 8; *BC* 6.2, 3 (July and August 1922), pp. 13-14; *BCF* 9.9 (February 1926), pp. 10-12; *BCF* 10.7 (December 1926), pp. 25-26; *FC* 1.7 (January 8, 1927), p. 8; *FC* 3.41 (September 4, 1929), p. 3; and *BCF* 13.10 (March 1930), pp. 11, 12, and 32.

Children[694] are identified as recipients of WB as well as persons considered to be elderly.[695]

While baptismal 'classes'[696] were often identified by the number to be baptized, it is unclear whether preparatory instruction classes were provided for baptismal candidates in North American churches and missions. It appears to be the case that the sermons elucidated the meaning of WB during the baptismal service.[697]

A more robust approach to teaching candidates about the meaning and significance of WB before the event seems to have been practiced by missionaries in Africa:

> We are preparing our first class for water baptism now. There are forty-three of them, and in order that they might better understand the true significance of this ordinance we hold a special class of instruction for an hour every day. They learn a Scripture verse on water baptism every day and are looking forward with much enthusiasm and joy to the blessing received when they shall be buried with their Lord in the waters of baptism.[698]

Due to the inclination to emphasize the positive aspects of Christian discipleship and downplay the challenges inherent in following Jesus, there is a limited acknowledgment of the hardships encountered by believers. Exceptions are made when reporting the challenges posed by the weather. For example, Rev. and Mrs. Sidney Correll held their first revival meeting at Elba, CO, where 'thirteen souls were saved and seven baptized in the Spirit. The baptismal service was very cold, for the wind was blowing a gale'.[699] Similarly,

---

[694] *BC* 4.4 (September 1920), p. 9; *BC* 7.1 (June 1923), pp. 14-15; *FC* 5.2 (December 3, 1930), p. 3; and *FC* 3.46 (Oct 9, 1929), pp. 5, 14.

[695] *BC* 7.1 (June 1923), pp. 14-15; *FC* 2.12 (February 15, 1928), p. 3.

[696] *FC* 1.40 (August 24, 1927), p. 4; *FC* 1.51 (November 9, 1927), p. 8; and *FC* 2.4 (December 4, 1927), p. 5.

[697] *BCF* 9.9 (February 1926), pp. 10-12; *BCF* 10.4 (September 1926), pp. 26, 32; *BCF* 10.7 (December 1926), pp. 25-26; *FC* 1.33 (July 9, 1927), pp. 3-5; *FC* 1.40 (August 24, 1927), p. 4; *FC* 2.12 (February 15, 1928), p. 3; *FC* 3.4 (December 19, 1928), pp. 2, 8, and 12; *FC* 3.13 (February 20, 1929), p. 5; *FC* 3.41 (September 4, 1929), p. 3; *FC* 5.2 (February 26, 1930), pp. 1-2; *BCF* 13.10 (March 1930), pp. 11, 12, and 32; *FC* 4.18 (March 26, 1930), p. 7.

[698] *FC* 5.12 (February 11, 1931), p. 5.

[699] *FC* 2.7 (January 11, 1928), p. 8.

reporting on baptisms in the Philippines: 'we baptized fifteen new converts, and if it had not been for the weather because it is still raining, we would have more than thirty who will be baptized'.[700]

Formula

Questions regarding McPherson's stand on the New Issue controversy were first reported in the July 1918 issue of the *BC*. McPherson frames the inquiries as persons 'asking us as to the stand we take regarding the new teaching, which advocates water baptism in Jesus' Name and denies the tri-personality of the God-Head'.[701] Asserting her desire to avoid 'controversy and doctrinal issues', McPherson states that 'after two years of prayerful study we still believe more firmly than ever in the Father, and in His Son Jesus Christ, and in the Holy Spirit as three persons and in water baptism according to our Lord's commission. Mt. 28:19'.[702]

Sister Aimee's preference for the Trinitarian formula is periodically reasserted from April 1919 until August 1930.[703] One of the most forceful statements regarding the widely accepted Trinitarian formula is a statement linking the baptismal formula with the pledge of baptismal candidates. In response to a query regarding 'why'? use of Father, Son, and HS, McPherson states 'because there is a triune God: God the Father, God the Son, and God the Holy Spirit'. Furthermore, they have all united in this wonderful work of redemption which has culminated in the glorious finish, in the death of Jesus Christ, typified by water baptism'.[704]

Meaning of Water Baptism

In her typical dramatic style of painting vivid imagery with her words, Sister Aimee proffered to readers that 'Jesus adopted a universal language – the sign language. Through this, He expressed the

---

[700] *FC* 6.8 (December 9, 1931), p. 5.
[701] *BC* 2.2 (July 1918), p. 10.
[702] *BC* 2.2 (July 1918), p. 10.
[703] *BC* 2.2 (July 1918), p. 10; *BC* 2.11 (April 1919), p. 16; *BC* 5.5 (Oct 1921), pp. 8-9; *BCF* 8.8 (January 1925), p. 22; *BCF* 10.11 (April 1927), pp. 15-16; *BCF* 11.1 (June 1927), pp. 15-16, 30; *BCF* 12.3 (March 1928), p. 17; and *BCF* 14.3 (August 1930), pp. 5, 31.
[704] *BCF* 11.1 (June 1927), pp. 15-16, 30. Capitalization is original to the text.

principles of the teachings of His Word and the believers' acceptance thereof'.[705]

Sister Aimee asserts, 'there was really no one baptized until John the Baptist came to the River Jordan preaching repentance and baptism in water'. Employing 'types and shadows' interpretative approach, Sister Aimee avows that OT events foretold WB. Specifically, under the leadership of Moses, when the Israelites were led through the Red Sea, by God's hand, we read they 'were baptized in the sea and in the clouds'. 'As they left Egypt, the land of sin, and came over to the land of promise on the other side, the waters opened to let them pass through'. Per McPherson, 'the Red Sea was a type of baptism, the cloud over their heads a type of being covered with the waters'.[706]

Moreover, WB symbolizes a coming out of the old way of life and a coming through the Red Sea of separation and up toward the promised land.[707]

Sister Aimee's baptismal theology drank deeply from the Jn. 1.35-49[708] account of the baptism of Jesus by John the Baptist and Rom. 6.1-14. These two passages and their imagery echoed in McPherson's sermons and lessons. For example, one sermon from July 1927 provides an elucidation by Sister Aimee of the aforementioned sign of WB.

> Water baptism symbolizes death, burial and resurrection – a death to the old, sinful life which you reckon is nailed to the cross in the person of Jesus Christ, our substitute who died for us. Water baptism is the burial of that which we reckon dead … Water baptism also symbolizes resurrection from the dead of the new life, that which is newborn within us, that new life that is as different from the old as a butterfly is from a caterpillar. The old caterpillar, the sinner, used to go along only seeing the things of mud, creeping along the earth. Then there came that time of death, death to the old life and we were wrapped up and submerged even as that old caterpillar when he went into his

---

[705] *BC* 1.9 (February 1918), p. 2.
[706] *FC* 3.4 (December 19, 1928), pp. 2, 8, and 12.
[707] *FC* 1.33 (July 9, 1927), pp. 3-5.
[708] *FC* 6.11 (December 30, 1931), p. 6. See *FC* 3.13 (February 20, 1929), p. 5. It appears the same passage bore a strong impact on Evangelist Roxie Alford.

cocoon. So you go down and are submerged, wrapped about with this watery grave.[709]

Similarly, the ICFG Declaration of Faith gives clear expression to Pauline imagery in Rom. 6.1-14:

> We believe that water baptism (1) in the name of the Father and of the Son and of the Holy Ghost, according to the command of our Lord, is a blessed outward sign of an inward work; a beautiful and solemn emblem reminding us that even as our Lord died upon the cross of Calvary, (2) so we reckon ourselves now dead indeed unto sin, and the old nature nailed to the tree with Him; and that even as He was taken down from the tree and buried, (3) so we are buried with Him by baptism into death: that like as Christ was raised up from the dead by the glory of the Father.[710]

Accordingly, WB has no salvific effect, nor was it viewed sacramentally by McPherson, nor presumably, other ICFG ministers.[711] Positively stated, WB is an 'initiation service, as well as other things, meaning following our Lord and walking in His glorious footsteps'.[712]

Her theological support of progressive sanctification positioned Sister Aimee to proffer the Baptism of the HS as the next step in the *via salutis,* after WB. She states in December 1926 that the first step, then, was repentance, the second step was to be baptized in water, and the third was the baptism of the HS.[713] On occasion, baptism in the HS was located in the fourth position, and healing was placed in the third position.[714]

One question relative to WB appears to have dominated Pentecostal circles during the first 25 years of the movement. Specifically, inquirers want to know if it is necessary to be baptized in water to be 'saved' and get to Heaven? McPherson is direct and to

---

[709] *FC* 1.33 (Jul 9, 1927), pp. 3-5. Also, *BCF* 9.9 (February 1926), pp. 10-12; *BCF* 10.7 (December 1926), pp. 25-26; *FC* 3.13 (February 20, 1929), p. 5; *FC* 3.41 (September 4, 1929), p. 3; and *FC* 5.2 (February 26, 1930), pp. 1-2, 5.
[710] *FC* 3.23 (May 1, 1929), p. 13.
[711] *FC* 2.47 (October 17, 1928), p. 2.
[712] *FC* 1.33 (July 9, 1927), pp. 3-5.
[713] *BCF* 10.7 (December 1926), pp. 25-26.
[714] *FC* 1.49 (October 26, 1927), p. 4.

the point in her reply: 'Let us not stop to argue with the Lord and say it is not necessary, but let us have an understanding of what the Lord's will is concerning this beautiful water baptism ordinance'.[715] The understanding is that 'It isn't that water baptism washes away your sin. It isn't that water baptism is absolutely essential to get you to Heaven. The dying thief had no time to be baptised. It was faith that saved him'.[716]

A request is made of Sister Aimee in the January 1927 issue of the *FC* to clarify the assertion that salvation is not the same as the Baptism of the HS. Appealing to the chronology of the *via salutis*, she retorts that they are indeed different. According to 'Act 2:38', 'Repent and be baptized (in water) for the remission of your sins, and you shall receive the gift of the Holy Ghost'.[717]

Regarding the 'proper' order of WB and the baptism of the HS, McPherson posits that 'a person can receive the baptism of the Holy Ghost even before he is baptized in water'. Citing the example that while Peter preached in the house of Cornelius, 'the Holy Ghost fell on all that heard the word'.[718] They received the HS and spoke with other tongues as the Spirit gave utterance. Peter then asked if a man can 'forbid water that these should be baptized who have received the Holy Ghost as well as we'?[719]

Pentecostal Worship and Witness (Healing and Evangelism)

Prior to the dedication of the AT on January 1, 1923, reports reflected the same kind of Pentecostal worship found in other periodicals. For example, the report on the San Francisco meetings held in April 1919 reflects the movement of the HS readers would expect to see:

> Last night over twenty men and women came to Jesus for Salvation at the first invitation during baptismal services Friday night, so that those being baptized according to Jesus' command (Mt. 28:19), spoke, sang, and prophesied in the Spirit, whilst weeping, shouting and holy laughter prevailed throughout the

---

[715] *FC* 1.33 (July 9, 1927), pp. 3-5.
[716] *FC* 1.33 (July 9, 1927), pp. 3-5.
[717] *FC* 1.7 (January 8, 1927), p. 8.
[718] *FC* 1.7 (January 8, 1927), p. 8.
[719] *FC* 1.7 (January 8, 1927), p. 8. Also, *BCF* 10.11 (April 1927), pp. 15-16.

entire hall. The power fell on the Pastor, as he spoke in tongues, and the Spirit witnessed through interpretation whilst in the water.[720]

Similarly, a September 1920 report from Alton, IL echoes a familiar narrative:

> During the baptizing of men, women and children many of whom had been converted during the meetings, many citizens would interrupt by begging to be allowed to testify to the great change that Christ had wrought in their lives, then go down beneath the waves ... the radiant joy and shouting of those baptized as they came up from their watery grave; eyes and hands uplifted to the open heavens.[721]

There appears to have been a perceivable shift away from the Pentecostal worship just observed after the building dedication and inauguration of WB at AT. An early report of a baptismal service paints an aesthetically pleasing portrait with a more subdued tone in the service:

> As the lights brightened from break of day to mid-noon and the first candidates stepped into the river in their flowing robes of white, the congregation suddenly rose to their feet and began to clap their hands and shout aloud the praises of the Lord. Over eighty were buried in Christ in the waters of baptism, that first night.[722]

Further accounts of WB services from 1923-1931 echo the template provided above with slight additions. From November 1924, 'This service always closes with a powerful altar call and makes a great impression on the unsaved'.[723] A report from June 1923 adds, 'Hundreds are saying to each other, "Oh, I never saw anything so beautiful!" "It is glorious, Praise the Lord."'[724] In the same article, we read:

---

[720] *BC* 2.11 (April 1919), p. 15.
[721] *BC* 4.4 (September 1920), p. 9.
[722] *BC* 6.9 (February 1923), p. 18.
[723] *BCF* 8.6 (November 1924), p. 27.
[724] *BC* 7.1 (June 1923), pp. 14-15.

Two little children descend into the water, smiling testifying with uplifted hands. Little lambs they are, following the Shepherd, and are baptized. Then follows an old man, 103 years of age, and another, 97. As one of these goes down into the water he exclaims: 'Oh, I should have come to Jesus before. This should have been done years ago.' And as he came up out of the water, 'Thank God, I am home at last.'[725]

Lastly, a report from December 1930 captures the worship of the Thanksgiving baptismal service when 'twenty-two were baptized, and a shout of victory arose from the lips of each one. Young men, young women, fathers, mothers, grandfathers, and children took their stand for the Lord and followed His example'.[726]

Noteworthy is the fact that more expressive Pentecostal worship occurred in the ICFG outside the Los Angeles, CA area. For example, one report from New Baltimore, MI, in May 1931, reports that after baptizing 41 candidates, the 'audience cheered, wept, sang, and praised God as they saw those who had previously walked in darkness, then being raised to walk in light'.[727] Likewise, from Taft, CA, it is reported that at a July 4 baptismal service held at the river, there were 'Ladies dressed in beautiful silk dresses, hands bedecked with diamonds, and hair perfectly marceled [sic]' who took the step of WB 'without letting their beautiful clothes or dresses hinder them'. After the service they were forced to remain on the riverside so their clothes could dry since they did not have a change of clothes with them.[728] It appears to be the case that the Pentecostal worship reported after January 1, 1923, found a more subdued expression in the AT and reported to global readers. The emphasis on the dramatic presentation of the Gospel, the focused attention paid to the aesthetics of the five senses, and constrained worship, limited to 'shouts of praise' and 'rejoicing', signaled a change of trajectory for one expression of the nascent Pentecostal movement.

While the traditional Pentecostal manifestations appeared underreported from AT, such was not the case relative to prayers for healing. From the outset of her ministry, divine healing was a

---

[725] *BC* 7.1 (June 1923), pp. 14-15.
[726] *FC* 5.2 (December 3, 1930), p. 3. Also, *FC* 3.13 (February 20, 1929), p. 7.
[727] *FC* 5.24 (May 7, 1931), p. 5.
[728] *FC* 1.35 (July 23, 1927), p. 8.

cornerstone of Aimee Semple McPherson's ministry. In fact, WB and divine healing were often reported together in the *BC, BCF,* and *FC*.[729] It appears to be the case that as persons 'saw the power of God working miracles among the sick', they were drawn to hear the Gospel of Jesus Christ.[730]

Just as divine healing attracted people to the Gospel, so did WB draw the curious to hear the Good News of Jesus Christ. In the July 1927 issue of the *FC,* Sister Aimee posited that WB 'is a sermon that preaches to a whole world that looks on, and says, "I have renounced the old life. It is goodbye forever, and I am going down into this watery grave."'[731]

The following report captures a September 1920 baptismal service scene held on the shores of the Mississippi. At the same time, spectators on the banks sang, attempting to gain a vantage point and that commanded an improved view over peoples' heads:

> O that I had power and space to describe the scene, the multitudes assembled on the river's edge as in the days of Christ, the flotilla of little boats, drawn nearby those determined to see, the white-robed children were singing, eyes and hands uplifted to the open heavens ... Some stood in this posture for minutes at a time, looking raptly upward without moving a muscle, and afterwards told us they had seen the face of Jesus smiling down upon them, surrounded by an innumerable company of angels. Strong men wiped tears continually from their eyes, and declared that they had never witnessed such a scene before ... Several gave their hearts to Christ on the shore, and went right into the water clothes and all. One dear lady, who had battled with conviction at home, suddenly gave her heart to Christ in her kitchen; and ran all the way to the river, arriving just in time to be immersed. O! Glory to Jesus, what a Savior![732]

---

[729] *BC* 4.4 (September 1920), p. 7; *BC* 5.4 (September 1921), p. 11; *BC* 6.12 (May 1923), p. 25; *BC* 7.4 (September 1923), p. 14; *BCF* 9.1 (June 1927), pp. 15-16, 30; *FC* 2.25 (May 23, 1928), p. 3; *FC* 3.25 (May 15, 1929), p. 2; *FC* 3.46 (October 9, 1929), pp. 5, 14; *FC* 4.18 (March 26, 1930), p. 2; *FC* 4.23 (April 30, 1930), p. 8; and *FC* 6.9 (December 16, 1931), p. 6; and *FC* 6.11 (December 30, 1931), p. 5.

[730] *FC* 3.46 (October 9, 1929), pp. 5, 14.

[731] *FC* 1.33 (July 9, 1927), pp. 3-5.

[732] *BC* 4.4 (September 1920), p. 9. Also, *BCF* 8.6 (November 1924), p. 27.

Oneness Pentecostal Periodicals

The Good Report

Introduction

The Good Report, a self-identified 'Pentecostal and Missionary Paper',[733] was a free, monthly Pentecostal periodical published and edited from May 1911 to April 1914, according to the extant copies reviewed. Initially, the periodical's first two issues were printed in Ottawa, CA, by Randall, Lawler, and R.E. McAlister.[734] After McAlister's move to Los Angeles, CA, from Ottawa, he partnered with Frank J. Ewart to edit and publish *TGR*. The remaining eight issues were published and edited in Los Angeles, CA.[735] In addition to articles and editorials by Ewart and McAlister, contributors to the paper include Henry Morse, G.T. Haywood, Harvey McAlister, and D.W. Kerr.[736]

R.E. McAlister published a brief article, 'The Apostolic Faith', in the first issue of the paper in May 1911, aligning himself with the Holiness-Pentecostal heritage of William J. Seymour of the Azusa Street Revival. McAlister asserts that 'THIS MOVEMENT is preeminently scripture and stand for the same truths as the apostles taught and practiced in the primitive church'.[737] According to McAlister, the return to the truths of the primitive church is blessed and used by God 'as a soul-saving agency in the hands of God'. McAlister substantiates his claim by asserting that 'Thousands have been saved, sanctified, healed and baptized in the HOLY GHOST'.[738] In the April 1, 1914 issue, Frank Ewart appears to embrace The Apostolic Faith teachings, especially the position on sanctification as

---

[733] *TGR* 1.1 (May 1911), p. 4.

[734] *TGR* 1.1 (May 1911); *TGR* 1.3 (1912).

[735] *TGR* 2 (June 1, 1913); *TGR* 2 (August 1, 1913); *TGR* 2 (September 1, 1913); *TGR* 1.6 (November 1, 1913); *TGR* 1.7 (December 1, 1913); *TGR* 1.8 (January 1, 1914); *TGR* 1.10 (March 1, 1914); and *TGR* 1.11 (April 1, 1914).

[736] *TGR* 1.6 (November 1, 1913), p. 2.

[737] *TGR* 1.1 (May 1911); pp. 1, 4. Emphasis original. Also, on page one, the paper's motto declares, 'A Whole Gospel, for a Whole Man, and to the Whole World. No Law but Love, no creed but Christ Jesus our Savior, Keeper, Healer, Baptizer, Glorious Lord and Coming King. Everything in Jesus and Jesus in Everything.'

[738] *TGR* 1.1 (May 1911); p. 4. Emphasis original.

a second definite work.⁷³⁹ However, *TGR* also contains articles teaching against sanctification as a second definite work.⁷⁴⁰ The appearance of both positions in TGR captures the growing tension between the two camps. Ewart and McAlister's support of The Apostolic Faith movement is about to shift to the Finished Work camp.

Ewart and McAlister's support and adoption of William Durham's Finished Work position began to appear in *TGR* as early as 1912 (Ottawa).⁷⁴¹ *TGR* advertised a tract by Durham, titled, 'Salvation In Christ for All'.⁷⁴² Thus, it appears to be the case that *TGR* serves as a credible resource to document their transition from The Apostolic Faith movement to the Finished Work camp. It is also notable that several representatives from this nascent group will be instrumental in following Durham's position to its logical conclusion and become leaders in the Oneness Pentecostal movement. Frank J. Ewart will go on to publish the *MDS*,⁷⁴³ teaching and advocating for Oneness Pentecostalism. R.E. McAlister will ultimately serve as the Secretary-Treasurer of Pentecostal Assemblies of Canada, the Canadian representation of the Oneness Pentecostalism.⁷⁴⁴

---

⁷³⁹ *TGR* 1.11 (April 1, 1914), p. 4. Also, see *TGR* 1.1 (May 1911), p. 5 for a 1911 testimony that speaks of a man and women who both experienced sanctification as second definite work of grace: 'my husband was marvelously delivered from the Christian Science, saved, sanctified, healed and baptized in the Holy Ghost, and I was sanctified and received the baptism. We both received the baptism me on the day of Pentecost, the Holy Ghost testifying for Himself in other tongues.'

⁷⁴⁰ *TGR* 1.3 (1912), pp. 2, 13.

⁷⁴¹ *TGR* 1.3 (1912), pp. 3, 6, and 15; *TGR* 1.6 (November 1, 1913), p. 4; *TGR* 1.7 (December 1, 1913), pp. 2, 3; *TGR* 1.8 (January 1, 1914), p. 4; *TGR* 1.10 (March 1, 1914), pp. 1, 4; and *TGR* 1.11 (April 1, 1914), p. 3.

⁷⁴² *TGR* 1.6 (November 1, 1913), p. 2; *TGR* 1.7 (December 1, 1913), p. 2; *TGR* 1.8 (January 1, 1914), p. 2; and *TGR* 1.10 (March 1, 1914), p. 4.

⁷⁴³ J.L Hall, 'Ewart, Frank' in Stanley M. Burgess and Eduard M. van der Maas (eds.), *NIDPCM* (rev. and exp. edn; Grand Rapids, MI: Zondervan, 2002), pp. 623-24.

⁷⁴⁴ E.A. Wilson, 'McAlister, Robert Edward', in Stanley M. Burgess and Eduard M. van der Maas (eds.), *NIDPCM* (rev. and exp. edn; Grand Rapids, MI: Zondervan, 2002), p. 852.

The Practice of Water Baptism

The Good Report emphasizes WB through an assortment of articles, reports,[745] and statements that proffer WB is an ordinance[746] and to be practiced out of obedience to Jesus Christ (Mt. 28.19; Acts 10.48).[747] A word of warning is proffered to those who neglect baptism by immersion: 'baptism of a believer is positively necessary to obedience and should one fail to obey when his light comes to them, there is [sic] grave chances of backsliding'.[748] The above assertion is predicated on the pattern Jesus Christ set forth by his baptism in the Jordan by John the Baptist:

> It became Him to fulfill all righteousness by being baptized in the River Jordan: we are therefore enjoined to follow Him in this outward act – symbol or expression on an inward death, burial and resurrection. Thus through the liquid 'grave' we have 'the answer of a good conscience toward God by the resurrection of Jesus Christ.' (I Peter 3:21) planted in the likeness of His death, raised by the might of His power, to walk in the newness of His life. (Rom. 6:4).[749]

It appears to be the case that the availability of a body of water was a high priority when considering meeting places for camp meetings. The following announcement relative to the Fourth Annual Camp Meeting states that it 'will be held at the usual campgrounds, on the shore of Lake Singleton', since 'it is an ideal location, with a beautiful place for water Baptism'.[750] The other bodies of water noted

---

[745] *TGR* 1 (May 1911), pp. 3, 5; *TGR* 1.3 (1912), pp. 2, 4, and 7; *TGR* 2 (June 1, 1913), p. 4; *TGR* 2 (August 1, 1913), p. 1; *TGR* 2 (September 1, 1913), pp. 1, 2, 3, and 4; *TGR* 1.7 (December 1, 1913), pp. 1, 3, and 4; *TGR* 1.8 (January 1, 1914), pp. 1, 4; *TGR* 1.10 (March 1, 1914), p. 4; and *TGR* 1.11 (April 1, 1914), p. 1.

[746] *TGR* 1.3 (1912), pp. 2, 3, and 4; *TGR* 1.7 (December 1, 1913), p. 4; and *TGR* 1.8 (January 1, 1914), p. 4. The Lord's Supper was also considered an ordinance according to the following: *TGR* 1 (May 1911), p. 8; *TGR* 1.3 (1912), pp. 3, 5, and 11; *TGR* 2 (June 1, 1913), p. 1; *TGR* 1.8 (January 1, 1914), p. 1; and *TGR* 1.10 (March 1, 1914), pp. 3, 5.

[747] *TGR* 1.3 (1912), p. 4; *TGR* 1.8 (January 1, 1914), p. 4.

[748] *TGR* 1.8 (January 1, 1914), p. 4.

[749] *TGR* 1.3 (1912), p. 11.

[750] *TGR* 1 (May 1911), p. 4.

in *TGR* are the Nile River,⁷⁵¹ the River Joseph,⁷⁵² and the sea.⁷⁵³ Ensuring there was sufficient water in which to immerse candidates appears to have been a priority for those reporting.

Last, WB is emphasized in *TGR* because, according to Holy Scripture, it 'is the only thing required of a believer between conversion and the reception of the Holy Ghost'.⁷⁵⁴ This point is especially salient in light of the rejection of sanctification as a second definite work of grace in keeping with the Finished Work teaching. With the emphasis on receiving the Baptism of the Holy Ghost, it was crucial for hearers to know that another 'crisis experience' was not needed beyond conversion to qualify for the reception of the HS. Per R.E. McAlister, 'The normal New Testament experience would be, salvation from sin through Jesus demonstrated by the ordinance of baptism and sealed by the Holy Spirit of Promise, which is the Baptism of the Holy Ghost'.⁷⁵⁵

The Breadth of Practice and Mode

The importance of WB in *TGR* is established through the baptismal reports from around the globe. The reports contain the location of the baptisms and the exact number baptized during each baptismal service.⁷⁵⁶ The majority of reports originate from Asia. Specifically, they are received from Byculla, Bombay, India,⁷⁵⁷ Minya, Egypt,⁷⁵⁸ Ningpo, China,⁷⁵⁹ Cairo, Egypt,⁷⁶⁰ Nanpara, U.P., India,⁷⁶¹ No. 16 Komarasawmy, Naidu Road, Fraser Town, Bangalore, India⁷⁶² and

---

⁷⁵¹ *TGR* 2 (June 1, 1913), p. 1.
⁷⁵² *TGR* 2 (September 1, 1913), p. 1.
⁷⁵³ *TGR* 1.7 (December 1, 1913), p. 1.
⁷⁵⁴ *TGR* 1.3 (1912), pp.3-5.
⁷⁵⁵ *TGR* 1.3 (1912), pp.3-5.
⁷⁵⁶ *TGR* 1 (May 1911), pp. 3, 5; *TGR* 1.3 (1912), pp. 2, 4, and 7; *TGR* 2 (June 1, 1913), p. 4; *TGR* 2 (August 1, 1913), p. 1; *TGR* 2 (September 1, 1913), pp. 1, 2, 3, and 4; *TGR* 1.7 (December 1, 1913), pp. 1, 3, and 4; *TGR* 1.8 (January 1, 1914), pp. 1, 4; *TGR* 1.10 (March 1, 1914), p. 4; and *TGR* 1.11 (April 1, 1914), p. 1.
⁷⁵⁷ *TGR* 1.7 (December 1, 1913), p. 1.
⁷⁵⁸ *TGR* 2 (June 1, 1913), p. 1.
⁷⁵⁹ *TGR* 2 (August 1, 1913), p. 1.
⁷⁶⁰ *TGR* 2 (September 1, 1913), p. 1.
⁷⁶¹ *TGR* 1.8 (January 1, 1914), p. 1.
⁷⁶² *TGR* 1.10 (March 1, 1914), p. 1.

Ogawa Machi, Kanda, Tokyo, Japan.[763] Another report originated from the continent of Africa: Cape Palmas, Liberia, Africa.[764] In addition to reporting baptism that already occurred, some reports looked forward in anticipation of future baptismal services.[765]

In keeping with the imagery of Jesus' baptism by John, the accepted mode of WB appears to have been total immersion.[766] In addition to immersion, the following terms are also employed to describe baptism: buried,[767] burial,[768] and watery grave.[769] A testimony from Harvey McAlister, Cobden, ONT, CA, provides one believer's reflection on his baptismal experience of immersion: 'I received a wonderful blessing in following Jesus down into the water and up out of the water in baptism. Obedience is better than sacrifice. All glory to Jesus.'[770]

The practices of infant baptism and sprinkling are rejected due to the commonly held belief that 'There is no place in the New Testament where infant baptism was ever taught or practiced ... The same could be said of the mode of sprinkling.'[771] Also, baptismal regeneration is deemed erroneous.[772]

The strong position on believer's baptism by total immersion may be explained by the following assertion from 'Believer's Baptism' by E.A. Paul:

> Present-day Christendom is resting largely upon sandy-man-taught theories and dogmas of an apostatized church, instead of upon God's Word, with the result that we see on every hand a conglomeration of ideas, methods and beliefs on this important

---

[763] *TGR* 1.11 (April 1, 1914), p. 1.

[764] *TGR* 1.10 (March 1, 1914), p. 1.

[765] *TGR* 1.6 (November 1, 1913), p. 1; *TGR* 1.11 (April 1, 1914), p. 1.

[766] *TGR* 1.1 (May 1911), p. 5; *TGR* 1.3 (1912), pp. 4, 6, 7, and 12; *TGR* 1.6 (November 1, 1913), p. 2.

[767] *TGR* 1.3 (1912), pp. 6-7; *TGR* 2 (August 1, 1913), p. 1; *TGR* 2 (September 1, 1913), p. 2; *TGR* 1.8 (January 1, 1914), p. 4; *TGR* 1.10 (March 1, 1914), p. 3; and *TGR* 2 (September 1, 1913), p. 2.

[768] *TGR* 1.3 (1912), pp. 3-5, 6-7, 11, and 13; *TGR* 1.7 (December 1, 1913), p. 3; and *TGR* 1.8 (January 1, 1914), p. 4.

[769] *TGR* 2 (September 1, 1913), p. 2; *TGR* 1.10 (March 1, 1914), p. 3.

[770] *TGR* 1.1 (May 1911), p. 5.

[771] *TGR* 1.3 (1912), p. 4; *TGR* 1.8 (January 1, 1914), p. 4; and *TGR* 2 (August 1, 1913), p. 1.

[772] *TGR* 1.8 (January 1, 1914), p. 4.

question. It surely grieves the heart of God to see how and who are being baptized. Some christen, some pour, some sprinkle, some immerse once, some immerse three times, some are believers and some are sinners, some infants, while some think it is a matter of choice.[773]

Authority to Baptize and Candidate Requirements

On the one hand, *TGR* provides no explicit guidance relative to who is authorized to baptize. It seems to be the case, in light of the following inference, that only credentialed ministers enjoy the privilege to baptize: 'Therefore God's ministers have no right to baptize those who do not and cannot believe as is seen by the above article and other scriptures, which space forbids'.[774]

On the other hand, there is abundant guidance regarding the requirements to be met by baptismal candidates. Per the articles contained in *TGR*, the first requirement is that 'The Scriptures show clearly that it is for believers only'.[775] How does one become a believer? It is through belief or trust in Jesus Christ for the forgiveness of sins, built on the foundation of Jesus Christ's crucifixion, death, and resurrection. It is not belief alone. Rather, it is for 'only those who meet the conditions of repentance and faith' that will 'share the benefits of salvation'.[776]

It is due to the lack of repentance that infants and the unrepentant cannot meet the prerequisites for WB:

> A sinner or unconscious babe has no right to baptism, for first of all, the old man, sin principle has to be crucified. This a sinner has not done and a babe cannot do. The following scriptural illustrations will bear out the fact that believers are the subjects of baptism. Mark 16:16. 'Jesus said to His disciples to preach the

---

[773] *TGR* 1.8 (January 1, 1914), p. 4.
[774] *TGR* 1.8 (January 1, 1914), p. 4.
[775] *TGR* 1.8 (January 1, 1914), p. 4; *TGR* 1.3 (1912), pp. 3-5.
[776] *TGR* 1.7 (December 1, 1913), p. 3. See the following for references on 'repentance': *TGR* 1.3 (1912), pp. 3-5; *TGR* 2 (August 1, 1913), p. 4; and *TGR* 1.10 (March 1, 1914), p. 2. Also, see these references regarding 'remission of sins': *TGR* 1.3 (1912), pp. 3, 11; *TGR* 2 (August 1, 1913), p. 1; *TGR* 1.7 (December 1, 1913), p. 3; *TGR* 1.8 (January 1, 1914), p. 4; and *TGR* 1.10 (March 1, 1914), pp. 2, 3.

Gospel (1 Cor 15:14) he that (first) believeth and is (second) baptized, shall be saved'.⁷⁷⁷

Once a person becomes a believer, it is incumbent upon them to be baptized as quickly as possible after conversion in obedience to Christ's command:

> A good conscience comes from an obedient heart, and an obedient heart obeys all the commands of God. Our Lord's command is that believers alone should be buried with Him by baptism (Rom. 6:4; Col. 2:12) ... Jesus' last command was to baptize them, that is believers, not sinners, nor unconscious babes. He did not consider it unimportant or a matter of choice, for he commanded (Mat. 28:18-20) it to be done and submitted to it Himself as an example, thus becoming us to fulfill all righteousness. (Mat. 3:15.)⁷⁷⁸

Commitment and Consequences

The baptismal reports do not reflect any opposition on the field relative to conducting baptismal services. However, they did encounter resistance to the Finished Work message they proclaimed. One article offers the following reflection:

> Opposers of the truth which is now girdling the globe, termed the 'Finished Work of Calvary,' realizing the absence of scriptural proof to meet the issue, as a last, resort have followed in the footsteps of the makers of history, and have retreated largely to false accusations ... seeking to lead the Christian public to believe that those who advocate the finished work of calvary [sic] are latter day heretics.⁷⁷⁹

Conversely, candidates for WB and those recently baptized encounter opposition relative to following the command of Christ to 'be baptized'. Lillian Denney, reporting from Nanpara, India, provides understanding and insight of the realities faced by Muslims and Hindus who receive the Good News of Jesus Christ and publicly declared the same through the act of WB. Relative to a recently

---

⁷⁷⁷ *TGR* 1.8 (January 1, 1914), p. 4.
⁷⁷⁸ *TGR* 1.3 (1912), pp. 3-5.
⁷⁷⁹ *TGR* 1.3 (1912), pp. 3-5.

baptized 'Mohammedan' convert, she writes: 'Baptism is the real reproach of the cross to these people, for it's that which outcasts them from all their people, for they think they are disgraced forever, once they are baptized'.[780] The fear of exclusion is no mere supposition relative to being cast out of the family. Denney reports that they sent the 20-year-old Mohammedan away because 'he feared his people and said he would have to stay away until they got over their anger, or they would kill him'. His fear was not imaginary and had a realistic basis. According to Denney's article, the young man 'told of some of his own relatives who were killed some time back, by other realtives [sic] because they became Christians'.[781]

Baptismal Formula

Surprisingly, the baptismal reports and extant copies of *TGR* do not guide the preferred baptismal formula. There is no mention of a baptismal formula. It seems to be the case that during the period, 1911-1914, the preferred formula for WB was not a concern for the nascent Pentecostal Oneness movement. Rather, the Finished Work theology commanded the attention of the editors and contributors to *TGR*. Only as Oneness Pentecostal theology matured was the emphasis placed on baptizing in the 'name of Jesus only'.

Pentecostal Worship and Witness

There are relatively few baptismal reports that provide informative descriptions of the baptismal services. There is no mention of the size of the group in attendance for the services, only the number of persons baptized.[782]

Another descriptor in the reports concerns the worship atmosphere of the baptismal services. A few of the stories highlight the presence and power of God amid the gathered worshipping community. The following phrases provide a partial view of the services: 'it was a blessed time',[783] 'What a rejoicing and praise went

---

[780] *TGR* 1.8 (January 1, 1914), p. 1.
[781] *TGR* 1.8 (January 1, 1914), p. 1.
[782] *TGR* 1 (May 1911), pp. 3, 5; *TGR* 1.3 (1912), pp. 2, 4, and 7; *TGR* 2 (June 1, 1913), p. 4; *TGR* 2 (August 1, 1913), p. 1; *TGR* 2 (September 1, 1913), pp. 1, 2, 3, and 4; *TGR* 1.7 (December 1, 1913), pp. 1, 3, and 4; *TGR* 1.8 (January 1, 1914), pp. 1, 4; *TGR* 1.10 (March 1, 1914), p. 4; and *TGR* 1.11 (April 1, 1914), p. 1.
[783] *TGR* 2 (June 1, 1913), p. 1.

up from the people as we went and came from the water!',[784] and 'Some were shouting'.[785]

The reports also provide information regarding the impact of the HS on the candidates and others in attendance. A report from Byculla, Bombay, India offers the following account:

> Last Sunday we had another baptism service in the sea. One man who had been converted through the services in our Gospel Hall, sprang into the water, shouting joyfully, 'Hallelujah to Jesus. Hallelujah to Jesus'.[786]

While not identified as 'signs following' the baptismal reports include testimonies of healing and visions. First, the news of healing from Robert F. Cook, Bangalore, South India: 'Sick were healed and eight believers were baptized in water'.[787] Second, we read from Ningpo, China, a report by H.L. Lawler: 'We buried six of them with Christ … and each of them saw a beautiful light as they came up out of the water. Some were shouting and their faces all shone with the glory of God'.[788]

Similarly, the baptismal services also became opportunities to proclaim the Full Gospel without saying a word. The services bore witness to the reconciling ministry of Jesus Christ and the power of the HS, compelling onlookers to follow Christ more fully. Again, H.L. Lawler provides evidence:

> Quite a few of the Chinese who had been taught the mode of 'sprinkling' were present, and some were deeply impressed. The water baptism also created a deep hunger and desire in the hearts of all the children for the 'most excellent way' – the blessed Holy Ghost baptism.[789]

The Meaning of Water Baptism

R.E. McAlister posits in 'Confession of Faith' that WB is crucial to obey the commands of the Gospel in Mt. 28.19; Acts 10.48, and is

---

[784] *TGR* 1.10 (March 1, 1914), p. 1
[785] *TGR* 2 (August 1, 1913), p. 1.
[786] *TGR* 1.7 (December 1, 1913), p. 1.
[787] *TGR* 1.10 (March 1, 1914), p. 1. Also, see *TGR* 1.1 (May 1911), p. 5.
[788] *TGR* 2 (August 1, 1913), p. 1.
[789] *TGR* 2 (August 1, 1913), p. 1.

the 'answering of a good conscience toward God (I Pet 3:21)'.[790] He further asserts that baptism denotes death, burial, and resurrection and our identification with Jesus Christ, according to Rom. 6.3-5; Col. 2.12.[791] Another view of Rom. 6.3-5 is provided by Elder G.T. Haywood who posits the baptism of Jesus by John 'was only symbolical of the baptism of the Spirit' and after the resurrection of Christ the passage was employed to signify a burial. Per Haywood, Romans 6 is a record of the Apostle Paul engaging a church that is baptized 'with the Holy Ghost according to the primitive standard and is showing them their relationship with Christ in His death, burial and resurrection through identification'.[792] Haywood's focus on the Baptism of the Holy Ghost appears to overshadow his understanding of and appreciation for individuals' baptism in water.

The concept of 'identification with Jesus in His death, burial, and resurrection' is echoed in A.H. Argue's article, 'At Evening Time It Shall Be Light',[793] and E.A. Paul's 'Believer's Baptism'.[794] The emphasis on 'identification' is based on the concept of Federal Headship. Clarity relative to believers' identification with Jesus Christ and fallen humanity's identification with Adam, is provided by the following:

> Adam was the federal head of the first human creation and he fell and became the progenitor of a race of sinners. In the fulness of time God sent His Son in the likeness of sinful flesh, and for sin condemned it in His flesh. That is, He died for the sins of the world. The world died in Him at the Cross. All who believe in Him have been quickened out from among the dead, and risen with Christ, while the unbelieving race is still in death – in trespass and sins.[795]

---

[790] *TGR* 1.3 (1912), pp.3-5. Also, see *TGR* 1.3 (1912), p. 11; *TGR* 1.8 (January 1, 1914), p. 4.
[791] *TGR* 1.3 (1912), pp. 3-5.
[792] *TGR* 1.7 (December 1, 1913), p. 3.
[793] *TGR* 1.3 (1912), pp. 6-7.
[794] *TGR* 1.8 (January 1, 1914), p. 4.
[795] *TGR* 1.10 (March 1, 1914), p. 2. The article elaborates further on identification in the following citation:

R.E. McAlister echoes the above understanding in his treatment of the legal aspects of redemption when he proffers the below:

> We are not justified on the ground that God granted pardon, but on the ground that Jesus our representative has paid our penalty. He died unto sin once. He now lives unto God, by the exercise of saving faith in the great sin-bearer, we lose our identity and become united with him, who was delivered for our offenses, and raised again for our justification. If we have been planted in the likeness of his death, we shall also be raised in the likeness of his resurrection.[796]

McAlister eschews sanctification as a second definite work of grace, and uses his article to press his position. Reflecting upon Rom. 6.3-6, he proffers that WB 'demonstrates our complete deliverance from sin through Him' because the 'old man' is dead. Furthermore, he contends 'that if the old man is alive in a justified believer that baptism would be a mockery'.[797] While the 'old man' lacks clear definition, it seems to be the case that the 'old man' bears correlation with Adam, fallen humanity, and actual transgressions against God.[798]

In addition to emphasizing WB's symbolism of death and burial (Rom. 6.3-6) of the 'old man', *TGR* also addresses the 'newness of life' or resurrection to be enjoyed upon conversion. The promise of resurrection life is also found in Rom. 6.5-6. Unfortunately, *TGR* is

---

> Thus Jesus Christ was GOD'S LAMB which took away the sins of the world. He was the Second Man Adam (I Cor. 15, 45) the Quickening Spirit, who brought back, by obedience to God, that which the first Adam lost by disobedience. Thus He became the federal head of the NEW CREATION (Ephesians 2:10). All who are in Christ are a new creation (II Corin. 5:17), [sic] that is, Christ is in them (II Corin. 13; 5). [sic] All who are still unsaved are still condemned in Adam. (Capitalization in the original)

[796] *TGR* 1.7 (December 1, 1913), p. 3.
[797] *TGR* 1.3 (1912), pp.3-5. Also, see *TGR* 1.8 (January 1, 1914), p. 4.
[798] *TGR* 2 (August 1, 1913), p. 3. The editorial provides the following perspective:

> And it is because our old man was crucified in Christ, that just as soon as a sinner repents of actual transgressions and turns to God, his sins are forgiven, and he is cleansed from all unrighteousness, and God does not say a word to him about the old man. In fact there is not a single scripture in the Bible where God deals with the old man, save at Calvary, and not a single bit of instruction or admonition other than to bury the dead body by baptism.

relatively silent on what it means to live the resurrected life in view of WB.

However, references to Col. 2.11, 3.1-3, and 9-10 are employed to provide guidance in regard to living in 'newness of life'.[799] E.A. Paul asserts that 'When a sinner through grace accepts Christ he enters into a relationship with God; he becomes a new creature and has put off the sins of the flesh (Col. 2:11)'.[800]

Based on the restored relationship with Jesus Christ, A.H. Argue presents Paul's directive in regard to 'newness of life' for the redeemed:

> Therefore if you have been raised up with Christ, keep seeking the things above, where Christ is, seated at the right hand of God. Set your mind on the things above, not on the things that are on earth. For you have died and your life is hidden with Christ in God.[801]

In sum, WB by total immersion is crucial for persons desirous of following Jesus' command to be baptized. Second, the symbolism of WB portrays the movement concretely from death to life when a person is redeemed and restored to the 'likeness of Jesus Christ'.

Meat in Due Season

Introduction

Frank J. Ewart, the assistant pastor to William Durham in Los Angeles, replaced Durham after his death in 1912. In 1913, Ewart heard R.E. McAlester preach on WB in the name of Jesus at the Arroyo Seco, CA camp meeting. In 1914 he began preaching the use of the shorter formula and started rebaptizing Trinitarian Pentecostals. According to Hall, he was one of the first to reject the doctrine of the Trinity and preach/teach the Oneness of God instead.[802]

Ewart, who served as Editor and Publisher of *MDS*, reports that 'This little paper is not like any of the other Pentecostal papers that are in the field. They have their message, but ours is distinct in

---

[799] *TGR* 1.3 (1912), p. 13.
[800] *TGR* 1.8 (January 1, 1914), p. 4.
[801] *TGR* 1.3 (1912), pp. 6-7.
[802] Hall, 'Ewart, Frank', pp. 623-24.

itself.'[803] The message of *MDS* focused on proclamation of the Oneness of God and WB in the name of Jesus. To support the purpose of *MDS*, Ewart included a number of baptismal reports and articles by guest contributors who addressed either one of the topics or both in an article.

According to Ewart's editorial in the June 1916 issue of *MDS*, tensions arose within the Oneness Pentecostal movement due to his teaching of the Oneness of God. Ewart proffers the following to readers:

> The last issue of the paper bridged the gulf that had sprung up between us and many of our fellow Ministers who had been baptized in the name of Jesus, but because of the teaching that Jesus Christ the Son swallowed up the Father's identity in His own person, they had withdrawn from our fellowship.[804]

It appears to be the case that the message of baptizing in Jesus' name only experienced initial resistance.[805] Then the message moved to be widely accepted within Pentecostalism. There is no evidence in the baptismal reports that the teaching on the Oneness of God was initially rejected. However, the presence of an article, 'The One True God,' by G.T. Haywood, does support that the teaching was being promulgated and that it had detractors.[806]

The Practice of Water Baptism

The three available issues of *MDS* provide a sufficient number of baptismal reports to demonstrate the importance of WB within the arm of the Oneness Pentecostal movement led by Frank Ewart.[807] Specifically, the reports stress baptisms employing the phrases 'baptized into the name of Jesus,'[808] and 'baptized in Jesus' name'.[809] However, the reports are not limited to these two phrases alone to

---

[803] *MDS* 1.9 (December 1915), p. 3
[804] *MDS* 1.13 (June 1916), p. 2.
[805] *MDS* 1.9 (December 1915), p. 3
[806] *MDS* 1.9 (December 1915), p. 3.
[807] *MDS* 1.9 (December 1915), pp. 1, 2, 3, and 4; *MDS* 1.13 (June 1916), pp. 1, 2, and 4; and *MDS* 1.21 (August 1917), pp. 1, 2.
[808] *MDS* 1.9 (December 1915), 1. *MDS* 1.13 (June 1916), pp. 1, 2, and 4.
[809] *MDS* 1.9 (December 1915), pp. 2, 4; *MDS* 1.13 (June 1916), pp. 2, 4; and *MDS* 1.21 (August 1917). p. 4.

describe the baptismal event. While few in number, the other references utilized by reporters include the following: baptized in water;[810] 'went down into the watery grave in the precious name of Jesus';[811] and obey/obeying (the command to follow Christ in baptism).[812]

Reports from the field are inconsistent in their content, lacking a uniform template to follow in reporting baptismal activity to the editor, and then readers. In general, the reports name the formula employed, the reporter, locale, number baptized in water, and the HS. On occasion, reports include descriptions of the services. Noteworthy is the fact that reports lack reference to baptistries and bodies of water and where the baptismal services were conducted.

Reporters also announced plans for future baptismal services in their location. The stated commitments for future baptisms stressed the importance and centrality of WB 'in Jesus' name' and the progress of the Oneness message.[813]

The Breadth of Practice and Mode

It appears that Ewart, based in Los Angeles, CA, employed baptismal reports[814] to demonstrate the spread and success of the Oneness message of WB 'in the name of Jesus only'. Reports originated from various locales in North America. The new teaching was readily accepted in Canada according to the reports from Winnipeg;[815] Toronto;[816] and Tyndal.[817] In the U.S., reports are submitted from the Twin Cities (Minneapolis and Saint Paul, MN);[818] Oregon City, OR;[819] San Antonio, TX;[820] and Oakland, CA.[821]

---

[810] *MDS* 1.9 (December 1915), pp. 1, 3; *MDS* 1.13 (June 1916), p. 4.
[811] *MDS* 1.9 (December 1915), p. 2.
[812] *MDS* 1.9 (December 1915), p. 4.
[813] *MDS* 1.13 (June 1916), p. 2.
[814] *MDS* 1.9 (December 1915), pp. 1, 2, 3, and 4; *MDS* 1.13 (June 1916), pp. 1, 2, and 4; and *MDS* 1.21 (August 1917), pp. 1, 2.
[815] *MDS* 1.9 (December 1915), p. 2; *MDS* 1.13 (June 1916), p. 2.
[816] *MDS* 1.9 (December 1915), p. 4.
[817] *MDS* 1.13 (June 1916), p. 2.
[818] *MDS* 1.9 (December 1915), p. 2.
[819] *MDS* 1.13 (June 1916), p. 1.
[820] *MDS* 1.21 (August 1917). p. 1.
[821] *MDS* 1.9 (December 1915), p. 4.

From the descriptions of the baptismal events, it appears to be the case that total immersion in 'the name of Jesus' was the accepted mode of baptism. As previously mentioned, the two phrases, 'went down into the watery grave in the precious name of Jesus';[822] and obey/obeying (the command to follow Christ in baptism),[823] were employed to describe baptism. The phrase 'being buried in the name of the Lord'[824] was also employed for baptism. These phrases were utilized in previously reviewed Pentecostal periodicals, where immersion was clearly stated to be the accepted mode of baptism. Additionally, one reporter opines, 'It is a wonderful privilege to see people coming up out of the water speaking in other tongues and prophesying'.[825] The preceding supports WB as total immersion.

Since Oneness Pentecostals drank deeply from the same stream as Trinitarian Pentecostals, it is unlikely that total immersion as accepted mode would differ. The water became the stage for complete conversion through baptism by immersion and receiving the baptism of the HS, with the evidence of speaking in tongues.

Similarly, there is no mention of 'sprinkling' or 'infant baptism' in *MDS*. It seems to be the case that Ewart, like Opperman, embraced the AG's stance on WB, which stood for believer's baptism alone and rejected infant baptism and sprinkling.

Authority to Baptize and Candidate Requirements

The periodical is void of guidance regarding who may baptize and rebaptize candidates. It seems to be the case that the administrator of WB had to testify to receiving a revelation concerning the Oneness of God in Jesus Christ, and that WB was to be conducted in the 'name of Jesus only'.[826] *Meat in Due Season* lacks any account of women ministers being engaged in ministry in the movement led by Ewart. However, an article, 'Woman's Place in the Body', reprinted from *TGR* , published in June 1913, appears to affirm women in ministry as long as they do not attempt to rule over men.[827]

---

[822] *MDS* 1.9 (December 1915), p. 2.
[823] *MDS* 1.9 (December 1915), p. 4.
[824] *MDS* 1.13 (June 1916), p. 2
[825] *MDS* 1.13 (June 1916), p. 2.
[826] *MDS* 1.9 (December 1915), p. 2; *MDS* 1.13 (June 1916), pp. 1, 2.
[827] *MDS* 1.13 (June 1916), p. 3.

It appears that ministers who were first in opposition to the new teachings and later testified to receiving a revelation served as 'success stories' to validate the message and its claims. By 'falling in line' they became catalysts for others to embrace the new teachings. One example provided by a June 1916 Canadian reporter from Tyndal, describes the process of one minister transitioning from Trinitarian to Oneness Pentecostalism:

> Lately Brother Armstrong, the Pastor of the Mission there who has been opposing this message, received a revelation of the truth, and openly declared before the saints that he had taken a stand for baptism in the name of Jesus Christ. He prophesied that many would see the light and be baptized in the name of the Lord this summer. They are to hold a special baptismal service there at once.[828]

The journey of another minister reflects the same pattern of rejection, receiving a revelation, and then becoming an ardent advocate. Frank Bartleman rehearses his embrace of Oneness Pentecostalism in an article entitled, 'Why I was Rebaptized, in the Name of Jesus Christ'.[829] Bartleman avers that during a convention the following occurred:

> A brother gave a warning from the platform against standing in the way of others and the Lord said, that is for you. Now the fear changed to the other side, and I began to fear God if I resisted longer. I got up and declared myself. A few minutes later, with others, I went into the water 'in the name of Jesus.' As I came out the Lord met me. The old anointing came upon me and the heavenly song flowed from my lips. In the dressing room I could hardly change my clothing. I was drunk on the Spirit. I had obeyed God.[830]

It seems that the only requirement to be met by baptismal candidates was the repentance of sin.[831] However, repentance did not mean the person was converted. Conversion only occurred when

---

[828] *MDS* 1.13 (June 1916), p. 2.
[829] *MDS* 1.9 (December 1915), p. 1.
[830] *MDS* 1.9 (December 1915), p. 1.
[831] *MDS* 1.9 (December 1915), pp. 2, 4; *MDS* 1.13 (June 1916), pp. 1, 4.

people repented, had faith in Christ, and were baptized 'in Jesus' name, and received the baptism in the Holy Ghost, with the evidence of speaking in tongues. This was all to occur in the water on the occasion of being baptized 'in Jesus' name'.

Baptismal Formula

Ewart, publisher and editor of the periodical, in agreement with other Oneness Pentecostal leaders, asserted that WB was to be conducted in the 'name of Jesus only'. Support for the position is provided by baptismal reports[832] and several articles/testimonies addressing the correct formula and denying the validity of the Trinitarian formula.[833]

Pentecostal Worship and Witness

Previously reviewed periodicals provided vibrant descriptions of water baptismal services that portrayed Pentecostal worship without constraint. *Meat in Due Season* service descriptions focus on what God was doing in the service and the events transpiring in the water, exclusive of what was occurring with onlookers. For example, a report on activities at Tyndal, a nearby town to Winnipeg, Canada, offers the following account:

> God broke through in such power that out of twelve that sought the Holy Spirit, eight received Him with a clear definite language. Many also have embraced their privilege of being buried in the name of the Lord, and God confirmed His word by filling them with the Spirit according to the scriptures.[834]

While stating 'God broke through in such power', the report first emphasizes the baptism of the HS, and then, the dual baptism of water and the HS.[835] Additional reports of dual baptism appear in other submissions, stressing the veracity of baptizing 'in Jesus' name'.[836] One new feature in *MDS* baptismal reports, relative to

---

[832] *MDS* 1.9 (December 1915), pp. 1, 2, 3, and 4; *MDS* 1.13 (June 1916), pp. 1, 2, and 4; and *MDS* 1.21 (August 1917), pp. 1, 2.
[833] *MDS* 1.9 (December 1915), p. 1.
[834] *MDS* 1.13 (June 1916), p. 2.
[835] *MDS* 1.13 (June 1916), p. 2.
[836] *MDS* 1.9 (December 1915), p. 2; *MDS* 1.13 (June 1916), p. 2.

Pentecostal worship, is the act of 'prophesying'[837] upon being baptized in water and the HS. It appears that instead of cataloging the physical activity of worship participants or those baptized, the emphasis was placed on the operation of the Spiritual gifts.

Commitment and Consequences

Meat in Due Season exhibits transparency regarding opposition to the message of Oneness Pentecostalism, as represented by Ewart and his cohort. Opposition to Ewart's teaching on the Oneness of God does not explicitly appear in the periodical. Instead, the hostility seems to focus solely on the baptismal formula and the pedagogy surrounding the same.

In Ewart's report of events occurring at the Ninth Street mission in Oakland, CA, we read that before they were baptized in the name of Jesus, many 'were bitterly hostile to this truth at the commencement of the meetings'.[838] The opposition was not limited to the laity. Ministers also opposed the message and practice of baptism 'in Jesus' name'.[839] The opposition was not limited to the Oneness message. It was visited upon new converts. F.J. Ewart recounts the resistance received by a Catholic man from Napa, CA in the following statement:

> He was bound with cords and beaten by his own wife. The Catholics accused him of giving away his money to the Pentecostal people, and of being insane, but when his trial came off in court the Judge acquitted him of every charge, and so absolute was the vindication that his wife wept on his neck and asked forgiveness.[840]

The above story attests to the commitment of the man persecuted by his wife and others. Similarly, ministers who had received the revelation of the truth regarding baptism 'in Jesus' name' and the new understanding of conversion were committed to proclaiming the 'simple gospel' in the face of the opposition mentioned above. The baptismal reports reflect the results of their committed labor.

---

[837] *MDS* 1.9 (December 1915), p. 2; *MDS* 1.13 (June 1916), p. 2.
[838] *MDS* 1.9 (December 1915), p. 4.
[839] *MDS* 1.13 (June 1916), p. 2.
[840] *MDS* 1.9 (December 1915), p. 4.

The Meaning of Water Baptism

A clear articulation of the components of salvation is contained in the following statement:

> Jesus is the door. The door consists of 3 cardinal facts: Christ died; 2, Christ was buried; 3, Christ arose and this is the gospel, 1 Cor. 15:3,4, and we are not only expected to believe these facts but to obey them by dying with Him (baptism in water) and rise with Him, (receive the Holy Ghost.).[841]

From the preceding, it is apparent that for Oneness Pentecostals, WB and Spirit baptism are both necessary for conversion to occur in a new convert. Water baptism symbolizes 'dying with Him' and 'rising with Christ' means to be baptized in the HS, with the evidence of speaking in tongues. Ewart opines in the June 1916 issue, 'When a man is baptized in the name of Jesus Christ, he acknowledges before all that he was justly condemned to die, but Jesus Christ took his place in that death'.[842]

Building on the substitution of Jesus Christ, Ewart posits that once a person identifies with Jesus Christ, their debt of sin is remitted or canceled. A receipt is given to the believer, symbolizing the cancellation of the sin debt. According to Ewart, the receipt signifies the gift of the Holy Ghost or Eternal life.[843]

In contrast, Trinitarian Pentecostals posit the necessity of faith alone for conversion to occur. Moreover, WB is symbolic of the death and resurrection of Christ, calling attention to a new life in Christ that is to be lived in the 'public square' as a witness to Jesus Christ.[844] The differences between Trinitarian and Oneness Pentecostals concerning the meaning of WB were continuous during the early expansion of both movements.

The Blessed Truth

Introduction

Daniel C.O. Opperman was an influential leader in the AG, before his withdrawal and transition to leadership in the Oneness

---

[841] *MDS* 1.21 (August 1917), p. 2.
[842] *MDS* 1.13 (June 1916), p. 4.
[843] *MDS* 1.13 (June 1916), p. 4.
[844] *MDS* 1.21 (August 1917), p. 2. Emphasis added.

Pentecostal movement.[845] He resided in Eureka Springs, AR, from where he published and edited the semi-monthly *TBT*. Lee Floyd served as Associate Editor. The following influential persons supplied articles as Contributing Editors: L.C. Hall, Zion City, IL; F. Bartleman, Los Angeles, CA; H.A. Goss, Hot Springs, AR; W.E. Booth-Clibborn, St. Louis, MO; and R.C. Lawson, Columbus, OH.[846]

The *TBT* was employed to advance the message of Oneness Pentecostals. The publication included baptismal reports, testimonies, convention announcements, and articles defending, clarifying, and providing biblical exposition in support of 'getting back to the simple, powerful Apostolic order and gospel'.

The first issue was published circa 1916. The last existing copy of *TBT* is dated July 1, 1923. While the timespan of *TBT*'s publication is unknown, we do know that Opperman died in 1926.[847] There is no evidence to suggest *TBT* survived his death.

In the August 15, 1918, edition of the *TBT*, an informative, cautionary notice is provided by Associate Editor Lee Floyd, entitled, 'Condensive News'. In the article, Floyd reports that to 'accommodate all the brethren, we are obliged to condense reports. The important news is the thing needed to be reported'.[848] Consequently, it is unclear if the baptismal reports in *TBT* are redacted or complete originals. While it is probable the stories have been edited, we cautiously presume we are reading 'the important news'.

The Practice of Water Baptism

Opperman employs *TBT* to accentuate the import and facticity of WBs by including the reports received from the field. Reports were received from the Midwestern US,[849] The East South-Central US,[850]

---

[845] E.L. Blumhofer, 'Opperman, Daniel Charles Owen' in Stanley M. Burgess and Eduard M. van der Maas (eds.), *NIDPCM* (rev. and exp. edn; Grand Rapids, MI: Zondervan, 2002), pp. 946-47.

[846] *TBT* 3.11 (August 15, 1918), p. 2.

[847] Blumhofer, 'Opperman, Daniel Charles Owen', pp. 946-47.

[848] *TBT* 3.11 (August 15, 1918), p. 4.

[849] North Dakota, South Dakota, Nebraska, Minnesota, Iowa, Missouri, Michigan, Wisconsin, Illinois, Indiana, Kansas, and Ohio.

[850] Alabama, Kentucky, Mississippi, and Tennessee.

and the West South-Central US.[851] A single report from Colombo, Ceylon,[852] originated outside the US.

Reports typically identified the reporter, locale, number baptized, size of the group in attendance, formula employed, and number baptized in the HS, when appropriate. Less often, the reports included accounts of healing and descriptions of the services.[853] In addition to the reports of past baptismal services, reporters projected future baptismal services in their location. The stated commitments for future baptisms stressed the importance and centrality of WB 'in Jesus' name' and the progress of the 'gospel'.[854]

Curiously absent from the reports are references to bodies of water and baptistries where the baptismal services were conducted. The lone exception is the report from Carrollton, IL, by Joe Barnett, pastor. He recounts the following events:

> Also, sixteen were buried in Jesus' name. Yesterday afternoon, I never saw anything like it. We have a tank in our kitchen and had meetings in the afternoon also baptizing. Nine were baptized, among them Bro. and Sinter Carter, who received the baptism at Eureka Springs. You should have heard them shout.[855]

Breadth of Practice and Mode

The extent to which adherents practiced WB, according to Opperman's teaching is demonstrated by identifying the locations where the reports originated. Specifically, baptismal reports were received from the following locations: Mountain Valley, AR;[856] Truman, AR;[857] Owen Sound, ONT, Canada;[858] Colombo, Ceylon;[859]

---

[851] Arkansas, Louisiana, Oklahoma, and Texas.
[852] *TBT* 4.2 (January 15, 1919), p. 3.
[853] *TBT* 3.11 (August 15, 1918), p. 3; *TBT* 4.2 (January 15, 1919), pp. 1, 2, 3, and 4; and *TBT* 4.11 (June 1, 1919), p. 6, 7.
[854] *TBT* 4.2 (January 15, 1919), p. 2; TBT 4.11 (June 1, 1919), pp. 6, 7.
[855] *TBT* 4.2 (January 15, 1919), p. 4.
[856] *TBT* 3.11 (August 15, 1918), p. 3.
[857] *TBT* 4.2 (January 15, 1919), p. 2.
[858] *TBT* 3.11 (August 15, 1918), p. 3.
[859] *TBT* 4.2 (January 15, 1919), p. 3.

Louisville, KY;[860] Carrollton, IL;[861] Ligioner, IN;[862] South Bend, IN;[863] Jamestown, LA;[864] Oakdale, LA;[865] Sugartown, LA;[866] ST. Paul, MN;[867] Hollywood, MO;[868] Joplin, MO;[869] Reeds Spring, MO;[870] Monett, MO;[871] Portsmouth, NH;[872] Portsmouth, OH;[873] Upper Sandusky, OH;[874] Beacon, TN;[875] Bible Hill, TN;[876] Monteagle, TN;[877] MT. Tabor, TN;[878] and Doucette, TX.[879]

It appears that several states in the Midwestern US and portions of the Southern US were impacted by Oneness preachers who proclaimed the revelation that 'in this day of light we must all be baptized in Jesus' name'.[880] This assertion applied to new converts and those persons previously baptized under the Trinitarian formula of Mt. 28.19. The mode of baptism is not explicitly identified as 'total immersion' or 'immersion' in the reports. However, it seems to be the case that 'total immersion' is in view when reporters employ burial language, stating that candidates were 'buried in Jesus' name'.[881] Water baptism via sprinkling and infant baptism are not addressed explicitly in *TBT*. It appears to be the case that Opperman continued to

---

[860] *TBT* 3.11 (August 15, 1918), p. 3.
[861] *TBT* 4.2 (January 15, 1919), p. 4.
[862] *TBT* 3.11 (August 15, 1918), p. 3; *TBT* 4.2 (January 15, 1919), p. 4.
[863] *TBT* 4.11 (June 1, 1919), p. 6.
[864] *TBT* 4.11 (June 1, 1919), p. 6.
[865] *TBT* 3.11 (August 15, 1918), p. 3.
[866] *TBT* 4.11 (June 1, 1919), p. 7.
[867] *TBT* 4.11 (June 1, 1919), p. 6.
[868] *TBT* 3.11 (August 15, 1918), p. 3.
[869] *TBT* 4.11 (June 1, 1919), p. 6.
[870] *TBT* 4.11 (June 1, 1919), p. 6.
[871] *TBT* 4.11 (June 1, 1919), pp. 6-7.
[872] *TBT* 3.11 (August 15, 1918), p. 3.
[873] *TBT* 4.11 (June 1, 1919), p. 6.
[874] *TBT* 3.11 (August 15, 1918), p. 3.
[875] *TBT* 4.11 (June 1, 1919), p. 6.
[876] *TBT* 3.11 (August 15, 1918), p. 3.
[877] *TBT* 4.2 (January 15, 1919), p. 4.
[878] *TBT* 4.11 (June 1, 1919), p. 6.
[879] *TBT* 4.11 (June 1, 1919), p. 7.
[880] *TBT* 4.11 (June 1, 1919), p. 6. Documentation of the impact is found in the following: *TBT* 4.2 (January 15, 1919), pp. 1, 2, 3, and 4; *TBT* 4.11 (June 1, 1919), p. 6, 7.
[881] *TBT* 3.11 (August 15, 1918), p. 3; *TBT* 4.2 (January 15, 1919), p. 4; and *TBT* 4.11 (June 1, 1919), p. 6.

embrace the AG's stance on WB, which rejected infant baptism and sprinkling and stood for believer's baptism alone. The stance on these two issues appears settled since there is no evidence of the issues raised in the new movement.

Authority to Baptize and Candidate Requirements

The *TBT* lacks a clear statement regarding who may baptize and rebaptize candidates. The baptismal reports[882] appear to be authored by ministers who had conducted the baptismal services. On this basis, the implication is that only ordained ministers had the authority to baptize. There is no evidence of a woman conducting a baptismal service.

With a revised soteriology, Oneness Pentecostals rejected the Trinitarian Pentecostal position that conversion occurred at the time of 'confession of sin, repentance, and faith in Christ'. Being converted met the requirements for WB. However, repentance of sin was inadequate for Oneness ministers. According to H.E. Reed's article, 'The Birth of Water and Spirit', the new 'revelation' called for 'getting back to the simple, powerful Apostolic order and gospel'.[883] Returning to the Apostolic order meant that 'salvation', 'conversion', or 'getting saved' does not occur until one is baptized in water and 'speaks with other tongues'. Speaking in tongues provides the evidence they have been baptized in the HS.[884]

In support of his position, Reed opines the 'beautiful harmonization' between Jn 3.3-8 and Acts 2.2-4. He rejects the interpretation that 'born of water and spirit' refers to natural birth, and asserts that 'If to be born of water means to be baptized in water, then to be born of spirit means to be baptized in the Spirit'.[885] Reed presses his position home with the following statement:

> If people would only meet God's condition and do what the Word has said, they would be saved or born of the Spirit by being baptized into the one body. If they believe as the scriptures hath they will do so and if they believe not they will be damned. Some who had been seeking for years have seen this, got in real earnest,

---

[882] *TBT* 4.2 (January 15, 1919), pp. 1, 2, 3, and 4; *TBT* 4.11 (June 1, 1919), p. 6, 7.
[883] *TBT* 3.11 (August 15, 1918), pp. 1-2.
[884] *TBT* 3.11 (August 15, 1918), p. 2.
[885] *TBT* 3.11 (August 15, 1918), p. 2.

opened their hearts to God. He showed them the trouble and they yielded and were filled with the Holy Ghost, speaking in tongues to His glory.[886]

There are no explicit statements in the reports that persons baptized were being rebaptized to meet the requirement of being baptized 'in Jesus' name'. However, it does not seem prudent to negate the probability that rebaptisms occurred. Preachers proclaimed, 'We are getting back to the simple, powerful Apostolic order and gospel' and then elucidated the meaning of the 'simple gospel'. As noted in Reed's comments above, the possibility of damnation for not following the Bible was very real indeed.[887]

Therefore, it is probable that hearers responded positively to the new message and were baptized and rebaptized to be faithful and obedient to the new revelation presented to them. No one wants to be damned.

Baptismal Formula

Oneness Pentecostals base their practices upon those of the Apostles as recounted in the Acts of the Apostles. Consequently, they assert that WB is only to occur 'in the name of Jesus Christ' (Acts 2.38).[888]

To support this position, an article by Frank Bartleman, 'Some Blessed Items of Truth', is included in *TBT* to document the interpretations and the thinking behind the above-noted position:

> Thank God some have had the courage to face the seeming difficulty between Matt. 28:19 and Acts 2:38, etc. The only possible vindication of the Apostles' action in baptizing 'in the name of Jesus Christ' would seem to be the fact that Matt 28:19 was fulfilled in that baptism. There seems to be no other way to harmonize the record of the Book of Acts with Matt. 28:19. Jesus is the revelation of the Father, Son and Holy Ghost to us. The revelation of the true God is 'in His Name.'

---

[886] *TBT* 3.11 (August 15, 1918), p. 2.
[887] *TBT* 3.11 (August 15, 1918), p. 2. Reed asserts that 'If they believe as the scriptures hath they will do so and if they believe not they will be damned'.
[888] *TBT* 3.11 (August 15, 1918), pp. 1-2, 3; *TBT* 4.2 (January 15, 1919), pp. 1, 2, 3, and 4; and *TBT* 4.11 (June 1, 1919), pp. 6, 7.

The Son is not designated specifically in Mt. 28:19. He is not identified as Jesus Christ. John the Baptist did not identify Jesus in his baptism. He baptized with a view to their following him who should come after him. His baptism was 'unto repentance.' Hence Paul rebaptized his converts (Acts 19) and specified the Messiah as Jesus.[889]

Pentecostal Worship and Witness

As noted previously, baptismal reports from the field were submitted to the *TBT* to chronicle the spread and impact of the new revelation. Reports tended to capture the size of the crowds, number baptized in water, the name of the reporter, and the number of those baptized in the HS. Documentation of the HS's impact on worshippers and others witnessing the services appears limited; however, it did occur. Relative to attendance, the reports tend to be unremarkable. However, there are three exceptions. 'Mother' Barnes of Broken Arrow, OK, writes 'We are having an immense crowd. About fifteen hundred each Saturday and Sunday night'.[890] 'Large crowds' are reported by O.L. Pipkin from Altus, OK.[891] A report by L.C. Hall, Owen Sound, ONT, Canada specifies that 'Between sixty and seventy were baptized in Jesus' Name and some wonderful cases of healing'.[892]

The worship atmosphere during the baptismal services provides another descriptor in the reports. One report offers the following description of the impact and response to the HS in the meetings: 'The power began to fall at an early hour and lasted until 12 o'clock. There was leaping and jumping and dancing and shouting, praising God and talking in tongues'.[893] Lawrence McFarland reports from Monteagle, TN that 'during a baptismal service, a girl danced under the power and preached from the sixteenth to the twenty-seventh Psalm. This was done in another tongue as she ran her finger under each line of Scripture. A soldier from Honolulu said she was speaking Japanese. Oh, it was glorious'.[894]

---

[889] *TBT* 3.11 (August 15, 1918), pp. 1-2.
[890] *TBT* 3.11 (August 15, 1918), p. 3.
[891] *TBT* 3.11 (August 15, 1918), p. 3.
[892] *TBT* 3.11 (August 15, 1918), p. 3.
[893] *TBT* 4.2 (January 15, 1919), p. 2.
[894] *TBT* 4.2 (January 15, 1919), p. 4.

In keeping with the 'simple gospel', there were occasions when persons were baptized in the HS while still in the water. S.C. McClain reports from Mountain Valley, AR, that during a meeting held by Bro. Dave Kelley, in early July 1918, that 'Seven were buried in His Name and received the baptism in the water and others were wonderfully blessed'.[895]

Another manifestation of God's activity during the baptismal services was divine healing. Reports from Mountain Valley and Truman, AR; Sugartown, LA; Owen Sound, ONT, Canada; and Doucette, TX all document occurrences of healing in the context of baptismal services.[896]

T.B. Walker from Truman, AR documented events in his locale with the following: 'Some are being converted. Some are being baptized with the Holy Ghost, and some are getting healing for their bodies'.[897] Similarly, from Sugartown, LA, J.J. Havard declares the outcomes of WBs in his locale: 'The saints were built up and some blessed cases of healing. One brother was bitten on the foot by a most poisonous snake. God healed him instantly and he did not stop work'.[898]

It appears to be the case that at least one church sought to test one of the claims in Mk 16.18 which states, 'They shall take up serpents; and if they drink any deadly thing, it shall not hurt them; they shall lay hands on the sick, and they shall recover'. Mrs. J.E. Megge reports from Bible Hill, TN that during a meeting 'The power fell and there was a time of much rejoicing in the Spirit. An old serpent was brought in and we did to the glory of God handle him in Jesus' Name. The people were convinced that there "is power in His name"'.[899]

From the reports reviewed, it appears that baptismal services allowed evangelism during and after the services. Large tents were employed for revival meetings, enabling the gathering of large crowds of participants and onlookers.

---

[895] *TBT* 3.11 (August 15, 1918), p. 3.
[896] *TBT* 3.11 (August 15, 1918), p. 3; *TBT* 4.2 (January 15, 1919), p. 2; and *TBT* 4.11 (June 1, 1919), p. 7.
[897] *TBT* 4.11 (June 1, 1919), p. 7.
[898] *TBT* 4.11 (June 1, 1919), p. 7.
[899] *TBT* 3.11 (August 15, 1918), p. 3.

While not reporting on Pentecostal worship, the following two reports provide insight into the value placed on the Lord's Supper and Footwashing. Notable is the fact that the term 'sacrament' is utilized in one of the reports.

Arthur Caudill, Portsmouth, reports that after several days of baptismal activity, those gathered 'had the Lord's supper and foot washing last night and there was even forty that partook of the communion and feet washing'.[900] Similarly, J.B. Price reports from Hollywood, MO, that 'Six received the witness of the Holy Ghost by speaking in other tongues. The Lord wonderfully blessed the sacramental service at 3 o'clock'.[901]

Commitment and Consequences

The 'simple gospel message' communicated verbally and in print echoed the following position embraced and supported by Oneness Pentecostals:

> First the Holy Ghost, then the full merits of Jesus' blood, then the full revelation of Jesus, has been the order of restoration. All things are being summed up in Jesus. With Luther's and Wesley's revelation we have nothing to do today, except incidentally. Each message has been mixed with error and has been incomplete in itself, as is always the case. Much unnecessary opposition has been aroused always, because of abuse in ignorance. Some opposition has been honest. The order of restoration has been 'Pentecost,' 'finished work,' and the further revelation of today. We are getting back to the simple, powerful Apostolic order and gospel.[902]

The rejection of the Trinitarian Pentecostal positions on formula, the Trinity, and soteriology created opposition to the message and proclaimers of the message. It is difficult to differentiate between the targets of the hostility visited upon the messengers. Was it the message or the preacher/teacher, and who was being opposed? In one instance, C.A. Pyatt of Monett, MO reports that it was message and preacher:

---

[900] *TBT* 4.11 (June 1, 1919), p. 6.
[901] *TBT* 3.11 (August 15, 1918), p. 3.
[902] *TBT* 4.11 (June 1, 1919), p. 6.

Bro. George W. Brown is here and has the appearance of being a man of God. When he came out on these lines the General Council requested his papers, so he has applied for papers with us in the P.A.W. The Trinity people certainly are angry with him for accepting this message.[903]

Three other reports referring to the opposition are vague in identifying opponents. One author asserts that 'The power of God is falling and the devil is howling', attributing the opposition to the devil.[904] In another report, the opposition is attributed to a nondescript enemy: 'We are still on the firing line. The enemy is making a desperate stand, but we are pressing the battle and the enemy is being forced back'.[905] Last, we read a testimony by L.A. Smith of Upper Sandusky, OH, stating that he has 'had a terrible battle in this city, but God has given the message and the grace to stand. Praise to His precious name. I, by the grace of God, will not compromise.'[906]

The Meaning of Water Baptism

The review of WB reveals that the attention paid to WB in *TBT* is usually in concert with participants being baptized with the HS, with the evidence of speaking in tongues. This is understandable considering the revised soteriology of Oneness Pentecostals, which couples WB, Spirit baptism with faith in Christ to accomplish the work of conversion.

Conversely, the lack of attention to the meaning of WB for the life of the believer is surprisingly absent. The only reference to meaning is supplied in the August 15, 1918, issue of *TBT*. The reporter asserts that 'baptism in 'Jesus' name' means that we are identified with him in death, and we go free. He was sacrificed for us.[907] While drawing upon the concepts of Federal Headship and substitutionary atonement, the reference fails to elaborate on the resurrection aspect of Christ's death.

---

[903] *TBT* 4.11 (June 1, 1919), p. 6.
[904] *TBT* 4.11 (June 1, 1919), p. 6.
[905] *TBT* 4.11 (June 1, 1919), p. 6.
[906] *TBT* 3.11 (August 15, 1918), p. 3.
[907] *TBT* 3.11 (August 15, 1918), pp. 1-2.

The Present Truth

Introduction

The Present Truth, published in Indianapolis, IN by L.V. Roberts, who served as Editor, asserts the purpose of the periodical in his opening editorial. Namely, to disseminate the 'present message, which we believe to be God's messages for today for His people, before them as soon as possible, before God makes another move'.[908] The content of the paper includes fresh articles from the Editor's pen and materials that have been printed in other newspapers. The included pieces are from the pens of Winifred Westfield,[909] Frank Ewart,[910] Glenn A. Cook,[911] G.H. Studd,[912] G.T. Haywood,[913] L.C. Hall,[914] F. Small,[915] E.R. Bass,[916] A.H. Argue,[917] Harry Morse,[918] John Scheppe,[919] H.O. Scott,[920] B.S. Moore,[921] and F.F. Bosworth.[922]

Also, Roberts avers that since the periodical is not a missionary paper, reports from foreign fields will not be printed. Similarly, 'Neither will we print minor reports of the homeland or personal testimonies'. Consequently, we may find few, if any, baptismal stories.[923]

Roberts posits he will take a non-combative and non-defensive posture with those opposed to the Oneness message. Roberts proposes to take the 'high road' when he asserts the following: 'our weapons are not carnal, but mighty through God's word, and we are

---

[908] *TPT* 1.1 (1916), p. 4.
[909] *TPT* 1.1 (1916), pp. 1-2.
[910] *TPT* 1.1 (1916), pp. 2, 5, and 7.
[911] *TPT* 1.1 (1916), pp. 2, 5, 6, and 7.
[912] *TPT* 1.1 (1916), p. 2..
[913] *TPT* 1.1 (1916), p. 3.
[914] *TPT* 1.1 (1916), p. 3.
[915] *TPT* 1.1 (1916), p. 4.
[916] *TPT* 1.1 (1916), p. 4.
[917] *TPT* 1.1 (1916), p. 5.
[918] *TPT* 1.1 (1916), pp. 6, 7.
[919] *TPT* 1.1 (1916), p. 6.
[920] *TPT* 1.1 (1916), p. 7.
[921] *TPT* 1.1 (1916), p. 7.
[922] *TPT* 1.1 (1916), p. 7.
[923] *TPT* 1.1 (1916), p. 4.

determined to stay on Bible grounds and trust God to take us through'.[924]

The Practice of Water Baptism

The Present Truth documents that WB is an ordinance of the Church.[925] However, executing the rite is meaningless 'apart from the Holy Ghost and the name of Jesus is dead powerless formality'.[926] According to the Editor, 'Water baptism in the name of Jesus Christ is an imperative necessity both in Acts 2:38 and John 3:5'.[927] He posits Acts 2.38 is God's remedy for sin; however, it is not the gospel. Furthermore, every ingredient is essential for treating the disease. Because each ingredient is vital, 'you can no more cut out water baptism in the name of Jesus Christ than you can cut out repentance'.[928] This point is reinforced throughout the publication's one volume by over sixty references to the name of Jesus Christ in the baptismal formula. The following variations on the formula are found in the first volume: 'baptized into the name of Jesus Christ', 'baptized into the name of the Lord Jesus Christ', and baptized into 'the Lord Jesus', 'Jesus' name', and 'the name'.[929]

Similarly, A.H. Argue stresses the linkage between WB and Spirit baptism in a brief article titled, 'Salvation'. He emphasizes the similarities of baptismal accounts found in Acts 2.4, 10.46, 11.15, and 19.2-6, where WB and Spirit baptism occur during the same time frame.[930]

G.H. Studd confesses his confusion over 'one baptism' found in Eph. 4.5's reference to 'One Lord, one faith, one baptism', and the relationship between water and Spirit baptism. Studd submits an account of his discernment process and the resolution of his confusion. Employing the concept of the outward embodied person observed and the inner person hidden from view, Studd proffers that it takes both the inner and outer to make One person. In correlation

---

[924] *TPT* 1.1 (1916), p. 4.
[925] References to WB may be found on the following pages: *TPT* 1.1 (1916), pp. 2, 4, 6, 7 and 8.
[926] *TPT* 1.1 (1916), p. 4.
[927] *TPT* 1.1 (1916), p. 7.
[928] *TPT* 1.1 (1916), p. 7.
[929] *TPT* 1.1 (1916), pp. 1-2, 4, 6, and 7.
[930] *TPT* 1.1 (1916), p. 5.

to water and Spirit baptism, Studd asserts that 'There is the outward and visible immersion in water in the name of Jesus, and there is the true anti-type of it, the baptism with the Holy Ghost', with speaking in other tongues as the Spirit giveth utterance.[931]

The Breadth of Practice and Mode

It is impossible to ascertain the extent of where the baptismal practice 'in Jesus' name' occurred from one issue of a periodical. There is a solitary baptismal report in eight pages of articles, sermons, and announcements. The report, filed by B.S. Moore and wife, writing from Yokohama, Japan, is located in their article titled, 'Christ' or 'Antichrist' – Which?[932] In the article, the Moores champion the cause of Jesus Christ in sharp contrast to the 'Federated Churches and Missions of Japan' who they assert are strongly opposed to the HS, and many deny the Deity of Jesus Christ'. Moreover, since the majority of professing Christians and missionaries deny the authority of Jesus Christ, the Moores, as persons 'outside the camp', felt compelled 'to go forth with a Holy message of Pentecostal full salvation through Jesus Christ'. The results of their labor to magnify Jesus are the baptism of thirty persons 'of which nearly all are true'. In addition to the thirty, there were others ready to be baptized.[933]

Before proceeding, it must be noted that there is a question regarding the validity of the above report as an authentic representative of the Pentecostal Oneness movement. The Moores, stationed in Japan as missionaries, were sent by the nascent AG as early as 1915, according to a report from them located in the *WW*.[934] It was rumored that they had defected and aligned with the Oneness movement; however, there is no evidence that a defection occurred. A report from the Moores in Japan, in the October 18, 1919, issue of the *PE*, reflects their continued alignment with the AG.[935] The report is filed at a minimum of two years after their article was published in the *PT*. Furthermore, the description of the presence of God in the service appears to reflect a Trinitarian rather than a

---

[931] *TPT* 1.1 (1916), p. 2.
[932] *TPT* 1.1 (1916), p. 7.
[933] *TPT* 1.1 (1916), p. 7.
[934] *WW* 12.9 (September 1915), p. 2.
[935] *PE* 310, 311 (October 18, 1919), p. 10.

Oneness perspective. They report that the service 'was blessed of God' and the 'anointing of the Spirit was on the meeting and the presence of Jesus greatly felt'.⁹³⁶

Given the preceding, it seems appropriate to reject the above baptismal report as a valid representation of the Pentecostal Oneness movement. It is probable that their article was reproduced from another periodical and appropriated by the Editor as a representation of the Oneness movement in Japan.

The mode of WB espoused by the *TPT* is total immersion. Baptism by immersion is consistent with previously reviewed periodicals in which the accepted method of baptism is immersion.⁹³⁷ In addition to the explicit use of immersion, the *TPT* also includes burial language to remove any doubt regarding mode.⁹³⁸

Authority and Requirements

The authority to baptize appears to rest on those who have received the revelation of the only valid way of baptizing, and that is 'in Jesus' name'. They also understand the revised *via salutis* whereby repentance, WB, and Spirit baptism occur sequentially without a perceptual passage of time.⁹³⁹

Repentance is the one qualification that must occur before a person may be baptized in water.⁹⁴⁰ Repentance of sin appears to be an inviolable requirement throughout the Pentecostal movement.

A curious statement seems to imply that there may be another requirement placed on candidates. In an article titled, 'Do You Know', the author asserts the following question: 'Do You Know that you must get a revelation of this mystery, and receive it yourself from God before you can live a godly life?'⁹⁴¹ It is unclear who is being addressed by the Editor. Is it clergy, baptismal candidates, or those who have been baptized in the name of Jesus?

---

⁹³⁶ *TPT* 1.1 (1916), p. 7.
⁹³⁷ *TPT* 1.1 (1916), pp. 2, 3. The only exception is the IPHC, which allows sprinkling and infant baptism.
⁹³⁸ *TPT* 1.1 (1916), pp. 1-2.
⁹³⁹ *TPT* (1916), pp. 1-2.
⁹⁴⁰ *TPT* 1.1 (1916), pp. 1-2, 5, and 7.
⁹⁴¹ *TPT* 1.1 (1916), p. 1.

Baptismal Formula

From the comments, it appears to be clear that the accepted formula to be employed is 'baptize in Jesus' name' to the exclusion of references to the Father and the HS as found in Mt. 28.19. Moreover, single immersion is promulgated in opposition to those who propose triune immersion. One writer opines that 'If triune immersion is right, then Jesus must have been buried and raised from the dead three **times** instead of only one'. The rationale behind the comment is Rom. 6.4, 5, and Col. 2.12, where 'Paul tells us that our baptism is to be in the likeness of his burial and resurrection'.[942]

Pentecostal Worship and Witness

Given the rejection of the article by the Moores,[943] there are no baptismal reports to consider relative to Pentecostal worship and witness.

The Meaning of Water Baptism

The meaning of WB appears rich and multi-faceted in *TPT*. First, echoing previously reviewed periodicals, baptism symbolizes identification with Jesus Christ in His death and resurrection. As such, WB is a public declaration and confession that Jesus Christ is Lord and Savior. Furthermore, baptism is more than testimony and confession. It represents a renunciation of the kingdom, claims, and authority of Satan, and signifies entrance to the kingdom of God and the authority and claims of Jesus Christ.[944] Second, because of Oneness soteriology, WB, accompanied by repentance and reception of the HS with the evidence of speaking in other tongues, serves as proof that a person is saved.[945] Third, baptism is participation in the death and resurrection of Jesus Christ. In light of the linkage between Calvary, WB, and Pentecost, Winifred Westfield posits in 'What is Truth'? the following elucidation of the effects of WB:

> A repentant sinner (Acts 2:38) baptised [sic] into Jesus Christ is baptised [sic] into his death. (Ro. 6:3.) Through faith the 'operation of God' (Col. 2:12) is performed upon his heart at this

---

[942] *TPT* 1.1 (1916), p. 3. Emphasis original.
[943] *TPT* 1.1 (1916), p. 7.
[944] *TPT* 1.1 (1916), p. 4.
[945] *TPT* 1.1 (1916), p. 5.

time; his old man is crucified that the body of sin might be destroyed (Ro. 6:6), and, being planted in the likeness of his DEATH he is raised to walk in the newness of LIFE (Ro. 6:34), [sic] receiving the Spirit of life, which is none other than Christ himself, for he that hath the Son hath life. It is the Spirit that quickeneth (Jn. 6:63.) 'The Spirit giveth life.' (2 Cor. 3:6.).[946]

Findings and Assessment

Introduction

The lack of scholarly theological treatment of WB as taught and practiced by early Pentecostals in the WHP, FW, and OP streams is notable given the plethora of research published in scholarly journals, dissertations, and monographs on the Eucharist, sanctification, footwashing, SB, ecclesiology, glossolalia, soteriology, the Trinity, the theological roots, historical roots, and sociological roots of the movement, and the role of the HS in various biblical books. The relative absence of WB among treated topics may indicate an unarticulated assumption that the practice of WB was marginalized by early Pentecostals in favor of the new experience of SB with the evidence of speaking in tongues. My close reading of 21 Pentecostal periodicals, spanning 1906-1931 inclusive, reveals the exact opposite to be the case. In actuality, the practice of WB held a place of prominence in the movement, rather than being marginalized in the shadow of SB. The sheer volume of reports that recount the thousands of persons baptized in water, along with sermons, Sunday School lessons, and articles relative to WB in the periodical literature testifies to the robust practice of WB around the globe by Pentecostal evangelists and missionaries during the first 25 years of the movement. However, despite the emphasis placed on the practice of WB by the three streams, our review reveals the movement lacked cohesion and unanimity regarding the practice and theological meaning of WB. In fact, the WHP, FW, and OP streams found congruence regarding WB's theological meaning and practice on few points. When practice and meaning diverged, some differences became significant points of disputation within and between the streams. We now review the points of similarity regarding the

---

[946] *TPT* 1.1 (1916), pp. 1-2.

practices and theological meaning of WB, while noting the points of difference and disputation.

Early Pentecostal Theology and Practice of Water Baptism

It appears to be the case that early Pentecostals within the three streams employ a straightforward reading of the biblical text, reaching similar conclusions regarding the theological foundation of WB. The three streams agree that WB is an ordinance of the Church instituted by the Lord Jesus Christ until the end of the age (Mk. 16.16; Mt. 28.18-20). As such, WB is to be practiced, following Jesus' example (Mt. 3.13-17), and in obedience to his command (Mt. 28.18-20), after repentance, confession of sin, and faith in Jesus Christ as Lord and Savior (Acts 2.38). All three streams stress obedience to Christ's command, and none deem WB optional.[947]

The close linkage of WB with conversion appears to permeate all three streams, giving rise to the perspective on the field that WB is necessary for one to be saved. Consequently, WB is to be offered to candidates as soon as possible after repentance, confession of sin, and profession of faith in Christ. There appear to be two allowable

---

[947] *AF* 1.10 (September 1907), p. 2; TBM 2.37 (May 1, 1909), p. 1; *TBM* 9.185 (August 1, 1916), p. 1; *LRE* 1.6 (March 1909), pp. 22-23; *LRE* 6.4 (January 1914), pp. 20-21; *LRE* 6.8 (May 1914), pp. 10-11; *LRE* 9.7 (April 1917), p. 13; *LRE* 10.6 (March 1918), pp. 19-21; *LRE* 13.4 (January 1921), p. 8; *LRE* 17.6 (March 1925), p. 23; *LRE* 17.7 (April 1925), p. 14; *LRE* 17.8 (May 1925), p. 16; *LRE* 20.8 (May 1928), pp. 20, 23; *LRE* 23.10 (July 1931), p. 22; *COGE* 8.17 (May 5, 1917), p. 1; *COGE* 1.9 (July 1, 1910), p. 7; *COGE* 1.15 (Oct 1, 1910), p. 5; *COGE* 10.20 (May 17, 1919), p. 3; *COGE* 14.35 (September 1, 1923), p. 3; *COGE* 19.42 (Oct 20, 1928), p. 4; *COGE* 20.5 (March 30, 1929), p. 4; *COGE* 20.50 (February 22, 1930), p. 4; *COGE* 21.9 (April 26, 1930), p. 2; *COGE* 5.40 (Oct 4, 1914), p. 5; *COGE* 6.30 (July 24, 1915), p. 3; *COGE* 6.33 (August 14, 1915), p. 1; *COGE* 7.10 (March 4, 1916), p. 4; *COGE* 5.8 (February 21, 1914), pp. 5, 8; *COGE* 6.30 (July 24, 1915), p. 3; *COGE* 21.30 (September 20, 1930), p. 1; *COGE* 22.26 (August 29, 1931), p. 2; *WWM* 1.21 (July 12, 1924), p. 2; *PH* 4.5 (September 1918), p. 3; *PH* 4.10 (February 1919), p. 4; *PH* 5.4 (September 1919), p. 3; *PH* 2.11 (March 1917), p. 2; *PH* 5.1 (May 1919), p. 3; *PHA* 3.10 (July 3, 1919), pp. 2-3; *PHA* 4.40 (February 3, 1921), pp. 8-9; *PHA* 3.10 (July 3, 1919), pp. 2-3; *PHA* 9.35 (January 7, 1926), pp. 6-7; *WW* 9.6 (June 20, 1913), p. 2; *WW* 12.9 (September 1915), p. 7; *WW* 10.5 (May 20, 1914), p. 1; *WW* 12.9 (September 1915), p. 2; *WW* 8.6 (August 20, 1912), p. 2; *WW* 9.8 (August 20, 1913), p. 3; *PE* 111 (October 16, 1915), pp. 1, 2; *TGR* 1.3 (1912), pp. 3-5; *TGR* 1.3 (1912), p. 11; and *TGR* 1.8 (January 1, 1914), p. 4. See *WWM* 4.11 (May 21, 1927), p. 2. A.J. Tomlinson of the WHP stream, explicitly asserts that WB 'is so closely connected with salvation that everyone should be baptized'.

scenarios for delaying WB. Foreign missionaries invoked the first in their attempt to validate a candidate's suitability for WB in view of the consequences of publicly proclaiming faith in Jesus as Lord and Savior. Before being allowed to be baptized, candidates had to undergo catechesis,[948] a verbal 'examination' to ensure understanding of the meaning of their conversion and WB,[949] public profession of faith,[950] and demonstrable proof of a changed life that reflected faith in Jesus Christ.[951] The same scrutiny does not appear with baptismal candidates in the USA. The second situation for delaying WB was to ensure that a qualified administrator was available to conduct the rite.[952]

The three streams appear to ground salvation from sin in their Christology and soteriology, focusing on the doctrine of the atonement, in particular, avowing that WB has no saving efficacy apart from faith in the atoning death of Christ and his resurrection. Only repentance, confession of sin, and faith in Jesus Christ affects one's salvation from sin and death.[953] Consequently, all three streams

---

[948] *LRE* 6.3 (December 1913), p. 7; *LRE* 9.9 (June 1917), p. 18; *LRE* 12.10 (July 1920), p. 17; *LRE* 17.5 (February 1925), p. 13; *LRE* 18.4 (January 1926), p. 4; *LRE* 19.2 (November 1926), p. 17; and *LRE* 20.12 (September 1928), pp. 14-15.

[949] *LRE* 11.6 (March 1919), p. 8; *LRE* 13.8b (May 1921), p. 22; *LRE* 19.1 (October 1926), p. 13; *LRE* 20.11 (August 1928), p. 15; *LRE* 20.12 (September 1928), p. 15; *PE* 192 (June 2, 1917), p. 6; *PE* 788 (March 9, 1929), p. 11; *PE* 639 (March 20, 1926), p. 7; and *PE* 786 (February 23, 1929), p. 10.

[950] *LRE* 8.10 (July 1916), p. 9; *LRE* 9.6 (March 1917), p. 3; *LRE* 12.10 (July 1920), p. 17; *LRE* 17.5 (February 1925), p. 13; and *LRE* 23.8 (May 1931), p. 21.

[951] *TBM* 5.115 (August 1, 1912), p. 1; *LRE* 12.10 (July 1920), p. 17; *LRE* 20.7 (April 1928), p. 21; and *LRE* 20.12 (September 1928), p. 14.

[952] *COGE* 21.9 (April 26, 1930), p. 2. Also see *COGE* 7.10 (March 4, 1916), p. 4; *COGE* 18.37 (September 10, 1927), p. 3; *COGE* 19.28 (July 14, 1928), p. 1; *COGE* 20.26 (August 24, 1929), p. 2; *COGE* 21.9 (April 26, 1930), p. 2; and *COGE* 22.21 (July 25, 1931), p. 4.

[953] *AF* 1.7 (April 1907), p. 3; *AF* 1.1 (September 1906), p. 2, 3; *AF* 1.3 (November 1906), p. 3; *AF* 1.5 (January 1907), p. 2; *AF* 1.6 (February-March 1907), p. 7; *AF* 1.10 (September 1907), p. 2; *AF* 1.11 (October-January 1908, pp. 2, 3; *AF* 1.12 (January 1908), p. 2; *AF* II.12 (May 1908), p. 2, 3; *TBM* 6.136 (July 1913), p. 3; *LRE* 8.10 (July 1916), p. 9; *LRE* 20.12 (September 1928), p. 15; *LRE* 23.10 (Jul 1931), p. 22; *COGE* 5.8 (February 21, 1914), pp. 5, 8; *COGE* 6.4 (January 23, 1915), pp. 1, 4; *COGE* 6.28 (July 10, 1915), p. 4; *COGE* 14.2 (January 13, 1923), p. 3; *COGE* 21.46 (January 24, 1931), p. 3; *FC* 1.33 (July 9, 1927), pp. 3-5; *FC* 1.7 (January 8,

reject baptismal regeneration.[954]

As noted above, the three streams do not view WB as optional; however, opinions begin to diverge regarding the *necessity* of WB for the believer. Within the WHP and FW streams, it is not necessary for a person to be baptized to be saved, except when refusal to be baptized is deemed to be disobedience to God's directive. Then, the issue is escalated to questioning whether the person is truly saved if they are disobedient to Christ's command. The OP stream is unequivocal that WB is necessary for salvation, positing that after repentance, confession of sin, and profession of faith in Jesus Christ, the believer's conversion is not complete and proven until they are baptized in water and the HS, with the evidence of speaking in tongues.[955] The OP stream, thus, links WB to pneumatology, integrating its soteriology, Christology, and pneumatology into the baptismal event. The OP stream bases this theological move on its interpretation of and linking disparate Scripture to make their point.[956]

1927), p. 8; *WWM* 1.21 (July 12, 1924), p. 2; *PH* 5.1 (May 1919), p. 3; *PHA* 1.29 (November 15, 1917), pp. 4-5; *PHA* 13.46 (March 21, 1929), p. 9; *PHA* 5.15 (August 11, 1921), p. 2; *PHA* 1.29 (November 15, 1917), pp. 4-5; *PHA* 8.31 (November 27, 1924), pp. 4-5; *WW* 9.10 (October 20, 1913), p. 2; *WW* 10.5 (May 20, 1914), pp. 2, 3; *WW* 12.9 (September 1915), p. 2; *PT* 1.8 (1911), pp. 5-7; *PE* 170 (December 23, 1916), p. 8; *PE* 83 (March 27, 1915), pp. 1, 3; *PE* 386/387 (April 2, 1921), pp. 2-3; and *PE* 805 (July 6, 1929), pp. 6-9.

[954] *AF* 1.10 (September 1907), p. 2; *COGE* 5.8 (February 21, 1914), pp. 5, 8; *COGE* 6.4 (January 23, 1915), pp. 1, 4; *COGE* 6.28 (July 10, 1915), p. 4; *COGE* 14.2 (January 13, 1923), p. 3; and *COGE* 21.46 (January 24, 1931), p. 3; *PH* 9.16 (January 15, 1923), p. 4.; *WWM* 4.11 (May 21, 1927), p. 2; *PHA* 3.10 (July 3, 1919), pp. 2-3; *PHA* 1.35 (December 27, 1917), p. 16; *PHA* 5.5 (June 2, 1921), p. 10; *PHA* 8.31 (November 27, 1924), pp. 4-5; *PHA* 15.8 (June 18, 1931), p. 10; *PHA* 15.20 (September 10, 1931), p. 10; *PE* 83 (March 27, 1915), pp. 1, 3; and *TGR* 1.8 (January 1, 1914), p. 4.

[955] *MDS* 1.21 (August 1917), p. 2; *MDS* 1.13 (June 1916), p. 4; *TBT* 3.11 (August 15, 1918), p. 2; and *PT* 1.1 (1916), pp. 1-2, 5.

[956] Winifred Westfield posits in 'What is Truth'? the following elucidation of the effects of WB:

> A repentant sinner (Acts 2:38) baptised [sic] into Jesus Christ is baptised [sic] into his death. (Ro. 6:3.) Through faith the 'operation of God' (Col. 2:12) is performed upon his heart at this time; his old man is crucified that the body of sin might be destroyed (Ro. 6:6), and, being planted in the likeness of his DEATH he is raised to walk in the newness of LIFE (Ro. 6:34), [sic] receiving

In addition, it appears to be the case that the OP stream reflected on the impact of the presence and power of the HS during WB services on those being baptized and those bearing witness to candidates following the command of Jesus to be baptized. It may be the case that their theological reflection on HS-empowered embodied Pentecostal worship that permeated baptismal services across the movement may well be the experiential source that fueled their move to integrate soteriology, Christology, and pneumatology into the baptismal event. It is to a consideration of the HS-empowered embodied Pentecostal worship that permeated the movement from the outset that we turn our attention.

While the baptismal theology and practice of early Pentecostals were rooted deeply in Christology and soteriology and focused on the invisible spiritual work within the person baptized, there was also considerable attention paid to the HS-empowered embodied Pentecostal worship that accompanied baptismal services. The periodicals in all three streams contain reports from the field describing both the impact on persons being baptized and upon those celebrating the baptisms. However, the nature of the reports varies between and within the streams relative to the emphasis placed on certain aspects of Pentecostal worship. For example, within the WHP stream, the *AF, TBM, LRE, COGE, PHA,* and *WWM* place noteworthy emphasis on the HS's presence, power, and impact on participants that result in fervently embodied Pentecostal worship. Participants receiving WB and those gathered to witness the baptismal services are reported as worshipping God with rejoicing, shouting, singing, joyful expressions, receiving the baptism of the HS with the evidence of speaking in tongues, praising God, messages in tongues with interpretations being given, being shaken and slain by the HS, receiving visions, seeing angels, divine healing, and experiencing other manifestations of the HS.[957] In addition, favorite

---

the Spirit of life, which is none other than Christ himself, for he that hath the Son hath life. It is the Spirit that quickeneth (Jn. 6:63.) 'The Spirit giveth life.' (2 Cor. 3:6.).

[957] *AF* 1.1 (September 1906), p. 4; *AF* 1.2 (October 1906), p. 4; *AF* 1.4 (December 1906), p. 1; *AF* 1.5 (January 1907), p. 1; *AF* 1.6 (February-March 1907), p. 4; *AF* 1.7 (April 1907), p. 1; *AF* 1.8 (May 1907), p. 4; *AF* 1.9 (June-August 1907), p. 1; *AF* 1.10 (September 1907), p. 1; *AF* 2.13 (May 1908), p. 1; *TBM* 1.15 (June 1,

phrases, 'a blessed time', 'a blessed feast to our souls', 'a blessed service', and 'a sweet heavenly service' are employed as shorthand to

---

1908), p. 1; *TBM* 3.51 (December 1, 1909), p. 4; *TBM* 3.67 (August 1, 1910), p. 3; *TBM* 3.68 (August 15, 1910), p. 3; *TBM* 3.70 (September 15, 1910), p. 1; *TBM* 4.72 (October 15, 1910), p. 2; *TBM* 4.74 (November 15, 1910), pp. 1, 4; *TBM* 4.76 (December 15, 1910), p. 4; *TBM* 5.105 (March 1, 1912), p. 2; *TBM* 6.137 (August 1, 1913), p. 3; *TBM* 7.145 (December 1, 1913), p. 1; *TBM* 7.148 (January 15, 1914), p. 2; *TBM* 7.156 (June 1, 1914), p. 3; *TBM* 8.167 (February 1, 1915), p. 3; *TBM* 8.174 (September 1, 1915), p. 3; *TBM* 9.179 (February 1, 1916), p. 3; *TBM* 9.185 (August 1, 1916), p. 3; *TBM* 9.186 (September 1, 1916), p. 4; *TBM* 10.200 (June 1, 1917), p. 3; *TBM* 12.216 (September 1919), p. 3; *TBM* 19.259 (March-May 1926), p. 3; *TBM* 21.268 (March-April 1928), p. 3; *TBM* 22.270 (September-December 1928), p. 4; *TBM* 22.272 (April-June 1929), p. 11; *LRE* 9.6 (March 1917), pp. 3-5; *LRE* 9.7 (April 1917), p. 13; *LRE* 10.3 (December 1917), p.16; *LRE* 11.4 (January 1919), p. 9; *LRE* 16.12 (September 1924), p. 16; *LRE* 17.7 (April 1925), p. 14; *LRE* 18.4 (January 1926), p. 4; *LRE* 19.3 (December 1926), p. 8; *LRE* 23.5 (February 1931), pp. 17-18; *LRE* 23.10 (July 1931), p. 22; *COGE* 1.15 (Oct 1, 1910), p. 5; *COGE* 5.20 (May 16, 1914), p. 5; *COGE* 5.38 (September 19, 1914), p. 8; *COGE* 6.18 (May 1, 1915), p. 4; *COGE* 6.22 (May 29, 1915), p. 3; *COGE* 6.24 (June 12, 1915), p. 2; *COGE* 6.273, 1915), p. 3; *COGE* 6.30 (July 24, 1915, p. 3; *COGE* 6.33 (August 14, 1915), p. 2; *COGE* 6.35 (August 28, 1915), p. 4; *COGE* 6.36. (September 4, 1915), p. 4; *COGE* 6.37 (September 11, 1915), p. 4; *COGE* 7.38 (September 16, 1916), p. 3; *COGE* 8.25 (June 30, 1917), p. 4; *COGE* 8.30 (August 4, 1917), p. 1; *COGE* 8.36 (September 15, 1917), p. 4; *COGE* 9.15 (April 13, 1918), p. 2; *COGE* 9.22 (June 1, 1918), pp. 2, 4; *COGE* 9.23 (June 8, 1918), p. 3; *COGE* 9.28 (July 13, 1918), p. 2; *COGE* 9.31 (August 3, 1918), p. 2; *COGE* 9.35 (August 31, 1918), p. 4; *COGE* 9.47 (November 23, 1918), p. 3; *COGE* 10.28 (July 12, 1919), *COGE* 11.20 (May 15, 1920), p. 3; *COGE* 11.39 (September 25, 1920), p. 2; *COGE* 11.40 (Oct 2, 1920), p. 2; *COGE* 11.46 (November 20, 1920), p. 3; *COGE* 13.12 (March 25, 1922), p. 4; *COGE* 13.38 (September 23, 1922), p. 2; *COGE* 14.30 (July 28, 1923), p. 3; *COGE* 15.46 (December 6, 1924), p. 2; *COGE* 16.36 (September 5, 1925), pp. 1-2; *COGE* 17.30 (July 31, 1926), p. 3; *COGE* 19.42 (Oct 20, 1928), p. 4; *COGE* 20.3 (March 16, 1929), p. 4; *COGE* 21.9 (April 26, 1930), p. 2; *COGE* 21.12 (May 17, 1930), p. 1; *COGE* 21.13 (May 24, 1930), p. 3; *COGE* 21.16 (June 14, 1930), p. 4; *COGE* 21.17 (June 21, 1930), p. 1; *COGE* 21.22 (July 26, 1930), p. 3; *COGE* 21.36 (November 8, 1930), p. 3; *COGE* 22.26 (August 29, 1931), p. 2; *PH* 4.5 (September 1918), p. 3; *PH* 4.5 (September 1918), p. 3; *PH* 4.6 (October 1918), p. 4; *PH* 4.10 (February 1919), p. 4; *PH* 5.1 (May 1919), p. 3; *PH* 5.6 (November 1919), pp. 1, 3; *PH* 5.7 (December 1919), p. 3; and *PH* 8.18 (June 1, 1922), pp. 1, 2; *WWM* 1.20 (June 28, 1924), p. 1; *WWM* 1.31 (December 6, 1924) p. 1; *WWM* 2.13 (June 20, 1925), p. 3; *WWM* 2.14 (July 4, 1925), p. 4; *WWM* 2.18 (August 29, 1925), p. 4; *WWM* 3.21 (October 9, 1926), p. 4; *WWM* 4.13 (June 18, 1927), p. 1; *WWM* 6.13 (July 6, 1929), p. 3; *WWM* 7.19 (September 27, 1930), p. 2; *WWM* 8.15 (July 18, 1931), p. 1; and *WWM* 8.24 (December 5, 1931), p. 4.

communicate the presence and activity of the HS in the baptismal worship services.⁹⁵⁸

The publications⁹⁵⁹ of McPherson and the *PHA*, within the FW and WHP streams respectively, also contain reports of the activity and impact of the HS upon baptismal candidates and worshipping witnesses; however, significant restraint marks the *PHA's* five of 100 reports where embodied Pentecostal worship is limited to people shouting and praising God.⁹⁶⁰ Reporters also opined that participants appeared to have been blessed by the HS's presence.⁹⁶¹ While some of the overt expressions of embodied Pentecostal worship are not documented in the *PHA*, the occurrences of divine healing are highlighted by the editor.⁹⁶² After the dedication of and inauguration of WB at the Angelus Temple (AT) in 1923, reports of a baptismal service paint an aesthetically pleasing portrait and lack the descriptions of embodied fervent Pentecostal worship, taking on a more subdued tone in the service, focusing on the beauty of service and expressions of praise.⁹⁶³ While reports of embodied Pentecostal worship appear lacking after the dedication and opening of AT,

---

⁹⁵⁸ *TBM* 3.51 (December 1, 1909), p. 3; *TBM* 3.52 (December 15, 1909), p. 1; *TBM* 3.62 (May 15, 1910), p. 2; *TBM* 3.67 (August 1, 1910), p. 3; *TBM* 3.68 (August 15, 1910), p. 3; and *TBM* 7.156 (June 1, 1914), p. 3.

⁹⁵⁹ McPherson's publications are uneven in their reporting of embodied Pentecostal worship. Prior to the dedication of the Angelus Temple (AT) on January 1, 1923, reports reflected the same kind of Pentecostal worship found in other periodicals within the FW stream. For example, early reports rehearse the movement of the HS on baptismal candidates who spoke, sang, and prophesied in the Spirit, while laughing, weeping, and shouting. This occurred as the HS power fell on the Pastor who spoke in tongues and the HS provided the interpretation through a person in the water. *BC* 2.11 (April 1919), p. 15; *BC* 4.4 (September 1920), p. 9. Reports from churches outside the AT area and after its dedication, contain evidence of expressive HS-empowered embodied Pentecostal worship, asserting baptismal witnesses worshipped with cheering, weeping, singing, praising God, and responding immediately to the invitation for WB by being baptized in their street clothes. *FC* 5.24 (May 7, 1931), p. 5; *FC* 1.35 (July 23, 1927), p. 8.

⁹⁶⁰ *PHA* 2.27 (October 31, 1918), p. 12; *PHA* 13.23 (October 3, 1929), p. 12.

⁹⁶¹ *PHA* 2.16 (August 15, 1918), pp. 6-7; *PHA* 5.21 (September 22, 1921), pp. 6-7.

⁹⁶² *PHA* 3.12-13 (July 17-24, 1919), pp. 6-7; *PHA* 4.17 (August 26, 1920), pp. 6-7; *PHA* 14.15 (August 7, 1930), pp. 11-12; and *PHA* 14.41 (February 12, 1931), p. 5.

⁹⁶³ *BC* 7.1 (June 1923), pp. 14-15; *BCF* 8.6 (November 1924), p. 27.

reports of divine healing were often linked to WB in the *BC*, *BCF*, and *FC*.⁹⁶⁴

Reports of embodied Pentecostal worship during WB services within the FW stream reflect the same expressions as those discovered in the WHP stream. The *PT* contains one account of a baptismal service that simply attests to the power of the HS bearing witness upon the people.⁹⁶⁵ The *WW* reports emphasize the presence of the HS during baptismal services, highlighting the power and approval of God falling on those present.⁹⁶⁶ God's approval is confirmed with visions and divine healing and participants respond with shouting, rejoicing, dancing in the Spirit, and talking in tongues as they encounter the HS.⁹⁶⁷ Similar to the *WW* and *PT*, the *PE* contains references to embodied Pentecostal worship within baptismal reports. The worship was saturated with 'shouts of/shouting for joy'.⁹⁶⁸ Baptismal candidates, moved by the HS, rejoiced, danced in the HS, and prayed and spoke in tongues as they came out of the water.⁹⁶⁹ Moreover, candidates and worshippers alike

---

⁹⁶⁴ *BC* 4.4 (September 1920), p. 7; *BC* 5.4 (September 1921), p. 11; *BC* 6.12 (May 1923), p. 25; *BC* 7.4 (September 1923), p. 14; *BCF* 9.1 (June 1927), pp. 15-16, 30; *FC* 2.25 (May 23, 1928), p. 3; *FC* 3.25 (May 15, 1929), p. 2; *FC* 3.46 (October 9, 1929), pp. 5, 14; *FC* 4.18 (March 26, 1930), p. 2; *FC* 4.23 (April 30, 1930), p. 8; and *FC* 6.9 (December 16, 1931), p. 6; and *FC* 6.11 (December 30, 1931), p. 5.

⁹⁶⁵ *PT* 2.1 (January 1912), pp. 11-12.

⁹⁶⁶ *WW* 8.8 (October 20, 1912), p. 3; *WW* 9.9 (September 20, 1913), p. 1; *WW* 9.10 (October 20, 1913), p. 3; *WW* 12.8 (August 1915), pp. 1, 3 and 8; *WW* 10.10 (October 1914), p. 4; *WW* 12.9 (September 1915), pp. 1, 7.

⁹⁶⁷ *WW* 9.3 (March 20, 1913), p. 3; *WW* 9.5 (May 20, 1913), p. 3; *WW* 9.6 (June 20, 1913), p. 5; *WW* 9.8 (August 20, 1913), p. 3; *WW* 9.9 (September 20, 1913), p. 3; *WW* 10.7 (July 1914), p. 1; *WW* 12.8 (August 1915), pp. 1, 3; *WW* 12.9 (September 1915), pp. 3, 8; and *WW* 12.10 (October 1915), pp. 5, 8.

⁹⁶⁸ *PE* 2.19 (May 9, 1914), p. 6; *PE* 101 (July 31, 1915), p. 1; *PE* 181 (March 17, 1917), p. 16; *PE* 211 (October 20, 1917), p. 14; *PE* 212 (October 27, 1917), pp. 2, 3; *PE* 215 (November 17, 1917), p. 14; *PE* 298/299 (July 26, 1919), p. 10; *PE* 310/311 (October 18, 1919), p. 12; *PE* 436/437 (March 18, 1922), p. 11; *PE* 456/457 (August 5, 1922), p. 9; *PE* 501 (June 16, 1923), p. 11; *PE* 530 (January 19, 1924), p. 13; *PE* 587 (March 7, 1925), p. 12; *PE* 595 (May 2, 1925), p. 13; *PE* 645 (May 1, 1926), p. 13; *PE* 702 (June 18, 1927), p. 11; *PE* 751 (June 9, 1928), p. 12; *PE* 758 (August 4, 1928), p. 12; *PE* 862 (August 23, 1930), p. 10; *PE* 905 (July 4, 1931), p. 12; *PE* 910 (August 8, 1931), p. 12; *PE* 921 (October 31, 1931), p. 13; and *PE* 927 (December 12, 1931), p. 8.

⁹⁶⁹ *PE* 50 (July 18, 1914), p. 3; *PE* 56 (August 29, 1914), p. 1.

received visions as the HS moved during the services.[970] Lastly, embodied Pentecostal worship was evident through incidences of divine healing.[971]

The periodicals of the OP stream, *TGR, MDS,* and *TBT* contain relatively few baptismal reports; however, those available provide rich descriptions that provide evidence of the power and presence of the HS related to embodied Pentecostal worship. *The Good Report* recounts participants and witnesses shouting, praising God, and rejoicing while the candidates and administrator entered and departed the water. Candidates saw visions from God, and divine healing was experienced in the gathered community.[972] The *MDS* reports of embodied Pentecostal worship focus solely on the work of the HS during WB, focusing on God's presence and power as the candidate is baptized both in water and the HS with evidence of speaking in other tongues.[973] The *MDS* reports acts of 'prophesying' by candidates upon being baptized in water and the HS.[974] Additional reports of dual baptism appear, stressing the veracity of baptizing 'in Jesus' name'.[975] *The Blessed Truth*'s baptismal accounts note both the activity of the HS and participants in WB services, illustrating embodied Pentecostal worship. Accounts acknowledge the power of God falling for some duration and worshipers being moved to shout, leap, jump, dance, praise God, and speak in tongues and preach in known languages unknown to the speaker.[976] In addition to the accounts of dual baptism, the *MDS* contains accounts of divine healing occurring during the WB services.[977]

Thus, it appears from the preceding review that HS-empowered embodied Pentecostal worship, divine healing, and the manifestation

---

[970] *PE* 56 (August 29, 1914), p. 1; *PE* 146/147 (July 8, 1916), p. 15; *PE* 306/307 (September 20, 1919), p. 13; *PE* 645 (May 1, 1926), p. 13; and *PE* 648 (May 22, 1926), p. 11.

[971] *PE* 96 (June 26, 1915), p. 1; *PE* 102 (August 7, 1915), p. 1; *PE* 141 (May 27, 1916), p. 15; *PE* 159 (September 30, 1916), p. 4; *PE* 298/299 (July 26, 1919), p. 8; *PE* 438/439 (April 1, 1922), p. 14; and *PE* 460/461 (September 2, 1922), p. 13.

[972] *TGR* 1.10 (March 1, 1914), p. 1; *TGR* 2 (August 1, 1913), pp. 1, 5.

[973] *MDS* 1.13 (June 1916), p. 2.

[974] *MDS* 1.9 (December 1915), p. 2; *MDS* 1.13 (June 1916), p. 2.

[975] *MDS* 1.9 (December 1915), p. 2; *MDS* 1.13 (June 1916), p. 2.

[976] *TBT* 4.2 (January 15, 1919), p. 2.

[977] *TBT* 3.11 (August 15, 1918), pp. 1-3; *TBT* 4.2 (January 15, 1919), p. 2; and *TBT* 4.11 (June 1, 1919), p. 7.

of spiritual gifts, including prophecy, speaking in tongues, and interpretation of tongues during WB services was inherent in all three streams of the movement. However, it appears to be the case that it was the OP stream alone that reflected on the theological significance of the HS's activity that gave rise to their integration of soteriology, Christology, and pneumatology into the baptismal event.

Regarding the meaning of WB, the three steams concur that baptism publicly symbolizes or signifies a believer's identification and union with Christ in his life, death, burial, and resurrection (Rom. 6.3-7).[978] More specifically, WB symbolizes the believer is buried with Christ in death to the 'old life' and raised with him to walk in 'newness of life'.[979] William Seymour of the WHP stream, stresses WB's

---

[978] Not everyone embraced the importance of Rom. 6.1-7 for understanding the meaning of WB. For example, A.J. Tomlinson was not a strong proponent of this interpretation, preferring to treat WB as a command of Christ to be obeyed, yet other contributors stressed the merits of the meaning attached to Rom. 6.3-4 in the *COGE*. See *COGE* 8.17 (May 5, 1917), p. 1; *COGE* 5.48 (December 5, 1914), p. 6; and *COGE* 10.28 (July 12, 1919), p. 3. See *COGE* 14.2 (January 13, 1923), p. 3. *COGE* 21.46 (January 24, 1931), p. 3. Nonetheless, despite the variations noted above, the three streams agreed on the symbolic nature of WB and what took place within the 'heart' of the believer.

[979] *AF* 1.10 (September 1907), p. 2; *TBM* 9.183 (June 1, 1916), p. 4; *TBM* 5.105 (March 1, 1912), p. 2; *TBM* 8.167 (February 1, 1915), p. 3; *TBM* 9.176 (November 1, 1915), p. 1; *TBM* 9.183 (June 1, 1916), p. 4; *TBM* 16.242 (January 1923), p. 1; *LRE* 4.9 (June 1912), p. 18; *LRE* 8.1 (October 1915), p. 17; *LRE* 8.3 (December 1915), p. 12; *LRE* 9.10 (July 1917), p. 14; *LRE* 9.11 (August 1917), p. 22; *LRE* 11.10 (July 1919), pp. 21-22; *LRE* 12.10 (July 1920), p. 15; *LRE* 13.4 (January 1921), p. 8; *LRE* 13.6 (March 1921), p. 11; *LRE* 14.3 (December 1921), p. 19; *LRE* 15.10 (July 1923), p. 20; *LRE* 17.6 (March 1925), p. 13; *LRE* 17.10 (July 1925), p. 23; *LRE* 18.6 March 1926 p. 14; *LRE* 18.9 (June 1926), p. 12; *LRE* 19.7 (April 1927), p. 23; *LRE* 19.9 (June 1927), p. 8; *LRE* 20.2 (November 1927), p. 11; *LRE* 20.5 (February 1928), p. 23; *LRE* 20.6 (March 1928), p. 17; *LRE* 20.8 (May 1928), p. 20; *LRE* 20.11 (August 1928), p. 15; *LRE* 21.8 (May 1929), p. 12; *LRE* 21.10 (July 1929), p. 11; *LRE* 22.4 (January 1930), p. 21; *LRE* 23.5 (February 1931), p. 21; *LRE* 23.7 (April 1931), pp. 7, 21; *LRE* 23.10 (July 1931), p. 22; *COGE* 5.48 (December 5, 1914), p. 6; *COGE* 10.28 (July 12, 1919), p. 3; *COGE* 14.2 (January 13, 1923), p. 3. *COGE* 21.46 (January 24, 1931), p. 3; *FC* 1.33 (July 9, 1927), pp. 3-5; *BCF* 9.9 (February 1926), pp. 10-12; *BCF* 10.7 (December 1926), pp. 25-26; *FC* 3.13 (February 20, 1929), p. 5; *FC* 3.41 (September 4, 1929), p. 3; *FC* 5.2 (February 26, 1930), pp. 1-2, 5; *FC* 3.23 (May 1, 1929), p. 13; *PH* 5.1 (May 1919), p. 3; *PH* 9.10 (September 1, 1922), p. 3; *PHA* 9.35 (January 7, 1926), pp. 6-7; *WW* 8.6 (August 20, 1912), p. 2; *WW* 9.8 (August 20,

symbolic nature, asserting that it is 'Not the putting away of the filth of the flesh, but the answer of a good conscience toward God'.[980] (1 Pet. 3.21). As the movement matured and additional views were included in the periodicals, the meaning attached to WB began to be articulated more fully in the WHP and FW streams. While reflecting a Zwinglian view of the sacraments, WB was understood to focus on the candidate's symbolic identification with Jesus' death, burial, and resurrection through the act of WB by immersion (Rom. 6.1-11). When the term 'participation' was employed, William Durham spoke in terms of Federal Headship, and maintaining the symbolic nature of WB. Two notable early Pentecostals, J.H. King, and G.E. Taylor, writing in the *PHA* of the WPH stream, held a minority view, equating WB with sanctification. They asserted WB was symbolic of a 'baptism of death' or 'deeper spiritual truth'.[981] Aimee Semple McPherson avers WB is an 'initiation service … meaning following our Lord and walking in His glorious footsteps'.[982] With this statement, McPherson appears to connect WB with following Jesus as a disciple after WB has occurred.

The following statement from the *PH* well represents the three streams perspective on the symbolic meaning of WB:

> The Ordinance of Baptism by a burial in water which Christ should be observed as commanded in the Scriptures, by all who have really repented and in their hearts have truly believed on Christ as Savior and Lord. In so doing, they have the body washed in pure water as an outward symbol of cleansing while their heart has already been sprinkled with the Blood of Christ as an inner cleansing. Thus they declare to the world that they have died with

---

1913), p. 3; *WW* 12.8 (August 1915), p. 5; *WW* 10.5 (May 20, 1914), p. 3; *PT* 2.1 (January 1912), pp. 3, 9-10; *PE* 83 (March 27, 1915), pp. 1, 3; *PE* 176 (February 10, 1917), p. 9; *PE* 306/307 (September 20, 1919), p. 9; *PE* 484/485 (February 17, 1923), p. 8; *PE* 601 (June 13, 1925), p. 3; *PE* 851 (June 7, 1930), p. 2; *PE* 386/387 (April 2, 1921), pp. 2-3; *PE* 805 (July 6, 1929), pp. 6-9; *TGR* 1.3 (1912), pp. 3-7, 11; *TGR* 1.8 (January 1, 1914), p. 4; *MDS* 1.13 (June 1916), p. 4; *TBT* 3.11 (August 15, 1918), pp. 1-2; and *PT* 1.1 (1916), pp. 1-2.

[980] *AF* 1.10 (September 1907), p. 2.

[981] *PHA* 1.7 (June 15, 1917), pp. 2-4; *PHA* 2.2 (May 9, 1918), p. 16; *PHA* 5.22 (September 29, 1921), p. 6; *PHA* 13.33 (December 12, 1929), p. 9; and *PHA* 11.25 (October 20, 1927), pp. 9-11.

[982] *FC* 1.33 (July 9, 1927), pp. 3-5.

Jesus and that they have also been raised with Him to walk in newness of life. – Mt. 28:19; Acts 10:47-48; Rom. 6:4; Acts 20:21; Heb. 10:22.[983]

Oneness Pentecostals integrated conversion, WB, and SB with the evidence of speaking in tongues into one event, asserting that speaking in tongues was certain evidence that the person had been 'saved'.

Given the importance of the symbolism of Rom. 6.3-4 and Jesus' baptism great attention was focused on the mode of WB. The FW and OP streams mandate baptism by immersion and reject sprinkling and infant baptism.[984] Within the WHP stream, the sole exception to

---

[983] *PH* 5.1 (May 1919), p. 3.
[984] *AF* 1.1 (September 1906), p. 4; *AF* 1.4 (December 1906), p. 1; *AF* 1.6 (February-March 1907), p. 4; *AF* 1.7 (April 1907), p. 7; *AF* 1.8 (May 1907), p. 4; *AF* 1.9 (June-August 1907), p.1; *TBM* 2.37 (May 1909), p. 1; *TBM* 3.60 (April 1910), p. 1; *TBM* 5.109 (May 1912), p. 1; *TBM* 9.185 (August 1916), p. 1; *LRE* 6.8 (May 1914), p. 11; *LRE* 7.9 (June 1915), p. 16; *LRE* 8.8 (May 1916), p. 13; *LRE* 9.6 (March 1917), pp. 17-18; *LRE* 11.11 (August 1922), p. 14; *LRE* 12.4 (January 1920), p. 16; *LRE* 15.3 (December 1922), p. 13; *LRE* 18.10 (Jul 1926), p. 12; *LRE* 19.7 (April 1927), p. 23; *LRE* 20.3 (December 1927), p. 4; *LRE* 6.10 (July 1914), p. 4; *LRE* 10.3 (December 1917), p. 16; *LRE* 12.6 (March 1920), p. 15; *LRE* 16.4 (January 1924), p. 22; *LRE* 18.9 (June 1926), p. 12; and *LRE* 20.12 (September 1928), p. 15; *COGE* 7.17 (April 22, 1916), pp. 1-2; *COGE* 8.22 (June 9, 1917), p. 2; *COGE* 8.40 (Oct 13, 1917), p. 4; *COGE* 11.24 (June 12, 1920), p. 4; *COGE* 1.15 (Oct 1, 1910), p. 5; *COGE* 5.8 (February 21, 1914), pp. 5, 8; *COGE* 8.32 (August 18, 1917), p. 2; *COGE* 10.28 (July 12, 1919), p. 3; *COGE* 12.31 (July 30, 1921), p. 2; *COGE* 16.36 (September 5, 1925), pp. 1-2; *COGE* 21.22 (July 26, 1930), p. 3; *BCF* 8.6 (November 1924), p. 27; *BCF* 11.7 (November 1927), p. 22; *FC* 2.25 (May 23, 1928), p. 3; *FC* 3.25 (May 15, 1929), p. 2; *FC* 3.35 (July 24, 1929), p. 2; *BCF* 13.10 (March 1930), pp. 11, 12, and 32; *FC* 4.18 (March 26, 1930), pp. 1, 7; *FC* 5.19 (April 1, 1931), p. 9; *FC* 5.23 (April 29, 1931), p. 2; *FC* 5.36 (July 29, 1931), p. 5; and *FC* 5.50B (Oct 10, 1931), p. 2; *BC* 4.4 (September 1920), pp. 7, 9; *BC* 5.4 (September 1921), p. 11; *BC* 5.5 (Oct 1921), p. 7; *BC* 5.5 (Oct 1921), pp. 8-9; *BC* 5.10 (March 1922), p. 12; *BC* 6.2, 3 (July and August 1922), pp. 9-10; *BC* 6.2, 3 (July and August 1922), pp. 13-14; *BC* 6.4 (September 1922), pp. 10-11; *BCF* 9.4 (September 1925), p. 11; *BCF* 9.10 (March 1926), p. 17; *BCF* 9.11 (April 1926), p. 27; *BCF* 10.3 (August 1926), p. 13; *FC* 1.33 (July 9, 1927), pp. 3, 5; *FC* 1.39 (August 17, 1927), p. 3; *FC* 3.4 (December 19, 1928), p. 12; *FC* 3.37 (August 7, 1929), p. 3; *FC* 3.50 (November 6, 1929), p. 9; *BCF* 13.1 (June 1929), p. 20; *FC* 4.6 (January 1, 1930), p. 7; *BCF* 13.10 (March 1930), p. 17; *FC* 4.23 (April 30, 1930), p. 6; *BCF* 14.4 (September 1930), p. 12; *FC* 4.32 (July 1, 1931), p. 7; *BCF* 14.14 (July 1931), p. 14; *BCF* 15.3 (August 1931), p. 33; *FC* 4.42 (September 9, 1931), p. 8; *BCF* 15.5 (Oct 1931), p. 7; and *FC* 6.8 (December 9, 1931), p. 4; *BCF* 10.7 (December 1926), pp. 25-26; *FC* 1.33 (July 9, 1927), pp. 3-5; *FC* 3.13 (February 20, 1929), p. 2; and *FC* 5.2 (February 26, 1930), pp. 1-2; *FC* 3.25

immersion as the mandated mode is the *PHA*. This variation accounts for diversity within the WHP stream and between the three streams. The *PHA* does not mandate immersion, it is an option along with sprinkling and infant baptism afforded to the baptismal candidate, including infants.[985] While a variety of modes were deemed acceptable, it appears to be the case that baptism by immersion was the most widely utilized mode.[986] Moreover, the *PHA* requires WB

(May 15, 1929), p. 5; *FC* 4.18 (March 26, 1930), p. 7; *WWM* 1.2 (September 29, 1923), p. 1; *WWM* 5.9 (April 28, 1928), p. 4; *WWM* 4.7 (March 26, 1927), p. 2; *WWM* (January 3, 1931), p. 1; *WWM* 4.6 (March 12, 1927), p. 1; *WWM* 4.11 (May 21, 1927), p. 1; *PH* 4.4 (August 1918), p. 1; *PH* 4.5 (September 1918), p. 3; *PH* 4.6 (October 1918), p. 4;; *PH* 4.10 (February 1919), p. 4; *PH* 5.5 (October 1919), p. 3; *PH* 5.9 (February 1920), p. 3; *PH* 8.15 (April 15, 1922), pp. 3, 4; *PH* 8.18 (June 1, 1922), p. 3; *PH* 8.22 (August 1, 1922), p. 4; *PH* 10.2 (April 1, 1923), p. 4; *PH* 10.18 (March 1, 1923), p. 4; *PT* 1.5 (July 1, 1910), p. 15; *PT* 2.2 (1912), pp. 6, 7; *PE* 181 (March 17, 1917), p. 9; *PE* 308/309 (October 4, 1919), p. 5; *PE* 324/325 (January 24, 1920), p. 5; *PE* 348/349 (July 10, 1920), pp. 6-7; *PE* 83 (March 27, 1915), pp. 1, 3; *PE* 306/307 (September 20, 1919), p. 9; *PE* 520 (November 3, 1923), p. 3; *PE* 889 (March 14, 1931), pp. 1, 9; *PE* 660 (August 14, 1926), p. 4; *TGR* 1.1 (May 1911), p. 5; *TGR* 1.3 (1912), pp. 4, 6, 7, and 12; *TGR* 1.6 (November 1, 1913), p. 2; *TGR* 1.8 (January 1, 1914), p. 4; and *TGR* 2 (August 1, 1913), p. 1; *MDS* 1.9 (December 1915), p. 2; *MDS* 1.13 (June 1916), p. 2; *TBT* 3.11 (August 15, 1918), p. 3; *TBT* 4.2 (January 15, 1919), p. 4; *TBT* 4.11 (June 1, 1919), p. 6; and *PT* 1.1 (1916), pp. 1-3.

[985] *PHA* 4.47 (Mar 24, 1921), p. 9; *PHA* 5.9 (June 30, 1921), pp. 9-10; *PHA* 3.27 (October 30, 1919), p. 14; *PHA* 2.2 (May 9, 1918), p. 16; and *PHA* 13.32 (December 5, 1929), p. 10.

[986] *PHA* 1.4 (May 24, 1917), p. 13; *PHA* 1.9 (June 28, 1917), p. 6; *PHA* 1.51 (April 18, 1918), p. 6; *PHA* 2.2 (May 9, 1918), pp. 10-11; *PHA* 2.16 (August 15, 1918), pp. 6-7, 10-11, and 12; *PHA* 2.18 (August 29, 1918), p. 5; *PHA* 2.27 (October 31, 1918), p. 12; *PHA* 2.33-34 (December 19-26, 1918), pp. 14-15; *PHA* 3.12-13 (July 17-24, 1919), pp. 6-7; *PHA* 3.21 (September 18, 1919). p. 15; *PHA* 3.27 (October 30, 1919), p. 14; *PHA* 3.30 (November 20, 1919), pp. 11-12; *PHA* 3.46 (March 11, 1920), p. 10; *PHA* 4.8 (June 24, 1920), p. 14; *PHA* 4.8 (June 24, 1920), p. 14; *PHA* 4.14 (August 5, 1920), p. 15; *PHA* 4.17 (August 26, 1920), pp. 6-7; *PHA* 4.25 (October 21, 1920), pp. 6, 15; *PHA* 4.44/45 (March 3, 10, 1921), pp. 5, 6-7, and 13; *PHA* 5.15 (August 11, 1921), p. 11; *PHA* 5.21 (September 22, 1921), pp. 6-7; *PHA* 5.22 (September 29, 1921), p. 6; *PHA* 5.31 (December 1, 1921), p. 3; *PHA* 5.33 (December 15, 1921), pp. 4, 6; *PHA* 5.37 (January 12, 1922), p. 12; *PHA* 5.8 (June 22, 1922), p. 10, 1; *PHA* 6.32 (December 7, 1922), pp. 7, 15; *PHA* 7.5 (May 31, 1923), pp. 7, 10, 11, 12, and 13; *PHA* 7.16 (August 16, 1923), p. 6; *PHA* 7.26 (October 25, 1923), p. 11; *PHA* 7.27 (November 1, 1923), p. 11; *PHA* 7.31 (November 29, 1923), pp. 6-7; *PHA* 8.22 (September 25, 1924), p. 5; *PHA* 8.29 (November 13, 1924), pp. 12-13; *PHA* 8.44 (February 26, 1925), p. 11; *PHA* 9.30 (November 26, 1925), pp. 11-12; *PHA* 9.35 (January 7, 1926), pp. 12-13; *PHA* 9.45 (March 18, 1926), pp. 6, 7; *PHA* 10.8 (June 24, 1926), p. 14; *PHA* 11.44 (March 8, 1928), p. 11; *PHA* 12.10 (July 5, 1928), pp. 12, 13; *PHA* 12.14 (August 2, 1928), p.

for admission to church membership.[987]

Baptismal Formula

A point of significant disputation arose within the nascent movement regarding the correct baptismal formula to be employed during the rite. Overall, the WHP stream, except the *AF* which is the only publication in the WHP stream which is silent on the preferred baptismal formula, requires use of the Trinitarian baptismal formula, 'in the name of the Father and the Son and the Holy Spirit' (Mt. 28.19) during the baptismal rite.[988] Notwithstanding the requirement asserted within the stream, a few authors, writing with an irenic spirit, advocated for latitude in the use of a baptismal formula.[989] Within the FW stream, on the one hand, only McPherson and William H. Durham's *Pentecostal Testimony* stood firmly for use of the Trinitarian

---

13; *PHA* 12.33 (December 13, 1928), pp. 5, 7; *PHA* 12.45 (March 14, 1929), p. 13; *PHA* 13.37 (January 17, 1929), pp. 4-5; *PHA* 13.42 (February 20, 1930), p. 14; *PHA* 13.45 (March 13, 1930), pp. 7, 12-13; *PHA* 13.50 (April 17, 1930), p. 5; *PHA* 13.52 (May 1, 1930), p. 8; *PHA* 14.5 (May 29, 1930), pp. 3-5, 10-12; *PHA* 14.15 (August, 7, 1930), pp. 11-12; *PHA* 14.16 (August 14, 1930), pp. 7, 15; *PHA* 14.22 (September 25, 1930), p. 11; *PHA* 14.24 (October 9, 1930), p. 7; *PHA* 14.28 (November 6, 1930), p. 7; *PHA* 14.41 (February 12, 1931), p. 5; *PHA* 15.5 (May 28, 1931), p. 12; *PHA* 15.7 (June 11, 1931), pp. 6, 7; *PHA* 15.19 (September 3, 1931), p. 11; *PHA* 15.20 (September 10, 1931), p. 12; *PHA* 15.23 (October 1, 1931), pp. 6-7; *PHA* 15.27 (October 29, 1931), pp. 14-15; *PHA* 15.33 (December 10, 1931), pp. 10-11; *PHA* 15.34 (December 17, 1931), pp. 3-4; and *IH.PA* 15.35 (December 24, 1931), pp. 7, 11-12.

[987] *PHA* 4.47 (March 24, 1921), p. 9.

[988] *TBM* 9.185 (August 1, 1916), p. 1; *TBM* 9.186 (September 1, 1916), p. 4; *TBM* 18.256 (June-September 1, 1925), p. 4; *LRE* 7.9 (June 1915), p. 16; *LRE* 8.4 (January 1916), p. 16; *LRE* 8.8 (May 1916), p. 13; *LRE* 12.1 (October 1919), p. 10; *LRE* 13.10 (July 1921), p. 15; *LRE* 23.5 (February 1931), p. 17; *COGE* 5.37 (September 12, 1914), p. 5; *COGE* 6.32 (August 7, 1915), p. 2; *COGE* 12.30 (July 23, 1921), p. 3; *COGE* (August 27, 1921), p. 3; *COGE* 12.38 (September 17, 1921), p.3; *COGE* 12.45 (November 12, 1921), p. 2; *COGE* 12.46 (November 19, 1921), p. 3; *COGE* 13.8 (February 25, 1922), p. 2; *COGE* 13.38 (September 23, 1922), p. 3; *COGE* 14.21 (May 26, 1923), p. 1; *COGE* 15.45 (November 29, 1924), pp. 1, 3; *COGE* 20.41 (December 14, 1929), pp. 1, 3; *COGE* 21.33 (Oct 11, 1930), pp. 1, 3; *COGE* 21.44 (January 10, 1931), pp. 1, 3; *WWM* 4.10 (May 7, 1927), pp. 1, 2; *PH* 10.3 (May 1, 1923), p. 5; *PH* 5.5 (October 1919), p. 3; *PH* 4.10 (February 1919), pp. 3, 4; *PH* 4.12 (April 1919), p. 1; *PH* 8.17 (May 15, 1922), pp. 2, 3; *PHA* 1.18 (August 30, 1917), pp. 4-5; *PHA* 13.33 (December 12, 1929), p. 9; *PHA* 14.28 (November 6, 1930), p. 10; *PHA* 2.2 (May 9, 1918), p. 3; and *PHA* 13.5 (May 30, 1929), p. 9.

[989] *COGE* 8.29 (July 28, 1917), p. 4; *PH* 4.10 (February 1919), p. 3.

formula.⁹⁹⁰ On the other hand, the *WW* and *PE* reflect an impartial stance, allowing the use of any formula found in the 'following passages of Scripture should be accepted: Mt. 28:19; Acts 2:38; 8:16; 10:48; or 19:5'.⁹⁹¹ A similar dynamic is also found in in the OP stream. *The Good Report* (*TGR*) makes no mention of a preferred baptismal formula. Other publications in the OP stream reject the Trinitarian formula, asserting WB 'in Jesus' name' (Acts 2.38) as the correct and only acceptable baptismal formula.⁹⁹²

Rebaptism

A closely related subject to the preceding is the issue of rebaptism of believers that may have 'backslidden' and returned to the faith. The FW stream's held position was that WB was a once-for-all act that need not be repeated, except for the periodicals of Aimee Semple McPherson which are silent on the matter.⁹⁹³ Within the OP stream, emphasis was placed on ensuring that candidates be baptized in 'in Jesus' name', which would appear to require those who had been previously baptized with the Trinitarian formula to be baptized anew; however, the OP periodicals are strangely silent on the matter. A consensus regarding rebaptism within the WHP stream does not appear. The *AF* is silent on the topic. However, the reporting of rebaptizing was commonplace for various reasons in the other WHP periodicals.⁹⁹⁴

---

⁹⁹⁰ *BC* 2.2 (July 1918), p. 10; *BC* 2.11 (April 1919), p. 16; *BC* 5.5 (Oct 1921), pp. 8-9; *BCF* 8.8 (January 1925), p. 22; *BCF* 10.11 (April 1927), pp. 15-16; *BCF* 11.1 (June 1927), pp. 15-16, 30; *BCF* 12.3 (March 1928), p. 17; *BCF* 14.3 (August 1930), pp. 5, 31; and *PT* 2.2 (May 1912), pp. 6-7.

⁹⁹¹ *WW* 12.10 (October 1915), p. 4; *PE* 111 (October 16, 1915), pp. 1, 2.

⁹⁹² *MDS* 1.9 (December 1915), pp. 1-4; *MDS* 1.13 (June 1916), pp. 1, 2, and 4; *MDS* 1.21 (August 1917). p. 4; *TBT* 3.11 (August 15, 1918), pp. 1-2, 3; *TBT* 4.2 (January 15, 1919), pp. 1, 2, 3, and 4; and *TBT* 4.11 (June 1, 1919), pp. 6, 7; and *PT* 1.1 (1916), p. 3.

⁹⁹³ *WW* 12.10 (October 1915), p. 4; *PE* 111 (October 16, 1915), pp. 1, 2.

⁹⁹⁴ First, the *LRE* does not require rebaptism but appears to accommodate those new to Pentecost who had been previously sprinkled and are desirous to be immersed. *LRE* 14.7 (April 1922), p. 12. Second, the *COGE* addresses the question of rebaptism regarding those who have backslidden and returned to the fold. The unequivocal answer is in the affirmative. Reclaimed backsliders need to be rebaptized. *COGE* 15.8 (February 23, 1924), p. 3; *COGE* 15.46 (December 6, 1924), p. 2. Apparently, one pastor required persons desiring to join the COG to

Administrator

A topic that received considerable focus within the three streams addressed who could serve as an acceptable administrator of WB. Again, while there is widespread agreement within the FW and OP streams, diversity of perspective marks both streams. Generally speaking, the FW stream proffers the belief that only those who are duly ordained ministers or elders could properly administer WB. Again, McPherson is the exception within the FW stream. In effect, only males could administer WB since only males could be ordained in the FW stream.[995]

The OP stream finds its agreement in the stipulation that administrators of WB have to testify to receiving a revelation concerning the Oneness of God in Jesus Christ, and that WB is to be conducted in the 'name of Jesus only'.[996] There is no mention of women administering WB in the OP stream. Within the WHP

---

be rebaptized regardless of their prior baptism. *COGE* 6.33 (August 14, 1915), p. 4. While not mandated in the *COGE*, rebaptism also seemed to follow significant religious experiences at the request of the candidate. *COGE* 7.26 (June 24, 1916), p. 3; *COGE* 10.42 (October 18, 1919), p. 3. Third, the *WWM* contains several reports of rebaptism occurring when backsliders return to Jesus as Lord and Savior. *WWM* 1.22 (July 26, 1924), p. 4; *WWM* 3.19 (September 11, 1926), p. 4; and *WWM* 3.26 (December 18, 1926), p. 1. Fourth, the *PH* is relatively noncommittal on the topic except to convey the story of an anxious sister who was experiencing doubts and felt compelled to be rebaptized during a baptismal service. *PH* 5.4 (September 1919), p. 3. Finally, the *PHA* provides scant evidence of rebaptism. One reference is provided documenting the baptisms of some who had been baptized previously; however, the context and rationale are absent. *PHA* 2.16 (August 15, 1918), pp. 10-11. In view of the preceding, it appears to be the case that the *COGE* and *WWM* contain the strongest statements on the necessity of rebaptism for those who have backslidden and returned to Jesus Christ as Lord and Savior along. Similarly, they supply most of the reports regarding those who have been rebaptized. It is striking that it is A.J. Tomlinson, the chief architect of the *COGE* and *WWM*, who stresses the necessity of obeying Christ's command to be baptized, who is also the one who insists on rebaptism of those who have fallen and returned. Perhaps his stance on rebaptism would have softened if he had given greater emphasis and credence to the value of Rom. 6.1-4 with its emphasis on identification with Jesus Christ in his death, burial, and resurrection.

[995] *WW* 10.7 (July 1914), p. 4; *WW* 10.5 (May 20, 1914), p. 1; *PE* 121 (January 1, 1916), p. 8; *PE* 330/331 (March 6, 1920), p. 5; *PE* 374/375 (January 8, 1921), p. 10; *PE* 418/419 (November 12, 1921), p. 5; and *PE* 499 (June 2, 1923), p. 8.

[996] *MDS* 1.9 (December 1915), p. 2; *MDS* 1.13 (June 1916), pp. 1, 2; and *PT* (1916), pp. 1-2.

stream, the *AF* asserts WB should be administered 'by a disciple who is baptized with the Holy Ghost'.⁹⁹⁷ There is no restriction placed on gender of the administrator. Similarly, the *COGE* asserts only those baptized in the HS with the evidence of speaking in tongues could administer WB.⁹⁹⁸ It appears to be the case that baptism in the HS was also a requirement for the ordination of males who were then authorized to administer WB.⁹⁹⁹ The *LRE* and *PHA* appear to authorize only duly appointed males to baptize and the *TBM* and *PH* are relatively silent on the matter.¹⁰⁰⁰ The person in the FW stream who lifted the restriction of ordained males only as authorized administrators of WB is Aimee Semple McPherson, who ordained men and women and thereby negated the male-only limitation.¹⁰⁰¹ Interestingly, while significant attention was given to the human qualifications of the administrator of WB, scant attention was given to the role of the HS in WB. The FW stream proves to be the exception. E.N. Bell, addressing the relationship between WB and Spirit baptism, posits, 'No one can ever enter into all that is implied in Christian baptism without the quickening presence of the Holy Ghost'.¹⁰⁰² While allowing that being baptized in the HS typically follows WB, there are biblical examples of the reverse order. Per Bell, the HS plays a vital role in WB; however, the exact nature of the HS's role is not elucidated.

Analysis of Strengths

Early Pentecostals are to be applauded for their zeal and commitment to practicing and upholding the importance of WB for the Pentecostal movement and the Church, while spreading the message of SB. Their emphasis on WB as symbolic in nature appears to have directed their preoccupation with key transactional elements in the

---

⁹⁹⁷ *AF* 1.10 (September 1907), p. 2.
⁹⁹⁸ *COGE* 6.22 (May 29, 1915), p. 2; *COGE* 18.35 (August 27, 1927), pp. 1, 3.
⁹⁹⁹ *COGE* 7.10 (March 4, 1916), p. 4; *COGE* 18.37 (September 10, 1927), p. 3; *COGE* 19.28 (July 14, 1928), p. 1; *COGE* 20.26 (August 24, 1929), p. 2; *COGE* 21.9 (April 26, 1930), p. 2; *COGE* 22.21 (July 25, 1931), p. 4; *WWM* 6.17 (August 31, 1929), p. 1; and *WWM* 4.11 (May 21, 1927), p. 2.
¹⁰⁰⁰ *LRE* 10.9 (June 1918), pp. 12-16.
¹⁰⁰¹ *FC* 1.35 (July 23, 1927), p. 8; *FC* 5.19 (April 1, 1931). p. 11; *FC* 5.23 (April 29, 1931), pp. 2, 6; *FC* 5.38 (August 12, 1931), p. 4; and *FC* 6.11 (December 30, 1931), pp. 3, 5.
¹⁰⁰² *PE* 230 (March 9, 1918), p. 2.

practice of the ordinance. First, the candidate had to confess faith in Jesus Christ as Savior. Second, WB by immersion as the sole acceptable means was matched by their intentionality in securing sufficient water to ensure the total immersion of believers in water. The consistent identification of the bodies of water (ocean, creeks, streams, and baptisteries) employed for WB underscores the early Pentecostal dedication to the concrete elements of WB. The universality of providing sufficient water for baptism is substantiated by the reports from around the globe, accompanied by naming geographical locations.

The core strength of the early Pentecostal theology and practice of WB contained in each stream is the strong reliance on Scripture for guidance on the subject. As noted above, the importance of WB appears to have been established in the minds of the early Pentecostals by their straightforward reading of the biblical text and their acceptance of WB as an ordinance of the Church instituted by Jesus. Jesus Christ established the validity of WB through submission to John's baptism (Mt. 3.13) and his command to the embryonic Church that WB was a vital practice in the *via salutis* (Mt. 28.19). This emphasis by early Pentecostals on WB as an act of obedience cannot be overstated. In fact, the focus on obedience in following the example of Jesus and his command to baptize new believers appears to have firmly established WB as a key element in the life of the movement.[1003]

Similarly, early Pentecostals' straightforward reading of Rom. 6.1-11 provided a rich theological resource for their understanding of the meaning of WB. The correspondence of Christ's death, burial, and resurrection to the new spiritual reality of the person who has repented of, confessed their sin, and claimed faith in Jesus Christ served to ground WB in the believer's *via salutis* beyond an act of pure obedience. WB appears to have reminded candidates and witnesses that spiritually speaking, they had been dead in their trespasses and sins and that through repentance and confession of sin, and faith in

---

[1003] 'Sacrament' was employed sparingly by early Pentecostals and when employed it was used interchangeably with 'ordinance'. Both ordinance and sacrament were viewed as symbolic in meaning. Symbolic is using, employing, or exhibiting a symbol. Water baptism symbolizes the death, burial, and death of Jesus Christ without ontological significance.

Christ they had been raised to new life and would be resurrected to spend eternity in heaven.

It seems to be the case that early Pentecostals' fervor to evangelize the 'lost' and spread the message of SB across the world grew from their straightforward reading of the Bible and personal experiences of transformed lives and SB. Their personal and corporate encounters of the HS appear to have sensitized them to take note of the Spirit's movement in various contexts. The occasion of WB services received special attention as early Pentecostals were keenly aware of and celebrated the power and presence of the HS in their baptismal services as people worshipped, praised God, danced, received the baptism of the HS with the evidence of speaking in tongues, numbers were healed, and the spiritual gifts operated. In sum, early Pentecostals appear to have taken particular note of the HS's impact during WB services as persons responded with embodied worship.

The preaching, teaching, and articles in the various periodicals appeared to provide the primary means of educating their hearers regarding the meaning of WB for early Pentecostals in the USA. Foreign missionaries seem to have developed catechetical processes that advanced their understanding of WB beyond symbolic act to include WB as a formative event in the changed lives of the candidates. WB was restricted to those who understood the meaning of WB, grasped the consequences of their public proclamation of allegiance to Jesus Christ as Lord and Savior, and gave evidence in their lives that they truly were disciples of Jesus.

Underdeveloped Areas

Despite their theological differences, the WHP and FW streams were univocal in their positions that WB was understood to be an ordinance, even when sacramental language was employed. Thus, WB is understood and valued from Christological and soteriological categories, largely devoid of pneumatology. There appear to be several factors that mitigated against their consideration of WB as anything more than an act of obedience and symbolic of the believer's transformation into a new relationship with God through faith or trust in Jesus Christ.

First, the lack of theological precision and reflection is observed in the adoption of Christological and soteriological schemas from

Luther, Wesley, and the Holiness streams with their focus on individual salvation by faith alone so a person can 'go to heaven'. The adoption of a gospel of forgiveness and sin management in order to 'go to heaven' effectively shifted the Gospel of the Kingdom preached by Jesus away from Jesus' strong emphasis on discipleship and following him by making other disciples.

When disputations arose during the first 25 years, the focus was on the transactional elements of employing a 'preferred' baptismal formula and the casuistic arguments regarding the necessity of WB for individual 'salvation of the soul'. While debate emerged regarding the relationship of WB to SB, the deeper exploration of the relationship between WB and soteriology rarely arose beyond the symbolic nature of WB and the act of obedience to the command of Christ. The attempt to relate WB, soteriology, and pneumatology was made by OPs who appeared to walk the tightrope of avoiding baptismal regeneration while recognizing the role of the HS in WB. Yet, by combining conversion, WB, and SB, OPs seemed to fail in differentiating SB from the indwelling of the HS championed by other Pentecostals. Moreover, their adoption of baptism in the name of Jesus alone appeared to overshadow their contribution with the result that their theological refinement of connecting pneumatology to WB was lost on Trinitarian Pentecostals.

Second, the apparent wholesale adoption of the Zwinglian view on WB and the Eucharist, as being symbolic in nature, appears to have mitigated against considering the ontological dimensions of the ordinances. On the one hand, early Pentecostals were suspicious of the term 'sacrament', equating the perceived errors of the High Churches' *ex opere operato* with the term. On the other hand, they staunchly rejected the Church of Christ's assertion of WB as a requirement for salvation. Consequently, they held to the symbolic meaning of WB espoused in the groups with which they had formerly been affiliated prior to joining the Pentecostal movement. There appears to be an implicit exploration of ontology in the *TBM* and *PHA*, specifically in the writings of King and Taylor on WB and sanctification, providing a glimmer of awareness of deeper theological questions in need of consideration; however, these were not developed.

Third, their passion for spreading the Gospel and the message of SB along with fighting the battle of the preferred formula left little time, energy, or leisure to explore questions of anthropology beyond those raised by soteriology and pneumatology. Moreover, questions of soteriology tended to focus on salvation of the 'soul' without reflection on the relationship between the mind, body, and soul. It appears theological praxis took precedence over theological reflection for the first generation of the movement.

Fourth, while significant attention is focused on the role of the HS in relation to embodied Pentecostal worship and divine healing during WB services, the lack of focus on the body *per se* appears to reflect the ongoing Neoplatonic devaluation of the body within Protestant theology, in general, and within early Pentecostalism, in particular. This is demonstrably clear when it comes to the lack of theological reflection on the human body. This relative silence reflects the disembodying ethos of the Holiness-Pentecostal theological tradition. The ethos grew out of a double layer of denial about the true nature of bodies. First, is a layer of negativity about the body; second, is the layer of relative silence on the body. The first may be observed in the various 'Holiness codes' that enumerate proper dress, appropriate and inappropriate activities, acceptable entertainment, etc. Moreover, teachings on abstinence from the use of alcohol, tobacco, soft drinks, recreational drugs, all signal the body is to be controlled and kept in check and not fall under the influence of foreign substances. While abstinence served as a prophylactic against abuse and addiction, it also appears to reflect the Neoplatonic view that the body as physical matter is bad and to be subjected to the control of the mind and HS. The second layer of the disembodying ethos is observable in the silence on the body and the lack of theological reflection on the body even though numerous accounts of early Pentecostal worship and divine healing during baptismal services capture what is occurring in and with participants' bodies. The reports chronicle people receiving the baptism of the HS with speaking in tongues, rejoicing, shouting, singing, joyful worship, manifestations of the Spirit of God, visions, persons being shaken by the HS, and praising God. Moreover, numerous reports of persons being healed through prayer, the laying on of hands, and anointings with oil, prayer clothes, and publications are found in the early periodicals.

Fifth, while the Bible-reading approach afforded early Pentecostals the ability to identify the outpouring of the HS in the Latter Rain as foretold by the prophet Joel, the approach appears to have failed them in providing a close reading of the biblical text regarding WB and its meaning for the Christ-follower's call to discipleship. The biblical texts referring to WB in Matthew are viewed without differentiation and are consequently treated as interchangeable. It appears that the understanding of WB from Matthew is then projected onto WB in Romans, and WB is understood in purely individualistic symbolic terms.

Further Attention Needed

The preceding enumeration of the mitigating factors that inhibited a fuller apprehension of the meaning of WB with the consequent implications for praxis is not meant to imply early Pentecostals did not reflect theologically on what they were teaching, preaching, and practicing. Rather, it is to acknowledge their passion for spreading the Gospel of personal salvation from, the message of SB, and the vision of individuals embracing Christian spiritual practices, took precedence over delving into theological categories that appeared to fall outside their practical agendas. Moreover, it is to acknowledge the gifts and restrictions of the Bible-reading approach to Scripture employed by the movement. On the one hand, the approach yielded fruit in grounding the Pentecostal understanding of HS baptism. On the other hand, the approach appeared to interpret the biblical texts referring to WB in Matthew and Romans without due appreciation for the theological development within each book and within the broader context of the canon. Consequently, the Matthean and Pauline texts were interpreted without differentiation, as interchangeable and understood in symbolic terms.

Also, the movement seemed to ground WB in Christology and soteriology and the inherited Neoplatonic theological traditions that negated the human body and tended to view the *via salutis* as a series of transactional or crisis events instead of relational transformative processes. Consequently, 'making disciples' was equated to people 'being saved', baptized in WB, and receiving the baptism of the HS. It appears to be the case that the same factors identified above that led the early Pentecostals to neglect serious theological reflection on WB have also had a deleterious impact on Pentecostal scholarship's theological reflection during the last half of the twentieth century with the veiled embrace of Neoplatonism and the devaluation of the human body.

Inherent in the above acknowledgement resides the necessity to revision a Pentecostal theology of WB that rejects Neoplatonism, embraces a more holistic Pentecostal embodied spirituality, and views soteriology as dynamic process that affects ontological change in the believer and gathered community as the HS and humans mediate transformative experiences within the believer and church. In other words, a revisioned Pentecostal theology of WB must reconsider the evidence that WB plays a vital soteriological and pneumatological role and function in the disciple-making process and growth of the local worshipping community. It is to that endeavor that we turn our attention, beginning with a reconsideration of relevant Scriptures.

Part II
Hearing the Voices of The Word

In addition to the *Wirkungsgeschichte* approach attempted in chapters 2 and 3 above, I will employ a narrative/theological reading/hearing of the canonical text. This approach engages the text as it stands within the canon: inspired, preserved, and illuminated by the HS. The narrative approach is congruent with a Pentecostal approach to Scripture since concerns related to historical criticism are tangential to the heart of their worldview. Pentecostals enter into and experience the story of Scripture through their reading and hearing. The goal is to *hear* the Word of God and encounter the God of the Scriptures.

5

READING THE NEW TESTAMENT

Introduction

I am not approaching the text as literature to be mastered, utilizing the tools of modernity. Instead, I will engage the text as a reader/hearer with eyes to see and ears to hear the theological truth and meaning that is to be apprehended and responded to for further transformation into the image of Jesus Christ. As a member of the Pentecostal community, I will then submit my reading/hearing of the texts to the larger Pentecostal community for discernment, correction, encouragement, and additional perspectives.

The focus of my reading/hearing is guided by three NT texts most frequently cited in the reviewed early Pentecostal periodical literature and the bibliographic review about WB. Specifically, the texts being considered focus on the baptism of Jesus (Mt. 3.13-17), the command of Jesus to baptize new converts (Mt. 28.16-20), and the meaning of WB (Rom. 6.1-7). In order to hear all Matthew reports about baptism, Mt. 21.25-27, which addresses John's authority to baptize, will also be considered. Providing a narrative/theological reading/hearing of these texts will allow separate voices from the biblical choir to sing solos before reassembling with the choir to add their distinctive voices to enhance the sound of the gathered choir.[1] It is to the reading/hearing of the texts that we now turn attention.

The Gospel of Matthew's Witness of Water Baptism

The placement of Matthew's Gospel in the Bible's canonical order provides canonical linkage between the OT and NT. Chronicles' placement as the final book in the Hebrew Bible provides insight relative to the relationship between the two testaments and Matthew's position as the first book of the NT. Chronicles[2] contains a genealogy from a/the human being, Adam, followed by a narrative of the history of ancient Israel and Egypt until the proclamation of King Cyrus the Great in 538 BCE. The chronicler ends the record on a note of hope since God's present time of punishment for Israel and Judah had run its course. The last words of Chronicles remind hearers that God is superintending the events of earth's history for his glory and the redemption of all creation, Israel, in particular. Exiled Israel was now blessed with the prospect of returning to the 'promised land' so they could enjoy a restored relationship with God while rebuilding both the temple of God and the city of Jerusalem.[3]

The hope provided by Chronicles sets the stage for the Gospel of Matthew, the first book in the NT. By bridging the four-hundred-year gap between the testaments, Matthew's genealogy links the two testaments, signaling the remainder of Israel's story is being revealed in Jesus Christ. Additionally, while Chronicles and Matthew share theological themes, they are also connected narratively in the broader canon, inviting readers/hearers of Matthew's Gospel to listen for the

---

[1] I am utilizing Thomas' metaphor of reading/hearing the voices of the various books of the Bible as the diverse voices in a Black gospel choir. See Thomas, 'What the Spirit is Saying to the Church', pp. 125-26.

[2] Chronicles, as placed in the Tanakh, holds the final place of the third section of Ketuvim, closing the Hebrew Bible. Chronicles was divided into two books in the Septuagint. In Christian contexts, it is known as the books of Chronicles, after the Latin name chronikon given to the text by the scholar Jerome. In the Christian Bible, the books (commonly referred to as 1 Chronicles and 2 Chronicles) usually follow the two books of Kings and precede Ezra–Nehemiah; thus, they conclude the history-oriented books of the OT.

[3] Ezra and Nehemiah recount the rebuilding of the temple and Jerusalem.

echoes of Israel's history in the unfolding of Matthew's account of Jesus.

For Matthew's readers,[4] places, events, and persons of Israel's history become paradigmatic for what occurs later. By juxtaposing the original contexts of the quotations with the new contexts of Jesus' life, while allowing they are not precisely the same, a framework of recapitulation is created where 'certain events of crucial significance to an earlier stage of salvation history (e.g., the exodus from Egypt) are repeated in the events of Jesus' life (e.g. his sojourn as an infant to and from Egypt)'.[5] However, the emphasis is about more than repetition since Jesus 'fills full' the previous occurrence and completes the redemptive work of God aligned with the prior event.[6] In other words, Matthew portrays Jesus as recapitulating the history of Israel without disobedience, grumbling, and rebellion.[7] On the contrary, empowered by the Spirit of God, Jesus represents

---

[4] Readers/hearers will be shortened to readers or hearers and should be understood as inclusive of readers and hearers.

[5] Blaine Charette, *Restoring Presence: The Spirit in Matthew's Gospel* (JPTSup 18; Sheffield, UK: Sheffield Academic Press; 2000), p. 13. C. Mitch and E. Sri, *The Gospel According to Matthew* (CCSS; Grand Rapids: MI, Baker Academic, 2010), p. 56, posit 'Egypt was a fitting place for the royal family to flee to. In the first century Egypt was under Roman rule but outside Herod's jurisdiction. It was a traditional place of refuge for Jews (1 Kings 11:40; 2 Macc 5:8; Jer 26:21; 42:15 – 44:30).'

[6] C.L. Blomberg, *Matthew* (NAC 22; Nashville: Broadman & Holman Publishers, 1992), p. 57, 'a text that may well have had a previous historical referent is seen as being completed or filled full, a common meaning of the verb *plēroō* ("fulfill.")'.

[7] Ulrich Luz, *Matthew 1-7* (Hermeneia, Minneapolis: Fortress Press, 2007), p. 82. According to Luz,

The history of Israel passes before their eyes in concentrated form. Thus, the genesis of Jesus Christ begins with Israel's history: it continues that history and includes it as its beginning. Its point of departure is Abraham. The genealogy, first, elucidates what 'Son of Abraham' means. Jesus the Messiah is an Israelite, Abraham's descendant. He is a descendant of the patriarchs. That is not a banality; it is part of God's plan in history. The genealogy also elucidates Jesus' Davidic sonship. Jesus is David's descendant and thus a Messiah of royal descent. That is why v. six also emphasizes David as king and then lets the kings on David's throne with whom the readers were familiar pass before their eyes. Thus, the genealogy puts Jesus at the center of Israel's history. He is Abraham's Son and royal Messiah and thus the bearer of all of Israel's messianic hopes per God's plan. This is the fundamental affirmation of the genealogy.

Israel's call and commissioning in detail so that he might be a light to all nations with the news that only God is King.

Readers of chapters 1–2[8] discover five major unifying themes that demonstrate that Jesus is more than a historical figure.[9] He is the hoped-for *Christos* of Israel.[10] Second is the identity of Jesus. He is identified as the *Christos*, the Son of David,[11] the Son of Abraham, and Immanuel in the first chapter.[12] In the second chapter, readers encounter Bethlehem, Egypt, and Nazareth as notable locations

---

[8] Luz, *Matthew 1-7*, p. 82 designates 1.2–4.22 as the prelude to the Gospel of Matthew, asserting 'It is a Christological and salvation-history prelude and at the same time the beginning and anticipation of Jesus' entire way from the city of David, Bethlehem, to "Galilee of the Gentiles"'.

[9] R.E. Brown, *The Birth of the Messiah: A Commentary on the Infancy Narratives in the Gospels of Matthew and Luke* (New York: Doubleday, 1993. New Updated Edition). See pp. 74-84 for Brown's supporting argument to his assertion that the genealogy is 'artificial' rather than 'historical'. Cf. D.A. Carson, *Matthew* (EBC; Grand Rapids, MI: Zondervan Academic, rev. end, 2010), p. 95: 'In the ancient world, letters serve not only as building blocks of words but also as symbols of numbers. Hence any word has a numerical value. The use of such symbolism is known as gematria. In Hebrew, David is 14.' Cf. R.T. France, *The Gospel of Matthew* (NICNT; Grand Rapids, MI: Eerdmans, 2007), p. 31. For discussions of Matthew's inclusion on women in the genealogy, see: Charles H. Talbert, *Matthew* (PCNT: Grand Rapid, MI: Baker Academic, 2010), pp. 32-33; pp. 73-77; Luz, *Matthew 1-7*, pp. 83-85; and Brown, *Birth of the Messiah*, pp. 71-74.

[10] See Charette, *Restoring*, pp. 22-27 for a discussion of Jesus the *Christos* in Matthew. From the first verse, hearers are drawn into the narrative to determine for themselves if Jesus is indeed Messiah. The eschatological significance of Jesus is seen in the five OT quotations or allusions (1.23; 2.6, 15, 18, 23) that assert Jesus is the Christ or Messiah (*Christos*) of Israel. Talbert, *Matthew*, p. 32 offers that 'To speak of Jesus as messiah at the end of this genealogy would be to insert him into a history and a people'. Talbert, *Matthew*, p. 32, posits 'In Jesus, the climax of the list, the genealogy says, these promises have been fulfilled. This establishes the point of view in terms which the following narrative about Jesus is to be understood (Bauer, 1990, 464).' In short, 'Jesus brings to realization all that was implicit in the events, persons, and declarations of Israel's history'. The actions surrounding the birth of Jesus are ascribed to the HS (1.18).

[11] For a fuller discussion of 'son of David', see Talbert, *Matthew*, pp. 31-32 who offers that in the First Gospel references to Jesus as son of David, 'both messianic and healing overtones are found'. Also, D. Senior, C.P., *The Gospel of Matthew* (IBT; Nashville: Abingdon Press, 1997), pp. 59-61; J.D. Kingsbury, *Matthew As Story* (rev. and enlarged end; Philadelphia: Fortress Press, 1988), pp. 45-48.

[12] Each of these names was associated with unfulfilled promises of deliverance, favor, and restoration for readers.

related to the birth and childhood of Jesus.[13] Third, the reference to Babylon (1.17) reminds readers of the travails of the Exile, which will end with the final return and birth of the Messiah. Fourth, the sharp contrast between the appointed, illegitimate King Herod[14] and the legitimate born King Jesus is impressed on readers.[15] Last, the Father's divine protection of the Son from his birth to the arrival in Nazareth[16] through Joseph, a 'righteous man', plays a prominent role.[17] Readers are now prepared and expectant for the appearance of Jesus as the Anointed One, Son of God, Son of Abraham, and Son of David.

Matthew 3.13-17 The Baptism of Jesus Christ

The baptismal scene focuses on the identity of Jesus. Readers might be surprised by Jesus' appearance at the Jordan River.[18] The last reference to him was in Nazareth (2.23), where he had settled after the return from Egypt with Mary and Joseph, prior. Jesus is revealed to readers as 'he who is coming' (3.11). Jesus initiated the seventy-mile trip from Galilee to the Jordan River for the sole purpose of

---

[13] Egypt reminds readers of the Patriarchs and the Exodus, and Bethlehem stirs echoes of David the King and the promise of an enduring David dynasty.

[14] According to Blomberg, *Matthew*, pp. 62-64, Herod the Great was a half-Idumean, half-Jew who, through collusion with the Romans, rose to power as client-ruler of Israel 37 BCE. He was known as a great builder, an astute politician with Romans and Jews, and heavy-handed taxations of the Jewish laborers. It appears that as Herod aged, his paranoia increased regarding perceived threats against his person and throne. He had several wives, sons, and others put to death due to his anxiety and fear associated with plots to usurp his power and control.

[15] The contrast between Jesus and Herod would have stirred the recollection of both honorable and unfaithful kings in Israel's history.

[16] For a detailed discussion of 'Nazarene' see J. Nolland, *The Gospel of Matthew: A Commentary on the Greek Text* (Grand Rapids, MI; Carlisle: Eerdmans; Paternoster Press, 2005), pp. 128-31.

[17] D. Senior, C.P., *What Are They Saying About Matthew* (New York/Mahwah, NJ, rev. and expanded edn, 1996), p. 38. Joseph plays a prominent role in the protection of Jesus, from infancy onward. France, *Matthew*, p. 51 states, 'That Joseph was "righteous" is sometimes thought to explain his avoidance of a public scandal because he was "merciful" or "considerate," but the more basic of the word is of one who is careful to keep the law'. Similarly, Blomberg, *Matthew*, p. 58, avers Joseph 'is called a "righteous" man, which for Matthew does not imply sinless perfection but regularly refers to one who is law-abiding, upright in character, and generally obedient and faithful to God's commandments'.

[18] For a discussion of the significance of the Jordan River see J.E. Taylor, *The Immerser: John the Baptist within Second Temple Judaism* (Grand Rapids, MI: Eerdmans, 1997), pp. 44-46.

being baptized by John[19] who had appeared in the wilderness of Judea proclaiming, 'Repent, for the kingdom of heaven is at hand' (3.1).[20]

According to Mt. 3.3, John is the 'Voice of one crying in the wilderness', who proclaims, 'Make ready the way of the Lord, make his paths straight!' (Isa. 40.3). John's preparation of the way for the Lord was through calling Israel to repent for their sins and be baptized in the Jordan in view of the Kingdom of heaven or 'the rule and reign of God' being at hand.[21] In traditional Greek usage,

---

[19] The vivid portrait of John captures readers' imagination due to the Baptist's attire, diet, message, his location in the wilderness of Judea, and baptizing the repentant in the Jordan River. John's physical description is reminiscent of the prophet Elijah (2 Kgs 1.8); however, readers do not know that John is Elijah-redivivus until 11.14. John's message and manner served as a reminder of the previous prophets of Israel, who foretold the judgment of God and called the people to repentance from their sinful, rebellious ways. For an excellent study of John the Baptist see Taylor, *The Immerser*. For a detailed discussion of the administration and functions of John's baptism see R.L. Webb, *John the Baptizer and Prophet: A Socio-historical Study* (Eugene, OR: Wipf and Stock Publishers, 2006), pp. 163-216.

[20] Blomberg, *Matthew*, p. 74 posits that while the Kingdom of heaven or Kingdom of God is not a geographical realm it is manifested 'in space and time in the community of those who accept the message John and Jesus proclaimed and who begin to work out God's purposes on earth – personally, socially, and institutionally'. In other words, the present reality of the Kingdom of heaven with the coming of Jesus means that 'the decisive establishment or manifestation of the divine sovereignty has drawn so near to men that they are now confronted with the possibility and the ineluctable necessity of repentance and conversion'. An in-depth examination of the meaning of the 'kingdom of heaven' is beyond the purview of this study; however, the interpretation provided above is in keeping with those offered by Blomberg, Luz, and France. For more detailed discussion of 'kingdom of heaven' and 'Kingdom of God' see Blomberg, *Matthew*, p. 71; Luz, *Matthew 1-7*, p. 113; and France, *Matthew*, pp. 101-104. Matthew employs 'kingdom of heaven' extensively (33 times) in the Gospel; however, on occasion, he utilizes 'kingdom of God' (Mt. 12.28; 19.24; 21.31, 43). Unanimity regarding the two terms is elusive among Matthean scholars. J.C. Thomas, 'The Kingdom of God in the Gospel According to Matthew' in *The Spirit of the New Testament* (Blandford Forum, Dorset, UK: Deo Publishing, 2011), pp. 48-61 provides a helpful survey of the scholars who distinguish between the two terms, and those who view the terms as synonymous. Employing narrative analysis, Thomas argues that 'for Matthew kingdom of God is a literary device used to draw the reader's attention to passages of special significance', p. 55.

[21] The reference to the 'wilderness of Judea' and the Jordan River would have evoked powerful individual and collective memories for Matthew's readers. First, the 'wilderness of Judea' stirred echoes of the Exodus, forty years of Israel's wilderness wanderings, the exile, and God's promise that it was in the wilderness

repentance implied a change of mind or attitude. Influenced by the OT, repentance took on 'the sense of a change of action as well'.[22] Readers would have surmised that John was asking his hearers 'to change their way of life due to a complete change of thought and attitude concerning sin and righteousness'.[23] In essence, repentance called for ontological change to be evidenced in the disposition and behavior of those responding to John's message.[24] While the introduction of WB by John was new to his audience, it was requisite to demonstrate that repentance of sin had occurred and a commitment to right living had been made. Matthew's hearers would have perceived that John was proclaiming the return of God's presence or Spirit to the land was imminent. Readers possibly understood baptism by John in the Jordan to signal that a new exodus was about to occur. Hearers would apprehend the gravity of the situation and that they too needed to repent and be baptized to return from their exile of sinfulness and disobedience. However, not everyone was receptive to John's message as his exchange with the Pharisees and Sadducees reveals.[25]

---

where he would lead his people to establish a new covenant with them (Hos. 2.16, 20-21). Second, the Jordan River, as the place of John's baptism, would have stirred recollections of Israel's connection to the Jordan River, where God had done great things. Specifically, God healed Naaman, the Syrian, of his leprosy (2 Kgs 5.1-14) and took Elijah the prophet to heaven (2 Kgs 2.1-11). Most importantly, by crossing the Jordan, God's people could enter the promised land and end 40 years of wilderness wandering. Hence, the setting of the wilderness and the Jordan River, accompanied by the message of repentance, followed by WB, served to call John's hearers to re-enact the Exodus story through WB. Thus, John's appearance in the wilderness at the Jordan would have signalled to readers that the horrors of exile are soon to be replaced with hope, healing, and forgiveness. Impressed on Matthew's readers as well is the importance of baptism, an event that will surface again in Mt. 28.19.

[22] Blomberg, *Matthew*, p. 73.

[23] Blomberg, *Matthew*, p. 73.

[24] Furthermore, Matthew's readers would have heard the call to repentance for themselves as well. No one was excluded from the call to repentance. Israelites were keenly aware from the Hebrew Bible and history that confession, repentance, and sacrifice were prerequisites for entrance into God's presence. 1 Sam. 15.22; Mic. 6.6-8.

[25] See Nolland, *Matthew*, p. 143: 'Offspring of vipers' is quite similar in imagery to the LXX phrase 'offspring of asps', which is regularly concerned with the mortal threat posed by snake venom. Matthew's Jesus will label the Pharisees 'offspring of vipers' in 12.34 and 23.33. In the latter, the imagery is linked with the killing and crucifying of prophets, sages, and scribes who are to be sent by Jesus. Matthew

John sharpens his prophetic message as the religious leaders of Israel appear before him.[26] Per John, it is a time of judgment. Jesus will bring judgment. His coming is an eschatological event. Moreover, Jesus will execute judgment since he is the coming King and possesses the power and authority to do so.[27] John offers that they need to repent and produce fruit 'worthy of their repentance'. John's summons to produce fruit 'worthy of repentance' flows organically from the call to repentance. The production of 'fruit' is not an addition to 'repentance'. Instead, the two are inextricably linked. Readers appear to be aware of the need for repentance and the production of 'fruit' that reflects true repentance. John's specific call to the religious leaders appears to differentiate them from the penitent people who come to be baptized. Like everyone else, they, too, need to repent and be set free from spiritual bondage to sin. They are to produce the 'fruit of repentance' or righteousness like that demonstrated by Joseph in 1.18-2.23. The call for them to produce fruit after their confession and baptism appears to be a rebuke of them as leaders in 'name only'.

While the intent of Jesus' presence at the Jordan is to be baptized by John, like the repentant sinners, John strongly and repeatedly protests to prevent the baptism from occurring.[28] In Mt. 3.11, readers discover the differences between John and the one who is 'to come' through John's clarifying comments. First is the contrast that the person who follows John is 'mightier' than he and that John is not

---

probably thinks already of the threat to Jesus' own life which will be posed by the Jewish leaders. Cf. S. Hauerwas, *Matthew* (BTCB; Grand Rapids, MI: Brazos Press, 2006), p. 47. 'It is not what the Pharisees and Sadducees say that John and Jesus condemn; but rather it is the inconsistency between their lives and what they commend'; and B. Charette, *The Theme of Recompense in Matthew's Gospel* (JSNTSup 79: Sheffield: JSOT Press, 1992), p. 119.

[26] It appears to readers that John did not view them as truly repentant. It may have been that their refusal to participate in WB was the determining factor in John's assessment. Presented as a question, John makes a charge against the 'brood of vipers' (offspring of vipers), asserting that if they possessed the knowledge, character, and spiritual sensitivity that enabled them 'to know' the Scriptures, they would know what was happening.

[27] The threshing floor's image evokes the memory of chaff sifting from the wheat, a sorting that will result in salvation and separation. As at the end of v. 7, v. 10 again predicts imminent judgment for those who reject John's call to repentance. The fire, as v. 12 makes clear, stands for eternal punishment.

[28] For an informed discussion of the relationship between Jesus and John, see Taylor, *The Immerser*, pp. 162-80.

worthy of being Jesus' slave, much less removing his sandals.[29] It is likely readers would have grasped the incomparable superiority of the one who is 'to come' as divine since 'no mere mortal could pour out the Spirit, this was the gift of God alone … just as no mere mortal would baptize in fire (which in this context means to judge the wicked)'.[30] Second is the contrast between their respective baptisms. The contrast between their baptisms exemplifies for readers how the one who is to follow is greater than John. For readers, John is the herald, the one who precedes the one who will have a more significant ministry than his. He is the baptizer who beckons hearers to repent, confess their sins, and be baptized. The one 'who is coming' is greater than John since he will baptize with the HS-and-fire. The one who is 'to come' is the leader who will bring judgment, disruption, and salvation to the repentant. He 'who is coming' is linked with the HS just as Jesus was at his conception along with Mary and Joseph. The readers' anticipation grows, but their expectations of a *Christos* like King David will soon be disappointed.

John's hesitancy and outright resistance to baptizing Jesus may have surprised readers as well. John's call to repentance, followed by WB, to those born as Jews was unprecedented. By doing so, John asserted that the 'contemporary Jewish society (w)as no longer genuinely constituting the holy people of God'.[31] Jewish ancestry was inadequate to ensure a relationship with God.[32] The readers would likely understand that John discerned intuitively or through the HS more about who Jesus was than he knew concretely. On the one hand, John perceived Jesus did not need repentance. It seems to be the case that John knows by this point that Jesus is the one who will forgive sins. On the other hand, John claimed he was needful of Jesus' baptism since he would baptize in HS-and-fire. Readers have before them a reversal of religious and cultural norms that will mark the ministry of Jesus.

---

[29] While the comment may communicate a sense of lower status, it may be that John is referring to the greater impact of the person's future ministry.

[30] C.S. Keener, *A Commentary on the Gospel of Matthew* (Grand Rapids, MI: Eerdmans, 1999), p. 130. See Isa. 44.3; 59.21; Ezek. 36.27; 37.14; 39.29; Joel 2.29; Zech. 12.10).

[31] France, *Matthew*, p. 109.

[32] Blomberg, *Matthew*, p. 75.

Nonetheless, Jesus responds that he 'needs' to be baptized to fulfill 'all righteousness', asserting himself as a prophet. The fact that there is no mention of confession and repentance in connection with Jesus' baptism would not have been lost on Matthew's readers. Jesus' submission to John's baptism was an endorsement of John's mission of calling Israel to repentance given the arrival of God's kingship. Through his baptism, Jesus indicates his solidarity with John and identifies with those who John has baptized in their declared desire for a new beginning with God. In short, by submitting himself to John's baptism, Jesus establishes that his ministry will be in continuity with that of John. Jesus, too, will call people to repent and be reconciled with God.[33] Furthermore, readers would have grasped that Jesus' baptism represented his identification with the people of Israel at the 'climactic stage in her history: confessing her sins to prepare for the kingdom (3:2, 6)'.[34] If this is correct, readers would have understood Jesus' baptism as vicarious since he represented Israel.[35]

The mention of 'righteousness' (3.15) is the initial time readers encounter the term in Matthew. In Matthew, 'righteousness' carries the 'basic meaning of the conduct God expects of his "people"'.[36] Matthew's readers would have made the connection to Joseph (Mt. 1.19), who is known as a righteous man due to his obedience, compassion, humility, trust, and proper behavior. Righteousness is marked by trust, obedience, and correct behavior or action. Just as Joseph was deemed righteous in view of his obedience to divine mandates through the 'angel of the Lord', so was it the intent of Jesus to be obedient to his heavenly Father, bringing fulfillment to

---

[33] See, Charette, *Restoring*, pp. 58-97 for a detailed exploration of Jesus' redemptive work in Matthew.

[34] Keener, *Matthew*, p. 132.

[35] G.W.H. Lampe, *The Seal of the Spirit* (New York: Longmans, Green & Company, 1951), p. 39. Readers discover the necessity of Jesus' baptism after he is baptized and before he leaves the baptismal scene.

[36] France, *Matthew*, p. 119. Also, Senior, *Matthew*, p. 94. Cf. M.E. Boring, 'Matthew's Narrative Christology: Three Stories', *Interpretation* 64.4 (Oct 2010), pp. 356-67 (p. 365), who asserts

> Thus, in Matthew, when Jesus comes to be baptized, it is a matter of doing righteousness, the revealed will of God – a central Matthean theme (e.g., 1:19; 3:15; 5:6,10,20,45; 6:1, and combined with the kingdom of God in 6:33). Of the evangelists, only Matthew makes doing the will of God a matter of the coming of the kingdom (6:10).

God's ancient promises proclaimed by the prophets. Therefore, it seems to be the case that the fulfillment of 'all righteousness' applied equally to John and Jesus. Readers would have recognized that John and Jesus were key figures in Israel's history. Jesus was retracing Israel's actions, places, and events, thereby recapitulating the history of Israel, and bringing it to its intended telos by practicing obedience at every turn. Similarly, John was obedient to God's call to serve as the 'Voice of one crying in the wilderness', who proclaims, 'Make ready the way of the Lord, make his paths straight!' (Mt. 3.3). The contrast between Jesus and John and their opponents would have made an indelible impression on Matthew's readers.[37] They both needed to obey God's plan of salvation which included the baptism of Jesus. 'The involvement of John and Jesus in the latter's baptism "is action which is part of the process whereby the kingdom of heaven is to be inaugurated." It is a onetime event that is a necessary condition of the fulfillment of God's purposes.'[38]

Matthew's hearers, to this point, have become aware of Jesus's multi-faceted identity.[39] Readers are then made eyewitness to Jesus' baptism as Matthew describes Jesus' baptism and events immediately. While there have been various understandings of the events, readers would have perceived the scene as a public revelation of Jesus as the Son of God.[40] Jesus is presumably baptized by immersion by John

---

[37] Together, their obedience stood in sharp contrast to Herod's neglect and disobedience and the religious and political foes as well as Israel and its self-preoccupation with privilege and prominence.

[38] Talbert, *Matthew*, p. 55. 'In this way both function in their roles in a way that is faithful to their covenant relationship with God (fulfillment of righteousness). One should not think, however, that this act that fulfills all righteousness is meant to be exhaustive. It is rather a beginning ... Matthew 21:32 indicates that righteousness is not a moment but a way'.

[39] On the one hand, Jesus is the Messiah (1.17), king of the Jews (2.1-12), and a son of David (1.1-16). On the other, he is God's son begotten by the HS (1.20, 25; 2.15).

[40] France, *Matthew*, pp. 118-19. See Luz, *Matthew 1-7*, p. 144 for his 'Excursus: Son of God' in which he states, 'Here we come upon the second basic christological inclusion of the Gospel of Matthew: alongside "God with us" (1:23; 28:20) it is the obedient Son of God who provides the christological framework for the entire Gospel'. For explorations of the titles of Jesus see J.D. Kingsbury, *Matthew: Structure, Christology, Kingdom* (Philadelphia: Fortress Press, 1975), pp. 40-

and immediately came out of the water. The heavens were opened or rent asunder, and Jesus saw the 'Spirit of God descending as a dove and lighting on Him' (3.16).[41] The event conveys God's public self-revelatory act. Readers observe Jesus seeing the Spirit of God descend 'as a dove'[42] and light on him, providing an observable physical manifestation of the HS.[43] Just as Jesus was conceived by the HS, now the HS anoints the mature man Jesus. The contact between the HS and Jesus stresses the full embrace of Jesus the *Christos* by the

---

127; J.D. Kingsbury, *Jesus Christ in Matthew, Mark, and Luke* (Proclamation Commentaries; Philadelphia: Fortress Press, 1981), pp. 64-73; *Matthew, As Story*, pp. 49-51, 95-103. Kingsbury asserts 'Son of God' is the pre-eminent title of Jesus, subsuming all other titles beneath it.

[41] It is possible that Matthew's readers perceived the above events as a visionary experience like that in Ezek. 1.1-4:

> Now it came about in the thirtieth year, on the fifth day of the fourth month, while I was by the river Chebar among the exiles, the heavens were opened and I saw visions of God. (On the fifth of the month in the fifth year of King Jehoiachin's exile, the word of the Lord came expressly to Ezekiel the priest, Son of Buzi, in the land of the Chaldeans by the river Chebar; and there the hand of the Lord came upon him.) As I looked, behold, a storm wind was coming from the north, a great cloud with fire flashing forth continually and a bright light around it, and in its midst something like glowing metal in the midst of the fire.

Another possible intertext is Isa. 64.1, where the prophet asks God to 'rend the heavens and come down, That the mountains might quake at Your presence'. The opening of the heavens is the prelude to the divine communication that will occur through the descent of the HS. The rending asunder of the heavens also signals the importance and rank of Jesus for readers.

[42] For possible interpretations of 'as a dove' see Charette, *Restoring*, p. 47. Cf. Y. Phanon, 'The Work of the Holy Spirit in the *Conception, Baptism and Temptation of Christ: Implications for the Pentecostal Christian Part I*', in *AJPS* 20.1 (Feb 2017), pp. 37-55.

[43] The manifestation of the HS in the form 'as a dove may' remind readers of the dove's descent on the Ark after the great flood (Gen. 8.8-12). In that case, the dove symbolized new creation and new life. Here, the descent of the HS in the form 'as a dove' could well signal to readers that new creation and new life were coming through Jesus. Another possible meaning for the 'dove' is an allusion to Psalm 74, where the 'dove' came 'to symbolize Israel in all its sufferings at the hands of its enemies'. If this is the case, the 'dove' signals for Matthew's readers Jesus' role as sufferer. The 'dove' 'lighting on him' places the HS in direct contact with the body of Jesus, emphasizing the HS's total embrace of Jesus. D.C. Capes, 'Intertextual Echoes in the Matthean Baptismal Narrative', *BBR* 9 (1999), pp. 37-49 (47-48).

Father and HS.⁴⁴ Jesus is the one 'in whom and through whom the eschatological Spirit fully operates'.⁴⁵ Moreover, the descent of the HS on Jesus may remind readers of the Spirit's descent on David when he was anointed king by Samuel (1 Sam. 16.13).⁴⁶

The third manifestation of God's approval is 'a voice from heaven' that reveals the Father's pleasure in his son: 'This is My beloved Son, in whom I am well-pleased' (3.17). Readers would understand that God's pleasure in his 'beloved Son' is because he has proven himself 'by walking the way of obedience to his Father'.⁴⁷ The proclamation officially declares Jesus' identity to the bystanders: 'This is my Son'. Readers are possibly reminded by the Father's words from heaven of the OT theme of Israel as God's 'son' found in Isa. 42.1 and Jer. 38.20 (LXX).⁴⁸ Readers observing the scene would have

---

⁴⁴ Carson, *Matthew*, p. 138, argues, 'The Spirit's descent in v.16 needs to be understood in the light of v. 17. The Spirit is poured out on the servant in Isaiah 42:1, to which v.17 alludes.'

⁴⁵ Charette, *Restoring*, p. 21.

⁴⁶ In David's situation, after he was anointed with oil, 'the Spirit of the Lord came mightily upon David from that day forward', depicting the possession as permanent. R.D. Bergen, *1, 2 Samuel* (NAC 7: Nashville: Broadman & Holman Publishers, 1996), p. 180, posits that

> In David's case more than mere symbolism was present in the anointing ceremony: 'The Spirit of the Lord came upon David in power' (v. 12), even as had been the case previously with Saul (cf. 10:10). What is more, it stayed with him 'from that day on'; this made David's anointing superior to Saul's (cf. v. 14). The coming of the Spirit, an event that was primarily spiritual in nature, had major implications for the political future of Israel; after this event the political landscape of Israel would be forever different.

> However, there was a delay between David's anointing as king in 1 Sam. 16.13 and when he began to reign over Judah in 2 Sam. 2.4, 7 and over Israel in 2 Sam. 5.3-4. With the descent of the HS on Jesus, in essence, 'God has anointed and empowered Jesus as messianic king'. Readers have been made aware of the presence of the HS throughout the narrative with particular attention focused on the conception and birth of Jesus (1.18). The descent of the HS in the form of a dove on Jesus is a clear signal that God's presence has returned to the land and his people in a significant fashion in the embodied Son of God, Jesus. Readers may have anticipated 'there would be an interval between Jesus' anointing as messiah and the beginning of his reign (Matt. 28:18-20), as was the case with David'. Talbert, *Matthew*, p. 57.

⁴⁷ U. Luz, *Studies in Matthew* (Grand Rapids, MI: Eerdmans, 2005), p. 93.

⁴⁸ J.A. Gibbs, 'Israel Standing with Israel: The Baptism of Jesus in Matthew's Gospel (Matt 3:13-17)', *CBQ* 64.3 (2002), pp. 511-26 (511-12). Gibbs advances his

grasped the import of the Father's proclamation that 'this one', Jesus, is his son, and he is well-pleased with his son. Jesus is the Son of God. Moreover, these verses assert that at his baptism Jesus is 'the Isaianic Servant upon whom Yahweh's spirit rests as well as the embodiment of Israel',[49] also, identified as 'son of God'. The pronouncement would have left no doubt for readers that Jesus, Son of David, Son of God, who has fulfilled all righteousness to this point, was the promised deliverer of Israel's sin.[50]

Thus, the meaning, necessity, and propriety of Jesus' baptism by John becomes clearer. For Matthew's readers, Jesus is 'the 'son of God' who has come to save 'the son of God,' that is, the lost sheep of the house of Israel (Mt. 10.6; 15.24)'.[51] In receiving John's baptism, Jesus identifies himself as 'son of God' with Israel that needs to repent and produce fruit reflective of said repentance. In essence, in his baptism Jesus stands with and for sinners with the promise that he will save from sin.[52] God is anointing and initiating Jesus' public ministry to the entire world. The Anointed One, empowered by the HS, is to establish the Kingdom of heaven through his person and ministry; all conducted according to the Father's will. God's pleasure

---

argument by demonstrating that there is scant reason to discern an allusion to Ps. 2.7 in Mt. 3.17, pp. 512-15, and making a case that Jer. 38.20 (LXX) is in the background of the Father's pronouncement, pp. 515-20. A similar concern was raised earlier by D.C. Allison, 'The Son of God as Israel: A Note on Matthean Christology', *IBS* 9 (1987), pp. 74-81. I find Gibb's argument compelling and in keeping with Matthew's view of Jesus' recapitulation of Israel's history and intended purpose of being a light to the nations. This view stands in contrast to Blomberg, *Matthew*, p. 82; Nolland, *Matthew*, p. 157; and *France*, Matthew, p. 123, who all prefer Ps. 2.7 coupled with Isa. 42.1.

[49] Gibbs, 'Israel Standing', p. 521.

[50] Senior, *Matthew*, p. 93, 'The emphatic description of Jesus as God's Son at the moment of baptism continues what was already declared in the infancy narratives: Jesus' origin is from God and he has a profound bond of kinship with God'.

[51] Gibbs, 'Israel Standing', p. 521.

[52] H.S. An, 'Reading Matthew's Account of the Baptism and Temptation of Jesus (Matt. 3:5-4:1) with the Scapegoat Rite on the Day of Atonement (Lev. 16:20—22)', *Canon & Culture* 12.1 (2018), pp. 5-31 (23), argues that

> In this exegetical framework, Jesus offered to be baptized by John the Baptist to fulfill one of the major prophetic expectations of the Old Testament embodied in the sacrificial ritual of the Day of Atonement. As an atoning sacrifice of the scapegoat rite, Jesus became God's perfect sacrificial provision, who carried away all of the sins of Israel and beyond for their remission.

may be connected to Jesus' righteousness reflected by obedience to the will of the Father, just as Joseph was deemed a righteous man due to his faithful obedience. It may be that the declaration of God's pleasure in Jesus evoked memories of God's displeasure with people who disobeyed and hid from God because of their guilt and shame.

In Mt. 3.16-17, the Father, the Son, and the HS appear to readers acting in concert as Jesus is anointed or commissioned before beginning his public ministry. The divine activity of the Father, Son, and HS is not new to readers. Rather, Mt. 2.15 makes explicit that Jesus was regarded as God's Son from infancy since the HS conceived Jesus. Similarly, Mt. 1.23 identifies him as Immanuel or 'God with us' from birth.[53] The ongoing presence of the King will be reiterated for readers in Mt. 28.20 when the disciples are called to remember 'that I am with you always, even to the end of the age'.

The theme of fulfillment continues for Matthew's readers. Jesus is the one in whom the hopes of Israel merge, but God's promises must be appropriated by repentance, confession, obedience, and commitment to a new way of living and relating to God.[54] If the Jewish leaders reject him, others will respond more positively. Up to this point, readers have learned the conception and birth of Jesus is through the HS. Now, Jesus is anointed by the HS at his WB and receives the pleasure of God the Father because of his obedience. He is to be led by the HS into the wilderness where he will face the temptations of the Accuser, just as Adam and Eve in the garden and the children of Israel had done under the leadership of Moses. While

---

[53] Blomberg, *Matthew*, p. 82.
[54] See Charette, *Recompense*, p. 87. Charette asserts,

One might observe that, just as the beneficiaries of the promise are no longer the physical descendants of Abraham, so also the object of the promise is no longer the physical land of Israel. In the purpose of God, the promise has outgrown its original categories. This is consistent with the pattern of fulfillment as it is described elsewhere in Matthew. The one in whom the restoration takes place is the son of David, in accordance with prophetic expectation. Yet, for Matthew, he is much more than the son of David. He is, in fact, the Son of God (3.17; 16.16). The dark exile from which Jesus rescues his own is spiritual rather than physical. He has come to save his people from their sins (1.21). Moreover, the return from exile is itself undertaken at a spiritual level. Through repentance and obedience to the way prescribed by Jesus, the righteous reach the inheritance prepared for them. For the accomplishment of the promised return of the people of God, the physical and terrestrial give way to the spiritual and transcendent.

hearers would well know the failures of Adam and Eve and Israel at this point, Jesus' obedience, and reliance on the HS to this juncture provide hope for a different outcome in Israel's story and all creation.

Readers discover the turning point for both John and Jesus is the imprisonment of John. At that point, Jesus withdrew from Galilee and settled in Capernaum. Readers learn that Jesus' relocation to Capernaum is the fulfillment of Isaiah's prophecy. Just as John called people to repentance, so too does Jesus. Readers are reminded of John by Jesus' preaching: 'Repent, for the kingdom of heaven is at hand'.[55] From Mt. 1.1 through Mt. 4.17, the theme of the salvation of God's people through Immanuel, the Messiah, the Anointed One, receives ever-sharpening focus on Jesus who embodies trust in the Father, obedience that is expressed through the worship of God alone, and the promise that the Kingdom has come. Hearers are invited to hear the Good News and follow in the steps of Jesus. Jesus' proclamation found fertile soil in four fishermen (Simon, who was called Peter, Andrew his brother, and James and John, the sons of Zebedee) who dropped their nets and followed Jesus' call to discipleship. The call and response of the four fishermen invite readers to understand themselves as witnesses and participants as well. They, too, are called to follow Jesus.

By following the story to this point, readers would have understood that Jesus' baptism was a watershed event, marking a significant change in his life and the lives of all people. First, Jesus submits himself to baptism by John so they may both fulfill 'all righteousness' by their obedience to the Father. Second, it is the occasion of Jesus' anointing by the HS and his commissioning to public ministry as the Son of God, according to the OT prophets. Third, his baptism is the public proclamation of his wholehearted commitment to the one true God alone, followed by a life of faith, trust, obedience, and allegiance to God.[56]

---

[55] Hauerwas, *Matthew*, p. 45. Hauerwas writes, 'The repentance for which John calls, the same repentance that Jesus calls for in Matt. 4:17, is the call for Israel to again live as God's holy people, a holiness embodied in the law, requiring Israel to live by gift, making possible justice restored'.

[56] In Mt 4.1-28.15, readers encounter the temptation of Jesus, his preaching, teaching, and healing ministry, which provides sufficient evidence for their discernment that the Kingdom of Heaven was indeed present in the life and

Matthew 21.23-27 John's Baptism

The next Matthean text of relevance is Mt. 21.23-27 that addresses the authority of Jesus, which is called into question by the 'chief priests and the elders of the people'. They question Jesus in the temple about the origin of his authority and the authority by which he was 'doing these things'. The content of 'these things' is not articulated; however, readers would have recollected Jesus' ministry of healing, exorcising demons, forgiving sins, and cleansing the temple, all conducted without the sanction of the religious leaders. In fact, Jesus' cleansing of the temple serves as a prophetic symbolic action of 'the temple's destruction, implying that he has authority over the temple that is greater than their own'.[57] Jesus responds with a counterquestion to them regarding the authority by which John baptized. 'Was the authority from heaven or from men?'

The mention of John's baptism would not have been lost on readers. John's baptism signified a new beginning for a repentant Israel (3.1-12). Moreover, 'John's baptism' is a way of referring to his entire ministry of preparing the way for the 'coming one' by calling Israel to repentance and WB as an indicator of true repentance. This is borne out by the reference 'believe him' in 21.25b, not just be baptized by John.[58] Also, Jesus' reference to John's baptism emphasizes the legitimacy and significance of John's baptism (entire ministry) and appears to endorse the ongoing validity of his baptism.

---

ministry of Jesus Christ, who was Israel redivivus as well as the promised heir of the Davidic dynasty. They also see the opposition Jesus faced from the political, religious, and spiritual realms that would ultimately put him to death and attempt a coverup to neutralize the message and meaning of the bodily resurrection of Jesus Christ.

[57] Mitch and Sri, *Matthew*, p. 274. Cf. Hauerwas, *Matthew*, pp. 183-84. Hauerwas asserts that in cleansing the Temple,

> Jesus' enactment of the jubilee now shapes the worship of God at [the] very center of Israel's life, that is, the temple itself. Jesus has restored the temple not only for the blind and lame, but for the poor. Those who sold doves did so because in Lev. 5:7 it was permitted for the poor to substitute doves and pigeons if they could not afford sheep. That provision became but another way for some to exploit the poor. Jesus cleanses the temple, and even the children, who had always been excluded from the temple, are heard praising Jesus in the temple, singing, 'Hosanna to the Son of David.'

[58] Carson, *Matthew*, p. 505 offers '"John's baptism" (v. 25) is a way of referring to the Baptist's entire ministry (cf. v25b and the reference to believing John, not simply being baptized by him)'.

Caught on the horns of a dilemma, the religious leaders refuse to answer, and Jesus reciprocates in kind. Yet, the answer is inescapable for readers who have observed 'these things' previously mentioned and remembered John's baptism. His authority is from God, just as the authority of John, who served prophetically to call Israel to repentance as preparation for the arrival of the Kingdom of heaven. The contrast between the understanding of the chief priests and elders and the readers is noteworthy.

Matthew 28.16-20 Building the Temple[59]

As directed by Jesus through the women, 'Mary Magdalene and the other Mary', the disciples return to Galilee, bringing readers full circle to where it all began.[60] Readers have anticipated the return to Galilee since Jesus' prediction in 26.32 and the instructions given in vv. 7 and 10. The momentous event of the resurrected Jesus' meeting with the disciples in Galilee provides readers with additional testimony that Jesus is indeed the divine Son of God. The eleven disciples fell down and worshiped him just as the magi from the East had worshiped him at this birth. Yet, some doubt or are hesitant. The identity of those doubting or hesitating is not noted. Were the ones who worshipped

---

[59] See Charette, *Restoring*, pp. 110-13 for an examination of the parallels between 2 Chron. 36.22-23 and Mt. 28.16-20 relative to the building of God's temple. Also, E. Krentz, 'Missionary Matthew: Matthew 28: 16-20 as Summary of the Gospel', *Currents in Theology and Mission* 31 (2002), pp. 24-41 (26-27), who argues for the similarities between the texts.

[60] In the return to Galilee, a reversal of Jesus' movement from North to South, readers would recall the arrival in Nazareth of Galilee where Joseph, the righteous man, Mary, and Jesus settled upon their return from Egypt (1.22), and possibly all that preceded their arrival: the conception of Jesus through the HS; the obedience of Joseph, the righteous man, to the HS at every turn; the opposition from Herod, the appointed King; the escape to Egypt. It is in Galilee where Jesus grew into manhood (2.22-23), where the message of the Kingdom of heaven was first proclaimed, and where the first disciples were called by Jesus (4.18-22). It is from Galilee that Jesus arrived at the Jordan to be baptized by John and was anointed or commissioned by the Father to begin his ministry (3.13). It is back to Galilee that Jesus returns to preach and teach about the Kingdom of heaven/God, demonstrate the reality of the Kingdom of heaven through healing, exorcisms, and the forgiveness of sins, and face the forces of evil (4.23). In Galilee, on an anonymous mountain, Jesus was transfigured before Peter, James, and John (17.1-8).

Jesus also the ones who doubted or hesitated or were these different persons?[61]

Undeterred by their doubt or hesitancy, Jesus asserts that 'All authority has been given to Me in heaven and on earth' (28.18). Through Jesus' resurrection from the dead, his absolute authority is expanded to include all heaven and earth or the entire universe.[62] Jesus' receipt of authority from the Father reminds readers of the royal power bestowed on the Son of Man in Dan. 7.13-14. This means for readers that Jesus is now empowered with his Father's authority over heaven and earth. In essence, it is in the person of the resurrected Jesus, through the power of the HS, that heaven and earth intermingle and overlap. The Kingdom of heaven has come through Jesus the *Christ*, while he is yet under the authority of the Father. Jesus is King just as the Father is King. They are co-regents, as it were. God's promises to Abraham and David have been fulfilled in Jesus. Since all authority has been granted to him by the Father, Jesus has the power to lead and direct those who follow him through his Spirit. Since he is the center of the new community of faith, the new messianic community, the people of *all* nations will be '*his* followers, obeying *his* commandments, and sustained by *his* unending presence among them'.[63] Just as Joseph was a righteous or good man and faithfully obeyed divine direction through visions, dreams, and the 'angel of the Lord', Jesus recapitulated Israel's history and purpose and 'filled full' OT prophecies. So too, are the disciples of Jesus to follow his direction for the expansion of the Kingdom of heaven and the reign of God.

---

[61] Talbert, *Matthew*, p. 312. For an opposing view, see Carson, *Matthew*, pp. 263-64. Readers would be mindful that all during Jesus' time with them, the eleven grew in their faith and understanding of who Jesus was. Readers would have grasped that worship and doubt were not incompatible and understandable given the newly experienced resurrection of Jesus from the dead. It seems to be the case that after the resurrection, followers of Jesus the Christ continued to learn and grow in their understanding of Jesus. The experience of worship and hesitation would have resonated with readers.

[62] Carson, *Matthew*, p. 665. Cf. Mitch and Sri, *Matthew*, p. 370, who assert Jesus 'never ceased to be omnipotent in his divinity, of course, but now he exercises his lordship over the universe through his risen humanity (see Eph 1:20-21; Phil 2:9)'. Cf. Ulrich Luz, *Matthew 21-28* (Hermeneia; Minneapolis: Fortress Press, 2005), p. 624.

[63] France, *Matthew*, p. 1108. Emphasis original.

Jesus is now the center of the new community of faith by virtue of his death and resurrection which displaced the Jerusalem temple as the symbolic dwelling place of God's presence under the old covenant. The resurrected Christ formed a new covenant people indwelled by his Spirit.[64] As such, the new covenant community, the church, represents the presence of God among people and, in effect, constitutes the new eschatological temple of God. Throughout the Gospel of Matthew readers have been alerted to the fact that in Jesus, the restoration of the 'eschatological people of God is taking place'.[65] Consequently, instead of a physical rebuilding of God's temple being in view, readers would have grasped the Messiah's task of temple building focused on Jesus' followers, current and future. As the church, or the reconfigured temple of God, the eleven disciples are commanded to participate in the expansion of the kingdom of God through building the temple of God.[66] Specifically, the disciples are commanded to 'make disciples of all the nations' (28.19) for him. The reference to all nations does not exclude Israel.[67] Readers would have understood that his disciples and they, by implication, were to make disciples for Jesus alone and not themselves.[68] The scope of the

---

[64] See Charette, *Restoring*, pp. 103-26 for a discussion of 'The Church as the New Temple in Matthew'. W. Klaiber, 'The Great Commission of Matthew 28:16-20', *American Baptist Quarterly* 37.2 (2018), pp. 108-22 (114), echoes the same understanding, stating:

> Historically it can only be said that after Easter when the disciples started to proclaim Jesus as Messiah of Israel and Savior of the world it was clear to them that they had to call people to be baptized, not only as an act of repentance but as a means which connects those who are baptized with all what Jesus has done for them. Therefore the first step of introducing human beings into the discipleship of Jesus for Matthew and his tradition is to include them through baptism into the saving communion with the triune God – the God who has created them, the God who has saved them, and the God who will fill and mould their lives with his overflowing love: Father, Son and Holy Ghost.

[65] Charette, *Restoring*, p. 98. See pp. 98-139 for an exploration of the relationship between the Spirit and the new community of God in Matthew.

[66] Cf. K.L. Sparks, 'Gospel as Conquest: Mosaic Typology in Matthew 28:16-20', *CBQ* 68.4 (2006), pp. 651-63, for an alternative interpretation of Mt. 28.16-20.

[67] Luz, *Studies*, p. 26; Talbert, *Matthew*, p. 313. Cf. Charette, *Recompense*, p. 156 avers, 'It might be observed that, as a consequence of the judgment pronounced against the Jewish nation in 21.43, Israel is now regarded as merely one among the other nations which need to be evangelized (cf. 28.19) and which will be judged on the basis of their response to disciples.'

[68] Keener, *Matthew*, p. 716.

disciples' ministry exceeds his. Theirs is to be a universal mission to all people, which implies crossing all boundaries of race, culture, ethnicity, gender, and religion. Rather than understand the command as a passive 'as you are going, make disciples', readers would grasp the imperative to 'make disciples' and requisite actions necessary: going, baptizing, and teaching. Just as the eleven were called to 'follow Jesus' and become his disciples, so too are they mandated to make disciples in like manner. Just as Jesus had traveled Judea and the surrounding countryside to preach and teach the Gospel of the Kingdom, heal the sick, forgive sins, and exorcise demons, so too are the eleven, and by inference, the readers as well.[69]

Matthew's readers would have found it necessary to reflect on Jesus' life and ministry with the twelve to ensure a proper understanding of discipleship and what it meant to be a disciple. It was more than trying to emulate the peripatetic ministry of Jesus. Crucial was the spiritual formation of the disciples that came through 'being with him'. It was through being with Jesus that they were transformed by his presence, teaching, and miracles.[70] Before the twelve could perform the works of Jesus, they needed the spiritual grounding and relationship with the Father modeled for them by Jesus. They, too, needed to practice the spiritual disciplines of prayer (6.9-13); fasting (6.16-18); and giving (6.2-4), as taught by Jesus. Jesus called them to himself as a teacher so they might learn of/from him. Before the twelve, he lived a life of total dependence on the Father

---

[69] Keener, *Matthew*, pp. 718-21.

[70] Talbert, *Matthew*, pp. 20-24 identifies four types of teachers with adult learners based on the writing of the first century period: philosophers, sages, interpreters of Jewish law, and prophets. He asserts the closest analogy between Jesus and his disciples is that of the philosopher and his disciples and draws on the analogy to assert:

> Hence, the disciples' being 'with him' has not only the philosophic frame of reference but also the overtones of being changed by beholding deity. In Matthew, then, for the disciples to be 'with Jesus' is for them to be transformed by their vision of God-with-us ... After Jesus's departure, they could have been with him early on, in part, through their memory and recollection of him. Later it would have been through their reading of the First Gospel. They were with Jesus as they moved through the narrative plot with him. The being with him made possible by the story powered their transformation ... Being with him and experiencing the vision of God-with-us – in person, by means of recollection, or by means of the book (the First Gospel) – powerfully assisted their life of obedience.

and the Scriptures, seeking guidance and strength before each ministry foray. They were called/invited to take on his yoke of authoritative instruction and accept what he said was true because he said it.[71] Also, they were called to listen, submit to his requirements because he made them. Readers understood that disciples hear, learn, obey, and grow in understanding Jesus' teaching and are transformed by them. However, the lives of the twelve were also marked by partial understanding, disbelief, and betrayal. Despite their lapses, all but one of the twelve committed themselves to Jesus before Jesus' resurrection from the dead.

The appearance of 'baptizing' in 28.19 perhaps comes as a surprise to readers since WB has not been mentioned since the baptism of Jesus by John in 3.16, save for Mt. 21.25, which refers to John's baptism. By this point, readers understand the relationship between Jesus' baptism, his authority as the Son of God, and his power to command his followers. Water baptism receives renewed attention by Jesus as he commissions (Mt. 28.19-20) his disciples to continue the missionary expansion of the Kingdom of heaven. Specifically, Jesus' commission is 'baptizing them in the name of the Father and the Son and the Holy Spirit' (28.19). The formula signals that the baptism commanded by Jesus moves beyond that of John the Baptist. This is not the readers' first exposure to the Father, Son, and HS's appearance in one setting. The reference undoubtedly evoked the story of Jesus' baptism by John (3.13-17). He was anointed/commissioned by the Spirit for his role as *Christos* to fulfill the OT prophecies and bring salvation to all creation. But what would it mean for the newly converted to be baptized 'in the name' of the Father, Son, and HS?

Matthew's readers would have recognized that to baptize in the name of the Father, Son, and HS is to place Jesus on the same level with the Father and the HS. Jesus is divine, just as the Father and the HS. In view of all that has preceded, readers' understanding of God's nature would be radically challenged and expanded. 'The singular "name" followed by the threefold reference to "Father, Son, and Holy Spirit" suggests both unity and plurality in the Godhead'.[72] To be baptized in the name of the Father, Son, and HS is to declare

---

[71] Carson, *Matthew*, p. 669.
[72] Blomberg, *Matthew*, p. 432.

allegiance to each person mentioned. Each is worthy of worship, and praise for each is divine and instrumental in the salvation of humanity. Readers may have recollected the strong connection between the temple as the dwelling place of the name of God under the old covenant.[73] Now, it is within followers of Jesus the Christ, the eschatological people of God, who constitute the temple of God where God dwells through the Spirit. Thus, to be baptized into the name of the 'Father, Son, and HS' is to be understood in an ontological sense. The focus is on what occurs in baptism. It is through WB that a believer 'in entering a relationship with God, becomes part of that community in which the name of God or God's Spirit now dwells'.[74] To undergo Jesus' baptism is to participate in a 'boundary event' designed to demarcate life before/after. To be baptized in water is to signify that through faith in Christ and confession that 'Jesus is Lord' an ontological change has been affected whereby people have moved from exile to restoration since they are now indwelled by the Spirit of God through their repentance, confession, and reorientation to God. To be baptized is

---

[73] Charette, *Restoring*, pp. 118-19 asserts that when the temple was constructed on Mt. Zion under Solomon, 'From that day forward it is identified as the place of Yahweh's name ... This conviction that the temple is the dwelling place of God's name and thus the locus of the divine presence is the essential theological premise that gave authority and legitimacy to the temple institution'. Nolland, *Matthew*, pp. 1268–69 offers that the nearest parallel in Mt. 28.19 is 18.20:

> In 18:20 'in the name' is an expression of solidarity with Jesus. Matthew intends a comprehensive commitment, together, to Jesus and what he has brought and done and stands for. Loyalty, belonging to, submission to, and intention to act on behalf of all may be involved. A similar kind of solidarity is likely intended for the baptized in 28:19. In 18:20 only Jesus is involved, but now we have reference to 'the name of the Father and of the Son and of the Holy Spirit'. Are we to think of them as sharing one name? The use of the singular 'the name' could mean that, and it would mean that if allusion to the divine name were intended. But there is clearly no allusion to the divine name in 18:20, and there is none in the references in Acts to baptism in the name of Jesus. This is not like the putting of God's name on people in the priestly blessing in Nu. 6:22–27. And if there is no allusion to the divine name, then there is no particular reason for thinking in terms of one name. Matthew's language is equivalent to 'in the name of the Father and the name of the Son and the name of the Holy Spirit'.

Cf. Carson, *Matthew*, pp. 668-69; Keener, *Matthew*, pp. 716-17; and France, *Matthew*, pp. 1116-18. discussions of the full Trinitarian 'formula'.

[74] Charette, *Restoring*, p. 119.

to become a member of the church, the messianic community or reconstituted temple of God. As such, WB appears as an eschatological event, 'to represent a once-for-all, decisive action into the community Jesus envisioned for his disciples'.[75] Moreover, for readers, to be baptized in water in the name of the Father, Son, and HS is to be 'gifted by the same Spirit which had directed and empowered him'.[76] Narratively, of course, the disciples' anointing with the HS is a future event, subsequent to Jesus' resurrection (Mt. 28.16-20). The readers of Matthew's gospel know that WB does not operate mechanically, it is only on the basis of confession, repentance, and trust/faith in Jesus Christ. For readers, it is essential that baptism in the name of the Father, the Son, and the HS occurs in order to become one of Jesus' disciples (Mt. 28.19). Through baptism, a disciple 'enters into a covenant relationship with God ... and [it] associates the disciple with the baptismal experience of Jesus'.[77] Finally, to become a disciple of Jesus is to come into 'covenant relationship with God and this finds expression through participation in the eschatological community in which God is present'.[78]

---

[75] Blomberg, *Matthew*, p. 431.

[76] Charette, *Restoring*, p. 119.

[77] Charette, *Restoring*, p. 126.

[78] Charette, *Restoring*, p. 119. While it is beyond the scope of this reading to address thoroughly the various views held by scholars regarding the interpretation of Mt. 28.19, a distinct voice in the field will serve as a representative. In J.D.G. Dunn, *Baptism in the Holy Spirit: A Re-examination of the New Testament Teaching on the Gift of the Spirit in relation to Pentecostalism today* (Philadelphia: The Westminster Press, 1970), p. 4, the author establishes the purpose of his study and outlines his position on WB in the following:

> I hope to show that for the writers of the NT the baptism in or gift of the Spirit was part of the event (or process) of becoming a Christian, together with the effective proclamation of the Gospel, belief in (*eis*) Jesus as Lord, and water-baptism in the name of the Lord Jesus; that it was the chief element in conversion-initiation so that only those who had received the Spirit could be called Christians; that the reception of the Spirit was a very definite and often dramatic experience, the decisive and climactic experience in conversion-initiation, to which the Christian was usually recalled when reminded of the beginning of his Christian faith and experience. We shall see that while the Pentecostal's belief in the dynamic and experiential nature of Spirit-baptism is well-founded, his separation of it from conversion-initiation is wholly unjustified; and that, conversely, while water-baptism is an important element

Readers are challenged with the message that while WB is crucial to being a disciple, so are living obedient lives according to his teachings and making disciples, just as Jesus did. Also, new disciples are recipients of the same power and responsibility the original twelve received when they were sent out in pairs of two (Mt. 10.7-8): 'And as you go, preach, saying, "The Kingdom of heaven is at hand. Heal the sick, raise the dead, cleanse the lepers, cast out demons. Freely you received, freely give"'.

It appears that teaching and modeling obedience to all of Jesus' commands forms the heart of disciple-making. Jesus' instructions 'teaching them to observe all that I commanded you' stimulates Matthew's readers to reflect on the content to be learned, practiced, and taught. Likely, readers would have recollected the five discourses[79] dispersed throughout Matthew's Gospel:

---

in the complex of conversion-initiation, it does neither to be equated or confused with Spirit-baptism nor to be given the most prominent part in that complex event. The high point in conversion-initiation is the gift of the Spirit, and the beginning of the Christian life is to be reckoned from the experience of spirit baptism.

Contra Dunn see Howard M. Ervin, *Conversion-Initiation and the Baptism in the Holy Spirit* (Peabody, MA: Hendrickson Publishers, 1985); Howard M. Ervin, *Spirit Baptism: A Biblical Investigation* (Peabody, MA: Hendrickson, 1987).

From my perspective, Dunn's work seems to suffer from a lack of attention to the narrative of the text he investigates, Matthew, in particular, and from his sole reliance on the historical-critical method.

[79] A.T. Lincoln, 'Matthew – A Story for Teachers?', in D.J.A. Clines, S.E. Fowl, and S.E. Porter (eds.), *The Bible in Three Dimension: Essays in celebration of forty years of Biblical Studies in the University of Sheffield* (JSOTSup, 87: Sheffield: JSOT Press, 1990), p. 115. Lincoln comments that

And what are they to teach? Jesus informs them (28.20) that the nations are to be taught to keep not the commandments of the Torah but 'all that I have commanded you'. The disciples are to pass on what they have been taught by the supremely authoritative interpreter of the Torah, Jesus himself. Where have they received this teaching? Above all, in the five great teaching discourses, which can now be seen to have been integral to the completion of the narrative plot. Knowing all Jesus' teaching, the disciples are also now in fact able to be the sort of teachers who meet with Jesus' approval according to the very first mention of their teaching task in The Sermon on the Mount in 5.19 – Those who teach and do even one of the least of his Commandments ... Although they seemed to disrupt the flow of the narrative and to have little to do with advancing the action, the five teaching discourses were in fact all the time preparing the disciples to be authoritative teachers of all that Jesus commanded

Mt. 5.1-7.29 The Discourse on Discipleship

Mt. 9.35-11.1 The Discourse on Mission

Mt. 13.1-35 The Parable Discourse on the Kingdom of Heaven

Mt. 18.1-19.2 The Discourse on Relationships in the Kingdom of Heaven

Mt. 24.3-25.46 The Discourse on the Future

The content of the discourses constitutes the body of 'commandments' given by Jesus. The new 'commandments' given by Jesus, not the Torah, establishes the foundation of Kingdom living for the followers of Jesus the Messiah. 'Jesus' teaching has given a new interpretation to the old law, and it is by obedience to *his* words that salvation is henceforth to be found (7:24-27).'[80]

The final words of Jesus before his departure, 'I am with you always, even to the end of the age' (28.20), takes readers back to the beginning of Matthew where it is foretold that Jesus will be called Immanuel, meaning 'God with us' (1.23). The same idea is expressed in both verses. The time of exile has ended for those in a relationship with Jesus. God's presence is once again guaranteed for those in covenant with the Father through the death and resurrection of Jesus. The disciples will not be left alone nor expected to accomplish the mission by themselves as they proclaim the Gospel of the Kingdom. Jesus will be present with them spiritually until the end of the age, that is, until he returns. The promise yet to be fulfilled for Matthew's readers is that prophesied by John about Jesus: 'He will baptize you with the Holy Spirit and fire' (3.11).

There is only one appropriate response to make for the reader who has followed the unfolding story of Jesus' genesis through his death and resurrection and commissioning of the eleven disciples; namely, to follow the eleven in the worship of and obedience to Jesus the *Christos*, Son of David, Son of Abraham, Son of Man, and Lord of heaven and earth and participate in proclaiming the Gospel of the Kingdom of heaven/God to all the nations and making disciples of

---

them, the climactic commissioning to which the narrative builds up and its major two-part movement (cf. 16.17-19; 28.16-20).

[80] France, *Matthew*, pp. 1118-19. Also, U. Luz, 'Empowerment and Commission in the New Testament', *JEPTA* 26.1 (2006), pp. 49-62 (54-55).

Jesus through WB and teaching Jesus's commandments. Making disciples is to be done in full assurance of Jesus' continued presence until his return and that he will yet baptize with the HS and fire.

Summary

In summary, a narrative reading of Matthew reveals that each reference (Mt. 3.13-17; 21.25-27; 28.19) to WB is highly nuanced and does not support undifferentiated interpretation and usage of the texts. First, John's baptism for repentance in which ontological change was expected was preparatory for God's return to the land and the end of exile for Israel due to their sin of idolatry and rebellion against God. Those baptized are to confess, repent from their sin, and demonstrate their repentance through changed lives and affections, the fruit 'meet for repentance' (Mt. 3.8).

Second, Jesus' baptism by John served several purposes in Matthew's narrative. Jesus' baptism serves as his anointing by the HS for his ministry. Jesus is empowered by the HS to carry out his mission. Through baptism Jesus identifies with God's people. Jesus embodies God's presence and return after Israel's repentance and production of fruit – changed lives (Mt. 3.13-17). Jesus is identified as one who will baptize in the HS and fire in the future. Jesus is the HS baptizer (Mt. 3.11).

Third, the command by Jesus for new disciples to be baptized in water following confession, repentance of their sin, and faith in the person of the crucified and risen Christ, appears as an act of incorporation into the life of God the Father, God the Son, and God the HS. To be baptized into the life of the Triune God is possible since believers have received the Good News of the Kingdom of Heaven. Since Jesus is revealed in Matthew as the new temple of God, believers become new temple people in which God dwells by the HS. Through WB, new believers are incorporated to the new temple people of God. Water baptism coupled with repentance, confession, and belief/trust in Jesus Christ is then a public proclamation of believers being incorporated into the life of God effecting an ontological change in their being. To be baptized into the life of God is an embodied experience that changes the person in every aspect of their being (Mt. 28.19).

Romans 6.1-11 Water Baptism – Death and Life in Jesus Christ[81]

As noted above, early Pentecostals in the WHP, FW, and OP streams relied heavily on Rom. 6.1-11 in their preaching and teaching on WB. It is to a fresh narrative reading of the text that we turn our focus.

In Rom. 6.1-3, readers are challenged to reject the absurd idea that those who have been justified by faith may continue in sin or remain under the dominion of sin, so grace may increase.[82] With the mention of sin in 6.1, 2, readers may have recollected Rom. 1.18-32's assertion that God's wrath was being revealed due to the guilt, unrighteousness, and godlessness of the Gentiles. Readers are apprised the process begins with an act of the will in that humans have suppressed the truth of the knowledge of God (1.18-23) in exchange for a 'lie', the opposite of truth (1.25). The desire to hide from their mortality compels humans to suppress the truth of God. Instead of glorifying God and expressing gratitude to God based on their intuitive knowledge, they opted for delusion, became futile in their

---

[81] Evidence regarding the practice of WB is scant in Romans, outside the author's mention in 6.1-14. The author of Romans assumes WB has been practiced and is understood by the readers. The argument advanced by the author hinges on their shared knowledge. C.K. Barrett, *The Epistle to the Romans* (BNTC; London: A & C Black [Publishers] Limited, 1991), p. 113; J.D.G. Dunn, *Romans 1-8* (WBC 38a: Dallas: Word Books, 1988), p. 327. While commentators assert 'that baptism is not the subject of the passage', Dunn, Romans 1-8, p. 308, posits Rom. 6.1-11 has become the locus classicus for Paul's baptismal theology. See H. Boers, 'The Structure and Meaning of Romans 6:1-14', *CBQ 63* (2001), pp. 664-82 (665-71), who provides a helpful history of interpretation for Rom. 6.1-14. Two articles, utilizing a ritual-theoretical approach to interpreting Romans 6, effectively escape some of the interpretative and epistemological problems associated with current interpretation of Pauline baptismal theology: A.K. Petersen, 'Shedding new Light on Paul's Understanding of Baptism: a Ritual-Theoretical Approach to Romans 6', *Studia Theologica,* 52.1 (1998), pp. 3-28; P.B. Smit, 'Ritual failure in Romans 6', *HTS Hervormde Theologiese Studies/Theological Studies* 72.4 (2016), pp. 1-13.

[82] Noteworthy for readers are the questions and answers contained in Romans. They reflect issues or concerns an interlocutor might ask in debate. In each case the author responds with the terse disclaimer, 'By no means'! (3.4, 6, 31), 'not at all' (3.9). The assertion/question in 3.8, suggesting 'doing evil so good will come of it later' is met with the brief, 'Their condemnation is deserved'. This question is repeated in Rom. 6.1 immediately following the stark comparison between Adam and Jesus Christ.

minds/thinking, which, in turn, resulted in darkened hearts or affections (1.21) and placed them under the wrath of God.[83]

Romans 1.22-23 captures for hearers the further devolution of humans as their thinking deteriorated and their self-understanding was clouded by rebellion against God.[84] The result of the suppression of the truth is God's releasing humans to the consequences of their sins (1.24-32). Readers are aware of the stages of malformation and shame by the thrice-repeated phrase 'God handed them over' (1.24, 26, 28) to moral degradation'.[85] Again, it is because they exchanged

---

[83] 'God's wrath' is derived from the prophetic voices of the OT that warned against idolatry or turning away from God as the center of human existence. The underlying assumption is that humans can know God from creation itself since it is the result of the Creator's originative activity. Creation points to God's attributes of eternal power and divinity in the created world known by humans. Since God is the originator of all, he has a claim on all that is created. The desire to hide from their mortality compels humans to suppress the truth of God. Instead of glorifying God and expressing gratitude to God based on their intuitive knowledge, they opted for delusion, became futile in their minds/thinking, which, in turn, resulted in darkened hearts or affections (1.21). C.S. Keener, *Romans* (Eugene, OR: Cascade Books, 2009), pp. 32-33, posits that Gentile intellectuals could have followed the author's argument, citing several Greek and Roman philosophers who espoused similar views. J.A. Fitzmyer, S.J., *Romans: A New Translation with Introduction and Commentary* (ABC 33: New Haven, CN: Yale University Press, 2008), pp. 279-80, argues for a distinction between the revelation of God through nature and the revelation of God through Jesus Christ. He states,

> Yet Paul does not mean that 'only by an act of revelation from above – God 'making it known' – can people understand God as He is.' For precisely this reason he uses a different verb, phaneroun, 'make evident,' for example, in and through material creation itself, as distinct from *apokalyptein*, 'reveal,' namely, through the Gospel. It is important to note this distinction. Paul admits that 'God's uprightness' is revealed in the Gospel, but he also maintains that people can perceive or come to a certain awareness of God's 'eternal power and divinity' from reflection on what he has made evident in material creation.

[84] Readers may have been reminded of Gen. 1.26-27, where the first humans were created in the image and likeness of God, which enabled them to perceive reality itself following God's mind, revealed in the shape of creation. That capability was exchanged for the created order, which was then worshipped instead of Creator God.

[85] Fitzmyer, *Romans*, pp. 272-74. 'When Paul says that God *paredōken*, "delivered (them) over" (1.24, 26, 28), he is speaking protologically; he is seeking to give a logical explanation of the dire condition of pagan humanity; in a primitive way,

the truth about God for a lie (1.25) that they receive in their persons the penalty for their error (1.27). Humans were given to follow their impure hearts, which led to dishonoring their bodies, resulting in men and women being driven by their demeaning passions.[86]

In view of the readers' former lives with the accompanying promise of God's wrath, the suggestion to continue in sin or remain under the dominion of sin is refuted with an absolute 'By no means'! A question follows, asking how a believer could continue to live in sin after already dying to sin, possibly referring to conversion.[87] It

---

which echoes OT thinking, he attributes that condition to an action of God who punishes pagan humanity in his divine wrath'.

[86] In addition to humans being handed over to impure hearts and demeaning passions, they are handed over by God to depraved minds or distorted thinking. The distorted passions, mind, and heart and consequences of a distorted will result in despicable behavior enumerated in the 'vice list' of Rom. 1.29-32. S. McKnight, *Reading Romans Backwards: A Gospel of Peace in the Midst of Empire* (Waco, TX: Baylor University Press, 2019, p. 161, asserts that

> In Pauline theology, perhaps, the best explanation for this connection of sinners to the cosmic decay and bondage is emergence theory. That is, sins become the causal basis for the emergence not just of human-sin-based sinful patterns in our world but of some kind of Sin-Self or Sin-Person that is aligned with an evil spiritual force. The alliance of Sin with Satan, then, works back on sinners to keep them in sinful behaviors so that Sin and Satan can guide humans to Death.

Also, see M. Croasmun, *The Emergence of Sin: The Cosmic Tyrant in Romans* (New York: Oxford University Press, 2017).

[87] Barrett, *Romans*, p. 113, asserts 'The definite past tense, "we died", points to a particular moment; conversion and (as the next verse shows) baptism must be in mind'. The concept of grace which undergirds the author's argument is introduced in Rom. 1.16-17, where readers learn the author is desirous to preach the Gospel of God, which is the Gospel of God's Son, Jesus Christ, due to its accosting transformative power to save everyone who believes. The mention of the nations, Greeks, and barbarians emphasizes for readers that salvation is social and has universal and eschatological significance and relevance. The Gospel of God is to be preached to all nations for them to be included and belong to the people of God. Moreover, salvation occurs in this life. The Gospel of the righteousness of God is revealed from or by faith to faith. Readers probably grasped the phrase to mean that 'God's righteousness revealed in the Gospel is a matter of faith from start to finish'. Keener, *Romans*, p. 29. The righteousness of God is Christ Jesus who died in obedience to the Father and was raised by the HS. God's righteousness or justice is accessed through faith and will work in the life of a believer to the end. Faith is not a human work of any kind, physical or mental; faith is total dependence on God's righteousness. God alone will and can make things right. Through faith, the 'gift of Christ Jesus human beings come to believe in him, belong to him, and share

seems that sin is to be understood as a personification, 'an actor on the stage of human history, the character that would enslave even Christians as a result of Adamic influence'.[88] Readers are instructed that God's grace accomplishes more than deliverance from wrath; grace also delivers from sin's power and transforms those who believe/trust in Jesus. It is God's grace that produces genuine righteousness from the heart, not the Law.[89]

---

in the uprightness that has been revealed through him and the gospel about him'. The meaning of this phrase, 'from faith to faith' is debated among scholars. Fitzmyer, *Romans,* pp. 263-65, posits the following possible interpretations and reasons for each:

> The double prep. phrase with ek ... eis is found in Ps 84:8, where the preps. express passage from one degree to another, a meaning that Paul uses elsewhere (2 Cor 2:16; 3:18) and which is also possible here: God's economy of salvation is shared more and more by a person as faith grows: from a beginning faith to a more perfect or culminating faith. By the coupling of the two prepositional phrases, Paul means that there is room only for faith, not deeds, in the process of justification. Another possible meaning is 'through faith (and) for faith,' understanding the prep. ek instrumentally and eis purposively; this reading would be in line with the development in 3:21–22. 'Through faith' would express the means by which a person shares in salvation; 'for faith' would express the purpose of the divine plan ... In either case Paul would be suggesting that salvation is a matter of faith from start to finish, whole and entire.

Habakkuk 2.4 now appears reminding readers that 'he who is righteous by faith shall live by faith'. Scholars also debate whose faith(fulness) is in view in this Habakkuk quotation. L.T. Johnson, *Reading Romans: A Literary and Theological Commentary* (Macon, GA: Smith & Helwys Publishing, 2001), pp. 29-30, provides the following analysis, which appears to reflect the author's desired impact on readers:

> Paul's first quotation concludes the thesis statement from Scripture Habakkuk 2.4. It is introduced to provide scriptural warrant for the phrase 'from faith to faith,' because it contains the Greek phrase ek pistis ('out of faith'). A literal translation of the Hebrew of Habakkuk is, 'the righteous shall live by his faith', meaning the person who has faith. The LXX itself, however, has the 'righteous one will live out of my faith,' meaning God's fidelity. Paul uses the Greek text, but his understanding seems to be closer to the Hebrew ... Whichever rendering seems better, it is clear that Paul's use of the citation here (as in Gal 3:11) establishes a thematic connection between life, righteousness, and faith.

[88] Fitzmyer, *Romans*, p. 430; F.J. Matera, *Romans* (PCNT: Grand Rapid, MI, 2010), p. 148.

[89] In Rom. 3:21–5:11, hearers may have discovered that due to the unrighteousness of Jews and Gentiles, God made provision for the righteousness or justice of all people, reflecting his faithfulness to the covenant

The readers' depth of knowledge and understanding of the significance and meaning of WB is called into question in 6.3, 'do you not know that all of us who have been baptized into Christ Jesus have been baptized into His death?'[90] Readers may have well understood WB as the dramatic symbol of the new exodus whereby believers 'are characterized as the new wilderness generation, on their way home to the promised land, accompanied by the presence of God through the Spirit'.[91] Since they have been 'baptized into Christ',

---

first initiated with Abraham. First, the righteousness of God has been revealed through the faith of Jesus Christ. The meaning of 'through faith in Jesus Christ') in Rom. 3. 22, 26 is disputed among scholars. For a detailed exploration of the various views see Keener, *Romans*, pp. 57-59 and Fitzmyer, *Romans*, pp. 345-46. I have opted for the subjective genitive reading, 'faith of Jesus', following Keener, *Romans*, p. 57:

> In favor of it referring to Jesus's own faith(fulness) is the centrality of his work (3:24–25); the parallel expression regarding God's faithfulness earlier in the chapter (3:3); and most compellingly, the precisely parallel expression to believers being of the faith of Jesus (3:26) and the faith of Abraham (4:16)'. Jesus' life was one of faithful obedience to the will of the Father, culminating in bearing God's wrath through his sacrificial crucifixion. It is through God's grace that 'redemption that is in Christ Jesus' (3.24) has been granted to all who put their trust or believe in Jesus Christ (3.21-26). In these verses, readers hear the effects of Jesus Christ's crucifixion and death: justification, redemption, and expiation, and possibly pardon for those who have faith in him. Second, the priority of faith over the Law and circumcision is proven by the life of Abraham (4.1-25), whose spiritual offspring are justified by faith, not by Law (4.13-17, 23-25). Abraham, considered the Father of the Jews and Greeks, is a type of those saved by faith. This is illuminated by evidence that Abraham was not justified by works (4.1-8), circumcision (4.9-12), but by faith in God's promises (4.18-25).

Readers may have been taken aback by the assertion that the justice of God came through the crucified and risen Jewish Messiah, Jesus, under the leadership of Caesar. Readers would have perceived the assertion as a direct challenge to Roman pretension. N.T. Wright, *Romans* (NIB vol. IX: Nashville, TN: Abingdon Press, 2015), p. 325.

[90] Barrett, *Romans*, p. 114, avers

> The point that Paul developed, or possibly introduced, in the understanding of baptism arose out of his insistence that Christ must always be understood as Christ crucified and interpreted in terms of crucifixion and resurrection. It followed from this that baptism into Christ must mean 'baptism into Christ crucified'; there was no other Christ.

[91] Wright, *Romans*, p. 446. Wright posits 'the death of Jesus at Passover time, and the meal he shared with his followers on the night he was betrayed, so

they are, as new exodus people, representatives of the Messiah. The incorporative language reminds readers of the nature of the Messiah. 'The Messiah represents his people, so that what is true of him becomes true of his people.'[92] Thus, readers are his people and share in his death and resurrection through WB. They are brought into the historical narrative of the new exodus through WB which constituted them as the new people of God.[93] Readers are thus alerted that they

---

interwove the theme of new exodus with the fact of Jesus' death that the two became inextricable'.

[92] Wright, *Romans*, p. 447.

[93] See Wright, *Romans*, p. 446, argues, 'We may suppose that the earliest Christian assumption about baptism was that it was both a dramatic symbol of the new exodus and a sign of Jesus' death'. Wright further asserts and I believe rightly so, that

> The master-narrative had been enacted when Israel's history was focused on the Messiah and his death and resurrection. The life-stories of individual people, Jews and Greeks alike, needed then to be brought within this larger narrative by the appropriate symbolic means. Just as faith in the God who raised Jesus was common for all, Jew and Gentile alike, so baptism in the name of Jesus had to be undergone by all ... Since what was at stake was the renewal of the people of God, and indeed of the whole creation (8:18-30), the event that brought together the individual life-story and the larger story of God, Israel and Jesus would itself be tangible and physical. That event, clearly, was baptism.

J.A. Adewuya, *Transformed by Grace: Paul's View of Holiness in Romans 6–8* (Eugene, OR: Cascade Books, 2004), p. 23, posits 'Baptism is a pictorial representation of spiritual regeneration. It declares personal faith in Jesus Christ, who died and was buried and rose again from the dead. Baptism represents the believer's confession of having died to sin and of having been raised up spiritually to a new life'. In contrast, Dunn, *Romans 1-8*, p. 328, appears to equate WB with Spirit baptism; Barrett, *Romans*, p. 114, argues 'baptized into Christ Jesus' is a shortened version of 'baptized into the name of Jesus Christ' which communicates to readers that those who are baptized 'into the name of' become the possession of Christ. Thus, baptized believers are the 'adherents, the property, of one whose death, resurrection, and ascension marked the dawn of the Age to Come'; and D.J. Moo, *The Epistle to the Romans* (NICNT: Grand Rapids, MI: Eerdmans, 1996), asserts that

> Baptism, rather, functions as shorthand for the conversion experience as a whole. As such, it is the instrument (note the 'through' in v. 4) by which we are put into relationship with the death and burial of Christ. It is not, then, that baptism is a symbol of dying and rising with Christ; nor is it that baptism is the place at which we die and rise with Christ. Dying and rising with Christ refers to the participation of the believer in the redemptive events themselves; and the ultimate basis for Paul's appeal in this chapter is not what happened when we were baptized, but what happened when Christ died and rose again.

need to remember[94] their status as members of the people of God, the new Israel, based on their baptism.[95]

Readers may have grasped WB as an eschatological event in that while the Age to Come[96] had dawned in the resurrection of Jesus the

---

[94] The act of remembering or recalling is not to be understood as an exercise in pure cognition. Instead, my use of 'remember', 'recalling', and 'remembering' carries with it the meaning of whole-person engagement. For support of my view, see K. Sutton and K. Williamson, 'Embodied Cognition', in L. Shapiro (ed), *The Routledge Handbook of Embodied Cognition* (London: Routledge, Taylor & Francis Group, 2014), pp. 315-25:

> Human beings are unusual in the variety of ways we relate to our history. Past events can be explicitly and consciously recollected, or can have more implicit influences on body, mind, and action. As well as the many respects in which the cumulative effects of the past drive our biology and our behaviour, we also have the peculiar capacity to think about our histories ... Recent psychological studies of autobiographical remembering emphasize that tracking the past is not necessarily its key function.

> Remembering also plays important and heavily context-sensitive roles in maintaining and renegotiating self-narratives, in promoting social relations, and in directing future action ... recent work especially stresses the future-oriented role of memory in guiding simulations of possible future events ... Personal narratives, social interactions, and future planning are often expressed and embodied in rich social and material settings. So autobiographical recall is embodied in that it is often for action and communication ... even though the specific past experiences I now remember may be long gone and may have left little or no trace on my current environment.

[95] Stanley E. Porter, *The Letter to the Romans: A Linguistic and Literary Commentary* (Sheffield: Sheffield Phoenix Press, 2015), p. 131, avers that in this section the author 'is concerned with the issue of ownership of the person who has placed one's faith in Christ'.

[96] A. Nygren, *Commentary on Romans* (Philadelphia: Fortress Press, 1949), p. 210, posits 'The idea of the two aeons has formed the background for all this; but it has not yet been explicitly stated ... But now it breaks out of the background into full view. Adam is the head of the old aeon, the age of death; Christ is the head of the new aeon, the age of life'. Similarly, Fitzmyer, *Romans*, p. 406, argues that 'In making this comparison, Paul establishes once more the basis for Christian hope (5:5): as Adam's sin introduced baleful consequences for all historical humanity, so the justification brought by Christ Jesus has affected those consequences for good and for salvation. Thus Adam and Christ are type and antitype.'

The precise meaning of 'because all sinned' is hotly debated among scholars. R.H. Mounce, *Romans* (NAC 27: Nashville: Broadman & Holman Publishers, 1995), pp. 141-42, summarizes the three prevailing views and their rebuttals in the following summary:

Christ, their restored relationship with Christ, through conversion and baptism, made them partakers of the Age to Come. Since the Age to Come has not arrived in fulness, baptized believers continue to live in the present age, marked by sin and death, and participate in the Age to Come, simultaneously. The readers' daily existential struggle to live in the already/not yet of the Age to Come in the face of the power of sin can be engaged by remembering the transformative event of their WB.

Readers seem to be able to grasp the participatory representation of the death, burial, and resurrection of Christ as candidates descend into, are covered by, and then emerge from the water into new life. In the baptismal event participants go through the experience of dying to sin, being buried, and rising to new life, just as Christ Jesus had done. Readers remember that their baptism associates them 'with a historical event, the death and burial of Jesus the Christ'.[97] The

---

First, one approach is to regard the prepositional phrase (lit., 'upon which/whom'), which the NIV translates 'because,' as introducing a relative clause with the pronoun referring to Adam. Employing the Old Testament concept of corporate personality, this would mean that death came to all because all sinned in Adam. Bruce writes that for Paul, Adam was not only the first man but was in a sense what his name means ('humanity'); the whole of humanity is viewed as having originally sinned in Adam. The major problem with this approach is that if Paul had intended to say 'in whom,' he would have used a simpler and more obvious construction. This construction does not take this meaning elsewhere (cf. Luke 5:25; Acts 7:33; 2 Cor 5:4; Phil 3:12; 4:10).

A second way to take the expression is to regard it as a conjunction. Death, the inevitable consequence of sin, made its way to each individual member of the race because everyone, in fact, has sinned. Although Adam's transgression determined human nature with its propensity to sin, the spread of that evil virus is the result of every person's decision to sin. We are responsible not for what Adam did but for what we have done. The problem with this approach is that there are no certain examples in early Greek secular literature where the words are taken as the equivalent of a causal conjunction.

The third possibility, which I am following,

is that the Greek words serve as a consecutive conjunction meaning 'with the result that.' In this case the primary cause of our sinful nature would be the sin of Adam; the result of that sin would be the history of sinning on the part of all who enter the human race and in fact sin of their own accord. This interpretation does justice to the language involved and conforms to the apostle's theological outlook as he is building his case in the Book of Romans.

[97] Matera, *Romans*, p. 150.

occurrence of 'co-buried' presses the point that due to their co-burial, the believer lives in union with the risen Jesus Christ.[98]

The incompatibility of continuing in sin because of their organic union with Christ in his death and life is further illustrated through the twin imagery of WB and burial (6.4-11).

Readers are made aware that through WB, believers have been buried with Christ Jesus into his death. The readers come to learn that WB introduces believers into union with the suffering and dying of Jesus Christ, emphasizing the act of crucifixion by which Christ has overcome sin. This idea will reappear in 6.11 when it is asserted, 'Even so consider yourselves to be dead to sin'.

Death and burial are followed by resurrection. On the one hand, the text asserts in Rom. 5.12-21 that all people are born into sin and death due to their solidarity with Adam. On the other hand, solidarity with Jesus Christ begins through baptism into him because of his death and resurrection (6.3–4).

At this point, readers may have perceived a tension in the letter's argument regarding faith and WB. Romans 1.16-17 and 3.25-26 has powerfully emphasized a person's need to respond to the righteousness of God[99] through Jesus Christ by faith/trust in Jesus.

---

[98] Fitzmyer, *Romans*, p. 434. Cf. A.E. Klich, OSU, 'Baptism as Unification with the Death and Resurrection of Christ (Romans 6:1-14)', *Ruch Biblijny i Liturgiczny* 70.2 (2017), pp. 147-61 (151), asserts

> In the pericope under study, Paul did not write 'buried like Christ' but 'buried with Him [Christ].' This means that the believer was laid in the tomb in Jerusalem together with Him. His death on the Cross and burial were at the same time the death and burial of Christians. Through this act, the faithful experience death for sin, burial, and resurrection like Christ. Paul uses one of his favorite verbs συνθάπτω ('buried'), which he writes with συν ('with'), 'buried with.' In this way, he expresses that the Christian lives in unity with the resurrected Christ; he or she will find fulfillment when a certain day he or she finds him or herself 'with Christ' in glory.

[99] The 'righteousness of God' has been widely interpreted by NT scholars. Keener's comments on the subject are deemed accurate by this researcher. I understand his references to Paul to refer to the author of Romans. Keener, *Romans*, pp. 27-29:

> In common Greek, dikaiosunē normally meant 'justice.' In what sense would God's 'justice' or 'righteousness' (Rom 1:17; 3:5, 21–22; 10:3) put people right with him (cf. 3:26)? Scripture often connects God's righteousness with his faithfulness and/or covenant love (e.g., Pss 36:5–6, 10; 40:10; 88:11–12; 98:2–3; 103:17; 111:3–4; 119:40–41; 141:1; 143:1, 11–12; 145:7). In the Psalms, God's

Now, it appears to underscore the necessary response as baptism. Per the argument, union with Jesus the Messiah is through an act that must be performed. However, the seeming tension is never addressed since it is only supposed; there is no contradiction. Those who have put their faith/trust in Jesus Christ are assumed readily to undergo WB. Readers would have grasped that apart from faith there was no provision for union with Christ.[100] WB is not viewed as optional or supplemental. Rather, it is through WB that readers are 'identified

righteousness causes him to act justly (e.g., Pss 31:1; 35:24) or mercifully (Pss 5:8; 71:2, 15–16, 19, 24; 88:12) in favor of his servant ... In the Greek version of the OT, the cognate verb dikaioō did not imply a legal fiction, but recognizing one as righteous, including in forensic contexts (cf. Gen 44:16; Isa 43:9, 26; Ezek 44:24): judges must not 'acquit the guilty' (Exod 23:7), but must 'justify,' i.e., pronounce righteous, the innocent (Deut 25:1). God himself would punish the guilty but 'justify' and vindicate the righteous (1 Kgs 8:32; 2 Chr 6:23); he himself was 'justified,' or 'shown to be right,' when he pronounced just judgment, even against the psalmist (Ps 51:4, in Rom 3:4). Thus for God to 'justify,' 'acquit,' or 'vindicate' someone who was a morally guilty person, as in Rom 4:5, might shock hearers. Nevertheless, those immersed in Scripture could also understand God rendering judgment in favor of someone based on his mercy ... Israel hoped for God's promise of sins (Is 53:11; cf. Rom 4:25). God being 'righteous' meant that he would honor the promise to Abraham, whom he found 'faithful' (Neh 9:8). For Paul, God's righteousness is incompatible with dependence on mere human righteousness (Rom 9:30–10:6; Phil 3:9). Divine righteousness is not a goal to be reached by human effort, but a relational premise that should dictate the new life of faithfulness to Christ. Often Romans uses the verb cognate (dikaioō) for God putting believers right with himself, reinforcing the possibility that this is how Paul uses the noun here. This verb can signify just vindication; in a forensic context it may entail 'justification' ... or acquittal. Those who argue for legal acquittal rightly emphasize God's generosity, or 'grace,' as opposed to human achievement ... Paul does not think only of 'acquittal,' which is only one element of the term's normal sense. Acquittal does not dominate the entire letter, which goes on to address conduct (Rom 6; 12:1–15:7); moreover, when God pronounces something done, one expects this to happen, not merely produce a legal fiction (Gen 1:3; 2 Cor 4:6). In Romans, righteousness is a transforming gift. It is a divine gift rather than human achievement (Rom 5:17, 21), but God's gift also enables obedience (cf. 1:5; 2:8; 5:19; 15:18), i.e., right living (6:16–18; 8:2–4; 13:14). In theological terms, justification is inseparable from regeneration. (Emphasis original)

[100] Barrett, *Romans,* pp. 114-15, asserts 'There is no sacramental opus operatum by means of which Christians can assure themselves, independently of faith and of their own moral seriousness, that they have risen from death to enjoy the life of the Age to Come'.

with Christ's death and resurrection, and their very being or "self" is transformed'.[101]

Through WB believers are incorporated into the people of God and participate in the new exodus that has been inaugurated by Jesus's death. Through WB readers are transported from people who are under wrath to the new covenant people of God. It appears to be the case that through conversion and WB an ontological change is affected in the person baptized into Christ. The organic metaphor involves the transfer of allegiance and identity. It seems readers would understand WB as a public act of conversion or transformation based on the act of obedience of faith to demonstrate commitment to Messiah Jesus as the 'last Adam' who has successfully recapitulated Israel's history and has now ushered them into his people marked by grace and reconciliation. As such, WB serves as an act of demarcation between two allegiances and identities. The former life, marked by sin and death, is left behind, and a new identity of righteousness and life is initiated by Christ (Rom. 5.18–19). Moreover, solidarity with Christ and his body includes sharing his death and burial with Adam and new life based on Jesus' resurrection.

As Christ was raised from the dead by the Father's glory, so those who have faith in Christ are raised from death through baptism. The ascription of resurrection to the Father's glory possibly reminds readers of the Exodus miracles assigned to Yahweh's glory (Exod. 16.7, 10). Readers may have also understood the reference to the 'glory' of the Father as a word rich with eschatological meaning in that God's glory will be revealed at the last day. Thus, for Christ to be

---

[101] Fitzmyer, *Romans*, p. 429. Klich, 'Baptism as Unification', p. 159, captures the change wrought in WB with the following:

In conclusion, we must state that Paul presents the power of God's grace, which overcomes all sin. Through baptism, the Christian is immersed in Christ's paschal mystery and is gifted the grace of redemption. This paraklesis presents Christians who went from death to life and have become 'new persons.' The 'old person' overcome with sin was buried with Christ once and for good. In baptism, the Christian comes into union with Christ, His death and resurrection, and glorious life in God. The Christian is therefore capable of openness to obedience to God and to throwing off bad tendencies related to sin. He or she becomes God's soldier, serving in an army fighting for the freedom of God's children and for justice. This is possible because he or she is open to God's grace.

raised by God's glory readers would perceive Christ's resurrection as an eschatological event, 'ushering in the time of the fulfilment of God's purpose'.[102]

Specifically, believers are raised to walk in newness of life as new exodus people through their union with Christ effectuated by their conversion and WB. The Greek expression translated 'newness of life' is better rendered 'a new sphere which is life'.[103] 'To walk in a new sphere which is life' evokes OT imagery of following God's direction, the Law, in how God's people are to live (Isa. 30.21, 42.5; Jer. 7.23, 26.4, Ezek. 11.20, 20.19; Dan. 4.37; Hos. 14.9).

Raised from the dead through faith in Christ, readers enter a new sphere of existence, a new life of obedience. In Christ, believers' lives are to be as different from their lives in Adam, as life is from death.[104]

Entrance into a new sphere of life is made possible through the believer's solidarity with Christ through the participatory act of WB in which the believer identifies with the glorified Jesus and is incorporated into the new people of God, the church. The phrase 'become united with' is from the idea of grafting[105] in which 'a young branch grafted onto a tree grows together with it in an organic unity and is nourished by its life-giving sap' to communicate the believer's new relationship with Jesus Christ.[106] Accordingly, union with Christ enables the believer to live with the life of Jesus Christ in the church.

---

[102] Barrett, *Romans*, p. 115.

[103] Mounce, *Romans*, p. 150. Boers, 'Structure', pp. 681-82, rightly asserts 'The real issue, however, is not the new life in Christ as such, but that the new life in Christ is a death to sin'.

[104] Barrett, *Romans,* p. 114, asserts

Baptized Christians are thus the adherents, the property, of one whose death, resurrection, and ascension marked the dawn of the Age to Come. Baptism thus finds its setting in Christian eschatology; but Christian eschatology is no simple matter, for though, in some sense, the Age to Come has come, it is manifest that the present age still persists, and that the general resurrection and renewal of creation have not yet taken place. It follows that baptism is the gateway not to heaven, or to the fully 'realized' kingdom of God, but to a life which is empirically related both to the present age, which is marked by sin and death, and to the Age to Come, which is 'righteousness, peace, and joy in the Holy Spirit' (14:17). This fact lies behind much of the present paragraph; but we must allow Paul to develop it in his own way.

[105] Barrett, *Romans,* pp. 115-16.

[106] Fitzmyer, *Romans*, p. 435.

In 5.12-21 it is stated that before conversion, readers shared the 'image' or 'likeness' of Adam, but now they share the 'likeness' of Jesus' death and will share in his resurrection. The author posits that since readers have been united with Christ in his death, it only follows they are united with Christ in his resurrection. As Jesus was raised victor over death, so also are readers set free from the bondage of sin. Their resurrection is present and future. In Rom. 6.5, the believers are said to live in a period of 'eschatological tension' since they have been delivered from sin and already walk in newness of life yet await the resurrection of their bodies (6.5).

In Romans 6.6-7, readers are introduced to the slave metaphor, which will be developed in 6.12–21.[107] Readers may have understood the slave metaphor in reference to the old and new exodus with their respective differences of liberation from bondage. It has already been established that sin was the source of death (5.12–21) and now it is asserted that death ends one's slavery to sin (6.6). Since readers have been freed from sin by Christ's death (6.6–7), their union with Christ, who died and is now alive forever, guarantees them future resurrection and eternal life (6.8–10).

Another reason readers should not remain under the dominion of sin is that their 'old self' or 'old man' was co-crucified or 'put to death with' Jesus on the cross.[108] The 'old man' does not refer to some 'particular part of the human person, but rather the whole person, the entire self, *seen as someone "in Adam"*'.[109] Hearers are reminded by 'body of sin' that the whole person is prone to sin and closed to acknowledging God, and having a relationship with the Father, Son, and HS. Readers would likely think of the opening description (1.18-23) of humanity's turning away from God to idols and the subsequent devolution into the depravity of mind, heart, and body. In Rom. 7.24, it will be called the 'body of death'. Readers' assurance of a resurrected life rests upon the certainty that the 'old self' as been put to death with Christ, once and for all. They are no longer slaves

---

[107] Matera, *Romans*, pp. 151-53.

[108] The NASB's 'might be done away with' translates καταργέω which means 'to make completely inoperative' or 'to put out of use'. G. Delling, 'ἀργός, ἀργέω, καταργέω,' in G. Kittel, G.W. Bromiley, & G. Friedrich (eds.), *Theological Dictionary of the New Testament* (Grand Rapids, MI: Eerdmans, electronic edn, Vol. 1), p. 453.

[109] Wright, *Romans*, p. 454. Italics original.

to sin, but new exodus people who have entered the 'promised land' that will reach fulfillment at the consummation of the Age to Come.

Again, sin is personified as a master that reigns over the whole person in Rom. 6.6. Sin dominates human life with an alien power that overcomes humanity. Readers are made aware that death fulfills the demands of sin and opens the way for the resurrection, which lies beyond the control of death. Once liberated from that master, believers can no longer focus their sights on sin. Resurrection is the victor over death. Since the 'old self' has been rendered powerless, it is no longer necessary for a believer to continue in bondage to sin. In union with Christ, believers, those who have been justified, are set free since sin is powerless to overcome new life. Readers may have been reminded of the Israelites' exodus from Egypt with its accompanying liberation from slavery with the hope of the promised land and freedom before them.

Readers would not be unaware of the repetition in this section. Thus, in 6.8, there again appears the fundamental proposition that those who have died in union with Christ will also live with him since they were united with Jesus in his resurrection. To live with Christ is to live life 'in him' in the here and now. While a future life with Christ after death is promised in the NT, it does not appear to be the thrust of this passage. Instead, as new exodus people readers are already participating in the resurrected life of the Messiah as they live in the sphere of his resurrected existence. Readers are to conduct their lives accordingly in the here and now.

In Rom. 6.9–10, appeal is made to a point of common knowledge among the readers. Since Christ has been raised from the dead, he cannot die again. Christ's resurrection rendered powerless the tyranny of death, rendering defeat to sin forever in kind. In contrast, Christ died to sin once for all and as victor over sin, he lives now in unbroken fellowship with God.[110] The reference, 'but the life that He lives, He lives to God' may remind readers of the obedience of Jesus

---

[110] According to Barrett, *Romans*, p. 118, verse nine 'emphasizes that the resurrection of Christ was an eschatological event, an anticipation of the resurrection of the last day; hence Christ will not die again. He (and he alone) has begun the resurrection life of the Age to Come; but those who are joined with him in his death and resurrection anticipate it by faith.'

to the Father that led him to the cross to secure the salvation of his people (Rom. 3.22-26).

Thus, it has clearly been established for readers that Christ is their example. Through his death, Christ finished his relationship with sin once for all. By his resurrection, Christ lives eternally in unbroken intimacy with God the Father. Christ's death and resurrection has demonstrated God's faithfulness and justice. Readers are then exhorted by 'So you too' are to 'consider' or 'reckon themselves' dead to sin and alive to God through Jesus Christ. The previous argument of chapter 4, where 11 times God is spoken of as 'crediting' righteousness to someone's account (4.3-11, 22-24), is once again invoked. Here, the readers are called to recognize and act on God's perspective since God has 'considered' or 'credited' them righteous. They are righteous because through their faith/trust in Christ they are in union with God through Christ, 'in whom they both died to their identity as sinners in Adam and were raised to a new master, God'.[111] As new exodus people readers must truly know their identities as those who have died to and been raised to new life in Christ and live accordingly. They are exhorted to live lives that are congruent with their new standing in Christ that has been explained in 6.2–10.[112]

Summary

In summary, readers are reminded in Rom. 6.1-11 of why they should not remain under the dominion of sin. First, they have been baptized into Christ's death. Second, their 'old self' or 'old man' has been crucified with Christ, so their sin-dominated self has been put to death. Third, the pattern for their lives, Christ, has died to sin and death, once and for all.[113] They are no longer under God's wrath, but are new exodus people who have entered the kingdom of

---

[111] Keener, *Romans*, pp. 81-82. Cf. J.R. Wagner, 'Baptism "Into Christ Jesus" and the Question of Universalism in Paul', *Horizons in Biblical Theology* 33 (2011), pp. 45-61.

[112] Fitzmyer, *Romans*, p. 438. 'Ontologically united with Christ through faith and baptism', they 'must deepen their faith continually to become more and more psychologically aware of that union'.

[113] Matera, *Romans*, p. 153.

righteousness and grace from the kingdom of sin and death through their faith and baptism.[114]

Conclusion: Results of Narrative Reading

It is beyond the scope of this project to propose a synthesis of Matthew and Romans with regard to their perspective on WB; however, it appears to be the case that they are closely aligned despite their distinct emphases. Both texts treat WB as an eschatological pneumatologically mediated event in which candidates who have repented, confessed, and proclaimed faith/trust in the death of resurrection of Jesus Christ are incorporated into the life of God and participate in the death and resurrection of Jesus Christ. In WB candidates experience an ontological change and receive a new identity that is to be reflected in transformed lives that more fully reflect the image of Jesus Christ in character, word, and deed. The ongoing process of transformation and ontological change is mediated through the Scriptures and the HS as disciples of Jesus integrate his teaching into their daily lives.

---

[114] See Y. Kwon, 'Baptism or Gospel of Grace?: Romans 6 Revisited', *ExpTim* 128.5 (2017), pp. 222-30, for his argument that a

> proper understanding of the gospel of grace includes: that everyone belongs to one of the two domains of authority (either under the domain of law/sin or under the domain of grace/Christ); that by the grace of God believers have experienced the transfer of lordship; and that despite this transfer, both aspects of 'already' and 'not yet' are creatively working together in Christian life.

PART III
DISCERNING THE VOICE OF THE SPIRIT

Up to this point, we have attempted to employ the Word-Spirit-Community Pentecostal hermeneutic in our project. First, we endeavored to hear the often-disparate voices of the Community relative to the theology and praxis of WB. Second, we sought to engage the Gospel of Matthew and Romans 6, via a close narrative reading, to hear the voice of the Word. The third part and sixth chapter attempt to construct a Pentecostal theology of WB, incorporating the voices of the Community and Word with voices from the larger scholarly community in an attempt to hear the voice of the Spirit leading forward.

6

EMBODIED PENTECOSTAL SPIRITUALITY

Introduction

Recent scholarship has argued for appreciating early Pentecostal theology through the lens of spirituality with emphases on orthopathy (right affections-affectivity), orthopraxy (right practices), and orthodoxy (right belief). In relationship to WB, Eucharist, footwashing, and Glossolalia, scholarly contributions have been offered that advance consideration of the ordinances as sacramental in nature.[1]

The contributions have employed a variety of approaches, all focusing on the person and work of the HS as an active participant in the administration and effect of the symbol or sign, *spiritually speaking*. While these contributions demonstrate the sanctifying effect of the sacraments on believer's affections scant attention was paid to the mind and human body and concept of embodiment in relation to the sacraments and soteriology. During the last ten years, Stephen Mills[2] and David Trementozzi[3] have independently offered contributions in theological anthropological ontology and soteriology that bridge the dualistic separation of mind and body

---

[1] Green, *Toward a Pentecostal Theology*.

[2] Stephen H. Mills, 'Renewal of the Mind: The Cognitive Sciences and a Pneumatological Anthropology of Transformation' (PhD dissertation, Regent University, 2014).

[3] David Trementozzi, 'Renewing the Christian Doctrine of Salvation: Toward a Dynamic & Transformational Soteriology' (PhD dissertation, Regent University, 2013).

through engagement of the cognitive sciences and psychology. Their research effectively demonstrates that envisioning faith (knowing God) and salvation are better construed as embodied and dynamic. By placing ontology and epistemology in conversation with the cognitive sciences and psychology they separately produce a holistic anthropology that effectively integrates reason, emotions, feelings, behaviors, learning, and embodiment. Furthermore, their revisioned anthropologies placed in dialogue with Pentecostal spirituality with its emphases on orthodoxy, orthopathy, and orthopraxy yield a more holistic soteriology that reflects salvation as dynamic, holistic, and multidimensional. While neither scholar fully addresses the meaning and importance of WB, it is my contention that a project of revisioning a Pentecostal theology of WB must incorporate insights from the cognitive sciences and psychology which place embodiment as a central tenet of what it means to be a person. It is to the findings of the cognitive sciences that we now turn our attention.

Cognitive Scientific Perspectives

David Trementozzi has demonstrated that conservative evangelicals have historically conceptualized soteriology primarily as an intellectual or cognitive activity, resulting in a restrictive focus on right belief, doctrine, or right knowledge (orthodoxy). Since 1993 with the publication of *Pentecostal Spirituality*[4] by Steven J. Land some Pentecostal scholars have expanded their treatments of soteriology to include orthopathy and orthopraxis. Nonetheless, emphasis on the intellectual or cognitive activity involved in belief in Jesus remains prominent in the above-mentioned theological traditions.

In the face of an intellectualized approach to anthropology and soteriology the results of cognitive and neurological research provide resources that enable a fuller understanding and appreciation for cognition that is more than a purely intellectual activity. The recent discoveries in the neurosciences suggest that practices, emotions, and embodiment are essential to human cognition. Lackoff and Johnson posit how research in the cognitive sciences provides a new way of conceptualizing human cognition:

---

[4] Land, *Pentecostal Spirituality*.

Cognitive science, the science of the mind and the brain, has in its brief existence been enormously fruitful. It has given us a way to know ourselves better, to see how our physical being – flesh, blood, sinew, hormone, cell, and synapse – and all things we encounter daily in the world make us who we are.[5]

Trementozzi, following Lackoff and Johnson, asserts that 'Such research has helped set the stage for alternative construals of cognition in which rationality, emotions, and behaviors are integrated and inseparable'.[6] Antonio Damasio and Reuven Feuerstein, representing neuroscience and psychology respectively, are major contributors who have provided 'alternative construals of cognition'. Damasio's contribution on the neurobiology of feelings and emotions stresses the embodied and emotional state of human cognition as well as Feuerstein's contribution in learning theory emphasizes the embodiment of cognition with the transformational potential of behavioral and neurological change in the learning process through Mediated Learning Experiences (MLE). It is to further consideration of the contributions of Damasio and Feuerstein that we turn attention.

Antonio Damasio[7]

In *Descartes' Error*, Damasio challenges the legacy of the 17th century French philosopher, Rene Descartes, who posited a separation between body, brain, mind, and emotion (Cartesian dualism). Damasio overtly rejects dualism between emotion and intellect. He asserts that emotion and feeling are vital aspects of rationality, identifying Descartes' error as

> the abyssal separation between body and mind, between the sizable, dimensioned, mechanically operated, infinitely divisible body stuff, on the one hand, and the unsizable, undimensioned,

---

[5] G. Lackoff and M. Johnson, *Philosophy in the Flesh: The Embodied Mind and its Challenge to Western Thought* (New York: Basic Books, 1999), p. 568.

[6] Trementozzi, 'Renewing the Christian Doctrine of Salvation', p. 48.

[7] Antonio Damasio (born February 25, 1944) is the University Professor of Psychology, Philosophy and Neurology, and David Dornsife Chair in Neuroscience at the University of Southern California (USC); he is also an adjunct professor at the Salk Institute in La Jolla, CA. Damasio has made seminal contributions to the understanding of brain processes underlying, emotions, feelings, decision-making, and consciousness.

un-pushpullable, nondivisible mind stuff; the suggestion that reasoning, and moral judgment, and the suffering that comes from physical pain or emotional upheaval might exist separately from the body. Specifically: the separation of the most refined operations of the mind from the structure and operation of a biological organism.[8]

Damasio bases the rejection of Cartesian dualism on his discovery that brain-damaged patients with unscathed intellectual capacities but with decreased or nonexistent emotional responsiveness were seriously impacted in their abilities to function socially. While patients did not lack the intellectual content, they were impotent to process their knowledge in a way that granted them the ability to thrive personally or interact socially in a meaningful fashion.[9] Damasio expands on the importance of emotion, positing

> The process of learning and recalling emotionally competent events is different with conscious feelings from what it would be without feelings. Some feelings optimize learning and recall. Other feelings, extremely painful feelings in particular, perturb learning and protectively suppress recall. In general, memory of the felt situation promotes, consciously or not, the avoidance of events associated with negative feelings and the seeking of situations that may cause positive feelings.[10]

Thus, Damasio, argues that cognition does not operate independently from emotions but depends on key brain systems that also process emotion.[11] Additionally, Damasio challenges contemporary versions of dualism that acknowledge integration between the mind and brain but disregard the relationship between mind and body.[12] For Damasio emotions and cognition are inextricably linked.

---

[8] A. Damasio, *Descartes' Error: Emotion, Reason, and the Human Brain* (London: Vintage Books, 2006), pp. 249-50.

[9] Damasio provides specific examples of this claim in his discussion of Phineas Gage and his modern counterpart 'Elliott' in chapters one and three of *Descartes' Error*.

[10] A. Damasio, *Looking for Spinoza: Joy, Sorrow, and the Feeling Brain* (New York: Harcourt, Inc., 2003), p. 178.

[11] Damasio, *Descartes' Error*, p. 245.

[12] Damasio, *Descartes' Error*, pp. 247-48.

Moreover, Damasio contends emotions do not just act upon cognition but are integral to cognition.[13]

According to Damasio, as the body maintains homeostasis, it continually employs information from the emotions correlated to the body-proper.[14] He contends that feelings emerge and correspond with certain body states of the organism and that certain modes of thinking network with particular emotions derived from its corresponding body state.[15] Furthermore, Damasio attests that 'a feeling is the perception of a certain state of the body along with the perception of a certain mode of thinking and of thoughts with certain themes'.[16] Hence, at a neurological level, Damasio argues that dualism between intellect and emotion must be rejected. Similarly, dualism between the body and intellect must be rejected since emotion and reason are both neurologically emergent realities totally dependent on human embodiment. In sum, per Damasio, without the body, there is no emotion; without the body, there is no mind.

Another reason Damasio is significant for this project is because he portrays how emotions are not only integral to cognitive function but are also indivisible from the body. The Cartesian bifurcation of brain and body and separation between the mind and body are both rejected. Damasio posits: 'It is not only the separation between mind and brain that is mythical: the separation between mind and body is probably just as fictional. The mind is embodied, in the full sense of the term, not just embrained'.[17] Damasio contends cognitive scientists must impartially grant the mind-body relationship for what it is:

> In the most popular and current of the modem views, the mind and brain go together, on one side, and the body (that is, the entire organism minus the brain) goes on the other side. Now the split

---

[13] Per Damasio, *Descartes' Error*, p. 200, The action of biological drives, body states, and emotions may be an indispensable foundation for rationality. The lower levels in the neural edifice of reason are the same that regulate the processing of emotions and feelings, along with global functions of the body proper such that the organism can survive.

[14] Damasio, *Looking for Spinoza*, pp. 30-40.

[15] Damasio, *Looking for Spinoza*, p. 85.

[16] Damasio, *Looking for Spinoza*, p. 86.

[17] Damasio, *Descartes' Error*, p. 118.

separates brain and 'body-proper' and the explanation of how mind and brain are related becomes more difficult when the brain-part of the body is divorced from the body-proper.[18]

Damasio avers that conjoining the brain with the mind is common practice in the cognitive sciences. However, Damasio acknowledges this does not automatically dismiss the charge of dualism. Per Damasio, the 'body' must refer to the entire body (i.e., body-proper), not just the brain. Based on his work with neurological patients, Damasio asserts that cognition is inseparable from embodiment.[19] Damasio posits

> What I am suggesting is that the mind arises from activity in neural circuits ... and that a normal mind will happen only if those circuits contain basic representations of the organism. I am not saying that the mind is in the body. I am saying that the body contributes more than life support and modulatory effects to the brain. It contributes a content that is part and parcel of the workings of the normal mind.[20]

Damasio asserts that while the mind, body, and brain can be separated under a microscope they are part of a single organism that is intact in 'normal operating circumstances'.[21] In short, Damasio deconstructs two dualistic premises, emotion vs. reason and mind vs. body, which have contributed to modern intellectualism and disembodiment.

Similarly, Damasio parts company with other neuroscientists in relation to the separation of mind from body when they explain the

---

[18] Damasio, *Looking for Spinoza*, p. 190.

[19] Damasio, *Descartes' Error,* pp. 173-75. Damasio's Somatic Marker Hypothesis maintains that the body is a 'topographic map' upon which the limbic system spreads out and perceives various bodily sensations (body states) in conjunction with certain conditions and situations. These body states form the fundamental background feeling from which emotions develop. In other words, somatic markers are a special instance of feelings generated from secondary emotions. Those emotions and feelings have been connected, by learning, to predicted future outcomes of certain scenarios. Accordingly, the physiological context from which emotions result and reasoning arises is provided by the body proper.

[20] Damasio, *Descartes' Error*, p. 226.

[21] Damasio, *Looking for Spinoza*, p. 195.

mind 'solely in terms of brain events'.[22] He rejects such a reduction as 'unnecessarily incomplete, and humanly unsatisfactory'.[23] Trementozzi, echoing Damasio, asserts, 'It is one thing when a person scientifically identifies the myriad processes of cognitive function; it is another when that person treats these functions as anything but holistic in design'.[24]

In addition to the contributions of neuroscience are the findings of cognitive psychology which contribute additional perspectives on the embodied scope of reasoning and learning. In the following section, I explore the work of cognitive psychologist and learning theorist, Reuven Feuerstein, and his research in embodied mediated learning.

Reuven Feuerstein[25]

Reuven Feuerstein (1921-2014), an Israeli clinical, developmental, and cognitive psychologist, specialized in the study of learning theory, and provided an alternative account for the subjectivity and embodiment of the human mind. Before exploring Feuerstein's contribution to the field of cognitive psychology, I acknowledge that some may argue that applying the findings from the cognitive psychology to Scripture appears anachronistic. However, I proffer that such an objection is premature, especially because Feuerstein's optimism regarding the modifiability of intelligence, the intellect emotion, and body in particular, flows from a faith perspective grounded in the OT.[26]

---

[22] Damasio, *Descartes' Error*, pp. 250-51.
[23] Damasio, *Descartes' Error*, p. 251.
[24] Trementozzi, 'Renewing the Christian Doctrine of Salvation', p. 53.
[25] Reuven Feuerstein, Refael S. Feuerstein, and Louis H. Falik, *Beyond Smarter* (New York: Teachers College Press, 2010), p. 24. Professor Reuven Feuerstein was the founder of the Feuerstein Institute and served as its chairman until his passing in 2014. A clinical, developmental, and cognitive psychologist, Professor Feuerstein is responsible for the vision, essence, ideas, and practices that make up the Feuerstein Institute.
[26] Feuerstein asserts his belief in the modifiability of the two components of intelligence, the intellect, and the emotion, is an expression of *faith*. He offers,

> The word is used despite the fact that from a position of *science* one has the inclination and training to divest oneself completely from such an 'unscientific' term. But the point we wish to emphasize is that in the beginning there must be a need – a need that will generate the belief in human modifiability. I must

As a devout orthodox Jew and theist, Feuerstein believed humanity was created as the *imago Dei* (Gen. 1.26-27). Moreover, humanity can be renewed in knowledge and in the image of his Creator, which involves the mind and heart. The image of God includes the whole person, in structure and function. Feuerstein assumed the dynamic capacity of cognition, positing that reasoning is inseparable from and interdependent with emotions and embodied behaviors.[27]

Feuerstein, trained under the renowned cognitive psychologist Jean Piaget, concurred with his mentor that individuals learn and progress through various learning stages. In a major departure from Piaget, Feuerstein rejected the concept of a 'fixed stages' level of cognitive skills. Rather, Feuerstein asserted the plasticity of cognitive abilities could be structurally modifiable through the intervention of human mediation in the learning process throughout a person's lifetime.[28] Also, Feuerstein claimed that the brain can exhibit plasticity and physically modify itself, despite biological and cultural

---

have the need to have my students and those with who I am engaged reach higher potentials of functioning. This need energizes me to act and motivates my faith (belief) that there are positive, effective, and meaningful alternatives to be found, to fight for, and to bring this faith into being. I believe that the student is a modifiable being who is capable of change and capable of changing according to his or her will and decisions. Human beings' modifiability differentiates them from other creatures and, according to the Rabbinic Midrash, 'even from the angels.' Herein lies the main uniqueness of human beings. Feuerstein, Feuerstein, and Falik, *Beyond Smarter*, p. 6. Italics original.

[27] Also, Shmuel Feuerstein, *Biblical and Talmudic Antecedents of Mediated Learning Experience Theory: Educational and Didactic Implications for Inter-Generational Cultural Transmission* (Israel: The International Center for the Enhancement of Learning Potential, 2002), pp. 6-13. R. Feuersteins's work was directed toward improving the cognitive abilities of children deprived of healthy reasoning abilities. The children suffered from genetically derived intellectual or mental disabilities or from cultural or physical deprivation. His theories have been tested and proven applicable across a wide range of populations, ranging from a sixty-five-year-old retiree returning to school to a child struggling with Down Syndrome.

[28] Piaget asserted that unless individuals successfully learned certain cognitive skills within specified age ranges, they were not likely to learn them later. See Ruth Burgess, 'Reuven Feuerstein: Propelling Change, Promoting Continuity', in Alex Kozulin and Yaacov Rand (eds), *Experience of Mediated Learning: An Impact of Feuerstein's Theory in Education and Psychology* (New York: Pergamon, 2000), p. 7. Burgess clarifies that Feuerstein rejected Piaget's notion of fixed stages, asserting 'that the order and timing of cognitive development is set, not by maturation, but by mediated social experiences'.

deprivations.[29] Thus, as the brain exhibits plasticity, it has the capacity to transcend deprivations sustained at earlier stages of cognitive development. Feuerstein's work directly progressed from this awareness of brain plasticity through his practice of mediated learning. Based on his vast experience and research, Feuerstein formulated the theory of Structural Cognitive Modifiability (SCM) that avers three basic ideas:

1. Three forces shape human beings: environment, human biology, and mediation.

2. Temporary states determine behavior: How someone behaves – namely emotional, intellectual, and even habitually learned activities – represents a temporary state, not a permanent trait. This means that intelligence is adaptive. In other words, intelligence can change; it is not fixed once and for all.

3. The brain is plastic: because all behaviors are open and developing, the brain can generate new structures through a combination of external and internal factors.[30]

The central hypothesis of Feuerstein's SCM is that cognition is more adequately understood as potential rather than accumulated knowledge. His theory maintains that a person's cognitive potential is modifiable regardless of heredity, genetic disorder, chromosomal disorders, age, social, physical, and psychological causes responsible for impairment. Feuerstein's theory challenges the modern intellectualist's exclusive attention on rational activity abstracted from performative[31] relationships and behavior and invites a more

---

[29] When the brain is called upon to adapt, activities generated by the interaction between the organism and one's culture change the structure of the brain. This involves the neural networks, the relationships between parts of the cortical system, relay systems, blood flow, electrical activities of the brain – in short, the entire range of neuro-physiological functions of the brain and its related systems. Reuven Feuerstein, Y. Rand, Louis H. Falik, and Refael. S. Feuerstein, *The Dynamic Assessment of Cognitive Modifiability* (Jerusalem, Israel: International Center for the Enhancement of Learning Potential, 2002), p. 73.

[30] Reuven Feuerstein et al., *The Feuerstein Instrumental Enrichment Program* (Jerusalem: ICELP Publications, 2006), pp. 25–27.

[31] Performativity is the power of language to effect change in the world: language does not simply describe the world but may instead (or also) function as

embodied and holistic model of learning. Feuerstein asserts the ability for a person to increase cognitive development depends on adequate exposure to mediated learning.[32] He posits that since human learning is dynamic and multidimensional, exposing individuals solely to unmediated learning encounters limits them in the degree to which they can fully actualize that encounter. In other words, learning suffers when embodiment and subjectivity are limited in cognition. Moreover, Feuerstein posits that individuals can rise above obstacles and modify their cognitive capabilities even if they have been deprived by lack of educational opportunities or faced physical or mental handicaps, tragedies, sickness, or disaster.[33] While many cognitive scientists argue that human cognition is locked in by genetic endowments and the ability to change is greatly limited, Feuerstein discovered a greater degree of cognitive modifiability in students experiencing significant deficiencies than many neuroscientists might be willing to cede.[34] Trementozzi asserts that Feuerstein challenges the static epistemology of modem intellectualism that envisions knowledge as accumulated facts and pieces of information; rather,

---

a form of social action. The concept of performative language was first described by the philosopher J.L. Austin who asserted that there was a difference between constative language, which describes the world and can be evaluated as true or false, and performative language, which does something in the world. For Austin, performative language included speech acts such as promising, swearing, betting, and performing a marriage ceremony. For a discussion of Performativity see A. McKinlay, 'Performativity: From J.L. Austin to Judith Butler', in Peter Armstrong and Geoff Lightfoot (eds), *The Leading Journal in the Field': Destabilizing Authority in the Social Sciences of Management* (London: MayFlyBooks, 2010), pp. 119-42.

[32] Rafi S. Feuerstein, 'Dynamic Cognitive Assessment and the Instrumental Enrichment Program: Origins and Development,' in Kozulin and Rand (eds.), *Experience of Mediated Learning,* p. 158.

[33] Feuerstein's early work was with Holocaust survivors who had experienced significant deprivation, hardship, and trauma, adversely impacting their cognitive and emotional development.

[34] Consequently, Feuerstein eschews static IQ tests since they only measure how much a person has already learned rather than their potential to learn. He takes issue with the highly influential book, *Bell Curve,* by Hernstein and Murray, from which the standard practice of IQ testing has largely derived (Richard J. Hernstein and Charles Murray, T*he Bell Curve: Intelligence and Class Structure in American Life* (New York: Simon & Shuster, 1996). Feuerstein contests that these authors 'present human beings as unmodifiable entities for whom the cognitive intellectual factor (as measured by IQ tests) is what determines their place in the world' (Feuerstein, Feuerstein, and Falik, *Beyond Smarter,* p. 86).

he recommends a dynamic construal of cognition more in terms of potential that associates knowledge with skills, intentionality, and practices.[35]

Based on his theory of SCM, Feuerstein's Mediated Learning Experience (MLE) delineates the dynamic interplay between a teacher serving as the mediator and a learner. Specifically, MLE is an interaction in which a teacher/mediator who possesses knowledge intends to convey a particular meaning or skill and encourages the student/recipient to transcend, that is, to relate the meaning to some other thought or experience. Mediation is intended to help the recipient expand their cognitive capacity, especially when ideas are new or challenging. Moreover, mediated learning incorporates intersubjective items like appreciation of culture, interests, likes and dislikes, in such a way that as curiosity is raised, so too is the motivation to learn and the ability to make sense of the subject matter.[36]

As noted above, Feuerstein's MLE learning is better understood in terms of potential rather than as a determined cognitive ability. Through the embodied practice of mediation, a person's reasoning ability can be transformed, regardless of psychometric measures.[37] With MLE, the learner is physically and emotionally engaged in the learning process through specific behaviors loaded with subjective meaning. For our purposes it is important to consider how MLE works, per Feuerstein.[38]

In mediated learning a human mediator can transform direct learning into mediated learning when they intervene in the learning

---

[35] Trementozzi, 'Renewing the Christian Doctrine of Salvation', pp. 59-60.

[36] Feuerstein, Feuerstein, and Falik, *Beyond Smarter*, p. 24.

[37] (i.e., IQ tests).

[38] It is informative to note the differences between the approaches of Piaget and Feuerstein. Piaget argued for a natural progression of learning through direct exposure to stimuli, or the 'stimulus-organism-response (S-O-R)' model, which posits that it is sufficient for a person to dialogue directly with nature and the environment for cognitive development to occur. In contrast to Piaget, Feuerstein asserted a human mediator is needed, or 'stimulus-human-organism-human-response (S-H-O-H-R)', allowing the mediator to take the learner beyond the natural limitations to reaching their full cognitive potential. Reuven Feuerstein, Louis H. Falik, and Refael S. Feuerstein, *Changing Minds & Brains—The Legacy of Reuven Feuerstein: Higher Thinking and Cognition Through Mediated Learning* (New York: Teachers College Press, 2015), pp. 5-11.

encounter and locate themselves between the learner and the stimulus and between the learner and the response. The mediator selects, adjusts, amplifies, and interprets the stimuli that come to the learner and the learner's responses in terms that are culturally, ethnically, and intellectually discernible. When there is a deficiency in MLE, there tends to be an underdevelopment in an individual's cognitive functions and direct learning strategies. However, when mediated learning is present, a person's cognitive deficiency may improve and the individual will eventually progress into an independent and self-regulating learner.[39]

Feuerstein's pedagogical approach flows from his vision of cognition that recognizes the vital role that emotions and subjective features exert on the cognitive process. In a section where he speaks about early cognitive development in children, Feuerstein says, 'It is undoubtedly true that, for MLE to occur, affection and emotional involvement of parents and siblings are important'.[40] Moreover, Feuerstein places significant impact on the influence of affective motivational causes impinging on the cognitive process. Where such motivation is missing, cognitive function is hindered, and when present it is improved.[41] It is critical to note that while Feuerstein often speaks about the influence of behavior (relative to MLE) it is never separated from the affective and emotional context that either increase or decrease motivation for the particular behavior. The very practice of MLE presupposes an affective context for mediation to occur effectively.

Feuerstein employs an embodied cognitive paradigm because his pedagogy is known for the prominent role that behaviors play on the reasoning process. The place of behavior is directly seen in his MLE as both the student and mediator engage one another with various behaviors and practices that foster the mediation of the targeted learning content. The types of behaviors that characterize Feuerstein's MLE exhibit at least four qualities. The significance of the qualities is that they all require specific emotional attributes and unique pedagogical practices (behaviors) embodied in the mediator

---

[39] Feuerstein, Falik, and Feuerstein, *Changing Minds*, pp. 5-11.

[40] R. Feuerstein, *Instrumental Enrichment: An Intervention Program for Cognitive Modifiability* (Baltimore, MD: University Park Press, 1980), p. 47.

[41] Feuerstein, *Instrumental Enrichment*, pp. 74-75.

and learner. As the mediator mediates or transfers these qualities to the learner and the learner internalizes them as part of their cognitive experience, learning becomes transformational.[42]

Concisely, brain plasticity is the underlying cognitive belief from which all of Feuerstein's research proceeds. While Feuerstein illustrates cognitive modifiability at behavioral and intellectual levels,

---

[42] See R. Feuerstein, Y. Rand, and J. E. Rynders, *Don't Accept Me as I Am: Helping 'Retarded' People to Excel* (New York: Plenum Press, 1988), pp. 64-66 for the following points of discussion. The authors describe eleven characteristics that distinguish MLE from other types of learning interaction. Mediated learning is marked by 1.) Intentionality and reciprocity, 2.) Transcendence, 3.) Mediation of meaning, 4.) Mediation of feelings of competence, 5.) Mediated regulation and control of behavior, 6.) Mediated sharing behavior, 7.) Mediation of individuation and psychological differentiation, 8.) Mediation of goal seeking, goal setting, goal planning, and achieving behavior 9.) Mediation of challenge: The search for novelty and complexity, 10.) Mediation of awareness of the human being as a changing entity, 11.) Mediation of an optimistic alternative. When these qualities are integrated in the learning encounter (via a mediator) a host of subjective items contribute to the cognitive process that not only allow learning to occur but also leads to transformation (i.e., modification) of the learner. Only the first four noted above are addressed below as they are sufficient for the purposes of this project. First and second, intentionality and reciprocity characterize mediated learning. They alternately speak of commitment by the mediator and demonstration of learning by the learner. Feuerstein avers that mediated learning can only be demonstrated to have occurred if the mediator is certain the message (i.e., learning content) truly reached the intended learner. Intentionality and reciprocity refer to the emotional state of the mediator and learner via a specific attitudinal mindset of motivation. Third, transcendence marks MLE in that the mediator produces flexibility in the learner so learning can transcend the immediate context in which it was received. Transcendence is the ability to apply learning to new contexts through linking subjectively relevant content to the learning encounter. Fourth, MLE mediates meaning to the learner that transforms an abstract or random learning context into one that is relevant and meaningful to the learner. Feuerstein posits that mediation of meaning requires subjectivity since it involves the 'energetic, affective, and emotional power' needed to make the meditational encounter overcome the normal resistance exerted by a learner and assures that the 'stimuli mediated will indeed be experienced' by the learner. Thus, a multidimensional and transformational belief about cognition undergirds Feuerstein's pedagogy. He maintains that learning consists of significantly more than an intellectual accumulation of facts and that emotions and behaviors are just as crucial as intellectual ability. Education is more than the sole accumulation of knowledge or skills because it (via MLE) has the potential to transform and modify an individual.

it is also indicated at the physiological level. In other words, Feuerstein's paradigm of cognition demonstrates that the subjective factors of emotion and behavior (via MLE) as central to cognitive function produce physical change in the brain structure. Echoing Damasio, Feuerstein posits that neuroscience can finally provide a physiological basis for SCM.[43]

Thus, solid neurological evidence and support now extends to the concepts of SCM and MLE. Therefore, Feuerstein's research demonstrates an embodied cognition, illustrating how emotions, feelings, and behaviors profoundly influence reasoning (MLE), and establishes how a mediated pedagogy is transformational at all levels. Furthermore, Feuerstein contends that learning is more effective when intellectual content is mediated.[44] Finally, Feuerstein maintains that emotionally laden knowledge not only transforms the learning capacities of 'mediated learners', but so too can affectively charged experiences physically transform the brain.[45] Accordingly, presupposing an affective context for mediation, Feuerstein uncovers how a mediated pedagogy is physiologically transformational.

Summary

In summary, the contributions of Antonio Damasio and Reuven Feuerstein explored above, represent new developments in the cognitive neurosciences and psychology that invite a more holistic

---

[43] Feuerstein, Feuerstein, and Falik, *Beyond Smarter*, p. 134. Feuerstein posits:
Today, however, the neurosciences bring us evidence not only of the modifiability of the individual's mental functions, but also that the changes that can be produced are changes in both the hardware and the software of the neural system. It is now no exaggeration to state that the neural system is modified by the behavior, no less than the behavior is determined by the neural system.

[44] Through his Mediated Learning Experience (MLE), the learner is physically and emotionally engaged in the pedagogical process through a mediator who fills particular behaviors with subjective meaning. The mediator selects, adjusts, amplifies, and interprets the stimuli that come to the learner and the learner's responses in terms that are culturally, ethnically, and intellectually meaningful. In other words, as the mediator translates knowledge to the learner in ways that are emotionally relevant and familiar, learning is more effective. Feuerstein, Feuerstein, and Falik, *Beyond Smarter*, p. 24.

[45] Feuerstein, Feuerstein, and Falik, *Beyond Smarter*, 139. Feuerstein reports:
Research is suggesting that the human brain can generate new brain cells, even into old age. If the brain is stimulated, at any stage in the life span, it will adapt, regenerate, and become more efficient. It reinforces our initial and ongoing theoretical hypotheses and confirms our methodological developments.

understanding of humanity, in general, and of learning and knowing as cognitive, affective, and embodied. Their research demonstrates that cognition, affectivity, and embodiment in a natural and social world are inextricably intertwined. More specifically, Damasio and Feuerstein are relevant for this project since it shows how cognition is an embodied and interpersonal-social phenomenon involving subjective realities that is accompanied by meaning making. Building on the work of R. Feuerstein, Shmuel Feuerstein has argued that a more holistic understanding of learning and knowing as embodied, cognitive, and affective is found throughout the history of the people of God as reflected in the OT. It is to an exploration of S. Feuerstein argument that we next turn attention.

Embodied Cognition and Ontological Change in the Hebrew Scripture and Tradition

The theistic foundations to MLE are further developed by Shmuel Feuerstein, colleague, and brother of Reuven Feuerstein. S. Feuerstein elucidates the foundations of the theory of MLE, asserting that mediated learning is central, both explicitly and implicitly, in the OT narratives, commandments, rituals, experiences, rites, festivals. Furthermore, he demonstrates the relationships between events, religious precepts, and conduct with a modern psycho-educational theory. S. Feuerstein posits that within the OT there is a strong emphasis on the process of identification in Judaism, and mediation is the vehicle through which a sense of identity is instilled.[46] He asserts

> There are a whole series of qualities and attributes related to God which the human being learns to aspire to. The individual is asked

---

[46] Feuerstein, *Biblical and Talmudic Antecedents*, p. 11. Cf., Adrian Hinkle, Pentecostal scholar, and Dean of College of Theology & Ministry at Oral Roberts University has combined OT studies with the educational theories of Howard Gardner (Multiple Intelligences theory) and Neil Fleming's VARK learning styles (visual, aural, reading/writing, kinesthetic) in an attempt to engage issues of pedagogy within ancient Israel. See, Adrian E. Hinkle, *Pedagogical Theory of the Hebrew Bible: An Application of Education Theory to Biblical Texts* (Eugene, OR: Wipf & Stock, 2016) and Adrian E. Hinkle, *Pedagogical Theory of Wisdom Literature: An Application of Education Theory to Biblical Texts* (Eugene, OR: Wipf & Stock, 2017).

to act in the image of God as is stated: God made man in his image. This image becomes the rationale for identification with characteristics that are attributed to the image of God. Identification is not only an emotional, volitional or motivational act but is probably one of the first and strongest requirements placed on the Jewish person.[47]

Noteworthy for our project is Feuerstein's assertion that the events, rites, and narratives contained in the Torah are designed to fulfill three functions: First, they convey an *explicit* message; i.e., the description of the historical events themselves, which are at the core of the development of the Jewish nation since its inception, starting with Abraham, Isaac, and Jacob and continuing through slavery in Egypt, redemption, the Divine revelation at Mount Sinai and the wanderings in the desert until the children of Israel reach the Holy Land. Second, they transmit an *implicit* message; namely, the transmission of a value system based upon justice, social involvement, identification with the community, care for the needy and handicapped and so forth. Third, they orient the individual to a *mode of perception* that can be applied in the variety of situations he or she may encounter in the future. This feature of cultural transmission is ensured by the mediated quality of the transmission, marked by the intentionality and reciprocity built into the transmission, and the mediation of meeting and transcendence.[48]

Our close narrative reading of the Gospel of Matthew appears to reveal a similar OT pattern and usage of narrative, rite, and event relative to WB. Jesus' command to his disciples in Mt. 28.19-20, 'Go, therefore, and make disciples of all the nations, baptizing them in the name of the Father and the Son and the Holy Spirit, teaching them to follow all that I commanded you; and behold, I am with you always, to the end of the age', seems to focus on the process of identification with Jesus Christ and becoming conformed to the likeness of Jesus through learning from his teachings as well as the way he taught. The goal of learning is not to amass information, but to be changed or transformed. Also, Rom. 6.1-11 appears to employ the usage of narrative, rite, and event to stress identification with

---

[47] Feuerstein, *Biblical and Talmudic Antecedents*, pp. 11-12.
[48] Feuerstein, *Biblical and Talmudic Antecedents*, pp. 162-63.

Jesus' death, burial, and resurrection and the transformative effect of the mediated rite. It appears to be the case that WB as a mediated event serves as a vehicle through which a sense of identity is instilled in the new disciple. Moreover, the formation and instillation of identity is transformative. Echoing Feuerstein, I assert there are a whole series of qualities and attributes related to Jesus Christ to which the new disciple of Jesus learns to aspire – to become like Jesus Christ in terms of character, thought, word, and deed. The disciple is asked to act in the image of Jesus Christ. The image of Jesus Christ becomes the rationale for identification with characteristics that are attributed to his person and image. Consequently, identification with Jesus Christ is the first and strongest requirements placed on the new disciple of Jesus. In other words, identification with the death, burial, and resurrection effects ontological change because it is an emotional, volitional, cognitive, or motivational act. Moreover, identification with Jesus is transformative for the body since cognition, affectivity, and embodiment are inextricably intertwined.

Embodied Pentecostal Soteriology

While it appears that early Pentecostals had an appreciation for the importance of the human body as the loci for the work of the HS, especially in relation to SB as evidenced by speaking in other tongues and manifested in worship, it does not appear they reflected theologically on the dynamic and embodied nature of soteriology, nor, on the ordinances of WB and the Eucharist as more than mere symbol.[49] In constructing a revisioned Pentecostal theology of WB, informed and resourced by our close reading of early Pentecostal literature, the contributions of Pentecostal scholars and church leaders, the cognitive and neurological sciences, and the narrative reading of Matthew and Romans, it appears that theological reflection on WB mandates a revisioning of WB that incorporates embodied human experience, a dynamic pneumatic soteriology, and apprehending WB as an ontologically eschatological transformative event that impacts the person in all aspects of his or her being.

---

[49] While some early Pentecostals valued footwashing as an ordinance, early Pentecostals unanimously viewed WB and the Eucharist as the ordinances of the Church.

As noted previously, Damasio argues for a more holistic understanding of persons that disavows Cartesian dualism and R. Feuerstein demonstrates learning and knowing as cognitive, embodied, affective, and relational. S. Feuerstein demonstrates that OT educational models reflect mediated learning that addresses people holistically and relationally in terms of their cognition, embodied selves, and affections, designed to effect ontological change in the people of God through ceremony, teaching, preaching, and ritual. From the work of the above-mentioned scholars, it seems reasonable to anticipate that MLE would be found in the NT as well, since the NT reflects a Hebraic worldview and theological grounding in the OT. It is my contention, based on the narrative reading of Matthew and Romans, that the practice of WB does indeed bear all the marks of a MLE, the same as those found in the OT, and that WB as mediated rite of the church effects ontological change in the candidate as he or she confesses faith in Christ and is born anew of the HS through the HS. It is to a brief consideration of Pentecostal soteriology as embodied that we first turn our attention.

Scholarly appreciation for the embodied nature of Pentecostal spirituality, experience worship, and practice was first articulated in Steve Land's ground-breaking *Pentecostal Spirituality*, where he opines the point of Pentecostal spirituality is 'to experience life as part of a biblical drama of participation in God's history'. Moreover, 'their concern was not so much with an *ordo salutis* as a *via salutis*. The narrative of salvation provided the structure for formation within the missionary movement.'[50] Per Land, 'the gathered community was engaged in the formation process in which all the elements of corporate worship ... contributed to preparing people to be called to new birth, sanctification, HS baptism, and a life of missionary engagement and witness'.[51] Land asserts that 'these ways of remembering the biblical Word mediated the biblical realities in a kind of Pentecostal sacramentality',[52] 'where learning about God and

---

[50] Land, *Pentecostal Spirituality*, p. 67. Land identifies the elements of corporate worship as – 'singing, preaching, testifying, witnessing, and the ordinances of water baptism, the Lord's Supper, and footwashing, altar calls, prayer meetings, and the exercise of the gifts of the Spirit'.

[51] Land, *Pentecostal Spirituality*, p. 67.

[52] Land, *Pentecostal Spirituality*, p. 67.

directly experiencing God perpetually inform and depend upon one another'.[53] Learning about God and directly experiencing God were body-mind-spirit engagements with the HS. The total embodied experience was necessary since spirituality encompassed the person's whole being, every aspect of his or her personhood. Moreover, 'the correspondence between Spirit and body is evident in a great variety of psychomotor celebration'.[54] Land posits that 'when the congergation gathered for worship they moved as one body-mind-spirit in response to the Holy Spirit'.[55] Furthermore, Land posits Spirit-body correspondence was also evidenced in the ordinances of the Lord's Supper, WB, and footwashing. However, baptism was not a converting sacrament of initiation, according to Land. Rather, WB, was viewed as a means of grace in that it represented following Jesus Christ in public and was performed in acknowledgment of an individual's conversion and that all righteousness had been fulfilled Mt. 3.15. While Land addressed the embodied nature of Pentecostal spirituality in his references to 'psychomotor celebration', his argument appears to be weakened by his treatment of WB as symbol/sacrament without ontological impact even though he acknowledges the mediation of the HS in the baptismal event.

Similarly, K. Archer, building on the work of Land, provides a more nuanced view of WB as a means of grace, echoing a Wesleyan perspective, in his assertion that the 'sacraments are significant symbolic signs that bring transformative grace by bringing people into closer contact with the saving action of Jesus'.[56] Per Archer, 'the sacramental ordinances become means of grace for the receptive individuals-in-community'.[57] Moreover, they are not 'magical actions' or 'symbols of human response'. Rather, the sacramental ordinances are 'effective means of grace when inspired by the Holy Spirit and received by genuine human response in faith'.[58] He, therefore, calls for a revisioning of the 'historical' Pentecostal understanding of ordinances into 'sacramental' ordinances 'because in Pentecostal

---

[53] Moore, 'A Pentecostal Approach to Scripture', pp. 1, 2.
[54] Land, *Pentecostal Spirituality*, pp. 108-109.
[55] Land, *Pentecostal Spirituality*, p. 108.
[56] Archer, 'Nourishment for our Journey', p. 82.
[57] Archer, 'Nourishment for our Journey', p. 86.
[58] Archer, 'Nourishment for our Journey', p. 86.

worshipping communities these rites provide sacramental experiences for the faith-filled participants'.[59]

While it is beyond the scope of this project to investigate fully the relationship between WB and ecclesiology, I agree with Archer's position that the worshipping community is the proper context for engaging theological reflection and that WB should be placed within the theological framework of the way of salvation since the Pentecostal *via salutis* is a dynamic pneumatic soteriology.[60] Our close reading of the early Pentecostal periodicals reveals that great joy and celebration attended the WBs as the HS would come close and those gathered would praise God for another person had come to join them on the missionary journey to the kingdom of God. Thus, WB was individual, as well as corporate, since it served to remind the previously baptized of their own death and resurrection in Jesus Christ, and call to become a holy witness in the power of the HS.

Per Archer, the sacramental ordinances are redemptive experiences since they provide ongoing spiritual formation of being conformed to the image of Christ through the participatory reenactment of various parts of the story of Jesus Christ. To the dismay of Archer, there are some Pentecostals who 'deny any "real grace" being mediated through the participatory ordinance to the community'.[61] Consequently, these 'mysteries' are reduced to memorial rituals for cognitive reflection and emotional machinations devoid of the HS's presence and power.

According to Archer, WB is the sacramental ordinance that publicly proclaims a person's new identity in Jesus Christ and his community of disciples. New converts are baptized by immersion in water because Jesus commanded his followers to do so in Mt. 28.18-20. It is 'by immersion' since it best reenacts 'the salvific experience of identifying with the death and resurrection of Jesus (Rom. 6.4) for the forgiveness of sins (Acts 2.38)'.[62] Archer posits that WB

---

[59] Archer, 'Nourishment for our Journey', p. 85. See Archer, 'Nourishment for our Journey', p. 84 where Archer follows the lead of evangelical scholar Stanley Grenz, who argues for retaining the term ordinance and asserts the ordinances are channels for the HS to work in the lives of Christians, thereby serving as more than memorial rites.

[60] Archer, 'Nourishment for our Journey', pp. 81-82.

[61] Archer, 'Nourishment for our Journey', p. 84.

[62] Archer, 'Nourishment for our Journey', p. 91.

'recapitulates the protection of Noah and his family from divine judgment sent upon the wicked (Gen, 6-9; 1 Pet. 3.20-21) and also the Israelites' exodus deliverance through the waters of the Red Sea'.[63] Through their deliverance from the Red Sea, they emerged as 'a people belonging to God on "the way" to the promised land. Water baptism is the sacramental sign initiating one into the corporate *via salutis*.'[64]

While the focus of WB is on the candidate, it is not on the candidate alone. The community members witness the candidate's baptism and are also beckoned by the HS to relive their own initiatory salvific experiences. Thus, they are called to reidentify themselves as part of the redemptive community – the body of Jesus Christ.

Archer offers that baptism also functions to direct us to the 'ultimate goal of salvation – glorification and the redemption of creation. It is a promise that creates hope and reshapes our identity as we proleptically participate in the redemptive experience.'[65] Archer states that 'We are the eschatological community of God and, as this community, we function as a redemptive sacrament for the world – the body of Christ broken for the healing of the nations'.[66]

From our above review of Land and Archer it appears that embodied spirituality is in view in their writings. On the one hand, while Land acknowledges and presses for embodied spirituality through various Pentecostal experiences, including the ordinances or sacramental ordinances, through which persons encounter the grace of God through the HS, he stops short of acknowledging ontological change in the participants or gathered community through the ordinances. Archer, on the other hand, speaks of WB as a sacramental act that effects ontological change in candidates and the witnessing community; however, he stops short of addressing the nature of the ontological changes.

In view of the findings of Damasio and Feuerstein and the writings of Land and Archer, it appears to be the case that a more robust understanding of WB whereby ontological change occurs in the embodied candidate and gathered community as embodied

---

[63] Archer, 'Nourishment for our Journey', p. 91.
[64] Archer, 'Nourishment for our Journey', p. 91.
[65] Archer, 'Nourishment for our Journey', p. 91.
[66] Archer, 'Nourishment for our Journey', p. 91.

participants is in order. I find significant assistance in this endeavor in the work of Amos Yong. It is to a consideration of Yong that we turn our attention.

My argument for advancing a Pentecostal theology of WB that is sacramental pneumatologically, whereby ontological change is effected in the baptismal candidate, finds coherence with Amos Yong's views on WB, who articulates his views with the assistance of the ecumenical *BEM*. First, Yong asserts the invocation of the HS at the occurrence of the WB, in the context of worship and celebration, should proclaim the event as explicitly Christian and locate the sacramentality in the presence, power, and activity of the HS and not in the materiality of the consecrated water.[67]

A second point highlighted by the *BEM* is that WB 'enacts our participation in the death and resurrection of Christ and our conversion/cleansing but also represents our reception of the gift of the Holy Spirit'.[68] According to Yong, 'Baptism is, in this sense, a concrete experiencing of the death and life of Jesus (the body of Christ) (cf. Rom. 6:4; Gal. 3:27; Col. 2:12). It is both an invitation to identify with the death and life of Jesus and an actualization of this reenactment.'[69] Yong's 'concrete experiencing of the death and life of Jesus' is experienced by the whole person. To employ Wesleyan and Pentecostal language, WB becomes the 'crisis experience' or the historical point in time when one experiences the life of Jesus Christ by the power of the HS.[70]

Last, Yong avers that if WB is understood as a 'living and transformative act of the Spirit of God on the community of faith, then baptism is ... fully sacramental in the sense of enacting the life and grace of God to those who need and receive it by faith'.[71] It appears to be the case that the HS is the source of the life and grace of God who receive it by faith/trust in Jesus, highlighting the pneumatological nature of WB. More specifically, concerning WB, the Christological, pneumatological, and relational core is kept in focus. Again, the relational core of the individual is as an embodied

---

[67] Yong, *The Spirit Poured Out on All Flesh*, p. 158.
[68] Yong, *The Spirit Poured Out on All Flesh*, p. 159.
[69] Yong, *The Spirit Poured Out on All Flesh*, p. 159.
[70] Yong, *The Spirit Poured Out on All Flesh*, p. 159.
[71] Yong, *The Spirit Poured Out on All Flesh*, p. 160.

person. The focus on the relational core echoes the findings of Feuerstein and Feuerstein who argued for the relational nature of MLE. While WB is followed on the basis of Jesus' command (Mt. 28.19) and Jesus' example of being baptized by John (Mt. 3.16) – which Pentecostals seem to have picked up on – Jesus' baptism of the Spirit which stresses the pneumatological core of WB, appears to have been minimized by many Pentecostals.[72] The apparent minimization may be due to the differentiation made by Pentecostals between reception of the HS at conversion from HS baptism, since Matthew's portrayal of Jesus as the HS baptizer points beyond his resurrection and ascension to a future event independent of WB. Nonetheless, this differentiation in no way diminishes the pneumatological nature of WB.

It is crucial for Yong that in addition to focusing on the Christological and pneumatological aspects of the Christian practices it is remembered that there 'is identification of the trinitarian [sic] God as the one who has initiated such charismatic and redemptive encounters for human beings and has chosen to reveal himself in precisely these events'.[73] Per Yong, 'it is these ecclesial practices of the body of Christ and the fellowship of the Spirit ... (that) constitute the normal matrix within or through which people encounter God's saving actions'.[74] The sacramentality of the ecclesial practices issues from the fact that they are instances through which God's salvific grace meets human beings. Grace-filled encounters occur not because certain words, formulas, or actions are performed. Rather, God's saving power is made manifest to the embodied body of Christ as long as they are represented relationally in Jesus Christ through the power of the HS.

Yong avers that while the triune God initiates the Christian practices, their reception by humans must be involved to maintain their relational character. Therefore, there is a performative aspect to the practices in general and WB, in particular. By baptizing in the

---

[72] While many scholars, including Pentecostals Tomberlin and A.R. Williams, argue for making Jesus' WB paradigmatic for Christian baptism, especially in regard to SB at the time of baptism, it appears to be the case that the sui generis nature of Christ's WB is minimized in an attempt to harmonize the biblical accounts.

[73] Yong and Anderson, *Renewing Christian Theology*, p. 154.

[74] Yong and Anderson, *Renewing Christian Theology*, p. 154.

name of Jesus Acts 2.38; 8.16; 10.48 or in the name of the Triune God Mt. 28.19 'Christians as historically embodied creatures are tangibly and kinesthetically both receiving from God and simultaneously bearing witness to the world'.[75] It is through receiving from God and bearing witness to the world as an embodied person that the WB candidate and gathered community are changed ontologically.

Based on our findings to this point, I offer that the ecclesial rite of WB be conceptualized as a soteriological, pneumatological, Christocentric, relational MLE whereby ontological change occurs in the candidate and the gathered community. For our purposes, the human facilitator, duly authorized by the church, functions as a mediator in the MLE in the context of a congregation with the goal of performing a religious ritual, accompanied by teaching or preaching regarding the meaning and significance of the event with the intent of advancing the identity formation of the candidate and his or her into the life of God and new community based on the candidate's repentance, confession, and faith/trust in Jesus Christ as Lord and Saviour. While many Pentecostals have minimized the role of the HS in WB, focusing instead on the qualifications of the human mediator, I argue that it is in invoking the HS, honoring the HS's role as mediator, and acknowledging the pneumatological nature of WB, albeit in unseen yet perceivable fashion, that candidates and witnesses experience ontological change due the soteriological nature of the baptismal event. As a learning experience mediated by the HS and human agent, WB impacts the body, cognition, and affections of the person baptized, restructures the brain, and calls for a refocused bodily experience in view of the candidates participating of the death and resurrection of Jesus Christ. This construal honors the pneumatological, relational, Christological nature of soteriology. Moreover, the person baptized is not the only person impacted by the event. Water Baptism as a mediated event takes place within the context of a gathered embodied community of faith whereby the community bears witness to and celebrates the baptism rite. In addition, those present are also changed ontologically as the Body of Christ realigns as a new member is added to the Body of Christ through the HS. The presence and movement of the HS during WB

---

[75] Yong and Anderson, *Renewing Christian Theology*, p. 155.

service is well-documented in the periodical literature of the first quarter century of the 1900s. Typically preceded by a sermon or lesson on the meaning of WB the worshipping community, candidate, and mediator are cognitively, affectively, and physically moved. The employment of the WB formula, 'I now baptize you in the name of the Father, Son, and Holy Spirit' provides additional cognitive material to apprehend, aided by the HS. The deep learning and ontological change that has taken place previously in WB is called to the present by remembering one's baptism and is registered by praise and worship of God by the gathered community. Participation in the MLE of WB effects transformational or ontological change in all gathered.

Close examination of the NT passages explored in our narrative reading above reveals that they too appear to fulfill the aims of events, rites, and narratives contained in the Torah identified by S. Feuerstein. In short, the biblical narratives of Matthew and Romans convey *explicit* messages; the description of the historical events themselves, which are at the core of the development of the new Israel through the life, death, and resurrection of Jesus the Messiah. The description of the historical events then serves to foster Christian identity, values, and culture for the reader. Second, the events reported in the NT appear to contain *de facto* examples of mediated learning for the participants. Of note regarding the second category is the proclamation and baptismal activity of John the Baptist and the baptism of new followers commanded by Jesus. It seems to be the case that the practice of WB with the accompanying teaching and meaning of the practice fits well within the framework of MLE that engages the whole person with resultant ontological change.

Five-fold Gospel

As mentioned in the chapter on Pentecostal Hermeneutics, early Pentecostals located themselves in Acts 2 and the Gospels, perceiving they were participants in the closing drama of God's redeeming work, leading them to apprehend they were the eschatological people of God. As such, early Pentecostals viewed themselves as channels of Jesus Christ, given form in the community of God, created, and sustained by the HS. This, in turn, propelled them to embrace and proclaim the Fivefold Gospel with Jesus Christ as the center. Jesus was proclaimed as Savior, Sanctifier, Spirit Baptizer, Healer, and Coming King. Per Archer, the early Pentecostals' proclamation of the Fivefold Gospel served as the central means of grace that the redemptive activity of God through Jesus Christ through the HS to the Pentecostal community and to the world.[76]

In his 1998 Society of Pentecostal Studies Presidential Address, Pentecostal NT scholar John Christopher Thomas asserts the fivefold gospel stands at the theological heart of Pentecostalism. He further posits that 'when a Pentecostal theology is written from the ground up, it will be structured around these central tenets of Pentecostal faith and preaching'.[77] Thomas connects each doxological confession of Jesus with a particular biblical-sacramental sign act. Thus, 'Jesus is our Savior' is connected with the ecclesiastical rite of WB, 'Jesus is our Sanctifier' with footwashing, Spirit Baptizer with glossolalia speech, Healer with praying for and anointing the sick with oil, and Jesus as Coming King with the Lord's Supper. Thus, Thomas has set forth a proposal that is more integrative theologically by interconnecting ecclesiology and soteriology with Christology and pneumatology.[78]

I proffer that my argument that WB is a pneumatic Christologically focused, soteriological mediated event, facilitated by the HS/human agent within and by the ecclesia that affects ontological change in the embodied candidate and the gathered witnesses advances the possibility of conceptualizing each corresponding rite to the remaining doxological confessions as ecclesial rites that effect embodied ontological transformation in the participants. Thus conceived, the rites pneumatically empower and transform believers to be conformed to the image of Christ in every aspect of their being. Also, ecclesial rites apprehended from an embodied participant viewpoint moves the rites from the Cartesian

---

[76] Archer, 'Nourishment for Our Journey', *JPT* 13 (2004), pp. 79–96, especially p. 83.

[77] John Christopher Thomas, '1998 Presidential Address: Pentecostal Theology in the Twenty-First Century', *Pneuma* 20 (1998), pp. 3–19, especially pp. 17–19.

[78] Thomas, '1998 Presidential Address', pp. 18-19. For a narrative expansion on Thomas' proposal and further development concerning the sacramental nature of the signs see Archer, 'Nourishment for Our Journey', pp. 79– 96.

and Neoplatonic treatment of mere symbols and a focus on the 'soul' to a biblical treatment that honors the embodied nature of human existence and reclaims the whole person as the focus of God's soteriological agenda through Jesus Christ in the power of the HS. Thus, WB, footwashing, glossolalic speech, praying for and anointing the sick with oil, and the Lord's Supper all attend to embodied persons and God's restorative efforts in preparation for the resurrection and the coming of the Kingdom of God in its fullness.[79]

Practical and Ecclesiological Implications

Considering the contributions of this study, what are the implications for Pentecostal spiritual life, ministry, and worship? While space does not permit me to engage adequately all relevant matters, I hope to highlight some constructive proposals for Pentecostal practice. Therefore, I want to suggest that this constructive contribution implies needed reformulations of and clarifications on baptismal (1) practice, (2) context, (3) catechesis, and (4) pastoral concerns.

Baptismal Practice

Mode

This study has suggested that the mode of WB most widely and frequently practiced in the reviewed periodicals and the Scriptural witness is immersion. While there is evidence that pouring and sprinkling occurred in the periodicals, they are in a minority position and do not reflect the general practice within Pentecostalism nor Scripture. The biblical witness claims priority within Pentecostalism and it appears to be the case that immersion was the practice of John the Baptist, and it was to immersion by John that Jesus submitted himself. Similarly, Rom. 6.1-11 on which the majority of Pentecostals rely to explicate the meaning of WB, appears to reflect immersion

---

[79] Robert P. Pope, 'Why the Church Needs a Full Gospel: A Review and Reaction to Pentecostal Ecclesiology', in John Christopher Thomas (ed.), *Toward a Pentecostal Ecclesiology: The Church and the Fivefold Gospel* (Cleveland, TN: CPT Press, 2010), pp. 272-84 (278), offers that these sacramental acts 'possess sacramental significance because they are *ecclesial* acts and as the product of God's creative Word, and thus as the "ontological witness to the world", the Church is God's means of proclaiming his grace and embodying it in the world.' Emphasis original.

when employing the imagery of death, burial, and resurrection. Consequently, for these reasons, I proffer immersion be the standard baptismal mode among Pentecostals.

Formula

The historical debates and tensions regarding the preferred baptismal formula within the various streams during the first 25 years of the movement provide evidence that the trinitarian preference was not unanimous. Nonetheless, our study has revealed that within early Pentecostalism the preferred baptismal formula by the majority of early Pentecostals is trinitarian. Moreover, the trinitarian preference is informed by the Scriptural witness which emphases the trinitarian nature of Jesus' baptism and his command to baptize 'in the name of the Father, the Son, Jesus Christ, and the Holy Spirit'. (Mt. 28:19). In view of the evidence, our construction is offered from a trinitarian perspective. Therefore, I recommend a trinitarian formula be employed in baptismal liturgies. While more could be said regarding how to engage ecumenists and OPs I have restricted my construction to setting forth a revisioning of a Pentecostal theology of WB, anticipating engagement with those noted to be a matter for additional research.

Authorized Minister

Our study of early Pentecostal baptismal practice reveals that the issue of authorization to baptize candidates received a variety of responses and lacked unanimity. Many opinions asserted only ordained persons could baptize and others posited any Christian possessed the authority to baptize. However, the preponderance of evidence weighed heavily in favor of persons who were baptized in the HS and credentialed by their ecclesiastical bodies since WB was viewed as an ordinance of the Church and was to be administered by a duly recognized authority within a local church. The question of women baptizing was addressed by the polity of each ecclesial body within the movement. It appears to be the case that only the Foursquare Gospel Church, founded by Aimee Semple McPherson, ordained women and authorized them to baptize. Based on our study and position that WB is an ordinance or sacrament of the Church and is to be conducted only within a local church by those duly credentialed, I offer that only those persons credentialed by that church are to conduct baptisms. I will address this issue further below relative to the baptismal context.

Baptismal Context

From our study of the early Pentecostal periodicals, it appears to be the case that WB was practiced wherever there was sufficient water to immerse candidates. It appears minimal consideration was given to the context besides the necessity of having sufficient water. The physical context, the composition and spiritual significance of the gathered witnesses present for the baptismal activity received minimal consideration besides estimating the size of the crowd. Consequently, scant attention was paid to the theological meaning and significance for the ongoing discipleship of the candidate in relationship to an established and organized faith community, a local church. Similar practice may be found today after youth camps and college/university convocations where WB services are offered for those desiring to proclaim faith in Jesus Christ publicly without connection to a local church.

Our study has argued that Jesus Christ's command for new disciples to be baptized in water following confession, repentance of their sin, and faith in the person of the crucified and risen Christ, appears as an act of incorporation into the life of the triune God, Father, Son, and HS. Since Jesus is revealed in Matthew as the new temple of God, believers become new temple people in which God dwells by the HS. Through WB, new believers are incorporated to the new temple people of God. Moreover, to be baptized into the life of God is an embodied experience that changes the person in every aspect of their being (Mt. 28.19). Water baptism coupled with repentance, confession, and belief/trust in Jesus Christ is then a public proclamation of believers being incorporated into the life of God effecting an ontological change in their being. Furthermore, WB provides occasion for those baptized to undergo identity formation, characterological change, and incorporation into the life of God and a localized community of embodied believers. However, the person baptized is not the only person impacted by the event. Water Baptism as a mediated event is to occur within the context of a localized ecclesia whereby the community bears witness to and celebrates the baptism rite as executed by the duly authorized representative of the congregation. Also, the HS serves as an unseen mediator who impacts the body, cognition, and affections of the person baptized as well as those gathered to bear witness. Members of the local Body of Christ are changed ontologically as the Body of Christ realigns as a new member is added to the Body of Christ through the HS. Thus, this construction asserts the sole acceptable baptismal context is the local church.

Baptismal Catechesis
As this study has suggested in both the review of the periodical literature and our close reading of the NT passages, there is an immediate relationship between WB and being/becoming a disciple of Jesus Christ. On the one hand, within the USA it appears that instruction regarding the importance and meaning of WB was limited to baptismal sermons, Sunday School lessons, and published sermons. On the other hand, missionaries in nations outside the USA went beyond the delivery of information through the above means and focused on a personalized approach to discipleship whereby baptismal candidates progressed through graduated phases before they were baptized. Converts were instructed and then examined to ensure they understood the importance and meaning of WB, as well as the implications for their lives. Successfully moving through this process prepared converts to have their testimonies tested against their daily lives which were examined by their spiritual leaders. It appears to be the case that in the face of actual opposition and potential persecution encountered by new converts from their families and cultures, the missionaries were committed to WB as a momentous event and wanted to ensure converts were equipped to count the cost of following Jesus as Lord and Savior and demonstrate congruence between their professions of faith and their lived witness.

The above comments are not to deny that there are some within Pentecostalism who currently provide catechesis and examination for new converts regarding the importance and meaning of WB. Rather, based on this study, it appears to be the case that collectively Pentecostals would benefit from following the discipling model provided by foreign missionaries who attempted to ensure that converts were bearing the anticipated fruit anticipated to follow their confession and repentance. Moreover, adhering to the model would underscore the 'believer's baptism' perspective that has and is highly valued by Pentecostals. This approach may inhibit spontaneous baptisms that have been well-documented within the movement; however, a closer linkage between WB and discipleship enables new converts and the Church to more closely align with the Scriptural model.

While age parameters for candidates do not appear in the USA or on the mission field, it would appear arbitrary to insist on chronological limits for candidates presently. Rather, I submit that persons who possess the developmental capacity to make responsible decisions and are cognizant of the implications of their actions might be considered in assessing the candidate's readiness for baptism. This approach would provide an opportunity to strengthen the linkage between WB and discipleship.

Pastoral Concerns

Our study revealed the diverse positions regarding the proper course of action to follow with persons who had 'backslidden', returned to faith, and desired to be baptized again. In view of our theological arguments regarding baptismal practice and context and the clear implication that WB is 'once-for-all' sacramental rite effecting ontological change in the candidate, congregation, and very life of the triune God, I assert that rebaptism need not occur. Rather, another ordinance or sacrament of the Church, footwashing, may be considered as rite of the Church to celebrate and commemorate a person's removal of sin and restoration to Christ and the Body of Christ. While space prohibits a fuller exploration of footwashing, John Christopher Thomas' treatment of the topic lays the groundwork for consideration of footwashing as a soteriological sanctifying embodied act of worship whereby ontological change is affected in participants so they may more effectively reflect the image of Christ.

7

CONTRIBUTIONS AND SUGGESTIONS FOR FURTHER RESEARCH

Contributions

First, this exhaustive, first-of-its-kind study on WB, spans the first 25 years of the Pentecostal movement and investigates 21 early Pentecostal periodicals published in the USA, providing an in-depth exploration of the baptismal theology and practices within the WHP, FW, and OP streams of the movement. During the course of my investigation, I read and reviewed over 3,730 issues from the 21 periodicals. The periodicals varied on the number of pages per issue; however, using an average of five pages per issue, the number of pages read and reviewed approximate 18,650. As noted above, I applied an inductive approach to allow the *AF* and *TBM* to establish the categories that would be employed for reading the remaining periodicals. After the initial close review of the *AF*-Los Angeles and the *TBM,* I undertook a second reading to assess if the categories were sufficient to the evidence and if relevant material had been overlooked. Upon refinement, the succeeding categories were established to employ in a close reading[1] of the remaining 19 periodicals: the number of persons baptized; the geographical location and the body of water utilized in WB; authorized administrator of WB; qualifications for WB; presence of Pentecostal

---

[1] I read each page of the 21 reviewed periodicals out of a concern that crucial data would be missed by a word search. Only later did I employ a search engine to double-check my close reading.

embodied worship; mode of baptism; baptismal formula; obstacles and commitment to WB; the size of crowds present at baptismal services; use of WB for witness and evangelism; stance on infant baptism; rebaptism; and the meaning of WB. By and large, the categories held throughout the review. In some instances, categories were combined due to the shortage of baptismal reports, sermons, and articles on WB.

Second, while space does not permit a full recounting of discoveries from a close reading of 21 periodicals, the following observations and insights are contributions to the field regarding WB, embodied Pentecostal worship, theology, praxis, and gender inclusivity during the first 25 years of the movement: (1) the practice of WB held a place of prominence in the movement, rather than being marginalized in the shadow of SB; (2) the movement lacked cohesion and unanimity regarding the practice and theological meaning of WB; (3) early Pentecostals within the three streams employ a straightforward reading of the biblical text, agreeing that WB is an ordinance of the Church instituted by the Lord Jesus Christ and is to be practiced, following Jesus' example in obedience to his command, after repentance, confession of sin, and faith in Jesus Christ as Lord and Savior; (4) none deem WB optional; (5) opinions diverge regarding the *necessity* of WB for the believer; (6) the three streams ground salvation from sin in their Christology and soteriology, focusing on the doctrine of the atonement, and reject baptismal regeneration; (7) only the OPs attempted to integrate soteriology, Christology, and pneumatology into the baptismal event; (8) foreign missionaries were more scrupulous to validate a candidate's suitability for WB than their counterparts in the USA; (9) baptism by immersion was the preferred mode, while the IPHC allowed sprinkling and infant baptism; (10) unity within and among the three streams was evasive regarding rebaptism; (11) the responses to questions regarding WB tended to focus on legal casuistry rather than integrated theological reasoning; (12) reflecting a Zwinglian view of the sacraments, the three steams concur that WB publicly symbolizes a believer's identification and union with Christ in his life, death, burial, and resurrection (Rom. 6.3-7); (13) in view of emphasis placed on WB, the OP stream periodicals contain relatively few baptismal reports; (14) perspectives and attitudes regarding baptismal formula varied widely among the three streams; (15) there was disagreement within and between the three streams regarding who could serve as the baptismal administrator, especially regarding to gender with preference given to males; (16) despite the subordination of women within the three steams, Aimee Semple McPherson played a significant role in the growth of Pentecostalism and the elevation of WB; (17) only the IPHC made WB a requirement for church membership and this appears to reflect the influence of previous denominational affiliations; and (18) the theological relationship between WB and ecclesiology was larger ignored except in terms of obedience to Christ's command.

Third, our research has shown that early Pentecostals viewed soteriology primarily as pertaining to the salvation of the 'soul,' preparing a person to go to heaven and avoid hell after death. While divine healing of the body was preached and taught there was minimal attention given to the body and soteriology. Attention was given to the resurrection of the body at the end of the age; however, there appeared to be little reflection and appreciation given to the body 'between the ages' besides that already noted. This study has challenged the Neo-Platonic and Cartesian viewpoints that operate within Pentecostalism and have adversely impacted Christian theological valuation of the human body and its place in the *via salutis* and in theological reflection. In particular, the study has questioned the spiritualization of soteriology that is concerned with the salvation of the 'soul' so a believer can go to heaven after death.

Fourth, in response to the disembodied soteriology of the early Pentecostals my research has integrated findings from the neurosciences and cognitive psychology for a re-visioned understanding of persons as embodied spiritual beings who are encountered in every aspect of their being by the redeeming God through the HS. Closely connected to arguing for embodiment is the assertion that ontological change occurs in persons through HS/human mediated learning experiences. Furthermore, I have argued that WB be construed as an MLE that affects ontological change in candidates and the gathered ecclesial community. To my knowledge this has not been attempted within Pentecostalism previously, especially in regard to WB.

Fifth, while OPs do not appear to have fully developed their soteriological and pneumatological integration with the concept of embodiment, their nascent approach of integration reflects their discernment that the human body cannot be ignored in the *via salutis*. I offer that the results of this study may provide a way forward for rapprochement between OPs and other Pentecostals as theological perspectives are re-visioned in view of embodiment.

Sixth, our research has demonstrated that HS-empowered embodied Pentecostal worship, divine healing, and the manifestation of spiritual gifts, including prophecy, speaking in tongues, and interpretation of tongues during WB services were inherent in all three streams of the movement; however, there is no evidence that theological reflection occurred regarding the body and any of the key doctrines. It went unnoticed that without embodiment there is no Christology, pneumatology, and soteriology. This study has attempted to place embodiment in conversation with soteriology and ecclesiology.

Seventh, while the close linkage between WB and conversion was acknowledged by early Pentecostals, WB was reduced to an act of obedience, except for the OP stream, without fully exploring the soteriological and ecclesial value of WB. This study has attempted to address this oversight constructively by placing WB in dialogue with soteriology, ecclesiology, pneumatology, and Christology.

Eighth, the WHP and FW streams were univocal in their positions that WB was understood to be an ordinance, even when sacramental language was employed. Thus, WB is understood and valued from Christological and soteriological categories, largely devoid of pneumatology. This study has attempted to place the person and work of the HS in direct dialogue with WB, emphasizing the indispensable role of the HS in the transformation of the candidate and congregation through the baptismal rite, thereby connecting soteriology, Christology, and pneumatology.

Ninth, the Bible-reading approach appears to have failed the early Pentecostals in discerning the function and meaning of WB for candidates and members of the ecclesia, especially in regard to the call to discipleship on the *via salutis*. Matthew's texts are viewed without differentiation and are consequently treated as interchangeable. Their interpretation of Matthew is then projected onto Paul's treatment in Romans, and WB is understood in purely individualistic symbolic terms. This study has attempted to provide a close theological narrative reading of relevant baptismal texts in Matthew and Romans in order to discern the subtleties and nuances of the texts. This approach has allowed us to discern the nature and function of John's baptism, the significance of Jesus' baptism, and the difference from believer's baptism, effectively challenging interpretations that treat the text without differentiation. To my knowledge, this is the first attempt at such an endeavor.

Suggestions for Further Research

Considering the contributions of this study, several opportunities present themselves as points of entry for further research.

First, attention must be focused on embodiment in dialogue with traditional anthropological models to ascertain their suitability and compatibility with a Pentecostal theological anthropology that integrates embodiment.

Second, once a revisioned Pentecostal theological anthropology that integrates embodiment has been established, the major theological doctrines will merit revisioning to move beyond the Neo-Platonic and Cartesian dualism that has characterized Christian theology for almost two millennia. For example, how are we to think of soteriology, hamartiology, pneumatology, sanctification, discipleship, divine healing, and the baptism of the HS in relationship to embodiment.

Third, what are the implications of this study for the Five-fold gospel and a subsequent re-visioned Pentecostal ecclesiology?

Fourth, it would be beneficial to: (1) engage U.S. Pentecostal periodicals that were excluded from the study; (2) undertake a study of periodicals published external to the U.S. context during the same time frame; and (3) expand the investigation time frame to engage periodicals published within and external to the U.S. context from 1932 to the present or other limiting date.

Fifth, based on this study how might we understand sacramentality?

Sixth, how might a theological narrative reading of other NT texts (Mk 16.15-16; Jn 3.3-7; Acts 2.38-39, 8.35-38; 22.12-16; 1 Cor. 6.9-

11; Gal. 3.24-27; Eph. 5.25-27; Col. 2.11-15; Tit. 3.4-7; and 1 Pet. 3.18-22) support and challenge the results of this study?

Seventh, R. Feuerstein's educational model stresses the importance of mediated learning for persons of all ages and potential, including persons with disabilities and cognitive impairment. What are the implications for preaching, teaching, education, and catechesis within the Pentecostal traditions?

Eighth, based on the results of this study, what are the implications for Pentecostals in relationship to racism, sexism, ageism, disability, terrorism, ecology, social issues, addiction, abuse, immigration, and additional topics that are based on erroneous assumptions and presuppositions of human beings?

Appendix A

The Bridegroom's Messenger

Chronological Order of Baptismal Service Location

Arcadia, FL;[1] Chattanooga, TN;[2] Alto, GA;[3] Chillicothe, OH;[4] Smith, AR;[5] Amarillo, TX;[6] Johannesburg, Transvaal, South Africa;[7] Bombay, India;[8] Cheng Ting Fu, China;[9] Krugersdorp, Transvaal, South Africa;[10] Malvern, AR;[11] Guatemala, Central America;[12] Winnipeg, Canada;[13] Shanghai, China;[14] Middelburg, Transvaal, South Africa;[15] Stouffville, Ontario, Canada;[16] Noma, FL;[17] Fort Worth, TX;[18] Topeka, KS;[19] Paterson, NJ;[20] Faizabad, Uttar Pradesh, India;[21] Dhond, Maharashtra, India;[22] Karagampitiya, Dehiwala, Ceylon;[23] Basti, Basti District, India;[24] North Melbourne, Victoria, Australia;[25] Kong-p'i-t'au, China;[26] Warrior, AL;[27] Darjeeling, India;[28] Preston, MD;[29]

---

[1] *TBM* 1.15 (June 1, 1908), p. 1.
[2] *TBM* 1.15 (June 1, 1908), p. 1.
[3] *TBM* 1.16 (June 15, 1908), p. 3.
[4] *TBM* 2.29 (January 1, 1909), p. 1.
[5] *TBM* 2.33 (March 1, 1909), p. 2.
[6] *TBM* 2.42 (July 15, 1909), p. 3.
[7] *TBM* 3.49 (November 1, 1909), p. 2; *TBM* 4.72 (October 15, 1910), p. 2; and *TBM* 5.105 (March 1, 1912), p. 2.
[8] *TBM* 3.49 (November 1, 1909), p. 2; *TBM* 3.71 (October 1, 1910), p. 4; *TBM* 4.85 (May 1, 1911), p. 1; *TBM* 5.102 (January 15, 1911), p. 3; *TBM* 5.117 (September 1, 1912), p. 4; *TBM* 6.136 (July 1, 1913), p. 3; *TBM* 7.15 (February 15, 1914); *TBM* 9.180 (March 1, 1916), p. 3; *TBM* 10.199 (May 1, 1917), p. 3; and *TBM* 10.200 (June 1, 1917), p. 3.
[9] *TBM* 3.51 (December 1, 1909), p. 3.
[10] *TBM* 3.51 (December 1, 1909), p. 4.
[11] *TBM* 3.52 (December 15, 1909), p. 1; *TBM* 5.96 (October 15, 1911), p. 2.
[12] *TBM* 3.53 (January 1, 1910), p. 4.
[13] *TBM* 3.54 (January 15, 1910), p. 2.
[14] *TBM* 3.60 (April 15, 1910), p. 4; *TBM* 8.173 (August 1, 1915), p. 3; *TBM* 22.272 (April-June, 1929), p. 11; and *TBM* 24.280 (April-June 1931), p. 6.
[15] *TBM* 3.61 (May 1, 1910), p. 2; *TBM* 3.70 (September 15, 1910), p. 4; *TBM* 4.74 (November 15, 1910), p. 3; *TBM* 4.81 (March 1, 1911), p. 4; *TBM* 5.115 (August 1, 1912), p. 1; *TBM* 6.134 (June 1, 1913), p. 1; *TBM* 6.134 (June 1, 1913), p. 1; and *TBM* 10.199 (May 1, 1917), p. 3.
[16] *TBM* 3.65 (July 1, 1910), p. 4.
[17] *TBM* 3.68 (August 15, 1910), p. 3.
[18] *TBM* 3.69 (September 1, 1910), p. 3.
[19] *TBM* 3.70 (September 15, 1910), p. 1.
[20] *TBM* 4.72 (October 15, 1910), p. 2.
[21] *TBM* 4.74 (November 15, 1910), pp. 1, 4; *TBM* 24.280 (April-June 1931), p. 6.
[22] *TBM* 4.75 (December 1, 1910), p. 2.
[23] *TBM* 4.75 (December 1, 1910), p. 4.
[24] *TBM* 4.76 (December 15, 1910), p. 4.
[25] *TBM* 4.83 (April 1, 1911), p. 1.
[26] *TBM* 4.83 (April 1, 1911), p. 4.
[27] *TBM* 4.94 (September 15, 1911), p. 3.
[28] *TBM* 4.94 (September 15, 1911), p. 3.
[29] *TBM* 5.96 (October 15, 1911), p. 3.

Pleasant Grove, NC;[30] Canton, China;[31] Northern India;[32] Florida;[33] Ningpo, China;[34] Minia, Egypt;[35] Hong Kong, China;[36] Wang Kong, China;[37] Petersburg, Transvaal, South Africa;[38] Ahuachapan, Salvador, Central America;[39] Queenstown, South Africa;[40] Travancore, South India;[41] Mc Bean, Quebec;[42] Doddballapur, Mysore State, South India;[43] Bangalore, South India;[44] Cape Palmas, Liberia, West Africa;[45] Dallas, TX;[46] Saskatchewan, Canada;[47] Cumberland, MD;[48] Madras, South India;[49] Sai Nam, S. China;[50] Sham Shui, South China;[51] Tokyo, Japan;[52] borders of Nepal;[53] Central Asian Pioneer Mission, Abbottabad, India;[54] Firth, ND;[55] Coban, Guatemala, Central America;[56] Peking, China;[57] Gualeguaychu, Argentina, South America;[58] Kingsville, TX;[59] Pilgrim's Rest, Transvaal, S. Africa;[60] Gonda, Uttar Pradesh, India;[61] Taianfu, Shantung, China;[62] Durban, Natal, South Africa;[63] Kentucky;[64] Benares, Uttar Pradesh, India;[65] Kandy, Ceylon;[66] Olympia, WA;[67]

---

[30] *TBM* 5.98 (November 15, 1911), p. 4.
[31] *TBM* 5.104 (February 15, 1912), p. 4; *TBM* 8.167 (February 1, 1915), p. 3.
[32] *TBM* 6.132 (May 1, 1913), p. 4.
[33] *TBM* 6.133 (May 15, 1913), p. 2.
[34] *TBM* 6.135 (June 15, 1913), p. 3; *TBM* 22.271 (January-March 1929), p. 10.
[35] *TBM* 6.136 (July 1, 1913), p. 2.
[36] *TBM* 6.136 (July 1, 1913), p. 3.
[37] *TBM* 6.137 (August 1, 1913), p. 2.
[38] *TBM* 6.137 (August 1, 1913), p. 3.
[39] *TBM* 6.140 (September 15, 1913), p. 3.
[40] *TBM* 7.141 (October 1, 1913), p. 1
[41] TBM 7.145 (December 1, 1913), p. 1
[42] *TBM* 7.147 (January 1, 1914), p. 1.
[43] *TBM* 7.148 (January 15, 1914), p. 2.
[44] *TBM* 7.150 (February 15, 1914), p. 3.
[45] *TBM* 7.156 (June 1, 1914), p. 2.
[46] *TBM* 7.156 (June 1, 1914), p. 3
[47] *TBM* 7.160 (August 15, 1914), p. 2.
[48] *TBM* 8.164 (November 1, 1914), p. 2.
[49] *TBM* 8.164 (November 1, 1914), p. 2.
[50] *TBM* 8.165 (December 1, 1914), p. 1; *TBM* 8.172 (July 1, 1915), p. 2.
[51] *TBM* 8.167 (February 1, 1915), p. 1.
[52] *TBM* 8.167 (February 1, 1915), p. 3; *TBM* 8.167 (February 1, 1915), p. 3; and *TBM* 12.216 (September 1, 1919), p. 3.
[53] *TBM* 8.167 (February 1, 1915), p. 3.
[54] *TBM* 8.174 (September 1, 1915), p. 3.
[55] *TBM* 8.175 (October 1, 1915), p. 5.
[56] *TBM* 9.177 (December 1, 1915), p. 2.
[57] *TBM* 9.185 (August 1, 1916), p. 3.
[58] *TBM* 9.186 (September 1, 1916), p. 4; *TBM* 9.187 (October 1, 1916), p. 3; *TBM* 10.191(February 1, 1917), p. 3; and *TBM* 10.200 (June 1, 1917), p. 3.
[59] *TBM* 10.200 (June 1, 1917), p. 4.
[60] *TBM* 14.226 (October-November 1, 1920), p. 3.
[61] *TBM* 14.229 (April-May 1, 1921), p. 3.
[62] *TBM* 18.253 (September-November 1, 1924), p. 3.
[63] *TBM* 18.256 (June-September 1, 1925), p. 3; *TBM* 19.258 (January-February 1926), p. 3.
[64] *TBM* 19.257 (October-December 1925), p. 2.
[65] *TBM* 19.259 (March-May 1926), p. 3; *TBM* 20.261. (September-October 1926), p. 3.
[66] *TBM* 19.259 (March-May 1926), p. 3.
[67] *TBM* 20.263 (March-April 1927), p. 4.

Atlanta, GA;[68] Barquisimeto, Venezuela;[69] Colombo, Ceylon;[70] Berea Tabernacle, Detroit, MI;[71] Russia;[72] Siquisique, Lara, Venezuela;[73] and Sharannager Mission, Gonda, Uttar Pradesh, India.[74]

Appendix B

Latter Rain Evangel

Chronological Order of Baptismal Service Locations

Water baptism is practiced globally as the reports originate in Lake St. Thomas, outside of Halifax, Nova Scotia, Canada;[75] Altadena, CA;[76] Luebo and Ibanji, Congo;[77] India;[78] Liberia, West Africa;[79] West Africa;[80] Yokohama, Japan;[81] Kovilpatti, India;[82] British West Indies;[83] Egypt;[84] Nanking Mission, China;[85] India;[86] Fiji Islands and Solomon Islands;[87] Kansu Province, China;[88] Sierra Leone, West Africa;[89] Sai Nam, China;[90] Johannesburg, South Africa;[91] Kwangsi Province, China;[92] Soudan;[93] Nigeria, Northern Africa;[94] Madras, India;[95] Pak Nai, South China;[96] Abiengama, Congo;[97] Canton, China;[98] Zion City, IL;[99] Newaka,

---

[68] *TBM* 21.266 (November-December 1927), p. 1.
[69] *TBM* 21.268 (March-April 1928), p. 3.
[70] *TBM* 21.269 (May-August 1928), p. 3.
[71] *TBM* 22.270 (September-December 1928), p. 4.
[72] *TBM* 22.271 (January-March 1929), p. 16.
[73] *TBM* 23.275 (January-March 1930), p. 12.
[74] *TBM* 29.278 (October-December 1930), p. 9.
[75] *LRE* 4.9 (June 1912), p. 18.
[76] *LRE* 4.10 (July 1912), p. 10.
[77] *LRE* 5.7 (April 1913), p. 15.
[78] *LRE* 6.3 (December 1913), p. 7.
[79] *LRE* 6.5 (February 1914), p. 14.
[80] *LRE* 6.8 (May 1914), p. 12.
[81] *LRE* 11.10 (July 1919), p. 22.
[82] *LRE* 6.11 (August 1914), p. 17.
[83] *LRE* 7.4 (January 1915), p. 15.
[84] *LRE* 7.9 (June 1915), p. 16; *LRE* 20.2 (November 1927), p. 6.
[85] *LRE* 8.11 (August 1916), p. 13.
[86] *LRE* 9.9 (June 1917), p. 18; *LRE* 18.6 (March 1926), p. 15.
[87] *LRE* 9.10 (July 1917), p. 14.
[88] *LRE* 11.1 (October 1918), p. 9.
[89] *LRE* 11.1 (October 1918), p. 10; *LRE* 15.9 (June 1923), p. 18.
[90] *LRE* 11.6 (March 1919), p. 16; *LRE* 14.5 (February 1922), p. 18; and *LRE* 17.5 (February 1925), p. 13.
[91] *LRE* 11.9 (June 1919), p. 15; *LRE* 20.12 (September 1928), p. 16.
[92] *LRE* 11.11 (August 1919), p. 14.
[93] *LRE* 12.1 (October 1919), p. 10.
[94] *LRE* 12.5 (February 1920), p. 19.
[95] *LRE* 12.6 (March 1920), p. 14.
[96] *LRE* 12.10 (July 1920), p. 15.
[97] *LRE* 12.10 (July 1920), p. 17.
[98] *LRE* 12.12 (September 1920), p. 20.
[99] *LRE* 13.5 (February 1921), p. 10.

Liberia;[100] Tao-Yuan, China;[101] Ch'ang-te-fu, China;[102] Bulgaria;[103] Lo Pau, SouthChina;[104] The Stone Church, Chicago, IL;[105] Buenos Aires, Argentina;[106] Gorakhpur, India;[107] Shanghai, China;[108] Yuanchow, Hunan, China;[109] Bergen, Norway;[110] West River, China;[111] Luchnow, India;[112] Colombo, Ceylon;[113] Bethel Orphanage, Wei Hsien. Chihli, North China;[114] Waitsap, China;[115] Mwanza, Tanzania;[116] Galesburg, IL;[117] Barquisimeto, Venezuela;[118] Kotchiu, Yunnan Province, China;[119] Olympia, Washington;[120] Athens, Greece;[121] Leung Tsuen, China;[122] Kansu, Tibet;[123] Bolivar, Argentina;[124] Poona, South India;[125] Bethel Temple, Williamsport, MD;[126] Monmau, China;[127] China;[128] Peru;[129] Potgietersrus, South Africa;[130] The Springs, Transvaal, South Africa;[131] Sharannagar, India;[132] Transvaal, South Africa;[133] Detroit, MI;[134] Mechling, SD;[135] Bettiah, Bihar, India;[136]

---

[100] LRE 13.6 (March 1921), p. 11.
[101] LRE 13.8 (May 1921), p. 22.
[102] LRE 13.8 (May 1921), p. 22.
[103] LRE 13.10 (July 1921), p. 15.
[104] LRE 14.3 (December 1921), p. 19; LRE 14.6 (March 1922), p. 22.
[105] LRE 14.7 (April 1922), p. 12; LRE 15.3 (December 1922), p. 13; LRE 19.6 (March 1927), p. 12; and LRE 19.9 (June 1927), p. 12.
[106] LRE 15.3 (December 1922), p. 23.
[107] LRE 15.10 (July 1923), p. 20.
[108] LRE 15.11 (August 1923), p. 17; LRE 18.6 (March 1926), p. 14; LRE 20.2 (November 1927), p. 11; and LRE 21.11 (August 1929), p. 17.
[109] LRE 16.7 (April 1924), p. 2.
[110] LRE 16.12 (September 1924), p. 14.
[111] LRE 17.4 (January 1925), p. 21
[112] LRE 17.8 (May 1925), p. 16.
[113] LRE 17.8 (May 1925), p. 16.
[114] LRE 17.10 (July 1925), p. 23.
[115] LRE 17.11 (August 1925), p. 15; LRE 18.12 (September 1926), p. 11
[116] LRE 17.11 (August 1925), p. 17.
[117] LRE 18.1 (October 1925), p. 23.
[118] LRE 18.4 (January 1926), pp. 4-5; LRE 20.6 (March 1928), p. 17.
[119] LRE 18.6 (March 1926), p. 16.
[120] LRE 18.10 (July 1926), p.12.
[121] LRE 18.11 (August 1920), p. 22.
[122] LRE 19.2 (November 1926), p. 17.
[123] LRE 19.5 (February 1927), p.11.
[124] LRE 19.8 (May 1927), p. 16.
[125] LRE 19.8 (May 1927), p. 16.
[126] LRE 19.9 (June 1927), p. 8.
[127] LRE 19.12 (September 1927), p. 3.
[128] LRE 20.3 (December 1927), p. 4; LRE 20.11 (August 1928), p. 12.
[129] LRE 20.3 (December 1927), p. 15.
[130] LRE 20.3 (December 1927), p. 17.
[131] LRE 20.7 (April 1928), pp. 21-22; LRE 22.11 (August 1930), p. 16; and LRE 23.5 (February 1931), p. 21.
[132] LRE 20.8 (May 1928), p. 20.
[133] LRE 21.1 (October 1928), p. 15; LRE 21.7 (April 1929), p. 13.
[134] LRE 20.8 (May 1928), p. 23.
[135] LRE 20.8 (May 1928), p. 23.
[136] LRE 20.10 (July 1928), pp. 20; 23.4 (January 1931), p. 18.

Uska Bazar, India;[137] Kisumu, East Africa;[138] Gombari, Congo-Belge;[139] Nawabganj, India;[140] Bangalore, India;[141] Assiout, Egypt;[142] Hamadan, Persia;[143] Enkweme Mission Station, Transvaal, South Africa;[144] Lucknow, India;[145] Wei Hsein, Hopei Province, China;[146] Madras, South India;[147] Ougadouga, West Africa;[148] Washington, D.C.;[149] Gombari, Congo-Belge;[150] Cairo, Egypt;[151] Nawabganj, India;[152] Vrededorp, Johannesburg, South Africa;[153] Middleburg and Hendrina, South Africa;[154] Ngau Piu Leng, South China;[155] Matagalpa, Nicaragua;[156] Jeannette, PA;[157] Debra Dun, North India;[158] Rupaidiha, North India;[159] Santa Ana, El Salvador;[160] Brakpan, South Africa;[161] and Minia, Egypt.[162]

Appendix C

Church of God Evangel
States and Cities in Alphabetical Order
Alabama
Abernant;[163] Alabama City;[164] Altoona;[165] Anniston;[166]

---

[137] *LRE* 20.11 (August 1928), p. 15.
[138] *LRE* 20.12 (September 1928), pp. 13-14.
[139] *LRE* 20.12 (September 1928), p. 14.
[140] *LRE* 20.12 (September 1928), pp. 14-15.
[141] *LRE* 20.12 (September 1928), p. 15.
[142] *LRE* 20.12 (September 1928), p. 18.
[143] *LRE* 21.2 (November 1928), p. 14.
[144] *LRE* 21.7 (April 1929), p. 14.
[145] *LRE* 21.8 (May 1929), p. 12.
[146] *LRE* 21.12 (September 1929), p. 9; *LRE* 22.10 (July 1930), p. 19.
[147] *LRE* 22.1 (October 1929), p. 21.
[148] *LRE* 22.4 (January 1930), p. 14.
[149] *LRE* 22.4 (January 1930), p. 21.
[150] *LRE* 22.5 (February 1930), p. 19.
[151] *LRE* 22.6 (March 1930), p. 10.
[152] *LRE* 22.11 (August 1930), p. 15.
[153] *LRE* 23.5 (February 1931), p. 20.
[154] *LRE* 23.5 (February 1931), p. 20.
[155] *LRE* 23.6 (March 1931), p. 19.
[156] *LRE* 23.7 (April 1931), p. 7.
[157] *LRE* 23.7 (April 1931), p. 21.
[158] *LRE* 23.8 (May 1931), p. 21.
[159] *LRE* 23.10 (July 1931), p. 22.
[160] *LRE* 23.10 (July 1931), p. 22.
[161] *LRE* 23.12 (September 1931), p. 22.
[162] *LRE* 24.1 (October 1931), p. 14.
[163] *COGE* 16.37 (September 12, 1925), p. 2; *COGE* 17.35 (September 4, 1926), p. 2; *COGE* 18.43 (October 22, 1927), p. 1; *COGE* 20.29 (September 14, 1929), p. 4; and COGE 22.24 (August 15, 1931), p. 1.
[164] *COGE* 12.31 (July 30, 1921), p. 2; *COGE* 13.29 (July 22, 1922), p. 2; *COGE* 16.24 (June 13, 1925), p.3; *COGE* 18.35 (August 27, 1927), p. 1; and *COGE* 21.22 (July 26, 1930), p. 2.
[165] *COGE* 13.34 (August 26, 1922), p. 2; COGE 22.33 (October 24, 1931), p. 4; and COGE 22.35 (November 7, 1931), p. 1.
[166] *COGE* 12.26 (June 25, 1921), p. 2; *COGE* 15.39 (October 11, 1924), p. 3.

Arkadelphia;[167] Arley;[168] Bankston;[169] Bear Creek;[170] Bessemer;[171] Blountsville;[172] Boaz;[173] Bradford;[174] Braverton;[175] Bridgeport;[176] Buhl;[177] Carbon Hill;[178] Castleberry;[179] Chavies;[180] Clanton;[181] Clearwater;[182] Coalburg;[183] Coaldale;[184] Corinth;[185] Cottondale;[186] Covin;[187] Crumley's Chapel;[188] Dixiana;[189] Dora;[190] Double Springs;[191] Ensley;[192] Empire;[193] Flat Creek;[194] Flat Top;[195] Flat Wood;[196] Fyffe;[197] Gadsden;[198] Gordo;[199] Grove Oak;[200] Hamilton;[201] Hartselle;[202] Heflin;[203] Hendrix;[204] Hollywood;[205] Hurricane;[206] Jacksonville;[207]

---

[167] *COGE* 21.34 (October 18, 1930), p. 3.
[168] *COGE* 21.30 (September 20, 1930), p. 3.
[169] *COGE* 18.43 (October 22, 1927), p. 3.
[170] *COGE* 19.39 (September 29, 1928), p. 1.
[171] *COGE* 16.46 (November 14, 1925), p. 4; *COGE* 21.32 (October 4, 1930), p. 3; and COGE 22.28 (September 12, 1931), p. 2.
[172] COGE 20.34 (October 19, 1929), p. 4.
[173] COGE 22.30 (September 26, 1931), p. 2.
[174] *COGE* 19.31 (August 4, 1928), p. 1.
[175] *COGE* 21.34 (October 18, 1930), p. 4.
[176] *COGE* 12.29 (July 16, 1921), p. 2; *COGE* 13.25 (June 24, 1922), p. 2.
[177] *COGE* 20.17 (June 22, 1929), p. 1; *COGE* 21.25 (August 16, 1930), p. 3.
[178] *COGE* 10.44 (November 8, 1919), p. 3; *COGE* 12.39 (September 24, 1921), p. 2; *COGE* 15.39 (October 11, 1924), p. 3; *COGE* 16.22 (May 30, 1925), p. 1; *COGE* 16.25 (June 20, 1925), p. 2; *COGE* 16.34 (August 22, 1925), p. 1; *COGE* 16.36 (September 5, 1925), p. 3; and *COGE* 17.27 (July 10, 1926), p. 4.
[179] *COGE* 18.44 (November 5, 1927), p. 3.
[180] *COGE* 13.31 (August 5, 1922), p. 2; *COGE* 13.37 (September 16, 1922), p. 2; *COGE* 15.34 (September 6, 1924), p. 3; and *COGE* 18.42 (October 15, 1927), p. 1.
[181] *COGE* 15.35 (September 13, 1924), p. 1.
[182] *COGE* 8.22 (June 9, 1917), p. 4.
[183] *COGE* 1.9 (July 1, 1910), p. 7; *COGE* 1.15 (October 1, 1910), p. 5.
[184] *COGE* 22.34 9October 31, 1931), p. 3.
[185] *COGE* 13.39 (September 30, 1922), p. 3.
[186] COGE 22.28 (September 12, 1931), p. 2.
[187] *COGE* 22.11 (May 16, 1931), p. 1.
[188] *COGE* 17.37 (September 18, 1926), p. 3; *COGE* 17.39 (October 2, 1926), p. 4.
[189] *COGE* 13.34 (August 26, 1922), p. 2; *COGE* 13.41 (October 14, 1922), p. 2.
[190] *COGE* 8.25 (June 30, 1917), p. 2; *COGE* 10.23 (June 7, 1919), p. 2; *COGE* 19.29 (July 21, 1928), p. 1; *COGE* 20.13 (May 25, 1929), p. 1; and COGE 20.31 (September 28, 1929), p. 2.
[191] *COGE* 21.25 (August 16, 1930), p. 4.
[192] *COGE* 19.35 (September 1, 1928), p. 3.
[193] *COGE* 12.30 (July 23, 1921), p. 2; *COGE* 15.38 (October 4, 1924), p. 1.
[194] *COGE* 16.28 (July 11, 1925), p. 1.
[195] *COGE* 17.29 (July 24, 1926), p. 3.
[196] *COGE* 9.29 (July 20, 1918), p. 3.
[197] *COGE* 18.44 (November 5, 1927), p. 4.
[198] *COGE* 17.39 (October 2, 1926), p. 4.
[199] *COGE* 21.16 (June 14, 1930), p. 2.
[200] *COGE* 18.44 (November 5, 1927), p. 4; COGE 20.30 (September 21, 1929), p. 4.
[201] *COGE* 11.20 (May 15, 1920), p. 3.
[202] *COGE* 21.28 (September 6, 1930), p. 4.
[203] *COGE* 15.36 (September 20, 1924), p. 1; *COGE* 21.26 (August 23, 1930), p. 3.
[204] *COGE* 14.38 (September 15, 1923), p. 3; *COGE* 22.37 (November 21, 1931), p. 1.
[205] *COGE* 12.35 (August 27, 1921), p. 2.
[206] *COGE* 13.41 (October 14, 1922), p. 2; *COGE* 15.38 (October 4, 1924), p. 4.
[207] *COGE* 8.23 (June 16, 1917), p. 4; *COGE* 11.41 (October 9, 1920), p. 2; and *COGE* 17.28 (July 17, 1926), p. 3.

Kellerman;[208] Kennedy;[209] Kimberly;[210] Larkinsville;[211] Madrid;[212] Magnolia;[213] Majestic;[214] Mentone;[215] Montague;[216] Montgomery;[217] Natural Bridge;[218] Nauvoo;[219] New Georgia;[220] Oneonta;[221] Opelika;[222] Pell City;[223] Phenix City;[224] Praco;[225] Pratt City;[226] Red Bay;[227] Sibleyville;[228] Smith's Chapel, Winston County;[229] Springvillle;[230] Sulphur Springs;[231] Sumiton;[232] Sylacauga;[233] Tallassee;[234] Taylor;[235] Thomasville;[236] Town Creek;[237] Trafford;[238] Tuscumbia;[239] Verbena;[240] Wannville;[241] Warrior;[242] Wedowee;[243]

---

[208] *COGE* 18.26 (June 25, 1927), p. 2.
[209] *COGE* 7.39 (September 23, 1916), p. 3; *COGE* 16.40 (October 3, 1925), p. 2; *COGE* 17.40 (October 9, 1926), p. 1; *COGE* 19.47 (December 1, 1928), p. 3; and *COGE* 21.31 (September 27, 1930), pp. *2,* 4.
[210] *COGE* 13.3 (January 21, 1922), p. 3; *COGE* 14.30 (July 28, 1923), p. 3; and *COGE* 16.36 (September 5, 1925), p. 3.
[211] *COGE* 16.47 (November 21, 1925), p. 3.
[212] *COGE* 1.16 (October 15, 1910), p. 7.
[213] *COGE* 11.40 (October 2, 1920), p. 2.
[214] *COGE* 15.38 (October 4, 1924), p. 1; *COGE* 22.23 (August 8, 1931), p. 2.
[215] *COGE* 6.32 (August 7, 1915), p. 4; *COGE* 20.1 (March 2, 1929), p. 3.
[216] COGE 22.31 (October 3, 1931), p. 3.
[217] COGE 22.34 9October 31, 1931), p. 4.
[218] *COGE* 10.20 (May 17, 1919), p. 3.
[219] *COGE* 12.39 (September 24, 1921), p. 2.
[220] *COGE* 11.44 (October 30, 1920), p. 3.
[221] *COGE* 22.36 (November 14, 1931), p. 1.
[222] *COGE* 19.29 (July 21, 1928), p. 1.
[223] *COGE* 12.26 (June 25, 1921), p. 2; *COGE* 16.31 (August 1, 1925), p. 3.
[224] *COGE* 16.20 (May 16, 1925), p. 2; *COGE* 18.30 (July 23, 1927), p. 4.
[225] *COGE* 19.44 (November 10, 1928), p. 3.
[226] *COGE* 17.35 (September 4, 1926), p. 2; *COGE* 18.44 (November 5, 1927), p. 2; *COGE* 20.4 (March 23, 1929), p. 3; *COGE* 20.13 (May 25, 1929), p. 3; COGE 20.30 (September 21, 1929), p. 2; and *COGE* 21.22 (July 26, 1930), p. 2.
[227] *COGE* 12.25 (Junee 18, 1921), p. 3; *COGE* 20.30 (September 21, 1929), p. 3; and *COGE* 22.29 (September 19, 1931), p. 3.
[228] *COGE* 12.41 (October 8, 1921), p. 2; *COGE* 18.44 (November 5, 1927), p. 2; *COGE* 20.33 (October 12, 1929), p. 2; *COGE* 20.35 (November 2, 1929), p. 4; and *COGE* 22.31 (October 3, 1931), p. 1.
[229] *COGE* 17.42 (November 6, 1926), p. 4.
[230] *COGE* 21.27 (August 30, 1930), p. 3.
[231] *COGE* 19.45 (November 17, 1928), p. 2.
[232] COGE 22.35 (November 7, 1931), p. 1; *COGE* 22.39 (December 5, 1931), p. 2.
[233] *COGE* 19.18 (May 15, 1928), p. 1.
[234] *COGE* 22.28 (September 12, 1931), p. 2.
[235] *COGE* 21.28 (September 6, 1930), p. 3.
[236] *COGE* 21.24 (August 9, 1930), p. 3; *COGE* 21.25 (August 16, 1930), p. 2; and COGE 22.22 (August 1, 1931), p. 1.
[237] *COGE* 12.36 (September 3, 1921), p. 2.
[238] *COGE* 9.24 (Junee 15, 1918), p. 4; *COGE* 19.37 (September 15, 1928), p. 1; and COGE 22.34 9October 31, 1931), p. 3.
[239] *COGE* 15.35 (September 13, 1924), p. 1.
[240] *COGE* 21.32 (October 4, 1930), p. 3.
[241] *COGE* 11.37 (September 11, 1920), p. 2.
[242] *COGE* 19.45 (November 17, 1928), p. 2; *COGE* 21.21 (July 19, 1930), p. 3.
[243] *COGE* 10.34 (August 23, 1919), p. 2; *COGE* 16.34 (August 22, 1925), p. 4; *COGE* 19.42 (October 20, 1928), p. 3; and *COGE* 22.11 (May 16, 1931), p. 2.

Wehadkee;[244] Whitney;[245] and Zion.[246]

Arkansas

Aubrey;[247] Bald Knob;[248] Bauxite;[249] Bay Village;[250] Black Rock;[251] Bradford;[252] Caraway;[253] Clarendon;[254] Dewey;[255] Forchin;[256] Harrisburg;[257] Haynes;[258] Haywood Chapel;[259] Hickory Flat;[260] Higden;[261] Hosie;[262] Jericho;[263] Lepanto;[264] Lepanto Junction;[265] Marianna;[266] Marmaduke;[267] Nettleton;[268] Omaha;[269] Pangburn;[270] Paragould;[271] Quitman;[272] Roosevelt;[273] Smithville;[274] Truman;[275] Tyronza;[276] Vanndale;[277] Whitlow Grove;[278] and Widener.[279]

---

[244] *COGE* 22.11 (May 16, 1931), p. 3.
[245] *COGE* 22.20 (July 18, 1931), p. 2.
[246] *COGE* 15.38 (October 4, 1924), p. 3.
[247] COGE 22.33 (October 24, 1931), p. 3.
[248] *COGE* 15.36 (September 20, 1924), p. 2.
[249] *COGE* 22.23 (August 8, 1931), p. 3; *COGE* 22.35 (November 7, 1931), p. 4.
[250] *COGE* 16.45 (November 7, 1925), p. 3.
[251] *COGE* 6.33 (August 14, 1915), p. 1.
[252] *COGE* 15.36 (September 20, 1924), p. 2.
[253] *COGE* 22.25 (August 22, 1931), p. 2; *COGE* 22.28 (September 12, 1931), p. 2.
[254] *COGE* 8.21 (Junee 2, 1917), p. 4.
[255] *COGE* 14.38 (September 15, 1923), p. 3.
[256] *COGE* 21.38 (November 22, 1930), p. 4.
[257] *COGE* 21.31 (September 27, 1930), p. 3.
[258] *COGE* 14.35 (September 1, 1923), p. 3; *COGE* 15.38 (October 4, 1924), p. 3.
[259] *COGE* 13.30 (July 29, 1922), p. 2.
[260] *COGE* 13.36 September 9, 1922), p. 2.
[261] *COGE* 13.21 (May 27, 1922), p. 2; *COGE* 21.35 (November 1, 1930), p. 3.
[262] *COGE* 16.34 (August 22, 1925), p. 4.
[263] *COGE* 11.24 (June 12, 1920), p. 4.
[264] *COGE* 16.34 (August 22, 1925), p. 3; *COGE* 17.15 (April 17, 1926), p. 3; *COGE* 21.26 (August 23, 1930), p. 4; and *COGE* 22.16 (Junee 20, 1931), p. 1.
[265] *COGE* 16.42 (October 17, 1925), p. 2.
[266] *COGE* 22.11 (May 16, 1931), p. 2.
[267] *COGE* 17.31 (August 7, 1926), p. 3.
[268] *COGE* 21.18 (Junee 28, 1930), p. 2.
[269] *COGE* 13.28 (July 15, 1922), p. 2; *COGE* 16.39 (September 26, 1925), p. 3; and *COGE* 21.18 (Junee 28, 1930), p. 4.
[270] *COGE* 12.26 (Junee 25, 1921), p. 2; *COGE* 12.31 (July 30, 1921), p. 2; *COGE* 12.36 (September 3, 1921), p. 2; *COGE* 14.44 (October 27, 1923), p. 4; *COGE* 16.26 (Junee 27, 1925), p. 3; and *COGE* 21.33 (October 11, 1930), p. 3.
[271] *COGE* 14.27 (July 7, 1923), p. 3; *COGE* 17.36 (September 11, 1926), p. 3.
[272] *COGE* 18.38 (September 17, 1927), p. 1; COGE 22.36 (November 14, 1931), p. 4.
[273] *COGE* 13.33 (August 19, 1922), p. 2.
[274] *COGE* 13.47 (December 9, 1922), p. 3.
[275] *COGE* 12.37 (September 10, 1921), p. 2; *COGE* 22.21 (July 25, 1931), p. 1.
[276] *COGE* 10.32 (August 9, 1919), p. 3; *COGE* 13.37 (September 16, 1922), p. 2.
[277] *COGE* 13.34 (August 26, 1922), p. 3; *COGE* 18.43 (October 22, 1927), p. 2.
[278] *COGE* 14.44 (October 27, 1923), p. 4.
[279] *COGE* 16.36 (September 5, 1925), p. 3; *COGE* 17.18 (May 8, 1926), p. 2; and *COGE* 21.32 (October 4, 1930), p. 1.

California
Baldwin Park;[280] Blythe.[281]

Colorado
Segundo.[282]

Delaware
Wilmington.[283]

Florida
Alachua;[284] Alva;[285] Arcadia;[286] Avon Park;[287] Bell;[288] Boyd;[289] Boyette;[290] Bradentown;[291] Brandon;[292] Brewster;[293] Brooksville;[294] Brownville;[295] Canal Point;[296] Chiefland;[297] Clear Mount;[298] Clearwater;[299] Cocoa;[300] Coconut Grove;[301] Coleman;[302] Cortez;[303] Cross City;[304] Culler;[305] Dade City;[306] Daytona;[307] Deerfield;[308] Echo;[309] Erwin Hill;[310] Eustis;[311] Ferndale;[312]

---

[280] *COGE* 13.43 (October 28, 1922), p. 4.
[281] *COGE* 22.7 (April 18, 1931), p. 2.
[282] *COGE* 9.40 (October 5, 1918), p. 3.
[283] *COGE* 17.29 (July 24, 1926), p. 3; *COGE* 20.20 (July 13, 1929), p. 4.
[284] *COGE* 20.13 (May 25, 1929), p. 4.
[285] *COGE* 7.25 (Junee 17, 1916), p. 3.
[286] COGE 22.33 (October 24, 1931), p. 4.
[287] *COGE* 21.34 (October 18, 1930), p. 4.
[288] *COGE* 11.42 (October 16, 1920), p. 2
[289] *COGE* 7.18 (April 29, 1916), p. 2.
[290] *COGE* 5.8 (February 21, 1914), pp. 5, 8.
[291] *COGE* 7.11 (March 11, 1916), p. 2; *COGE* 8.27 (July 14, 1917), p. 4; *COGE* 12.31 (July 30, 1921), p. 2; and *COGE* 13.36 September 9, 1922), p. 3.
[292] *COGE* 5.28 (July 11, 1914), p. 5.
[293] *COGE* 21.26 (August 23, 1930), p. 4; *COGE* 22.25 (August 22, 1931), p. 1.
[294] *COGE* 12.11 (March 12, 1921), p. 3.
[295] *COGE* 13.37 (September 16, 1922), p. 2.
[296] *COGE* 13.37 (Sep 16, 1922), p. 2.
[297] *COGE* 9.30 (July 27, 1918), p. 2; *COGE* 17.36 (September 11, 1926), p. 3.
[298] *COGE* 12.29 (July 16, 1921), p. 2.
[299] *COGE* 6.4 (January 23, 1915), p. 4.
[300] *COGE* 7.30 (July 22, 1916), p. 3.
[301] *COGE* 13.34 (August 26, 1922), p. 2; *COGE* 20.18 (Junee 29, 1929), p. 4; and *COGE* 21.13 (May 24, 1930), p. 3.
[302] *COGE* 18.46 (November 19, 1927), p. 3; *COGE* 22.21 (July 25, 1931), p. 1.
[303] *COGE* 5.41 (October 10, 1914), p. 3; *COGE* 22.19 (July 11, 1931), p. 1.
[304] *COGE* 17.44 (November 20, 1926), p. 4.
[305] *COGE* 14.47 (November 17, 1923), p. 3.
[306] *COGE* 16.39 (September 26, 1925), p. 4.
[307] *COGE* 16.28 (July 11, 1925), p. 3.
[308] *COGE* 15.42 (November 8, 1924), p. 4.
[309] *COGE* 9.35 (August 31, 1918), p. 3.
[310] *COGE* 17.44 (November 20, 1926), p. 4.
[311] *COGE* 15.23 (Junee 21, 1924), p. 3.
[312] *COGE* 15.38 (October 4, 1924), p. 1; *COGE* 19.33 (August 18, 1928, p. 2.

Fessenden;[313] Fort Green;[314] Fort Lauderdale;[315] Fort Myers;[316] Fort Meade;[317] Fort White;[318] Gasparilla;[319] Glen Saint Mary;[320] Haines City;[321] Hamilton County;[322] High Springs;[323] Hudson;[324] Jacksonville;[325] Jennings;[326] Jensen;[327] Judson;[328] Jupiter;[329] Kathleen;[330] Key West;[331] LaBelle;[332] Lake Wales;[333] Largo;[334] Lawtey;[335] Linden;[336] Live Oak;[337] McAlpin;[338] Manatee;[339] Marco;[340] Mayo Junction;[341] Miami;[342] Midway;[343] Milton;[344] Nocatee;[345] O'brien;[346] Okeechobee;[347]

---

[313] *COGE* 15.20 (May 31, 1924), p. 3.
[314] *COGE* 22.31 (October 3, 1931), p. 4.
[315] *COGE* 11.46 (November 20, 1920), p. 3; *COGE* 13.34 (August 26, 1922), p. 2; *COGE* 16.26 (Junee 27, 1925), p. 2; *COGE* 18.28 (July 9, 1927), p. 2; and *COGE* 19.15 (April 14, 1928), pp. 3, 4.
[316] *COGE* 5.38 (September 19, 1914), p. 5; *COGE* 6.3 (January 16, 1915), p. 3; *COGE* 21.15 (Junee 7, 1930), p. 3; and *COGE* 21.49 (February 14, 1931), p. 4.
[317] *COGE* 12.25 (Junee 18, 1921), p. 3.
[318] *COGE* 11.40 (October 2, 1920), p. 2.
[319] *COGE* 21.10 (May 3, 1930), p. 1.
[320] *COGE* 8.26 (July 7, 1917), p. 3.
[321] *COGE* 21.23 (August 2, 1930), p. 1.
[322] *COGE* 22.31 (October 3, 1931), p. 3.
[323] *COGE* 14.41 (October 6, 1923), p. 4.
[324] *COGE* 21.26 (August 23, 1930), p. 4.
[325] *COGE* 15.16 (May 3, 1924), p. 4; *COGE* 18.5 (January 29, 1927), p. 1.
[326] *COGE* 10.35 (August 30, 1919), p. 2.
[327] *COGE* 21.36 (November 8, 1930), p. 3.
[328] *COGE* 20.26 (August 24, 1929), p. 2.
[329] *COGE* 16.5 (January 31, 1925), p. 1; *COGE* 17.20 (May 22, 1926), p. 4; and *COGE* 20.39 (November 30, 1929), p. 4.
[330] *COGE* 16.7 (February 14, 1925), p. 4; *COGE* 22.15 (Junee 13, 1931), p. 2.
[331] *COGE* 6.30 (July 24, 1915, p. 3; *COGE* 16.5 (January 31, 1925), p. 1; and *COGE* 20.27 (August 31, 1929), p. 1
[332] *COGE* 18.28 (July 9, 1927), p. 1; *COGE* 18.30 (July 23, 1927), p. 3; and *COGE* 18.35 (August 27, 1927), p. 1.
[333] *COGE* 18.34 (August 20, 1927), p. 1; COGE 22.34 9October 31, 1931), p. 3.
[334] *COGE* 18.26 (Junee 25, 1927), p. 4.
[335] *COGE* 21.34 (October 18, 1930), p. 4.
[336] *COGE* 5.18 (May 2, 1914), p. 6; *COGE* 7.18 (April 29, 1916), p. 2; *COGE* 17.23 (Junee 12, 1926), p. 4; and COGE 22.27 (September 5, 1931), p. 2.
[337] *COGE* 10.19 (May 10, 1919), p. 3; *COGE* 12.18 (April 30, 1921), p. 2; *COGE* 13.36 September 9, 1922), p. 2; COGE 20.30 (September 21, 1929), p. 1; *COGE* 22.22 (August 1, 1931), p. 1; and COGE 22.31 (October 3, 1931), p. 3.
[338] *COGE* 7.30 (July 22, 1916), p. 2.
[339] *COGE* 17.22 (Junee 5, 1926), p. 4; *COGE* 20.26 (August 24, 1929), p. 4; and *COGE* 21.19 (July 5, 1930), p. 1.
[340] *COGE* 5.18 (May 2, 1914), p. 6.
[341] *COGE* 14.15 (April 14, 1923), p. 2.
[342] *COGE* 6.11 (March 13, 1915), p. 2; *COGE* 11.27 (July 3, 1920), p. 2; *COGE* 11.29 (July 17, 1920), p. 1; *COGE* 12.40 (October 1, 1921), p. 2; *COGE* 13.12 (March 25, 1922), p. 4; *COGE* 17.30 (July 31, 1926), p. 3; and *COGE* 22.9 (May 2, 1931), p. 3.
[343] *COGE* 14.22 (Junee 2, 1923), p. 2.
[344] *COGE* 15.44 (November 22, 1924), p. 2.
[345] *COGE* 16.17 (April 25, 1925), p. 4; *COGE* 19.33 (August 18, 1928, p. 2; *COGE* 20.9 (April 27, 1929), p. 2; and COGE 21.9 (April 26, 1930), p. 1.
[346] *COGE* 11.37 (September 11, 1920), p. 3; *COGE* 19.42 (October 20, 1928), p. 4.
[347] *COGE* 13.15 (April 15, 1922), p. 2.

Olustee;[348] Orlando;[349] Pensacola;[350] Perry;[351] Peters;[352] Plant City;[353] Reddick;[354] Riviera;[355] Salerno;[356] Saint Petersburg;[357] Sarasota;[358] Scanlon;[359] Sulphur Spring;[360] Tampa;[361] Tarpon Springs;[362] Wauchula;[363] Webster;[364] West Palm Beach;[365] Williston;[366] Wimauma;[367] Winter Garden;[368] Zellwood;[369] and Zolfo.[370]

Georgia

Acworth;[371] Albany;[372] Alma;[373] Arber Hill;[374] Atlanta;[375] Augusta;[376] Baxley;[377] Berryton;[378] Blairsville;[379] Brentwood;[380] Bristol;[381]

---

[348] *COGE* 18.32 (August 6, 1927), p. 1.
[349] *COGE* 7.38 (September 16, 1916), p. 2; *COGE* 16.44 (October 31, 1925), p 4; *COGE* 17.24 (Junee 19, 1926), p. 4; *COGE* 19.1 (January 7, 1928), p. 1; *COGE* 19.32 (August 11, 1928), p. 2; and *COGE* 21.42 (December 20, 1930), p. 1.
[350] *COGE* 21.13 (May 24, 1930), p. 3.
[351] *COGE* 7.18 (April 29, 1916), p. 2; *COGE* 15.32 (August 23, 1924), p. 1.
[352] *COGE* 19.12 (March 24, 1928), p. 1.
[353] *COGE* 16.22 (May 30, 1925), p. 4; *COGE* 22.4 (March 28, 1931), p. 3.
[354] *COGE* 16.34 (August 22, 1925), p. 3.
[355] *COGE* 19.19 (May 22, 1928), p. 4; *COGE* 20.5 (March 30, 1929), p. 4; *COGE* 20.23 (August 3, 1929), p. 4; and *COGE* 21.25 (August 16, 1930), p. 4.
[356] COGE 22.26 (August 29, 1931), p. 3.
[357] *COGE* 5.37 (September 12, 1914), p. 5; *COGE* 18.29 (July 16, 1927), p. 1.
[358] *COGE* 16.7 (February 14, 1925), p. 1; *COGE* 19.18 (May 15, 1928), p. 1.
[359] *COGE* 7.20 (May 13, 1916), p. 3.
[360] *COGE* 18.37 (September 10, 1927), p. 3.
[361] *COGE* 11.39 (September 25, 1920), p. 2; *COGE* 12.22 (May 28, 1921), p. 3; *COGE* 13.16 (April 22, 1922), p. 2; *COGE* 13.42 (October 21, 1922), p. 4; *COGE* 16.15 (April 11, 1925), p. 1; and *COGE* 16.46 (November 14, 1925), p. 3.
[362] *COGE* 6.33 (August 14, 1915), p. 4; *COGE* 12.15 (April 9, 1921), p. 3; *COGE* 17.39 (October 2, 1926), p. 4; *COGE* 19.31 (August 4, 1928), p. 1; *COGE* 21.13 (May 24, 1930), p. 1; and *COGE* 22.14 (Junee 6, 1931), p. 1.
[363] *COGE* 15.31 (August 16, 1924), p. 1.
[364] *COGE* 22.36 (November 14, 1931), p. 4.
[365] *COGE* 12.12 (March 19, 1921), p. 2; *COGE* 12.44 (October 29, 1921), p. 2; and *COGE* 18.31 (July 31, 1927), p. 1.
[366] *COGE* 15.46 (December 6, 1924), p. 2; *COGE* 15.47 (December 13, 1924), p. 3.
[367] *COGE* 5.42 (October 17, 1914), p. 3, 4; *COGE* 12.26 (Junee 25, 1921), p. 2; *COGE* 12.31 (July 30, 1921), p. 2; *COGE* 13.26 (July 1, 1922), p. 1; *COGE* 13.45 (November 18, 1922), p. 3; *COGE* 14.27 (July 7, 1923), p. 4; and *COGE* 15.44 (November 22, 1924), p. 1.
[368] *COGE* 17.19 (May 15, 1926), p. 1.
[369] *COGE* 15.32 (August 23, 1924), p. 3; *COGE* 20.28 (September 7, 1929), p. 2.
[370] *COGE* 14.16 (April 21, 1923), p. 4.
[371] *COGE* 21.31 (September 27, 1930), p. 4; COGE 22.35 (November 7, 1931), p. 2.
[372] *COGE* 20.13 (May 25, 1929), p. 1.
[373] *COGE* 22.12 (May 23, 1931), p. 4; *COGE* 22.24 (August 15, 1931), p. 2; and COGE 22.26 (August 29, 1931), p. 2.
[374] *COGE* 20.33 (October 12, 1929), p. 1.
[375] *COGE* 7.21 (May 20, 1916), p. 2.
[376] *COGE* 12.39 (September 24, 1921), p. 2; *COGE* 18.3 (January 15, 1927), p. 2.
[377] *COGE* 19.31 (August 4, 1928), p. 1; COGE 22.34 9October 31, 1931), p. 3.
[378] *COGE* 11.40 (October 2, 1920), p. 2; *COGE* 17.35 (September 4, 1926), p. 3; and *COGE* 19.44 (November 10, 1928), p. 3.
[379] *COGE* 14.50 (December 8, 1923), p. 3.
[380] *COGE* 15.43 (November 15, 1924), p. 1.
[381] *COGE* 16.42 (October 17, 1925), p. 4.

Broxton;[382] Brunswick;[383] Cairo;[384] Carrollton;[385] Calhoun;[386] Canton;[387] Cedartown;[388] Clayton;[389] Cohutta Springs;[390] Crandall;[391] Crane Eater Church of God, near Calhoun;[392] Cobbtown;[393] Dalton;[394] Davisboro;[395] Douglasville;[396] Due;[397] Eldorado;[398] Erwin Hill;[399] Fairmount;[400] Fitzgerald;[401] Hartwell;[402] Hazelhurst;[403] Hiwassee;[404] Jessup;[405] Kennesaw;[406] Lake Park;[407] La Fayette;[408] Lenox;[409] Lindale;[410] Ludville;[411] Lumber City;[412] Macon;[413] Madry Springs;[414] Marietta;[415] Medford;[416] Melrose;[417]

---

[382] *COGE* 14.46 (November 10, 1923), p. 3.

[383] *COGE* 16.44 (October 31, 1925), p 4; *COGE* 21.28 (September 6, 1930), p. 3.

[384] *COGE* 21.16 (Junee 14, 1930), p. 1; *COGE* 21.18 (Junee 28, 1930), p. 4; *COGE* 22.19 (July 11, 1931), p. 3; and COGE 22.30 (September 26, 1931), p. 3.

[385] COGE 22.35 (November 7, 1931), p. 1.

[386] *COGE* 20.29 (September 14, 1929), p. 1.

[387] COGE 22.30 (September 26, 1931), p. 4.

[388] *COGE* 20.37 (November 16, 1929), p. 1; COGE 22.35 (November 7, 1931), p. 4.

[389] COGE 20.31 (September 28, 1929), p. 1; COGE 20.34 (October 19, 1929), p. 4.

[390] *COGE* 13.40 (October 7, 1922), p. 2.

[391] *COGE* 8.34 (September 1, 1917), p. 4.

[392] *COGE* 5.38 (September 19, 1914), p. 7; *COGE* 6.32 (August 7, 1915), p. 2; *COGE* 9.34 (August 24, 1918), p. 2; and *COGE* 10.43 (October 25, 1919), p. 3.

[393] COGE 22.34 (October 31, 1931), p. 3.

[394] *COGE* 12.33 (August 13, 1921), p. 3; *COGE* 15.42 (November 8, 1924), p. 2; *COGE* 15.44 (November 22, 1924), p. 2; *COGE* 16.18 (May 2, 1925), p. 2; *COGE* 16.36 (September 5, 1925), p. 3; *COGE* 17.2 (January 16, 1926), p. 4.; *COGE* 17.36 (September 11, 1926), p. 3; *COGE* 18.39 (September 24, 1927), p. 3; and *COGE* 21.30 (September 20, 1930), p. 3.

[395] *COGE* 11.33 (August 14, 1920), p. 2; *COGE* 14.50 (December 8, 1923), p. 3.

[396] *COGE* 11.21 (May 22, 1920), p. 2.

[397] *COGE* 13.8 (February 25, 1922), p. 3.

[398] *COGE* 12.24 (Junee 11, 1921), p. 3.

[399] *COGE* 22.30 (September 26, 1931), p. 2.

[400] *COGE* 14.44 (October 27, 1923), p. 2; *COGE* 16.35 (August 29, 1925), p. 3.

[401] *COGE* 11.28 (July 10, 1920), p. 2; *COGE* 14.34 (August 25, 1923), p. 2; *COGE* 18.44 (November 5, 1927), p. 3; *COGE* 22.20 (July 18, 1931), p. 1; COGE 22.27 (September 5, 1931), p.1; and *COGE* 22.28 (September 12, 1931), p. 1.

[402] *COGE* 15.38 (October 4, 1924), p. 2; *COGE* 16.39 (September 26, 1925), p. 2; *COGE* 18.6 (February 5, 1927), p. 4; *COGE* 18.38 (September 17, 1927), p. 1; *COGE* 20.37 (November 16, 1929), p. 1; *COGE* 21.25 (August 16, 1930), p. 3; and *COGE* 21.27 (August 30, 1930), p. 3.

[403] *COGE* 11.33 (August 14, 1920), p. 2; *COGE* 13.29 (July 22, 1922), p. 4; and *COGE* 16.24 (Junee 13, 1925), p. 4.

[404] COGE 22.29 (September 19, 1931), p. 1.

[405] *COGE* 12.21 (May 21, 1921), p. 3.

[406] *COGE* 21.32 (October 4, 1930), p. 3.

[407] *COGE* 7.47 (November 18, 1916), p. 2; *COGE* 12.25 (Junee 18, 1921), p. 3.

[408] *COGE* 17.42 (November 6, 1926), p. 4; *COGE* 18.37 (September 10, 1927), p. 3.

[409] *COGE* 13.38 (September 23, 1922), p. 2; *COGE* 21.26 (August 23, 1930), p. 2.

[410] *COGE* 10.43 (October 25, 1919), p. 4; *COGE* 18.33 (August 13, 1927), p. 1; *COGE* 20.19 (July 6, 1929), p. 3; *COGE* 21.28 (September 6, 1930), p. 3; and COGE 22.31 (October 3, 1931), p. 1.

[411] *COGE* 22.24 (August 15, 1931), p. 3; COGE 22.35 (November 7, 1931), p. 3.

[412] *COGE* 19.22 (Junee 2, 1928), p. 3.

[413] *COGE* 20.26 (August 24, 1929), p. 4.

[414] *COGE* 12.35 (August 27, 1921), p. 2; *COGE* 12.36 (September 3, 1921), p. 2.

[415] *COGE* 19.47 (December 1, 1928), p. 2; *COGE* 20.22 (July 27, 1929), p. 3; and *COGE* 21.30 (September 20, 1930), p. 1.

[416] *COGE* 17.29 (July 24, 1926), p. 4; *COGE* 17.31 (August 7, 1926), p. 3.

[417] *COGE* 6.36. (September 4, 1915), p. 3.

Millen;[418] Mountain City;[419] Naugatuck;[420] Nichols;[421] Newtown;[422] Oconee;[423] Odessa; [424] Odum;[425] Offerman;[426] Patterson;[427] Pine Park;[428] Pineview;[429] Quartz;[430] Rocky Ford;[431] Rome;[432] Roswell;[433] Royston;[434] Scaly;[435] Shaw;[436] Sonoraville;[437] Spring Place;[438] Statesboro;[439] Suches;[440] Surrency;[441] Tennille;[442] Thomaston;[443] Toonigh;[444] Valdosta;[445] Varnell;[446] Vidalia;[447] Waresboro;[448] Waycross;[449] West Green;[450] Whigham;[451] Whitegrove;[452] White Stone;[453] Winokur;[454] and Winter Garden.[455]

---

[418] *COGE* 17.24 (Junee 19, 1926), p. 3; *COGE* 17.30 (July 31, 1926), p. 4.
[419] *COGE* 18.43 (October 22, 1927), p. 1.
[420] *COGE* 21.30 (September 20, 1930), p. 1.
[421] *COGE* 16.15 (April 11, 1925), p. 1.
[422] *COGE* 16.34 (August 22, 1925), p. 3; *COGE* 17.37 (September 18, 1926), p. 2.
[423] *COGE* 19.38 (September 22, 1928), p. 2.
[424] *COGE* 12.40 (October 1, 1921), p. 2; COGE 22.27 (September 5, 1931), p. 2.
[425] *COGE* 12.11 (March 12, 1921), p. 3; *COGE* 12.18 (April 30, 1921), p. 3; *COGE* 12.21 (May 21, 1921), p. 3; *COGE* 17.24 (Junee 19, 1926), p. 1; *COGE* 20.28 (September 7, 1929), p. 4; *COGE* 21.26 (August 23, 1930), p. 4;*COGE* 21.31 (September 27, 1930), p. 3; and *COGE* 21.32 (October 4, 1930), p. 1.
[426] *COGE* 11.7 (February 14, 1920), p. 2; *COGE* 12.23 (Junee 4, 1921), p. 3; COGE 21.2 (March 8, 1930), p. 2; and *COGE* 21.48 (February 7, 1931), p. 1.
[427] *COGE* 22.19 (July 11, 1931), p. 3.
[428] *COGE* 22.29 (September 19, 1931), p. 2.
[429] *COGE* 20.30 (September 21, 1929), p. 2; *COGE* 21.29 (September 13, 1930), p. 4.
[430] *COGE* 18.41 (October 8, 1927), p. 2.
[431] *COGE* 21.24 (August 9, 1930), p. 1.
[432] *COGE* 5.35 (August 29, 1914), p. 8; *COGE* 7.40 (September 30, 1916), p. 4; and *COGE* 18.33 (August 13, 1927), p. 1.
[433] *COGE* 17.41 (October 16, 1926), p. 4; *COGE* 19.39 (September 29, 1928), p. 2.
[434] *COGE* 21.30 (September 20, 1930), p. 1.
[435] *COGE* 19.40 (October 6, 1928), p. 1.
[436] *COGE* 18.41 (October 8, 1927), p. 1.
[437] *COGE* 13.34 (August 26, 1922), p. 2.
[438] *COGE* 7.42 (October 14, 1916), p. 3.
[439] *COGE* 13.43 (October 28, 1922), p. 2; and *COGE* 16.34 (August 22, 1925), p. 3.
[440] *COGE* 12.37 (September 10, 1921), p. 2; *COGE* 14.40 (September 29, 1923), p. 3.
[441] *COGE* 13.36 September 9, 1922), p. 2.
[442] *COGE* 22.20 (July 18, 1931), p. 3.
[443] *COGE* 20.12 (May 18, 1929), p. 2; *COGE* 21.27 (August 30, 1930), p. 3; *COGE* 22.21 (July 25, 1931), pp. 3; and COGE 22.30 (September 26, 1931), p. 3.
[444] *COGE* 16.39 (September 26, 1925), p. 3.
[445] *COGE* 14.21 (May 26, 1923), p. 2.
[446] *COGE* 12.23 (June 4, 1921), p. 3; *COGE* 13.35 (September 2, 1922), p. 2.
[447] *COGE* 22.34 (October 31, 1931), p. 3.
[448] *COGE* 12.44 (October 29, 1921), p. 2; *COGE* 13.33 (August 19, 1922), p. 2; *COGE* 14.31 (August 4, 1923), p. 2; and *COGE* 21.24 (August 9, 1930), p. 1.
[449] *COGE* 19.34 (August 25, 1928), p. 3; *COGE* 22.6 (April 11, 1931), p. 3; *COGE* 22.33 (October 24, 1931), p. 2; and COGE 22.35 (November 7, 1931), p. 3.
[450] *COGE* 21.34 (October 18, 1930), p. 4.
[451] *COGE* 18.29 (July 16, 1927), p. 1; *COGE* 18.44 (November 5, 1927), p. 1.
[452] *COGE* 5.42 (October 17, 1914), p. 6.
[453] *COGE* 17.39 (October 2, 1926), p. 4.
[454] *COGE* 21.33 (October 11, 1930), p. 4.
[455] *COGE* 15.27 (July 19, 1924), p. 4.

Illinois

Bridgeport;[456] Cherry Hill;[457] Chicago;[458] Christopher;[459] Dorrisville;[460] East Alton;[461] Eldorado;[462] Harrisburg;[463] Heyworth;[464] Johnston City;[465] Karbers Ridge;[466] Lawrenceville;[467] Logan;[468] Marcoe;[469] McLeansboro;[470] Newport;[471] Olney;[472] Pittsburg;[473] Seminary;[474] Sesser;[475] Sugar Grove;[476] Sumner;[477] and West Frankfort.[478]

Indiana

Lewis;[479] Linton;[480] and Muncie.[481]

Kentucky

Ages;[482] Alton;[483] Arjay;[484] Baizetown;[485] Barbourville;[486] Bowling Green;[487] Brandenburg;[488] Brodhead;[489] Carrie;[490] Cawood;[491]

---

[456] *COGE* 18.41 (October 8, 1927), p. 2; *COGE* 22.19 (July 11, 1931), p. 3.
[457] *COGE* 12.38 (September 17, 1921), p. 2.
[458] *COGE* 21.9 (April 26, 1930), p. 2; *COGE* 20.26 (August 24, 1929), p. 2.
[459] *COGE* 17.20 (May 22, 1926), p. 2; *COGE* 19.48 (December 8, 1928), p. 1.
[460] *COGE* 13.23 (June 10, 1922), p. 2.
[461] *COGE* 21.28 (September 6, 1930), p. 2.
[462] *COGE* 15.29 (August 2, 1924), p. 3; *COGE* 21.15 (June 7, 1930), p. 3; *COGE* 22.14 (June 6, 1931), p. 3; and COGE 22.35 (November 7, 1931), p. 4.
[463] *COGE* 14.48 (November 24, 1923), p. 3; *COGE* 15.13 (March 29, 1924), p. 3.
[464] *COGE* 21.39 (November 29, 1930), p. 3.
[465] *COGE* 11.35 (August 28, 1920), p. 2; *COGE* 21.11 (May 10, 1930), p. 1.
[466] *COGE* 16.24 (June 13, 1925), p. 1.
[467] *COGE* 15.25 (July 5, 1924), p. 4; *COGE* 17.38 (September 25, 1926), p. 3.
[468] *COGE* 12.43 (October 22, 1921), p. 2; *COGE* 18.24 (June 11, 1927), p. 2.
[469] *COGE* 12.47 (November 26, 1921), p. 2.
[470] *COGE* 10.42 (October 18, 1919), p. 4.
[471] *COGE* 12.38 (September 17, 1921), p. 2.
[472] *COGE* 15.25 (July 5, 1924), p. 4; *COGE* 16.39 (September 26, 1925), p. 3
[473] *COGE* 14.39 (September 22, 1923), p. 3.
[474] *COGE* 16.44 (October 31, 1925), p. 4.
[475] *COGE* 11.35 (August 28, 1920), p. 4; *COGE* 18.29 (July 16, 1927), p. 2; and *COGE* 18.31 (July 31, 1927), p. 4.
[476] *COGE* 22.15 (June 13, 1931), p. 2.
[477] *COGE* 18.44 (November 5, 1927), p. 3.
[478] *COGE* 10.26 (June 28, 1919), p. 3; *COGE* 15.16 (May 3, 1924), p. 4; *COGE* 16.30 (July 25, 1925), p. 3; and *COGE* 21.14 (May 31, 1930), p. 2.
[479] *COGE* 22.11 (May 16, 1931), p. 1.
[480] *COGE* 21.23 (August 2, 1930), p. 4.
[481] *COGE* 19.43 (November 3, 1928), p. 3; *COGE* 19.50 (December 22, 1928), p. 1
[482] *COGE* 12.14 (April 2, 1921), p. 3; *COGE* 18.14 (April 2, 1927), p. 4.
[483] *COGE* 14.38 (September 15, 1923), p. 3.
[484] *COGE* 14.15 (April 14, 1923), p. 2.
[485] *COGE* 13.26 (July 1, 1922), p. 2; *COGE* 14.38 (September 15, 1923), p. 3
[486] COGE 22.38 (November 28, 1931), p. 3.
[487] *COGE* 18.43 (October 22, 1927), p. 4; *COGE* 19.41 (October 13, 1928), p. 1.
[488] *COGE* 12.42 (October 15, 1921), p. 2.
[489] *COGE* 21.30 (September 20, 1930), p. 2.
[490] *COGE* 14.1 (January 6, 1923), p. 2.
[491] *COGE* 19.34 (August 25, 1928), p. 2; *COGE* 21.13 (May 24, 1930), p. 4.

Chavies;[492] Christopher;[493] Corbin;[494] Cromwell;[495] Cropper;[496] Dekoven;[497] Eastern;[498] Echols;[499] Elizabethtown;[500] Evarts;[501] Flemingsburg;[502] Fonde;[503] Fordsville;[504] Grangertown;[505] Harlan;[506] Harris;[507] Hazard;[508] Hazelgreen;[509] Hode;[510] Louisville;[511] Heidelberg;[512] High Splint;[513] Hollingsworth;[514] Lawrenceburg;[515] Leighton;[516] Lejunior;[517] Linda;[518] McHenry;[519] McVeigh;[520] Mater;[521] Middlesboro;[522] Millstone;[523] Morganfield;[524] Nancy;[525] Nigh;[526] Oak Grove;[527] Oppy;[528] Pinson Fork;[529] Providence;[530] Quicksand;[531] Ravenna;[532] Saint Helen;[533]

---

[492] *COGE* 18.16 (April 15, 1927), p. 4.
[493] *COGE* 13.38 (September 23, 1922), p. 3; *COGE* 15.28 (July 26, 1924), p. 2; and *COGE* 17.12 (March 27, 1926), p. 4.
[494] *COGE* 6.26 (June 26, 1915), p. 3; *COGE* 14.5 (February 3, 1923), p. 3.
[495] *COGE* 13.31 (August 5, 1922), p. 2; *COGE* 19.37 (September 15, 1928), p. 4.
[496] *COGE* 18.7 (February 12, 1927), p. 1.
[497] *COGE* 11.9 (February 28, 1920), p. 4.
[498] *COGE* 17.45 (November 27, 1926), p. 4.
[499] *COGE* 13.36 September 9, 1922), p. 2.
[500] *COGE* 14.31 (August 4, 1923), p. 2.
[501] *COGE* 21.33 (October 11, 1930), p. 4.
[502] *COGE* 14.50 (December 8, 1923), p. 3.
[503] *COGE* 11.50 (December 26, 1920), p. 3; *COGE* 14.52 (December 22, 1923), p. 2.
[504] *COGE* 11.22 (May 29, 1920), p. 4.
[505] *COGE* 11.31 (July 31, 1920), p. 2.
[506] *COGE* 17.24 (June 19, 1926), p. 4; *COGE* 21.27 (August 30, 1930), p. 1; and COGE 22.24 (August 15, 1931), p. 3.
[507] *COGE* 18.44 (November 5, 1927), p. 1; *COGE* 21.28 (September 6, 1930), p. 3.
[508] *COGE* 12.16 (April 16, 1921), p. 2.
[509] *COGE* 11.9 (February 28, 1920), p. 1.
[510] *COGE* 21.37 (November 15, 1930), p. 3.
[511] *COGE* 11.27 (July 3, 1920), p. 3; *COGE* 13.44 (November 11, 1922), p. 1; and *COGE* 15.41 (October 25, 1924), p. 2.
[512] *COGE* 18.47 (November 26, 1927), p. 4.
[513] *COGE* 19.4 (January 28, 1928), p. 3.
[514] *COGE* 18.27 (July 2, 1927), p. 2.
[515] *COGE* 14.38 (September 15, 1923), p. 3.
[516] *COGE* 18.29 (July 16, 1927), p. 4.
[517] *COGE* 17.25 (June 26, 1926), p. 4.
[518] *COGE* 20.33 (October 12, 1929), p. 3; *COGE* 21.39 (November 29, 1930), p. 3.
[519] *COGE* 11.28 (July 10, 1920), p. 1.
[520] *COGE* 17.32 (August 14, 1926), p. 3; *COGE* 18.28 (July 9, 1927), p. 1; and *COGE* 19.50 (December 22, 1928), p. 4.
[521] *COGE* 13.44 (November 11, 1922), p. 2; *COGE* 16.14 (April 4, 1925), p. 3.
[522] *COGE* 22.9 (May 2, 1931), p. 1.
[523] *COGE* 21.41 (December 13, 1930), p. 1.
[524] *COGE* 12.39 (September 24, 1921), p. 2.
[525] *COGE* 21.26 (August 23, 1930), p. 2.
[526] *COGE* 21.27 (August 30, 1930), p. 4.
[527] *COGE* 21.29 (September 13, 1930), p. 2.
[528] *COGE* 11.42 (October 16, 1920), p. 2.
[529] *COGE* 18.37 (September 10, 1927), p. 3.
[530] *COGE* 13.28 (July 15, 1922), p. 2.
[531] *COGE* 12.2 (January 8, 1921), p. 3.
[532] *COGE* 16.30 (July 25, 1925), p. 1.
[533] *COGE* 12.36 (September 3, 1921), p. 2.

Salem;[534] Shamrock;[535] Soloma;[536] Somerset;[537] Stithton;[538] Straight Creek;[539] Stringtown;[540] Sturgis;[541] Tribbey;[542] Twila;[543] Wess;[544] Willisburg;[545] Winchester;[546] Windyville;[547] Worley;[548] and Yancey.[549]

Louisiana

Archibald;[550] Bogalusa;[551] Covington;[552] Dunn;[553] Epps;[554] Folsom;[555] Forest;[556] Kentwood;[557] Monroe;[558] Onlive;[559] Rayville;[560] Shepherd's Fold;[561] and Uneedus.[562]

Maine

Portland.[563]

Maryland

Eden;[564] Frederickstown;[565] Fruitland;[566] and

---

[534] *COGE* 14.42 (October 13, 1923), p. 3; *COGE* 20.34 (October 19, 1929), p. 3.
[535] *COGE* 12.10 (March 5, 1921), p. 2.
[536] *COGE* 21.46 (January 24, 1931), p. 4.
[537] *COGE* 10.29 (July 19, 1919), p. 4; *COGE* 10.31 (August 2, 1919), p. 2; *COGE* 16.39 (September 26, 1925), p. 1; *COGE* 17.26 (July 3, 1926), p. 4; *COGE* 20.29 (September 14, 1929), p. 3; and *COGE* 21.20 (July 12, 1930), p. 4.
[538] *COGE* 11.21 (May 22, 1920), p. 4.
[539] *COGE* 13.44 (November 11, 1922), p. 4.
[540] *COGE* 14.30 (July 28, 1923), p. 3.
[541] *COGE* 12.31 (July 30, 1921), p. 2; *COGE* 12.32 (August 6, 1921), p. 2; and *COGE* 13.36 September 9, 1922), p. 2.
[542] *COGE* 21.34 (October 18, 1930), p. 1.
[543] *COGE* 15.13 (March 29, 1924), p. 4; *COGE* 18.44 (November 5, 1927), p. 1.
[544] *COGE* 12.12 (March 19, 1921), p. 2; *COGE* 12.25 (June 18, 1921), p. 3; and *COGE* 13.42 (October 21, 1922), p. 2.
[545] *COGE* 11.39 (September 25, 1920), p. 2; *COGE* 13.41 (October 14, 1922), p. 2.
[546] *COGE* 15.41 (October 25, 1924), p. 2.
[547] *COGE* 12.48 (December 3, 1921), p. 2.
[548] *COGE* 18.44 (November 5, 1927), p. 3.
[549] *COGE* 19.37 (September 15, 1928), p. 4.
[550] *COGE* 22.30 (September 26, 1931), p. 1.
[551] *COGE* 13.44 (November 11, 1922), p. 1.
[552] *COGE* 12.21 (May 21, 1921), p. 3; *COGE* 14.11 (March 17, 1923), p. 4; and *COGE* 12.29 (July 16, 1921), p. 2.
[553] *COGE* 11.28 (July 10, 1920), p. 3; *COGE* 13.32 (August 12, 1922), p. 2; *COGE* 17.14 (April 10, 1926), p. 2; *COGE* 17.24 (June 19, 1926), p. 4; and *COGE* 20.16 (June 15, 1929), p. 4.
[554] *COGE* 20.30 (September 21, 1929), p. 4.
[555] *COGE* 12.17 (April 23, 1921), p. 2; *COGE* 19.41 (October 13, 1928), p. 1.
[556] *COGE* 22.23 (August 8, 1931), p. 1.
[557] *COGE* 5.38 (September 19, 1914), p. 5; *COGE* 7.17 (April 22, 1916), p. 3; *COGE* 12.21 (May 21, 1921), p. 3; *COGE* 18.43 (October 22, 1927), p. 1; and *COGE* 22.11 (May 16, 1931), p. 2.
[558] *COGE* 16.19 (May 9, 1925), p. 4; *COGE* 16.47 (November 21, 1925), p. 3.
[559] *COGE* 12.18 (April 30, 1921), p. 2; *COGE* 14.46 (November 10, 1923), p. 3.
[560] *COGE* 20.18 (June 29, 1929), p. 4.
[561] *COGE* 13.34 (August 26, 1922), p. 3.
[562] *COGE* 21.21 (July 19, 1930), p. 3.
[563] *COGE* 21.24 (August 9, 1930), p. 3.
[564] *COGE* 12.19 (May 7, 1921), p. 3.
[565] *COGE* 13.44 (November 11, 1922), p. 2.
[566] *COGE* 12.33 (August 13, 1921), p. 3.

Preston.[567]

Michigan

Lake Odessa;[568] Detroit;[569] and Pontiac.[570]

Mississippi

Booneville;[571] Bradley;[572] Charleston;[573] Cascilla;[574] Cebastorpol;[575] Chapel Hill;[576] Conehatta;[577] Darbun;[578] Delta;[579] Drew;[580] Eupora;[581] Hardy;[582] Houston;[583] Indianola;[584] Isola;[585] Joyess;[586] Lodi;[587] Liberty;[588] Longview;[589] McCall;[590] McCall Creek;[591] Magee;[592] Mendenhall;[593] Merigold;[594] Mize;[595] Mooresville;[596] Morgantown;[597] Neshoba;[598] Philadelphia;[599] Pickwick;[600] Ratliff;[601] Reid;[602]

---

[567] *COGE* 8.34 (September 1, 1917), p. 2.
[568] *COGE* 16.28 (July 11, 1925), p. 1; and *COGE* 19.19 (May 22, 1928), p. 3.
[569] *COGE* 21.50 (February 21, 1931), p. 2.
[570] COGE 22.36 (November 14, 1931), p. 4; COGE 22.37 (November 21, 1931), p. 4.
[571] *COGE* 21.30 (September 20, 1930), p. 1; COGE 22.31 (October 3, 1931), p. 2.
[572] *COGE* 21.27 (August 30, 1930), p. 3.
[573] *COGE* 1.16 (October 15, 1910), p. 4.
[574] *COGE* 1.18 (November 15, 1910), p. 8.
[575] *COGE* 18.16 (April 15, 1927), p. 1.
[576] *COGE* 12.41 (October 8, 1921), p. 2.
[577] *COGE* 22.11 (May 16, 1931), p. 2.
[578] *COGE* 6.37 (September 11, 1915), p. 4; *COGE* 7.42 (October 14, 1916), p. 4.
[579] *COGE* 11.39 (September 25, 1920), p. 3.
[580] *COGE* 17.23 (June 12, 1926), p. 2.
[581] *COGE* 8.22 (June 9, 1917), p. 2; *COGE* 17.38 (September 25, 1926), p. 3; *COGE* 17.40 (October 9, 1926), p. 3; *COGE* 19.47 (December 1, 1928), p. 4; *COGE* 22.28 (September 12, 1931), p. 2; and *COGE* 22.33 (October 24, 1931), p. 4.
[582] *COGE* 8.31 (August 11, 1917), p. 4.
[583] *COGE* 20.28 (September 7, 1929), p. 1.
[584] *COGE* 12.17 (April 23, 1921), p. 2.
[585] *COGE* 20.29 (September 14, 1929), p 4.
[586] *COGE* 8.22 (June 9, 1917), p. 3.
[587] *COGE* 11.39 (September 25, 1920), p. 3.
[588] *COGE* 13.31 (August 5, 1922), p. 3; *COGE* 18.40 (October 1, 1927), p. 1.
[589] *COGE* 20.36 (November 9, 1929), p. 1; *COGE* 21.18 (June 28, 1930), p. 3; *COGE* 21.27 (August 30, 1930), p. 3; and *COGE* 22.30 (September 26, 1931), p. 1.
[590] *COGE* 22.31 (October 3, 1931), p. 2.
[591] *COGE* 12.21 (May 21, 1921), p. 3.
[592] *COGE* 21.32 (October 4, 1930), p. 4; COGE 22.35 (November 7, 1931), p. 3.
[593] *COGE* 21.28 (September 6, 1930), p. 2.
[594] *COGE* 18.38 (September 17, 1927), p. 1.
[595] *COGE* 20.26 (August 24, 1929), p.2; *COGE* 21.25 (August 16, 1930), p.1.
[596] *COGE* 12.38 (September 17, 1921), p. 2.
[597] *COGE* 19.41 (October 13, 1928), p. 1; *COGE* 19.45 (November 17, 1928), p. 2; *COGE* 21.25 (August 16, 1930), p. 4; *COGE* 22.12 (May 23, 1931), p. 4; and *COGE* 22.13 (May 30, 1931), p. 2.
[598] *COGE* 17.42 (November 6, 1926), p. 3.
[599] *COGE* 16.41 (October 10, 1925), p. 3.
[600] *COGE* 12.34 (August 20, 1921), p. 3; *COGE* 13.39 (September 30, 1922), p. 3.
[601] *COGE* 21.32 (October 4, 1930), p. 4.
[602] *COGE* 12.36 (September 3, 1921), p. 2.

Reform;[603] Richburg;[604] Ruleville;[605] Sebastopol;[606] Summit;[607] Thorn;[608] Webb;[609] Weir;[610] and Winborn.[611]

Missouri

Bonne Terre;[612] Brighton;[613] Broadwater;[614] Cantwell;[615] Desloge;[616] Fredericktown;[617] Graniteville;[618] Harmony;[619] Joplin;[620] Lamar;[621] Leadwood;[622] Marble Hill;[623] Mountain Grove;[624] North St. Joseph;[625] Qulin;[626] and St. Joseph.[627]

Montana

Big Timber;[628] Boulder;[629] Joliet;[630] and Lewiston.[631]

New Jersey

Swedesboro;[632] Woodbury.[633]

New Mexico

Albuquerque;[634] Raton.[635]

---

[603] *COGE* 16.39 (September 26, 1925), p. 3.
[604] *COGE* 12.32 (August 6, 1921), p. 2.
[605] *COGE* 13.37 (September 16, 1922), p. 2.
[606] *COGE* 20.28 (September 7, 1929), p.1.
[607] *COGE* 13.25 (June, 24, 1922), p. 2.
[608] *COGE* 12.39 (September 24, 1921), p. 2.
[609] *COGE* 16.20 (May 16, 1925), p. 3.
[610] *COGE* 7.42 (October 14, 1916), p. 3
[611] *COGE* 22.33 (October 24, 1931), p. 3.
[612] *COGE* 11.33 (August 14, 1920), p. 2.
[613] *COGE* 12.37 (September 10, 1921), p. 2; *COGE* 13.47 (December 9, 1922), p. 3; and COGE 22.31 (October 3, 1931), p. 3.
[614] *COGE* 15.39 (October 11, 1924), p. 1.
[615] *COGE* 12.10 (March 5, 1921), p. 2; *COGE* 15.39 (October 11, 1924), p. 1; *COGE* 19.22 (June 2, 1928), p. 2; and *COGE* 22.14 (June 6, 1931), p. 1.
[616] *COGE* 21.25 (August 16, 1930), p. 3.
[617] *COGE* 13.32 (August 12, 1922), p. 2; *COGE* 13.37 (September 16, 1922), p. 2.
[618] *COGE* 16.27 (July 4, 1925), p. 1.
[619] *COGE* 16.21 (May 23, 1925), p. 3.
[620] *COGE* 20.3 (March 16, 1929), p. 4.
[621] *COGE* 12.18 (April 30, 1921), p. 3.
[622] *COGE* 18.41 (October 8, 1927), p. 2.
[623] *COGE* 13.41 (October 14, 1922), p. 2.
[624] *COGE* 12.34 (August 20, 1921), p. 3.
[625] *COGE* 22.21 (July 25, 1931), p. 1.
[626] *COGE* 12.34 (August 20, 1921), p. 3.
[627] *COGE* 18.38 (September 17, 1927), p. 1.
[628] *COGE* 21.38 (November 22, 1930), p. 2.
[629] *COGE* 18.34 (August 20, 1927), p. 2.
[630] *COGE* 22.7 (April 18, 1931), p. 3.
[631] *COGE* 21.32 (October 4, 1930), p. 4.
[632] *COGE* 12.31 (July 30, 1921), p. 2.
[633] *COGE* 10.21 (May 24, 1919), p. 2; *COGE* 12.26 (June 25, 1921), p. 2.
[634] *COGE* 12.20 (May 14, 1921), p. 2.
[635] *COGE* 8.40 (October 13, 1917), p. 4.

Appendices 425

New York

Brooklyn.[636]

North Carolina

Adley;[637] Alarka;[638] Albermarle;[639] Andrews;[640] Asheville;[641] Belmont;[642] Bessemer City;[643] Charlotte;[644] Clyde;[645] Draper;[646] Dunn;[647] East Laport;[648] Ela;[649] Erwin;[650] Fayetteville;[651] Gastonia;[652] Greenville;[653] Hayesville;[654] Hope Mills;[655] Kannapolis;[656] Mooresville;[657] North Wilkesboro;[658] Reeds Cross Roads;[659] Ryder;[660] Scaly;[661] Selma;[662] Shooting Creek;[663] Shooting Rock;[664] Smithfield;[665] Sunburst;[666] Tusquittee;[667] Washington;[668] and Wilmington.[669]

---

[636] *COGE* 12.23 (June 4, 1921), p. 2.
[637] *COGE* 16.39 (September 26, 1925), p. 3.
[638] *COGE* 18.37 (September 10, 1927), p. 1; *COGE* 22.36 (November 14, 1931), p. 4.
[639] *COGE* 13.30 (July 29, 1922), p. 2; *COGE* 12.36 (September 3, 1921), p. 2.
[640] COGE 22.33 (October 24, 1931), p. 2.
[641] *COGE* 20.20 (July 13, 1929), p. 1; *COGE* 22.17 (June 27, 1931), p. 4; and *COGE* 22.33 (October 24, 1931), p. 3.
[642] *COGE* 11.46 (November 20, 1920), p. 2; *COGE* 16.44 (October 31, 1925), p 4; *COGE* 17.35 (September 4, 1926), p. 2; *COGE* 18.40 (October 1, 1927), p. 1; *COGE* 19.18 (May 15, 1928), p. 1; *COGE* 20.24 (August 10, 1929), p. 4; and *COGE* 20.50 (February 22, 1930), p. 4.
[643] *COGE* 7.30 (July 22, 1916), p. 2.
[644] *COGE* 18.25 (June 18, 1927), p. 2; *COGE* 18.31 (July 31, 1927), p. 1; *COGE* 18.43 (October 22, 1927), p. 1; *COGE* 19.32 (August 11, 1928), p. 2; and *COGE* 21.16 (June 14, 1930), p. 3.
[645] COGE 22.33 (October 24, 1931), p. 3.
[646] *COGE* 21.24 (August 9, 1930), p. 3.
[647] *COGE* 8.31 (August 11, 1917), p. 3
[648] *COGE* 15.22 (June 14, 1924), p. 3.
[649] *COGE* 21.32 (October 4, 1930), p. 4.
[650] *COGE* 21.33 (October 11, 1930), p. 2.
[651] *COGE* 12.28 (July 9, 1921), p. 4.
[652] *COGE* 17.35 (September 4, 1926), p. 3; *COGE* 20.15 (June 8, 1929), p. 1.
[653] *COGE* 20.18 (June 29, 1929), p. 1.
[654] *COGE* 8.21 (June 2, 1917), p. 4; *COGE* 10.38 (September 20, 1919), p. 3; *COGE* 15.39 (October 11, 1924), p. 1; and *COGE* 18.43 (October 22, 1927), p. 1.
[655] *COGE* 22.15 (June 13, 1931), p. 1.
[656] *COGE* 8.32 (August 18, 1917), p. 4; *COGE* 13.29 (July 22, 1922), p. 3; *COGE* 14.39 (September 22, 1923), p. 3; *COGE* 19.31 (August 4, 1928), p. 4; and *COGE* 21.19 (July 5, 1930), p. 3.
[657] *COGE* 22.17 (June 27, 1931), p. 1.
[658] *COGE* 19.41 (October 13, 1928), p. 4.
[659] *COGE* 22.35 (November 7, 1931), p. 4.
[660] *COGE* 21.28 (September 6, 1930), p. 3
[661] *COGE* 20.33 (October 12, 1929), p. 2; *COGE* 21.21 (July 19, 1930), p. 4.
[662] *COGE* 16.42 (October 17, 1925), p. 3.
[663] *COGE* 15.36 (September 20, 1924), p. 3; *COGE* 21.35 (November 1, 1930), p. 2; and COGE 22.33 (October 24, 1931), p. 2.
[664] *COGE* 16.36 (September 5, 1925), pp. 1-2.
[665] *COGE* 18.36 (September 5, 1927), p. 1.
[666] *COGE* 10.14 (April 5, 1919), p. 2; *COGE* 13.29 (July 22, 1922), p. 2.
[667] *COGE* 11.35 (August 28, 1920), p. 2; *COGE* 16.44 (October 31, 1925), p. 3; and *COGE* 18.38 (September 17, 1927), p. 1.
[668] *COGE* 16.39 (September 26, 1925), p. 3; COGE 20.30 (September 21, 1929), p. 3.
[669] *COGE* 19.32 (August 11, 1928), p. 1; *COGE* 21.33 (October 11, 1930), p. 4.

North Dakota

Berthold;[670] Golden Valley;[671] Hartland;[672] Ree;[673] and Shell Creek.[674]

Ohio

Akron;[675] Archers Fork;[676] Canton;[677] Cincinnati;[678] Columbus;[679] Circleville;[680] Dayton;[681] Findlay;[682] Hamilton;[683] Ironton;[684] Jackson;[685] Kenmore;[686] Lancaster;[687] Lawndale;[688] Magnolia;[689] Marietta;[690] Middletown;[691] Roanoke;[692] South Lebanon;[693] Toledo;[694] Walbridge;[695] Wellston;[696] and Youngstown.

Oklahoma

Ardmore;[697] Bold Springs;[698] Butler;[699] Corn;[700]

---

[670] *COGE* 19.26 (June 30, 1928), p. 3; *COGE* 19.28 (July 14, 1928), p. 1.
[671] *COGE* 14.47 (November 17, 1923), p.4; *COGE* 15.30 (August 9, 1924), p. 3; and *COGE* 15.39 (October 11, 1924), p. 1.
[672] *COGE* 21.37 (November 15, 1930), p. 1.
[673] *COGE* 17.25 (June 26, 1926), p. 1; *COGE* 17.37 (September 18, 1926), p. 3.
[674] *COGE* 18.35 (August 27, 1927), p. 3.
[675] *COGE* 12.41 (October 8, 1921), p. 2; *COGE* 17.29 (July 24, 1926), p. 4; *COGE* 18.35 (August 27, 1927), p. 1; *COGE* 18.40 (October 1, 1927), p. 3; COGE 21.8 (April 19, 1930), p. 4; *COGE* 21.41 (December 13, 1930), p. 4; and *COGE* 21.43 (January 3, 1931), p. 4.
[676] *COGE* 14.5 (February 3, 1923), p. 3.
[677] *COGE* 15.45 (November 29, 1924), p. 1; *COGE* 17.15 (April 17, 1926), p. 3; and COGE 22.31 (October 3, 1931), p. 1.
[678] *COGE* 16.22 (May 30, 1925), p. 3; *COGE* 17.7 (February 20, 1926), p. 2; *COGE* 18.28 (July 9, 1927), p. 1; *COGE* 20.21 (July 20, 1929), p. 1; and *COGE* 21.15 (June 7, 1930), p. 3.
[679] *COGE* 21.24 (August 9, 1930), p. 2.
[680] *COGE* 13.3 (January 21, 1922), p. 3; *COGE* 13.31 (August 5, 1922), p. 2; and *COGE* 14.43 (October 20, 1923), p. 4.
[681] *COGE* 16.42 (October 17, 1925), p. 1; *COGE* 16.47 (November 21, 1925), p. 3; and *COGE* 18.16 (April 15, 1927), p. 2.
[682] *COGE* 19.34 (August 25, 1928), p. 2.
[683] *COGE* 16.41 (October 10, 1925), p. 2; *COGE* 21.33 (October 11, 1930), p. 1.
[684] *COGE* 18.52 (December 24, 1927), p. 3.
[685] *COGE* 17.24 (June 19, 1926), p. 4; *COGE* 19.36 (September 8, 1928), p. 2.
[686] *COGE* 15.44 (November 22, 1924), p. 1.
[687] *COGE* 17.16 (April 24, 1926), p. 1.
[688] *COGE* 16.6 (February 7, 1925), p. 1.
[689] *COGE* 18.28 (July 9, 1927), p. 1; *COGE* 19.30 (July 28, 1928), p. 4.
[690] *COGE* 15.16 (May 3, 1924), p. 4; *COGE* 21.15 (June 7, 1930), p. 3; and COGE 22.27 (September 5, 1931), p. 2.
[691] *COGE* 11.17 (April 24, 1920), p. 3; *COGE* 12.14 (April 2, 1921), p. 3; *COGE* 12.40 (October 1, 1921), p. 2; *COGE* 14.14 (April 7, 1923), p. 3; *COGE* 19.49 (December 15, 1928), p. 1; and *COGE* 21.7 (April 12, 1930), p. 1.
[692] *COGE* 21.27 (August 30, 1930), p. 1.
[693] *COGE* 14.25 (June 23, 1923), p. 3; *COGE* 21.2 (March 8, 1930), p. 1
[694] COGE 20.31 (September 28, 1929), p. 4.
[695] *COGE* 9.28 (July 13, 1918), p. 2.
[696] *COGE* 18.42 (October 15, 1927), p. 2.
[697] *COGE* 15.25 (July 5, 1924), p. 4.
[698] *COGE* 14.42 (October 13, 1923), p. 3.
[699] *COGE* 16.34 (August 22, 1925), p. 3.
[700] *COGE* 20.29 (September 14, 1929), p. 4; *COGE* 21.35 (November 1, 1930), p. 2.

Crescent;[701] Depew;[702] Finley;[703] Lawton;[704] Maud;[705] Murphy;[706] Ravia;[707] Seminole;[708] Snyder;[709] Stillwell;[710] Tellor;[711] and Weatherford.[712]

Pennsylvania

Emlenton;[713] Harrisburg;[714] Norristown;[715] Pittsburgh;[716] Six Points;[717] Somerset;[718] Underhill;[719] and Williamsburg.[720]

South Carolina

Aiken;[721]; Anderson;[722] Blacksburg;[723] Bunker Hill;[724] Charleston;[725] Cherokee Falls;[726] Columbia;[727] Crow Creek;[728] Dillon;[729] Easley;[730] Fork;[731] Gaffney;[732] Greenville;[733]

---

[701] *COGE* 10.40 (October 4, 1919), p. 2.
[702] *COGE* 21.6 (April 5, 1930), p. 4; *COGE* 21.30 (September 20, 1930), p. 1.
[703] *COGE* 21.44 (January 10, 1931), p. 2.
[704] *COGE* 12.34 (August 20, 1921), p. 3.
[705] *COGE* 18.42 (October 15, 1927), p. 1; *COGE* 21.22 (July 26, 1930), p. 1; and COGE 22.28 (September 12, 1931), p. 3.
[706] *COGE* 21.18 (June 28, 1930), p. 2.
[707] *COGE* 12.39 (September 24, 1921), p. 2; *COGE* 13.29 (July 22, 1922), p. 4; *COGE* 21.27 (August 30, 1930), p. 2; and *COGE* 21.28 (September 6, 1930), p. 3.
[708] *COGE* 21.27 (August 30, 1930), p. 3.
[709] *COGE* 21.30 (September 20, 1930), p. 1.
[710] *COGE* 15.37 (September 27, 1924), p. 2.
[711] *COGE* 14.34 (August 25, 1923), p. 2.
[712] *COGE* 12.34 (August 20, 1921), p. 3.
[713] *COGE* 13.36 September 9, 1922), p. 2.
[714] COGE 20.33 (October 12, 1929), p. 4.
[715] *COGE* 17.43 (November 13, 1926), p. 4; *COGE* 21.31 (September 27, 1930), p. 3.
[716] *COGE* 19.24 (June 16, 1928), p. 3; *COGE* 16.29 (July 18, 1925), p. 4.
[717] *COGE* 14.40 (September 29, 1923), p. 3.
[718] *COGE* 18.44 (November 5, 1927), p. 3.
[719] *COGE* 22.21 (July 25, 1931), p. 3.
[720] *COGE* 22.12 (May 23, 1931), p. 4.
[721] *COGE* 21.25 (August 16, 1930), p. 2; *COGE* 21.31 (September 27, 1930), p. 4.
[722] *COGE* 15.34 (September 6, 1924), p. 2; *COGE* 15.42 (November 8, 1924), p. 2; *COGE* 18.35 (August 27, 1927), p. 1; and *COGE* 21.32 (October 4, 1930), p. 3.
[723] *COGE* 17.18 (May 8, 1926), p. 2.
[724] *COGE* 12.40 (October 1, 1921), p. 2.
[725] *COGE* 19.47 (December 1, 1928), p. 1.
[726] *COGE* 22.24 (August 15, 1931), p. 1.
[727] *COGE* 13.40 (October 7, 1922), p. 3; *COGE* 16.36 (September 5, 1925), p. 4; and *COGE* 21.3 (March 15, 1930), p. 4.
[728] *COGE* 16.39 (September 26, 1925), p. 3.
[729] *COGE* 12.21 (May 21, 1921), p. 3; *COGE* 12.31 (July 30, 1921), p. 2; *COGE* 13.44 (November 11, 1922), p. 4; *COGE* 14.32 (August 11, 1923), p. 3; *COGE* 17.30 (July 31, 1926), p. 3; and *COGE* 17.35 (September 4, 1926), p. 3.
[730] *COGE* 16.42 (October 17, 1925), p. 3.
[731] *COGE* 11.21 (May 22, 1920), p. 2; *COGE* 11.46 (November 20, 1920), p. 1.
[732] *COGE* 22.31 (October 3, 1931), p. 1.
[733] *COGE* 11.38 (September 18, 1920), p. 3; *COGE* 13.42 (October 21, 1922), p. 4; *COGE* 15.27 (July 19, 1924), p. 3; *COGE* 21.36 (November 8, 1930), p. 1; *COGE* 22.31 (October 3, 1931), p. 2; and *COGE* 22.37 (November 21, 1931), p. 4.

Hamer;[734] Honea Path;[735] LaFrance;[736] Lando;[737] McColl;[738] Pendleton;[739] Piedmont;[740] Rock Hill;[741] Ruby;[742] Townville;[743] Walhalla;[744] Warrenville;[745] Westminster;[746] West Union;[747] and Winnsboro.[748]

Tennessee

Afton;[749] Aetna Mountain;[750] Alcoa;[751] Baggett's Chapel;[752] Bald Hill;[753] Belltown;[754] Birchwood;[755] Black Oak;[756] Bone Cave;[757] Bristol;[758] Brockdell;[759] Bybee;[760] Campaign;[761] Carson Springs;[762] Cedar Hill;[763] Chattanooga;[764]

---

[734] *COGE* 14.34 (August 25, 1923), p. 2.
[735] *COGE* 13.30 (July 29, 1922), p. 2.
[736] *COGE* 20.31 (September 28, 1929), p. 2; *COGE* 22.16 (June 20, 1931), p. 1; and *COGE* 22.21 (July 25, 1931), p. 2.
[737] *COGE* 14.6 (February 10, 1923), p. 2.
[738] *COGE* 13.36 September 9, 1922), p. 2.
[739] *COGE* 18.43 (October 22, 1927), p. 1; *COGE* 19.30 (July 28, 1928), p. 1.
[740] *COGE* 14.28 (July 14, 1923), p. 2.
[741] *COGE* 10.43 (October 25, 1919), p. 4; *COGE* 17.39 (October 2, 1926), p. 3; and *COGE* 21.31 (September 27, 1930), p. 3.
[742] *COGE* 14.42 (October 13, 1923), p. 3.
[743] *COGE* 16.44 (October 31, 1925), p. 4; *COGE* 20.34 (October 19, 1929), p. 2.
[744] *COGE* 8.35 (September 8, 1917), p. 2; *COGE* 12.38 (September 17, 1921), p. 2; *COGE* 13.36 September 9, 1922), p. 2; *COGE* 13.40 (October 7, 1922), p. 2; *COGE* 14.18 (May 5, 1923), p. 3; *COGE* 16.35 (August 29, 1925), p. 4; *COGE* 19.30 (July 28, 1928), p. 3; *COGE* 20.15 (June 8, 1929), p. 1; *COGE* 20.34 (October 19, 1929), p. 1; *COGE* 21.16 (June 14, 1930), p. 2; *COGE* 21.39 (November 29, 1930), p. 2; *COGE* 22.17 (June 27, 1931), p. 2; *COGE* 22.23 (August 8, 1931), p. 1; and *COGE* 22.36 (November 14, 1931), p. 4.
[745] *COGE* 22.38 (November 28, 1931), p. 3.
[746] *COGE* 13.37 (September 16, 1922), p. 2.
[747] *COGE* 5.32 (August 8, 1914), p. 8; *COGE* 21.24 (August 9, 1930), p. 3.
[748] *COGE* 21.12 (May 17, 1930), p. 1.
[749] *COGE* 14.34 (August 25, 1923), p. 2.
[750] *COGE* 12.35 (August 27, 1921), p. 2.
[751] *COGE* 12.52 (December 31, 1921), p. 3; *COGE* 14.39 (September 22, 1923), p. 3; and *COGE* 16.42 (October 17, 1925), p. 4.
[752] *COGE* 13.34 (August 26, 1922), p. 2.
[753] *COGE* 16.37 (September 12, 1925), p. 2.
[754] *COGE* 14.38 (September 15, 1923), p. 3.
[755] *COGE* 16.41 (October 10, 1925), p. 2; *COGE* 20.37 (November 16, 1929), p. 1; and *COGE* 21.30 (September 20, 1930), p. 3.
[756] *COGE* 16.39 (September 26, 1925), p. 3.
[757] *COGE* 14.41 (October 6, 1923), p. 4; *COGE* 21.33 (October 11, 1930), p. 2.
[758] *COGE* 12.31 (July 30, 1921), p. 2; *COGE* 12.45 (November 12, 1921), p. 2; and *COGE* 20.32 (October 5, 1929), p. 3.
[759] *COGE* 10.29 (July 19, 1919), p. 2; *COGE* 12.20 (May 14, 1921), p. 2; and *COGE* 16.34 (August 22, 1925), p. 3.
[760] *COGE* 12.35 (August 27, 1921), p. 2.
[761] *COGE* 21.24 (August 9, 1930), p. 3.
[762] *COGE* 18.43 (October 22, 1927), p. 1; *COGE* 21.33 (October 11, 1930), p. 3.
[763] *COGE* 7.40 (September 30, 1916), p. 4.
[764] *COGE* 6.27 (July 3, 1915), p. 3; *COGE* 7.35 (August 26, 1916), p. 4; *COGE* 14.30 (July 28, 1923), p. 3; and *COGE* 22.23 (August 8, 1931), p. 1.

Cleveland;[765] Coalfield;[766] Copperhill;[767] Crab Orchard;[768] Creston;[769] Cunningham;[770] Daisy;[771] Dayton;[772] Dividing Ridge;[773] Dunlap;[774] East Chattanooga;[775] Elizabethton;[776] Erwin;[777] Etowah;[778] Fox Bluff;[779] Goin;[780] Grasshopper;[781] Graysville;[782] Harriman;[783] Helenwood;[784] Hendon;[785] Henning;[786] Hiwassee;[787] Humboldt;[788] Jefferson City;[789] Jellico;[790] Johnson Grove;[791] Johnson's Chapel;[792] Kelly's Ferry;[793]

---

[765] *COGE* 10.42 (October 18, 1919), p. 2; *COGE* 11.42 (October 16, 1920), p. 2; *COGE* 13.18 (May 6, 1922), p. 2; *COGE* 14.41 (October 6, 1923), p. 4; *COGE* 16.29 (July 18, 1925), p. 1; *COGE* 20.16 (June 15, 1929), p. 1; *COGE* 20.28 (September 7, 1929), p. 2; *COGE* 20.43 (January 4, 1930), p. 1; *COGE* 21.27 (August 30, 1930), p. 2; *COGE* 22.6 (April 11, 1931), p. 4; *COGE* 22.21 (July 25, 1931), p. 4; and *COGE* 22.31 (October 3, 1931), p. 2.

[766] *COGE* 9.28 (July 13, 1918), p. 3.

[767] *COGE* 14.43 (October 20, 1923), p. 4; *COGE* 17.35 (September 4, 1926), p. 3; and *COGE* 21.24 (August 9, 1930), p. 3.

[768] *COGE* 12.21 (May 21, 1921), p. 3; *COGE* 16.42 (October 17, 1925), p. 4; *COGE* 16.45 (November 7, 1925), p. 1; *COGE* 16.52 (December 26, 1925), p. 2; and *COGE* 18.37 (September 10, 1927), p. 1.

[769] *COGE* 13.44 (November 11, 1922), p. 2.

[770] *COGE* 8.35 (September 8, 1917), p. 1.

[771] *COGE* 6.36. (September 4, 1915), p. 2; *COGE* 13.36 September 9, 1922), p. 2; *COGE* 14.38 (September 15, 1923), p. 3; *COGE* 20.15 (June 8, 1929), p. 4; *COGE* 20.17 (June 22, 1929), p. 1; *COGE* 20.22 (July 27, 1929), p. 1; *COGE* 21.13 (May 24, 1930), p. 1; and *COGE* 22.7 (April 18, 1931), p. 1.

[772] *COGE* 6.28 (July 10, 1915), p. 2; *COGE* 9.37 (September 14, 1918), p. 3; *COGE* 12.28 (July 9, 1921), p. 4; and *COGE* 18.45 (November 12, 1927), p. 1.

[773] *COGE* 10.43 (October 25, 1919), p. 2.

[774] *COGE* 9.36 (September 7, 1918), p. 2; *COGE* 21.36 (November 8, 1930), p. 1.

[775] *COGE* 12.28 (July 9, 1921), p. 4; *COGE* 15.29 (August 2, 1924), p. 3; *COGE* 16.32 (August 8, 1925), p. 1; *COGE* 17.24 (June 19, 1926), p. 4; *COGE* 17.37 (September 18, 1926), p. 3; *COGE* 19.37 (September 15, 1928), p. 2; and *COGE* 22.26 (August 29, 1931), p. 3.

[776] *COGE* 11.20 (May 15, 1920), p. 3; *COGE* 14.20 (May 19, 1923), p. 3.

[777] *COGE* 20.30 (September 21, 1929), p. 2; *COGE* 20.31 (September 28, 1929), p. 1; *COGE* 21.45 (January 17, 1931), p. 1; *COGE* 22.19 (July 11, 1931), p. 2.

[778] *COGE* 22.37 (November 21, 1931), p. 1; *COGE* 21.25 (August 16, 1930), p. 2; and *COGE* 21.33 (October 11, 1930), p. 2.

[779] *COGE* 9.27 (July 6, 1918), p. 3.

[780] *COGE* 22.10 (May 9, 1931), p. 2.

[781] *COGE* 13.37 (September 16, 1922), p. 3; *COGE* 14.34 (August 25, 1923), p. 2.

[782] *COGE* 5.39 (September 26, 1914), p. 5; *COGE* 11.46 (November 20, 1920), p. 3; and *COGE* 17.40 (October 9, 1926), p. 3.

[783] *COGE* 7.35 (August 26, 1916), p. 2; *COGE* 10.22 (May 31, 1919), p. 3; and *COGE* 17.29 (July 24, 1926), p. 3.

[784] *COGE* 13.42 (October 21, 1922), p. 2; *COGE* 14.32 (August 11, 1923), p. 3.

[785] *COGE* 20.32 (October 5, 1929), p. 1.

[786] *COGE* 22.26 (August 29, 1931), p. 1; *COGE* 13.34 (August 26, 1922), p. 2.

[787] *COGE* 10.38 (September 20, 1919), p. 2; *COGE* 11.36 (September 4, 1920), p. 2; and *COGE* 15.35 (September 13, 1924), p. 1.

[788] *COGE* 22.4 (March 28, 1931), p. 1.

[789] *COGE* 12.25 (June 18, 1921), p. 3; *COGE* 21.15 (June 7, 1930), p. 3; and *COGE* 22.3 (March 21, 1931), p. 4.

[790] *COGE* 15.23 (June 21, 1924), p. 4.

[791] *COGE* 14.43 (October 20, 1923), p. 4.

[792] *COGE* 14.44 (October 27, 1923), p. 4.

[793] *COGE* 10.32 (August 9, 1919), p. 4.

Knoxville;[794] LaFollette;[795] Lawrenceburg;[796] Lenoir City;[797] Lone Oak;[798] McDonald;[799] McMinnville;[800] Madisonville;[801] Martha Washington;[802] Maryville;[803] Memphis;[804] Mineral Park;[805] Morristown;[806] Mount Vail;[807] Nashville;[808] New Hope;[809] Newport;[810] New River;[811] North Chattanooga;[812] Oliver Springs;[813] Ooltewah;[814] Persia;[815] Pikeville;[816] Pleasant Hill;[817] Portland;[818] Pruden;[819] Ravenscroft;[820] Ripley;[821] Roope Spring;[822] Sale Creek;[823] Salt Creek;[824] Sevierville;[825] Short Mountain;[826] Silver Point;[827]

---

[794] *COGE* 10.42 (October 18, 1919), p. 2; *COGE* 10.43 (October 25, 1919), p. 4; *COGE* 21.34 (October 18, 1930), p. 2; *COGE* 12.11 (March 12, 1921), p. 3; *COGE* 18.27 (July 2, 1927), p.1; *COGE* 19.34 (August 25, 1928), p. 4; and *COGE* 21.33 (October 11, 1930), p. 2

[795] *COGE* 15.37 (September 27, 1924), p. 1; *COGE* 21.8 (April 19, 1930), p. 4.

[796] *COGE* 11.34 (August 21, 1920), p. 2.

[797] *COGE* 16.23 (June 6, 1925), p. 4; *COGE* 16.39 (September 26, 1925), p. 2; *COGE* 18.32 (August 6, 1927), p. 1; and *COGE* 22.23 (August 8, 1931), p. 3.

[798] *COGE* 10.32 (August 9, 1919), p. 2; *COGE* 20.22 (July 27, 1929), p. 3.

[799] *COGE* 20.33 (October 12, 1929), p. 3.

[800] *COGE* 13.38 (September 23, 1922), p. 4; *COGE* 20.28 (September 7, 1929), p. 2; and *COGE* 22.27 (September 5, 1931), p. 2.

[801] *COGE* 13.36 September 9, 1922), p. 2.

[802] *COGE* 13.42 (October 21, 1922), p. 2.

[803] *COGE* 12.45 (November 12, 1921), p. 2; *COGE* 15.38 (October 4, 1924), p. 3; and *COGE* 18.43 (October 22, 1927), p. 4.

[804] *COGE* 16.48 (November 28, 1925), p. 3; *COGE* 18.36 (September 5, 1927), p. 3; and *COGE* 22.29 (September 19, 1931), p. 3.

[805] *COGE* 7.43 (October 21, 1916), p. 2.

[806] *COGE* 14.30 (July 28, 1923), p. 3.

[807] *COGE* 12.41 (October 8, 1921), p. 2.

[808] *COGE* 11.30 (July 24, 1920), p. 2; *COGE* 11.46 (November 20, 1920), p. 3; *COGE* 12.23 (June 4, 1921), p. 3; *COGE* 12.34 (August 20, 1921), p. 3; and *COGE* 13.32 (August 12, 1922), p. 2.

[809] *COGE* 12.40 (October 1, 1921), p. 2.

[810] *COGE* 18.47 (November 26, 1927), p. 4; *COGE* 22.27 (September 5, 1931), p. 2.

[811] *COGE* 15.40 (October 18, 1924), p. 4.

[812] *COGE* 13.36 September 9, 1922), p. 3; *COGE* 17.21 (May 29, 1926), p. 4; *COGE* 17.23 (June 12, 1926), p. 4; *COGE* 20.30 (September 21, 1929), p. 3; and *COGE* 21.32 (October 4, 1930), p. 2.

[813] *COGE* 9.27 (July 6, 1918), p. 3.

[814] *COGE* 6.34 (August 21, 1915), p. 4; *COGE* 20.28 (September 7, 1929), p. 2.

[815] *COGE* 13.44 (November 11, 1922), p. 2; *COGE* 14.6 (February 10, 1923), p. 4.

[816] *COGE* 10.32 (August 9, 1919), p. 3; *COGE* 11.43 (October 23, 1920), p. 2; *COGE* 17.36 (September 11, 1926), p. 3; and *COGE* 18.28 (July 9, 1927), p. 1.

[817] *COGE* 11.27 (July 3, 1920), p. 2; *COGE* 11.28 (July 10, 1920), p. 2.

[818] *COGE* 13.39 (September 30, 1922), p. 4.

[819] *COGE* 22.9 (May 2, 1931), p. 1 .

[820] *COGE* 16.42 (October 17, 1925), p. 3.

[821] *COGE* 10.20 (May 17, 1919), p. 3; *COGE* 11.31 (July 31, 1920), p. 3; *COGE* 13.37 (September 16, 1922), p. 2; *COGE* 14.37 (September 8, 1923), p. 2; *COGE* 18.47 (November 26, 1927), p. 1; and *COGE* 20.30 (September 21, 1929), p. 2.

[822] *COGE* 13.37 (September 16, 1922), p. 2.

[823] *COGE* 13.42 (October 21, 1922), p. 2; *COGE* 19.45 (November 17, 1928), p. 1.

[824] *COGE* 21.14 (May 31, 1930), p. 1.

[825] *COGE* 14.43 (October 20, 1923), p. 4; *COGE* 21.31 (September 27, 1930), p. 1.

[826] *COGE* 12.36 (September 3, 1921), p. 2; *COGE* 13.38 (September 23, 1922), p. 2; *COGE* 14.38 (September 15, 1923), p. 3; *COGE* 15.35 (September 13, 1924), p. 1; and *COGE* 16.42 (October 17, 1925), p. 4.

[827] *COGE* 18.33 (August 13, 1927), p. 1.

Soddy;[828] South Pittsburg;[829] Southside;[830] Sparta;[831] Speedwell;[832] Spring City;[833] Sweetwater;[834] Talbott;[835] Tate Springs;[836] Townsend;[837] Unicoi;[838] Victoria;[839] White Oak Flat;[840] White Oak Mountain;[841] Whiteside;[842] Whitwell;[843] and Zion.[844]

Texas

Abilene;[845] Alamo;[846] Bonham;[847] Bowie;[848] Bronson;[849] Brownfield;[850] Burk Burnett;[851] Clark's Chapel;[852] Colorado;[853] Comanche;[854] Crockett;[855] Desdemona;[856] Dodd City;[857] Electra;[858] Fort Worth;[859] Glenwood;[860] Kennard;[861] Ladonia;[862] Lannius;[863] Lone Elm;[864] Lubbock;[865] Lyra;[866] Mobeetie;[867] Mount

---

[828] *COGE* 20.29 (September 14, 1929), p. 3.
[829] *COGE* 13.34 (August 26, 1922), p. 2.
[830] *COGE* 7.42 (October 14, 1916), p. 3.
[831] *COGE* 17.42 (November 6, 1926), p. 4; *COGE* 22.10 (May 9, 1931), p. 4; and *COGE* 22.31 (October 3, 1931), p. 2.
[832] *COGE* 16.26 (June 27, 1925), p. 4.
[833] *COGE* 5.46 (November 21, 1914). p. 3.
[834] *COGE* 10.47 (November 29, 1919), p. 4.
[835] *COGE* 22.18 (July 4, 1931), p. 1.
[836] *COGE* 14.43 (October 20, 1923), p. 4.
[837] *COGE* 21.21 (July 19, 1930), p. 1.
[838] *COGE* 20.35 (November 2, 1929), p. 4; *COGE* 22.6 (April 11, 1931), p. 4.
[839] *COGE* 21.28 (September 6, 1930), p. 2.
[840] *COGE* 7.39 (September 23, 1916), p. 4; *COGE* 8.30 (August 4, 1917), p. 2.
[841] *COGE* 5.32 (August 8, 1914), p. 8.
[842] *COGE* 18.34 (August 20, 1927), p. 1; *COGE* 20.30 (September 21, 1929), p. 2.
[843] *COGE* 11.40 (October 2, 1920), p. 2; *COGE* 12.38 (September 17, 1921), p. 2; *COGE* 17.50 (December 25, 1926), p. 4; and *COGE* 21.12 (May 17, 1930), p. 1.
[844] *COGE* 16.42 (October 17, 1925), p. 1.
[845] *COGE* 18.35 (August 27, 1927), p. 1.
[846] COGE 22.28 (September 12, 1931), p. 3.
[847] *COGE* 12.25 (June 18, 1921), p. 3; *COGE* 12.38 (September 17, 1921), p. 2.
[848] COGE 22.23 (August 8, 1931), p. 1.
[849] *COGE* 15.19 (May 24, 1924), p. 4.
[850] *COGE* 19.41 (October 13, 1928), p. 4.
[851] *COGE* 20.22 (July 27, 1929), p. 2.
[852] *COGE* 12.35 (August 27, 1921), p. 2.
[853] *COGE* 21.23 (August 2, 1930), p. 4.
[854] *COGE* 22.16 (June 20, 1931), p. 4.
[855] *COGE* 12.39 (September 24, 1921), p. 2; *COGE* 18.22 (May 28, 1927), p. 4; *COGE* 18.34 (August 20, 1927), p. 1; *COGE* 21.25 (August 16, 1930), p. 4; and *COGE* 22.29 (September 19, 1931), p. 3.
[856] *COGE* 20.11 (May 11, 1929), p. 3; *COGE* 21.12 (May 17, 1930), p. 3.
[857] *COGE* 14.33 (August 18, 1923), p. 3.
[858] *COGE* 18.39 (September 24, 1927), p. 1; *COGE* 19.44 (November 10, 1928), p. 3; and *COGE* 19.46 (November 24, 1928), p. 4.
[859] *COGE* 17.32 (August 14, 1926), p. 3.
[860] *COGE* 13.29 (July 22, 1922), p. 3.
[861] *COGE* 18.14 (April 2, 1927), p. 2.
[862] *COGE* 12.30 (July 23, 1921), p. 2.
[863] *COGE* 13.38 (September 23, 1922), p. 2; *COGE* 16.34 (August 22, 1925), p. 3.
[864] *COGE* 11.46 (November 20, 1920), p. 3; *COGE* 12.16 (April 16, 1921), p. 2; and *COGE* 12.35 (August 27, 1921), p. 2.
[865] *COGE* 13.38 (September 23, 1922), p. 2; *COGE* 14.46 (November 10, 1923), p. 3.
[866] *COGE* 10.27 (July 5, 1919), p. 2.
[867] *COGE* 14.27 (July 7, 1923), p. 3; *COGE* 16.42 (October 17, 1925), p. 3.

Sterling;[868] Mount Vernon;[869] Palmer;[870] Paris;[871] Point;[872] Ranger;[873] Rochester;[874] Shamrock;[875] Shepherds Chapel;[876] Silver Point;[877] Slaton;[878] Sulphur Bluff;[879] Thurber;[880] Trinity;[881] Weatherford;[882] and Wichita Falls.[883]

Virginia

Altavista;[884] Appalachia;[885] Bedford;[886] Cliffview;[887] Cripple Creek;[888] Glamorgan;[889] Grant;[890] Gunton Park;[891] Jericho;[892] Kaymoor;[893] Leesville;[894] Lynchburg;[895] Marion;[896] Max Meadows;[897] Monarat;[898] Norton;[899] Parrott;[900] Pulaski;[901] Richland;[902] Roanoke;[903]

---

[868] *COGE* 12.39 (Se p 24, 1921), p. 2; *COGE* 14.35 (September 1, 1923), p. 4; and COGE 22.37 (November 21, 1931), p. 4.
[869] *COGE* 15.32 (August 23, 1924), p. 3.
[870] *COGE* 20.30 (September 21, 1929), p. 1.
[871] *COGE* 8.32 (August 18, 1917), p. 2; *COGE* 19.30 (July 28, 1928), p. 1.
[872] *COGE* 10.35 (August 30, 1919), p. 3; *COGE* 13.34 (August 26, 1922), p. 3; *COGE* 20.28 (September 7, 1929), p. 4; and COGE 22.38 (November 28, 1931), p. 4.
[873] *COGE* 11.20 (May 15, 1920), p. 3; *COGE* 11.27 (July 3, 1920), p. 2; *COGE* 13.34 (August 26, 1922), p. 2; and *COGE* 18.40 (October 1, 1927), p. 1.
[874] *COGE* 21.18 (June 28, 1930), p. 1.
[875] *COGE* 18.43 (October 22, 1927), p. 1.
[876] *COGE* 13.36 September 9, 1922), p. 2.
[877] *COGE* 18.43 (October 22, 1927), p. 2; *COGE* 18.44 (November 5, 1927), p. 1.
[878] *COGE* 21.24 (August 9, 1930), p. 1.
[879] *COGE* 22.27 (September 5, 1931), p. 1.
[880] *COGE* 12.14 (April 2, 1921), p. 3; *COGE* 17.41 (October 16, 1926), p. 4.
[881] *COGE* 12.26 (June 25, 1921), p. 2; *COGE* 17.42 (November 6, 1926), p. 4; and *COGE* 22.24 (August 15, 1931), p. 3.
[882] *COGE* 13.39 (September 30, 1922), p. 3; *COGE* 14.4 (January 27, 1923), p. 3; *COGE* 15.40 (October 18, 1924), p. 3; *COGE* 16.28 (July 11, 1925), p. 4; *COGE* 20.31 (September 28, 1929), p. 4.
[883] *COGE* 22.16 (June 20, 1931), p. 1.
[884] *COGE* 10.32 (August 9, 1919), p. 3; *COGE* 11.29 (July 17, 1920), p. 3; and *COGE* 13.44 (November 11, 1922), p. 2.
[885] *COGE* 22.38 (November 28, 1931), p. 4.
[886] *COGE* 22.28 (September 12, 1931), p. 2.
[887] *COGE* 21.24 (August 9, 1930), p. 1.
[888] *COGE* 7.33 (August 12, 1916), p. 3; *COGE* 8.28 (July 21, 1917), p. 4.
[889] *COGE* 22.3 (March 21, 1931), p. 3.
[890] *COGE* 22.14 (June 6, 1931), p. 1.
[891] *COGE* 12.39 (September 24, 1921), p. 2.
[892] *COGE* 8.44 (November 10, 1917), p. 4.
[893] *COGE* 11.43 (October 23, 1920), p. 3.
[894] *COGE* 10.40 (October 4, 1919), p. 3; *COGE* 13.34 (August 26, 1922), p. 2.
[895] *COGE* 19.34 (August 25, 1928), p. 4; *COGE* 21.37 (November 15, 1930), p. 1, 3; and *COGE* 21.41 (December 13, 1930), p. 3.
[896] *COGE* 16.15 (April 11, 1925), p. 1.
[897] *COGE* 11.46 (November 20, 1920), p. 3.
[898] *COGE* 8.24 (June 23, 1917), p. 4; *COGE* 15.28 (July 26, 1924), p. 1; and *COGE* 16.22 (May 30, 1925), p. 2.
[899] *COGE* 18.10 (March 5, 1927), p. 2; *COGE* 18.44 (November 5, 1927), p. 1.
[900] *COGE* 6.22 (May 29, 1915), p. 3.
[901] *COGE* 10.41 (October 11, 1919), p. 4; *COGE* 20.24 (August 10, 1929), p. 2.
[902] *COGE* 21.24 (August 9, 1930), p. 1.
[903] *COGE* 11.27 (July 3, 1920), p. 4.

Salem;[904] and Schoolfield.[905]

West Virginia

Barnabus;[906] Bluefield;[907] Cannelton;[908] Cedar Grove;[909] Charleston;[910] Clarksburg;[911] Clear Fork;[912] Coalwood;[913] Crown;[914] Crown Hill;[915] Cyclone;[916] Dan;[917] Davis;[918] Dearing;[919] Deep Valley;[920] Delbarton;[921] Dola;[922] East Lynn;[923] Eccles;[924] Elkins;[925] Garrison;[926] Gary;[927] Glen Morrison;[928] Hiawatha;[929] Highcoal;[930] Holden;[931] Hovaca;[932] Huntington;[933] Kellysville;[934] Kermit;[935] Keyser;[936] Keystone;[937] Lax;[938] Leckie;[939] Lego;[940] Lenore;[941]

---

[904] *COGE* 21.29 (September 13, 1930), p. 2.
[905] *COGE* 19.30 (July 28, 1928), p. 4.
[906] *COGE* 16.9 (February 28, 1925), p. 4; *COGE* 19.15 (April 14, 1928), p. 1; and *COGE* 22.20 (July 18, 1931), p. 3.
[907] COGE 22.23 (August 8, 1931), p. 1.
[908] *COGE* 16.13 (March 28, 1925), p. 3.
[909] *COGE* 12.14 (April 2, 1921), p. 3.
[910] *COGE* 21.33 (October 11, 1930), p. 4; COGE 22.29 (September 19, 1931), p. 2.
[911] *COGE* 20.8 (April 20, 1929), p. 1.
[912] *COGE* 20.27 (August 31, 1929), p. 3.
[913] *COGE* 17.37 (September 18, 1926), p. 3.
[914] *COGE* 21.24 (August 9, 1930), p. 4.
[915] *COGE* 12.37 (September 10, 1921), p. 2; *COGE* 15.22 (June 14, 1924), p. 3; and *COGE* 22.11 (May 16, 1931), p. 2.
[916] COGE 22.31 (October 3, 1931), p. 3.
[917] *COGE* 20.8 (April 20, 1929), p. 1.
[918] *COGE* 22.36 (November 14, 1931), p. 2.
[919] *COGE* 19.41 (October 13, 1928), p. 2.
[920] *COGE* 22.38 (November 28, 1931), p. 1.
[921] *COGE* 21.2 (March 8, 1930), p. 3.
[922] *COGE* 22.11 (May 16, 1931), p. 1.
[923] COGE 22.24 (August 15, 1931), p. 2.
[924] COGE 22.24 (August 15, 1931), p. 2.
[925] *COGE* 17.40 (October 9, 1926), p. 2; *COGE* 17.45 (November 27, 1926), p. 4; and *COGE* 21.14 (May 31, 1930), p. 1.
[926] *COGE* 21.8 (April 19, 1930), p. 4; *COGE* 22.7 (April 18, 1931), p. 2.
[927] *COGE* 18.35 (August 27, 1927), p. 1.
[928] *COGE* 21.19 (July 5, 1930), p. 4; *COGE* 21.25 (August 16, 1930), p. 4; and COGE 22.23 (August 8, 1931), p. 2.
[929] *COGE* 18.13 (March 26, 1927), p. 3.
[930] *COGE* 21.10 (May 3, 1930), p. 4
[931] *COGE* 13.39 (September 30, 1922), p. 3.
[932] *COGE* 15.15 (April 26, 1924), p. 3.
[933] *COGE* 15.1 (January 5, 1924), p. 2; *COGE* 16.20 (May 16, 1925), p. 3; and *COGE* 20.35 (November 2, 1929), p. 1.
[934] *COGE* 14.33 (August 18, 1923), p. 3.
[935] *COGE* 22.39 (December 5, 1931), p. 3.
[936] *COGE* 13.37 (September 16, 1922), p. 2.
[937] *COGE* 21.31 (September 27, 1930), p. 2; *COGE* 21.33 (October 11, 1930), p. 1.
[938] *COGE* 20.22 (July 27, 1929), p. 1.
[939] *COGE* 12.26 (June 25, 1921), p. 2.
[940] *COGE* 18.4 (January 22, 1927), p. 4.
[941] *COGE* 22.22 (August 1, 1931), p. 4.

Lester;[942] Logan;[943] Mc Beth;[944] Mallory;[945] Mead Poca;[946] Monclo;[947] Morgantown;[948] Naugatuck;[949] Oakvale;[950] Packsville;[951] Paden City;[952] Parkersburg;[953] Pemberton;[954] Petersburg;[955] Pierce;[956] Pike Fork;[957] Powhatan;[958] Princeton;[959] Rhodell;[960] Roderfield;[961] Saint Albans;[962] Shegon;[963] Smithers;[964] Stone Branch;[965] Taplin;[966] Ury;[967] Verdunville;[968] War;[969] Ward;[970] Webb;[971] West Huntington;[972] Whitesville;[973] and Wilsondale.[974]

---

[942] *COGE* 12.18 (April 30, 1921), p. 3; *COGE* 16.26 (June 27, 1925), p. 4; *COGE* 16.48 (November 28, 1925), p. 3; *COGE* 20.28 (September 7, 1929), p. 1; *COGE* 21.36 (November 8, 1930), p. 2; and *COGE* 22.18 (July 4, 1931), p. 4.

[943] *COGE* 13.33 (August 19, 1922), p. 2; *COGE* 15.16 (May 3, 1924), p. 4; *COGE* 16.3 (January 17, 1925), p. 1; *COGE* 16.37 (September 12, 1925), p. 1; *COGE* 18.27 (July 2, 1927), p.1; *COGE* 19.23 (June 9, 1928), p. 3; and *COGE* 20.27 (August 31, 1929), p. 3.

[944] *COGE* 22.14 (June 6, 1931), p. 4.

[945] *COGE* 21.33 (October 11, 1930), p. 3; *COGE* 22.14 (June 6, 1931), p. 1; and *COGE* 22.30 (September 26, 1931), p. 1.

[946] *COGE* 16.26 (June 27, 1925), p. 4; *COGE* 17.28 (July 17, 1926), p. 2.

[947] COGE 20.30 (September 21, 1929), p. 1; *COGE* 22.19 (July 11, 1931), p. 3.

[948] *COGE* 16.19 (May 9, 1925), p. 2.

[949] *COGE* 20.12 (May 18, 1929), p. 4; *COGE* 21.12 (May 17, 1930), p. 4.

[950] *COGE* 13.23 (June 10, 1922), p. 2.

[951] *COGE* 21.32 (October 4, 1930), p. 4.

[952] *COGE* 21.11 (May 10, 1930), p. 4.

[953] *COGE* 6.18 (May 1, 1915), p. 4; *COGE* 9.47 (November 23, 1918), p. 3; *COGE* 13.22 (June 3, 1922), p. 4; *COGE* 14.24 (June 16, 1923), p. 4; *COGE* 15.9 (March 1, 1924), p. 3; *COGE* 15.46 (December 6, 1924), p. 2; *COGE* 16.18 (May 2, 1925), p. 1; and *COGE* 22.27 (September 5, 1931), p. 2.

[954] *COGE* 22.20 (July 18, 1931), p. 1.

[955] *COGE* 18.32 (August 6, 1927), p. 1; *COGE* 19.33 (August 18, 1928, p. 1.

[956] *COGE* 21.38 (November 22, 1930), p. 4.

[957] *COGE* 21.47 (January 31, 1931), p. 2.

[958] *COGE* 10.37 (September 13, 1919), p. 2.

[959] *COGE* 13.39 (September 30, 1922), p. 2; *COGE* 15.36 (September 20, 1924), p. 3; *COGE* 16.22 (May 30, 1925), p. 3; *COGE* 17.29 (July 24, 1926), p. 3; and *COGE* 21.28 (September 6, 1930), p. 1.

[960] *COGE* 22.34 9October 31, 1931), p. 4.

[961] *COGE* 20.17 (June 22, 1929), p. 1; *COGE* 21.33 (October 11, 1930), p. 4; and *COGE* 21.34 (October 18, 1930), pp. 1, 2.

[962] *COGE* 22.6 (April 11, 1931), p. 1.

[963] *COGE* 16.27 (July 4, 1925), p. 3; *COGE* 19.25 (June 23, 1928), p. 1.

[964] *COGE* 21.48 (February 7, 1931), p. 1.

[965] *COGE* 22.35 (November 7, 1931), p. 4.

[966] *COGE* 22.2 (March 14, 1931), p. 1.

[967] *COGE* 22.21 (July 25, 1931), p. 1.

[968] *COGE* 16.25 (June 20, 1925), p. 2; *COGE* 20.15 (June 8, 1929), p. 1.

[969] *COGE* 19.40 (October 6, 1928), p. 1; *COGE* 22.12 (May 23, 1931), p. 3.

[970] *COGE* 21.10 (May 3, 1930), p. 1.

[971] *COGE* 17.35 (September 4, 1926), p. 3.

[972] *COGE* 21.2 (March 8, 1930), p. 3.

[973] *COGE* 21.10 (May 3, 1930), p. 4.

[974] *COGE* 17.14 (April 10, 1926), p. 4.

APPENDIX D

Church of God Evangel

Countries/cities in Alphabetical Order

Argentina

Argentina.[1]

Bahamas

Current, Eleuthera Island;[2] Green Turtle Cay;[3] Coopers Town, Abaco;[4] Mastic Point, Andros Island;[5] and Nassau.[6]

Canada

Consul, Saskatchewan.[7]

China

Tsinanfu.[8]

Jamaica:

Borobridge;[9] Cedar Valley;[10] Chapleton;[11] Dry Harbour;[12] Frankfield;[13] Grantham;[14] Grantstown;[15] Kingston;[16] Largo;[17]

and Leicesterfield.[18]

---

[1] *COGE* 11.27 (July 3, 1920), p. 2.
[2] *COGE* 8.10 (March 10, 1917), p. 3.
[3] *COGE* 8.18 (May 12, 1917), p. 3; *COGE* 17.25 (June 26, 1926), p. 1.
[4] *COGE* 17.39 (October 2, 1926), p. 1.
[5] *COGE* 21.20 (July 12, 1930), p. 4.
[6] *COGE* 8.10 (March 10, 1917), p. 3; *COGE* 21.30 (September 20, 1930), p. 3.
[7] *COGE* 22.31 (October 3, 1931), p. 3.
[8] *COGE* 12.50 (December 17, 1921), p. 3.
[9] *COGE* 12.40 (October 1, 1921), p. 2.
[10] *COGE* 21.2 (March 8, 1930), p. 1; *COGE* 21.31 (September 27, 1930), p. 1.
[11] *COGE* 20.2 (March 9, 1929), p. 1; *COGE* 20.46 (January 25, 1930), p. 2.
[12] *COGE* 16.32 (August 8, 1925), p. 1; *COGE* 22.33 (October 24, 1931), p. 4.
[13] *COGE* 21.16 (June 14, 1930), p. 4; *COGE* 21.17 (June 21, 1930), p. 1; and *COGE* 22.10 (May 9, 1931), p.
[14] *COGE* 20.34 (October 19, 1929), p. 2.
[15] *COGE* 21.44 (January 10, 1931), p. 4.
[16] *COGE* 20.37 (November 16, 1929), p. 1. *COGE* 20.37 (November 16, 1929), p. 1.
[17] *COGE* 10.38 (September 20, 1919), p. 4; *COGE* 11.44 (October 30, 1920), p. 3; *COGE* 13.6 (February 11,1922), p. 2; *COGE* 13.22 (June 3, 1922), p. 4; *COGE* 13.25 (June 24, 1922), p. 2; and *COGE* 19.18 (May 15,1928), p. 4.
[18] *COGE* 22.25 (August 22, 1931), p. 2.

Japan
Osaka[19]

Appendix E

Church of God Evangel
Baptismal Terminology

'Baptized' references:
COGE 1.5 (May 1, 1910), p. 7; *COGE* 1.16 (October 15, 1910), p. 4; *COGE* 5.23 (June 6, 1914), p. 5; *COGE* 5.34 (August 22, 1914), p. 3; *COGE* 5.40 (October 4, 1914), p. 5; *COGE* 5.42 (October 17, 1914), p. 5; *COGE* 5.48 (December 5, 1914), p. 5; *COGE* 6.18 (May 1, 1915), p. 4; *COGE* 6.20 (May 15, 1915), p. 2; *COGE* 6.25 (June 19, 1915), p. 2; *COGE* 6.27 (July 3, 1915), p. 3; *COGE* 6.33 (August 14, 1915), p. 1; *COGE* 6.50 (December 11, 1915), p. 3; *COGE* 7.10 (March 4, 1916), p. 4; *COGE* 7.12 (March 18, 1916), p. 3; *COGE* 7.25 (June 17, 1916), p. 3; *COGE* 7.27 (July 1, 1916), p. 3; *COGE* 7.48 (November 25, 1916), p. 2; *COGE* 8.13 (March 31, 1917), p. 4; *COGE* 8.22 (June 9, 1917), p. 3; *COGE* 8.25 (June 30, 1917), p. 4; *COGE* 8.26 (July 7, 1917), p. 4; *COGE* 8.27 (July 14, 1917), p. 4; *COGE* 8.30 (August 4, 1917), p. 1; *COGE* 8.34 (September 1, 1917), p. 2; *COGE* 8.37 (September 22, 1917), p. 3; *COGE* 8.40 (October 13, 1917), p. 4; *COGE* 9.14 (April 6, 1918), p. 4; *COGE* 9.15 (April 13, 1918), p. 2; *COGE* 9.22 (June 1, 1918), p. 2; *COGE* 9.23 (June 8, 1918), p. 3; *COGE* 9.28 (July 13, 1918), p. 4; *COGE* 9.30 (July 27, 1918), p. 3; *COGE* 9.31 (August 3, 1918), p. 2; *COGE* 9.33 (August 17, 1918), p. 4; *COGE* 9.35 (August 31, 1918), p. 4; *COGE* 10.22 (May 31, 1919), p. 3; *COGE* 10.26 (June 28, 1919), p. 3; *COGE* 10.28 (July 12, 1919), pp. 3, 4; *COGE* 10.34 (August 23, 1919), p. 2; *COGE* 10.38 (September 20, 1919), p. 3; *COGE* 10.40 (October 4, 1919), p. 2; *COGE* 10.41 (October 11, 1919), p. 3; *COGE* 10.46 (November 22, 1919), p. 4; *COGE* 10.50 (December 20, 1919), p. 4; *COGE* 11.9 (February 28, 1920), p. 1; *COGE* 11.21 (May 22, 1920), p. 2; *COGE* 11.27 (July 3, 1920), pp. 2, 4; *COGE* 11.28 (July 10, 1920), pp. 3, 4; *COGE* 11.32 (August 7, 1920), p. 2; *COGE* 11.33 (August 14, 1920), p. 1; *COGE* 11.35 (August 28, 1920), p. 2; *COGE* 11.40 (October 2, 1920), p. 2; *COGE* 12.21 (May 21, 1921), p. 3; *COGE* 12.23 (June 4, 1921), p. *COGE* 12.38 (September 17, 1921), p. 2; *COGE* 12.39 (September 24, 1921), p. 2; *COGE* 12.44 (October 29, 1921), p. 2; *COGE* 12.50 (December 17, 1921), p. 3; *COGE* 13.3 (January 21, 1922), p. 3; *COGE* 13.22 (June 3, 1922), p. 4; *COGE* 13.23 (June 10, 1922), p. 1; *COGE* 13.28 (July 15, 1922), p. 2; *COGE* 13.37 (September 16, 1922), p. 1; *COGE* 14.32 (August 11, 1923), p. 3; *COGE* 14.37 (September 8, 1923), p. 4; *COGE* 15.16 (May 3, 1924), p. 4; *COGE* 15.22 (June 14, 1924), p. 3; *COGE* 15.42 (November 8, 1924), p. 2; *COGE* 15.43 (November 15, 1924), p. 1; *COGE* 16.26 (June 27, 1925), p. 1; *COGE* 16.28 (July 11, 1925), p. 1; *COGE* 16.32 (August 8, 1925), p. 1; *COGE* 16.34 (August 22, 1925), p. 1; *COGE* 16.36 (September 5, 1925), pp. 1-2; *COGE* 16.37 (September 12, 1925), p. 1; *COGE* 16.39 (September 26, 1925), p. 3; *COGE* 16.42 (October 17, 1925), p. 3; *COGE* 17.15 (April 17, 1926), p. 3; *COGE* 17.16 (April 24, 1926), p. 1; *COGE* 17.18 (May 8, 1926), p. 2; *COGE* 17.24 (June 19, 1926), p. 1; *COGE* 17.28 (July 17, 1926), p. 3; *COGE* 17.37 (September 18, 1926), p. 3; *COGE* 17.39 (October 2, 1926), p. 4; *COGE* 17.40 (October 9, 1926), p. 2; *COGE* 17.42 (November 6, 1926), p. 4; *COGE* 17.44 (November 20, 1926), p. 4; *COGE* 18.7 (February 12, 1927), p. 1; *COGE* 18.27 (July 2, 1927), p. 2; *COGE* 18.36 (September 5, 1927), p. 3; *COGE* 18.37 (September 10, 1927), p. 1; *COGE* 18.39 (September 24, 1927), p. 1; *COGE* 18.44 (November 5, 1927), p. 2; *COGE* 18.45 (November 12, 1927), p. 1; *COGE* 19.29 (July 21, 1928), pp. 1, 3; *COGE* 19.37 (September 15, 1928), pp. 1, 2; *COGE* 19.45 (November 17, 1928), p. 1; *COGE* 20.22 (July 27, 1929), p. 3; *COGE* 20.26 (August 24, 1929), p. 2; *COGE* 20.30 (September 21, 1929), pp. 1, 3; *COGE* 21.2 (March 8, 1930), p. 2; *COGE* 20.32 (October 5, 1929), p. 3; *COGE* 20.34 (October 19, 1929), p. 1; *COGE* 21.9 (April 26, 1930), p. 2; *COGE* 21.10 (May 3, 1930), p. 4; *COGE* 21.12 (May 17, 1930), p. 3; *COGE* 21.15 (June 7, 1930), p. 3; *COGE* 21.16 (June 14, 1930), pp. 2, 3; *COGE* 21.20 (July 12, 1930), p. 4; *COGE* 21.23 (August 2, 1930), p. 4; *COGE* 21.24 (August 9, 1930), p. 3; *COGE* 21.25 (August 16, 1930), p. 2; *COGE* 21.27 (August 30, 1930), pp. 2, 3; *COGE* 21.28 (September 6, 1930), p. 2; *COGE* 21.30

---

[19] *COGE* 12.40 (October 1, 1921), p. 2.

(September 20, 1930), pp. 1, 3; *COGE* 21.34 (October 18, 1930), p. 4; *COGE* 21.36 (November 8, 1930), p. 1; *COGE* 21.46 (January 24, 1931), p. 4; *COGE* 22.11 (May 16, 1931), pp. 1, 2; *COGE* 22.16 (June 20, 1931), p. 1; *COGE* 22.17 (June 27, 1931), pp. 1, 2, and 4; *COGE* 22.21 (July 25, 1931), p. 1, 4; COGE 22.24 (August 15, 1931), p. 1; *COGE* 22.25 (August 22, 1931), p. 1; COGE 22.26 (August 29, 1931), p. 3; COGE 22.27 (September 5, 1931), p. 3; *COGE* 22.28 (September 12, 1931), p. 2; COGE 22.29 (September 19, 1931), p. 2; COGE 22.31 (October 3, 1931), pp. 1, 2; COGE 22.35 (November 7, 1931), pp. 3, 4; and *COGE* 22.37 (November 21, 1931), p. 1.

Appendix F

Church of God Evangel

Baptismal Terminology

'Baptized in water' references
COGE 1.9 (July 1, 1910), p. 7; *COGE* 1.12 (August 15, 1910), p. 7; *COGE* 1.18 (November 15, 1910), p. 3; *COGE* 3.14 (September 15, 1912), p. 6, 7; *COGE* 5.8 (February 21, 1914), p. 5, 8; *COGE* 5.13 (March 28, 1914), p. 7; *COGE* 5.20 (May 16, 1914), p. 5; *COGE* 5.21 (May 23, 1914), pp. 6, 8; *COGE* 5.23 (June 6, 1914), p. 5; *COGE* 5.27 (July 4, 1914), p. 8; *COGE* 5.28 (July 11, 1914), p. 8; *COGE* 5.34 (August 22, 1914), p. 5; *COGE* 5.35 (August 29, 1914), pp. 6, 8; *COGE* 5.37 (September 12, 1914), p. 5; *COGE* 5.38 (September 19, 1914), pp. 4, 8;; *COGE* 5.40 (October 4, 1914), pp. 4, 5; *COGE* 5.42 (October 17, 1914), pp. 4, 6; *COGE* 5.49 (December 12, 1914), p. 1; *COGE* 6.2 (January 9, 1915), p. 2; *COGE* 6.7 (February 13, 1915), p. 1; *COGE* 6.20 (May 15, 1915), p. 3; *COGE* 6.22 (May 29, 1915), p. 3; *COGE* 6.24 (June 12, 1915), p. 3; *COGE* 6.27 (July 3, 1915), p. 2; *COGE* 6.28 (July 10, 1915), pp. 3, 4; *COGE* 6.29 (July 17, 1915), pp. 2, 3, and 4; *COGE* 6.30 (July 24, 1915), p. 3; *COGE* 6.31 (July 31, 1915), p. 4; *COGE* 6.32 (August 7, 1915), p. 2; *COGE* 6.33 (August 14, 1915), pp. 2, 3; *COGE* 6.34 (August 21, 1915), pp. 2, 3; *COGE* 6.35 (August 28, 1915), pp. 2, 4; *COGE* 6.36. (September 4, 1915), p. 4; *COGE* 6.37 (September 11, 1915), p. 4; *COGE* 6.38 (September 18, 1915), p. 4; *COGE* 6.39 (September 25, 1915), pp. 2, 3, and 5; *COGE* 6.40 (October 2, 1915), p. 4; *COGE* 6.42 (October 16, 1915), p. 4; *COGE* 6.43 (October 23, 1915), p. 4; *COGE* 6.44 (October 30, 1915), pp. 2, 4; *COGE* 6.47 (November 20, 1915), p. 4; *COGE* 6.51 (December 18, 1915), pp. 3, 4; *COGE* 7.2 (January 8, 1916), p. 3; *COGE* 7.17 (April 22, 1916), p. 3; *COGE* 7.20 (May 13, 1916), p. 3; *COGE* 7.21 (May 20, 1916), p. 4; *COGE* 7.25 (June 17, 1916), p. 2; *COGE* 7.26 (June 24, 1916), pp. 2, 3; *COGE* 7.27 (July 1, 1916), p. 3; *COGE* 7.28 (July 8, 1916), p. 4; *COGE* 7.31 (July 29, 1916), p. 4; *COGE* 7.32 (August 5, 1916), p. 2; *COGE* 7.33 (August 12, 1916), p. 3; *COGE* 7.34 (August 19, 1916), p. 3; *COGE* 7.35 (August 26, 1916), p. 2; *COGE* 7.37 (September 9, 1916), p. 2.; *COGE* 7.38 (September 16, 1916), pp. 1, 3, and 4; *COGE* 7.39 (September 23, 1916), p. 2; *COGE* 7.40 (September 30, 1916), p. 4; *COGE* 7.43 (October 21, 1916), p. 3; *COGE* 7.46 (November 11, 1916), p. 4; *COGE* 7.47 (November 18, 1916), p. 3; *COGE* 7.56 (December 16, 1916), p. 3; *COGE* 8.5 (February 3, 1917), p. 2; *COGE* 8.13 (March 31, 1917), p. 4; *COGE* 8.14 (April 14, 1917), p. 2; *COGE* 8.15 (April 22, 1917), p. 4;; *COGE* 8.22 (June 9, 1917), p. 4; *COGE* 8.24 (June 23, 1917), p. 4; *COGE* 8.26 (July 7, 1917), pp. 2, 3; *COGE* 8.28 (July 21, 1917), pp. 2, 4; *COGE* 8.29 (July 28, 1917), p. 4; *COGE* 8.30 (August 4, 1917), p. 4; *COGE* 8.31 (August 11, 1917), p. 3; *COGE* 8.32 (August 18, 1917), p. 4; *COGE* 8.33 (August 25, 1917), pp. 2, 3, and 4; *COGE* 8.34 (September 1, 1917), p. 2; *COGE* 8.35 (September 8, 1917), p. 3; *COGE* 8.36 (September 15, 1917), pp. 2, 4; *COGE* 8.37 (September 22, 1917), pp. 2, 3; *COGE* 8.39 (October 6, 1917), p. 2; *COGE* 8.40 (October 13, 1917), p. 2; *COGE* 8.41 (October 20, 1917), p. 2; *COGE* 8.44 (November 10, 1917), pp. 3, 4; *COGE* 8.45 (November 17, 1917), p. 4; *COGE* 8.46 (November 24, 1917), p. 3; *COGE* 8.47 (December 1, 1917), p. 3; *COGE* 9.5 (February 2, 1918), p. 2; *COGE* 9.18 (May 4, 1918), p. 4; *COGE* 9.20 (May 18, 1918), p. 4; *COGE* 9.22 (June 1, 1918), pp. 2, 3, and 4; *COGE* 9.23 (June 8, 1918), p. 3; *COGE* 9.25 (June 22, 1918), p. 3; *COGE* 9.26 (June 29, 1918), p. 3; *COGE* 9.27 (July 6, 1918), p. 2; *COGE* 9.29 (July 20, 1918), p. 4; *COGE* 9.31 (August 3, 1918), pp. 3, 4; *COGE* 9.32 (August 10, 1918), p. 2; *COGE* 9.33 (August 17, 1918), p. 4; *COGE* 9.34 (August 24, 1918), p. 3; *COGE* 9.35 (August 31, 1918), p. 4; *COGE* 9.37 (September 14, 1918), p. 4; *COGE* 9.38 (September 21, 1918), p. 3; *COGE* 9.40 (October 5, 1918), pp. 2, 3; *COGE* 9.41 (October 12, 1918), pp. 2, 4; *COGE* 9.43 (October 26, 1918), p. 2; *COGE* 10.8 (February 22, 1919), p. 2; *COGE* 10.15 (April 12, 1919), pp. 3, 4; *COGE* 10.19 (May 10, 1919), p. 3; *COGE* 10.21 (May 24, 1919), p. 3; *COGE* 10.22 (May 31, 1919), pp. 2, 3; *COGE* 10.24 (June 14, 1919), p. 4; *COGE* 10.26 (June 28, 1919), p. 3; *COGE* 10.27 (July 5, 1919), p. 2; *COGE* 10.28 (July 12, 1919), p. 4; *COGE* 10.29 (July 19, 1919), p. 2; *COGE* 10.30 (July 26, 1919), p. 4; *COGE* 10.31 (August 2, 1919), pp. 3, 4; *COGE* 10.32 (August 9, 1919), pp. 2, 4; *COGE* 10.34 (August 23, 1919), p. 2; *COGE* 10.36 (September 6, 1919), p. 2; *COGE* 10.37 (September

13, 1919), p. 3; *COGE* 10.40 (October 4, 1919), p. 4; *COGE* 10.41 (October 11, 1919), p. 2; *COGE* 10.42 (October 18, 1919), pp. 3, 4; *COGE* 10.43 (October 25, 1919), pp. 2, 4; *COGE* 10.44 (November 8, 1919), pp. 2, 4; *COGE* 10.46 (November 22, 1919), p. 4; *COGE* 10.47 (November 29, 1919), p. 4; *COGE* 11.7 (February 14, 1920), p. 2; *COGE* 11.17 (April 24, 1920), p. 3; *COGE* 11.20 (May 15, 1920), pp. 2, 3; *COGE* 11.21 (May 22, 1920), pp. 2, 4; *COGE* 11.22 (May 29, 1920), p. 4; *COGE* 11.24 (June 12, 1920), p. 4; *COGE* 11.26 (June 26, 1920), p. 4; *COGE* 11.27 (July 3, 1920), p. 2; *COGE* 11.28 (July 10, 1920), pp. 2, 3; *COGE* 11.29 (July 17, 1920), p. 2; *COGE* 11.31 (July 31, 1920), pp. 2, 3; *COGE* 11.32 (August 7, 1920), p. 2; *COGE* 11.33 (August 14, 1920), p. 2; *COGE* 11.34 (August 21, 1920), p. 2; *COGE* 11.35 (August 28, 1920), p. 2; *COGE* 11.36 (September 4, 1920), pp. 2, 3; *COGE* 11.37 (September 11, 1920), p. 3; *COGE* 11.38 (September 18, 1920), pp. 3, 4; *COGE* 11.39 (September 25, 1920), p. 3; *COGE* 11.40 (October 2, 1920), p. 2; *COGE* 11.42 (October 16, 1920), p. 2; *COGE* 11.43 (October 23, 1920), p. 2; *COGE* 11.44 (October 30, 1920), p. 3; *COGE* 11.46 (November 20, 1920), p. 2; *COGE* 12.8 (February 19, 1921), p. 2; *COGE* 12.10 (March 5, 1921), p. 2; *COGE* 12.11 (March 12, 1921), p. 3; *COGE* 12.12 (March 19, 1921), p. 2; *COGE* 12.14 (April 2, 1921), p. 3; *COGE* 12.15 (April 9, 1921), p. 3; *COGE* 12.16 (April 16, 1921), p. 2; *COGE* 12.17 (April 23, 1921), p. 2; *COGE* 12.18 (April 30, 1921), pp. 2, 3; *COGE* 12.19 (May 7, 1921), p. 3; *COGE* 12.20 (May 14, 1921), p. 2; *COGE* 12.21 (May 21, 1921), p. 3; *COGE* 12.23 (June 4, 1921), p. 3; *COGE* 12.24 (June 11, 1921), p. 3; *COGE* 12.25 (June 18, 1921), p. 3; *COGE* 12.26 (June 25, 1921), p. 2; *COGE* 12.28 (July 9, 1921), p. 4; *COGE* 12.29 (July 16, 1921), p. 2; *COGE* 12.30 (July 23, 1921), p. 2; *COGE* 12.31 (July 30, 1921), p. 2; *COGE* 12.32 (August 6, 1921), p. 2; *COGE* 12.33 (August 13, 1921), p. 3; *COGE* 12.34 (August 20, 1921), p. 3; *COGE* 12.35 (August 27, 1921), p. 2; *COGE* 12.36 (September 3, 1921), p. 2; *COGE* 12.37 (September 10, 1921), p. 2; *COGE* 12.38 (September 17, 1921), p. 2; *COGE* 12.38 (September 17, 1921), p. 2; *COGE* 12.39 (Se p 24, 1921), p. 2; *COGE* 12.40 (October 1, 1921), p. 2; *COGE* 12.41 (October 8, 1921), p. 2; *COGE* 12.42 (October 15, 1921), p. 2; *COGE* 12.45 (November 12, 1921), p. 2; *COGE* 12.52 (December 31, 1921), p. 3; *COGE* 13.3 (January 21, 1922), p. 3; *COGE* 13.6 (February 11, 1922), p. 2; *COGE* 13.15 (April 15, 1922), p. 2; *COGE* 13.16 (April 22, 1922), p. 2;*COGE* 13.21 (May 27, 1922), p. 2; *COGE* 13.23 (June 10, 1922), p. 2; *COGE* 13.25 (June, 24, 1922), p. 2; *COGE* 13.26 (July 1, 1922), pp. 1, 2; *COGE* 13.28 (July 15, 1922), p. 2; *COGE* 13.29 (July 22, 1922), pp. 2, 3, and 4; *COGE* 13.30 (July 29, 1922), p. 2; *COGE* 13.31 (August 5, 1922), p. 2; *COGE* 13.32 (August 12, 1922), p. 2; *COGE* 13.33 (August 19, 1922), p. 2; *COGE* 13.34 (August 26, 1922), pp. 2, 3; *COGE* 13.36 September 9, 1922), pp. 2, 3; *COGE* 13.37 (September 16, 1922), p. 2; *COGE* 13.38 (September 23, 1922), pp. 2, 4; *COGE* 13.39 (September 30, 1922), pp. 2, 3; *COGE* 13.40 (October 7, 1922), p. 2; *COGE* 13.41 (October 14, 1922), p. 2; *COGE* 13.42 (October 21, 1922), p. 2; *COGE* 13.43 (October 28, 1922), p. 4; *COGE* 13.44 (November 11, 1922), p. 1; *COGE* 13.44 (November 11, 1922), pp. 1, 2, and 4; *COGE* 13.45 (November 18, 1922), p. 3; *COGE* 13.47 (December 9, 1922), p. 3; *COGE* 14.4 (January 27, 1923), p. 3; *COGE* 14.5 (February 3, 1923), p. 3; *COGE* 14.6 (February 10, 1923), pp. 2, 4; *COGE* 14.11 (March 17, 1923), p. 4; *COGE* 14.14 (April 7, 1923), p. 3; *COGE* 14.15 (April 14, 1923), p. 2; *COGE* 14.16 (April 21, 1923), p. 4; *COGE* 14.21 (May 26, 1923), p. 2; *COGE* 14.25 (June 23, 1923), p. 3; *COGE* 14.28 (July 14, 1923), p. 2; *COGE* 14.30 (July 28, 1923), p. 3; *COGE* 14.31 (August 4, 1923), p. 2; *COGE* 14.32 (August 11, 1923), p. 3; *COGE* 14.33 (August 18, 1923), p. 3; *COGE* 14.34 (August 25, 1923), p. 2; *COGE* 14.35 (September 1, 1923), p. 4; *COGE* 14.38 (September 15, 1923), p. 3; *COGE* 14.39 (September 22, 1923), p. 3; *COGE* 14.39 (September 22, 1923), p. 3; *COGE* 14.41 (October 6, 1923), p. 4; *COGE* 14.42 (October 13, 1923), p. 3; *COGE* 14.43 (October 20, 1923), p. 4; *COGE* 14.44 (October 27, 1923), pp. 2, 4; *COGE* 14.47 (November 17, 1923), p.4; *COGE* 14.48 (November 24, 1923), p. 3; *COGE* 14.50 (December 8, 1923), p. 3; *COGE* 14.52 (December 22, 1923), p. 2; *COGE* 15.1 (January 5, 1924), p. 2; *COGE* 15.9 (March 1, 1924), p. 3; *COGE* 15.19 (May 24, 1924), p. 4; *COGE* 15.22 (June 14, 1924), p. 3; *COGE* 15.23 (June 21, 1924), p. 4; *COGE* 15.25 (July 5, 1924), p. 4; *COGE* 15.27 (July 19, 1924), p. 3; *COGE* 15.28 (July 26, 1924), p. 2; *COGE* 15.29 (August 2, 1924), p. 3; *COGE* 15.30 (August 9, 1924), p. 3; *COGE* 15.31 (August 16, 1924), p. 1; *COGE* 15.34 (September 6, 1924), p. 3; *COGE* 15.35 (September 13, 1924), p. 1; *COGE* 15.36 (September 20, 1924), pp. 2, 3; *COGE* 15.38 (October 4, 1924), pp. 1, 2, and 3; *COGE* 15.39 (October 11, 1924), p. 1; *COGE* 15.41 (October 25, 1924), p. 2; *COGE* 15.42 (November 8, 1924), p. 2; *COGE* 15.44 (November 22, 1924), pp. 1, 2; *COGE* 15.46 (December 6, 1924), p. 2; *COGE* 15.47 (December 13, 1924), p. 3; *COGE* 16.3 (January 17, 1925), p. 1; *COGE* 16.6 (February 7, 1925), p. 1; *COGE* 16.7 (February 14, 1925), pp. 1, 4; *COGE* 16.9 (February 28, 1925), p. 4; *COGE* 16.10 (March 7, 1925), p. 4; *COGE* 16.14 (April 4, 1925), p. 3; *COGE* 16.15 (April 11, 1925), p. 1; *COGE* 16.17 (April 25, 1925), p. 4; *COGE* 16.18 (May 2, 1925), p. 2; *COGE* 16.19 (May 9, 1925), p. 2; *COGE* 16.20 (May 16, 1925), pp. 2, 3; *COGE* 16.21 (May 23, 1925), p. 3; *COGE* 16.22 (May 30, 1925), pp. 2, 3, and 4; *COGE* 16.24 (June 13, 1925), p.4; *COGE* 16.25 (June 20, 1925), p. 2; *COGE* 16.27 (July 4, 1925), pp. 1, 3; *COGE* 16.28 (July 11, 1925), pp. 3, 4; *COGE* 16.29 (July 18, 1925), p. 1; *COGE* 16.30 (July 25, 1925), pp. 1, 3; *COGE* 16.31 (August 1, 1925), p. 3; *COGE* 16.32 (August 8, 1925), p. 1; *COGE* 16.34 (August 22, 1925), p. 3; *COGE* 16.35 (August 29, 1925), p. 4; *COGE* 16.36 (September 5, 1925), pp. 3, 4; *COGE* 16.37 (September 12, 1925), p. 2; *COGE* 16.39 (September 26, 1925), pp. 1, 2, and 3; *COGE* 16.40 (October 3, 1925), p. 2; *COGE* 16.41 (October 10, 1925), p. 2; *COGE* 16.42 (October 17, 1925), pp. 1, 2, 3, and 4; *COGE* 16.44 (October 31, 1925), pp. 3, 4; *COGE* 16.45 (November 7, 1925), p. 1; *COGE* 16.46 (November 14, 1925), pp. 3, 4; *COGE* 16.47 (November 21, 1925), p. 3; *COGE* 16.48 (November 28, 1925), p. 3; *COGE* 17.2 (January 16, 1926), p. 4; *COGE* 17.7 (February 3, 20, 1926), p. 2; *COGE* 17.12 (March 27, 1926), p. 4; *COGE* 17.14 (April 10, 1926), pp. 2, 4; *COGE* 17.15 (April 17, 1926), p. 3; *COGE* 17.22 (June 5, 1926), p. 4; *COGE* 17.24 (June 19, 1926), pp. 3, 4; *COGE* 17.25 (June 26, 1926), p. 1; *COGE* 17.26 (July 3, 1926), p. 4; *COGE* 17.28 (July 17, 1926), p. 2; *COGE* 17.29 (July 24, 1926), pp. 3, 4; *COGE* 17.31 (August 7, 1926), p. 3; *COGE* 17.32 (August 14, 1926), p. 3; *COGE* 17.35 (September 4, 1926), pp. 2, 3; *COGE* 17.36 (September 11, 1926), p. 3; *COGE* 17.37 (September 18, 1926), p. 3; *COGE* 17.38 (September 25, 1926), p. 3; *COGE* 17.39 (October 2, 1926), p. 4; *COGE* 17.40 (October 9, 1926), p. 1; *COGE* 17.41 (October 16, 1926), p. 4; *COGE* 17.42 (November 6, 1926), p. 4; *COGE* 17.45 (November 27, 1926), p. 4; *COGE* 18.3 (January 15, 1927), p. 2; *COGE* 18.6 (February 5, 1927), p. 4; *COGE* 18.13 (March 26, 1927), p. 3; *COGE* 18.14 (April 2, 1927), pp. 2, 4; *COGE* 18.16 (April 15, 1927), pp. 2, 4; *COGE* 18.24 (June 11, 1927), p. 2; *COGE* 18.26 (June 25, 1927), p. 4; *COGE* 18.27 (July 2, 1927), p.1; *COGE* 18.28 (July 9, 1927), p. 1; *COGE* 18.29 (July 16, 1927), pp. 1, 2; *COGE* 18.30 (July 23, 1927), p. 3; *COGE* 18.31 (July 31, 1927), p. 1; *COGE* 18.32 (August 6, 1927), p. 1; *COGE* 18.33 (August 13, 1927), p. 1; *COGE* 18.34 (August 20, 1927), pp. 1, 2; *COGE* 18.35 (August 27, 1927), p. 1; *COGE* 18.36 (September 5, 1927), pp. 1, 3; *COGE* 18.37 (September 10, 1927), p. 3; *COGE* 18.38 (September 17, 1927), p. 1; *COGE* 18.40 (October 1, 1927), pp. 1, 3; *COGE* 18.41 (October 8, 1927), p. 2; *COGE* 18.42 (October 15, 1927), p. 2; *COGE* 18.43 (October 22, 1927), pp. 1, 2, 3, and 4; *COGE* 18.44 (November 5, 1927), pp. 1, 3, and 4; *COGE* 18.47 (November 26, 1927), p. 4; *COGE* 18.52 (December 24, 1927), p. 3; *COGE* 19.15 (April 14, 1928), p. 1; *COGE* 19.18 (May 15, 1928), p. 1; *COGE* 19.22 (June 2, 1928), pp. 2, 3; *COGE* 19.25 (June 23, 1928), p. 1; *COGE* 19.27 (July 7, 1928), p. 4; *COGE* 19.28 (July 14, 1928), p. 1; *COGE* 19.29 (July 21, 1928), p. 1; *COGE* 19.30 (July 28, 1928), pp. 1, 3, and 4; *COGE* 19.31 (August 4, 1928), p. 1; *COGE* 19.32 (August 11, 1928), pp. 1, 2; *COGE* 19.33 (August 18, 1928, pp. 1, 2; *COGE* 19.34 (August 25, 1928), pp. 2, 3, and 4; *COGE* 19.35 (September 1, 1928), p. 3; *COGE* 19.36 (September 8, 1928), p. 2; *COGE* 19.37 (September 15, 1928), p. 4; *COGE* 19.38 (September 22, 1928), p. 2; *COGE* 19.39 (September 29, 1928), p. 1; *COGE* 19.40 (October 6, 1928), p. 1; *COGE* 19.41 (October 13, 1928), p. 1, 4; *COGE* 19.42 (October 20, 1928), pp. 3, 4; *COGE* 19.43 (November 3, 1928), p. 3; *COGE* 19.44 (November 10, 1928), p. 3; *COGE* 19.45 (November 17, 1928), p. 2; *COGE* 19.46 (November 24, 1928), p. 4;*COGE* 19.47 (December 1, 1928), pp. 1, 3; *COGE* 19.48 (December 8, 1928), p. 1; *COGE* 19.49 (December 15, 1928), p. 1; *COGE* 19.50 (December 22, 1928), pp. 1, 4; *COGE* 20.8 (April 20, 1929), p. 1; *COGE* 20.11 (May 11, 1929), p. 3; *COGE* 20.12 (May 18, 1929), p. 4; *COGE* 20.13 (May 25, 1929), pp. 1, 3; *COGE* 20.15 (June 8, 1929), p. 1; *COGE* 20.26 (August 24, 1929), p. 4; *COGE* 20.16 (June 15, 1929), p. 1; *COGE* 20.17 (June 22, 1929), p. 1; *COGE* 20.18 (June 29, 1929), p. 1; *COGE* 20.20 (July 13, 1929), pp. 1, 4; *COGE* 20.21 (July 20, 1929), p. 1; *COGE* 20.22 (July 27, 1929), pp. 1, 2, and 3; *COGE* 20.23 (August 3, 1929), p. 4; *COGE* 20.4 (March 23, 1929), p. 3; *COGE* 20.27 (August 31, 1929), p. 3; *COGE* 20.28 (September 7, 1929), pp. 1, 2; *COGE* 20.29 (September 14, 1929), pp. 1, 3, and 4; *COGE* 20.30 (September 21, 1929), pp. 1, 2, 3, and 4; *COGE* 20.31 (September 28, 1929), pp. 1, 2, and 4; *COGE* 20.32 (October 5, 1929), pp. 1, 3; *COGE* 20.33 (October 12, 1929), pp. 2, 3, and 4; *COGE* 20.34 (October 19, 1929), pp. 1, 3, and 4; *COGE* 20.35 (November 2, 1929), p. 4; *COGE* 20.36 (November 9, 1929), p. 1; *COGE* 20.37 (November 16, 1929), p. 1; *COGE* 20.39 (November 30, 1929), p. 4; *COGE* 20.43 (January 4, 1930), p. 1; *COGE* 21.2 (March 8, 1930), pp. 1, 3; *COGE* 21.6 (April 5, 1930), p. 4; *COGE* 21.7 (April 12, 1930), p. 1; *COGE* 21.8 (April 19, 1930), p. 4; *COGE* 21.9 (April 26, 1930), p. 1; *COGE* 21.10 (May 3, 1930), p. 1; *COGE* 21.11 (May 10, 1930), pp. 1, 4; *COGE* 21.12 (May 17, 1930), p. 4; *COGE* 21.13 (May 24, 1930), pp. 1, 3, and 4; *COGE* 21.14 (May 31, 1930), pp. 1, 2; *COGE* 21.15 (June 7, 1930), p. 3; *COGE* 21.16 (June 14, 1930), pp. 1, 2; *COGE* 21.18 (June 28, 1930), pp.1, 2, 3, and 4; *COGE* 21.19 (July 5, 1930), pp. 1, 4; *COGE* 21.20 (July 12, 1930), p. 4; *COGE* 21.21 (July 19, 1930), pp. 3, 4; *COGE* 21.22 (July 26, 1930), pp. 1, 2; *COGE* 21.23 (August 2, 1930), pp. 1, 4; *COGE* 21.24 (August 9, 1930), pp. 1, 2, 3, and 4; *COGE* 21.25 (August 16, 1930), p. 2, 3, and 4; *COGE* 21.26 (August 23, 1930), pp. 2, 4; *COGE* 21.27 (August 30, 1930), pp. 1, 2, 3, and 4; *COGE* 21.28 (September 6, 1930), pp. 1, 3; *COGE* 21.29 (September 13, 1930), p. 2; *COGE* 21.30 (September 20, 1930), p. 2; *COGE* 21.31 (September 27, 1930), pp. 1, 2, 3, and 4; *COGE* 21.32 (October 4, 1930), pp. 1, 2, 3, and 4; *COGE* 21.33 (October 11, 1930), pp. 1, 2, 3, and 4; *COGE* 21.34 (October 18, 1930), pp. 1, 2, and 4; *COGE* 21.35 (November 1, 1930), p. 2; *COGE* 21.36 (November 8, 1930), pp. 1, 2; *COGE* 21.37 (November 15, 1930), pp. 1, 3; *COGE* 21.38 (November 22, 1930), pp. 1, 2, 4; *COGE* 21.39 (November 29, 1930), pp. 2, 3; *COGE* 21.41 (December 13, 1930), pp. 1, 3, and 4; *COGE* 21.42 (December 20, 1930), p. 1; *COGE* 21.43 (January 3, 1931), p. 4; *COGE* 21.44 (January 10, 1931), p. 2; *COGE* 21.47 (January 31, 1931), p. 2; *COGE* 21.48 (February 7, 1931), p. 1; *COGE* 21.49 (February 14, 1931), p. 4; *COGE* 21.50 (February 21, 1931), p. 2; *COGE* 22.2 (March 14, 1931), p. 1; *COGE* 22.3 (March 21, 1931), pp. 3, 4; *COGE* 22.4 (March 28, 1931), pp. 1, 3; *COGE* 22.6 (April 11, 1931), pp. 1, 3, and 4; *COGE*

22.7 (April 18, 1931), pp. 1, 2; *COGE* 22.9 (May 2, 1931), pp. 1, 3; *COGE* 22.11 (May 16, 1931), pp. 1, 2, and 3; *COGE* 22.12 (May 23, 1931), p. 4; *COGE* 22.13 (May 30, 1931), p. 2; *COGE* 22.14 (June 6, 1931), pp. 1, 4; *COGE* 22.15 (June 13, 1931), p. 2; *COGE* 22.16 (June 20, 1931), p. 1; *COGE* 22.18 (July 4, 1931), p. 4; *COGE* 22.19 (July 11, 1931), p. 3; *COGE* 22.20 (July 18, 1931), pp. 1, 2, and 3; *COGE* 22.21 (July 25, 1931), pp. 1, 3; *COGE* 22.22 (August 1, 1931), pp. 1, 4; COGE 22.23 (August 8, 1931), pp. 1, 2, and 3; *COGE* 22.24 (August 15, 1931), pp. 1, 2, and 3; COGE 22.25 (August 22, 1931), p. 2; COGE 22.26 (August 29, 1931), p. . COGE 22.27 (September 5, 1931), pp. 1, 2; COGE 22.28 (September 12, 1931), pp. 2, 3; COGE 22.29 (September 19, 1931), p. 2; *COGE* 22.30 (September 26, 1931), pp. 1, 2; COGE 22.31 (October 3, 1931), pp. 1, 2, 3, and 4; COGE 22.33 (October 24, 1931), p. 19, pp. 2, 3, and 4; *COGE* 22.34 (October 31, 1931), pp. 3, 4; COGE 22.35 (November 7, 1931), pp. 1, 2, 3, and 4; *COGE* 22.36 (November 14, 1931), pp. 1, 3, and 4; COGE 22.37 (November 21, 1931), p. 4; *COGE* 22.38 (November 28, 1931), pp. 1, 3, and 4; and *COGE* 22.39 (December 5, 1931), p. 2.

Appendix G

Church of God Evangel

Baptismal Terminology

'followed the Lord in water baptism' references:
COGE 1.16 (October 15, 1910), p. 7; *COGE* 5.18 (May 2, 1914), p. 6; *COGE* 5.28 (July 11, 1914), p. 5; *COGE* 5.33 (August 15, 1914), p. 5; *COGE* 5.38 (September 19, 1914), p. 7; *COGE* 5.39 (September 26, 1914), p. 5; *COGE* 5.41 (October 10, 1914), p. 3; *COGE* 5.42 (October 17, 1914), pp. 4, 6; *COGE* 5.46 (November 21, 1914). p. 3; *COGE* 6.4 (January 23, 1915), p. 4; *COGE* 6.11 (March 13, 1915), p. 2; *COGE* 6.18 (May 1, 1915), p. 4; *COGE* 6.22 (May 29, 1915), p. 3; *COGE* 6.24 (June 12, 1915), p. 2; *COGE* 6.26 (June 26, 1915), p. 3; *COGE* 6.27 (July 3, 1915), p. 3; *COGE* 6.28 (July 10, 1915), p. 2; *COGE* 6.32 (August 7, 1915), pp. 2, 4; *COGE* 6.33 (August 14, 1915), p. 4; *COGE* 6.36. (September 4, 1915), pp. 2, 3; *COGE* 7.11 (March 11, 1916), p. 2; *COGE* 7.17 (April 22, 1916), p. 3; *COGE* 7.18 (April 29, 1916), p. 2; *COGE* 7.20 (May 13, 1916), p. 3; *COGE* 7.25 (June 17, 1916), p. 3; *COGE* 7.30 (July 22, 1916), pp. 2, 3; *COGE* 7.31 (July 29, 1916), p. 3; *COGE* 7.35 (August 26, 1916), pp. 2, 4; *COGE* 7.38 (September 16, 1916), p. 2; *COGE* 7.39 (September 23, 1916), pp. 4; *COGE* 7.40 (September 30, 1916), p. 4; *COGE* 7.42 (October 14, 1916), pp. 3, 4; *COGE* 7.43 (October 21, 1916), p. 2; *COGE* 7.47 (November 18, 1916), p. 2; *COGE* 8.10 (March 10, 1917), p. 3; *COGE* 8.18 (May 12, 1917), p. 3; *COGE* 8.21 (June 2, 1917), p. 4; *COGE* 8.22 (June 9, 1917), pp. 2, 4; *COGE* 8.23 (June 16, 1917), p. 4; *COGE* 8.24 (June 23, 1917), p. 4; *COGE* 8.25 (June 30, 1917), p. 2; *COGE* 8.26 (July 7, 1917), p. 3; *COGE* 8.27 (July 14, 1917), p. 4; *COGE* 8.30 (August 1917), p. 2; *COGE* 8.31 (August 11, 1917), p. 3; *COGE* 8.31 (August 11, 1917), p. 4; *COGE* 8.32 (August 18, 1917), p. 4; *COGE* 8.34 (September 1, 1917), p. 2; *COGE* 8.34 (September 1, 1917), p. 4; *COGE* 8.35 (September 8, 1917), p. 1; *COGE* 8.35 (September 8, 1917), p. 2; *COGE* 8.40 (October 13, 1917), p. 4; *COGE* 8.44 (November 10, 1917), p. 4; *COGE* 9.24 (June 15, 1918), p. 4; *COGE* 9.27 (July 6, 1918), p. 3; *COGE* 9.28 (July 13, 1918), pp. 2, 3; *COGE* 9.29 (July 20, 1918), p. 3; *COGE* 9.34 (August 24, 1918), p. 2; *COGE* 9.35 (August 31, 1918), p. 3; *COGE* 9.36 (September 7, 1918), p. 2.; *COGE* 9.37 (September 14, 1918), p. 3; *COGE* 9.39 (September 28, 1918), p. 2; *COGE* 9.40 (October 5, 1918), p. 3; *COGE* 10.14 (April 5, 1919), p. 2; *COGE* 10.19 (May 10, 1919), p. 3; *COGE* 10.20 (May 17, 1919), p. 3; *COGE* 10.21 (May 24, 1919), pp. 2; *COGE* 10.22 (May 31, 1919), p. 3; *COGE* 10.23 (June 7, 1919), p. 2; *COGE* 10.26 (June 28, 1919), p. 3; *COGE* 10.27 (July 5, 1919), p. 2; *COGE* 10.29 (July 19, 1919), pp. 2, 4; *COGE* 10.31 (August 2, 1919), p. 2; *COGE* 10.32 (August 9, 1919), p. 2, 3, and 4; *COGE* 10.35 (August 30, 1919), pp. 2, 3; *COGE* 10.37 (September 13, 1919), p. 2; *COGE* 10.38 (September 20, 1919), pp. 2, 3, and 4; *COGE* 10.40 (October 4, 1919), pp. 2, 3; *COGE* 10.41 (October 11, 1919), p. 4; *COGE* 10.42 (October 18, 1919), pp. 2, 4; *COGE* 10.43 (October 25, 1919), pp. 2, 3, and 4; *COGE* 10.44 (November 8, 1919), p. 3; *COGE* 10.47 (November 29, 1919), p. 4; *COGE* 11.1 (January 3, 1920), p. 4; *COGE* 11.9 (February 28, 1920), p. 4; *COGE* 11.27 (July 3, 1920), p. 3; *COGE* 11.28 (July 10, 1920), p. 2; *COGE* 11.29 (July 17, 1920), pp. 1, 3; *COGE* 11.30 (July 24, 1920), p. 2; *COGE* 11.31 (July 31, 1920), pp. 2, 3; *COGE* 11.33 (August 14, 1920), p. 2; *COGE* 11.34 (August 21, 1920), p. 2; *COGE* 11.35 (August 28, 1920), pp. 2, 4; *COGE* 11.36 (September 4, 1920), p. 2; *COGE* 11.37 (September 11, 1920), pp, 2, 3; *COGE* 11.38 (September 18, 1920), p. 3; *COGE* 11.39 (September 25, 1920), pp. 2, 3; *COGE* 11.40 (October 2, 1920), p. 2; *COGE* 11.41 (October 9, 1920), p. 2; *COGE* 11.42 (October 16, 1920), p. 2; *COGE* 11.43 (October 23, 1920), pp. 2, 3; *COGE* 11.46 (November 20, 1920), p. 3; *COGE* 11.50 (December 26, 1920), p. 3; *COGE* 12.5 (January 8, 1921), p. 3; *COGE* 12.8 (February 19, 1921), pp. 2, 4; *COGE* 12.12 (March 19, 1921), p. 2; *COGE* 12.14 (April 2, 1921), p. 3; *COGE* 12.16 (April 16, 1921),

p. 2; *COGE* 12.17 (April 23, 1921), p. 2.; *COGE* 12.20 (May 14, 1921), p. 2; *COGE* 12.21 (May 21, 1921), p. 3; *COGE* 12.25 (June 18, 1921), p. 3; *COGE* 12.26 (June 25, 1921), p. 2; *COGE* 12.28 (July 9, 1921), p. 4; *COGE* 12.29 (July 16, 1921), p. 2; *COGE* 12.31 (July 30, 1921), p. 2; *COGE* 12.32 (August 6, 1921), p. 2; *COGE* 12.33 (August 13, 1921), p. 3; *COGE* 12.34 (August 20, 1921), p. 3; *COGE* 12.35 (August 27, 1921), p. 2; *COGE* 12.36 (September 3, 1921), p. 2; *COGE* 12.37 (September 10, 1921), p. 2; *COGE* 12.38 (September 17, 1921), p. 2; *COGE* 12.39 (September 24, 1921), p. 2; *COGE* 12.40 (October 1, 1921), p. 2; *COGE* 12.41 (October 8, 1921), p. 2; *COGE* 12.43 (October 22, 1921), p. 2; *COGE* 12.44 (October 29, 1921), p. 2; *COGE* 12.47 (November 26, 1921), p. 2; *COGE* 12.48 (December 3, 1921), p. 2; *COGE* 13.8 (February 25, 1922), p. 3; *COGE* 13.12 (March 25, 1922), p. 4; *COGE* 13.23 (June 10, 1922), p. 2; *COGE* 13.25 (June, 24, 1922), p. 2; *COGE* 13.29 (July 22, 1922), p. 2; *COGE* 13.30 (July 29, 1922), p. 2; *COGE* 13.31 (August 5, 1922), pp. 2, 3; *COGE* 13.32 (August 12, 1922), p. 2; *COGE* 13.34 (August 26, 1922), pp. 2, 3; *COGE* 13.35 (September 2, 1922), p. 2; *COGE* 13.36 September 9, 1922), pp. 2, 3; *COGE* 13.37 (September 16, 1922), pp. 2, 3; *COGE* 13.38 (September 23, 1922), pp. 2, 3; *COGE* 13.39 (September 30, 1922), p. 4; *COGE* 13.40 (October 7, 1922), p. 3; *COGE* 13.41 (October 14, 1922), p. 2; *COGE* 13.42 (October 21, 1922), pp. 2, 4; *COGE* 13.43 (October 28, 1922), p. 2; *COGE* 13.44 (November 11, 1922), p. 2; *COGE* 13.47 (December 9, 1922), p. 3; *COGE* 14.1 (January 6, 1923), p. 2; *COGE* 14.18 (May 5, 1923), p. 3; *COGE* 14.20 (May 19, 1923), p. 3; *COGE* 14.22 (June 2, 1923), p. 2; *COGE* 14.24 (June 16, 1923), p. 4; *COGE* 14.27 (July 7, 1923), p. 3; *COGE* 14.30 (July 28, 1923), p. 3; *COGE* 14.31 (August 4, 1923), p. 2; *COGE* 14.34 (August 25, 1923), p. 2; *COGE* 14.34 (August 25, 1923), p. 2; *COGE* 14.35 (September 1, 1923), p. 3; *COGE* 14.37 (September 8, 1923), p. 2; *COGE* 14.38 (September 15, 1923), p. 3; *COGE* 14.39 (September 22, 1923), p. 3; *COGE* 14.40 (September 29, 1923), p. 3; *COGE* 14.43 (October 20, 1923), p. 4; *COGE* 14.44 (October 27, 1923), p. 4; *COGE* 14.46 (November 10, 1923), p. 3; *COGE* 14.47 (November 17, 1923), p. 3; *COGE* 14.50 (December 8, 1923), p. 3; *COGE* 15.13 (March 29, 1924), p. 4; *COGE* 15.15 (April 26, 1924), p. 3; *COGE* 15.16 (May 3, 1924), p. 4; *COGE* 15.20 (May 31, 1924), p. 3; *COGE* 15.23 (June 21, 1924), p. 3; *COGE* 15.25 (July 5, 1924), p. 4; *COGE* 15.27 (July 19, 1924), p. 4; *COGE* 15.28 (July 26, 1924), p. 1; *COGE* 15.29 (August 2, 1924), p. 3; *COGE* 15.32 (August 23, 1924), pp. 1, 3; *COGE* 15.34 (September 6, 1924), p. 2; *COGE* 15.35 (September 13, 1924), p. 1; *COGE* 15.36 (September 20, 1924), pp. 1, 2, and 3; *COGE* 15.37 (September 27, 1924), pp. 1, 2; *COGE* 15.38 (October 4, 1924), p. 4; *COGE* 15.39 (October 11, 1924), pp. 1, 3; *COGE* 15.40 (October 18, 1924), p. 3; *COGE* 15.41 (October 25, 1924), p. 2; *COGE* 15.42 (November 8, 1924), p. 4; *COGE* 15.44 (November 22, 1924), p. 2; *COGE* 15.45 (November 29, 1924), p. 1; *COGE* 15.46 (December 6, 1924), p. 2; *COGE* 16.5 (January 31, 1925), p. 1; *COGE* 16.13 (March 28, 1925), p. 3; *COGE* 16.15 (April 11, 1925), p. 1; *COGE* 16.18 (May 2, 1925), p. 1; *COGE* 16.19 (May 9, 1925), p. 4; *COGE* 16.20 (May 16, 1925), p. 3; *COGE* 16.23 (June 6, 1925), p. 4; *COGE* 16.24 (June 13, 1925), p. 3; *COGE* 16.26 (June 27, 1925), pp. 2, 4; *COGE* 16.28 (July 1925), p. 1; *COGE* 16.34 (August 22, 1925), pp. 3, 4; *COGE* 16.36 (September 5, 1925), pp. 1-2, and 3; *COGE* 16.37 (September 1925), p. 2; *COGE* 16.39 (September 26, 1925), p. 4; *COGE* 16.41 (October 10, 1925), p. 3; *COGE* 16.42 (October 17, 1925), pp. 3, 4; *COGE* 16.44 (October 31, 1925), p. 4; *COGE* 16.45 (November 7, 1925), p. 3; *COGE* 16.47 (November 21, 1925), p. 3; *COGE* 16.52 (December 26, 1925), pp. 2, 4; *COGE* 17.18 (May 8, 1926), p. 2; *COGE* 17.19 (May 15, 1926), p. 1; *COGE* 17.23 (June 12, 1926), p. 4; *COGE* 17.25 (June 26, 1926), p. 4; *COGE* 17.27 (July 10, 1926), p. 4; *COGE* 17.29 (July 24, 1926), p. 3; *COGE* 17.30 (July 31, 1926), pp. 3, 4; *COGE* 17.31 (August 7, 1926), p. 3; *COGE* 17.32 (August 14, 1926), p. 3; *COGE* 17.35 (September 4, 1926), p. 3; *COGE* 17.36 (September 11, 1926), p. 3; *COGE* 17.37 (September 18, 1926), p. 3; *COGE* 17.38 (September 25, 1926), p. 3; *COGE* 17.39 (October 2, 1926), pp. 3, 4; *COGE* 17.40 (October 9, 1926), p. 3; *COGE* 17.41 (October 16, 1926), p. 4; *COGE* 17.42 (November 6, 1926), pp. 3, 4; *COGE* 17.43 (November 13, 1926), p. 4; *COGE* 17.44 (November 20, 1926), p. 4; *COGE* 17.45 (November 27, 1926), p. 4; *COGE* 17.50 (December 25, 1926), p. 4; *COGE* 18.4 (January 22, 1927), p. 4; *COGE* 18.5 (January 29, 1927), p. 1; *COGE* 18.10 (March 5, 1927), p. 2; *COGE* 18.16 (April 15, 1927), p. 1; *COGE* 18.26 (June 25, 1927), p. 2; *COGE* 18.28 (July 9, 1927), p. 2; *COGE* 18.29 (July 16, 1927), p. 4; *COGE* 18.31 (July 31, 1927), pp. 1, 4; *COGE* 18.34 (August 20, 1927), p. 1; *COGE* 18.35 (August 27, 1927), pp. 1, 3; *COGE* 18.37 (September 10, 1927), pp. 1, 3; *COGE* 18.38 (September 17, 1927), p. 1; *COGE* 18.39 (September 24, 1927), p. 3; *COGE* 18.41 (October 8, 1927), pp. 1, 2; *COGE* 18.42 (October 15, 1927), p. 1; *COGE* 18.43 (October 22, 1927), pp. 1, 2, and 4; *COGE* 18.44 (November 5, 1927), pp. 1, 2, and 4; *COGE* 18.46 (November 19, 1927), p. 3; *COGE* 18.47 (November 26, 1927), p. 1; *COGE* 19.1 (January 7, 1928), p. 1; *COGE* 19.4 (January 28, 1928), p. 3; *COGE* 19.12 (March 24, 1928), p. 1; *COGE* 19.15 (April 14, 1928), pp. 3, 4; *COGE* 19.18 (May 15, 1928), pp. 1, 4; *COGE* 19.19 (May 22, 1928), p. 4; *COGE* 19.23 (June 9, 1928), p. 3; *COGE* 19.30 (July 28, 1928), pp. 1, 4; *COGE* 19.31 (August 4, 1928), pp. 1, 4; *COGE* 19.37 (September 15, 1928), p. 4; *COGE* 19.39 (September 29, 1928), p. 2; *COGE* 19.41 (October 13, 1928), pp. 1, 2, and 4; *COGE* 19.44 (November 10, 1928), p. 3; *COGE* 19.45 (November 17, 1928), p. 2; *COGE* 19.47 (December 1, 1928), p. 2; *COGE* 20.1 (March 2, 1929), p. 3; *COGE* 20.3 (March 16, 1929), p. 4; *COGE* 20.9 (April 27, 1929), p. 2; *COGE* 20.13 (May 25, 1929), p. 4; *COGE* 20.15 (June 8, 1929), p. 4; *COGE* 20.16 (June 15, 1929), p. 4; *COGE* 20.18 (June 29, 1929), p. 4; *COGE* 20.19

(July 6, 1929), p. 3; *COGE* 20.22 (July 27, 1929), p. 1; *COGE* 20.24 (August 10, 1929), p. 2; *COGE* 20.24 (August 10, 1929), p. 4; *COGE* 20.26 (August 24, 1929), pp. 2, 4; *COGE* 20.27 (August 31, 1929), p. 1; *COGE* 20.28 (September 7, 1929), pp. 1, 4; *COGE* 20.29 (September 14, 1929), pp. 3, 4; *COGE* 20.30 (September 21, 1929), pp. 1, 2; *COGE* 20.31 (September 28, 1929), pp. 1, 2, and 4; *COGE* 20.33 (October 12, 1929), pp. 1, 2, and 3; *COGE* 20.34 (October 19, 1929), p. 2; *COGE* 20.35 (November 2, 1929), p. 1; *COGE* 20.46 (January 25, 1930), p. 2; *COGE* 21.8 (April 19, 1930), p. 4; *COGE* 21.12 (May 17, 1930), p. 1; *COGE* 21.12 (May 17, 1930), p. 1; *COGE* 21.13 (May 24, 1930), p. 1; *COGE* 21.16 (June 14, 1930), p. 4; *COGE* 21.17 (June 21, 1930), p. 1; *COGE* 21.18 (June 28, 1930), p. 4; *COGE* 21.19 (July 5, 1930), p. 3; *COGE* 21.21 (July 19, 1930), pp. 1, 3; *COGE* 21.25 (August 16, 1930), pp. 3, 4; *COGE* 21.26 (August 23, 1930), pp. 3, 4; *COGE* 21.27 (August 30, 1930), pp. 1, 3; *COGE* 21.28 (September 6, 1930), pp. 2, 3, and 4; *COGE* 21.29 (September 13, 1930), pp. 1, 2, and 4; *COGE* 21.30 (September 20, 1930), pp. 1, 3; *COGE* 21.31 (September 27, 1930), pp. 3, 4; *COGE* 21.32 (October 4, 1930), pp. 1, 3; *COGE* 21.33 (October 11, 1930), pp. 1, 4; *COGE* 21.34 (October 18, 1930), pp. 3, 4; *COGE* 21.35 (November 1, 1930), p. 3; *COGE* 21.36 (November 8, 1930), p. 3; *COGE* 21.38 (November 22, 1930), p. 4; *COGE* 21.45 (January 17, 1931), p. 1; *COGE* 22.6 (April 11, 1931), p. 4; *COGE* 22.7 (April 18, 1931), p. 3; *COGE* 22.10 (May 9, 1931), pp. 2, 4; *COGE* 22.12 (May 23, 1931), pp. 3, 4; *COGE* 22.14 (June 6, 1931), pp. 1, 3; *COGE* 22.15 (June 13, 1931), pp. 1, 2; *COGE* 22.16 (June 20, 1931), p. 4; *COGE* 22.18 (July 4, 1931), p. 1; *COGE* 22.19 (July 11, 1931), pp. 1, 2, and 3; *COGE* 22.20 (July 18, 1931), p. 1; *COGE* 22.21 (July 25, 1931), pp. 1, 3; *COGE* 22.22 (August 1, 1931), p. 1; *COGE* 22.23 (August 8, 1931), pp. 1, 2; *COGE* 22.24 (August 15, 1931), pp. 2, 3; *COGE* 22.25 (August 22, 1931), p. 2; *COGE* 22.26 (August 29, 1931), pp. 1, 3; *COGE* 22.27 (September 5, 1931), pp. 1, 2; *COGE* 22.28 (September 12, 1931), pp. 1, 2; *COGE* 22.29 (September 19, 1931), pp. 1, 3; *COGE* 22.30 (September 26, 1931), pp. 1, 2, 3, and 4; *COGE* 22.31 (October 3, 1931), pp. 1, 2, and 3; *COGE* 22.33 (October 24, 1931), pp. 2, 4; *COGE* 22.34 (October 31, 1931), p. 3; *COGE* 22.35 (November 7, 1931), pp. 1, 3, and 4; *COGE* 22.36 (November 14, 1931), pp. 2, 4; *COGE* 22.37 (November 21, 1931), p. 4; *COGE* 22.38 (November 28, 1931), p. 3; and *COGE* 22.39 (December 5, 1931), p. 3.

Appendix H

The Pentecostal Herald

Geographical locations listed alphabetically according to state/city, country/city:

Arkansas

Black Rock;[20] Blytheville;[21] Boonville;[22] Harrison;[23] and London.[24]

California

Willow Creek;[25] Oakland.[26]

Colorado

Colorado Springs;[27]

---

[20] *PH* 5.7 (December 1919), p. 4.
[21] *PH* 4.4 (August 1918), p. 4.
[22] *PH* 10.9 (October 1, 1923), p. 5.
[23] *PH* 5.4 (September 1919), p. 4.
[24] *PH* 4.6 (October 1918), p. 3.
[25] *PH* 5.6 (November 1919), p. 4.
[26] *PH* 9.15 (January 1, 1923), p. 4.
[27] *PH* 5.5 (October 1919), p. 3.

Denver;[28] Rocky Ford;[29] Superior.[30]

Florida/Georgia

Florida and Georgia.[31]

Hawaii

Pahoe.[32]

Illinois

Chicago;[33]

Ramsey.[34]

Indiana

Indianapolis.[35]

Iowa

Chester;[36] Davis City;[37] and Van Wert.[38]

Kansas

Northwest Kansas.[39]

Kentucky

Brooks;[40] Middle Creek.[41]

Michigan

Iron Mountain;[42] Petoskey.[43]

---

[28] *PH* 10.4 (June 1, 1923), p. 5.
[29] *PH* 10.18 (March 1, 1923), p. 4.
[30] *PH* 9.9 (August 15, 1922), p. 3; *PH* 10.2 (April 1, 1923), p. 4.
[31] *PH* 7.4 (June 1921), p. 2.
[32] *PH* 6.11 (February 1921), p. 3.
[33] *PH* 5.3 (August 1919), p. 3; *PH* 8.22 (August 1, 1922), p. 4; and *PH* 9.10 (September 1, 1922), p. 1.
[34] *PH* 5.5 (October 1919), p. 3.
[35] *PH* 4.5 (September 1918), p. 3; *PH* 4.10 (February 1919), p. 4; *PH* 5.1 (May 1919), p. 3; *PH* 5.4 (September 1919), p. 3; *PH* 5.6 (November 1919), pp. 1, 3; *PH* 6.11 (February 1921), p. 3; *PH* 8.15 (April 15, 1922), p. 3; *PH* 8.18 (June 1, 1922), pp. 1, 2; and *PH* 10.3 (May 1, 1923), p. 5.
[36] *PH* 4.4 (August 1918), p. 3.
[37] *PH* 3.10 (February 1918), p. 3
[38] *PH* 8.9 (January 1, 1922), p. 1; and *PH* 8.17 (May 15, 1922), p. 4.
[39] *PH* 4.5 (September 1918), p. 3; *PH* 5.5 (October 1919), p. 1.
[40] *PH* 5.4 (September 1919), p. 1.
[41] *PH* 6.3 (June 1920), p. 3.
[42] *PH* 5.9 (February 1920), p. 3.
[43] *PH* 6.11 (February 1921), p. 1.

Minnesota

Doran;[44] Grayling;[45] Minneapolis;[46] and Trail.[47]

Missouri

Moberly;[48] Princess Ann;[49] and St. Louis.[50]

Nebraska

Freemont;[51] Naper.[52]

North Dakota

Noonan.[53]

Ohio

Akron;[54] Cincinnati;[55] and Steubenville.[56]

Oklahoma

Bidding Springs.[57]

Oregon

Portland.[58]

Pennsylvania

Dover;[59] Fallen Timber;[60] Lancaster;[61] and Philadelphia.[62]

---

[44] *PH* 4.4 (August 1918), p. 3.
[45] *PH* 4.4 (August 1918), p. 1.
[46] *PH* 4.12 (April 1919), p. 4.
[47] *PH* 4.12 (April 1919), p. 4.
[48] *PH* 4.7 (November 1918), p. 3.
[49] *PH* 8.16 (May 1, 1922), p. 4.
[50] *PH* 9.13 (November 1, 1922), p. 3.
[51] *PH* 9.11 (September 15, 1922), p. 4.
[52] *PH* 8.20 and 21 (July 1 and 15, 1922), p. 4.
[53] *PH* 5.4 (September 1919), p. 4.
[54] *PH* 7.4 (June 1921), p. 4.
[55] *PH* 5.4 (September 1919), p. 3.
[56] *PH* 6.3 (June 1920), p. 4
[57] *PH* 5.5 (October 1919), p. 4.
[58] *PH* 4.6 (October 1918), p. 4.
[59] *PH* 7.4 (June 1921), p. 2.
[60] *PH* 10.7 (September 1, 1923), p. 7.
[61] *PH* 5.5 (October 1919), p. 1.
[62] *PH* 9.9 (August 15, 1922), p. 3.

South Dakota

Lemmon.[63]

Tennessee
Cool Springs.[64]

Texas
Cedar Hill;[65] Dripping Springs;[66] Greenville;[67] Houston;[68] and Ladonia.[69]

Washington
Seattle.[70]

Wisconsin

Elton.[71]

Africa

Gatooma, South Rhodesia Apostolic Faith Mission;[72] Transvaal, South Africa.[73]

Canada

Edmonton, Alta;[74] Winnipeg.[75]

China

Canton;[76] Hong Kong;[77] and Sam Shui.[78]

---

[63] *PH* 4.6 (October 1918), p. 4.
[64] *PH* 5.7 (December 1919), p. 3.
[65] *PH* 5.5 (October 1919), p. 4.
[66] *PH* 6.10 (January 1921), p. 4.
[67] *PH* 6.11 (February 1921), p. 2.
[68] *PH 6.11 (February 1921), p. 2.*
[69] *PH* 4.5 (September 1918), p. 4.
[70] *PH* 5.5 (October 1919), p. 1.
[71] *PH* 5.5 (October 1919), p. 1; *PH* 5.7 (December 1919), p. 4.
[72] *PH* 6.3 (June 1920), p. 2.
[73] *PH* 8.15 (April 15, 1922), p. 4.
[74] *PH* 4.5 (September 1918), p. 3; *PH* 4.7 (November 1918), p. 2; and *PH* 5.3 (August 1919), p.4.
[75] *PH* 5.5 (October 1919), p. 4.
[76] *PH* 8.18 (June 1, 1922), p. 3.
[77] *PH* 8.15 (April 15, 1922), p. 4; *PH* 8.22 (August 1, 1922), p. 4.
[78] *PH* 3.10 (February 1918), p. 3.

England

> Grimsby.[79]

India

> Sharannagar Mission of Nawabganj (Gonda), U.P.[80]

Japan

> Osaka.[81]

Appendix I

White Wing Messenger

Geographical locations by state/city:

Alabama

Alabama;[82] Birmingham;[83] Collins;[84] Collinsville;[85] Detroit;[86] Ensley;[87] Goddard;[88] Hackleburg;[89] Haleyville;[90] Kennedy;[91] Moulton;[92] and Mount Hope.[93]

Arkansas

Arkansas;[94] Black Creek;[95] Cleveland;[96] Clinton;[97] Fisher;[98] Higden;[99]

---

[79] *PH* 10.4 (June 1, 1923), p. 6.
[80] *PH* 8.15 (April 15, 1922), p. 3; *PH* 8.16 (May 1, 1922), p. 4.
[81] *PH* 7.4 (June 1921), p. 4.
[82] *WWM* 6.17 (August 31, 1929), p.
[83] *WWM* 7.21 (October 25, 1930), p. 1.
[84] *WWM* 6.18 (September 28, 1929), p. 1.
[85] *WWM* 8.23 (November 21, 1931), p. 2.
[86] *WWM* 8.19 (September 26, 1931), p. 2; *WWM* 8.21 (October 24, 1931), p. 4.
[87] *WWM* 8.19 (September 26, 1931), p. 2.
[88] *WWM* 8.15 (July 18, 1931), p. 2.
[89] *WWM* 7.21 (October 25, 1930), p. 1.
[90] *WWM* 4.15 (July 16, 1927), p. 3.
[91] *WWM* 8.23 (November 21, 1931), p. 1.
[92] *WWM* 7.20 (October 11, 1930), p. 2.
[93] *WWM* 6.23 (December 7, 1929), p. 2; *WWM* 8.19 (September 26, 1931), p. 2.
[94] *WWM* 5.20 (August 18, 1928), p. 3.
[95] *WWM* 5.21 (September 1, 1928), p. 3.
[96] *WWM* 5.21 (September 1, 1928), p. 3.
[97] *WWM* 4.13 (June 18, 1927), p. 4.
[98] *WWM* 4.11 (May 21, 1927), p. 1; *WWM* 4.8 (April 9, 1927), p. 1; and *WWM* 4.14 (July 2, 1927), p. 2.
[99] *WWM* 6.17 (August 31, 1929), p. 2.

Horatio;[100] Marchvin;[101] and Trumann;[102]

Colorado

Colorado[103]

Florida

Florida;[104] Hallandale;[105] Hollywood;[106] Homestead;[107] Key West;[108] Miami;[109] Perry;[110] Sanford;[111] and South Bay.[112]

Georgia

Acworth;[113] Atlanta;[114] Cogdell;[115] Columbus;[116] Dahlonega;[117] Dalton;[118] Fairfax;[119] Kennesaw;[120] Lithonia;[121] Manor;[122] Marietta;[123] Mount Green;[124] Nichols;[125] Pittman;[126] and Rossville.[127]

---

[100] *WWM* 8.17 (August 15, 1931), p. 1.
[101] *WWM* 8.22 (November 7, 1931), p. 2.
[102] *WWM* 3.26 (December 18, 1926), pp. 1, 2; *WWM* 4.19 (September 10, 1927), p. 3; and *WWM* 4.20 (October 1, 1927), p. 3.
[103] *WWM* 8.21 (October 24, 1931), p. 2.
[104] *WWM* 3.21 (October 9, 1926), p. 4.
[105] *WWM* 4.1 (January 1, 1927), p. 2; *WWM* 5.13 (June 23, 1928), p. 3.
[106] *WWM* 3.18 (August 28, 1926), p. 3; *WWM* 4.18 (August 27, 1927), p. 1.
[107] *WWM* 5.20 (August 18, 1928), p. 1.
[108] *WWM* 5.15 (July 21, 1928), p. 3; *WWM* 5.25 (November 17, 1928), p. 2.
[109] *WWM* 1.20 (June 28, 1924), p. 2; *WWM* 3.20 (September 25, 1926), p. 2; *WWM* 4.12 (June 4, 1927), p. 1; and *WWM* 5.9 (April 28, 1928), p. 3.
[110] *WWM* 7.19 (September 27, 1930), p. 1.
[111] *WWM* 8.22 (November 7, 1931), p. 1.
[112] *WWM* 5.13 (June 23, 1928), p. 2.
[113] *WWM* 4.20 (October 1, 1927), p. 3.
[114] *WWM* 1.32 (December 20, 1924), p. 4; *WWM* 4.20 (October 1, 1927), p. 3.
[115] *WWM* 5.9 (April 28, 1928), p. 1.
[116] *WWM* 7.2 (January 18, 1930), p. 2.
[117] *WWM* 8.19 (September 26, 1931), p. 4.
[118] *WWM* 2.13 (June 20, 1925), p. 3; *WWM* 2.19 (September 26, 1925), p. 3; *WWM* 5.23 (October 6, 1928), p. 3; and *WWM* 8.15 (July 18, 1931), p. 1.
[119] *WWM* 5.15 (July 21, 1928), p. 3.
[120] *WWM* 2.13 (June 20, 1925), p. 3.
[121] *WWM* 4.19 (September 10, 1927), p. 2.
[122] *WWM* 1.14 (April 5, 1924), p. 3; *WWM* 1.22 (July 26, 1924), p. 2; *WWM* 4.18 (August 27, 1927), p. 3; *WWM* 7.11 (May 24, 1930), p. 3; and *WWM* 8.24 (December 5, 1931), p. 4.
[123] *WWM* 8.20 (October 10, 1931), p. 1.
[124] *WWM* 8.10 (May 9, 1931), p. 4; *WWM* 7.25 (December 20, 1930), p. 3.
[125] *WWM* 8.15 (July 18, 1931), p. 4.
[126] *WWM* 8.10 (May 9, 1931), p. 4.
[127] *WWM* 1.2 (September 29, 1923), p. 3; *WWM* 1.2 (September 29, 1923), p. 3; *WWM* 4.8 (April 9, 1927), p. 1; and *WWM* 8.20 (October 10, 1931), p. 1.

Illinois

Eldorado;[128] Harco;[129] and Johnston.[130]

Indiana

Gas City;[131] Indianapolis.[132]

Kansas

Lawrence;[133] Pittsburg.[134]

Kentucky

Adolphus;[135] Ages;[136] Arjay;[137] Barthell;[138] Buckner;[139] Burdine;[140] Burnside;[141] Central City;[142] Chapel Hill;[143] Corbin;[144] Dahl;[145] Elizabethtown;[146] Good Water;[147] Granger Town;[148] Highland Park;[149] Holt;[150] Hoover;[151] Kentenia;[152] Kentucky;[153] Lick Creek;[154] Longmont;[155] Louisville;[156] McHenry;[157] Mitchell Hill;[158] Moorman;[159]

---

[128] *WWM* 2.13 (June 20, 1925), p. 3.
[129] *WWM* 4.13 (June 18, 1927), p. 1.
[130] *WWM* 4.8 (April 9, 1927), p. 3.
[131] *WWM* 1.2 (September 29, 1923), p. 2.
[132] *WWM* 7.17 (August 16, 1930), p. 1.
[133] *WWM* 8.8 (April 11, 1931), p. 1;
[134] *WWM* 1.21 (July 12, 1924), p. 3; *WWM* 1.24 (August 23, 1924), p. 3; and *WWM* 6.13 (July 6, 1929), p. 3.
[135] *WWM* 6.15 (August 3, 1929), p. 1; *WWM* 7.21 (October 25, 1930), p. 1.
[136] *WWM* 1.3 (October 13, 1923), p. 3.
[137] *WWM* 3.9 (April 24, 1926), p. 3; *WWM* 4.17 (August 13, 1927), p. 2.
[138] *WWM* 7.14 (July 5, 1930), p. 1.
[139] *WWM* 3.18 (August 28, 1926), p. 2.
[140] *WWM* 6.13 (July 6, 1929), p. 3.
[141] *WWM* 6.18 (September 28, 1929), p. 2; *WWM* 7.18 (August 30, 1930), p. 2; *WWM* 7.25 (December 20, 1930), p. 1; and *WWM* 8.1 (January 3, 1931), p. 1.
[142] *WWM* 1.3 (October 13, 1923), p. 3; *WWM* 6.19 (October 12, 1929), p. 1; and *WWM* 8.21 (October 24, 1931), p. 2.
[143] *WWM* 7.19 (September 27, 1930), p. 1.
[144] *WWM* 3.18 (August 28, 1926), p. 2; *WWM* 4.19 (September 10, 1927), p. 1
[145] *WWM* 3.24 (November 20, 1926), p. 2.
[146] *WWM* 7.14 (July 5, 1930), p. 2.
[147] *WWM* 5.11 (May 26, 1928), p. 2;
[148] *WWM* 2.7 (March 28, 1925), p. 2; *WWM* 2.24 (December 5, 1925), p. 1; *WWM* 4.14 (July 2, 1927), p. 1; and *WWM* 5.11 (May 26, 1928), p. 2.
[149] *WWM* 3.26 (December 18, 1926), p. 1; *WWM* 3.16 (July 31, 1926), p. 2; and *WWM* 4.16 (July 30, 1927), p. 3.
[150] *WWM* 4.26 (December 24, 1927), p. 3.
[151] *WWM* 7.23 (November 22, 1930), p. 1.
[152] *WWM* 1.29 (November 8, 1924), p. 4; *WWM* 2.9 (April 25, 1925), p. 3.
[153] *WWM* 5.21 (September 1, 1928), p. 1; *WWM* 8.20 (October 10, 1931), p. 2.
[154] *WWM* 8.22 (November 7, 1931), p. 4.
[155] *WWM* 4.14 (July 2, 1927), p. 3.
[156] *WWM* 2.6 (March 14, 1925), p. 4; *WWM* 4.13 (June 18, 1927), p. 1; *WWM* 4.18 (August 27, 1927), p. 1; and *WWM* 6.19 (October 12, 1929), p. 4.
[157] *WWM* 3.20 (September 25, 1926), p. 1.
[158] *WWM* 1.21 (July 12, 1924), p. 3.
[159] *WWM* 6.17 (August 31, 1929), p. 1; *WWM* 8.15 (July 18, 1931), p. 3.

Morganfield;[160] Mount Eden;[161] Owensboro;[162] Paint Cliff;[163] Quinton;[164] Somerset;[165] Sturgis;[166] and Willisburg.[167]

Louisiana

Louisiana;[168] Morgan City.[169]

Maryland

Deals Island Beach;[170] Maryland;[171] Salisbury;[172] and Whiteburg.[173]

Mississippi

Boyle;[174] Cary;[175] Catchings;[176] Causey's Chapel;[177] Chapel Hill;[178] Cleveland;[179] Drew;[180] Hollandale;[181] Kosciusko;[182] Liberty;[183] Long Shot;[184] Lucre;[185] Lyon;[186] Money;[187] Okolona;[188] Panther Burn;[189] and Taylor.[190]

---

[160] *WWM* 1.20 (June 28, 1924), p. 3; *WWM* 1.21 (July 12, 1924), p. 3; and *WWM* 2.20 (October 10, 1925), p. 3
[161] *WWM* 4.16 (July 30, 1927), p. 3.
[162] *WWM* 5.23 (October 6, 1928), p. 3.
[163] *WWM* 7.11 (May 24, 1930), p. 3.
[164] *WWM* 6.19 (October 12, 1929), p. 2.
[165] *WWM* 7.13 (June 21, 1930). p. 1; *WWM* 7.14 (July 5, 1930), p. 2; and *WWM* 7.18 (August 30, 1930), p. 1.
[166] *WWM* 4.16 (July 30, 1927), p. 3; *WWM* 8.22 (November 7, 1931), p. 1.
[167] *WWM* 1.2 (September 29, 1923), p. 1; *WWM* 8.24 (December 5, 1931), p. 2.
[168] *WWM* 7.7 (March 29, 1930), p. 2.
[169] *WWM* 1.22 (July 26, 1924), p. 4; *WWM* 2.14 (July 4, 1925), p. 3; and *WWM* 2.17 (August 15, 1925), p. 2.
[170] *WWM* 4.11 (May 21, 1927), p. 1
[171] *WWM* 7.17 (August 16, 1930), p. 2.
[172] *WWM* 8.22 (November 7, 1931), p. 2.
[173] *WWM* 5.15 (July 21, 1928), p. 4.
[174] *WWM* 4.17 (August 13, 1927), p. 2; *WWM* 8.24 (December 5, 1931), p. 1.
[175] *WWM* 8.25 (December 19, 1931), p. 3.
[176] *WWM* 1.2 (September 29, 1923), p. 3.
[177] *WWM* 1.24 (August 23, 1924), p. 3; *WWM* 7.24 (December 6, 1930), p. 3
[178] *WWM* 5.25 (November 17, 1928), p. 1.
[179] *WWM* 6.19 (October 12, 1929), p. 1.
[180] *WWM* 4.17 (August 13, 1927), p. 1.
[181] *WWM* 7.24 (December 6, 1930), p. 4.
[182] *WWM* 1.24 (August 23, 1924), p. 3; *WWM* 1.26 (September 27, 1924), p. 3; and *WWM* 3.24 (November 20, 1926), p. 1.
[183] *WWM* 3.16 (July 31, 1926), p. 1; *WWM* 4.23 (November 12, 1927), p. 3.
[184] *WWM* 5.15 (July 21, 1928), p. 3.
[185] *WWM* 3.20 (September 25, 1926), p. 4.
[186] *WWM* 2.20 (October 10, 1925), p. 4; *WWM* 1.31 (December 6, 1924) p. 1; *WWM* 7.13 (June 21, 1930). p. 2; and *WWM* 8.23 (November 21, 1931), p. 2.
[187] *WWM* 6.18 (September 28, 1929), p. 2.
[188] *WWM* 4.20 (October 1, 1927), p. 3
[189] *WWM* 5.22 (September 15, 1928), p. 3.
[190] *WWM* 4.1 (January 1, 1927), p. 3.

Missouri

Banner;[191] Birchtree;[192] Bonne Terre;[193] Delta;[194] House's Creek;[195] Jobe;[196] Turkey Oak;[197] and Winona.[198]

New York

Jamaica Beach;[199] New York.[200]

North Carolina

Bogue;[201] Clyde;[202] Cooper;[203] Gastonia;[204] Gold Valley;[205] Louisburg;[206] New Hope;[207] Selma;[208] and Wade.[209]

North Dakota

Center;[210] Golden Valley.[211]

Ohio

Akron;[212] Canton;[213] Cincinnati;[214] and Ohio.[215]

Oklahoma

Ada;[216] Allen;[217] Bristow;[218]

---

[191] *WWM* 8.23 (November 21, 1931), p. 4.
[192] *WWM* 4.11 (May 21, 1927), p. 2.
[193] *WWM* 5.15 (July 21, 1928), p. 2.
[194] *WWM* 6.25 (December 21, 1929), p. 3
[195] *WWM* 8.15 (July 18, 1931), p. 3.
[196] *WWM* 2.18 (August 29, 1925), p. 3.
[197] *WWM* 7.23 (November 22, 1930), p. 1.
[198] *WWM* 8.15 (July 18, 1931), p. 1.
[199] *WWM* 2.18 (August 29, 1925), p. 4.
[200] *WWM* 7.7 (March 29, 1930), p. 2; *WWM* 1.30 (November 22, 1924), p. 4; *WWM* 3.19 (September 11, 1926), p. 4; and *WWM* 3.22 (October 23, 1926), p. 3
[201] *WWM* 8.20 (October 10, 1931), p. 4.
[202] *WWM* 4.20 (October 1, 1927), p. 2.
[203] *WWM* 7.13 (June 21, 1930. p. 3; *WWM* 7.14 (July 5, 1930), p. 1.
[204] *WWM* 4.8 (April 9, 1927), p. 1.; *WWM* 5.27 (December 15, 1928), p. 3.
[205] *WWM* 7.23 (November 22, 1930), p. 2.
[206] *WWM* 3.15 (July 17, 1926), p. 3.
[207] *WWM* 8.1 (January 3, 1931), p. 1.
[208] *WWM* 7.24 (December 6, 1930), p. 3.
[209] *WWM* 5.11 (May 26, 1928), p. 2.
[210] *WWM* 4.17 (August 13, 1927), p. 1.
[211] *WWM* 8.17 (August 15, 1931), p. 1.
[212] *WWM* 4.7 (March 26, 1927), p. 1; *WWM* 7.9 (April 26, 1930), p. 3; and *WWM* 7.11 (May 24, 1930), p. 2.
[213] *WWM* 4.24 (November 26, 1927), p. 1.
[214] *WWM* 8.15 (July 18, 1931), p. 1.
[215] *WWM* 4.22 (October 29, 1927), p. 1; *WWM* 6.18 (September 28, 1929), p. 2.
[216] *WWM* 8.10 (May 9, 1931), p. 3; *WWM* 8.20 (October 10, 1931), p. 1.
[217] *WWM* 7.13 (June 21, 1930. p. 2; *WWM* 7.15 (July 19, 1930), p. 1; and *WWM* 8.17 (August 15, 1931), p. 1.
[218] *WWM* 2.11 (May 23, 1925), p. 4; *WWM* 6.12 (June 22, 1929), p. 3; *WWM* 7.16 (August 2, 1930), p. 3; *WWM* 8.17 (August 15, 1931), p. 2; and *WWM* 8.20 (October 10, 1931), p. 1.

Oklahoma;[219] Oklahoma City;[220] Porter;[221] and Sapulpa.[222]

Pennsylvania

Cowansville;[223] Emlenton;[224] Huey;[225] Parkers Landing;[226] Red Bank;[227] Six Points;[228] and Youngstown.[229]

South Carolina

South Carolina.[230]

Tennessee

Baggett's Chapel;[231] Baggs Chapel;[232] Bowling Branch;[233] Cleveland;[234] Cotton Wood;[235] Cumberland City;[236] Dyersburg;[237] Fork Ridge;[238] Greeneville;[239] Harriman;[240] Hickman;[241] Kingsport;[242] Lancaster;[243] Noah's Chapel;[244] Oneida;[245] Pleasant Grove;[246] Portland;[247] Ridgedale;[248] Slayden;[249] Springville;[250] Tennessee;[251]

---

[219] *WWM* 3.2 (January 16, 1926), p. 2.
[220] *WWM* 2.11 (May 23, 1925), p. 2.
[221] *WWM* 7.19 (September 27, 1930), p. 2; *WWM* 7.20 (October 11, 1930), p. 1; *WWM* 8.15 (July 18, 1931), p. 2; and *WWM* 8.19 (September 26, 1931), p. 3.
[222] *WWM* 1.23 (August 9, 1924), p. 3; *WWM* 2.3 (January 31, 1925), p. 1; and *WWM* 8.21 (October 24, 1931), p. 3.
[223] *WWM* 5.20 (August 18, 1928), p. 2.
[224] *WWM* 3.20 (September 25, 1926), p. 2.
[225] *WWM* 8.10 (May 9, 1931), p. 4.
[226] *WWM* 1.20 (June 28, 1924), p. 3; *WWM* 3.20 (September 25, 1926), p. 4
[227] *WWM* 5.21 (September 1, 1928), p. 3; *WWM* 6.15 (August 3, 1929), p. 2.
[228] *WWM* 1.30 (November 22, 1924), p. 1.
[229] *WWM* 8.17 (August 15, 1931), p. 1.
[230] *WWM* 4.22 (October 29, 1927), p. 1.
[231] *WWM* 8.20 (October 10, 1931), p. 1; *WWM* 5.22 (September 15, 1928), p. 3; and *WWM* 7.18 (August 30, 1930), p. 4.
[232] *WWM* 5.22 (September 15, 1928), p. 2.
[233] *WWM* 4.23 (November 12, 1927), p. 1.
[234] *WWM* 2.19 (September 26, 1925), p. 2.
[235] *WWM* 8.17 (August 15, 1931), p. 1.
[236] *WWM* 2.14 (July 4, 1925), p. 3.
[237] *WWM* 5.27 (December 15, 1928), p. 2; *WWM* 7.21 (October 25, 1930), p. 2.
[238] *WWM* 1.8 (December 29, 1923), p. 3.
[239] *WWM* 2.20 (October 10, 1925), p. 4.
[240] *WWM* 8.22 (November 7, 1931), p. 4; *WWM* 1.29 (November 8, 1924), p. 1.
[241] *WWM* 3.22 (October 22, 1926), p. 1; *WWM* 3.25 (December 4, 1926), p. 3; and *WWM* 4.19 (September 10, 1927), p. 2.
[242] *WWM* 7.15 (July 19, 1930), p. 1.
[243] *WWM* 4.20 (October 1, 1927), p. 2; *WWM* 5.21 (September 1, 1928), p. 2.
[244] *WWM* 8.17 (August 15, 1931), p. 2.
[245] *WWM* 4.6 (March 12, 1927), p. 1.
[246] *WWM* 2.11 (May 23, 1925), p. 3.
[247] *WWM* 4.21 (October 15, 1927), p. 3.
[248] *WWM* 6.19 (October 12, 1929), p. 4.
[249] *WWM* 8.19 (September 26, 1931), p. 4.
[250] *WWM* 7.16 (August 2, 1930), p. 1.
[251] *WWM* 4.26 (December 24, 1927), p. 3; *WWM* 8.22 (November 7, 1931), p. 1.

Trout;[252] Westmoreland;[253] and White Bluff.[254]

Virginia
Allenslevel;[255] Altavista;[256] Clift;[257] Coeburn;[258] Danville;[259] Dry Branch;[260] Fries;[261] Leesville;[262] Lowmoor;[263] Lynchburg;[264] Norfolk;[265] Roanoke;[266] Sand Mountain, near Wytheville;[267] Schoolfield;[268] Sharron Springs;[269] and Shawsville.[270]

West Virginia
Big Creek;[271] Deepwater;[272] Elkins;[273] Hendricks;[274] Laneville;[275] Moundsville;[276] Okley;[277] Summerlee;[278] West Virginia;[279] Wevaco;[280] and Whipple.[281]

---

[252] *WWM* 6.23 (December 7, 1929), p. 3.
[253] *WWM* 5.23 (October 6, 1928), p. 3; *WWM* 8.21 (October 24, 1931), p. 3.
[254] *WWM* 7.17 (August 16, 1930), p. 3.
[255] *WWM* 5.22 (September 15, 1928), p. 3.
[256] *WWM* 2.11 (May 23, 1925), p. 1; *WWM* 7.16 (August 2, 1930), p. 2.
[257] *WWM* 7.1 (January 4, 1930), p. 3.
[258] *WWM* 2.14 (July 4, 1925), p. 3; *WWM* 6.10 (May 18, 1929), p. 1.
[259] *WWM* 3.18 (August 28, 1926), p. 1.
[260] *WWM* 5.15 (July 21, 1928), p. 2.
[261] *WWM* 3.18 (August 28, 1926), p. 1; *WWM* 3.25 (December 4, 1926), p. 1; *WWM* 4.25 (December 10, 1927), p. 1; *WWM* 4.25 (December 10, 1927), p. 3; *WWM* 6.10 (May 18, 1929), p. 1; and *WWM* 7.25 (December 20, 1930), p. 1.
[262] *WWM* 7.16 (August 2, 1930), p. 1.
[263] *WWM* 7.21 (October 25, 1930), p. 1.
[264] *WWM* 7.13 (June 21, 1930. p. 2.
[265] *WWM* 1.2 (September 29, 1923), p. 3.
[266] *WWM* 2.19 (September 26, 1925), p. 3; *WWM* 4.16 (July 30, 1927), p. 4; *WWM* 4.18 (August 27, 1927), p. 3; *WWM* 5.13 (June 23, 1928), p. 2; and *WWM* 7.25 (December 20, 1930), p. 2.
[267] *WWM* 8.22 (November 7, 1931), p. 1.
[268] *WWM* 2.14 (July 4, 1925), p. 2.
[269] *WWM* 8.19 (September 26, 1931), p. 3;
[270] *WWM* 8.19 (September 26, 1931), p. 2.
[271] *WWM* 8.19 (September 26, 1931), p. 3.
[272] *WWM* 8.17 (August 15, 1931), p. 3; *WWM* 8.19 (September 26, 1931), p. 3.
[273] *WWM* 6.13 (July 6, 1929), p. 1.
[274] *WWM* 7.1 (January 4, 1930), p. 3.
[275] *WWM* 5.23 (October 6, 1928), p. 2.
[276] *WWM* 8.17 (August 15, 1931), p. 1.
[277] *WWM* 7.24 (December 6, 1930), p. 4; *WWM* 7.23 (November 22, 1930), p. 2.
[278] *WWM* 6.12 (June 22, 1929), p. 4.
[279] *WWM* 6.10 (May 18, 1929), p. 3.
[280] *WWM* 7.17 (August 16, 1930), p. 1.
[281] *WWM* 1.20 (June 28, 1924), p. 1.

Appendix J

White Wing Messenger

Geographical locations in alphabetical order by country/city:

Bahamas
Acklins Island;[1] Bahamas;[2] Cat Island;[3] Crooked Island;[4] Eleuthera;[5] Nassau;[6] and Pleasant Bay.[7]

Barbados
Barbados.[8]

Jamaica
Brough Bridge;[9] Jamaica.[10]

Virgin Islands
St. Thomas.[11]

China
China.[12]

Appendix K

White Wing Messenger

Exact reporting references to baptismal services:

WWM 1.2 (September 29, 1923), pp. 1, 2, and 3; *WWM* 1.3 (October 13, 1923), p. 3; *WWM* 1.8 (December 29, 1923), p. 3; *WWM* 1.14 (April 5, 1924), p. 3; *WWM* 1.20 (June 28, 1924), pp. 1, 2 and 3; *WWM* 1.21 (July 12, 1924), p. 3; *WWM* 1.22 (July 26, 1924), pp. 2, 4; *WWM* 1.23 (August 9, 1924), p. 3; *WWM* 1.24 (August 23, 1924), p. 3; *WWM* 1.26 (September 27, 1924), p. 3; *WWM* 1.30 (November 22, 1924), pp. 1, 4; *WWM* 1.32 (December 20, 1924), p. 4; *WWM* 2.3 (January 31, 1925), p. 1; *WWM* 2.6 (March 14, 1925), p. 2; *WWM* 2.7 (March 28, 1925), p. 2; *WWM* 2.9 (April 25, 1925), p. 3; *WWM* 2.11 (May 23, 1925), pp. 1, 2, 3, and 4; *WWM* 2.13 (June 20, 1925), p. 3; *WWM* 2.14 (July 4, 1925), p. 2, 3, and 4; *WWM* 2.18 (August 29, 1925), pp. 3, 4; *WWM* 2.19 (September 26, 1925), pp. 2, 3; *WWM* 2.20

---

[1] *WWM* 7.7 (March 29, 1930), p. 3.
[2] *WWM* 4.6 (March 12 ,1927), p. 3.
[3] *WWM* 2.6 (March 14, 1925), p. 2.
[4] *WWM* 7.17 (August 16, 1930), p. 2; *WWM* 7.25 (December 20, 1930), p. 4.
[5] *WWM* 6.13 (July 6, 1929), p. 3; *WWM* 7.19 (September 27, 1930), p. 2.
[6] *WWM* 2.14 (July 4, 1925), p. 4; *WWM* 4.6 (March 12 ,1927), p. 4; and *WWM* 8.8 (April 11, 1931), p. 1.
[7] *WWM* 7.16 (August 2, 1930), p. 3; *WWM* 7.16 (August 2, 1930), p. 3
[8] *WWM* 4.7 (March 26, 1927), p. 1.
[9] *WWM* 1.8 (December 29, 1923), p. 3.
[10] *WWM* 1.2 (September 29, 1923), p. 1.
[11] *WWM* 3.25 (December 4, 1926), p. 1.
[12] *WWM* 8.18 (August 29, 1931), p. 1.

(October 10, 1925), pp. 3, 4; *WWM* 2.24 (December 5, 1925), p. 1; *WWM* 3.2 (January 16, 1926), p. 2; *WWM* 3.9 (April 24, 1926), p. 3; *WWM* 3.15 (July 17, 1926), p. 3; *WWM* 3.16 (July 31, 1926), pp. 1, 2; *WWM* 3.18 (August 28, 1926), pp. 1, 2; *WWM* 3.19 (September 11, 1926), p. 4; *WWM* 3.20 (September 25, 1926), pp. 1, 2, and 4; *WWM* 3.21 (October 9, 1926), p. 4; *WWM* 3.22 (October 22, 1926), pp. 1, 3; *WWM* 3.24 (November 20, 1926), pp. 1, 2; *WWM* 3.25 (December 4, 1926), pp. 1, 3; *WWM* 3.26 (December 18, 1926), pp. 1, 2; *WWM* 4.1 (January 1, 1927), p. 3; *WWM* 4.6 (March 12 ,1927), pp. 1, 4; *WWM* 4.7 (March 26, 1927), p. 1; *WWM* 4.8 (April 9, 1927), p. 1; *WWM* 4.11 (May 21, 1927), pp. 1, 2; *WWM* 4.12 (June 4, 1927), p. 1; ;*WWM* 4.13 (June 18, 1927), p. 1; *WWM* 4.14 (July 2, 1927), p. 1, 2, and 3; *WWM* 4.15 (July 16, 1927), p. 3; *WWM* 4.16 (July 30, 1927), pp. 3; 4; *WWM* 4.17 (August 13, 1927), pp. 1, 2; *WWM* 4.18 (August 27, 1927), pp. 1, 3; *WWM* 4.19 (September 10, 1927), pp. 1, 2, and 3; *WWM* 4.20 (October 1, 1927), pp. 2, 3; *WWM* 4.21 (October 15, 1927), p. 2, 3; *WWM* 4.22 (October 29, 1927), p. 1; *WWM* 4.23 (November 12, 1927), pp. 1, 2, and 3; *WWM* 4.24 (November 26, 1927), p. 1; *WWM* 4.25 (December 10, 1927), pp. 1, 3; *WWM* 4.26 (December 24, 1927), pp. 2, 3; *WWM* 5.4 (February 18, 1928), p. 2; *WWM* 5.7 (March 31, 1928), p. 2; *WWM* 5.9 (April 28, 1928), p. 1; *WWM* 5.11 (May 26, 1928), p. 2; *WWM* 5.13 (June 23, 1928), p. 2; *WWM* 5.15 (July 21, 1928), p. 2, 3, and 4; *WWM* 5.20 (August 18, 1928), pp. 1, 2; *WWM* 5.21 (September 1, 1928), pp. 1, 2, and 3; *WWM* 5.22 (September 15, 1928), pp. 2, 3; *WWM* 5.23 (October 6, 1928), pp. 2, 3; *WWM* 5.25 (November 17, 1928), pp. 1, 2; *WWM* 5.27 (December 15, 1928), pp. 2, 3; *WWM* 6.10 (May 18, 1929), pp. 1, 3; *WWM* 6.12 (June 22, 1929), pp. 3, 4; *WWM* 6.13 (July 6, 1929), p. 1, 2, and 3; *WWM* 6.15 (August 3, 1929), pp. 1, 2; *WWM* 6.17 (August 31, 1929), pp. 1, 2, and 3; *WWM* 6.18 (September 28, 1929), pp. 1, 2; *WWM* 6.19 (October 12, 1929), pp. 1, 2, and 4; *WWM* 6.23 (December 7, 1929), pp. 2, 3; *WWM* 6.25 (December 21, 1929), p. 3; *WWM* 7.1 (January 4, 1930), p. 3; *WWM* 7.2 (January 18, 1930), p. 2; *WWM* 7.3 (February 1, 1930), p. 2; *WWM* 7.7 (March 29, 1930), pp. 2, 3; *WWM* 7.8 (April 12, 1930), p. 2; *WWM* 7.9 (April 26, 1930), p. 3; *WWM* 7.11 (May 24, 1930), pp. 2, 3; *WWM* 7.13 (June 21, 1930. pp. 1, 2, and 3; *WWM* 7.14 (July 5, 1930), pp. 1, 2; *WWM* 7.15 (July 19, 1930), p. 1; *WWM* 7.16 (August 2, 1930), pp. 1, 2, and 3; *WWM* 7.17 (August 16, 1930), pp. 1, 2, and 3; *WWM* 7.18 (August 30, 1930), p. 1, 2, and 4; *WWM* 7.19 (September 27, 1930), pp. 1, 2; *WWM* 7.20 (October 11, 1930), pp. 1, 2; *WWM* 7.21 (October 25, 1930), pp. 1, 2; *WWM* 7.23 (November 22, 1930), pp. 1, 2; *WWM* 7.24 (December 6, 1930), pp. 3, 4; *WWM* 7.25 (December 20, 1930), pp. 1, 2, and 3; *WWM* 8.1 (January 3, 1931), p. 1; *WWM* 8.8 (April 11, 1931), p. 1; *WWM* 8.10 (May 9, 1931), pp. 3, 4; *WWM* 8.15 (July 18, 1931), pp. 1, 2, 3, and 4; *WWM* 8.17 (August 15, 1931), pp. 1, 2, and 3; *WWM* 8.18 (August 29, 1931), p. 1; *WWM* 8.19 (September 26, 1931), pp. 2, 3, and 4; *WWM* 8.20 (October 10, 1931), p. 1, 2, and 4; *WWM* 8.21 (October 24, 1931), pp. 2, 3, and 4; *WWM* 8.22 (November 7, 1931), pp. 1, 2, and 4; *WWM* 8.23 (November 21, 1931), pp. 1, 2, and 4; *WWM* 8.24 (December 5, 1931), pp. 1, 2, and 4; and *WWM* 8.25 (December 19, 1931), p. 3.

Baptismal reports without exact numbers:

WWM 1.31 (December 6, 1924) p. 1; *WWM* 2.17 (August 15, 1925), p. 2; *WWM* 2.18 (August 29, 1925), p. 4; *WWM* 3.26 (December 18, 1926), p. 1; *WWM* 4.13 (June 18, 1927), p. 1; *WWM* 4.16 (July 30, 1927), p. 3; *WWM* 4.20 (October 1, 1927), p. 2; *WWM* 5.20 (August 18, 1928), p. 3; *WWM* 7.15 (July 19, 1930), p. 1; and *WWM* 8.10 (May 9, 1931), p. 4.

Baptismal services planned for the future:

WWM 1.2 (September 29, 1923), pp. 1, 3; *WWM* 1.8 (December 29, 1923), p. 3; *WWM* 1.22 (July 26, 1924), p. 3; *WWM* 1.29 (November 8, 1924), pp. 1, 4;*WWM* 2.6 (March 14, 1925), p. 4; *WWM* 2.20 (October 10, 1925), p. 4; *WWM* 3.18 (August 28, 1926), p. 3; *WWM* 4.1 (January 1, 1927), p. 2; *WWM* 4.7 (March 26, 1927), p. 1; *WWM* 4.8 (April 9, 1927), p. 3; *WWM* 4.13 (June 18, 1927), p. 4; *WWM* 4.16 (July 30, 1927), p. 3; *WWM* 4.18 (August 27, 1927), p. 3; *WWM* 7.19 (September 27, 1930), p. 1; *WWM* 7.25 (December 20, 1930), p. 4; *WWM* 8.10 (May 9, 1931), p. 4; and *WWM* 8.23 (November 21, 1931), p. 2.

Appendix L

White Wing Messenger

Usage of 'Followed the Lord in water baptism':

WWM 1.2 (September 29, 1923), pp. 1, 2, and 3; *WWM* 1.3 (October 13, 1923), p. 3; *WWM* 1.14 (April 5, 1924), p. 3; *WWM* 1.20 (June 28, 1924), p. 2; *WWM* 1.21 (July 12, 1924), p. 3; *WWM* 1.24 (August 23, 1924), p. 3; *WWM* 1.30 (November 22, 1924), p. 1; *WWM* 2.3 (January 31, 1925), p. 1; *WWM* 2.6 (March 14, 1925), p. 2; *WWM* 2.7 (March 28, 1925), p. 2; *WWM* 2.9 (April 25, 1925), p. 3; *WWM* 2.11 (May 23, 1925), pp. 1, 3; *WWM* 2.13 (June 20, 1925), p. 3; *WWM* 2.14 (July 4, 1925), pp. 2, 3; *WWM* 2.18 (August 29, 1925), p. 3; *WWM* 2.19 (September 26, 1925), p. 3; *WWM* 3.2 (January 16, 1926), p. 2; *WWM* 3.16 (July 31, 1926), p. 2; *WWM* 3.19 (September 11, 1926), p. 4; *WWM* 3.20 (September 25, 1926), p. 4; *WWM* 3.24 (November 20, 1926), p. 2; *WWM* 4.6 (March 12, 1927), p. 1; *WWM* 4.8 (April 9, 1927), p. 1; *WWM* 4.11 (May 21, 1927), p. 1; *WWM* 4.13 (June 18, 1927), p. 1; *WWM* 4.14 (July 2, 1927), p. 2; *WWM* 4.15 (July 16, 1927), p. 3; *WWM* 4.16 (July 30, 1927), p. 3; *WWM* 4.17 (August 13, 1927), pp. 1, 2; *WWM* 4.18 (August 27, 1927), pp. 1, 3; *WWM* 4.19 (September 10, 1927), p. 3; *WWM* 4.20 (October 1, 1927), pp. 2, 3; *WWM* 4.21 (October 15, 1927), p. 3; *WWM* 4.22 (October 29, 1927), p. 1; *WWM* 4.25 (December 10, 1927), p. 3; *WWM* 4.26 (December 24, 1927), p. 3; *WWM* 5.11 (May 26, 1928), p. 2; *WWM* 5.13 (June 23, 1928), pp. 2, 3; *WWM* 5.15 (July 21, 1928), pp. 2, 3, and 4; *WWM* 5.22 (September 15, 1928), pp. 2, 3; *WWM* 5.23 (October 6, 1928), pp. 2, 3; *WWM* 5.25 (November 17, 1928), pp. 1, 2; *WWM* 5.27 (December 15, 1928), p. 3; *WWM* 6.10 (May 18, 1929), p. 1; *WWM* 6.12 (June 22, 1929), pp. 3, 4; *WWM* 6.17 (August 31, 1929), pp. 2, 3; *WWM* 6.19 (October 12, 1929), pp. 1, 4; *WWM* 6.23 (December 7, 1929), p. 2; *WWM* 7.9 (April 26, 1930), p. 3; *WWM* 7.13 (June 21, 1930). p. 2; *WWM* 7.16 (August 2, 1930), pp. 1, 3; *WWM* 7.17 (August 16, 1930), pp. 1, 2; *WWM* 7.18 (August 30, 1930), p. 4; *WWM* 7.19 (September 27, 1930), pp. 1, 2; *WWM* 7.20 (October 11, 1930), p. 2; *WWM* 7.21 (October 25, 1930), p. 1; *WWM* 8.8 (April 11, 1931), p. 1; *WWM* 8.17 (August 15, 1931), pp. 1, 2; *WWM* 8.19 (September 26, 1931), p. 2; *WWM* 8.21 (October 24, 1931), pp. 3, 4; *WWM* 8.22 (November 7, 1931), p. 1; and *WWM* 8.24 (December 5, 1931), p. 2.

Appendix M

White Wing Messenger

References to 'baptized in water':

WWM 1.3 (October 13, 1923), p. 3; WWM 1.8 (December 29, 1923), p. 3; WWM 1.20 (June 28, 1924), pp. 1, 3; WWM 1.22 (July 26, 1924), pp. 2, 3, and 4; WWM 1.23 (August 9, 1924), p. 3; WWM 1.26 (September 27, 1924), p. 3; WWM 1.32 (December 20, 1924), p. 4; WWM 2.11 (May 23, 1925), pp. 2, 4; WWM 2.14 (July 4, 1925), p. 3; WWM 2.18 (August 29, 1925), p. 4; WWM 2.19 (September 26, 1925), p. 3; WWM 2.20 (October 10, 1925), pp. 1, 3, and 4; WWM 2.24 (December 5, 1925), p. 1; WWM 3.9 (April 24, 1926), p. 3; WWM 3.15 (July 17, 1926), p. 3; WWM 3.16 (July 31, 1926), p. 1; WWM 3.18 (August 28, 1926), pp. 1, 2, and 3; WWM 3.19 (September 11, 1926), p. 4; WWM 3.20 (September 25, 1926), pp. 1, 2, and 4; WWM 3.22 (October 22, 1926), pp. 1, 3; WWM 3.24 (November 20, 1926), p. 1; WWM 3.25 (December 4, 1926), pp. 1, 3; WWM 3.26 (December 18, 1926), pp. 1, 2; WWM 4.1 (January 1, 1927), p. 3; WWM 4.11 (May 21, 1927), p. 2; WWM 4.12 (June 4, 1927), p. 1; WWM 4.14 (July 2, 1927), pp. 1, 3; WWM 4.16 (July 30, 1927), p. 4; WWM 4.17 (August 13, 1927), p. 2; WWM 4.18 (August 27, 1927), p. 3; WWM 4.19 (September 10, 1927), pp. 1, 2; WWM 4.20 (October 1, 1927), pp. 2, 3; WWM 4.23 (November 12, 1927), pp. 1, 2; WWM 4.24 (November 26, 1927), p. 1; WWM 4.25 (December 10, 1927), p. 1; WWM 4.26 (December 24, 1927), p. 2; WWM 5.4 (February 18, 1928), p. 2; WWM 5.7 (March 31, 1928), p. 2; WWM 5.9 (April 28, 1928), p. 1; WWM 5.11 (May 26, 1928), p. 2; WWM 5.13 (June 23, 1928), p. 2; WWM 5.15 (July 21, 1928), pp. 2, 3; WWM 5.20 (August 18, 1928), p. 2; WWM 5.21 (September 1, 1928), pp. 1, 2, and 3; WWM 5.22 (September 15, 1928), pp. 2, 3; WWM 5.23 (October 6, 1928), p. 2; WWM 5.27 (December 15, 1928), p. 2; WWM 6.10 (May 18, 1929), pp. 1,

3; WWM 6.12 (June 22, 1929), p. 3; WWM 6.13 (July 6, 1929), pp. 1, 2, and 3; WWM 6.15 (August 3, 1929), pp. 1, 2; WWM 6.17 (August 31, 1929), pp. 1, 3; WWM 6.18 (September 28, 1929), pp. 1, 2; WWM 6.19 (October 12, 1929), pp. 2, 4; WWM 6.23 (December 7, 1929), p. 3; WWM 6.25 (December 21, 1929), p. 3; WWM 7.1 (January 4, 1930), p. 3; WWM 7.2 (January 18, 1930), p. 2; WWM 7.3 (February 1, 1930), p. 2; WWM 7.7 (March 29, 1930), pp. 2, 3; WWM 7.8 (April 12, 1930), p. 2; WWM 7.11 (May 24, 1930), pp. 2, 3; WWM 7.13 (June 21, 1930, pp. 1, 2, and 3; WWM 7.14 (July 5, 1930), pp. 1, 2; WWM 7.16 (August 2, 1930), pp. 2, 3; WWM 7.17 (August 16, 1930), pp. 1, 3; WWM 7.18 (August 30, 1930), pp. 1, 2; WWM 7.19 (September 27, 1930), p. 2; WWM 7.20 (October 11, 1930), pp. 1, 2; WWM 7.21 (October 25, 1930), pp. 1, 2; WWM 7.23 (November 22, 1930), pp. 1, 2; WWM 7.24 (December 6, 1930), pp. 3, 4; WWM 7.25 (December 20, 1930), pp. 1, 2, and 3; WWM 8.1 (January 3, 1931), p. 1; WWM 8.8 (April 11, 1931), p. 1; WWM 8.10 (May 9, 1931), pp. 3, 4; WWM 8.15 (July 18, 1931), pp. 1, 2, 3, and 4; WWM 8.17 (August 15, 1931), pp. 1, 2, and 3; WWM 8.19 (September 26, 1931), pp. 2, 3, and 4; WWM 8.20 (October 10, 1931), pp. 1, 2, and 4; WWM 8.21 (October 24, 1931), p. 2; WWM 8.22 (November 7, 1931), pp. 1, 2, and 4; WWM 8.23 (November 21, 1931), pp. 2, 4; and WWM 8.25 (December 19, 1931), p. 3.

Appendix N

Word and Witness

Geographical locations by state/city:

Alabama

Brockton;[1] Clintonville;[2] Coffee Springs;[3] Crichton;[4] Florala;[5] Geneva;[6] Pearce;[7] Prichard;[8] Roberstdale;[9] and Slocomb.[10]

Arkansas

Arkansas;[11] Benton;[12] Beverly;[13] Boynton;[14] Corning;[15] Douglas;[16] Earle;[17] Fir;[18] Havana;[19] Hiram;[20] Hot Springs;[21] Lonoke;[22] Malvern;[23]

---

[1] *WW* 9.6 (June 20, 1913), p. 8.
[2] *WW* 9.11 (November 20, 1913), p. 2.
[3] *WW* 9.5 (May 20, 1913), p. 3.
[4] *WW* 12.10 (October 1915), p. 5; *WW* 12.10 (October 1915), p. 6.
[5] *WW* 12.9 (September 1915), p. 1.
[6] *WW* 9.5 (May 20, 1913), p. 2.
[7] *WW* 12.7 (July 1915), p. 5.
[8] *WW* 9.5 (May 20, 1913), p. 3.
[9] *WW* 12.7 (July 1915), p. 1; *WW* 12.10 (October 1915), p. 7.
[10] *WW* 9.7 (July 20, 1913), p. 1.
[11] *WW* 9.12 (December 20, 1913), p. 3.
[12] *WW* 8.8 (October 20, 1912), p. 2; *WW* 9.1 (January 20, 1913), p. 3; *WW* 9.5 (May 20, 1913), p. 3.
[13] *WW* 10.10 (October 1914), p. 2.
[14] *WW* 12.7 (July 1915), p. 7.
[15] *WW* 12.6 (June 1915), p. 5.
[16] *WW* 9.1 (January 20, 1913), p. 3.
[17] *WW* 8.8 (October 20, 1912), p. 1.
[18] *WW* 12.9 (September 1915), p. 5.
[19] *WW* 10.10 (October 1914), p. 4.
[20] *WW* 12.7 (July 1915), p. 1.
[21] *WW* 10.10 (October 1914), p. 4; *WW* 10.1 (January 20, 1914), p. 1.
[22] *WW* 12.9 (September 1915), p. 1.
[23] *WW* 12.10 (October 1915), p. 8.

Nimmons;[24] Opal;[25] Pangburg;[26] Paragould;[27] Parma;[28] Pleasant Valley;[29] Shoal Creek;[30] and Willow.[31]

California
Los Angeles;[32] San Bernadino.[33]

Florida
Allentown;[34] Laurel Hill;[35] Milton;[36] and Paxton.[37]

Georgia
Atlanta.[38]

Idaho
Star.[39]

Illinois
Golden Gate;[40] Macedonia;[41] Marion;[42] Maud;[43] and Ramsey.[44]

Indiana
Evansville;[45] Sparksville;[46] and Terre Haute.[47]

Iowa
Ottumwa;[48] Russell;[49]
Kansas

---

[24] *WW* 9.8 (August 20, 1913), p. 1.
[25] *WW* 12.11 (November 1915), p. 3.
[26] *WW* 12.9 (September 1915), p. 1.
[27] *WW* 9.10 (October 20, 1913), p. 3.
[28] *WW* 9.9 (September 20, 1913), p. 1.
[29] *WW* 12.8 (August 1915), p. 8; *WW* 12.9 (September 1915), p. 3.
[30] *WW* 9.6 (June 20, 1913), p. 8; *WW* 12.11 (November 1915), p. 3.
[31] *WW* 10.8 (August 1914), p. 2.
[32] *WW* 9.3 (March 20, 1913), p. 3.
[33] *WW* 9.9 (September 20, 1913), p. 3.
[34] *WW* 12.9 (September 1915), p. 4.
[35] *WW* 12.8 (August 1915), p. 8.
[36] *WW* 9.8 (August 20, 1913), p. 3.
[37] *WW* 10.5 (May 20, 1914), p. 3.
[38] *WW* 12.10 (October 1915), p. 5.
[39] *WW* 9.1 (January 20, 1913), p. 3.
[40] *WW* 9.6 (June 20, 1913), p. 5.
[41] *WW* 12.5 (May 1915), p. 8.
[42] *WW* 12.9 (September 1915), p. 2.
[43] *WW* 12.9 (September 1915), p. 3.
[44] *WW* 12.11 (November 1915), p. 5.
[45] *WW* 10.7 (July 1914), p. 2.
[46] *WW* 10.7 (July 1914), p. 1.
[47] *WW* 12.6 (June 1915), p. 8.
[48] *WW* 8.8 (October 20, 1912), p. 3.
[49] *WW* 10.1 (January 20, 1914), p. 1.

Cedar;[50] Faulkner;[51] Great Bend;[52] Iola;[53] and Topeka.[54]

Kentucky
Fagan;[55] Louisville.[56]

Louisiana
Anacoco;[57] Elton;[58] Longville;[59] Louisiana;[60] Merryville;[61] and Sardis.[62]

Maryland
Cumberland;[63] Frostburg.[64]

Massachusetts
Chelsea.[65]

Michigan
Albion;[66] Detroit.[67]

Minnesota
Duluth;[68] Saint Paul.[69]

Mississippi
Meridian;[70] Neshoba;[71] and Quitman.[72]

---

[50] *WW* 9.8 (August 20, 1913), p. 3.
[51] *WW* 9.2 (February 20, 1913), p. 3.
[52] *WW* 9.9 (September 20, 1913), p. 1.
[53] *WW* 12.8 (August 1915), p. 3.
[54] *WW* 9.7 (July 20, 1913), p. 1; *WW* 10.10 (October 1914), p. 1.
[55] *WW* 12.9 (September 1915), p. 7.
[56] *WW* 9.7 (July 20, 1913), p. 1; *WW* 12.5 (May 1915), p. 7.
[57] *WW* 12.7 (July 1915), p. 1.
[58] *WW* 12.7 (July 1915), p. 5.
[59] *WW* 12.7 (July 1915), p. 7.
[60] *WW* 9.12 (December 20, 1913), p. 3.
[61] *WW* 12.7 (July 1915), p. 3.
[62] *WW* 10.7 (July 1914), p. 1.
[63] *WW* 9.10 (October 20, 1913), p. 3.
[64] *WW* 12.10 (October 1915), p. 8.
[65] *WW* 10.4 (April 20, 1914), p. 3.
[66] *WW* 12.9 (September 1915), p. 5.
[67] *WW* 12.9 (September 1915), p. 3.
[68] *WW* 12.8 (August 1915), p. 3.
[69] *WW* 9.8 (August 20, 1913), p. 3.
[70] *WW* 9.9 (September 20, 1913), p. 2.
[71] *WW* 9.11 (November 20, 1913), p. 1.
[72] *WW* 9.9 (September 20, 1913), p. 3.

Missouri

Cainsville;[73] Caruthersville;[74] Essex;[75] Hog Eye;[76] Joplin;[77] Monroe City;[78] Springfield;[79] and Vinson.[80]

Nebraska

Auburn.[81]

New Mexico

Bradshaw;[82] Red Tower;[83] and Texico.[84]

Oklahoma

Broken Bow;[85] Claremore;[86] Cowlington;[87] Cruce;[88] Dewar;[89] Oklahoma;[90] Paden;[91] Qualls;[92] Quinton;[93] Ryan;[94] and Shawnee.[95]

Oregon

Independence;[96] Portland.[97]

Tennessee

Bluff Springs;[98] Trenton.[99]

Texas

Austin;[100] Beckville;[101]

---

[73] *WW* 10.7 (July 1914), p. 1.
[74] *WW* 12.9 (September 1915), p. 4.
[75] *WW* 9.9 (September 20, 1913), p. 3.
[76] *WW* 12.8 (August 1915), p. 5.
[77] *WW* 12.8 (August 1915), p. 1.
[78] *WW* 12.9 (September 1915), p. 7.
[79] *WW* 9.10 (October 20, 1913), p. 3
[80] *WW* 12.8 (August 1915), p. 3.
[81] *WW* 9.9 (September 20, 1913), p. 3.
[82] *WW* 10.3 (March 20, 1914), p. 1.
[83] *WW* 10.3 (March 20, 1914), p. 1.
[84] *WW* 9.9 (September 20, 1913), p. 1.
[85] *WW* 12.9 (September 1915), p. 1.
[86] *WW* 9.7 (July 20, 1913), p. 1.
[87] *WW* 9.9 (September 20, 1913), p. 3.
[88] *WW* 9.10 (October 20, 1913), p. 3.
[89] *WW* 9.8 (August 20, 1913), p. 3.
[90] *WW* 9.9 (September 20, 1913), p. 1; *WW* 9.12 (December 20, 1913), p. 3.
[91] *WW* 12.7 (July 1915), p. 5; *WW* 12.8 (August 1915), p. 8.
[92] *WW* 12.11 (November 1915), p. 3.
[93] *WW* 9.9 (September 20, 1913), p. 3.
[94] *WW* 9.10 (October 20, 1913), p. 3
[95] *WW* 12.8 (August 1915), p. 8.
[96] *WW* 10.3 (March 20, 1914), p. 1.
[97] *WW* 9.9 (September 20, 1913), p. 4; *WW* 12.9 (September 1915), p. 7.
[98] *WW* 12.10 (October 1915), p. 2.
[99] *WW* 12.10 (October 1915), p. 2.
[100] *WW* 9.9 (September 20, 1913), p. 3; *WW* 12.8 (August 1915), p. 8.
[101] *WW* 12.9 (September 1915), p. 4.

Bronson;[102] Conroe;[103] Dallas;[104] Dripping Springs;[105] Dublin;[106] Electra;[107] George's Creek;[108] Glen Rose;[109] Goodrich;[110] Haskell;[111] Highland;[112] Kingsville;[113] Ladonia;[114] Mabank;[115] Midway;[116] Remington;[117] Ricardo;[118] Saratoga;[119] Sweet Water;[120] Tebo;[121] Thicket;[122] Tyler;[123] Warren;[124] Waxahachie;[125] and White Flat.[126]

Wisconsin
Wausau.[127]

Appendix O

Word and Witness

Alphabetical geographical listing of countries/cities:

Africa
Africa.[128]

Brazil
Para.[129]

---

[102] *WW* 12.7 (July 1915), p. 1.
[103] *WW* 12.10 (October 1915), p. 2.
[104] *WW* 8.8 (October 20, 1912), p. 3; *WW* 9.8 (August 20, 1913), p. 3; *WW* 9.9 (September 20, 1913), p. 3; and
WW 12.11 (November 1915), p. 5.
[105] *WW* 12.9 (September 1915), p. 4.
[106] *WW* 9.10 (October 20, 1913), p. 3.
[107] *WW* 9.10 (October 20, 1913), p. 3.
[108] *WW* 9.8 (August 20, 1913), p. 3; *WW* 9.10 (October 20, 1913), p. 3.
[109] *WW* 12.6 (June 1915), p. 3; *WW* 12.10 (October 1915), p. 7.
[110] *WW* 9.7 (July 20, 1913), p. 1.
[111] *WW* 12.11 (November 1915), p. 3.
[112] *WW* 12.9 (September 1915), p. 3.
[113] *WW* 12.8 (August 1915), p. 3.
[114] *WW* 12.8 (August 1915), p. 1; *WW* 12.10 (October 1915), p. 1.
[115] *WW* 12.10 (October 1915), p. 2.
[116] *WW* 12.9 (September 1915), p. 1.
[117] *WW* 9.10 (October 20, 1913), p. 3.
[118] *WW* 12.8 (August 1915), p. 1.
[119] *WW* 10.7 (July 1914), p. 2; *WW* 12.5 (May 1915), p. 7.
[120] *WW* 12.9 (September 1915), p. 4.
[121] *WW* 12.5 (May 1915), p. 8.
[122] *WW* 10.7 (July 1914), p. 2.
[123] *WW* 9.11 (November 20, 1913), p. 2.
[124] *WW* 8.6 (August 20, 1912), p. 3; *WW* 12.5 (May 1915), p. 7.
[125] *WW* 12.5 (May 1915), p. 3.
[126] *WW* 12.7 (July 1915), p. 7.
[127] *WW* 9.12 (December 20, 1913), p. 3.
[128] *WW* 10.4 (April 20, 1914), p. 4; *WW* 12.8 (August 1915), p. 5; and *WW* 12.9 (September 1915), p. 8.
[129] *WW* 9.10 (October 20, 1913), p. 2.

Canada

Trossachs, Saskatchewan;[130] Winnipeg.[131]

Chile

Chile.[132]

China

China;[133] Hongkong;[134] Shanghai,[135] and Yunnan Fu.[136]

Guatemala

Matagalpa.[137]

Egypt

Minya.[138]

India

India.[139]

Appendix P

Pentecostal Evangel

Entries on water baptism:

PE 2.19 (May 9, 1914), pp. 6, 8; *PE* 33 (May 9, 1914), p. 10; *PE* 49 (July 11, 1914), p. 3; *PE* 50 (July 18, 1914), pp. 3, 4; *PE* 51 (July 25, 1914), p. 4; *PE* 52 (August 1, 1914), pp. 3, 4; *PE* 54 (August 15, 1914), pp. 3, 4; *PE* 55 (August 22, 1914), pp. 1, 3; *PE* 56 (August 29, 1914), pp. 1, 3, and 4; *PE* 57 (September 5, 1914), pp. 1, 3, and 4; *PE* 58 (September 12, 1914), pp. 2, 3, and 4; *PE* 59 (September 19, 1914), pp. 1, 2; *PE* 60 (September 26, 1914), pp. 1, 4; *PE* 62 (October 10, 1914), pp. 2, 3, and 4; *PE* 63 (October 17, 1914), pp. 1, 3, and 4; *PE* 64 (October 24, 1914), pp. 2, 4; *PE* 65 (October 31, 1914), pp. 1, 4; *PE* 66 (November 7, 1914), pp. 2, 3, and 4; *PE* 67 (November 14, 1914), pp. 1, 2, and 3; *PE* 68 (November 21, 1914), p. 3; *PE* 69 (December 5, 1914), pp. 1, 2, and 4; *PE* 70 (December 12, 1914), pp. 1, 2, 3, and 4; *PE* 71 (December 19, 1914), pp. 3, 4; *PE* 72 (December 26, 1914), pp. 1, 2, and 3; *PE* 73 (January 9, 1915), p. 3; *PE* 74 (January 16, 1915), p. 4; *PE* 78 (February 20, 1915), pp. 3, 4; *PE* 79 (February 27, 1915), pp. 2, 4; *PE* 80 (March 6, 1915), pp. 1, 3; *PE* 81 (March 13, 1915), p. 3; *PE* 83 (March 27, 1915), p. 4; *PE* 85 (April 10, 1915), pp. 1, 4; *PE* 86 (April 17, 1915), pp. 1, 4; *PE* 88 (May 1, 1915), pp. 1, 4; *PE* 89 (May 8, 1915), pp. 1, 2, and 4; *PE* 90 (May 15, 1915), pp. 1, 3; *PE* 93 (June 5, 1915), p. 4; *PE* 94 (June 12, 1915), p. 4; *PE* 95 (June 19, 1915), pp. 1, 3; *PE* 96 (June 26, 1915), p. 1; *PE* 97 (July 3, 1915), pp. 1, 3; *PE* 98 (July 10, 1915), pp. 1, 3; *PE* 99 (July 17, 1915), pp. 1, 3, and 4; *PE* 100 (July 24, 1915), pp. 1, 2, 3, and 4; *PE* 101 (July 31, 1915), p. 1; *PE* 102 (August 7, 1915), pp. 1, 2; *PE* 103 (August 14, 1915),

---

[130] *WW* 10.8 (August 1914), p. 3.
[131] *WW* 8.6 (August 20, 1912), p. 3.
[132] *WW* 10.4 (April 20, 1914), p. 4.
[133] *WW* 10.4 (April 20, 1914), p. 4; *WW* 10.7 (July 1914), p. 4; WW 12.6 (June 1915), p. 6; *WW* 12.8 (August 1915), p. 7; and *WW* 12.9 (September 1915), p. 6.
[134] *WW* 9.11 (November 20, 1913), p. 4.
[135] *WW* 9.6 (June 20, 1913), p. 1; *WW* 9.10 (October 20, 1913), p. 2.
[136] *WW* 9.11 (November 20, 1913), p. 3.
[137] *WW* 10.10 (October 1914), p. 4.
[138] *WW* 9.6 (June 20, 1913), p. 1; *WW* 9.8 (August 20, 1913), p. 1.
[139] *WW* 9.11 (November 20, 1913), p. 4.

pp. 1, 2, 3, and 4; *PE* 104 (August 21, 1915), pp. 1, 2, and 3; *PE* 105 (August 28, 1915), pp. 1, 2, and 4; *PE* 106 (September 4, 1915), pp. 1, 2, 3, and 4; *PE* 107 (September 11, 1915), pp. 1, 2; *PE* 108 (September 18, 1915), pp. 1, 2, 3, and 4; *PE* 109 (September 25, 1915), p. 1; *PE* 110 (October 2, 1915), pp. 3, 4; *PE* 112 (October 23, 1915), p. 1; *PE* 113 (October 30, 1915), p. 1; *PE* 114 (November 6, 1915), pp. 1, 3; *PE* 115 (November 13, 1915), p. 1, 2, and 4; *PE* 116 (November 20, 1915), pp. 1, 4; *PE* 117 (November 27, 1915), pp. 1, 4; *PE* 120 (December 18, 1915), p. 4; *PE* 122 (January 8, 1916), pp. 8, 16; *PE* 123 (January 15, 1916), p. 13, 15, and 16; *PE* 124 (January 22, 1916), pp. 14, 16; *PE* 125 (February 5, 1916), pp. 12, 14; *PE* 126 (February 12, 1916), p. 12; *PE* 127 (February 19, 1916), pp. 12, 14; *PE* 128 (February 26, 1916), pp. 12, 13, and 14; *PE* 131 (March 18, 1916), pp. 13, 14; *PE* 132 (March 25, 1916), pp. 13, 14; *PE* 135 (April 15, 1916), p. 15; *PE* 136 (April 22, 1916), pp. 11; 15; *PE* 137 (April 29, 1916), p. 14; *PE* 138 (May 6, 1916), pp. 14, 15; *PE* 139 (May 13, 1916), pp. 11, 12, 13, 14, and 15; *PE* 141 (May 27, 1916), pp. 14, 15; *PE* 142 (June 3, 1916), p. 12; *PE* 143 (June 10, 1916), pp. 7, 11, 14, and 15; *PE* 144 (June 17, 1916), p. 15; *PE* 145 (June 24, 1916), pp. 8, 14, and 15; *PE* 146/147 (July 8, 1916), pp. 7, 11; *PE* 148 (July 15, 1916), p. 15; *PE* 149 (July 22, 1916), pp. 9, 11, 14, and 15; *PE* 150 (July 29, 1916), pp. 12, 14; *PE* 151 (August 5, 1916), pp. 14, 15; *PE* 152 (August 12, 1916), pp. 11, 14; *PE* 154 (August 26, 1916), pp. 14, 15; *PE* 155 (September 2, 1916), pp. 11, 13, and 15; *PE* 156 (September 9, 1916), pp. 11, 13, *PE* 157 (September 16, 1916), p. 14; *PE* 158 (September 23, 1916), pp. 4, 14; *PE* 159 (September 30, 1916), pp. 4, 14; *PE* 160 (October 14, 1916), p. 15; *PE* 161 (October 21, 1916), pp. 14, 15; *PE* 162 (October 28, 1916), pp. 14, 15; *PE* 163 (November 4, 1916), pp. 8, 13; *PE* 164 (November 11, 1916), pp. 12, 14, and 15; *PE* 165 (November 18, 1916), pp. 12, 14; *PE* 166 (November 25, 1916), pp. 11, 12; *PE* 167 (December 2, 1916), pp. 12, 14; *PE* 168 (December 9, 1916), pp. 12, 13, and 14; *PE* 170 (December 23, 1916), pp. 12, 13, 14, and 15; *PE* 171 (January 6, 1917), p. 14; *PE* 172 (January 13, 1917), pp. 12, 14, and 16; *PE* 173 (January 20, 1917), p. 14; *PE* 174 (January 27, 1917), pp. 14, 15, and 16; *PE* 177 (February 17, 1917), p. 4; *PE* 178 (February 24, 1917), p. 11; *PE* 181 (March 17, 1917), pp. 12, 16; *PE* 182 (March 24, 1917), p. 14; *PE* 184 (April 7, 1917), p. 3; *PE* 186 (April 21, 1917), p. 14; *PE* 187 (April 28, 1917), p. 15; *PE* 188 (May 5, 1917), pp. 12, 14; *PE* 190 (May 19, 1917), pp. 11, 12, and 14; *PE* 191 (May 26, 1917), p. 14; *PE* 193 (June 9, 1917), pp. 11, 14; *PE* 195 (June 23, 1917), p. 14; *PE* 196 (June 30, 1917), pp. 11, 14; *PE* 197 (July 7, 1917), p. 12, 13, and 14; *PE* 198 (July 14, 1917), pp. 13, 14; *PE* 199 (July 21, 1917), pp. 11, 14; *PE* 200 (July 28, 1917), pp. 13, 14; *PE* 201 (August 4, 1917), pp. 13, 14, and 16; *PE* 202 (August 11, 1917), pp. 12, 14; *PE* 203 (August 18, 1917), pp. 12, 14; *PE* 204 (August 25, 1917), pp. 12, 14, and 16; *PE* 206 (September 8, 1917), pp. 11, 12, and 14; *PE* 207 (September 15, 1917), pp. 12, 13, and 14; *PE* 208 (September 29, 1917), p. 14; *PE* 209 (October 6, 1917), pp. 12, 14, and 16; *PE* 210 (October 13, 1917), p. 14; *PE* 211 (October 20, 1917), p. 14; *PE* 212 (October 27, 1917), pp. 2, 3, and 14; *PE* 213 (November 3, 1917), pp. 13, 14; *PE* 214 (November 10, 1917), pp. 12, 13, and 14; *PE* 215 (November 17, 1917), pp. 12, 14; *PE* 216 (November 24, 1917), pp. 11, 14; *PE* 217 (December 1, 1917), p. 10; *PE* 218 (December 8, 1917), p. 14; *PE* 219 (December 15, 1917), p. 14; *PE* 220 (December 22, 1917), p. 11; *PE* 221 (January 5, 1918), p. 10; *PE* 223 (January 19, 1918), pp. 10, 14; *PE* 224 (January 26, 1918), p. 10; *PE* 225 (February 2, 1918), pp. 7, 8   ; *PE* 226 (February 9, 1918), p. 8; *PE* 227 (February 16, 1918), pp. 4-5, and 10; *PE* 230 (March 9, 1918), pp. 10, 15; *PE* 230 (March 9, 1918), p. 15; *PE* 233 (March 30, 1918), p. 13; *PE* 234/235 (April 6, 1918), pp. 14, 15; *PE* 236/237 (April 20, 1918), pp. 11, 15; *PE* 238/239 (May 4, 1918), pp. 9, 10, 14, and 15; *PE* 240/241 (May 18, 1918), pp. 11, 14; *PE* 242/243 (June 1, 1918), pp. 11, 14; *PE* 244/245 (June 15, 1918), pp. 12, 13, and 16; *PE* 246/247 (June 29, 1918), pp. 11, 14; *PE* 248/249 (July 27, 1918), pp. 3, 10, and 14; *PE* 250/251 (August 10, 1918), p. 14; *PE* 252/253 (August 24, 1918), pp. 14, 15; *PE* 254 (September 7, 1918), pp. 5, 7; *PE* 256/257 (October 5, 1918), pp. 1, 10, 11, and 14; *PE* 258/259 (October 19, 1918), pp. 1, 10, and 11; *PE* 260/261 (November 2, 1918), pp. 10, 14; *PE* 262/263 (November 16, 1918), pp. 1, 10; *PE* 266/267 (December 14, 1918), p. 10; *PE* 268/269 (December 28, 1918), pp. 8, 10; *PE* 270/271 (January 11, 1919), pp. 1, 11; *PE* 272/273 (January 25, 1919), pp. 1, 4; *PE* 274/275 (February 8, 1919), pp. 3, 12; *PE* 278/279 (March 8, 1919), pp. 10, 14, *PE* 280/281 (March 22, 1919), pp. 10, 11; *PE* 282/283 (April 5, 1919), pp. 10, 14; *PE* 284/285 (April 19, 1919), pp. 10, 11, and 15; *PE* 286/287 (May 3, 1919), pp. 14; 15; *PE* 288/289 (May 17, 1919), pp. 7, 10, 13, 14, and 15; *PE* 290/291 (May 31, 1919), p. 14; *PE* 292/293 (June 14, 1919), pp. 9, 10, 13, and 14; *PE* 294/295 (June 28, 1919), pp. 9, 10, 11, 14, and 19; *PE* 296/297 (July 12, 1919), pp. 6, 11, 14, and 15; *PE* 298/299 (July 26, 1919), pp. 8, 10, 11, 13, and 14; *PE* 300/301 (August 9, 1919), pp. 8, 10, 11, and 14; *PE* 302/303 (August 23, 1919), pp. 10, 11, 13, and 14; *PE* 304/305 (September 6, 1919), pp. 10, 11, 14, and 16; *PE* 306/307 (September 20, 1919), pp. 11, 12, 13, and 14; *PE* 308/309 (October 4, 1919), pp. 9, 12; *PE* 310/311 (October 18, 1919), pp. 11, 12, 13, and 14; *PE* 312/313 (November 1, 1919), pp. 23, 29; *PE* 314/315 (November 15, 1919), p. 7, 10, 11, 12, and 14; *PE* 316/317 (November 29, 1919), pp. 9, 13, 14, and 15; *PE* 318/319 (December 13, 1919), p. 14; *PE* 320/321 (December 27,

1919), pp. 9, 12, 13 pp. 13, and 14; *PE* 322/323 (January 10, 1920), pp. 12, 13, and 15; *PE* 324/325 (January 24, 1920), pp. 10, 12, and 14; *PE* 326/325 (February 7, 1920), p. 13; *PE* 328/329 (February 24, 1920), pp. 10, 12, and 14; *PE* 330/331 (March 6, 1920), p. 13; *PE* 332/333 (March 20, 1920), pp. 13, 14; *PE* 334/335 (April 13, 1920), pp. 13, 14; *PE* 336/337 (April 17, 1920), p. 13; *PE* 338/339 (May 1, 1920), pp. 13, 14; *PE* 340/341 (May 15, 1920), p. 14; *PE* 342/343 (May 29, 1920), p. 14; *PE* 344/345 (June 12, 1920), p. 14; *PE* 346/347 (June 26, 1920), pp. 11, 13, and 14; *PE* 348/349 (July 10, 1920), pp. 1, 11, and 13; *PE* 350/351 (July 24, 1920), pp. 13, 14; *PE* 352/353 (August 7, 1920), pp. 10, 13, and 14; *PE* 354/355 (August 21, 1920), pp. 9, 10, 12, 13, and 14; *PE* 356/357 (September 4, 1920), pp. 9, 10, 12, 13, and 14; *PE* 358/359 (September 18, 1920), pp. 7, 11, 12, 13, 14, and 15; *PE* 360/361 (October 2, 1920), pp. 10, 11, and 14; *PE* 362/363 (October 16, 1920), pp. 11, 13, and 14; *PE* 364/365 (October 30, 1920), pp. 11, 13, and 14; *PE* 366/367 (November 13, 1920), pp. 9, 10, and 14; *PE* 368/369 (November 27, 1920), pp. 3, 13, and 14; *PE* 370/371 (December 11, 1920), pp. 13, 14; *PE* 376/377 (January22, 1921), p. 12; *PE* 378/379 (February 5, 1921), p. 15; *PE* 380/381 (February 19, 1921), pp. 7, 22; *PE* 382/383 (March 5, 1921), pp. 11, 14; *PE* 384/385 (March 19, 1921), pp. 11, 15, and 22; *PE* 386/387 (April 2, 1921), p. 14; *PE* 388/389 (April 16, 1921), p. 13; *PE* 392/393 (May 14, 1921), pp. 9, 14; *PE* 394/395 (May 28, 1921), pp. 11, 14; *PE* 396/397 (June 11, 1921), pp. 12, 13, and 14; *PE* 398/399 (June 25, 1921), pp. 14, 15; *PE* 400/401 (July 9, 1921), p. 30; *PE* 402/403 (July 23, 1921), p. 14; *PE* 404/405 (August 6, 1921), pp. 11, 12, 13, 14, 15, and 16; *PE* 406/407 (August 20, 1921), pp. 12, 14; *PE* 408/409 (September 3, 1921), pp. 9, 12, 13, 14, and 15; *PE* 410/411 (September 17, 1921), pp. 9, 14, and 15; *PE* 412/413 (October 1, 1921), pp. 14, 15; *PE* 414/415 (October 15, 1921), pp. 12, 13, 14, and 15; *PE* 416/417 (October 29, 1921), pp. 10, 11, 14, and 15; *PE* 418/419 (November 12, 1921), pp. 13, 14; *PE* 420/421 (November 26, 1921), pp. 10, 11, 13, 14, and 15; *PE* 422/423 (December 10, 1921), pp. 28, 30; *PE* 424/425 (December 24, 1921), p. 14; *PE* 426/427 (January 7, 1922), pp. 9, 13, and 14; *PE* 428/429 (January 21, 1922), pp. 13, 14; *PE* 430/431 (February 4, 1922), p. 14; *PE* 432/433 (February 18, 1922), pp. 10, 15; *PE* 434/435 (March 4, 1922), pp. 13, 14; *PE* 436/437 (March 18, 1922), p. 11; *PE* 438/439 (April 1, 1922), pp. 9, 14; *PE* 440/441 (April 15, 1922), pp. 11, 14; *PE* 442/443 (April 29, 1922), pp. 15, 18, 20, and 21; *PE* 444/445 (May 13, 1922), pp. 10, 14; *PE* 446/447 (May 27, 1922), pp. 12, 14; *PE* 448/449 (June 10, 1922), pp. 14, 15; *PE* 450/451 (June 24, 1922), pp. 14, 15; *PE* 452/453 (July 8, 1922), pp. 4, 9, and 14; *PE* 454/455 (July 22, 1922), pp. 10, 11, 12, and 13; *PE* 456/457 (August 5, 1922), pp. 9, 12, 13, and 14; *PE* 458/459 (August 19, 1922), pp. 5, 10, 12, 13, 14, and 15; *PE* 460/461 (September 2, 1922), pp. 10, 11, and 13; *PE* 462/463 (September 16, 1922), pp. 10, 13; *PE* 464/465 (September 30, 1922), pp. 10, 11, and 14; *PE* 466/467 (October 14, 1922), pp. 8, 28, and 28; *PE* 468/469 (October 28, 1922), pp. 10, 11, 13, and 14; *PE* 470/471 (November 11, 1922), pp. 20, 21, and 22; *PE* 472/473 (November 25, 1922), pp. 5, 20, 27, and 28; *PE* 474/475 (December 9, 1922), p. 10; *PE* 476/477 (December 23, 1922), pp. 13, 14, and 16; *PE* 478/479 (January 6, 1923), pp. 10, 11, 12, and 13; *PE* 480/481 (January 20, 1923), p. 14; *PE* 482/483 (February 3, 1923), pp. 10, 11; *PE* 486/487 (March 3, 1923), pp. 14, 15, and 16; *PE* 488/489 (March 17, 1923), p. 14; *PE* 490 (March 31, 1923), pp. 9, 14; *PE* 491 (April 7, 1923), pp. 12, 13; *PE* 493 (April 21, 1923), p. 10; *PE* 494 (April 28, 1923), p. 10; *PE* 495 (May 5, 1923), pp. 10, 13, and 14; *PE* 496 (May 12, 1923), p. 13; *PE* 497 (May 19, 1923), pp. 13, 14; *PE* 498 (May 26, 1923), pp. 10, 11; *PE* 499 (June 2, 1923), p. 10; *PE* 500 (June 9, 1923), pp. 10, 11; *PE* 501 (June 16, 1923), pp. 11, 13; *PE* 502 (June 23, 1923), pp. 10, 11, and 13; *PE* 503 (June 30, 1923), pp. 10, 13; *PE* 504 (July 7 1923), p. 10, *PE* 505 (July 14, 1923), pp. 8, 10, and 11; *PE* 506 (July 21, 1923), pp. 10, 11; *PE* 507 (July 28, 1923), pp. 9, 10; *PE* 508 (August 4, 1923), p. 9, 10, 11, 12, and 13; *PE* 509 (August 11, 1923), pp. 9, 10, 11, and 12; *PE* 510 (August 18, 1923), pp. 10, 11, 13, and 15; *PE* 512 (September 1, 1923), pp. 10, 11; *PE* 513 (September 8, 1923), pp. 10, 11, 12, 13, and 15; *PE* 514 (September 15, 1923), pp. 10, 11; *PE* 515 (September 22, 1923), pp. 10, 11, 12, and 13; *PE* 516 (October 6, 1923), pp. 10, 11, 12, and 13; *PE* 517 (October 13, 1923), pp. 10, 11; *PE* 518 (October 20, 1923), p. 13; *PE* 519 (October 27, 1923), p. 12; *PE* 521 (November 10, 1923), pp. 8, 11, 12, and 13; *PE* 522 (November 17, 1923), p. 12; *PE* 523 (November 24, 1923), p. 26; *PE* 524 (December 1, 1923), p. 26; *PE* 525 (December 8, 1923), p. 13; *PE* 526 (December 15, 1923), pp. 10, 12; *PE* 527 (December 22, 1923), pp. 12, 13; *PE* 528 (January 5, 1924), p. 12; *PE* 529 (January 12, 1924), pp. 8, 14; *PE* 530 (January 19, 1924), pp. 10, 13; *PE* 531 (January 26, 1924), p. 12; *PE* 532 (February 2, 1924), pp. 12, 13; *PE* 533 (February 9, 1924), p. 12; *PE* 534 (February 16, 1924), p. 10; *PE* 535 (February 23, 1924), pp. 11, 13; *PE* 536 (March 1, 1924), pp. 11, 12, and 13; *PE* 538 (March 15, 1924), p. 12; *PE* 540 (March 29, 1924), p. 13; *PE* 541 (April 5, 1924), p. 13; *PE* 542 (April 12, 1924), p. 14; *PE* 543 (April 19, 1924), p. 12; *PE* 545 (May 3, 1924), p. 8, 12, and 13; *PE* 547 (May 17, 1924), pp. 11, 13; *PE* 548 (May 24, 1924), p. 10; *PE* 549 (June 7, 1924), pp. 12, 13; *PE* 550 (June 14, 1924), pp. 10, 12, and 13; *PE* 551 (June 21, 1924), pp. 9, 12; *PE* 552 (June 28, 1924), pp. 9, 10, 11, and 12; *PE* 553 (July 5, 1924), pp. 9, 11, and 12; *PE* 555 (July 19, 1924), pp. 3, 13; *PE* 556

(July 26, 1924), p. 12; *PE* 557 (August 2, 1924), pp. 12, 13; *PE* 558 (August 9, 1924), pp. 11, 12, and 13; *PE* 559 (August 16, 1924), pp. 7, 9, 11, and 12; *PE* 560 (August 23, 1924), pp. 11, 12, and 13; *PE* 561 (August 30, 1924), pp. 12, 14; *PE* 563 (September 13, 1924), pp. 9, 11, 12, and 13; *PE* 564 (September 20, 1924), pp. 11, 12, and 14; *PE* 565 (September 27, 1924), pp. 12, 13; *PE* 566 (October 4, 1924), pp. 8, 9, 11, 12, and 13; *PE* 567 (October 11, 1924), pp. 12, 14; *PE* 568 (October 18, 1924), pp. 10, 12, and 13; *PE* 569 (October 25, 1924), pp. 12, 13; *PE* 570 (November 1, 1924), p. 12; *PE* 571 (November 8, 1924), pp. 12, 13; *PE* 572 (November 15, 1924), pp. 9, 11, 12, and 13; *PE* 573 (November 22, 1924), p. 12; *PE* 574 (November 29, 1924), p. 28; *PE* 575 (December 6, 1924), pp. 12, 13; *PE* 576 (December 13, 1924), pp. 11, 13; *PE* 578 (January 3, 1925), pp. 11, 12, and 13; *PE* 579 (January 10, 1925), p. 12; *PE* 580 (January 17, 1925), pp. 9, 10, and 12; *PE* 584 (February 14, 1925), pp. 10, 12; *PE* 585 (February 21, 1925), pp. 10, 12, 13, and 14; *PE* 587 (March 7, 1925), p. 12; *PE* 588 (March 14, 1925), p. 12; *PE* 589 (March 21, 1925), pp. 10, 12; *PE* 590 (March 28, 1925), pp. 12, 13; *PE* 591 (April 4, 1925), pp. 11, 12; *PE* 592 (April 11, 1925), pp. 10, 12; *PE* 593 (April 18, 1925), p. 13; *PE* 594 (April 25, 1925), p. 12; *PE* 595 (May 2, 1925), pp. 11, 12, and 13; *PE* 596 (May 9, 1925), p. 12; *PE* 597 (May 16, 1925), p. 12; *PE* 598 (May 23, 1925), p. 12; *PE* 599 (May 30, 1925), p. 13; *PE* 600 (June 6, 1925), pp. 13, 14; *PE* 601 (June 13, 1925), p. 13; *PE* 602 (June 20, 1925), p. 13; *PE* 603 (June 27, 1925), p. 13; *PE* 604 (July 4, 1925), pp. 7, 13; *PE* 605 (July 11, 1925), pp. 9, 12, and 13; *PE* 606 (July 18, 1925), p. 13; *PE* 607 (July 26, 1925), pp. 10, 12; *PE* 608 (August 1, 1925), pp. 10, 12; *PE* 609 (August 8, 1925), pp. 9, 13; *PE* 610 (August 15, 1925), pp. 7, 11, and 12; *PE* 611 (August 22, 1925), pp. 9, 12; *PE* 612 (August 29, 1925), pp. 10, 12; *PE* 613 (September 5, 1925), pp. 11, 12, and 13; *PE* 614 (September 12, 1925), pp. 11, 12; *PE* 615 (September 19, 1925), pp. 10, 12, and 13; *PE* 616 (September 26, 1925), pp. 12, 13; *PE* 618 (October 17, 1925), pp. 12, 13; *PE* 619 (October 24, 1925), pp. 16, 17; *PE* 620 (October 31, 1925), p. 12; *PE* 621 (November 7, 1925), pp. 10, 12; *PE* 622 (November 14, 1925), p. 16; *PE* 623 (November 21, 1925), p. 12; *PE* 625 (December 5, 1925), p. 18; *PE* 626 (December 12, 1925), p. 12; *PE* 627 (December 19, 1925), p. 12; *PE* 628 (January 2, 1926), p. 6; *PE* 629 (January 9, 1926), pp. 6, 7, and 12; *PE* 630 (January 16, 1926), pp. 10, 11; *PE* 631 (January 23, 1926), p. 12; *PE* 632 (January 30, 1926), pp. 10, 12; *PE* 634 (February 13, 1926), p. 11; *PE* 635 (February 20, 1926), pp. 10, 12; *PE* 636 (February 27, 1926), p. 13; *PE* 637 (March 6, 1926), p. 12; *PE* 638 (March 13, 1926), pp. 12, 13; *PE* 639 (March 20, 1926), pp. 7, 12; *PE* 640 (March 27, 1926), pp. 10, 12, and 13; *PE* 642 (April 10, 1926), p. 12; *PE* 643 (April 17, 1926), pp. 11, 12; *PE* 644 (April 24, 1926), pp. 11, 13; *PE* 645 (May 1, 1926), pp. 11, 12, and 13; *PE* 646 (May 8, 1926), p. 10; *PE* 647 (May 15, 1926), p. 12; *PE* 648 (May 22, 1926), pp. 11, 12, and 13; *PE* 649 (May 29, 1926), pp. 10, 11, and 13; *PE* 650 (June 5, 1926), pp. 5, 6, 7, 10, and 12; *PE* 652 (June 19, 1926), pp. 2, 3, 11, 12, and 13; *PE* 653 (June 26, 1926), pp. 11, 12; *PE* 654 (July 3, 1926), pp. 10, 12; *PE* 655 (July 10, 1926), pp. 17, 18, 20, and 21; *PE* 656 (July 17, 1926), pp. 11, 12, and 13; *PE* 657 (July 24, 1926), pp. 8, 9, 11, 12, and 13; *PE* 658 (July 31, 1926), pp. 11, 12; *PE* 659 (August 7, 1926), p. 12; *PE* 660 (August 14, 1926), pp. 10, 13; *PE* 661 (August 21, 1926), pp. 10, 12, 13, and 14; *PE* 662 (August 28, 1926), pp. 5, 12, 13, and 14; *PE* 663 (September 4, 1926), pp. 3, 5, and 12; *PE* 664 (September 11, 1926), pp. 12, 13, and 14; *PE* 665 (September 18, 1926), pp. 3, 12, 13, and 14; *PE* 666 (September 25, 1926), pp. 5, 11, 12, and 13; *PE* 667 (October 2, 1926), pp. 11, 12, and 13; *PE* 668 (October 9, 1926), pp. 10, 12, and 14; *PE* 669 (October 23, 1926), pp. 5, 8, 9, 10, 11, and 12; *PE* 670 (October 30, 1926), p. 12; *PE* 671 (November 6, 1926), pp. 12, 13; *PE* 672 (November 13, 1926), pp. 4, 9, 12, and 13; *PE* 673 (November 20, 1926), pp. 19, 20, and 21; *PE* 674 (November 27, 1926), p. 16; *PE* 675 (December 4, 1926), pp. 5, 6, 19, and 20; *PE* 676 (December 11, 1926), pp. 12, 13; *PE* 677 (December 18, 1926), p. 12; *PE* 678 (January 1, 1927), pp. 12, 13; *PE* 679 (January 8, 1927), pp. 10, 13; *PE* 681 (January 22, 1927), pp. 4, 6, 12, and 13; *PE* 682 (January 29, 1927), p. 12; *PE* 683 (February 5, 1927), p. 13; *PE* 684 (February 12, 1927), p. 12; *PE* 685 (February 19, 1927), p. 12; *PE* 687 (March 5, 1927), pp. 2, 5, 19, and 20; *PE* 688 (March 12, 1927), pp. 10, 12, and 13; *PE* 690 (March 26, 1927), pp. 18, 20; *PE* 691 (April 2, 1927), pp. 10, 12; *PE* 692 (April 9, 1927), pp. 11, 12; *PE* 693 (April 16, 1927), p. 12; *PE* 694 (April 23, 1927), p. 1; *PE* 695 (April 30, 1927), p. 9; *PE* 696 (May 7, 1927), pp. 8, 15; *PE* 698 (May 21, 1927), p. 12; *PE* 699 (May 28, 1927), p. 12; *PE* 700 (June 4, 1927), pp. 9, 10, 12, and 13; *PE* 701 (June 11, 1927), pp. 9, 10, and 12; *PE* 702 (June 18, 1927), pp. 10, 11, 12, and 13; *PE* 703 (June 25, 1927), p. 12; *PE* 704 (July 2, 1927), p. 12; *PE* 705 (July 9, 1927), pp. 3, 8, 9, 12, and 13; *PE* 706 (July 16, 1927), pp. 20, 21; *PE* 707 (July 23, 1927), pp. 3, 12; *PE* 708 (July 30, 1927), pp. 8, 9, 11, and 12; *PE* 709 (August 6, 1927), pp. 4, 5, 17, 18, 19, 20, and 21; *PE* 710 (August 13, 1927), pp. 8, 10, 11, and 12; *PE* 711 (August 20, 1927), pp. 11, 12; *PE* 712 (August 27, 1927), pp. 11, 12; *PE* 713 (September 3, 1927), pp. 11, 12, and 13; *PE* 714 (September 10, 1927), pp. 11, 12, 13, and 15; *PE* 715 (September 17, 1927), pp. 8, 12; *PE* 716 (September 24, 1927), pp. 9, 12, and 13; *PE* 717 (October 8, 1927), pp. 10, 12; *PE* 718 (October 15, 1927), pp. 20, 21; *PE* 719 (October 22, 1927), p. 12; *PE* 720 (October 29, 1927), p. 20; *PE* 721 (November 5, 1927), pp. 10, 12; *PE* 722 (November 12, 1927), p. 12;

PE 723 (November 19, 1927), p. 12; *PE* 725 (December 3, 1927), pp. 20, 21; *PE* 726 (December 10, 1927), p. 20; *PE* 727 (December 17, 1927), pp. 10, 12, and 14; *PE* 728 (December 24, 1927), pp. 10, 12, and 13; *PE* 729 (January 7, 1928), pp. 4, 11, and 12; *PE* 730 (January 14, 1928), p. 13; *PE* 731 (January 21, 1928), p. 19; *PE* 732 (January 28, 1928), pp. 3, 12; *PE* 733 (February 4, 1928), pp. 10, 12; *PE* 734 (February 11, 1928), pp. 12, 13; *PE* 735 (February 18, 1928), pp. 3, 9, 11, and 12; *PE* 736 (February 25, 1928), pp. 12, 13; *PE* 737 (March 3, 1928), p. 12; *PE* 738 (March 10, 1928), pp. 12, 13; *PE* 739 (March 17, 1928), p. 10; *PE* 740 (March 24, 1928), p. 13; *PE* 741 (March 31, 1928), pp. 11, 12, and 13; *PE* 742 (April 7, 1928), pp. 9, 12, and 13; *PE* 743 (April 14, 1928), p. 12; *PE* 744 (April 21, 1928), p. 12; *PE* 745 (April 28, 1928), pp. 11, 12; *PE* 746 (May 5, 1928), pp. 11, 12; *PE* 748 (May 19, 1928), p. 2; *PE* 749 (May 26, 1928), p. 12; *PE* 750 (June 2, 1928), p. 12; *PE* 751 (June 9, 1928), pp. 12, 13; *PE* 752 (June 16, 1928), p. 12; *PE* 754 (June 30, 1928), pp. 9, 10, 12, and 13; *PE* 755 (July 7, 1928), pp. 14, 15, and 16; *PE* 756 (July 21, 1928), pp. 8, 12, and 16; *PE* 757 (July 28, 1928), p. 12; *PE* 758 (August 4, 1928), pp. 5, 11, and 12; *PE* 759 (August 11, 1928), pp. 3, 12; *PE* 760 (August 18, 1928), pp. 10, 11, and 12; *PE* 761 (August 25, 1928), pp. 12, 13; *PE* 762 (September 1, 1928), p. 12; *PE* 763 (September 8, 1928), pp. 9, 11, 12, and 13; *PE* 764 (September 15, 1928), pp. 11, 12, and 13; *PE* 765 (September 22, 1928), pp. 12, 13; *PE* 766 (September 29, 1928), pp. 15, 16; *PE* 767 (October 6, 1928), pp. 11, 12; *PE* 768 (October 13, 1928), pp. 12, 13; *PE* 769 (October 20, 1928), pp. 11, 12; *PE* 770 (October 27, 1928), pp. 5, 12, and 13; *PE* 771 (November 3, 1928), pp. 11, 12; *PE* 772 (November 10, 1928), pp. 10, 12; *PE* 773 (November 17, 1928), pp. 19, 20, and 21; *PE* 774 (November 24, 1928), pp. 10, 12; *PE* 775 (December 1, 1928), p. 19; *PE* 777 (December 15, 1928), p. 12; *PE* 778 (December 22, 1928), pp. 12, 13; *PE* 779 (January 5, 1929), pp. 5, 11; *PE* 780 (January 12, 1929), pp. 10, 12, and 13; *PE* 781 (January 19, 1929), p. 12; *PE* 782 (January 26, 1929), p. 12; *PE* 785 (February 16, 1929), p. 12; *PE* 786 (February 23, 1929), p. 10; *PE* 788 (March 9, 1929), pp. 11, 12; *PE* 789 (March 16, 1929), pp. 11, 12; *PE* 792 (April 6, 1929), pp. 11, 13; *PE* 793 (April 13, 1929), p. 10, 12, and 13; *PE* 794 (April 20, 1929), pp. 10, 12; *PE* 795 (April 27, 1929), p. 10; *PE* 796 (May 4, 1929), pp. 9, 12; *PE* 797 (May 11, 1929), pp. 11, 12; *PE* 798 (May 18, 1929), pp. 9, 12, 13, and 14; *PE* 799 (May 25, 1929), p. 12; *PE* 800 (June 1, 1929), p. 12; *PE* 802 (June 15, 1929), pp. 14, 15, and 16; *PE* 803 (June 22, 1929), p. 12; *PE* 804 (June 29, 1929), p. 16; *PE* 805 (July 6, 1929), pp. 12, 13; *PE* 806 (July 13, 1929), p. 12; *PE* 807 (July 20, 1929), p. 12; *PE* 808 (July 27, 1929), p. 14; *PE* 809 (August 3, 1929), p. 14; *PE* 810 (August 10, 1929), pp. 6, 10, 12, and 13; *PE* 811 (August 17, 1929), pp. 11, 12; *PE* 812 (August 24, 1929), pp. 11, 12; *PE* 813 (August 31, 1929), pp. 12, 13; *PE* 814 (September 7, 1929), pp. 12, 13; *PE* 815 (September 14, 1929), p. 12; *PE* 816 (September 21, 1929), p. 12; *PE* 817 (October 5, 1929), pp. 10, 11, and 12; *PE* 818 (October 12, 1929), pp. 13, 16, 17, and 18; *PE* 819 (October 19, 1929), p. 12; *PE* 821 (November 2, 1929), pp. 10, 11, and 12; *PE* 822 (November 9, 1929), p. 12; *PE* 823 (November 16, 1929), p. 12; *PE* 824 (November 23, 1929), pp. 5, 6, and 20; *PE* 825 (November 30, 1929), p. 20; *PE* 826 (December 7, 1929), p. 17; *PE* 829 (January 4, 1930), pp. 11, 12, and 13; *PE* 830 (January 11, 1930), p. 12; *PE* 831 (January 18, 1930), pp. 6, 7, and 11; *PE* 832 (January 25, 1930), p. 12; *PE* 833 (February 1, 1930), p. 13; *PE* 835 (February 15, 1930), pp. 10, 12; *PE* 836 (February 22, 1930), p. 12; *PE* 837 (March 1, 1930), pp. 11, 12; *PE* 838 (March 8, 1930), pp. 11, 12; *PE* 839 (March 15, 1930), p. 11; *PE* 840 (March 22, 1930), pp. 12, 13; *PE* 841 (March 29, 1930), p. 12; *PE* 842 (April 5, 1930), pp. 13, 18, and 19; *PE* 843 (April 12, 1930), p. 12; *PE* 844 (April 19, 1930), p. 12; *PE* 851 (June 7, 1930), p. 12; *PE* 852 (June 14, 1930), pp. 12, 13; *PE* 853 (June 21, 1930), p. 12; *PE* 854 (June 28, 1930), pp. 5, 10, and 12; *PE* 855 (July 5, 1930), pp. 11, 13; *PE* 856 (July 12, 1930), pp. 11, 12, and 14; *PE* 857 (July 19, 1930), p. 12; *PE* 858 (July 26, 1930), pp. 11, 12, and 13; *PE* 859 (August 2, 1930), pp. 5, 12; *PE* 860 (August 9, 1930), p. 12; *PE* 861 (August 16, 1930), pp. 9, 12; *PE* 862 (August 23, 1930), pp. 10, 12, and 13; *PE* 863 (August 30, 1930), pp. 9, 11, and 12; *PE* 864 (September 6, 1930), pp. 10, 12, and 14; *PE* 865 (September 13, 1930), pp. 10, 12; *PE* 866 (September 27, 1930), pp. 8, 12; *PE* 867 (October 4, 1930), pp. 10, 11, and 12; *PE* 868 (October 11, 1930), pp. 9, 11, 12, and 13; *PE* 869 (October 18, 1930), pp. 8, 12, and 13; *PE* 870 (October 25, 1930), pp. 10, 12; *PE* 871 (November 1, 1930), pp. 10, 12, and 13; *PE* 873 (November 15, 1930), pp. 15, 16, and 17; *PE* 874 (November 22, 1930), p. 20; *PE* 875 (November 29, 1930), pp. 17, 19, 20, and 21; *PE* 876 (December 6, 1930), p. 16; *PE* 877 (December 13, 1930), pp. 5, 8, 11, and 12; *PE* 878 (December 20, 1930), p. 12; *PE* 879 (January 3, 1931), p. 12; *PE* 880 (January 10, 1931), pp. 6-7, 9, 11, and 12; *PE* 882 (January 24, 1931), pp. 12, 13; *PE* 883 (January 31, 1931), p. 12; *PE* 884 (February 7, 1931), pp. 11, 12; *PE* 886 (February 21, 1931), pp. 10, 12; *PE* 887 (February 28, 1931), pp. 10, 12, and 13; *PE* 888 (March 7, 1931), pp. 11, 12, and 13; *PE* 889 (March 14, 1931), p. 13; *PE* 890 (March 21, 1931), pp. 3, 16; *PE* 891 (March 28, 1931), pp. 11, 12; *PE* 892 (April 4, 1931), pp. 11, 12, and 13; *PE* 893 (April 11, 1931), p. 12; *PE* 894 (April 18, 1931), p. 12; *PE* 895 (April 25, 1931), p. 12; *PE* 896 (May 2, 1931), pp. 11, 12; *PE* 897 (May 9, 1931), pp. 11, 12; *PE* 898 (May 16, 1931), pp. 11, 12, and 13; *PE* 899 (May 23, 1931), p. 12; *PE* 900 (May 30, 1931), p. 12; *PE* 901 (June 6, 1931), pp. 12, 13; *PE* 902

(June 13, 1931), p. 16; *PE* 903 (June 20, 1931), pp. 12, 13; *PE* 904 (June 27, 1931), pp. 2, 3, 17, 18, 19, 20, and 21; *PE* 905 (July 4, 1931), p. 12; *PE* 906 (July 11, 1931), pp. 12, 13; *PE* 907 (July 18, 1931), pp. 12, 13; *PE* 908 (July 25, 1931), pp. 11, 12; *PE* 909 (August 1, 1931), pp. 10, 11; *PE* 910 (August 8, 1931), p. 12; *PE* 911 (August 15, 1931), pp. 12, 13; *PE* 912 (August 22, 1931), pp. 10, 11, 12, and 13; *PE* 913 (August 29, 1931), p. 9; *PE* 914 (September 5, 1931), pp. 7, 14, 15, and 16; *PE* 915 (September 12, 1931), pp. 5, 13, 14, 15, and 16; *PE* 916 (September 26, 1931), pp. 6, 8, 15, 16, and 17; *PE* 917 (October 3, 1931), pp. 6, 16, 17, and 18; *PE* 918 (October 10, 1931), pp. 15, 16, and 18; *PE* 919 (October 17, 1931), pp. 15, 16, 17, and 18; *PE* 920 (October 24, 1931), pp. 13, 14, and 15; *PE* 921 (October 31, 1931), pp. 13, 16, and 17; *PE* 922 (November 7, 1931), p. 16; *PE* 923 (November 14, 1931), pp. 16, 17; *PE* 924 (November 21, 1931), pp. 18, 19; *PE* 925, 19, 20, and 21; *PE* 926 (December 5, 1931), pp. 18, 19, and 20; *PE* 927 (December 12, 1931), pp. 8, 12, and 13; *PE* 928 (December 19, 1931), pp. 10, 12.

Appendix Q

Pentecostal Evangel

References to 'baptized' 'baptized in water' and 'baptizing':

PE 2.19 (May 9, 1914), p. 6; *PE* 33 (May 9, 1914), p. 10; *PE* 49 (July 11, 1914), p. 3; *PE* 50 (July 18, 1914), p. 3; *PE* 51 (July 25, 1914), p. 4; *PE* 52 (August 1, 1914), pp. 3, 4; *PE* 54 (August 15, 1914), p. 3; *PE* 56 (August 29, 1914), pp. 1, 3, and 4; *PE* 57 (September 5, 1914), pp. 1, 3, and 4; *PE* 58 (September 12, 1914), pp. 2, 3, and 4; *PE* 59 (September 19, 1914), pp. 1, 2; *PE* 60 (September 26, 1914), pp. 1, 4; *PE* 61 (October 3, 1914), pp. 2, 3, and 4; *PE* 62 (October 10, 1914), pp. 2, 3, and 4; *PE* 63 (October 17, 1914), pp. 1, 3; *PE* 64 (October 24, 1914), p. 4; *PE* 65 (October 31, 1914), pp. 1, 4; *PE* 66 (November 7, 1914), pp. 3, 4; *PE* 67 (November 14, 1914), pp. 1, 2, and 3; *PE* 68 (November 21, 1914), p. 3; 69 (December 5, 1914), pp. 1, 2, 4; *PE* 70 (December 12, 1914), pp. 1, 2, 3, and 4; *PE* 71 (December 19, 1914), pp. 3, 4; *PE* 72 (December 26, 1914), pp. 1, 2, and 3; *PE* 73 (January 9, 1915), p. 3; *PE* 78 (February 20, 1915), pp. 3, 4; *PE* 79 (February 27, 1915), pp. 2, 4; *PE* 80 (March 6, 1915), pp. 1, 3; *PE* 81 (March 13, 1915), p. 3; *PE* 83 (March 27, 1915), p. 4; *PE* 85 (April 10, 1915), p. 1; *PE* 86 (April 17, 1915), p. 4; *PE* 88 (May 1, 1915), pp. 1, 4; *PE* 90 (May 15, 1915), pp. 1, 3; *PE* 93 (June 5, 1915), p. 4; *PE* 94 (June 12, 1915), p. 4; *PE* 95 (June 19, 1915), p. 1; *PE* 96 (June 26, 1915), p. 1; *PE* 97 (July 3, 1915), pp. 1, 3; *PE* 98 (July 10, 1915), p. 1; *PE* 99 (July 17, 1915), pp. 1, 3, and 4; *PE* 100 (July 24, 1915), pp. 1, 2, 3, and 4; *PE* 101 (July 31, 1915), p. 1; *PE* 102 (August 7, 1915), pp. 1, 2; *PE* 103 (August 14, 1915), pp. 1, 2, 3, and 4; *PE* 104 (August 21, 1915), pp. 1, 2; *PE* 105 (August 28, 1915), pp. 1, 2, and 4; *PE* 106 (September 4, 1915), pp. 1, 2, 3, and 4; *PE* 107 (September 11, 1915), pp. 1, 2; *PE* 108 (September 18, 1915), p. 4; *PE* 109 (September 25, 1915), p. 1; *PE* 110 (October 2, 1915), pp. 3, 4; *PE* 112 (October 23, 1915), p. 1; *PE* 113 (October 30, 1915), p. 1; *PE* 114 (November 6, 1915), pp. 1, 3; *PE* 115 (November 13, 1915), pp.1, 2, and 4; *PE* 116 (November 20, 1915), pp. 1, 4; *PE* 117 (November 27, 1915), pp. 1, 4; *PE* 120 (December 18, 1915), p. 4; *PE* 123 (January 15, 1916), pp. 13, 15, and 16; *PE* 124 (January 22, 1916), p. 14; *PE* 125 (February 5, 1916), pp. 12, 14; *PE* 127 (February 19, 1916), p. 14; *PE* 128 (February 26, 1916), p. 12; *PE* 131 (March 18, 1916), pp. 13, 14; *PE* 132 (March 25, 1916), p. 14; *PE* 135 (April 15, 1916), p. 15; *PE* 136 (April 22, 1916), pp. 11, 15; *PE* 137 (April 29, 1916), p. 14; *PE* 138 (May 6, 1916), pp. 14, 15; *PE* 139 (May 13, 1916), pp. 12, 14, and 15; *PE* 141 (May 27, 1916), pp. 14, 15; *PE* 142 (June 3, 1916), p. 12; *PE* 143 (June 10, 1916), pp. 7, 14; *PE* 145 (June 24, 1916), pp. 8, 14; *PE* 146/147 (July 8, 1916), pp. 7, 11, and 15; *PE* 149 (July 22, 1916), pp. 14, 15; *PE* 150 (July 29, 1916), pp. 12, 14; *PE* 151 (August 5, 1916), p. 15; *PE* 152 (August 12, 1916), pp. 11, 14; *PE* 154 (August 26, 1916), pp. 14, 15; *PE* 155 (September 2, 1916), pp. 11, 13, and 15; *PE* 156 (September 9, 1916), p. 11; *PE* 157 (September 16, 1916), p. 14; *PE* 158 (September 23, 1916), pp. 4, 14; *PE* 159 (September 30, 1916), pp. 4, 14; *PE* 160 (October 14, 1916), p. 15; *PE* 161 (October 21, 1916), pp. 14, 15; *PE* 162 (October 28, 1916), pp. 14, 15; *PE* 163 (November 4, 1916), pp. 8, 13; *PE* 164 (November 11, 1916), pp. 12, 14, and 15; *PE* 165 (November 18, 1916), pp. 12, 14; *PE* 166 (November 25, 1916), p. 11, 12; *PE* 167 (December 2, 1916), pp. 12, 14; *PE* 168 (December 9, 1916), pp. 12, 13, and 14; *PE* 170 (December 23, 1916), pp. 12, 13, and 14; *PE* 171 (January 6, 1917), p. 14; *PE* 172 (January 13, 1917), pp. 12, 14, and 16; *PE* 173 (January 20, 1917), p. 14; *PE* 174 (January 27, 1917), pp. 14, 15, and 16; *PE* 177 (February 17, 1917), p. 4; *PE* 178 (February 24, 1917), p. 11; *PE* 181 (March 17, 1917), pp. 12, 16; *PE* 182 (March 24, 1917), p. 14; *PE* 184 (April 7, 1917), p. 3; *PE* 186 (April 21, 1917), p. 14; *PE* 187 (April 28, 1917), p. 15; *PE* 188 (May 5, 1917), pp. 12,

14; *PE* 190 (May 19, 1917), p. 12, and 14; *PE* 191 (May 26, 1917), p. 14; *PE* 192 (June 2, 1917), p. 14; *PE* 193 (June 9, 1917), pp. 11, 14; *PE* 195 (June 23, 1917), p. 14; *PE* 196 (June 30, 1917), p. 14; *PE* 197 (July 7, 1917), pp. 12, 13, and 14; *PE* 198 (July 14, 1917), p. 14; *PE* 199 (July 21, 1917), p. 14; *PE* 200 (July 28, 1917), pp. 13, 14; *PE* 201 (August 4, 1917), p. 14; *PE* 202 (August 11, 1917), pp. 12, 14; *PE* 203 (August 18, 1917), pp. 12, 14; *PE* 204 (August 25, 1917), pp. 12, 14, and 16; *PE* 206 (September 8, 1917), pp. 11, 12, and 14; *PE* 207 (September 15, 1917), p. 14; *PE* 208 (September 29, 1917), p. 14; *PE* 209 (October 6, 1917), pp. 12, 14, and 16; *PE* 210 (October 13, 1917), p. 14; *PE* 211 (October 20, 1917), p. 14; *PE* 212 (October 27, 1917), pp. 2, 3, and 14; *PE* 213 (November 3, 1917), pp. 13, 14; *PE* 214 (November 10, 1917), pp. 12, 13, and 14; *PE* 216 (November 24, 1917), p. 11; *PE* 218 (December 8, 1917), p. 14; *PE* 219 (December 15, 1917), p. 14; *PE* 220 (December 22, 1917), p. 11; *PE* 221 (January 5, 1918), p. 10; *PE* 223 (January 19, 1918), pp. 10, 14; *PE* 224 (January 26, 1918), p. 10; *PE* 225 (February 2, 1918), pp. 7, 8; *PE* 226 (February 9, 1918), p. 8; *PE* 227 (February 16, 1918), pp. 4-5, 10; *PE* 230 (March 9, 1918), p. 10; *PE* 234/235 (April 6, 1918), pp. 14, 15; *PE* 236/237 (April 20, 1918), pp. 11, 15; *PE* 238/239 (May 4, 1918), pp. 9, 10, and 14; *PE* 240/241 (May 18, 1918), pp. 11, 14; *PE* 242/243 (June 1, 1918), p. 14; *PE* 244/245 (June 15, 1918), pp. 13, 16; *PE* 246/247 (June 29, 1918), pp. 11, 14; *PE* 248/249 (July 27, 1918), pp. 3, 10, 14; *PE* 250/251 (August 10, 1918), p. 14; *PE* 252/253 (August 24, 1918), pp. 14, 15; *PE* 254 (September 7, 1918), pp. 5, 7; *PE* 256/257 (October 5, 1918), pp. 1, 10, 11, and 14; *PE* 258/259 (October 19, 1918), pp. 1, 10, and 11; *PE* 260/261 (November 2, 1918), pp. 10, 14; *PE* 262/263 (November 16, 1918), pp. 1, 10; *PE* 268/269 (December 28, 1918), p. 10; *PE* 270/271 (January 11, 1919), pp. 1, 11; *PE* 272/273 (January 25, 1919), pp. 1, 4; *PE* 274/275 (February 8, 1919), pp. 3, 12; *PE* 278/279 (March 8, 1919), p. 14; *PE* 280/281 (March 22, 1919), p. 10; *PE* 282/283 (April 5, 1919), pp. 10, 14; *PE* 284/285 (April 19, 1919), pp. 10, 11; *PE* 286/287 (May 3, 1919), pp. 14; *PE* 288/289 (May 17, 1919), pp. 10, 13, and 15; *PE* 290/291 (May 31, 1919), p. 14; *PE* 292/293 (June 14, 1919), pp. 9, 10, 13, and 14; *PE* 294/295 (June 28, 1919), pp. 9, 10, 11, 14, and 19; *PE* 296/297 (July 12, 1919), pp. 11, 14, and 15; *PE* 298/299 (July 26, 1919), pp. 10, 11, 13, and 14; *PE* 300/301 (August 9, 1919), pp. 8, 10, 11, and 14; *PE* 302/303 (August 23, 1919), pp. 10, 11, 13, and 14; *PE* 304/305 (September 6, 1919), p. 10, 11, 14, and 16; *PE* 306/307 (September 20, 1919), pp. 10, 11, 12, 13, and 14; *PE* 308/309 (October 4, 1919), pp. 9, 12; *PE* 310/311 (October 18, 1919), pp. 11, 12, 13, and 14; *PE* 312/313 (November 1, 1919), pp. 23, 29; *PE* 314/315 (November 15, 1919), pp. 10, 11, 12, and 14; *PE* 316/317 (November 29, 1919), pp. 13, 14, and 15; *PE* 318/319 (December 13, 1919), p. 14; *PE* 320/321 (December 27, 1919), pp. 12, 13, and 14; *PE* 322/323 (January 10, 1920), p. 13; *PE* 324/325 (January 24, 1920), pp. 10, 12, and 14; *PE* 326/327 (February 7, 1920), p. 13; *PE* 328/329 (February 24, 1920), pp. 10, 12, and 14; *PE* 330/331 (March 6, 1920), p. 13; *PE* 334/335 (April 13, 1920), p. 13; *PE* 336/337 (April 17, 1920), p. 13; *PE* 338/339 (May 1, 1920), pp. 13, 14; *PE* 342/343 (May 29, 1920), p. 14; *PE* 344/345 (June 12, 1920), p. 12; *PE* 346/347 (June 26, 1920), pp. 13, 14; *PE* 348/349 (July 10, 1920), pp. 1, 11, and 13; *PE* 350/351 (July 24, 1920), pp. 13, 14; *PE* 352/353 (August 7, 1920), pp. 10, 13, and 14; *PE* 354/355 (August 21, 1920), pp. 10, 12, and 14; *PE* 356/357 (September 4, 1920), pp. 10, 12, 13, and 14; *PE* 358/359 (September 18, 1920), pp. 7, 11, 12, 14, and 15; *PE* 360/361 (October 2, 1920), pp. 10, 11, and 14; *PE* 362/363 (October 16, 1920), pp. 13, 14; *PE* 364/365 (October 30, 1920), pp. 11, 13, and 14; *PE* 366/367 (November 13, 1920), pp. 10, 14; *PE* 368/369 (November 27, 1920), pp. 13, 14; *PE* 370/371 (December 11, 1920), pp. 13, 14; *PE* 376/377 (January 22, 1921), p. 12; *PE* 378/379 (February 5, 1921), p. 15; *PE* 380/381 (February 19, 1921), pp. 7, 22; *PE* 382/383 (March 5, 1921), p. 11; *PE* 384/385 (March 19, 1921), pp. 11, 15, and 22; *PE* 386/387 (April 2, 1921), p. 14; *PE* 388/389 (April 16, 1921), p. 13; *PE* 392/393 (May 14, 1921), p. 14; *PE* 394/395 (May 28, 1921), pp. 11, 14; *PE* 396/397 (June 11, 1921), pp. 13, 14; *PE* 398/399 (June 25, 1921), pp. 14, 15; *PE* 400/401 (July 9, 1921), p. 30; *PE* 402/403 (July 23, 1921), p. 14; *PE* 404/405 (August 6, 1921), pp. 11, 13, 14, 15, and 16; *PE* 406/407 (August 20, 1921), pp. 12, 14; 408/409 (September 3, 1921), pp. 9, 12, 13, 14, and 15; *PE* 410/411 (September 17, 1921), pp. 9, 14, and 15; *PE* 412/413 (October 1, 1921), pp. 14, 15; *PE* 414/415 (October 15, 1921), pp. 12, 13, 14, and 15; *PE* 416/417 (October 29, 1921), pp. 10, 11, 14, and 15; *PE* 418/419 (November 12, 1921), pp. 13, 14; *PE* 420/421 (November 26, 1921), pp. 10, 13, and 14; *PE* 422/423 (December 10, 1921), pp. 28, 30; *PE* 424/425 (December 24, 1921), p. 14; *PE* 426/427 (January 7, 1922), pp. 9, 13; *PE* 428/429 (January 21, 1922), p. 14; *PE* 430/431 (February 4, 1922), p. 14; *PE* 432/433 (February 18, 1922), p. 15; *PE* 434/435 (March 4, 1922), p. 13; *PE* 436/437 (March 18, 1922), p. 11; *PE* 438/439 (April 1, 1922), p. 9; *PE* 442/443 (April 29, 1922), pp. 18, 20, and 21; *PE* 444/445 (May 13, 1922), p. 14; *PE* 446/447 (May 27, 1922), pp. 12, 14; *PE* 448/449 (June 10, 1922), p. 15; *PE* 450/451 (June 24, 1922), pp. 14, 15; *PE* 452/453 (July 8, 1922), p. 9, 14; *PE* 454/455 (July 22, 1922), pp. 10, 11, 12, and 13; *PE* 456/457 (August 5, 1922), pp. 9, 12, 13, and 14; *PE* 458/459 (August 19, 1922), pp. 10, 12, 13, 14, and 15; *PE* 460/461 (September 2, 1922), pp. 10, 11, and 13; *PE* 462/463 (September 16, 1922), pp. 10, 13; *PE* 464/465 (September 30,

1922), pp. 10, 11, and 14; *PE* 466/467 (October 14, 1922), pp. 28, 29; *PE* 468/469 (October 28, 1922), pp. 10, 11, and 14; *PE* 470/471 (November 11, 1922), pp. 20, 21, and 22; *PE* 472/473 (November 25, 1922), pp. 20, 22, 27, and 28; *PE* 476/477 (December 23, 1922), pp. 13, 14, and 16; *PE* 478/479 (January 6, 1923), pp. 10, 12, and 13; *PE* 480/481 (January 20, 1923), p. 14; *PE* 482/483 (February 3, 1923), pp. 10, 12; *PE* 484/485 (February 17, 1923), pp. 10, 11; *PE* 486/487 (March 3, 1923), pp. 14, 15, and 16; *PE* 488/489 (March 17, 1923), p. 14; *PE* 490 (March 31, 1923), pp. 9, 14; *PE* 493 (April 21, 1923), p. 10; *PE* 494 (April 28, 1923), p. 10; *PE* 495 (May 5, 1923), p. 14; *PE* 496 (May 12, 1923), p. 13; *PE* 497 (May 19, 1923), pp. 13, 14; *PE* 498 (May 26, 1923), p. 10; *PE* 499 (June 2, 1923), p. 10; *PE* 500 (June 9, 1923), pp. 10, 11; *PE* 501 (June 16, 1923), pp. 11, 13; *PE* 502 (June 23, 1923), pp. 10, 13; *PE* 503 (June 30, 1923), pp. 10, 13; *PE* 504 (July 7, 1923), p. 10; *PE* 505 (July 14, 1923), pp. 8, 10, and 11; *PE* 506 (July 21, 1923), p. 10; *PE* 507 (July 28, 1923), pp. 9, 10; *PE* 508 (August 4, 1923), pp. 9, 10, 11, and 12; *PE* 509 (August 11, 1923), pp. 9, 10, and 12; *PE* 510 (August 18, 1923), pp. 10, 11, and 15; *PE* 511 (August 25, 1923), pp. 10, 13; *PE* 512 (September 1, 1923), p. 10; *PE* 513 (September 8, 1923), pp. 10, 15; *PE* 514 (September 15, 1923), pp. 10, 11; *PE* 515 (September 22, 1923), pp. 10, 11, 12, and 13; *PE* 516 (October 6, 1923), pp. 10, 11, 12, and 13; *PE* 517 (October 13, 1923), pp. 10, 11; *PE* 518 (October 20, 1923), p. 13; *PE* 519 (October 27, 1923), p. 12; *PE* 521 (November 10, 1923), pp. 8, 12; *PE* 522 (November 17, 1923), p. 12; *PE* 523 (November 24, 1923), p. 26; *PE* 524 (December 1, 1923), p. 26; *PE* 525 (December 8, 1923), p. 13; *PE* 527 (December 22, 1923), pp. 12, 13; *PE* 528 (January 5, 1924), p. 12; *PE* 529 (January 12, 1924), pp. 8, 14; *PE* 530 (January 19, 1924), pp. 10, 13; *PE* 532 (February 2, 1924), p. 12; *PE* 533 (February 9, 1924), p. 12; *PE* 534 (February 16, 1924), p. 10; *PE* 535 (February 23, 1924), p. 11; *PE* 536 (March 1, 1924), pp. 11, 12, and 13; *PE* 540 (March 29, 1924), p. 13; *PE* 542 (April 12, 1924), p. 14; *PE* 543 (April 19, 1924), p. 12; *PE* 545 (May 3, 1924), pp. 8, 12; *PE* 547 (May 17, 1924), pp. 11, 13; *PE* 549 (June 7, 1924), p. 12; *PE* 550 (June 14, 1924), pp. 10, 12, and 13; *PE* 551 (June 21, 1924), pp. 9, 12; *PE* 552 (June 28, 1924), pp. 9, 10, 11, and 12; *PE* 553 (July 5 1924), pp. 9, 11, and 12; *PE* 555 (July 19, 1924), p. 3; *PE* 556 (July 26, 1924), p. 12; PE 557 (August 2, 1924), p. 12; *PE* 558 (August 9, 1924), pp. 11, 12, and 13; *PE* 559 (August 16, 1924), pp. 9, 11, and 12; *PE* 560 (August 23, 1924), pp. 11, 12; *PE* 561 (August 30, 1924), pp. 12, 14; *PE* 562 (September 6, 1924), p. 12; *PE* 563 (September 13, 1924), pp. 9, 12; *PE* 564 (September 20, 1924), pp. 12, 14; *PE* 565 (September 27, 1924), pp. 12, 13; *PE* 566 (October 4, 1924), pp. 8, 9, 11, 12, and 13; *PE* 567 (October 11, 1924), p. 12; *PE* 568 (October 18, 1924), pp. 10, 12, and 13; *PE* 569 (October 25, 1924), pp. 12, 13; *PE* 570 (November 1, 1924), p. 12; *PE* 571 (November 8, 1924), pp. 12, 13; *PE* 572 (November 15, 1924), pp. 9, 12, and 13; *PE* 573 (November 22, 1924), p. 12; *PE* 574 (November 29, 1924), p. 28; *PE* 575 (December 6, 1924), p. 13; *PE* 576 (December 13, 1924), pp. 11, 13; *PE* 578 (January 3, 1925), pp. 12, 13; *PE* 579 (January 10, 1925), p. 12; *PE* 580 (January 17, 1925), p. 10, 12; *PE* 584 (February 14, 1925), pp. 10, 12; *PE* 585 (February 21, 1925), pp. 12, 13; *PE* 586 (February 28, 1925), pp. 12, 14; *PE* 587 (March 7, 1925), p. 12; *PE* 589 (March 21, 1925), pp. 10, 12; *PE* 590 (March 28, 1925), p. 13; *PE* 591 (April 4, 1925), pp. 11, 12; *PE* 592 (April 11, 1925), p. 12; *PE* 593 (April 18, 1925), p. 13; *PE* 594 (April 25, 1925), p. 12; *PE* 595 (May 2, 1925), p. 13; *PE* 596 (May 9, 1925), p. 12; *PE* 597 (May 16, 1925), p. 12; *PE* 598 (May 23, 1925), p. 12; *PE* 599 (May 30, 1925), p. 13; *PE* 600 (June 6, 1925), pp. 13, 14; *PE* 601 (June 13, 1925), p. 13; *PE* 602 (June 20, 1925), p. 13; *PE* 603 (June 27, 1925), p. 13; *PE* 604 (July 4, 1925), p. 13; *PE* 605 (July 11, 1925), pp. 9, 13; *PE* 606 (July 18, 1925), p. 13; *PE* 607 (July 26, 1925), p. 12; *PE* 608 (August 1, 1925), p. 12; *PE* 609 (August 8, 1925), p. 13; *PE* 610 (August 15, 1925), pp. 7, 11, 12; *PE* 611 (August 22, 1925), pp. 9, 12; *PE* 612 (August 29, 1925), pp. 10, 12; *PE* 613 (September 5, 1925), pp. 11, 12, and 13; *PE* 614 (September 12, 1925), pp. 11, 12; *PE* 615 (September 19, 1925), pp. 10, 12, and 13; *PE* 616 (September 26, 1925), pp. 12, 13; *PE* 618 (October 17, 1925), pp. 12, 13; *PE* 619 (October 24, 1925), p. 16; *PE* 620 (October 31, 1925), p. 12; *PE* 621 (November 7, 1925), pp. 10, 12; *PE* 622 (November 14, 1925), p. 16; *PE* 625 (December 5, 1925), p. 18; *PE* 626 (December 12, 1925), p. 12; *PE* 627 (December 19, 1925), p. 12; *PE* 628 (January 2, 1926), p. 6; *PE* 629 (January 9, 1926), pp. 6, 7, and 12; *PE* 630 (January 16, 1926), p. 10; *PE* 631 (January 23, 1926), p. 12; *PE* 632 (January 30, 1926), p. 12; *PE* 635 (February 20, 1926), pp. 10, 12; *PE* 636 (February 27, 1926), p. 13; *PE* 638 (March 13, 1926), pp. 12, 13; *PE* 639 (March 20, 1926), p. 7; *PE* 640 (March 27, 1926), p. 13; *PE* 642 (April 10, 1926), p. 12; *PE* 643 (April 17, 1926), pp. 11, 12; *PE* 644 (April 24, 1926), p. 13; *PE* 645 (May 1, 1926), pp. 11, 13; *PE* 646 (May 8, 1926), p. 10; *PE* 647 (May 15, 1926), p. 12; *PE* 648 (May 22, 1926), pp. 11, 12, and 13; *PE* 649 (May 29, 1926), pp. 10, 11, and 13; *PE* 650 (June 5, 1926), pp. 5, 7, 10, and 12; *PE* 652 (June 19, 1926), pp. 11, 13; *PE* 653 (June 26, 1926), pp. 11, 12; *PE* 654 (July 3, 1926), pp. 10, 12; *PE* 655 (July 10, 1926), pp. 17, 20, and 21; *PE* 656 (July 17, 1926), pp. 11, 12, and 13; *PE* 657 (July 24, 1926), pp. 8, 9, 11, 12, and 13; *PE* 658 (July 31, 1926), pp. 11, 12; *PE* 659 (August 7, 1926), pp. 11, and 12; *PE* 660 (August 14, 1926), pp. 10, 13; *PE* 661 (August 21, 1926), pp. 10, 12, 13, and 14; *PE* 662 (August 28, 1926), pp. 5, 12, and 13; *PE* 663 (September 4, 1926), pp. 3, 5, and 12; *PE* 664 (September

11, 1926), pp. 12, 13; *PE* 665 (September 18, 1926), pp. 3, 12, 13, and 14; *PE* 666 (September 25, 1926), pp. 5, 11, 12, and 13; *PE* 667 (October 2, 1926), pp. 11, 12, and 13; *PE* 668 (October 9, 1926), p. 12, 14; *PE* 669 (October 23, 1926), pp. 5, 8, 9, 10, 11, and 12; *PE* 670 (October 30, 1926), p. 12; *PE* 671 (November 6, 1926), pp. 12, 13; *PE* 672 (November 13, 1926), pp. 12, 13; *PE* 673 (November 20, 1926), pp. 20, 21; *PE* 674 (November 27, 1926), p. 16; *PE* 675 (December 4, 1926), pp. 5, 19, and 20; *PE* 676 (December 11, 1926), p. 12; *PE* 677 (December 18, 1926), p. 12; *PE* 678 (January 1, 1927), pp. 12, 13; *PE* 679 (January 8, 1927), pp. 10, 13; *PE* 681 (January 22, 1927), pp. 4, 6, 12, and 13; *PE* 682 (January 29, 1927), p. 12; *PE* 683 (February 5, 1927), p. 13; *PE* 685 (February 19, 1927), p. 12; *PE* 687 (March 5, 1927), pp. 2, 5, and 20; *PE* 688 (March 12, 1927), pp. 10, 12, and 13; *PE* 690 (March 26, 1927), pp. 18, 20; *PE* 691 (April 2, 1927), pp. 10, 12; *PE* 692 (April 9, 1927), p. 11; *PE* 693 (April 16, 1927), p. 12; *PE* 694 (April 23, 1927), p. 1; *PE* 695 (April 30, 1927), p. 9; *PE* 696 (May 7, 1927), pp. 8, 15; *PE* 698 (May 21, 1927), p. 12; *PE* 699 (May 28, 1927), p. 12; *PE* 700 (June 4, 1927), pp. 9, 10, 12, and 13; *PE* 701 (June 11, 1927), pp. 10, 12; *PE* 702 (June 18, 1927), pp. 10, 2, and 13; *PE* 703 (June 25, 1927), p. 12; *PE* 704 (July 2, 1927), p. 12; *PE* 705 (July 9, 1927), pp. 3, 8, 9, 12, and 13; *PE* 706 (July 16, 1927), pp. 20, 21; *PE* 707 (July 23, 1927), pp. 3, 12; *PE* 708 (July 30, 1927), pp. 8, 9, 11, and 12; *PE* 709 (August 6, 1927), pp. 4, 5, 17, 18, 19, 20, and 21; *PE* 710 (August 13, 1927), pp. 8, 10, 11, and 12; *PE* 711 (August 20, 1927), p. 12; *PE* 712 (August 27, 1927), pp. 11, 12; *PE* 713 (September 3, 1927), pp. 11, 12, and 13; *PE* 714 (September 10, 1927), pp. 11, 12, 13, and 15; *PE* 715 (September 17, 1927), pp. 8, 12; *PE* 716 (September 24, 1927), pp. 9, 12, and 13; *PE* 717 (October 8, 1927), pp. 10, 12; *PE* 718 (October 15, 1927), pp. 20, 21; *PE* 719 (October 22, 1927), p. 12; *PE* 720 (October 29, 1927), p. 20; *PE* 721 (November 5, 1927), p. 12; *PE* 722 (November 12, 1927), p. 12; *PE* 723 (November 19, 1927), p. 12; *PE* 725 (December 3, 1927), pp. 20, 21; *PE* 726 (December 10, 1927), p. 20; *PE* 727 (December 17, 1927), pp. 10, 12; *PE* 728 (December 24, 1927), pp. 12, 13; *PE* 729 (January 7, 1928), pp. 4, 12; *PE* 731 (January 21, 1928), p. 19; *PE* 732 (January 28, 1928), p. 12; *PE* 733 (February 4, 1928), pp. 10, 12; *PE* 734 (February 11, 1928), p. 13; *PE* 735 (February 18, 1928), pp. 3, 11, 12; *PE* 736 (February 25, 1928), pp. 12, 13 *PE* 736 (February 25, 1928), pp. 12, 13; *PE* 737 (March 3, 1928), p. 12; *PE* 738 (March 10, 1928), pp. 12, 13; *PE* 741 (March 31, 1928), pp. 12, 13; *PE* 742 (April 7, 1928), pp. 12, 13; *PE* 743 (April 14, 1928), p. 12; *PE* 744 (April 21, 1928), p. 12; *PE* 745 (April 28, 1928), p. 12; *PE* 746 (May 5, 1928), pp. 11, 12; *PE* 748 (May 19, 1928), p. 2; *PE* 749 (May 26, 1928), p. 12; *PE* 750 (June 2, 1928), p. 12; *PE* 751 (June 9, 1928), pp. 12, 13; *PE* 752 (June 16, 1928), p. 12; *PE* 754 (June 30, 1928), pp. 9, 12, 13; *PE* 755 (July 7, 1928), pp. 14, 15, and 16; *PE* 756 (July 21, 1928), pp. 8, 12, and 16; *PE* 757 (July 28, 1928), p. 12; *PE* 758 (August 4, 1928), pp. 5, 12; *PE* 759 (August 11, 1928), pp. 3, 12; *PE* 760 (August 18, 1928), pp. 10, 11, and 12; *PE* 761 (August 25, 1928), pp. 12, 13; *PE* 762 (September 1, 1928), p. 12; *PE* 763 (September 8, 1928), pp. 9, 11, 12, and 13; *PE* 764 (September 15, 1928), pp. 12, 13; *PE* 765 (September 22, 1928), pp. 12, 13; *PE* 766 (September 29, 1928), p. 16; *PE* 767 (October 6, 1928), pp. 11, 12; *PE* 768 (October 13, 1928), pp. 12, 13; *PE* 769 (October 20, 1928), pp. 11, 12; *PE* 770 (October 27, 1928), pp. 5, 12, and 13; *PE* 771 (November 3, 1928), pp. 11, 12; *PE* 772 (November 10, 1928), p. 12; *PE* 773 (November 17, 1928), p. 19, 20, and 21; *PE* 774 (November 24, 1928), pp. 10, 12; *PE* 775 (December 1, 1928), p. 19; *PE* 777 (December 15, 1928), p. 12; *PE* 778 (December 22, 1928), pp. 12, 13; *PE* 779 (January 5, 1929), pp. 5, 11; *PE* 780 (January 12, 1929), pp. 10, 12, and 13; *PE* 781 (January 19, 1929), p. 12; *PE* 782 (January 26, 1929), p. 12; *PE* 785 (February 16, 1929), p. 12; *PE* 786 (February 23, 1929), p. 10; *PE* 788 (March 9, 1929), pp. 11, 12; *PE* 789 (March 16, 1929), pp. 11, 12; *PE* 792 (April 6, 1929), pp. 11, 13; *PE* 793 (April 13, 1929), pp. 12, 13; *PE* 794 (April 20, 1929), pp. 10, 12; *PE* 796 (May 4, 1929), pp. 9, 12; *PE* 797 (May 11, 1929), pp. 11, 12; *PE* 798 (May 18, 1929), pp. 12, 13, and 14; *PE* 799 (May 25, 1929), p. 12; *PE* 800 (June 1, 1929), p. 12; *PE* 802 (June 15, 1929), pp. 14, 16; *PE* 803 (June 22, 1929), p. 12; *PE* 804 (June 29, 1929), p. 16; *PE* 805 (July 6, 1929), pp. 12, 13; *PE* 806 (July 13, 1929), p. 12; *PE* 807 (July 20, 1929), p. 12; *PE* 808 (July 27, 1929), p. 14; *PE* 809 (August 3, 1929), p. 12; *PE* 810 (August 10, 1929), pp. 6, 12, and 13; *PE* 811 (August 17, 1929), pp. 11, 12; *PE* 812 (August 24, 1929), pp. 11, 12; *PE* 813 (August 31, 1929), pp. 12, 13; *PE* 814 (September 7, 1929), p. 12; *PE* 815 (September 14, 1929), p. 12; *PE* 816 (September 21, 1929), p. 12; *PE* 817 (October 5, 1929), p. 12; *PE* 818 (October 12, 1929), pp. 16, 17, and 18; *PE* 819 (October 19, 1929), p. 12; *PE* 820 (October 26, 1929), p. 16; *PE* 821 (November 2, 1929), pp. 10, 12; *PE* 822 (November 9, 1929), p. 12; *PE* 823 (November 16, 1929), p. 12; *PE* 824 (November 23, 1929), pp. 5, 6, and 20; *PE* 826 (December 7, 1929), p. 17; *PE* 829 (January 4, 1930), pp. 11, 12; *PE* 830 (January 11, 1930), p. 12; *PE* 833 (February 1, 1930), p. 13; *PE* 835 (February 15, 1930), pp. 10, 12; *PE* 836 (February 22, 1930), p. 12; *PE* 837 (March 1, 1930), p. 11; *PE* 838 (March 8, 1930), p. 12; *PE* 839 (March 15, 1930), p. 11; *PE* 840 (March 22, 1930), pp. 12, 13; *PE* 841 (March 29, 1930), p. 12; *PE* 842 (April 5, 1930), pp. 18, 19; *PE* 843 (April 12, 1930), p. 12; *PE* 844 (April 19, 1930), p. 12; *PE* 851 (June 7, 1930), p. 12; *PE* 852 (June 14, 1930), pp. 12, 13; *PE* 853 (June 21, 1930), p. 12; *PE* 854 (June 28,

1930), pp. 10, 12; *PE* 855 (July 5, 1930), p. 11; *PE* 856 (July 12, 1930), p. 11; *PE* 857 (July 19, 1930), p. 12; *PE* 858 (July 26, 1930), pp. 11, 12, and 13; *PE* 859 (August 2, 1930), pp. 5, 12; *PE* 860 (August 9, 1930), p. 12; *PE* 861 (August 16, 1930), pp. 9, 12; *PE* 862 (August 23, 1930), pp. 10, 12, and 13; *PE* 863 (August 30, 1930), pp. 11, 12; *PE* 864 (September 6, 1930), pp. 10, 12, and 14; *PE* 865 (September 13, 1930), p. 12; *PE* 866 (September 27, 1930), p. 12; *PE* 867 (October 4, 1930), pp. 10, 11, and 12; *PE* 868 (October 11, 1930), pp. 9, 11, 12, and 13; *PE* 869 (October 18, 1930), pp. 12, 13; *PE* 870 (October 25, 1930), pp. 10, 12; *PE* 871 (November 1, 1930), pp. 10, 12, and 13; *PE* 872 (November 8, 1930), p. 12; *PE* 873 (November 15, 1930), pp. 16, 17; *PE* 874 (November 22, 1930), p. 20; *PE* 875 (November 29, 1930), pp. 20, 21; *PE* 877 (December 13, 1930), pp. 5, 11, and 12; *PE* 878 (December 20, 1930), p. 12; *PE* 879 (January 3, 1931), p. 12; *PE* 880 (January 10, 1931), pp. 6, 7, 9, 11, and 12; *PE* 881 (January 17, 1931), p. 12; *PE* 883 (January 31, 1931), p. 12; *PE* 884 (February 7, 1931), pp. 11, 12; *PE* 886 (February 21, 1931), p. 10; *PE* 887 (February 28, 1931), p. 10; *PE* 888 (March 7, 1931), p. 13; *PE* 889 (March 14, 1931), p. 13; *PE* 890 (March 21, 1931), p. 3; *PE* 891 (March 28, 1931), p. 11; *PE* 892 (April 4, 1931), p. 11; *PE* 894 (April 18, 1931), p. 12; *PE* 896 (May 2, 1931), p. 12; *PE* 897 (May 9, 1931), p. 11; *PE* 898 (May 16, 1931), pp. 11, 12, and 13; *PE* 900 (May 30, 1931), p. 12; *PE* 901 (June 6, 1931), pp. 12, 13; *PE* 902 (June 13, 1931), p. 16; *PE* 903 (June 20, 1931), p. 13; *PE* 905 (July 4, 1931), p. 12; *PE* 907 (July 18, 1931), p. 13; *PE* 909 (August 1, 1931), pp. 10, 11; *PE* 910 (August 8, 1931), p. 12; *PE* 911 (August 15, 1931), p. 13; *PE* 912 (August 22, 1931), pp. 10, 13; *PE* 914 (September 5, 1931), pp. 1, 7, 14, 15, and 16; *PE* 915 (September 12, 1931), pp. 5, 14, 15, and 16; *PE* 916 (September 26, 1931), pp. 8, 15, and 17; *PE* 917 (October 3, 1931), p. 16; *PE* 918 (October 10, 1931), pp. 15, 16; *PE* 919 (October 17, 1931), pp. 15, 17, and 18; *PE* 920 (October 24, 1931), p. 14; *PE* 921 (October 31, 1931), pp. 13, 16; *PE* 922 (November 7, 1931), p. 16; *PE* 923 (November 14, 1931), p. 17; *PE* 925 (November 28, 1931), p. 20; and *PE* 928 (December 19, 1931), p. 10.

Appendix R

Pentecostal Evangel

References to 'immersed':

PE 2.19 (May 9, 1914), p. 6; *PE* 50 (July 18, 1914), p. 3; *PE* 67 (November 14, 1914), p. 1; *PE* 96 (June 26, 1915), p. 1; *PE* 101 (July 31, 1915), p. 1; *PE* 102 (August 7, 1915), p. 1; *PE* 104 (August 21, 1915), p. 3; *PE* 113 (October 30, 1915), p. 1; *PE* 156 (September 9, 1916), p. 11; *PE* 170 (December 23, 1916), p. 12; *PE* 172 (January 13, 1917), p. 16; *PE* 173 (January 20, 1917), p. 14; *PE* 201 (August 4, 1917), p. 16; *PE* 204 (August 25, 1917), p. 16; *PE* 207 (September 15, 1917), p. 12; *PE* 215 (November 17, 1917), p. 12; *PE* 219 (December 15, 1917), p. 14; *PE* 240/241 (May 18, 1918), p. 11; *PE* 250/251 (August 10, 1918), p. 14; *PE* 278/279 (March 8, 1919), p. 10; *PE* 296/297 (July 12, 1919), p. 6; *PE* 300/301 (August 9, 1919), p. 11; *PE* 306/307 (September 20, 1919), pp. 10, 11; *PE* 316/317 (November 29, 1919), p. 13; *PE* 322/323 (January 10, 1920), p. 13; *PE* 334/335 (April 13, 1920), p. 13; *PE* 338/339 (May 1, 1920), p. 13; *PE* 354/355 (August 21, 1920), p. 14; *PE* 356/357 (September 4, 1920), p. 9; *PE* 392/393 (May 14, 1921), p. 14; *PE* 412/413 (October 1, 1921), p. 15; *PE* 414/415 (October 15, 1921), p. 12; *PE* 448/449 (June 10, 1922), p. 14; *PE* 452/453 (July 8, 1922), pp. 9, 14; *PE* 468/469 (October 28, 1922), p. 13; *PE* 476/477 (December 23, 1922), p. 14; *PE* 486/487 (March 3, 1923), p. 16; *PE* 512 (September 1, 1923), p. 11; *PE* 517 (October 13, 1923), p. 11; *PE* 524 (December 1, 1923), p. 26; *PE* 535 (February 23, 1924), p. 13; *PE* 542 (April 12, 1924), p. 14; *PE* 548 (May 24, 1924), p. 10; *PE* 551 (June 21, 1924), p. 12; *PE* 552 (June 28, 1924), p. 10; *PE* 559 (August 16, 1924), p. 12; *PE* 586 (February 28, 1925), p. 12; *PE* 602 (June 20, 1925), p. 13; *PE* 605 (July 11, 1925), p. 12; *PE* 608 (August 1, 1925), p. 10; *PE* 609 (August 8, 1925), p. 9; *PE* 613 (September 5, 1925), p. 12; *PE* 614 (September 12, 1925), p. 12; *PE* 625 (December 5, 1925), p. 18; *PE* 656 (July 17, 1926), p. 11; *PE* 671 (November 6, 1926), p. 13; *PE* 676 (December 11, 1926), p. 13; *PE* 681 (January 22, 1927), p. 6; *PE* 684 (February 12, 1927), p. 12; *PE* 690 (March 26, 1927), p. 20; *PE* 700 (June 4, 1927), p. 12; *PE* 708 (July 30, 1927), p. 12; *PE* 717 (October 8, 1927), pp. 10, 12; *PE* 720 (October 29, 1927), p. 20; *PE* 729 (January 7, 1928), p. 4; *PE* 735 (February 18, 1928), p. 9; *PE* 745 (April 28, 1928), p. 11; *PE* 754 (June 30, 1928), p. 10; *PE* 758 (August 4, 1928), p. 11; *PE* 764 (September 15, 1928), p. 11; *PE* 766 (September 29, 1928), p. 15; *PE* 786 (February 23, 1929), p. 10; *PE* 793 (April 13, 1929), p. 10; *PE* 795 (April 27, 1929), p. 10; *PE* 798 (May 18, 1929), p. 12; *PE* 805 (July 6, 1929), p. 13; *PE* 806 (July 13, 1929), p. 12; *PE* 810 (August 10, 1929), p. 12; *PE* 811 (August 17, 1929),

p. 12; *PE* 816 (September 21, 1929), p. 12; *PE* 821 (November 2, 1929), pp. 10-11; *PE* 829 (January 4, 1930), p. 12; *PE* 837 (March 1, 1930), p. 11; *PE* 842 (April 5, 1930), p. 13; *PE* 843 (April 12, 1930), p. 12; *PE* 855 (July 5, 1930), p. 13; *PE* 856 (July 12, 1930), pp. 11, 12, and 14; *PE* 857 (July 19, 1930), p. 12; *PE* 858 (July 26, 1930), p. 12; *PE* 860 (August 9, 1930), p. 12; *PE* 861 (August 16, 1930), p. 12; *PE* 862 (August 23, 1930), pp. 12, 13; *PE* 863 (August 30, 1930), p. 12; *PE* 864 (September 6, 1930), p. 12; *PE* 865 (September 13, 1930), pp. 10, 12; *PE* 866 (September 27, 1930), p. 12; *PE* 867 (October 4, 1930), pp. 10, 12; *PE* 868 (October 11, 1930), pp. 11, 12; *PE* 869 (October 18, 1930), pp. 12, 13; *PE* 870 (October 25, 1930), p. 12; *PE* 871 (November 1, 1930), p. 12; *PE* 873 (November 15, 1930), p. 16; *PE* 875 (November 29, 1930), p. 19; *PE* 887 (February 28, 1931), p. 13; *PE* 890 (March 21, 1931), p. 16; *PE* 892 (April 4, 1931), pp. 12, 13; *PE* 893 (April 11, 1931), p. 12; *PE* 895 (April 25, 1931), p. 12; *PE* 896 (May 2, 1931), p. 11; *PE* 899 (May 23, 1931), p. 12; *PE* 900 (May 30, 1931), p. 12; and *PE* 927 (December 12, 1931), p. 13.

Appendix S

Pentecostal Evangel

References to 'Burial Language':

'Buried with Christ in baptism (Matt. 28:19)';[140] 'buried in baptism';[141] 'buried by baptism';[142]

---

[140] *PE* 286/287 (May 3, 1919), p. 15; *PE* 294/295 (Jun 28, 1919), p. 10; *PE* 296/297 (Jul 12, 1919), pp. 11, 14; *PE* 298/299 (Jul 26, 1919), p. 14; *PE* 300/301 (Aug 9, 1919), p. 14; *PE* 302/303 (Aug 23, 1919), p. 14; *PE* 304/305 (Sep 6, 1919), pp. 10, 11; *PE* 308/309 (Oct 4, 1919), p. 12; *PE* 310/311 (Oct 18, 1919), p. 12; *PE* 352/353 (Aug 7, 1920), p. 14; *PE* 366/367 (Nov 13, 1920), p. 9; *PE* 392/393 (May 14, 1921), p. 9; *PE* 442/443 (Apr 29, 1922), p. 15; *PE* 452/453 (Jul 8, 1922), p. 9; *PE* 456/457 (Aug 5, 1922), p. 9; *PE* 456/457 (Aug 5, 1922), p. 12; *PE* 462/463 (Sep 16, 1922), p. 10; *PE* 488/489 (Mar 17, 1923), p. 14; *PE* 498 (May 26, 1923), pp. 10, 11; *PE* 500 (Jun 9, 1923), p. 10; *PE* 506 (Jul 21, 1923), pp. 10, 11; *PE* 509 (Aug 11, 1923), pp. 10, 11; *PE* 513 (Sep 8, 1923), p. 11; *PE* 516 (Oct 6, 1923), p. 10; *PE* 521 (Nov 10, 1923), pp. 8, 11; *PE* 531 (Jan 26, 1924), p. 12; *PE* 545 (May 3, 1924), p. 13; *PE* 556 (Jul 26, 1924), p. 12; *PE* 613 (Sep 5, 1925), p. 12; *PE* 667 (Oct 2, 1926), p. 13; *PE* 668 (Oct 9, 1926), p. 10; *PE* 714 (Sep 10, 1927), pp. 12, 15; *PE* 729 (Jan 7, 1928), p. 4; *PE* 740 (Mar 24, 1928), p. 13; *PE* 741 (Mar 31, 1928), p. 11; *PE* 758 (Aug 4, 1928), p. 11; *PE* 762 (Sep 1, 1928), p. 12; *PE* 763 (Sep 8, 1928), p. 11; *PE* 788 (Mar 9, 1929), p. 12; *PE* 797 (May 11, 1929), p. 12; *PE* 800 (Jun 1, 1929), p. 12; *PE* 803 (Jun 22, 1929), p. 12; *PE* 810 (Aug 10, 1929), p. 10; *PE* 821 (Nov 2, 1929), p. 10; *PE* 823 (Nov 16, 1929), p. 12; *PE* 831 (Jan 18, 1930), p. 11; *PE* 863 (Aug 30, 1930), p. 12; *PE* 867 (Oct 4, 1930), pp. 10, 12; *PE* 868 (Oct 11, 1930), p. 13; *PE* 869 (Oct 18, 1930), pp. 12, 13; *PE* 871 (Nov 1, 1930), p. 12; *PE* 877 (Dec 13, 1930), p. 12; *PE* 887 (Feb 28, 1931), pp. 10, 12; *PE* 897 (May 9, 1931), p. 12; *PE* 898 (May 16, 1931), p. 11; *PE* 901 (Jun 6, 1931), p. 13; *PE* 902 (Jun 13, 1931), p. 16; *PE* 905 (Jul 4, 1931), p. 12; *PE* 906 (Jul 11, 1931), p. 13; *PE* 909 (Aug 1, 1931), p. 10; *PE* 913 (Aug 29, 1931), p. 9; *PE* 914 (Sep 5, 1931), p. 16; *PE* 916 (Sep 26, 1931), p. 15; *PE* 918 (Oct 10, 1931), pp. 15, 16, and 18; *PE* 919 (Oct 17, 1931), pp. 17, 18; *PE* 920 (Oct 24, 1931), pp. 13, 14; *PE* 921 (Oct 31, 1931), p. 16; *PE* 922 (Nov 7, 1931), p. 16; *PE* 923 (Nov 14, 1931), p. 16; *PE* 924 (Nov 21, 1931), p. 19; and *PE* 926 (Dec 5, 1931), p. 18.

[141] *PE* 49 (Jul 11, 1914), p. 3; *PE* 300/301 (Aug 9, 1919), p. 8; *PE* 306/307 (Sep 20, 1919), p. 14; *PE* 491 (Apr 7, 1923), pp. 12-13; *PE* 493 (Apr 21, 1923), p. 10; *PE* 512 (Sep 1, 1923), p. 11; *PE* 557 (Aug 2, 1924), p. 13; *PE* 876 (Dec 6, 1930), p. 16; *PE* 901 (Jun 6, 1931), p. 12; *PE* 909 (Aug 1, 1931), p. 10; *PE* 911 (Aug 15, 1931), p. 13; *PE* 917 (Oct 3, 1931), pp. 16, 17; *PE* 918 (Oct 10, 1931), p. 16; *PE* 919 (Oct 17, 1931), p. 18; *PE* 920 (Oct 24, 1931), p. 13; *PE* 921 (Oct 31, 1931), p. 16; and *PE* 922 (Nov 7, 1931), p. 16.

[142] *PE* 464/465 (Sep 30, 1922), p. 11; *PE* 466/467 (Oct 14, 1922), p. 8; *PE* 597 (May 16, 1925), p. 12; *PE* 619 (Oct 24, 1925), p. 17; *PE* 721 (Nov 5, 1927), p. 10; *PE* 829 (Jan 4, 1930), p. 13; *PE* 871 (Nov 1, 1930), p. 12; and *PE* 891 (Mar 28, 1931), p. 11.

'buried in water' or 'buried in the waters of baptism';[143] 'buried in the watery grave' or 'baptized in the water grave';[144] 'buried with Jesus in water baptism';[145] 'buried with the Lord Jesus';[146] 'buried into His death';[147] 'baptized' or 'buried with our Lord';[148] 'followed the Lord into the watery grave';[149] 'buried with Christ in the watery grave';[150] 'buried with our Lord in the liquid grave';[151] 'buried with our Lord by baptism';[152] 'buried with the Master in water baptism';[153] 'buried with the Lord in baptism';[154] 'buried them in water baptism';[155] 'buried with Him in water baptism' or 'buried with Him in the waters of baptism';[156] 'buried with Christ in water' or 'buried with Christ';[157] 'buried beneath the waters of baptism';[158] 'buried as in Romans 6:4';[159] 'buried into the likeness of His death';[160] 'buried with the Lord

---

[143] *PE* 567 (Oct 11, 1924), p. 12; *PE* 580 (Jan 17, 1925), p. 9; *PE* 601 (Jun 13, 1925), p. 13; *PE* 669 (Oct 23, 1926), p. 9; *PE* 730 (Jan 14, 1928), p. 13; *PE* 742 (Apr 7, 1928), p. 12; *PE* 756 (Jul 21, 1928), p. 12; *PE* 767 (Oct 6, 1928), p. 12; *PE* 779 (Jan 5, 1929), p. 11; *PE* 803 (Jun 22, 1929), p. 12; *PE* 822 (Nov 9, 1929), p. 12; and *PE* 832 (Jan 25, 1930), p. 12.

[144] *PE* 288/289 (May 17, 1919), p. 7; *PE* 422/423 (Dec 10, 1921), p. 28; *PE* 488/489 (Mar 17, 1923), p. 14; *PE* 904 (Jun 27, 1931), p. 19; and *PE* 926 (Dec 5, 1931), p. 19.

[145] *PE* 585 (Feb 21, 1925), p. 13

[146] *PE* 861 (Aug 16, 1930), p. 9; *PE* 915 (Sep 12, 1931), pp. 15, 16.

[147] *PE* 595 (May 2, 1925), p. 13.

[148] *PE* 312/313 (Nov 1, 1919), p. 23; *PE* 452/453 (Jul 8, 1922), p. 4; and *PE* 669 (Oct 23, 1926), p. 8.

[149] *PE* 901 (Jun 6, 1931), p. 13; *PE* 911 (Aug 15, 1931), p. 13; and *PE* 918 (Oct 10, 1931), p. 15.

[150] *PE* 508 (Aug 4, 1923), p. 13; *PE* 868 (Oct 11, 1930), p. 11; *PE* 870 (Oct 25, 1930), p. 12; *PE* 880 (Jan 10, 1931), p. 12; *PE* 916 (Sep 26, 1931), p. 16; and *PE* 917 (Oct 3, 1931), p. 18.

[151] *PE* 759 (Aug 11, 1928), p. 12.

[152] *PE* 530 (Jan 19, 1924), p. 13; *PE* 536 (Mar 8, 1924), p. 13.

[153] *PE* 758 (Aug 4, 1928), p. 12.

[154] *PE* 334/335 (Apr 13, 1920), p. 14; *PE* 495 (May 5, 1923), p. 14; *PE* 564 (Sep 20, 1924), p. 14; *PE* 586 (Feb 28, 1925), p. 12; *PE* 590 (Mar 28, 1925), p. 12; *PE* 607 (Jul 26, 1925), p. 12; *PE* 667 (Oct 2, 1926), p. 13; *PE* 708 (Jul 30, 1927), p. 12; *PE* 814 (Sep 7, 1929), p. 12; *PE* 839 (Mar 15, 1930), p. 11; and *PE* 909 (Aug 1, 1931), p. 10.

[155] *PE* 288/289 (May 17, 1919), p. 14; *PE* 406/407 (Aug 20, 1921), p. 12; *PE* 474/475 (Dec 9, 1922), p. 10; *PE* 513 (Sep 8, 1923), p. 10; and *PE* 518 (Oct 20, 1923), p. 13.

[156] *PE* 292/293 (Jun 14, 1919), p. 9; *PE* 298/299 (Jul 26, 1919), p. 10; *PE* 310/311 (Oct 18, 1919), p. 14; *PE* 338/339 (May 1, 1920), p. 13; *PE* 350/351 (Jul 24, 1920), p. 14; *PE* 478/479 (Jan 6, 1923), p. 10; *PE* 495 (May 5, 1923), p. 14; *PE* 521 (Nov 10, 1923), p. 13; *PE* 568 (Oct 18, 1924), p. 12; *PE* 571 (Nov 8, 1924), p. 12; *PE* 614 (Sep 12, 1925), p. 12; *PE* 615 (Sep 19, 1925), p. 13; *PE* 616 (Sep 26, 1925), p. 12; *PE* 632 (Jan 30, 1926), p. 10; *PE* 655 (Jul 10, 1926), p. 20; *PE* 662 (Aug 28, 1926), p. 14; *PE* 856 (Jul 12, 1930), p. 11; and *PE* 910 (Aug 8, 1931), p. 12.

[157] *PE* 559 (Aug 16, 1924), p. 7; *PE* 566 (Oct 4, 1924), p. 12; *PE* 590 (Mar 28, 1925), p. 13; *PE* 607 (Jul 26, 1925), p. 12; *PE* 610 (Aug 15, 1925), p. 11; *PE* 640 (Mar 27, 1926), p. 10; *PE* 656 (Jul 17, 1926), p. 12; *PE* 687 (Mar 5, 1927), p. 19; *PE* 720 (Oct 29, 1927), p. 20; *PE* 816 (Sep 21, 1929), p. 12; *PE* 900 (May 30, 1931), p. 12; and *PE* 912 (Aug 22, 1931), p. 13.

[158] *PE* 513 (Sep 8, 1923), p. 15.

[159] *PE* 49 (Jul 11, 1914), p. 3.

[160] *PE* 506 (Jul 21, 1923), p. 10.

in water';[161] 'buried into death with Christ by baptism';[162] 'baptized or buried with Christ in immersion';[163] 'we buried "them" in the waters of a running brook in the likeness of the death';[164] 'went through the water';[165] 'buried in Christian baptism';[166] 'Followed the Lord in Christian baptism' or 'received Christian baptism';[167] 'the ordinance of baptism was administered';[168] 'baptized in the name of the Lord Jesus Christ[169] 'followed their Lord in this way';[170] 'followed the Lord' and 'followed Christ' in baptism';[171] 'followed the Maste';[172] 'followed Jesus in water baptism';[173] and 'followed the Saviour in baptism'.[174]

Appendix T

Bridal Call/Bridal Call Foursquare, Foursquare Crusader
Geographical locations of water baptism services:
California
Huntington Park;[175] Lamar;[176] Long Beach;[177] Los Angeles (Angelus Temple);[178]

---

[161] *PE* 572 (Nov 15, 1924), p. 12.
[162] *PE* 584 (Feb 14, 1925), p. 12.
[163] *PE* 868 (Oct 11, 1930), p. 12; *PE* 920 (Oct 24, 1931), p. 14.
[164] *PE* 755 (Jul 7, 1928), p. 15.
[165] *PE* 549 (Jun 7, 1924), p. 13.
[166] *PE* 896 (May 2, 1931), p. 12; *PE* 900 (May 30, 1931), p. 12; and *PE* 923 (Nov 14, 1931), p. 16.
[167] *PE* 900 (May 30, 1931), p. 12; *PE* 901 (Jun 6, 1931), pp. 12, 13; *PE* 902 (Jun 13, 1931), p. 16; *PE* 903 (Jun 20, 1931), pp. 12, 13; *PE* 904 (Jun 27, 1931), pp. 19, 20, and 21; *PE* 905 (Jul 4, 1931), p. 12; *PE* 906 (Jul 11, 1931), pp. 12, 13; *PE* 907 (Jul 18, 1931), p. 12; *PE* 908 (Jul 25, 1931), pp. 11, 12; *PE* 909 (Aug 1, 1931), pp. 10, 11; *PE* 910 (Aug 8, 1931), p. 12; *PE* 911 (Aug 15, 1931), p. 12; *PE* 912 (Aug 22, 1931), pp. 11, 12; *PE* 913 (Aug 29, 1931), p. 9; *PE* 916 (Sep 26, 1931), p. 15; *PE* 916 (Sep 26, 1931), p. 17; *PE* 918 (Oct 10, 1931), p. 16, 18; *PE* 920 (Oct 24, 1931), p. 15; *PE* 921 (Oct 31, 1931), p. 13; *PE* 923 (Nov 14, 1931), pp. 16, 17; *PE* 924 (Nov 21, 1931), p. 18; *PE* 925 (Nov 28, 1931), pp. 20, 21; and *PE* 927 (Dec 12, 1931), p. 12.
[168] *PE* 86 (Apr 17, 1915), p. 1.
[169] *PE* 85 (Apr 10, 1915), p. 4.
[170] *PE* 922 (Nov 7, 1931), p. 16.
[171] *PE* 905 (Jul 4, 1931), p. 12; *PE* 906 (Jul 11, 1931), p. 12; *PE* 915 (Sep 12, 1931), p. 15; *PE* 916 (Sep 26, 1931), pp. 6, 8, 15, and 16; *PE* 917 (Oct 3, 1931), pp. 16, 17, and 18; *PE* 918 (Oct 10, 1931), p. 16, 18; *PE* 919 (Oct 17, 1931), pp. 16, 17, and 18; *PE* 920 (Oct 24, 1931), p. 13; *PE* 921 (Oct 31, 1931), pp. 16, 17; *PE* 922 (Nov 7, 1931), p. 16; *PE* 923 (Nov 14, 1931), pp. 16, 17; *PE* 925 (Nov 28, 1931), pp. 17, 20; and *PE* 926 (Dec 5, 1931), p. 20.
[172] *PE* 911 (Aug 15, 1931), p. 13.
[173] *PE* 912 (Aug 22, 1931), p. 10.
[174] *PE* 919 (Oct 17, 1931), p. 16.
[175] *FC* 5.12 (February 11, 1931), p. 4.
[176] *FC* 2.35 (July 23, 1930), p. 5.
[177] *FC* 5.24 (May 7, 1931), p. 2.
[178] *BC* 6.9 (February 1923), p. 18; *BC* 6.12 (May 1923), p. 25; *BC* 7.1 (June 1923), pp. 14-15, 19; *BC* 7.4 (September 1923), p. 14; *BC* 7.6 (November 1923), p. 19; *BCF* 8.4 (September 1924), pp. 19-22; *BCF* 8.6 (November 1924), p. 27; *BCF* 8.8 (January 1925), pp. 22, 23; *BCF* 8.9 (February 1925), p. 28; *BCF*

Oakland;[179] Ontario;[180] Pasadena;[181] Riverside;[182] Salinas;[183] San Bernadino;[184] San Francisco;[185] San Jose;[186] Santa Paula;[187] South Gate;[188] Taft;[189] and Watsonville.[190]

Colorado

Brighton;[191] Denver;[192] and Elbert.[193]

Illinois

Alton;[194] Chicago;[195] and Kewanee.[196]

Iowa

Cedar Rapids;[197] East Des Moines;[198] and Muscatine.[199]

Michigan

New Baltimore.[200]

Texas

Dallas.[201]

8.10 (March 1925), p. 20; *BCF* 8.11 (April 1925), p. 28; *BCF* 9.3 (August 1925), p. 20; *BCF* 10.4 (September 1926), pp. 26, 32; *BCF* 10.9 (February 1927), p. 26; *BCF* 11.6 (November 1927), p. 27; *BCF* 12.2 (February 1928), p. 20; *BCF* 12.3 (March 1928), pp. 9, 27; *BCF* 12.12 (May 1929), p. 18; *BCF* 14.4 (September 1930), p. 20; *FC* 1.22 (April 23, 1927), p. 2; *FC* 1.25 (May 14, 1927), p. 5; *FC* 1.28 (June 4, 1927), p. 5; *FC* 1.33 (July 9, 1927), pp. 4, 8; *FC* 1.49 (October 26, 1927), p. 4; *FC* 1.51 (November 9, 1927), pp. 3, 5, and 8; *FC* 2.4 (December 4, 1927), pp. 4, 5; *FC* 2.6 (January 4, 1928), p. 5; *FC* 2.7 (January 11, 1928), p. 2; *FC* 2.12 (February 15, 1928), p. 3; *FC* 2.25 (May 23, 1928), p. 3; *FC* 2.35 (July 23, 1930), p. 1; *FC* 3.13 (February 20, 1929), p. 7; *FC* 3.19 (April 3, 1929), p. 2; *FC* 3.23 (May 1, 1929), p. 8; *FC* 3.25 (May 15, 1929), p. 2; *FC* 3.35 (July 24, 1929), p. 1; *FC* 3.46 (October 9, 1929), pp. 5, 14; *FC* 4.18 (March 26, 1930), pp. 2, 7; *FC* 4.23 (April 30, 1930), p. 8; *FC* 5.2 (December 3, 1930), p. 3; *FC* 5.14 (February 25, 1931), p. 5; and *FC* 5.19 (April 1, 1931), p. 9.

[179] *BC* 6.4 (September 1922), p. 10; *FC* 3.13 (February 20, 1929), p. 6.
[180] *FC* 3.18 (March 27, 1929), p. 8.
[181] *FC* 2.24 (May 9, 1928), p. 4.
[182] *FC* 2.25 (May 23, 1928), p. 7; *FC* 5.23 (April 29, 1931), p. 2.
[183] *BC* 5.10 (March 1922), p. 12.
[184] *FC* 5.36 (July 29, 1931), p. 5.
[185] *BC* 2.11 (April 1919), p. 15.
[186] *BC* 5.4 (September 1921), p. 11; *BC* 5.5 (October 1921), pp. 7, 8-9.
[187] *FC* 5.23 (April 29, 1931), p. 5.
[188] *FC* 4.18 (March 26, 1930), p. 2.
[189] *FC* 1.35 (July 23, 1927), p. 8.
[190] *FC* 6.8 (December 9, 1931), p. 5.
[191] *FC* 5.23 (April 29, 1931), p. 6.
[192] *BC* 6.2, 3 (July and August 1922), pp. 9-10, 13-14; *FC* 5.50B (October 10, 1931), p. 4.
[193] *FC* 2.7 (January 11, 1928), p. 8.
[194] *BC* 4.4 (September 1920), pp. 7, 9.
[195] *BCF* 11.6 (November 1927), p. 32.
[196] *FC* 6.5 (November 18, 1931), p. 5.
[197] *FC* 6.9 (December 16, 1931), p. 6.
[198] *FC* 6.5 (November 18, 1931), p. 5.
[199] *FC* 2.35 (July 23, 1930), p. 5.
[200] *FC* 5.24 (May 7, 1931), p. 5.
[201] *FC* 3.25 (May 15, 1929), p. 8.

Washington
Vancouver;[202] Snoqualmie.[203]

Wisconsin
Kenosha.[204]

England
London.[205]

Philippines
Antique;[206] Philippine Islands.[207]

---

[202] *FC* 5.12 (February 11, 1931), p. 4.
[203] *FC* 5.18 (March 25, 1931), p. 2.
[204] *FC* 5.50B (October 10, 1931), p. 5.
[205] *FC* 3.35 (July 24, 1929), p. 2.
[206] *FC* 6.11 (December 30, 1931), p. 3.
[207] *FC* 6.8 (December 9, 1931), p. 5; *FC* 6.11 (December 30, 1931), p. 3.

BIBLIOGRAPHY

Early Pentecostal Periodicals

Apostolic Faith (Azusa Street Mission, Los Angeles, CA)
Bridal Call (ICFG, Los Angeles, CA)
Bridal Call Foursquare (ICFG, Los Angeles, CA)
Christian Evangel (AG, Plainfield, IN; Findley, OH)
Church of God Evangel (COG, Cleveland, TN)
Faithful Standard (Church of God, Cleveland, TN)
Foursquare Crusader (ICFG, Los Angeles, CA)
Latter Rain Evangel (Stone Church, Chicago, ILL)
Meat in Due Season (Frank J. Ewart, Los Angeles, CA)
Pentecostal Evangel (AG, Plainfield, IN; Findlay, OH: St. Louis, MO; and Springfield, MO)
Pentecostal Herald (Pentecostal Assemblies of the U.S.A., Chicago, IL)
Pentecostal Holiness Advocate (IPHC, Falcon, NC; Royston, GA; Franklin Springs, GA)
Pentecostal Testimony (William H. Durham, Chicago, IL; Los Angeles, CA)
The Blessed Truth (Daniel C. O. Opperman, Eureka Springs, AR)
The Bridegroom's Messenger (The Pentecostal Mission, Atlanta, GA)
The Good Report (R.E. McAlister and Frank J. Ewart, Ottawa, CA; Los Angeles, CA)
The Pentecost (J.R. Flower, Indianapolis, IN; Kansas City, MO)
The Present Truth (L. V. Roberts, Indianapolis, IN)
The Whole Truth (Justus Bowe, Argenta, AR)
Weekly Evangel (AG, St. Louis, MO; Springfield, MO)
White Wing Messenger (COGOP, Cleveland, TN)
Word and Witness (AG, Malvern, AR; Findley, OH; St. Louis, MO)

Other Works Cited

Adewuya, J.A., *Transformed by Grace: Paul's View of Holiness in Romans 6-8* (Eugene: OR, Cascade Books, 2004).
Ahn, Yongnan Jeon, 'Various Debates in the Contemporary Pentecostal Hermeneutics', *The Spirit & Church* 2.1 (May 2000), pp. 9-52.
Albrecht, Daniel E., 'Pentecostal Spirituality: Looking Through the Lens of Ritual', *Pneuma* 14.2 (1992), pp. 107-25.

—R. Israel, and R. McNally, 'Pentecostals and Hermeneutics: Texts, Rituals and Community', *Pneuma* 15 (1993), pp. 137-61.

—'Pentecostal Spirituality: Ecumenical Potential and Challenge', *Cyberjournal for Pentecostal-Charismatic Research* 2 (July 1997), <http://www. pctii.org/cyberj/cyberj2/albrecht.html>.

—*Rites in the Spirit: A Ritual Approach to Pentecostal/Charismatic Spirituality* (JPTSup 17; Sheffield: Sheffield University Press, 1999).

Alexander, Kimberly Ervin, *Pentecostal Healing: Models in Theology and Practice* (JPTSup 29; Blandford Forum, Dorset, UK; Deo, 2006).

—'The Pentecostal Healing Community', in John Christopher Thomas (ed.), *Toward a Pentecostal Ecclesiology: The Church and the Fivefold Gospel* (Cleveland, TN: CPT Press, 2010), pp. 183-206.

Allison, D.C., 'The Son of God as Israel: A Note on Matthean Christology', *Irish Biblical Studies* 9 (1987), pp. 74-81.

Althouse, Peter, and Robby Waddell, 'The Pentecostals and Their Scriptures', *Pneuma* 38.1-2 (2016), pp. 115-21.

An, H.S., 'Reading Matthew's Account of the Baptism and Temptation of Jesus (Matt. 3:5-4:1) with the Scapegoat Rite on the Day of Atonement (Lev. 16:20-22)', *Canon & Culture* 12.1 (2018), pp. 5-31.

Anderson, Allan, 'To All Points of the Compass': The Azusa Street Revival and Global Pentecostalism', *Enrichment: A Journal for Pentecostal Ministry* 11.2 (2006), pp. 164-72.

Anderson, G., 'Pentecostal Hermeneutics' (Annual Meeting of the Society for Pentecostal Studies, Springfield, MO, 1992).

Archer, K., 'Pentecostal Hermeneutics: Retrospect and Prospect', *JPT* 4.8 (April 1996), pp. 63-81.

—'Early Pentecostal Biblical Interpretation: Blurring the Boundaries' (Annual Meeting of the Society for Pentecostal Studies, Kirkland, WA, Mar 2000).

—'Early Pentecostal Biblical Interpretation', *JPT* 9.1 (2001), pp. 32-70.

—'Nourishment for our Journey: The Pentecostal *Via Salutis* and Sacramental Ordinances', *JPT* 13.1 (2004), pp. 76-96.

—'Pentecostal Story: The Hermeneutical Filter for the Making of Meaning', *Pneuma* 26.1 (Spring 2004), pp. 36-59.

—*A Pentecostal Hermeneutic for the Twenty-First Century: Spirit, Scripture, and Community* (JPTSup 28; London, UK: T&T Clark, 2004; Cleveland, TN; CPT Press, 2nd edn, 2009).

—'Pentecostal Hermeneutics and the Society for Pentecostal Studies: Reading and Hearing in One Spirit and One Accord', *Pneuma* 37.3 (2015), pp. 128–71.

Archer, K., and L. William Oliverio, Jr. (eds.), *Constructive Pneumatological Hermeneutics in Pentecostal Christianity* (New York: Palgrave Macmillan, 2016).

Archer, Melissa, *I Was in the Spirit on the Lord's Day: A Pentecostal Engagement with Worship in the Apocalypse* (Cleveland, TN: CPT Press, 2015).

Arrington, French L., *Christian Doctrine: A Pentecostal Perspective* (3 vols., Cleveland, TN, Pathway, 1992-94).

—'Hermeneutics', in S.M. Burgess and G.B. McGee (eds.), *DPCM* (Grand Rapids: Zondervan, 1988), pp. 376-89.

—'The Use of the Bible by Pentecostals', *Pneuma* 16 (1994), pp. 101-107.

Autry, A.C. 'Dimensions of Hermeneutics in Pentecostal Focus', *JPT* 3 (1993), pp. 29-50.

Baptism, Eucharist, and Ministry, Faith and Order Paper 111 (Geneva: World Council of Churches, 1982).

Barrett, C.K., *The Epistle to the Romans* (BNTC; London: A & C Black [Publishers] Limited, 1991).

Bartholomew, Craig G. and Heath A. Thomas (eds.), *A Manifesto for Theological Interpretation* (Grand Rapids, MI: Baker Academic, 2016).

Beasley-Murray, G.R., *Baptism in the New Testament* (London: McMillan & Co, 1963).

Becker, Matthias, 'A Tenet under Examination: Reflections on the Pentecostal Hermeneutical Approach', *JEPTA* 24.1 (2004), pp. 30-48.

Bergen, R.D., *1, 2 Samuel* (NAC 7: Nashville: Broadman & Holman Publishers, 1996).

Bicknell, Richard, 'The Ordinances: The Marginalized Aspects of Pentecostalism', in Keith Warrington (ed.), *Pentecostal Perspectives* (Carlisle: Paternoster, 1998), pp. 204-22.

Biddy, Wesley Scott, 'Re-envisioning the Pentecostal Understanding of the Eucharist: An Ecumenical Proposal', *Pneuma* 28.2 (2006), pp. 228-51.

Blomberg, C.L., *Matthew* (NAC 22; Nashville: Broadman & Holman Publishers, 1992).

Blumhofer, E.L, *The Assemblies of God: A Chapter in the Story of American Pentecostalism* (3 vols.; Springfield, MO: Gospel Publishing House, 1989).

—*Restoring the Faith: The Assemblies of God, Pentecostalism, and American Culture* (Chicago: University of Illinois Press, 1999).

—'Opperman, Daniel C.O.', in Stanley M. Burgess and Eduard M. van der Maas (eds.), *NIDPCM* (Grand Rapids, MI: Zondervan, rev. and exp. edn; 2002), pp. 946-47.

—'Piper, William Hamner' in Stanley M. Burgess and Eduard M. van der Maas (eds.), *NIDPCM* (Grand Rapids, MI: Zondervan, rev. and exp. edn; 2002), pp. 989-90.

Boers, H., 'The Structure and Meaning of Romans 6:1-14', *CBQ* 63 (2001), pp. 664-82.
Bond, John, 'What is Distinctive about Pentecostal Theology', in M.S. Clark and H.I. Lederle (eds.) *What is Distinctive about Pentecostal Theology?* (Pretoria: University of South Africa, 1989), pp. 133-42.
Boring, M.E., 'Matthew's Narrative Christology: Three Stories', *Interpretation* 64.4 (Oct 2010), pp. 356-67.
Bridges Johns, Cheryl, 'The Adolescence of Pentecostalism: In Search of a Legitimate Sectarian Identity', *Pneuma* 17.1 (Spring 1995), pp. 3-17.
——, 'The Light That Streams from the End: Worship Within the Coming Christendom', *The Living Pulpit* 12.3 (2003), pp. 14-15.
—'Partners in Scandal: Wesleyan and Pentecostal Scholarship', *Pneuma* 21.2 (Fall 1999), pp. 183-97.
—*Pentecostal Formation; A Pedagogy Among the Oppressed*, (JPTSup 2; Sheffield, UK: Sheffield Academic Press, 1993; Eugene, OR: Wipf & Stock, 2010).
Brown, Raymond E., S.S., *The Birth of the Messiah: A Commentary on the Infancy Narratives in the Gospels of Matthew and Luke* (New York: Doubleday, rev. edn, 1993).
Bryant, H.O., *Spirit Christology in the Christian Tradition: From the Patristic Period to the Rise of Pentecostalism in the Twentieth Century* (Cleveland, TN: CPT Press, 2015).
Bundy, D.D., 'Hollenweger, Walter Jacob', in Stanley M. Burgess and Eduard M. van der Maas (eds.), *NIDPCM* (Grand Rapids, MI: Zondervan, rev. edn, 2002), p. 729.
Burgess, Ruth, 'Reuven Feuerstein: Propelling Change, Promoting Continuity', in Alex Kozulin and Yaacov Rand (eds.), *Experience of Mediated Learning: An Impact of Feuerstein's Theory in Education and Psychology* (New York: Pergamon, 2000), pp. 3-20.
Burgess, S.M., and G.B. McGee (eds.), *DPCM* (Grand Rapids: Zondervan, 1988). Burgess, Stanley M., and Ed M. Van der Maas (eds.), *NIDPCM* (Grand Rapids, MI: Zondervan, rev. and exp. edn; 2002).
Byrd, J., 'Paul Ricoeur's Hermeneutical Theory and Pentecostal Proclamation', *Pneuma* 15.2 (1993), pp. 203-14.
Capes, D.C., 'Intertextual Echoes in the Matthean Baptismal Narrative', *BBR 9* (1999), pp. 37-49.
Cargal, T.B., 'Beyond the Fundamentalist-Modernist Controversy: Pentecostals and Hermeneutics in a Postmodern Age', *Pneuma* 15 (1993), pp. 163-87.
Cartledge, Mark J., *Testimony in the Spirit: Rescripting Ordinary Pentecostal Theology* (Burlington, VT: Ashgate Publishing Company, 2010).
—'Text-Community-Spirit: The Challenges Posed by Pentecostal Theological Method to Evangelical Theology', in K.L. Spawn and A.T.

Wright (eds.), *Spirit & Scripture: Examining a Pneumatic Hermeneutic* (London: T&T Clark, 2012), pp. 130-42.

Cartwright, D.W., 'Brewster, Percy Stanley', in Stanley M. Burgess and Eduard M. van der Maas (eds.), *NIDPCM* (Grand Rapids, MI: Zondervan, rev. and exp. edn; 2002), p. 442.

Carson, D.A., *Matthew* (EBC; Grand Rapids, MI: Zondervan Academic, rev. edn, 2010).

Chan, Simon, *Liturgical Theology: The Church as Worshiping Community* (Downers Grove, IL: InterVarsity Press, 2006).

—*Pentecostal Theology and the Christian Spiritual Tradition* (JPTSup 21; Sheffield: Sheffield Academic Publishing, 2001; Eugene: OR, Wipf and Stock, 2011).

—*Spiritual Theology: A Systematic Study of the Christian Life* (Downers Grove, IL: Intervarsity Press, 1998).

Charette, Blaine, *Restoring Presence: The Spirit in Matthew's Gospel,* (JPTSup 18; Sheffield, UK: Sheffield Academic Press; 2000).

—*The Theme of Recompense in Matthew's Gospel* (JSNTSup 79: Sheffield: JSOT Press, 1992).

Clark, Mathew S., 'Pentecostal Hermeneutics: The Challenge of Relating to (Post)-Modern Literary Theory', *The Spirit and Church* 2.1 (May 2000), pp. 67-93.

Clark, Matthew S., and H.I. Lederle (eds.), *What is Distinctive about Pentecostal Theology* (Pretoria: University of South Africa, 1989).

Conn, C.W., 'Church of God (Cleveland, TN)' in Stanley M. Burgess and Eduard M. van der Maas (eds.), *NIDPCM* (Grand Rapids, MI: Zondervan, rev. and exp. edn; 2002), pp. 530-34.

—*Like A Mighty Army: A History of the Church of God 1886-1996* (Cleveland, TN: Pathway Press, 2008).

Croasmun, M., *The Emergence of Sin: The Cosmic Tyrant in* Romans (New York: Oxford University Press, 2017).

Cross, Terry L., 'The Divine-Human Encounter: Towards a Pentecostal Theology of Experience', *Pneuma* 31 (2009), pp. 3-34.

Curtis, H.D. 'Pentecostal Missions and the Changing Character of Global Christianity', *International Bulletin of Missionary Research* 36.3 (2012), pp. 122–28.

Damasio, A., *Descartes' Error: Emotion, Reason, and the Human Brain* (London: Vintage Books, 2006).

—*Looking for Spinoza: Joy, Sorrow, and the Feeling Brain* (New York: Harcourt, Inc., 2003).

Davidson, C.T., *Upon This Rock* (3 vols., Cleveland, TN: White Wing Publishing House and Press, 1973-76).

Davies, E.W., *Biblical Criticism: A Guide for the Perplexed* (London: Bloomsbury, 2013).
Davies, M., 'Literary Criticism,' in R.J. Coggins and J.L. Houlden (eds.), *A Dictionary of Biblical Interpretation* (London: SCM, 1990).
—'Reader-Response Criticism,' in R.J. Coggins and J.L. Houlden (eds.), *A Dictionary of Biblical Interpretation* (London: SCM, 1990).
Dayton, D., *Theological Roots of Pentecostalism* (Peabody: MA, Hendrickson Publishers, 1991; Grand Rapids, MI: Baker, 2011.).
Delling, G., 'ἀργός, ἀργέω, καταργέω,' in G. Kittel, G.W. Bromiley, & G. Friedrich (eds.), *Theological Dictionary of the New Testament* (trans. and ed. Geoffrey W. Bromiley 10 vols.; Grand Rapids, MI: Eerdmans, electronic ed.), I, p. 453.
Deppe, Dean, 'Comparing Spirit Hermeneutics by Craig Keener with Classical Pentecostal Hermeneutics', *Calvin Theological Journal* 52.2 (2017), pp. 265–76.
Duffield, Guy P., and Nathaniel M. Van Cleave, *Foundations of Pentecostal Theology* (Los Angeles: L.I.F.E. Bible College at Los Angeles, 1983).
Dunn, James D. G. *Baptism in the Holy Spirit: A Re-Examination of the New Testament Teaching on the Gift of the Spirit in Relation to Pentecostalism Today* (London: SCM Press, 2010).
—*Romans 1-8*, Word Biblical Commentary (Dallas: Word Press, 1988).
Dusing, Michael, 'The New Testament Church', in Stanley M Horton (ed.), (Springfield, MO: Logion Press, rev. edn, 1995), pp. 525-66.
Ellington, Scott. 'Pentecostalism and the Authority of Scripture', *JPT* 4.9 (1996), pp. 16-38.
Ervin, Howard M. *Conversion-Initiation and the Baptism in the Holy Spirit* (Peabody, MA: Hendrickson Publishers, 1985).
—*Spirit Baptism: A Biblical Investigation* (Peabody, MA: Hendrickson, 1987).
Fackre, Gabriel, *The Christian Story: A Narrative of Basic Christian Doctrine* (2 vols.; Grand Rapids, MI: Eerdmans, 3rd edn, 1996).
Faupel, David William, *The Everlasting Gospel: The Significance of Eschatology in the Development of Pentecostal Thought* (JPTSup 10; Sheffield: Sheffield Academic Press 1996; Dorset, UK: Deo Publishing, 2009).
Fee, Gordon D., 'Hermeneutics and Historical Precedent—A Major Problem in Pentecostal Hermeneutics', in Russell P. Spittler (ed.), *Perspectives on the New Pentecostalism* (Grand Rapids, MI: Baker Book House, 1976), pp. 118-32.
Feuerstein, Rafi S., (2000). 'Dynamic cognitive assessment and the instrumental enrichment program: Origins and development', in A. Kozulin & Y. Rand (eds.), *Experience of Mediated Learning: An impact of Feuerstein's Theory in Education and Psychology* (New York: Pergamon Press, 2000), pp. 147–65.

Feuerstein, Reuven, *Instrumental Enrichment: An Intervention Program for Cognitive Modifiability* (Baltimore, MD: University Park Press, 1980).

—Y. Rand, and J. E. Rynders, *Don't Accept Me as I Am: Helping 'Retarded' People to Excel* (New York: Plenum Press, 1988).

—et al., *The Dynamic Assessment of Cognitive Modifiability* (Jerusalem, Israel: International Center for the Enhancement of Learning Potential, 2002).

—et al., *The Feuerstein Instrumental Enrichment Program* (Jerusalem: ICELP Publications, 2006).

—Rafael S. Feuerstein, and Louis H. Falik, *Beyond Smarter* (New York: Teachers College Press, 2010).

—Louis H. Falik, and Refael S. Feuerstein, *Changing Minds & Brains —The Legacy of Reuven Feuerstein: Higher Thinking and Cognition Through Mediated Learning* (New York: Teachers College Press, 2015).

Feuerstein, Shmuel, *Biblical and Talmudic Antecedents of Mediated Learning Experience Theory: Educational and Didactic Implications for Inter-Generational Cultural Transmission* (Israel: The International Center for the Enhancement of Learning Potential, 2002).

Fitzmyer, J.A., S.J., *Romans: A New Translation with Introduction and Commentary* (AB 33: New Haven, CT: Yale University Press, 2008).

Fowl, Stephen E. (ed.), *The Theological Interpretation of Scripture: Classic and Contemporary Readings* (Blackwell Reading in Modern Theology; Oxford: Blackwell, 1997).

—*Theological Interpretation of Scripture* (Cascade Companions; Eugene: OR, Cascade, 2009).

France, R.T., *The Gospel of Matthew* (NICNT; Grand Rapids, MI: Eerdmans, 2007).

Gibbs, J.A., 'Israel Standing with Israel: The Baptism of Jesus in Matthew's Gospel (Matt 3:13-17)', *CBQ* 64.3 (2002), pp. 511-26.

Gohr, G.W., 'Pearlman, Myer', in Stanley M. Burgess and Eduard M. van der Maas (eds.), *NIDPCM* (Grand Rapids, MI: Zondervan, rev. and exp. edn; 2003), p. 959.

Green, Chris E. W., *Sanctifying Interpretation: Vocation, Holiness, and* Scripture (Cleveland, TN: CPT Press, 2nd edn, 2020).

—*Toward a Pentecostal Theology of the Lord's Supper: Foretasting the Kingdom* (Cleveland, TN: CPT Press, 2012).

Green, Joel B., *Practicing Theological Interpretation: Engaging Biblical Texts for Faith and Formation* (Theological Explorations for the Church Catholic; Grand Rapids, MI: Baker Academic, 2011).

Hall, J.L, 'Ewart, Frank' in Stanley M. Burgess and Eduard M. van der Maas (eds.), *NIDPCM* (Grand Rapids, MI: Zondervan, rev. and exp. edn; 2002), pp. 623-24.

Harrington, Hannah K. and Rebecca Patten, 'Pentecostal Hermeneutics and Postmodern Literary Theory', *Pneuma* 16.1 (Spring 1994), pp. 109-14.

Hauerwas, S., *Matthew* (BTC; Grand Rapids, MI: Brazos Press, 2006).

Hernstein, Richard J. and Charles Murray, *The Bell Curve: Intelligence and Class Structure in American Life* (New York: Simon & Shuster, 1996).

Hinkle, Adrian E., *Pedagogical Theory of the Hebrew Bible: An Application of Education Theory to Biblical Texts* (Eugene, OR: Wipf & Stock, 2016).

—*Pedagogical Theory of Wisdom Literature: An Application of Education Theory to Biblical Texts* (Eugene, OR: Wipf & Stock, 2017).

Hocken, Peter, 'The Holy Spirit Makes the Church More Eschatological', in William K. Kay and Anne E. Dyer (eds.), *Pentecostal and Charismatic Studies: A Reader* (London: SCM Press, 2004), pp. 43-46.

Horton, Stanley M. (ed.), *Systematic Theology* (Springfield, MO: Logion Press, rev. edn,1995).

Hollenweger, Walter J., *The Pentecostals: The Charismatic Movement in the Churches* (Minneapolis, MN: Augsburg Publishing House, 1972; London: SCM Press, 1976; Peabody: MA, Hendrickson Publishers, 1988).

—*Pentecostalism: Origins and Developments* Worldwide (Peabody, MA: Hendrickson Publishers, Inc., 1997).

Hunter, H.D., 'Ordinances, Pentecostal', in Stanley M. Burgess and Eduard M. van der Maas (eds.), *NIDPCM* (Grand Rapids, MI: Zondervan, rev. and exp. edn; 2002), pp. 947-49.

—*Spirit-Baptism: A Pentecostal Alternative* (Lanham, MD: University Press of America, 1983).

—'Reflections by a Pentecostalist on Aspects of *BEM*', *JES* 29.3-4 (1992), pp. 317-45.

—'Ordinances, Pentecostal', in Stanley M. Burgess and Eduard M. van der Maas (eds.), *NIDPCM* (Grand Rapids, MI: Zondervan, rev. and exp. edn; 2002), pp. 947-49.

—'Tomlinson, Ambrose Jessup' in Stanley M. Burgess and Eduard M. van der Maas (eds.), *NIDPCM* (Grand Rapids, MI: Zondervan, rev. and exp. edn; 2002), pp. 1143-45.

—'Tomlinson, Milton Ambrose', in Stanley M. Burgess and Eduard M. van der Maas (eds.), *NIDPCM* (Grand Rapids, MI: Zondervan, rev. and exp. edn; 2002), p. 1147.

Hunter, H.D., and Cecil M. Robeck (eds.), *The Azusa Street Revival and Its Legacy* (Cleveland, TN: Pathway Press, 2006).

Hyatt, Eddie (ed.), *Fire on the Earth: Eyewitness Reports from the Azusa Street Revival* (Lake Mary, FL: Creation House, 2006).

Jackson, A.R., 'Wesleyan Holiness and Finished Work Pentecostal Interpretations of Gog and Magog Biblical Texts', *JPT* 25.2 (2016), pp. 168–83.

Johns, Jackie David, 'Pentecostalism and the Postmodern Worldview', *JPT* 7 (1995), pp. 73-96.

Johns, Jackie David, and C. Bridges Johns, 'Yielding to the Spirit: A Pentecostal Approach to Group Bible Study', *JPT* 1 (1992), pp. 109-34.

Johnson, David R., 'The Mark of the Beast, Reception History, and Early Pentecostal Literature', *JPT* 25.2 (2016), 184–202.

Johnson, Luke T., *Reading Romans: A Literary and Theological Commentary* (Macon, GA: Smith & Helwys Publishing, 2001).

Kärkkäinen, Veli-Matti, 'The Pentecostal View' in Gordon T. Smith (ed.), *The Lord's Supper: Five Views* (Downers Grove, IL: IVP Academic, 2008).

Keener, C.S., *A Commentary on the Gospel of Matthew* (Grand Rapids, MI: Eerdmans, 1999), p. 132.

—*Romans* (Eugene, OR: Cascade Books, 2009).

—*Spirit Hermeneutics: Reading Scripture in Light of Pentecost* (Grand Rapids, MI: Eerdmans, 2016).

King, J.H., *From Passover to Pentecost* (Franklin Springs, GA: Publishing House of the Pentecostal Holiness Church, 1955; Franklin Springs, GA: LifeSprings Resources, 2004).

Kingsbury, J.D., *Jesus Christ in Matthew, Mark, and Luke* (Proclamation Commentaries; Philadelphia: Fortress Press, 1981).

—*Matthew As Story* (Philadelphia: Fortress Press, rev. and enlarged edn, 1988).

—*Matthew: Structure, Christology, Kingdom* (Philadelphia: Fortress Press, 1975).

Klaiber, W., 'The Great Commission of Matthew 28:16-20', *American Baptist Quarterly* 37.2 (2018), pp. 108-22.

Klich, A.E., OSU, 'Baptism as Unification with the Death and Resurrection of Christ (Romans 6:1-14)', *Ruch Biblijny i Liturgiczny* 70.2 (2017), pp. 147-61.

Kwon, Y., 'Baptism or Gospel of Grace?: Romans 6 Revisited', *Expository Times* 128.5 (2017), pp. 222-30.

Lackoff, G. and M. Johnson, *Philosophy in the Flesh: The Embodied Mind and its Challenge to Western Thought* (New York: Basic Books, 1999).

Lamp, J.S., 'New Heavens and New Earth: Early Pentecostal Soteriology as a Foundation for Creation Care in the Present', *Pneuma* 36.1 (2014), pp. 64–80.

Lampe, G.W.H., *The Seal of the Spirit: A Study in the Doctrine of Baptism and Confirmation in the New Testament and the Fathers* (Eugene, OR: Wipf & Stock, 2004).

Lancaster, J., 'The Ordinances', in P.S. Brewster (ed.), *Pentecostal Doctrines* (Cheltenham: Elim, 1976), pp. 79-92.
Land, Steven J., *Pentecostal Spirituality: A Passion for the Kingdom* (JPTSup 1; Sheffield: Sheffield Academic Press, 1993; Cleveland, TN: CPT Press, 2010).
Land, Steven J., Rickie D. Moore, and John Christopher Thomas (eds), *Passover, Pentecost & Parousia: Studies in Celebration of the Life and Ministry of R. Hollis Gause* (JPTSup 35; Dorset, UK: Deo Publishing, 2010).
Landrus, H.L., 'Hearing 3 John 2 in the Voices of History', *JPT* 11.1 (2002), pp. 70–88.
Lincoln, A.T., 'Matthew – A Story for Teachers?', in D.J.A. Clines, S.E. Fowl, and S.E. Porter (eds), *The Bible in Three Dimension: Essays in Celebration of Forty Years of Biblical Studies in the University of Sheffield* (JSOTSup, 87: Sheffield: JSOT Press, 1990).
Luz, Ulrich, *Matthew in History: Interpretation, Influence, and Effects* (Minneapolis: Fortress Press, 1994).
—*Matthew 21-28* (Hermeneia; Minneapolis: Fortress Press, 2005).
—*Studies in Matthew* (Grand Rapids, MI: Eerdmans, 2005).
—'Empowerment and Commission in the New Testament', *JEPTA* 26.1 (2006), pp. 49-62.
—*Matthew 1-7* (Hermeneia; Minneapolis: Fortress Press, 2007).
Macchia, Frank D., 'Sighs Too Deep for Words: Towards a Theology of Glossolalia', *JPT* 1.1 (1992), pp. 47–73.
—'Tongues as a Sign: Towards a Sacramental Understanding of Pentecostal Experience', *Pneuma* 15.1 (1993), pp. 61-76.
—'Is Footwashing the Neglected Sacrament? A Theological Response to John Christopher Thomas', *Pneuma* 19.2 (1997), pp. 239-49.
—*Baptized in the Spirit: A Global Pentecostal Theology* (Grand Rapids: Zondervan, 2006).
—*Justified in the Spirit: Creation, Redemption, and the Triune God* Grand Rapids, MI: Eerdmans, 2010).
McCall, Bradford, 'The Pentecostal Reappropriation of Common Sense Realism', *JPT* 19.1 (January 1, 2010), pp. 59–75.
McKay, John W., 'When the Veil Is Taken Away: The Impact of Prophetic Experience on Biblical Interpretation', *JPT* 5 (1994), pp. 17-40.
McKnight, S., *Reading Romans Backwards: A Gospel of Peace in the Midst of Empire* (Waco, TX: Baylor University Press, 2019).
McKinlay, A., 'Performativity: From J.L. Austin to Judith Butler', in Peter Armstrong and Geoff Lightfoot (eds), *The Leading Journal in the Field': Destabilizing Authority in the Social Sciences of Management* (London: MayFlyBooks, 2010), pp. 119-42.

McLean, M.D., 'Toward a Pentecostal Hermeneutic', *Pneuma* 6.2 (1984), pp. 35-56.
McQueen, Larry R., *Joel and the Spirit: The Cry of a Prophetic Hermeneutic* (Cleveland, TN: CPT Press, 2009).
—*Toward a Pentecostal Eschatology: Discerning the Way Forward* (JPTSup 39; Dorset: Deo Publishing, 2012
Martin, Lee Roy (ed.), *Pentecostal Hermeneutics: A Reader* (Leiden: Brill, 2013).
—'The Function and Practice of Fasting in Early Pentecostalism', *Pharos Journal of Theology* 96 (2015), pp. 1–19.
—*The Unheard Voice of God: A Pentecostal Hearing of the Book of Judges* (JPTSup 32; Dorset, UK: Deo Publishing, 2008).
Matera, Frank J., *Romans* (PCNT: Grand Rapid, MI: Baker Academic 2010).
Menzies, R.P., 'Jumping Off the Postmodern Bandwagon', *Pneuma* 16 (1994), pp. 115-20.
Menzies, William W., and Stanley M. Horton, *Bible Doctrines: A Pentecostal Perspective* (Springfield, MO: Logion Press, 1993).
—*Anointed to Serve: The Story of the Assemblies of God* (Springfield, MO: Gospel Publishing House, 1971).
—'The Methodology of Pentecostal Theology: An Essay on Hermeneutics', in P. Elbert (ed.), *Essays on Apostolic Themes: Studies in Honor of Howard M. Ervin* (Peabody, MA: Hendrickson Publishers, 1985).
Mills, Stephen H., 'Renewal of the Mind: The Cognitive Sciences and a Pneumatological Anthropology of Transformation' (PhD dissertation, Regent University, 2014). Virginia Beach, VA.
Mitch, C. and E. Sri, *The Gospel According to Matthew* (CCSS; Grand Rapids: MI, Baker Academic, 2010).
Moo, D.J., *The Epistle to the Romans* (NICNT: Grand Rapids, MI: Eerdmans, 1996).
Moore, Rickie D., 'Altar Hermeneutics: Reflections of Pentecostal Biblical Interpretation', *Pneuma* 38.2 (2016), pp. 148–59.
— 'A Pentecostal Approach to Scripture', *The Seminary Viewpoint* 8.1 (1987), pp. 1-2.
—'Approaching God's Word Biblically: A Pentecostal Perspective' (Annual Meeting of the Society for Pentecostal Studies, Fresno, CA, 1989).
—'Canon and Charisma in the Book of Deuteronomy', *JPT* 1 (1992), pp. 75-92.
—'The Prophetic Calling: An Old Testament Profile and Its Relevance for Today', *JEPTA* 24 (2004), pp. 16-29.
Mounce, R.H., *Romans* (NAC 27: Nashville: Broadman & Holman Publishers, 1995).
Neumann, Peter D., *Pentecostal Experience: An Ecumenical Encounter* (PTMS 187; Eugene, OR: Pickwick Publications, 2012).

Newman, L.V., 'Pentecostal Hermeneutics: Suggesting a Model, Exploring the Problems' (Annual Meeting of the Society for Pentecostal Studies, Lakeland, FL, 1991).

Noel, Bradley Truman, *Pentecostal and Postmodern Hermeneutics: Comparisons and Contemporary Impact* (Eugene, OR: Wipf and Stock, 2010).

Nolland, J., *The Gospel of Matthew: A Commentary on the Greek Text* (Grand Rapids, MI; Carlisle: Eerdmans; Paternoster Press, 2005).

Nygren, A., *Commentary on Romans* (Philadelphia: Fortress Press, 1949), p. 210,

Oliverio, L. William, 'Reading Craig Keener: On Spirit Hermeneutics: Reading Scripture in Light of Pentecost', *Pneuma* 39.1–2 (2017), pp. 126–45.

—*Theological Hermeneutics in the Classical Pentecostal Tradition: A Typological Account* (Global Pentecostal and Charismatic Studies 12; Leiden: Brill, 2012).

Owens, Robert R., *The Azusa Street Revival: Its Roots and Its Message* (Longwood, FL: Xulon Press, 2005).

Pearlman, Myer, *Knowing the Doctrines of the Bible* (Springfield, MO: Gospel Publishing House, 1937). Revised 1981.

Perkins, Pheme, 'Crisis in Jerusalem? Narrative Criticism in New Testament Studies', *Theological Studies* 50 (1989), pp. 296-313.

Petersen, A.K., 'Shedding new Light on Paul's Understanding of Baptism: a Ritual-Theoretical Approach to Romans 6', *Studia Theologica*, 52.1 (1998), pp. 3-28.

Phanon, Y., 'The Work of the Holy Spirit in the *Conception, Baptism and Temptation of Christ: Implications for the Pentecostal Christian Part I*', *AJPS* 20.1 (Feb 2017), pp. 37-55.

Philemon, Leulseged, *Pneumatic Hermeneutics: The Role of the Holy Spirit in the Theological Interpretation of Scripture* (Cleveland, TN: CPT Press, 2019).

Pinnock, Clark H., *The Scripture Principle* (San Francisco: Harper & Row, Publishers, 1984).

—'The Work of the Holy Spirit in Hermeneutics', *JPT* 2 (1993), pp. 3-23.

—'The Work of the Holy Spirit from the Perspective of a Charismatic Biblical Theologian', *JPT* 18 (2009), pp. 157-71.

—'The Work of the Spirit in the Interpretation of Scripture from the Perspective of a Charismatic Biblical Theologian', in Lee Roy Martin (ed.), *Pentecostal Hermeneutics: A Reader* (Leiden: Brill, 2013), pp. 233-48.

Pope, Robert P., 'Why the Church Needs a Full Gospel: A Review and Reaction to Pentecostal Ecclesiology', in John Christopher Thomas (ed.), *Toward a Pentecostal Ecclesiology: The Church and the Fivefold Gospel* (Cleveland, TN: CPT Press, 2010), pp. 272-84.

Porter, S., *The Letter to the Romans: A Linguistic and Literary Commentary* (Sheffield: Sheffield Phoenix Press, 2015).

Powell, Mark Allen, *What is Narrative Criticism?* (Minneapolis, MN: Fortress Press, 1990).

Powery, Emerson B., 'Ulrich Luz's *Matthew in History*: A Contribution to Pentecostal Hermeneutics?' *JPT* 14 (1999), pp. 3-17.

Pruitt, Raymond M., *Fundamentals of the Faith* (Cleveland, TN: White Wing Publishing House and Press, 1981).

Reed, D.A., *'In Jesus Name': The History and Beliefs of Oneness* Pentecostals (JPTSup 31; Blandford Forum: Deo, 2008).

—'Oneness Pentecostalism', in Stanley M. Burgess and Eduard M. van der Maas (eds.), *NIDPCM* (Grand Rapids, MI: Zondervan, rev. and exp. edn; 2002), pp. 936-44.

Riss, R.M., 'Durham, William H.', in Stanley M. Burgess and Eduard M. van der Maas (eds.), *NIDPCM* (Grand Rapids, MI: Zondervan, rev. and exp. edn; 2002), pp. 594-95.

Robeck, Jr., C.M. and Jerry L. Sandidge, 'The Ecclesiology of *Koinonia* and Baptism: A Pentecostal Perspective', *JES* 27.3 (1990), pp. 504–34.

—'Angelus Temple' in Stanley M. Burgess and Eduard M. van der Maas (eds.), *NIDPCM* (Grand Rapids, MI: Zondervan, rev. and exp. edn; 2002), pp. 314-15.

—'Hocken, Peter Dudley', in Stanley M. Burgess and Eduard M. van der Maas (eds.), *NIDPCM* (Grand Rapids, MI: Zondervan, rev. and exp. edn; 2002), p. 723.

—'McPherson, Aimee Semple', in Stanley M. Burgess and Eduard M. van der Maas (eds.), *NIDPCM* (Grand Rapids, MI: Zondervan, rev. and exp. edn; 2002), pp. 856-59.

—'Seymour, William Joseph' in Stanley M. Burgess and Eduard M. van der Maas (eds.), *NIDPCM* (Grand Rapids, MI: Zondervan, rev. and exp. edn; 2002), pp. 1053-58.

—'Williams, Ernest Swing', in Stanley M. Burgess and Eduard M. van der Maas (eds.), *NIDPCM* (Grand Rapids, MI: Zondervan, rev. and exp. edn; 2002), pp. 1197-98.

—'Williams, J. Rodman', in Stanley M. Burgess and Eduard M. van der Maas (eds.), *NIDPCM* (Grand Rapids, MI: Zondervan, rev. and exp. edn; 2002), p. 1198

—*The Azusa Street Mission, and Revival: The Birth of the Global Pentecostal Movement* (Nashville, TN: Thomas Nelson, 2006).

Senior, D., C.P., *What Are They Saying About Matthew* (New York/Mahwah, NJ, rev. and exp. edn, 1996).

—*The Gospel of Matthew* (IBT; Nashville: Abingdon Press, 1997).

Sheppard, G.T., 'Pentecostalism and the Hermeneutics of Dispensationalism: Anatomy of an Uneasy Relationship', *Pneuma* 6.2 (1984), pp. 5-33.
—'Biblical Interpretation after Gadamer', *Pneuma* 16 (1994), pp. 121-41.
Slay, James L., *This We Believe* (Cleveland, TN: Pathway Press, 1963).
Smit, P.B., 'Ritual failure in Romans 6', *HTS Hervormde Theologiese Studies/ Theological Studies* 72.4 (2016), pp. 1-13.
Smith, J.K.A., *Thinking in Tongues: Pentecostal Contributions to Christian Philosophy* (Pentecostal Manifestos Series; Grand Rapids, MI: Eerdmans, 2010).
Sparks, K.L., 'Gospel as Conquest: Mosaic Typology in Matthew 28:16-20', *CBQ* 68.4 (2006), pp. 651-63.
Spawn, Kevin L. and Archie T. Wright (eds.), *Spirit and Scripture: Examining a Pneumatic Hermeneutic* (New York, NY: T&T Clark International, 2012).
Stronstad, Roger, 'Trends in Pentecostal Hermeneutics', *Paraclete* 22.3 (1988), pp. 1-12.
—'The Hermeneutic of Lucan Historiography', *Paraclete* 22.4 (1988), pp. 5-17.
—'Pentecostal Experience and Hermeneutics', *Paraclete* 26.1 (1992), pp. 14-30.
—*The Prophethood of All Believers: A Study in Luke's Charismatic Theology* (JPTSup 16; Sheffield: Sheffield Academic Press, 1999; Cleveland, TN: CPT Press, 2010).
Sutton, K. and K. Williamson, 'Embodied Cognition', in L. Shapiro (ed.), *The Routledge Handbook of Embodied Cognition* (London: Routledge, Taylor & Francis Group, 2014).
Synan, H.V., 'Pentecostalism', in Walter A. Elwell (ed.), *The Evangelical Dictionary of Theology* (Grand Rapids: Baker, 1984).
—'Taylor, George Floyd' in Stanley M. Burgess and Eduard M. van der Maas (eds.), *NIDPCM* (Grand Rapids, MI: Zondervan, rev. and exp. edn; 2002), pp. 1115-16.
—'Cashwell, Gaston Barnabas' in Stanley M. Burgess and Eduard M. van der Maas (eds.), *NIDPCM* (Grand Rapids, MI: Zondervan, rev. and exp. edn; 2002), pp. 457-58.
Tan, Simon G.H., 'Reassessing Believer's Baptism in Pentecostal Theology and Practice', *AJPS* 6.2 (2003), pp. 219-34.
Talbert, Charles H., *Matthew* (PCNT: Grand Rapid, MI: Baker Academic, 2010).
Taylor, J.E., *The Immerser: John the Baptist within Second Temple Judaism* (Grand Rapids, MI: Eerdmans, 1997).
Thomas, John Christopher, 'Women, Pentecostals and the Bible: An Experiment in Pentecostal Hermeneutics', *JPT* 5 (1994), pp. 41-56.

—'1998 Presidential Address: Pentecostal Theology in the Twenty-First Century', *Pneuma* 20.1 (1998), pp. 3–19.
—*The Spirit of the New Testament* (Blandford Forum: Deo Publishing, 2005).
—'Healing in the Atonement: A Johannine Perspective', *JPT* 14.1 (2005), pp. 175–89.
—'"Where the Spirit Leads": The Development of Pentecostal Hermeneutics', *Journal of Beliefs & Values: Studies in Religion & Education* 30.3 (December 2009), pp. 289–302.
—'The Kingdom of God in the Gospel According to Matthew' in *The Spirit of the New Testament* (Blandford Forum, Dorset, UK: Deo Publishing, 2011), pp. 48-61.
—'What the Spirit is Saying to the Church—The Testimony of a Pentecostal in New Testament Studies', in K.L. Spawn and A.T. Wright (eds.) *Spirit & Scripture: Examining a Pneumatic Hermeneutic* (London: T&T Clark, 2012), pp. 115-29.
—'Pentecostal Biblical Interpretation', in S.L. McKenzie (ed.), *Oxford Encyclopedia of Biblical Interpretation* (2 vols, Oxford: Oxford University Press, 2013).
—*Footwashing in John 13 and the Johannine Community* (Cleveland, TN: CPT Press, 2nd edn; 2014).
Thomas, John Christopher, and K.E. Alexander, '"And the Signs are Following": Mark 16.9– 20—A Journey into Pentecostal Hermeneutics', *JPT* 11.2 (2003), pp. 147–70;
Tomberlin, Daniel, *Pentecostal Sacraments: Encountering God at the Altar* (Cleveland, TN: Center for Pentecostal Leadership and Care, Pentecostal Theological Seminary, 2010; Cleveland, TN: Cherohala Press, rev. edn, 2019).
Tomlinson, M.A., *Basic Bible Beliefs* (Cleveland, TN: White Wing Publishing House and Press, 1961).
Treier, Daniel J., *Introducing Theological Interpretation of Scripture: Recovering a Christian Practice* (Grand Rapids, MI: Baker Academic, 2008).
Trementozzi, David, 'Renewing the Christian Doctrine of Salvation: Toward a Dynamic & Transformational Soteriology' (PhD dissertation, Regent University, 2013).
Valdez, Sr., A.C., *Fire on Azusa Street: An Eyewitness Account* (Costa Mesta, CA: Gift Publications, 1980).
Vanhoozer, Kevin J., (ed.), *Dictionary for Theological Interpretation of the Bible* (Grand Rapids, MI: Baker Academic, 2005).
Vondey, Wolfgang, *People of Bread: Rediscovering Ecclesiology* (Mahwah, NJ: Paulist Press, 2008).
—*Beyond Pentecostalism: The Crisis of Global Christianity and the Renewal of the Theological Agenda* (Grand Rapids, MI: Eerdmans, 2010).

—'Pentecostal Contributions to The Nature and Mission of the Church' in Wolfgang Vondey (ed.), *Pentecostalism and Christian Unity: Ecumenical Documents and Critical Assessments* (Eugene, OR: Pickwick Publications, 2010), pp. 256-68.

Waddell, Robby, *The Spirit of the Book of Revelation* (JPTSup 30; Blandford Forum: Deo Publishing, 2006).

Wagner, J.R., 'Baptism "Into Christ Jesus" and the Question of Universalism in Paul', *Horizons 33* (2011), pp. 45-61.

Warner, W.E., 'Bell, Eudorus N.' in Stanley M. Burgess and Eduard M. van der Maas (eds.), *NIDPCM* (Grand Rapids, MI: Zondervan, rev. and exp. edn; 2002), p. 369.

—'Church of God in Christ (White)' in Stanley M. Burgess and Eduard M. van der Maas (eds.), *NIDPCM* (Grand Rapids, MI: Zondervan, rev. and exp. edn; 2002), p. 537.

—'International Pentecostal Church of Christ' in Stanley M. Burgess and Eduard M. van der Maas (eds.), *NIDPCM* (Grand Rapids, MI: Zondervan, rev. and exp. edn; 2002), pp. 797-98.

—'Pentecostal Church of God' in Stanley M. Burgess and Eduard M. van der Maas (eds.), *NIDPCM* (Grand Rapids, MI: Zondervan, rev. and exp. edn; 2002), pp. 965-66.

Warrington, Keith, *Pentecostal Theology: A Theology of Encounter* (London: T & T Clark, 2008).

Webb, R.L., *John the Baptizer and Prophet: A Socio-historical Study* (Eugene, OR: Wipf and Stock Publishers, 2006).

Williams, Andrew Ray, *Washed in the Spirit: Toward a Pentecostal Theology of Water* Baptism (Cleveland, TN: CPT Press, 2021).

Williams, Ernest S., *Systematic Theology* (3 vols.; Springfield, MO: Gospel Publishing House, 1953).

Williams, J. Rodman, *Renewal Theology: The Church, the Kingdom, and Last Things* (Grand Rapids: MI: Zondervan Publishing House, 1992).

—*Renewal Theology: Systematic Theology from a Charismatic Perspective* (Grand Rapids: Zondervan, 1992).

Wilson, E.A., 'McAlister, Robert Edward', in Stanley M. Burgess and Eduard M. van der Maas (eds.), *NIDPCM* (Grand Rapids, MI: Zondervan, rev. and exp. edn; 2002), p. 852.

Work, T., *Ain't Too Proud to Beg: Living Through the Lord's Prayer* (Grand Rapids, MI: Eerdmans, 2007).

—*Deuteronomy* (Grand Rapids, MI: Brazos, 2009).

Wright, N.T., *Romans* (NIB; Nashville, TN: Abingdon Press, 2015).

Yong, Amos, *Spirit-Word-Community: Theological Hermeneutics in Trinitarian Perspective* (Eugene, OR: Wipf & Stock, 2002).

—*The Spirit Poured Out on All Flesh: Pentecostalism and the Possibility of Global Theology* (Grand Rapids, MI: Baker Academic, 2005).

—*Mission After Pentecost: The Witness of the Spirit from Genesis to Revelation* (Grand Rapids, MI: Baker Academic, 2019).

Yong, Amos, and Jonathan A. Anderson, *Renewing Christian Theology: Systematics for a Global Christianity* (Waco, TX: Baylor University Press, 2014).

Index of Biblical References

Genesis	
1.3	359
1.26-27	351, 376
6-9	89, 389
8.8-12	334
17.9-14	167
44.16	359

Exodus	
16.7	360
16.10	360
23.7	359

Leviticus	
5.7	339
16.20-22	336

Numbers	
6.22-27	345

Deuteronomy	
2.13	98
11.10-15	9
25.1	359

1 Samuel	
1.28	167
10.10	335
15.22	329
16.12	335
16.13	335
16.14	335

2 Samuel	
2.4	335
2.7	335
5.3-4	335

1 Kings	
8:32	359
11.40	325

2 Kings

1.8	328
2.1-11	329
5.1-14	329

2 Chronicles	
6.23	359
36.22-23	340

Nehemiah	
9.8	359

2 Maccabees	
5.8	325

Job	
29.29	9

Psalm	
2.7	336
5.8	359
31.1	359
35.24	359
36.5-6	358
36.10	358
40.10	358
51.4	359
71.2	359
71.15-16	359
71.19	359
71.24	359
74	334
84.8	353
88.11-12	358
88.12	359
98.2-3	358
103.17	358
111.3-4	358
119.40-41	358
141.1	358
143.1	358
143.11-12	358
145.7	358

Proverbs	
11.14	231
16.15	9
22:6	167

Isaiah	
30.21	361
40.3	328
42.1	335, 336
42.5	361
43.9	359
43.26	359
44.3	331
53.11	359
59.21	331
64.1	334

Jeremiah	
1.5	182
3.3	9
5.24	9
7.23	361
26.4	361
26.21	325
38.20	335, 336
42–44	325

Ezekiel	
1.1-4	334
11.20	361
20.19	361
36.25-27	238, 239
36.25	221
36.27	331
37.14	331
39.39	331
44.24	359

Daniel	
4.37	361
7.13-14	341

Hosea

2.16	329	3.7	330	18.1-19.2	348
2.20-21	329	3.8	349	18.20	345
6.3	9	3.10	330	19:13-15	167
14.9	361	3.11	327, 330, 348, 349	19.13	38
				19.14	38
Joel		3.12	330	19.24	328
2.23	9	3.13-16	47	21.23-27	339
2.29	331	3.13-15	41	21.25-27	10, 323, 349
		3.13-17	10, 298, 323, 327, 335, 344, 349	21.25	339, 344
Micah				21.31	328
6.6-8	329			21.32	333
		3.13	113, 123, 135, 314, 340	21.43	328, 342
Habakkuk				23.33	329
2.4	353	3.15	68, 270, 332, 387	24.3-25.46	348
				26.32	340
Zechariah		3.16-17	337	28.7	340
10.1	9	3.16	85, 334, 344, 391	28.10	340
12.10	331			28.16-20	10, 323, 340, 342, 346, 348
		3.17	335, 336, 337		
Matthew		4.1-28.15	338	28.18-20	47, 89, 176, 270, 298, 335, 388
1.1-4.17	338	4.17	338		
1.2-4.22	326	4.18-22	340		
1-2	326	4.23	340	28.18	341
1.1-16	333	5.1-7.29	348	28.19-20	344, 384
1.17	327, 333	5.6	332	28.19	37, 39, 40, 41, 43, 48, 50, 51, 54, 79, 85, 86, 95, 96, 114, 117, 121, 123, 133, 134, 137, 147, 151, 152, 157, 158, 165, 171, 174, 175, 188, 193, 194, 199, 200, 208, 209, 214, 230, 243, 257, 260, 266, 272, 285, 287, 288, 296, 308, 310, 311,
1.18-2.23	330	5.10	332		
1.18	326, 335	5.19	347		
1.19	332	5.20	332		
1.20	333	5.45	332		
1.21	337	6.1	332		
1.22	340	6.2-4	343		
1.23	326, 333, 337, 348	6.9-13	343		
		6.10	332		
1.25	333	6.16-18	343		
2.1-12	333	6.33	332		
2.6	326	7.24-27	348		
2.15	326, 333, 337	9.35-11.1	348		
2.18	326	10.6	336		
2.22-23	340	10.7-8	347		
2.23	326, 327	11.14	328		
3	165, 166	12.28	328		
3.1-12	339	12.34	329		
3.1	328	13.1-35	348		
3.2	332	15.24	336		
3.3	328, 333	16.16	337		
3.5-4.1	336	16.17-19	348		
3.6	332	17.1-8	340		

Index of Biblical References 495

	314, 329,	3.23	137	9.18	47
	342, 344,	3.26	223	10.44-48	163
	345, 346,	3.38	286	10.46	293
	349, 391,	4.1-2	176, 223	10.47-48	85, 158, 214,
	392, 396, 397	4.2	177		308
28.20	40, 41, 43,	4.12	177	10.47	47, 180, 243
	175, 333,	6.63	297, 301	10.48	47, 86, 96,
	337, 347, 348	13-17	22, 344		194, 200,
		13	74		230, 243,
Mark		13.1-20	55		266, 272,
1.9	137	13.10	55		311, 392
1.10	85, 95, 137	16.13	17	11.15	293
1.1-11	176, 191	17.1-8	340	11.24	205
8.26-40	176			15	15
10:13-16	167	Acts		16.31	165
16.9-20	27	1.4	110	16.33	47, 96, 166
16.15-16	405	2	8, 9, 393	18.18	48
16.15	47	2.2-4	286	19	288
16.16	40, 47, 51,	2.3	108	19.2-6	293
	113, 157,	2.4	108, 145, 293	19.3-5	48
	163, 180,	2.17	9, 197	19.4	243
	243, 269, 298	2.28	113	19.5-6	96
16.18	289	2.30	39	19.5	47, 96, 180,
16.19-20	163	2.37-40	104		200, 230, 311
		2.38-39	405	20.21	48, 158, 214,
Luke		2.38	37, 40, 43,		308
1.15	182		47, 51, 54,	20.27	50
3.22	85		85, 86, 89,	22.12-16	405
5.25	357		92, 96, 175,	22.16	239
14.47	158		180, 199,		
18:15-17	167		200, 229,	Romans	
			230, 239,	1.4	75
John			243, 260,	1.5	359
1.29-36	47		287, 293,	1.16-17	352, 358
1.32-34	85		296, 298,	1.17	358
1.35-49	258		300, 311,	1.18-32	350
3.2	40		388, 392	1.18-23	350, 362
3.3-8	286	2.41	51	1.21	351
3.3-7	405	2.42-47	90-91	1.22-23	351
3.5	164, 199,	2.42	213	1.24-32	351
	180, 237, 293	7.33	357	1.24	351
3.6	40	8.12	47	1.25	350, 352
3.10	180	8.16	86, 96, 200,	1.26	351
3.11	40		230, 311, 392	1.27	352
3.16	344			1.28	351
3.20-30	177	8.35-38	405	1.29-32	352
3.22	137	8.36-38	47, 137	2.8	359
		8.38-39	113, 123, 135		

3.3	354	6.1-4	37, 45, 50,	9.30-10.6	359
3.4	350, 359		53, 96, 130,	10.3	358
3.5	358		312	12.1-15.7	359
3.6	350	6.1-3	350	13.14	359
3.8	350	6.1	350	14.17	361
3.9	350	6.2-10	364	15.18	359
3.21-5.11	353	6.2	350	16.3	197
3.21-22	358	6.3-7	180, 306, 402		
3.21-26	354	6.3-6	39, 179, 180,	1 Corinthians	
3.21-22	353		181, 182,	1.10	213
3.22-26	364		205, 206, 274	6.9-11	405-406
3.22	354	6.3-5	113, 243, 273	7.14	167
3.24-25	354	6.3-4	123, 135,	10.1-11	56
3.24	354		151, 306,	10.1	167
3.25-26	358		308, 358	10.2	92, 167
3.26	354, 358	6.3-7	180, 402	11.26	91, 213
3.31	350	6.3	40, 58, 74,	12.7-11	51
4.1-25	354		148, 158,	12.12-13	206
4.1-8	354		200, 205,	12.13	45, 61, 96,
4.3-11	364		229, 296,		205, 206
4.5	359		300, 354	15.3	282
4.9-12	354	6.4-11	358	15.4	282
4.13-17	354	6.4-5	158	15.13-19	240
4.16	354	6.4	40, 74, 83,	15.14	270
4.18-25	354		85, 89, 158,	15.17	240
4.22-24	364		194, 200,	15.29	240
4.23-25	354		203, 214,	15.45	274
4.25	359		2.17, 229,		
5.5	356		236, 240,	2 Corinthians	
5.12-21	358, 362		266, 270,	2.16	353
5.17	359		296, 308,	3.6	297, 301
5.18-19	360		388, 390	3.18	353
5.19	359	6.5-6	274	4.6	359
5.21	359	6.5	296, 362	5.4	357
6	7, 33, 122,	6.6-7	362	5.17	92, 274
	148, 159,	6.6	180, 181,	11.2	205
	170, 180,		182, 297,	13.5	274
	229, 248,		300, 362, 363		
	273, 350, 359	6.8-10	362	Galatians	
6.1-14	236, 240,	6.8	363	2	182
	244, 258,	6.9-10	363	2.20	182
	259, 350, 358	6.11	358	3.11	353
6.1-11	10, 104, 307,	6.12-21	362	3.24-27	406
	314, 350,	6.16-18	359	3.26	48
	364, 384, 395	6.34	297, 300	3.27	39, 40, 43,
6.1-7	306, 323	7.24	362		48, 50, 58,
		8.2-4	359		83, 96, 113,

Index of Biblical References   497

	123, 135, 148, 206, 240, 390	2.11-15	406	12.2	88
		2.11-12	239		
		2.11	275	James	
		2.12	39, 58, 83, 123, 135, 148, 221, 239, 270, 273, 296, 300, 390	5.7	9

Ephesians
1.20-21   341
2.10   205, 274
4.5   39, 60, 61, 96, 293
4.17   99
4.22   99
5.8   92
5.25-27   406
5.26   48, 237

Philippians
2.9   341
3.9   359
3.12   357
4.10   357

Colossians
1.13   92
1.24   205

3.1-3   275
3.9-10   275

Titus
2.5   239
3.4-7   406
3.5   48, 82

Hebrews
6.2   174
7.16   74
9.10   174
9.14   74
10.22   158, 214, 239, 308

1 Peter
2.9-10   92
2.20-21   92
3.18-22   406
3.20-21   89, 389
3.21   40, 41, 82, 113, 178, 266, 273, 307, 389

1 John
5:7   154

3 John
2   27

Revelation
2.5   42

Index of Authors

Adewuya, J.A.   355
Ahn, Y.J.   12
Albrecht, D.E.   11, 79, 80, 81
Alexander, K.E.   3, 4, 27
Allison, D.C.   336
Althouse, P.   12
An, H.S.   336
Anderson, A.   125
Anderson, G.   11
Anderson, J.A.   84, 85, 86, 391, 392
Archer, K.   3, 5, 7, 8, 9, 12, 13, 16, 20, 21, 22, 25, 26, 27, 86, 87, 88, 89, 105, 387, 388, 389, 394
Archer, M. 15, 22, 25, 26, 27, 30
Arrington, F.   11, 59, 60, 61, 76, 105
Autry, A.C.   11
Barrett, C.K.   350, 352, 354, 355, 359, 361, 363
Bartholomew, C.G.   16
Beasley-Murray, B.R.   47
Becker, M.   12
Bergen, R.D.   335
Bicknell, R.   75, 76, 77, 78, 96
Biddy, W.S.   92, 93, 94, 95
Blomberg, C.L.   325, 327, 328, 329, 331, 336, 337, 344, 346
Blumhofer, E.L.   8, 36, 39, 125, 283
Boers, H.   350, 361
Bond, J.   51, 52
Boring, M.E.   332
Bridges Johns, C.   11, 13, 15, 30
Brown, R.   326
Bryant, H.O.   27
Bundy, D.D.   44
Burgess, R.   376
Burgess, S.M.   11
Byrd, J.   11
Capes, D.C.   334
Cargal, T.B.   11
Cartledge, M.J.   21, 100, 101, 102, 104
Cartwright, D.W.   45
Carson, D.A.   326, 335, 339, 341, 344, 345

Chan, S.   2, 3, 89, 90, 91, 92, 105
Charette, B.   8, 325, 326, 330, 332, 334, 335, 337, 340, 342, 345, 346
Clark, M.S.   12, 51
Conn, C.W.   43, 136
Croasmun, M.   352
Cross, T.L.   21, 25
Curtis, H.D.   125
Damasio, A.   5, 371, 372, 373, 374, 375, 382, 383, 386, 389
Davidson, C.T.   43
Davies, E.W.   14
Davies, M.   14
Dayton, D.   8, 9, 18, 56
Delling, G.   362
Deppe, D.   13
Duffield, G.P.   50, 51, 53, 104
Dunn, J.D.G.   46, 346, 347, 350, 355
Dusing, M.   53, 54, 55, 105
Ellington, S.   23
Ervin, H.M.   11, 347
Fackre, G.   8
Falik, L.H.   375, 376, 377, 378, 379, 380, 382
Faupel, D.W.   5, 8, 37
Fee, G.D.   11
Feuerstein, R.S.   378
Feuerstein, R.   371, 375, 376, 377, 379, 382, 383
Feuerstein, R.S.   375, 376, 377, 378, 379, 380, 382
Feuerstein, S.   376, 383
Fitzmyer, J.A.   351, 353, 354, 356, 358, 360, 361, 364
Fowl. S.E.   16, 347
France, R.T.   326, 327, 328, 331, 332, 333, 336, 341, 345, 348
Gibbs, J.A.   335, 336
Gohr, G.W.   36
Green, C.E.W.   3, 11, 12, 14, 16, 23, 25, 26, 27, 31, 32, 35, 71, 369
Green, J.B.   12, 16
Hall, J.L.   265, 275

Index of Authors

Harrington, H.K.   12, 14
Hauerwas, S.   330, 338, 339
Hernstein, R.J.   378
Hinkle, A.E.   383
Hocken, P.   69, 70
Horton, S.M.   53, 54, 105
Hollenweger, W.J.   1, 2, 44, 45, 107
Hunter, H.D.   8, 41, 64, 65, 66, 105, 136, 183
Hyatt, E.   8
Jackson, A.R.   27
Johns J.D.   9, 11
Johnson, D.R.   27
Johnson, L.T.   353
Johnson, M.   370, 371
Kärkkäinen, V-M.   12, 97, 98
Keener, C.S.   12, 13, 351, 332, 342, 343, 345, 351, 352, 354, 358, 364
King, J.H.   160, 180, 181, 307
Kingsbury, J.D.   326, 333, 334
Klaiber, W.   342
Klich, A.E.   358, 360
Kwon, Y.   365
Lackoff, G.   370, 371
Lamp, J.S.   27
Lampe, G.W.H.   332
Lancaster, J.   45, 46, 47, 48
Land, Steven J.   1, 5, 21, 22, 24, 30, 35, 56, 67, 68, 69, 370, 386, 387, 389
Landrus, H.L.   27
Lederle, H.I.   51
Lincoln, A.T.   347
Luz, U.   28, 29, 30, 325, 326, 328, 333, 335, 341, 342, 348
Macchia, F.D.   12, 24, 25, 71, 72, 73, 74, 75, 94, 105
McCall, B.   12
McGee, J.B.   11
McKay, J.W.   21, 23, 25
McKnight, S.   352
McKinlay, A.   378
McLean, M.D.   11
McQueen, L.R.   9, 16, 26, 27
Martin, L.R.   10, 12, 19, 20, 21, 25, 26, 27
Matera, F.J.   353, 357, 362, 364

Menzies, R.P.   12, 13
Menzies, W.W.   11, 36, 53, 54, 104
Mills, S.H.   369
Mitch, C.   325, 339, 341
Moo, D.J.   355
Moore, R.D.   9, 11, 12, 14, 16, 26, 31, 32, 68, 387
Mounce, R.H.   356, 361
Murray, C.   378
Newman, L.V.   11
Noel, B.T.   12, 13
Nolland, J.   327, 329, 336, 345
Nygren, A.   356
Oliverio, L.W.   12, 13
Owens, R.R.   8
Patten, R.   12, 14
Pearlman, M.   36, 37, 38, 39, 41, 53, 59, 60, 76, 104
Perkins, P.   14
Petersen, A.K.   350
Phanon, Y.   335
Philemon, L.   16, 17, 18, 19
Pinnock, C.H.   20, 21, 22, 23, 25
Pope, R.P.   395
Porter, S.   356
Powell, M.A.   14
Powery, E.B.   30
Pruitt, R.M.   49, 50, 53, 104
Reed, D.A.   199, 207
Riss, R.M.   206, 207
Robeck, C.M.   8, 37, 38, 39, 40, 57, 61, 62, 63, 64, 65, 69, 75, 105, 107, 241, 242
Sandidge, J.L.   37, 38, 40, 61, 62, 63, 64, 65, 75, 105
Senior, D.   326, 327, 332, 336
Sheppard, G.T.   11, 12
Slay, J.L.   42, 43, 44, 53, 104
Smit, P.B.   350
Smith, J.K.A.   13, 24
Sparks, K.L.   342
Spawn, K.L.   11, 12, 21
Sri, E.   325, 339, 341
Stronstad, R.   9, 11
Sutton, K.   356
Synan, H.V.   8, 114, 160
Tan, S.G.H.   78, 79

Talbert, C.H.   326, 333, 335, 341, 342, 343
Taylor, J.E.   327, 330
Thomas, H.A. 16
Thomas, J.C.   2, 3, 4, 10, 11, 12, 13, 15, 16, 20, 26, 27, 28, 31, 55, 56, 57, 73, 74, 86, 88, 324, 328, 394, 395, 399
Tomberlin, D.   102, 103, 105, 391
Tomlinson, M.A.   40, 41, 42, 49, 53, 60, 104
Treier, D.J.   16
Trementozzi, D.   369, 370, 371, 375, 378, 379
Valdez, Sr., A.C.   8
Vanhoozer, K.J.   16

Vondey, W.   99, 100
Waddell, R.   12, 14
Wagner, J.R.   364
Warner, W.E.   114, 149, 193
Warrington, K.   24, 25, 75, 95, 96, 97
Webb, R.L.   328
Williams, A.R.   103, 104, 105
Williams, E.S.   39, 40, 41, 53, 54, 60, 61
Williams, J.R.   57, 58, 59
Williamson, K.   356
Wilson, E.A.   265
Work, T.   98, 99
Wright, A.T.   11, 12, 21
Wright, N.T.   8, 354, 355, 362
Yong, A.   5, 12, 13, 16, 26, 81, 82, 83, 84, 85, 86, 105, 390, 391

www.ingramcontent.com/pod-product-compliance
Lightning Source LLC
Chambersburg PA
CBHW050416170426
43201CB00008B/434